£ 17.95

HISTORY OF THE AMERICAN CINEMA

Volume 5

1930-1939

Fred Astaire and Ginger Rogers dancing "The Carioca" in FLYING DOWN TO RIO *(RKO, 1933).*

HISTORY OF THE AMERICAN CINEMA

CHARLES HARPOLE, GENERAL EDITOR

5
GRAND DESIGN:
HOLLYWOOD AS A MODERN BUSINESS ENTERPRISE
1930-1939

Tino Balio

UNIVERSITY OF CALIFORNIA PRESS

Berkeley • Los Angeles • London

University of California Press
Berkeley and Los Angeles, California
University of California Press, Ltd.
London, England

First Paperback Printing 1995

Library of Congress Cataloging-in-Publication Data

Balio, Tino.
    Grand design : Hollywood as a modern business enterprise,
1930–1939 / Tino Balio.
        p.   cm.
    Originally published: New York : Scribner's ; Toronto : Maxwell
Macmillan Canada; New York : Maxwell Macmillan International,
© 1933. (History of the American cinema; v. 5)
    Includes filmographies, bibliographical references, and indexes.
    ISBN 0-520-20334-8 (pbk. : alk. paper)
    1. Motion picture industry—United States—History.   2. Motion
pictures—United States—History.   I. Title.   II. Series: History
of the American cinema ; v. 5.
PN1993.5.U6B28   1995
384'.8'0973—dc20
                                                                    95-30572
                                                                    CIP

Printed in the United States of America

1 2 3 4 5 6 7 8 9

Cover design by Ritter and Ritter, Inc.

History of the American Cinema

Charles Harpole, general editor of the History of the American Cinema, is a cinema historian, filmmaker, and consultant. Author of *Gradients of Depth in the Cinema Image* and articles on cinema and mass media, he has written animation for Sesame Street and directed a film in Russia. He has taught at New York University, the University of Texas–Dallas, the University of Georgia, and Ohio State University. He now teaches, writes, and makes films in Florida, where he also helped found the Florida film festival.

The Cinema History Project and the *History of the American Cinema* have been supported by grants from the National Endowment for the Humanities and the John and Mary R. Markle Foundation.

Contents

Acknowledgments

I wish to thank Charles Harpole whose perseverance and dedication made this publication project possible. My thanks also to David A. Cook and Jack Ellis for reading the book in manuscript and for making many valuable suggestions.

I am indebted to David Bordwell, Kristin Thompson, and Janet Staiger, whose *Classical Hollywood Cinema* established the foundation for any serious study of American film history. I am also indebted to the graduate students in my seminars at the University of Wisconsin, particularly Moya Luckett, Kevin Heffernan, Heidi Kenaga, and Teresa Becker, who asked the provocative questions that challenged accepted wisdom about Hollywood films.

I received research support from the National Endowment for the Humanities and from the Graduate School of the University of Wisconsin, for which I am grateful.

I would like to thank the following archives and their staffs for providing illustrations and research assistance for the book: the Wisconsin Center for Film and Theater Research, the State Historical Society of Wisconsin, George Eastman House/International Museum of Photography, the Motion Picture Division of the Library of Congress, and the Museum of Modern Art.

To my colleagues David Bordwell, Donald Crafton, Maxine Fleckner-Ducey, Lea Jacobs, Vance Kepley, and J. J. Murphy, my appreciation for their friendship and support. And to my wife, Mary Pinkerton, my gratitude for her patience and understanding.

TINO BALIO

Contributors

DAVID BORDWELL is Jacques Ledoux Professor of Film Studies at the University of Wisconsin–Madison. KRISTIN THOMPSON is Honorary Fellow, Department of Communication Arts, University of Wisconsin–Madison. With Janet Staiger, they are authors of *The Classical Hollywood Cinema: Film Style and Mode of Production to 1960* (1985). Among Bordwell's other books are *Narration in the Fiction Film* (1985) and *Making Meaning: Inference and Rhetoric in the Interpretation of Cinema* (1989). Thompson's books include *Exporting Entertainment: Hollywood in the World Film Market 1907–1934* (1985) and *Breaking the Glass Armor: Neoformalist Film Analysis* (1988).

JAN-CHRISTOPHER HORAK is Senior Curator, Film Collections, at the George Eastman House and Associate Professor of English at the University of Rochester. He is the author of *Film and Photo in the Twenties* (1979), *Helmer Lerski* (1982), and *Anti-Nazi Films by German Exiles: 1939–1945* (1984). He is currently completing *Lovers of Cinema: Early American Avant-Garde.*

RICHARD MALTBY is Senior Lecturer in Film in American and Commonwealth Arts at the University of Exeter. His publications include *Harmless Entertainment: Hollywood and the Ideology of Consensus* (1983) and *Passing Parade: Popular Culture in the Twentieth Century* (1989). His article "The King of Kings and the Czar of All the Rushes: The Propriety of the Christ Story" won the Arthur Miller Centre prize for American Studies in 1990. He is currently completing *Reforming the Movies: Politics, Censorship, and the Institutions of the American Cinema, 1908–1939.*

BRIAN TAVES received his Ph.D. in cinema critical studies from the University of Southern California and is on the staff of the Motion Picture Division of the Library of Congress. Taves is the author of *Robert Florey, The French Expressionist* (1987), and numerous articles. He is presently writing *The Romance of Adventure: The Genre of Historical Adventure in the Movies.*

CHARLES WOLFE is Associate Professor of Film Studies at the University of California, Santa Barbara. He is the author of *Frank Capra: A Guide to References and Resources* (1987), editor of *Meet John Doe* (1989), and co-editor (with Edward Branigan) of the American Film Institute Film Readers Series.

HISTORY OF THE AMERICAN CINEMA

Volume 5
1930-1939

Vivien Leigh as Scarlett O'Hara in GONE WITH THE WIND *(MGM, 1939).*

1

Introduction

*E*nding the decade on an upbeat, Hollywood proclaimed 1939 "The Greatest Year in Motion Pictures." Only vestiges of the Depression remained, and people were flocking to the theaters. To satisfy its fans, Hollywood turned out more "classics" that year than any other in the decade. A partial list of these films arranged in the order of their release includes JESSE JAMES (20th-Fox), GUNGA DIN (RKO), MADE FOR EACH OTHER (Selznick-UA), STAGECOACH (Wanger-UA), DARK VICTORY (Warners), WUTHERING HEIGHTS (Goldwyn-UA), ONLY ANGELS HAVE WINGS (Columbia), YOUNG MR. LINCOLN (20th-Fox), THE WIZARD OF OZ (MGM), MR. SMITH GOES TO WASHINGTON (Columbia), NINOTCHKA (MGM), DESTRY RIDES AGAIN (Universal), and GONE WITH THE WIND (Selznick-MGM). The stars of these pictures included Bette Davis, Tyrone Power, Henry Fonda, Cary Grant, Carole-Lombard, James Stewart, John Wayne, Merle Oberon, Laurence Olivier, Judy Garland, Jean Arthur, Greta Garbo, Marlene Dietrich, Clark Gable, and Vivien Leigh. "Taken all together," said Larry Swindell, "the films of 1939 are the best argument for the studio system."[1]

GONE WITH THE WIND, the last big picture of the decade and the greatest box-office hit of the sound era, "epitomized to a remarkable degree almost every trend and taste of the 1930s." A prestige picture produced in Technicolor by David O. Selznick, GONE WITH THE WIND cost more to make and had a longer running time than any previous American picture. Its marketing made it the first modern "event movie" and created the blockbuster syndrome, which has dominated the industry's thinking to this day. Based on Margaret Mitchell's Pulitzer Prize-winning classic, GONE WITH THE WIND depicts cataclysmic events of the Civil War from the perspective of a female protagonist, Scarlett O'Hara, "the most familiar fictional character in the history of womanhood." GONE WITH THE WIND, therefore, should be more accurately classified as a prestige "woman's picture." That the era's most successful production was targeted at women and employed a woman's perspective provides a starting point for an understanding of production trends during the thirties.[2]

The Movies as a Social Institution

The hoopla surrounding Selznick's two-year talent search for an actress to play Scarlett O'Hara, the epic scope of the production, and the staging of its premiere in Atlanta testify to the social status of motion pictures during the thirties. Just what function did motion pictures serve in American life in the thirties? The answer is elusive. But Margaret Thorp's *America at the Movies,* which was published in 1939, provides as good an introduction as any to contemporaneous thinking about the subject. Moviegoing had become ingrained during the thirties. Thorp estimated that 85 million people went to the movies every week in seventeen thousand theaters located in more than nine thousand cities, towns, and villages. Breaking down the 85 million figure, Thorp noted that many patrons were repeaters; at most, around 40 million out of the total U.S. population of 130 million had the movie habit. The audience was primarily middle-class whites between the ages of fourteen and forty-five, the most important segment of which was the adult female—the "average citizen's wife" who set the tone of the majority of American movies. According to Thorp, "audiences wanted to be cheered up when they went to the movies; they had no desire to see on the screen the squalor and misery of which there was all too much at home."[3]

The number of blacks in the United States was estimated at between 12 and 13 million; as a group they "seem to be the only considerable section of the population who cannot go to a movie whenever they have the price," said Thorp.[4] Around four hundred theaters catered to blacks, about one for every thirty thousand. In the South, some theaters had segregated sections for blacks, but most did not admit them at all.

As a central social institution, Hollywood ranked as the third-largest source of news in the country, surpassed only by Washington and New York. Hollywood satisfied the cravings of its fans by feeding tidbits about its comings and goings to more than three hundred newspaper, magazine, and radio correspondents from around the world permanently assigned to the movie capital. This fascination with the movies revealed itself not only in the public's preoccupation with the life-styles of the stars but also in the presumed power of the movies as a socializing force. Socialization is defined as "the process of transmitting information that assists individuals in becoming socially competent." Thorp noted that young people learned social skills from the movies, such as how to decline an invitation from a bore, how to accept a gift, how to avoid or accept a kiss, and how to light a friend's cigarette. Hollywood's ability to glamorize fashions persuaded women to think of themselves as certain types, such as a Claudette Colbert type, a Carole Lombard type, or a Norma Shearer type. Said Thorp, "No fashion magazine, however skillfully edited, can compete with [Hollywood] when it comes to making it seem imperative to own a particular hat or frock or necklace. Neither adjectives nor photographs nor drawings can make a women feel about an evening wrap as she feels when she sees it on the shoulders of Irene Dunne or in the arms of William Powell." Men, too, were influenced by the movies: "The story has been told so often that it must be true that the fashion of going without undershirts began when Clark Gable undressed in the tourist camp in IT HAPPENED ONE NIGHT. The sale of masculine underwear declined so sharply immediately afterwards that knitwear manufacturers and garment workers unions sent delegations to the producers asking them to take out the scene."[5]

Even politicians and civic leaders fell under the spell of the movies. When the mayor of Albany, New York, proclaimed a "SNOW WHITE Week," when the Illinois state legislature "passed a resolution calling for the appointment of a committee of seven senators and seven representatives to attend the Springfield premiere of YOUNG MR. LINCOLN," and when Georgia governor E. D. Rivers designated the day of GONE WITH THE WIND's premiere a state holiday, these officials basked in what Ian Jarvie calls the "charismatic authority" of the movies, which is to say, the ability of the movies to bestow charisma on others.[6]

The Movies as a Controlled Institution

In order for Clark Gable to say the line "Frankly, my dear, I don't give a damn" at the conclusion of GONE WITH THE WIND, David O. Selznick had to seek special dispensation from the Hays Office and pay a fine to use the word *damn*. The incident says a lot about the thirties and serves as a reminder that Hollywood was also a controlled institution. Hollywood liked to characterize itself as producing mere "harmless entertainment" that appealed to "the largest possible audience."[7] Pursuing this policy left the industry open to attacks from all sides.

The education establishment charged the movies with poisoning the minds of the nation's youth. In 1933 the Payne Fund, a private foundation, published the results of a five-year scientific study by a group of researchers in psychology, education, and sociology that assessed the influence of motion pictures on children. Collectively titled *Motion Pictures and Youth*, the studies gained some academic respect and were far from universally hostile to the movies, but a popular summary of the investigation by Henry James Forman published in 1933 and alarmingly titled *Our Movie-Made Children* produced a sustained attack on the movies and was widely synopsized, extracted, and reviewed in the popular press. Margaret Thorp summarized the contents of Forman's book as follows:

> By a variety of tests and experiments the investigators came to such conclusions as that motion pictures are a cause of delinquency and crime; that the pictures contain too much crime, love, and sex to make a wholesome diet for children; that the exhibition of gangster pictures in slum neighborhoods "amounts to the diffusion of poison"; that the conduct of screen characters is lower than the prevailing standards of morality; that children who go to the movies are likely to be less well behaved in school than non-moviegoers; that moviegoing is highly detrimental to children's sleep; that moviegoing produces "profound mental and psychological effects of an emotional order." (*America at the Movies*, p. 121)

Assessing the relevance of the movies to adults, pundits charged that Hollywood movies were dishonest, stupid, and banal, among other things. For example, Edmund Wilson said,

> In what sense does the United States lead the world in moving pictures? We make more of them and are more proficient mechanically, but . . . with the retrenchments imposed by the depression, the whole movie business seemed to harden into something immovably banal. The big producers nailed down their favorite formulas in all their obviousness, falsity and vulgarity, and almost entirely abandoned the attempt to make the old stock situations seem lifelike or to point them up with scenic distinction. The actors who were brought to

Hollywood were handled with extreme stupidity, and invariably, if they stayed there, ruined. A lot of talent has been fed into the studios, and what have our pictures got to show for it? How shall we ever know now whether John Barrymore would ever have amounted to anything? How shall we know whether Katharine Hepburn—or for that matter, Greta Garbo—ever really had anything to her? ("It's Terrible! It's Ghastly! It Stinks!" *New Republic*, 21 July 1937, p. 311)

At one time or another, church leaders charged that the movies were immoral; reactionaries charged that the movies advocated Communist causes; diplomats charged that the movies portrayed foreigners as villains and courtesans. To absolve themselves of any responsibility in showing such fare, independent exhibitors claimed that offensive pictures were foisted on them by the big distributors. Reformers took up the cause by petitioning Congress to outlaw the monopolistic trade practices and to impose federal censorship on the industry.

It is no wonder then that American film became the most controlled entertainment in the country. During the thirties, motion pictures were subjected to controls from three sources. The first was state and municipal censorship boards. Because the movies had yet to win First Amendment protection—which is to say, freedom of speech—censorship boards, vested with the simple statutory authority, could deny exhibition permits to any film they disliked. Since this form of censorship attempted to prevent so-called objectionable subject matter from reaching the screen, it was called "prior censorship."

The second source of control was pressure groups. Women's organizations and religious groups, such as the Daughters of the American Revolution, the Association of University Women, the National Congress of Parents and Teachers, the National Council of Jewish Women, and the Catholic Legion of Decency, had delegates looking over producers' shoulders to preview films and publish lists recommending or condemning new releases. The threat of a motion picture boycott by the Legion of Decency at the parish level constituted the chief "gun behind the door" and was generally credited with keeping Hollywood in line.[8]

The third form of control, self-regulation, was administered by the Production Code Administration (PCA), an arm of the industry's trade organization called the Motion Picture Producers and Distributors of America (MPPDA). Self-regulation entailed the scrutinizing of motion pictures at various stages of development by industry-appointed censors to ensure that motion-picture content conformed to the tenets of the Production Code. This practice was very different from prior censorship, which resulted in offensive elements being cut from a finished film after it had been placed into release. Self-regulation, said Lea Jacobs, was a defensive practice "operated at the level of the text" that involved two distinct but isolated stages: (1) evaluation, or the identification of films or elements within films likely to offend reform groups or provoke action by government regulatory agencies; and (2) negotiation, or the finding of ways to forestall the anticipated complaints and the minimizing of cuts that would be required by the state censorship boards once a picture had been placed in release.[9] To force producer compliance with the Production Code, the MPPDA promised to levy a $25,000 fine against any member company that released a picture without a PCA seal of approval. And to prove they meant business, the majors announced they would exhibit only those pictures approved by the PCA in their affiliated theater chains.

The Movies as an Economic Institution

Adept public relations by the industry kept the censors at bay and the channels of distribution open. An interesting thing about the distribution system was that whenever a major company produced a hit picture, such as GONE WITH THE WIND, all the majors made money. This phenomenon was not really understood by the public until the publication of Mae Huettig's *Economic Control of the Motion Picture Industry* in 1944. During the thirties, Hollywood was dominated by the Big Five—Loew's, Inc. (Metro-Goldwyn-Mayer), Warner Bros., Paramount, 20th Century–Fox, and RKO. The majors produced practically all the quality pictures; operated worldwide distribution networks; and owned the most important theaters in the country. Observing that the structure of the motion-picture industry was "a large inverted pyramid, top-heavy with real estate and theaters, resting on a narrow base of the intangibles which constitute films," Huettig concluded that the crux of the motion-picture business is not production but exhibition.[10]

If the brick-and-mortar branch of the industry constituted the bulk of the invested capital of a company and generated the most revenue, Huettig asked, "Who decides what films are made?" The headquarters of the major companies were located a continent away from Hollywood—in New York, close to Wall Street, publishing, and Broadway. There, top executives determined crucial issues concerning the quantity and quality of the films Hollywood produced. The men (and they were all men) in charge of exhibition wielded enormous clout. Having served more than likely on the front lines of the business, they knew from experience what the public wanted and called for surefire hits. The heads of distribution also had a say. Since they knew the kinds of pictures that exhibitors wanted, they might announce that such-and-such a star was box-office poison or that overland-bus pictures were hot. And since they knew marketing, they might place a cap on the number of roadshow pictures needed. However, at every studio it was the chief executive officer who made the crucial decisions. It was he who controlled the purse strings and determined how much the company could afford to spend on production. After settling on a figure, he divided the money between the class-A and class-B pictures first and then determined the budgets for the big pictures. Afterward, the front office prepared a tentative release schedule. At that point, the production department in Hollywood took over. To repeat, executives far removed from Hollywood were able to make key policy-making decisions affecting production because they were closest to the principal source of income—theater admissions.

Huettig asked, "What is the relationship between the operations of the majors, the kinds of people who run the companies, and the kinds of films produced?" Motion-picture production was but one of many activities of the majors and not necessarily the most important. Warner Bros., for example, owned more than a hundred subsidiaries, including a film laboratory, a radio manufacturer, music-publishing houses, a lithography company, a recording studio, and a

"Preview—Major Studio Feature Tonight."

theater accessory firm, in addition to its theater chain. Diversification affected the makeup of executive personnel, officers, and board members of a company because, as Huettig put it, "if the production of movies is but one aspect of the corporate existence, it follows that representation will be given to the other activities in proportion to their importance."[11] Paramount's board, for example, consisted of investment bankers, manufacturers, and businessmen of various stripes.

The presence of outside bankers and businessmen on boards of directors reflected the fact that the assests of the majors consisted chiefly of theaters. Although this had little significance in itself, the way majors acquired these chains did. The majors raised the capital to acquire their chains during the halcyon days before the 1929 crash through the public sale of stocks and bonds. Incurring long-term debt had an important effect on production, said Huettig: "The production of films, essentially fluid and experimental as a process, is harnessed to a form of organization which can rarely afford to be either experimental or speculative because of the regularity with which heavy fixed charges must be met."[12]

This led her to ask, "What kind of theaters do the majors own?" Affiliated chains ranged in size from two hundred to fifteen hundred theaters. Although these chains consisted only of around 20 percent of the theaters in the country, they contained nearly 80 percent of the first-run houses and the most profitable subsequent-run houses. It would be hard to overestimate the importance of first-run houses. Located in the hubs of major metropolitan areas, these motion-picture palaces generated anywhere from 50 to 80 percent of the box office in any market and had the potential as a group of returning more than half the production costs of a given picture.

Affiliated theater chains were situated in different regions of the country. The Loew's chain was located primarily in New England and greater New York, the Warner chain in Pennsylvania, the Paramount chain in the Midwest and the South, and so on. Only in the largest cities at the first-run level did these chains actually compete with one another, not in the hundreds of neighborhood theaters or in the thousands of houses outside these areas. Flagship theaters used in-house productions almost exclusively. In order to distribute pictures nation-wide, the majors pooled their product, which is to say, they exhibited one another's pictures in areas where they did not compete and gave one another the right to pick the best pictures on each other's roster. Thus, a hit picture like GONE WITH THE WIND redounded "to the benefit of each of the theater-owning majors since each shares in the box office," said Huettig.[13]

Because these chains generated most of the income of a company, Huettig concluded that production and distribution were important only to the extent that they enabled the majors to maintain their favored status in exhibition: "The production of films by the major companies is not really an end in itself, on the success or failure of which the company's existence depends; it is an instrument directed toward the accomplishment of a larger end, i.e., domination of the theater market."[14]

Huettig's final question was "What is the relationship between the Big Five and the Little Three?" No one studio had the capacity to produce a year's supply of pictures for its subsequent-run theaters, especially after the double-feature vogue. A subsequent-run theater typically showed double bills that changed two or three times a week. Because these theaters required as many as three hundred pictures a year, the majors needed supplemental products, particularly inexpensive class-B pictures to fill the bottom half of the double bill. This gap in film supply explains the existence of the Little Three—Columbia, Universal, and United Artists. The first two companies produced and distributed motion pictures and concentrated mainly on supplying B pictures for the low end of the market. United Artists, the smallest of the eight, functioned solely as a distributor for a small group of elite independent producers.

Production in a Era of Oligopoly

Delineating the institutions that intersected with Hollywood during the thirties suggests the range of forces impinging on the production of motion pictures. Movies had to support the political and social status quo, they had to reflect a certain moralistic worldview, and they had to satisfy audiences, among other things. More than anything else, movies had to keep theaters full.

During the Depression, the majors were nearly dragged down by their theaters, but stability was restored as the economy improved. The history of the industry in the thirties reveals that the majors, acting in concert through the MPPDA, succeeded in getting government sanction for the trade practices they had developed over the years through informal collusion. These trade practices guaranteed that studios operated at full capacity with the knowledge that every film produced would find a theatrical outlet. Moreover, these trade practices ensured that the affiliated theaters would be supplied first and could charge the highest ticket prices. As if that were not enough, these trade practices shut out the competition as well.

The thirties transformed the American film industry into a modern business enterprise. No longer run by their founders as family businesses, motion-picture companies were managed by hierarchies of salaried executives who rationalized operations to ensure long-term stability and profits. For a while during the Depression, investment bankers and industrialists acted as receivers for several stricken companies and proved themselves singularly inept in handling the business. Not until the boards of directors of these firms appointed executives who earned their stripes in motion pictures did the companies revive. Afterward, the relationship of banks to motion pictures changed. Investment bankers continued to serve as board members, but they were isolated from day-to-day operations, including production. Commercial bankers offered financial services, but they did not provide direct production loans or have a say in what Hollywood produced.

An obstacle to the smooth running of the business remained the contentiousness of pressure groups, particularly the Catholic Legion of Decency, and the threat of federal censorship. The public perceived that the Legion of Decency's "crusade for cleaner motion pictures" in 1934 forced Hollywood to clean up its pictures. For example, the *Christian Century* said,

> The producers, fearing that the crusade would eventuate in a cam-
> paign for legal censorship, acted quickly and set up a censorship of
> their own within the industry. Thus in 1934 they put into effect and

implemented the code of ethics which they signed so solemnly, ballyhooed so loudly, and ignored so contemptuously in 1930. They gave their hired defender, Mr. Will Hays, the authority to pass upon every picture released by the motion picture trust. ("The Legion of Decency's First Year," 27 March 1935, pp. 392–393)

But, in Chapter 3 Richard Maltby argues that no fundamental shift in policy occurred in 1934. Actually, the industry started enforcing the Production Code from the time of its adoption in 1930 and had been busy developing review procedures based on ad hoc precedents. The apparent changes in the Code after the Legion of Decency crusade were mainly cosmetic and had much more to do with the industry making a public show of atonement. Then why did Hollywood make such a fuss about creating the Production Code Administration in 1934 and appointing a prominent Catholic layman, Joseph Breen, to head it? Maltby demonstrates that Hollywood made a show of atonement in 1934 because a deal had been struck; in return for a public acknowledgment of misfeasance, the Catholic hierarchy agreed to drop its support for federal regulation of the industry. Thereafter, Hollywood distributed its pictures in peace.

Keeping theaters supplied with pictures meant that studios had to regulate every stage of production. During the Depression, the majors acceded to demands of rank-and-file craftsmen for higher wages, since, as a group, they represented a small percentage of production costs. But the majors fought bitterly to prevent talent groups from unionizing, fearing that their demands might throw production schedules out of kilter.

Three talent groups wanted recognition—directors, screenwriters, and actors. The rise in status of the producer came at the expense of the director. Having lost much of their autonomy, directors became cogs in a wheel, relegated essentially to the task of staging the action. The least militant of the talent groups and among the best paid, directors seemed relatively happy with their lot. In its fight for recognition, the Screen Directors Guild presented a modest set of demands; directors wanted more preparation time, a chance to read the script before going into production, and the right to assemble a film in its first rough form. The studios signed an accord with the Screen Directors Guild in 1939, but only a handful of elite directors were given more authority over their pictures.

The Screen Actors Guild won recognition in 1937. Because stars constituted the most important component of production, the majors waged a vicious public relations battle that ridiculed their demands. The majors established minimum wages for rank-and-file actors and made minor concessions to other classes of performers, but the basic employment agreement that tied the star to the studio—known in the business as the option contract—remained intact.

The most militant of the talent groups and the last to win recognition by the studios, the Screenwriters Guild was the group best equipped to express its discontent. Led by writers who had made names for themselves as members of the eastern literary establishment, screenwriters bitterly complained about their low status in the studio system, the speed at which they were forced to work, compulsory collaboration, and the unfair assigning of screen credits, among other things. Going for the jugular, a left-wing group in the guild demanded more creative authority over production and copyright protection that would make writers co-owners of the pictures based on their scripts. The majors responded to this platform by pitting politically conservative screenwriters against the militants, by threatening a blacklist, and by stonewalling. The Screenwriters Guild signed a pact with the studios in 1941 and won a few minor concessions, but the creative status of the writer remained as is.

Filmmaking in the era of the studio system is typically described as a collaborative process, but it might be more accurate to say that filmmaking was a group effort involving a strict division of labor with a producer at the helm. Curtis Bernhardt, who worked as a director in Germany, England, and France, contrasted working conditions in Europe and those he encountered when he joined Warners in 1940:

> My earliest memory of Warner Brothers . . . is of somebody handing me a script and saying: "You start shooting Monday." And I was used to having three, four, or five months' preparation: selecting the story, writing one shooting-script with the writers and then a second shooting-script, and when I was ready I went on the stage and started shooting. . . . When I declined, he took me to see Jack Warner who said: "Well, if you can't do it, take your release." That was my first impression of Hollywood. (Quoted in Charles Higham and Joel Greenberg, *The Celluloid Muse: Hollywood Directors Speak* [New York: New American Library, 1972], pp. 49–50)

Searching for ways to control production costs, while maintaining an acceptable level of quality, companies switched from the central-producer system to unit production. In the former, one executive oversaw the entire season's output of a studio; in the latter, several exectuives did. Like modern business enterprises, Hollywood had organized all phases of the production process in a rational manner, from story acquisition to editing. For example, in deciding what to produce in any given year, moguls did not rely on hunches or attempt to foist their personal tastes on the public; rather, studios organized story departments in New York, Hollywood, and London to keep in close contact with Broadway, publishing, and the literary world.

Analyzing the routines of motion-picture production, Chapter 4 focuses on the creation of a picture's visual style. By providing an overview of art direction, costume design, and cinematography, it suggests that powerful department heads, such as MGM's Cedric Gibbons and Paramount's Hans Dreier, and individual artists, such as Anton Grot, William Cameron Menzies, and Gregg Toland, exerted an enormous influence over the look of a picture, which sometimes extended to the way it was shot.

Harnessed to an industrial form of production, the studio system readily absorbed new technologies. Analyzing the aesthetic norms of the classical Hollywood style, Chapter 5 demonstrates that Hollywood adopted innovations in sound recording, camerawork, and cinematography that were made within the studios, service firms, and professional organizations. Adopting new technologies did not alter the structure of the industry the way the talkies did; rather, they enabled Hollywood to operate more efficiently and enhanced the techniques of conventional storytelling.

This brings up the issue of competition. How did the majors compete with one another? Or stated another way, how did companies differentiate their films?

Each studio developed a house style that was an amalgam of fiscal policy, specialty genres, and stars, among other factors. Studios attempted to differentiate their pictures at every level of production, from the humblest B Western to the most colossal epic. As a general rule, differentiation mattered most at the highest level, where a studio stood the chance of gaining (or losing) the most money.

Chapter 6 begins the discussion of product differentiation by focusing on the key ingredient studios used to sell their pictures to the public—the star system. Firmly in place by the thirties, the star system underwent considerable change as a result of the talkies and the Depression. After converting to the talkies, Hollywood scoured Broadway, vaudeville, and radio for fresh talent, a process that lasted the decade. However, signing a personality from a different line of show business was one thing; making him or her palatable to motion-picture audiences was another. The techniques Hollywood devised to accomplish this feat further rationalized the process of star development and made big names even more dependent on the studios.

Expanding its bag of tricks to advertise and promote its stars, Hollywood took advantage of radio. Starting out as potential competitors during the Depression, motion pictures and radio soon settled into a symbiotic relationship. Radio basked in the charismatic power of Hollywood, and Hollywood tapped the advertising potential of the new medium by developing radio programming to showcase its stars, to stimulate moviegoing, and to hype new releases.

Chapter 7 continues the discussion of product differentiation by analyzing feature-film production trends. Since the production strategies of the majors were designed to compete for the box-office dollar, the discussion rests on what was popular, when, and, whenever possible, why. The analysis relied on several barometers of public taste. *Variety*'s annual list of top-grossing films revealed people voting with their pocketbooks and gauged the relative drawing power of a star and a production cycle. Although the trade publication identified only six to eight winners a year, the data provided insights into the major trends (see Appendix 1).

Industry professionals expressed their preferences during the annual Academy Awards ceremonies. Although an Oscar did not affect a picture's box-office performance, as most nominated pictures had completed their runs well before the ceremonies, the Academy Awards became a standard against which to compare the critics' and the public's choices (see Appendix 2).

Film critics had their say not only in reviews but also in various "Ten Best" lists. The *New York Times* list, for example, consisted of personal picks of the newspaper's chief film critic and included an occasional foreign art film and documentary, in addition to mainstream Hollywood fare. *Film Daily*'s Ten Best, which represented a cross section of the print media, was compiled by polling reviewers and entertainment editors from newspapers, magazines, and the trade around the country. More than 300 critics participated in the nationwide poll in 1931; by 1939, the number had reached nearly 550, about half the daily and Sunday papers, large and small, across the country. Of these newspapers, about sixty conducted local polls to determine the correspondence between the house critics' and readers' tastes (see Appendix 3).

The polls and awards agreed often enough to indicate a consensus among the public and the critics and are therefore used as a basis for structuring the chapter on production trends. Placing production trends within the context of their times reveals that the public was often at odds with what film scholars today admire about the thirties and reveals more clearly Hollywood's marketing strategies.

The "other half" of Hollywood films, those unheralded class-B pictures relegated to the bottom half of the marquee, played a significant though thankless role in the business. Produced on meager budgets and sold at bargain prices, Bs collected enough as a group to lower studio overhead, which enabled the majors to operate year-round at full capacity. Without the Bs, the studio system would have rested on shaky ground indeed. Chapter 8 analyzes just how extensive this brand of production was. A staple of the majors (except United Artists), B films were also produced by the minor studios associated with the MPPDA, Monogram and Republic, and scores of fly-by-night companies operating on Poverty Row. If mainstream Hollywood targeted the white middle class, Poverty Row set its sights on less prepossessing filmgoers, including rural, black, and immigrant groups. Derided by the trade press and marginalized in film histories, B's are just now being recognized for the role they played in the social lives of what Michael Harrington called "the other America."

Alternative film practices, represented by documentaries and avant-garde films, functioned outside the commercial mainstream. Produced on shoestring budgets by individuals or small groups of collaborators with their own equipment, these films were often experimental in form and found outlets in art theaters, schools, churches, union halls, and civic groups. Chapter 9 analyzes, among other things, the work of politically committed filmmakers to record and render dramatic "the social trauma of unemployment, labor violence, and the erosion of American farmland, and to construct causal explanations for these disturbances and disasters." Hollywood imitated aspects of the documentary style when it produced social-problem pictures, but not the causal analysis, preferring instead to resolve crises within the norms of entertainment. Chapter 10 describes the personal filmmaking of the avant-garde. Without a political agenda of its own and barely noticed outside its own coterie, the avant-garde was kept alive by cineastes. Ever resourceful, Hollywood also absorbed elements of this film practice, but used them only for embellishment.

As his decisive first move to attack the Depression, newly elected President Franklin Roosevelt declared a four-day national bank holiday in March 1933. In closing the banks, FDR prevented further panic withdrawals and gave the Treasury Department time to draft emergency legislation. The effect on the motion-picture business was catastrophic. During the moratorium, box-office receipts fell about 45 percent, crippling theaters all over the country. To stay open, some operators were accepting IOUs, and others, produce, groceries, or almost anything in lieu of cash. Said *Variety,* "The decline was such that it leaves an open question whether the moving picture will ever again know the popularity of those peaks it reached in the silent era and then again with sound."[6]

Hollywood also felt the impact of the bank holiday. The cash flow dried up, which prevented the studios from meeting their payrolls. Production chiefs concluded that the studios could be kept open, temporarily at least, if employees earning $50 or more a week took a 50 percent cut for eight weeks. "Morale was already low," said *Variety,* "and the 50% cut to men who had already taken two or three cuts, seemed the last straw."[7]

As the Depression wore on, studios laid off more than 20 percent of their work force. Paramount shut down its Long Island studio and laid off almost five thousand employees who had been earning between $35 and $50 a week. General salary cuts for executives, contract people, and those who worked on a week-to-week basis were put into effect on practically all the major lots. The number of unemployed and underpaid extras in Hollywood became a national scandal. Wages for those lucky enough to find work dropped from $2 a day to $1.25. As a result of such economizing, the annual payroll of major companies dropped from $156 million in 1931 to an estimated $50 million in 1933.[8]

Exhibition was even harder hit. In 1930, more than twenty thousand theaters were operating in the United States. Two years later, an estimated four thousand had gone dark. The vast majority of these theaters seated an average of seven hundred and were owned by independents. The number of workers in this sector of the business dropped by a third, from 130,000 in 1929 to a low point of 87,000 in 1932.[9]

The impact of these conditions on the bottom lines of the major motion-picture corporations was as follows: after registering profits of $14.5 million in 1929 and $7 million in 1930, Warners lost nearly $8 million in 1931; Fox's earnings fell from $10 million in 1930 to minus $4 million in 1931; and RKO's $3.4 million surplus from 1930 turned to a $5.7 million deficit in one year. Paramount remained in the black in 1931, but Adolph Zukor saw his company's earnings fall from $18.4 million to $6.3 million and then, in 1932, to a record loss of $21 million.

The bottom fell out of the market in 1933. No longer able to avoid the ignominy of bankruptcy and receivership, RKO went down first, in January 1933, followed soon after by Paramount and Fox. Warners, battered by losses of $14 million in 1932 and $6 million in 1933, was fighting to stay afloat. Of the Big Five, only Loew's had yet to show a deficit; however, its earnings plunged from $15 million in 1930 to $4.3 million in 1933. As for the Little Three, Universal had gone into receivership, and Columbia and United Artists were wounded, but not down.[10]

Bankruptcies and receiverships were common enough during the Depression and enabled distressed companies to protect their assets for the benefit of investors while a court-approved plan was worked out to pay creditors in an orderly fashion. In the motion-picture industry, bankruptcies and receiverships occurred in the exhibition subsidiaries of the majors and not in the production and distribution ends and resulted from the ferocious battle for control of the nation's theaters at the end of the 1920s. During 1929, "hardly a week elapsed but that two or more of the giant interests were not amalgamating or absorbing one another," said *Variety*. Paramount, Warners, and RKO were particularly aggressive and built or acquired hundreds of theaters, thereby encumbering themselves with millions of dollars of debt. When the boom ended in 1931, the so-called deluxe theaters, built in flush times and at recklessly extravagant costs, became white elephants, at least for the duration of the Depression. In short, the major companies could not meet their fixed cost obligations, which simply meant they did not have the cash to pay their mortgage commitments, short-term obligations, and the heavy charges on their funded debts.[11]

RKO, a newcomer to the industry, was the most vulnerable. Founded in October 1928 as a holding company, Radio-Keith-Orpheum Corporation was created nearly overnight by RCA to exploit its Photophone sound system. The company amalgamated the Film Booking Office, a small Hollywood producer and distributor, the Keith-Albee-Orpheum vaudeville theater circuit, and Photophone into a vertically integrated giant containing a national chain of three hundred theaters, four studios, and assets of more than $100 million. RKO's receivership was caused by a 40 percent drop in attendance at its theaters and a paucity of successful films from Radio Pictures. RKO tried to compensate for its poor product by pushing vaudeville, but its circuit could not carry the burden.[12]

Paramount's bankruptcy was the second largest the country had ever known and one of the most complicated. During the 1920s, Paramount's theater chain, known as Publix, expanded to fifteen hundred houses. Most were acquired with money raised with bond issues underwritten by Kuhn, Loeb & Company. But according to *Fortune,* some theaters "were acquired in what seemed a shrewder way: exchange of stock, with a guarantee to repurchase at $80 a share. (Paramount stock never sold above 78.)" The repurchase agreements matured when Paramount's stock sold below $50 and when credit was tight; and when theater attendance plummeted, "not all the managerial resolution in the world could nick the fixed charges [that the company] had been so sanguinely accumulating. It required the judiciary ax."[13]

Fox's troubles began in 1929. The company was fully extended; by then, Fox had acquired extensive theater holdings, had become a leader in the innovation of sound, and had invested heavily in the construction of Movietone City, an all-sound studio facility in West Los Angeles. But in an audacious move, founder William Fox purchased a controlling interest in Loew's, Inc. from the estate of Marcus Loew and from Loew's management for $28 million. Fox borrowed the money from AT&T and Halsey, Stuart & Company, the La Salle Street investment firm. Fox's strategy was to merge his company with Loew's and create the world's largest motion-picture enterprise. But the Justice Department of the new Herbert Hoover administration blocked the move as a violation of the antitrust laws. As a result, Fox was forced to sequester the Loew's stock.[14]

Meanwhile, William Fox had been hit hard by the crash. To stay afloat, he sold off assets to AT&T and Halsey, Stuart, but in return for the cash, he had to relinquish control of his company. Dethroned from the company he founded, Fox sold his majority interest to Harley C. Clarke, the president of General Theatres

Equipment, in 1930. The takeover was financed largely by AT&T and the Chase National Bank. In 1931, Fox divested himself of the Loew's stock. As will be discussed later, Harley Clarke did not possess the know-how to revive a distressed film company. Fox Films lost nearly $11.5 million in 1931 and 1932, which pushed it to the brink.[15]

Universal Pictures, the only member of the Little Three to seek protection in the courts, entered the Depression with a chain of more than three hundred theaters. Unlike the Big Five's theaters, Universal's were mainly small neighborhood and rural houses. During the conversion to sound, Universal did not have the money to wire its houses and sold off most of its circuit. The remainder of the theaters were placed into receivership in 1933 and were soon sold.[16] Universal was chronically short of cash afterward. To raise production financing, Carl Laemmle, Sr., borrowed $750,000 from J. Cheever Cowdin's Standard Capital Company in 1935. As part of the loan agreement, Laemmle granted Standard a ninety-day option to purchase a majority interest in the studio for $5.5 million. Cowdin exercised the option in March 1936 and took over operating control of Universal Pictures. After selling his stock in the studio, Laemmle, who had founded the company in May 1912, retired from motion pictures.

The motion-picture companies that escaped the Depression unscathed—which is to say, weathered the Depression without bankruptcy, reorganization, or shake-up any kind—were Loew's, Inc., Warner Bros., Columbia Pictures, and United Artists. Of the group, Loew's was the strongest. Considered by Wall Street as the Tiffany's of motion-picture corporations, Loew's earned profits every year of the Depression. Two factors were responsible for Loew's outstanding achievement. The first was the company's fiscal conservatism. Loew's had branched out into production during the 1920s by absorbing Metro Pictures, Goldwyn Pictures, and Louis B. Mayer Productions to form MGM, but stood pat with its chain of 125 high-class theaters, which founder Marcus Loew had earlier acquired. The second was MGM's singlar success in gauging public tastes. During the thirties, MGM produced more hits than any other company. Of the twenty-four films that made it to *Variety*'s annual list of top-grossing films from 1930 to 1933, MGM produced nine, or more than a third. As *Fortune* put it, MGM was "encrusted with more stars and triumphs than Hollywood had seen in one place."[17]

The Depression hit Warner Bros. hard, but the company refused to seek protection in the courts. Warners was the only member of the Big Five still run by the original founders: Harry Warner was president of the company; Albert Warner, treasurer and vice-president; and Jack Warner, vice-president in charge of production. Warners entered the thirties having just completed a spending spree the likes of which had never been seen, even in the movie business. By being the first to innovate sound, Warners generated extraordinary profits, which it used to solidify its position in the industry. Beginning in late 1928, Warners acquired First National Pictures, the Stanley chain of three hundred theaters, music publishing houses, and other investments that boosted its assets from $5 million to $230 million. In a few short years, Warners had become a leading company in the industry. Forced to retrench during the Depression, the company sold or closed more than half of its theaters, cut wages, and pared production budgets to the lowest level among the majors. In 1930, Warners was $113 million in debt, but as a result of Harry Warner's bloodletting, the debt had been greatly reduced (to $29 million) by 1938, and by 1943 it was fully retired.[18]

Columbia Pictures, the healthiest member of the Little Three, was also a family-run business. Under the direction of brothers Harry and Jack Cohn, who held most of the equity and voting stock in the company, Columbia won the admiration of Wall Street for its restraint; the studio neither tried to acquire theaters nor encumbered itself with long-term contracts with high-priced talent. Columbia stayed afloat during the Depression by sticking to its strategy of producing and distributing shorts, programmers (low-budget films that could fill either the A or B position on a bill), and B pictures for the low end of the market. In 1934, Columbia won recognition as a full-fledged member of the Little Three by producing two surprise hits, Frank Capra's IT HAPPENED ONE NIGHT and Victor Schertzinger's ONE NIGHT OF LOVE.[19]

United Artists, the smallest major, had always led a precarious existence. As a distributor of independent productions, UA's livelihood depended solely on the ability of its producers to secure a steady flow of financing, which in turn would allow UA to keep its pipeline full. Without an adequate number of features to distribute, UA could not meet the fixed costs of operating an international sales organization. A decline both in box-office admissions and in the number of independent productions during the early 1930s forced UA into the red in 1932, but improved conditions thereafter stabilized the company's business.

The Code of Fair Competition

In a comprehensive attempt to revive the economy, President Roosevelt drafted the National Industrial Recovery Act (NIRA), which became law in June 1933.[20] Administered by the National Recovery Administration (NRA), the act assumed that cooperative action among trade organizations was superior to cutthroat competition and that the business community would be willing to put aside selfish interests for the good of the nation. Specifically, the act mandated that industries were to draw up codes of fair competition that would be enforceable by law. The government was willing to waive antitrust laws, but in return, industries had to make concessions guaranteeing labor the right of collective bargaining and establishing minimum wages and maximum hours.

The Code of Fair Competition for the Motion Picture Industry was signed into law on 27 November 1933. The major film companies quickly embraced the Code. Reflecting the vertically integrated structure of the industry, the Code regulated labor at the production level and trade practices at the distribution and exhibition levels. Concerning labor, the Code banned company unions, set minimum rates of pay, and allowed workers to organize and bargain collectively. The studios readily acceded to the demands of the craft unions and the army of stagehands and technicians that were organized by the International Alliance of Theatrical Stage Employees (IATSE), who received a reduction in hours, increased wages, and greater job security. One hundred and forty different labor unions in the industry approved and signed the Code without controversy. These concessions cost management relatively little, since the salaries paid to these workers constituted a small percentage of the cost of production.

In the mind of the public, Hollywood's chief industrial imbalance was not the underpayment of labor, but the overpayment of executives and talent. Concerning executives' salaries, the majors rewarded their managements "far in excess of the normal standards of far larger corporations," said Douglas Gomery.[21] For example, MGM's top management had personal service contracts that paid them large salaries plus a fixed percentage of the company's profits. Washington bureaucrats and others believed that the extraordinary salaries Hollywood paid its top people contributed to the bankruptcies and receiverships that were plaguing the industry.

To quell public indignation, MGM's Louis B. Mayer and other industry moguls took temporary cuts in pay, so that during the turbulence of preparing the Code, they capitalized on the situation by blaming stars for the financial difficulties of their businesses. When the finished version of the Code appeared, the moguls had succeeded in writing in provisions barring star raiding, curbing the activities of agents, and limiting the salaries of artistic personnel.

Talent reacted by forming the Screen Writers Guild in April 1933 and the Screen Actors Guild that June. Actors and writers bombarded Washington with telegrams, held mass meetings, and launched publicity campaigns opposing the control of salaries on any basis other than an open market. A threat of a strike and intensive lobbying of the White House resulted in the permanent suspension of the obnoxious provisions of the Code. However, as will be explained in chapter 4, the guilds failed to receive recognition as bargaining agents for actors and writers or to substantially improve the status of their members in the industry.

Although the bitterness of the fight over salaries turned Hollywood into a union-minded town—to the chagrin of the studios—the majors were victorious in the larger and more significant battle over the marketplace. They succeeded in receiving government sanction for the trade practices that they spent ten years developing through informal collusion and that enabled them to make the highest possible profits. In short, the Motion Picture Code legalized the monopolistic structure of the industry.

On one side of the battle line stood the Motion Picture Producers and Distributors of America (MPPDA), better known as the Hays Office after its head, Will H. Hays. On the other stood the Allied States Association of Motion Picture Exhibitors, a trade association representing small unaffiliated exhibitors headed by Abram Meyers, a former member of the Federal Trade Commission. The battle was really no contest. Allied dropped out early in the negotiations, charging that the interests of independent exhibitors were not being safeguarded. To resolve the demands of the independents, the Hays group met privately with Allied and made concessions, the most important of which deleted the ban on double features.

The trade practices sanctioned by the Code comprised the block-booking system, clearance and zoning, and admission price discrimination. In the minds of small independent exhibitors, these trade practices had been used to wrest the greatest possible profits from the market and to keep them in a subordinate position. Block booking was the most controversial trade practice. All the important companies sold their pictures in blocks of varying size, often consisting of an entire season's output. These were offered to exhibitors on an all-or-nothing basis before the pictures had actually been produced. In contracting for a block of pictures, an exhibitor was required to take short subjects as well. This practice of linking shorts to features was known as full-line forcing. A congressional investigating committee remarked, "This is the only industry in which the buyer, having no idea of what he is buying, underwrites blindly all the product offered him."[22]

The independent exhibitor was not against the practice of block booking per se, since he needed a large number of pictures to fill the playing time of his theater, which typically showed double features and changed programs two or three times a week. But he did object to having all the pictures of a studio foisted on him, regardless of their quality or desirability. And he felt particularly victimized in noting that compulsory block booking did not apply to the affiliated circuits; in dealing with one another, the major chains negotiated selective contracts allowing them to pick and choose the best of each other's pictures.

The benefits of compulsory block booking for the majors were real. Knowing that even the poorest picture would find an outlet, the studios could operate at full capacity. In the process, the majors shifted the risks of production financing to the independent exhibitor. The long-term effects of the policy also stifled competition by foreclosing the market to independent producers and distributors. In short, block booking allowed the majors to wrest the greatest amount of profits from the marketplace. Before it was endorsed by the NRA, block booking had been attacked by consumer groups, congressmen, and the Federal Trade Commission, in addition to independent exhibitors, so in drafting the Motion Picture Code, the majors made a few concessions, in the hope of quelling the controversy. But the block-booking system remained pretty much intact.

By dominating the clearance and zoning boards established by the Code, the majors also succeeded in protecting the favored status of their theaters. These boards took over the function of the local film boards of trade, which were established before the NRA and dominated by the Big Five to arrange theaters in their respective regions into a marketing pattern consisting of run, clearance, and zoning. Organizing distribution, the majors had divided the country into thirty markets, with each market subdivided into zones. Theaters within each zone were classified by run. Located in the downtowns of the largest cities, first-run theaters seated thousands and charged the highest admission prices. Second-run houses were typically located in neighborhood business districts and charged lower prices. Subsequent-run theaters, going down the scale to fifth-, sixth-, seventh-run, and more, were located in outlying communities and charged still less. A film would move from zone to zone like clockwork, with each zone separated by a clearance ranging from fourteen days to forty-two days or more. In a large market, a picture might remain in distribution for as long as a year.

Since the value of a motion picture to an exhibitor depended on its novelty, the granting of excessive clearance to prior-run houses had the effect of increasing their drawing power and keeping patronage in subsequent-run houses at low levels. Practically every legal action independent exhibitors or the government filed against affiliated circuits contained charges of inequitable clearance and zoning. With the creation of the clearance and zoning boards, the majors now had the power to adjudicate these matters for themselves.

The same held true for complaints of admission price discrimination heard by the grievance boards. In their rental contracts with exhibitors, distributors stipulated minimum admission prices for each playdate. This practice prevented price rivalry among theaters and guaranteed that the distributor would collect the optimum revenues from rentals.

The affiliated circuits, which operated first- and second-run theaters primarily, had a vested interest in seeing later-run independents subjected to strict admission-price control, since if these houses cut prices, the affiliates would stand to lose business. To drum up business at the outset of the Depression, independents offered prizes, coupons, two-for-one admissions, and the like, which indirectly reduced the cost of admission. To prevent these practices, grievance boards were vested with extraordinary power. They could punish exhibitors found violating Code admission-price provisions by ordering a boycott by the distributors.

Leaders of the motion-picture industry behaved probably no better and no worse than their counterparts in other American businesses. Frederick Lewis Allen, in his social history of the thirties, has described a probe into the NRA that appeared in *Harper's Magazine* in the autumn of 1933. The article concluded that "the spirit and intent of the National Industrial Recovery Act and the codes are being frustrated, openly or in secret." The article also demonstrated, in Allen's words, "that the governments's aim to raise wages was being defeated, either by the sheer refusal of employers to obey the minimum-wage provisions of the blanket code, or by their raising some wages up to the minimum and lowering others down to it."[23]

On 27 May 1935 the Supreme Court invalidated the NRA. In a unanimous decision, the Court declared that the NRA was unconstitutional on two grounds: first, Congress had violated the constitutional principles of the separation of powers by delegating its powers to the executive; and second, Congress had overstepped its authority by enacting laws regulating the business practices of firms engaged in interstate trade. "The decision implied that it would be unconstitutional for the Federal government to deal with a national industrial or social or agricultural problem by dictating to individual factories, stores, or farmers what they should do," said Allen. FDR was outraged by the decision and told a press conference afterward that "we have been relegated to the horse-and-buggy definition of interstate commerce."[24]

The NRA clearly had failed as a recovery measure. Understanding this, FDR devoted his second term to reform, believing that big industries, such as steel, oil, and aluminum, had not cooperated with the NRA and were now obstacles to economic recovery. Working through the Department of Justice, he launched an antitrust crusade; one of the principal targets was the motion-picture industry.

Wall Street and Hollywood

Receiverships and bankruptcies changed Wall Street's relationship to the motion-picture industry. During the first two decades of its history, the film industry was financed almost exclusively from earnings or from private capital. When the movies proved their potential as big business, the great Wall Street and La Salle Street investment houses vied for the underwriting of new stock issues for capital expansion, which they sold to the public. Kuhn, Loeb & Company, for example, financed Famous Players' acquisition of a theater chain beginning in 1919; Goldman, Sachs & Company bankrolled Warners' acquisition of Vitagragh, First National, and Stanley Theatres during the conversion to sound; and Halsey, Stuart & Company enabled Fox Films to construct the Fox Movietone Studio and to acquire theaters during the same period. The wiring of the nation's theaters

Moviegoers outside Chaplin's CITY LIGHTS *(UA, 1931)*.

and the construction of sound studios in Hollywood was financed largely by the Morgan and Rockefeller banking groups. In underwriting these stock issues, investment houses placed representatives on the boards of directors of the respective film companies, where they worked hand in hand with top management to oversee fiscal matters. When motion-picture firms went under during the Depression, these same bankers installed themselves in the top management positions and took charge of the distressed companies.

Bankers and financiers proved singularly inept in managing motion-picture businesses. They were skillful at cutting costs, but they did not have the know-how or the temperament to make pictures audiences liked. Take the case of Fox Films. After William Fox sold his interest in the company to Harley C. Clarke, the board appointed Clarke the new president and chief executive officer. Clarke's credentials in addition to his post as head of General Theatres included the presidency of a Chicago-based holding company that owned or controlled more than fifty gas and electric companies in the United States and Great Britain. According to Gomery, Clarke "felt he could 'clean up' the mess by applying techniques of scientific business management which had worked so well in the utilities industry. But . . . standard business practices did not always work in the motion picture business. During the Great Depression they produced only debt. Clarke resigned in 1931 after only one year on the job."[25]

Clarke was succeeded by Edward R. Tinker, the former board chairman of the Chase National Bank. Tinker also failed to clean up the financial mess, and within a year the theater division of Fox filed for bankruptcy. Exit Tinker. Neither a former utility executive nor a former bank chairman had been able to cure the ailing motion-picture corporation.

Finally, the board chose a veteran of the movie business to direct the company. Sidney Kent, the former head of distribution at Paramount and "one of the driving forces behind Paramount's rise to power," said Gomery, used his considerable managerial skills to reorganize the theater chain, to put distribution back on the right track, and even to clear the company of debts.[26] But Kent understood that the long-term health of the company depended on a steady supply of popular films. Kent therefore revamped studio operations on the West Coast in 1935 by negotiating a merger of the Fox Film Corporation and Twentieth Century Pictures.

Twentieth Century was a highly successful independent production company that had been distributing through United Artists. Founded in 1933 by Joseph M. Schenck, UA's chairman, the production unit revolved around the talents of Darryl F. Zanuck, the former production chief at Warners, and his associate, William Goetz, the son-in-law of Louis B. Mayer and a former RKO producer. Zanuck had joined Warner Bros. in 1924 at the age of twenty-two to become one of the most prolific scriptwriters in Hollywood. After making a name for himself creating the incredibly successful Rin Tin Tin series, he became studio manager and helped to guide operations through the transition to sound. In 1930 he was made head of production. In this position, Zanuck developed the formula for action-filled, fast-paced, and topical pictures that characterized the Warner output during the early thirties. Zanuck walked off the lot in 1933 when, at the conclusion of the bank moratorium, Harry Warner went back on his word to restore the salaries of studio employees who had taken cuts.

Schenck took advantage of the situation by going into partnership with Zanuck to supply United Artists with badly needed product. In his first year with Twentieth Century, Zanuck demonstrated his production skills by delivering twelve pictures, most of which were hits. Because of personality differences with UA's owners, particularly with Mary Pickford and Charlie Chaplin, UA did not offer Zanuck a partnership in the company, as was its custom with successful producers. Schenck thereupon resigned from UA, taking Twentieth Century with him.

As part of the merger with Fox, Schenck was named chairman of the board of the newly named 20th Century–Fox Film Corporation, and Zanuck, vice-president in charge of production. Although the net worth of the former UA production unit was placed at $5 million, its earning capacity surpassed the huge Fox Film Corporation, which had assets of more than $50 million. Because of this, Twentieth Century appeared first in the composite name.[27]

Paramount offers another case of Wall Street mismanagement. When the Depression hit the box office in 1931, Paramount named John Hertz, a retired Chicago taxicab millionaire and partner in Wall Street's Lehman Brothers, to the board and appointed him chairman of the finance committee. Hertz slashed production budgets by a third, reduced salaries across the board, and stream-lined distribution. But cost cutting could not attract people to Paramount's theaters. Paramount was awash in red ink by 1933, convincing Hertz to step down just as the company opted for receivership.

During the receivership, "fifty-three different law firms, banks, protective committees, and experts yammered and bled for two and one-half years over the sick giant and its 500 subsidiaries," said *Fortune.* After the court approved Paramount's reorganization plan in July 1935, the new board of directors was led by former debtors and bankers, including Lehman Brothers, Electrical Research Products, Inc. (ERPI), and the Royal Insurance Company of Great Britain. Of the fifteen men on the board, only Adolph Zukor, the founder of the company, and one other member had any experience in motion pictures. Seeking to vindicate his tenure at the helm, Hertz convinced the board to name ERPI president John Otterson the chief executive of the company. Another solid businessman, Otterson, imitating Harley Clarke at Fox, tried to run Paramount like a public utility. Otterson bombarded the studio with cost-accounting procedures, effi-ciency schemes, and personnel forms, and morale sank to a new low.[28]

To investigate the situation, Paramount's board sought the advice of the prominent businessman and former film executive Joseph P. Kennedy, the father of future president John F. Kennedy. In his report to the board, Kennedy stated "that negative costs were exceeding their budgets by $7,000,000; that shooting schedules were being disregarded; that one scenario (average cost, $15,000) was junked for every one that could be charged to productions; that the planning of the 1936–37 program was hopelessly inchoate, costly stars were being alienated, writers were loafing, truck drivers were sulking, and things generally were in one hell of a mess." Concluding his investigation, Kennedy told the board "to get rid of their quality businessmen or prepare for another receivership."[29]

Stanton Griffis, who headed the financiers and real estate men on Paramount's board, acted in the summer of 1936. To replace the "quality businessmen" at the helm, Griffis installed a show-business management headed by Barney Balaban, a founding partner of the Chicago-based Balaban & Katz theater chain that had become a Paramount subsidiary in 1926. "In putting Balaban into the pilothouse at Par," said *Variety,* "a theatre operator had been given the presidency of a dominant producer-distributor for the first time." Adolph Zukor, who had been moved up to honorary chairman of the board, was placed in charge of the studio. Simultaneously, Griffis shook up the board by making ten new appointments. Leaving production entirely in Zukor's hands, Balaban went to work putting Paramount's house in order. Within six months, he had turned the company around and Paramount entered a new era of prosperity. Commenting on the reorganization, *Fortune* said, Paramount's postbankruptcy directors "capped an era of Wall Street influence on management that had reduced the once accurate name of Paramount to a symbol of all that was ludicrous, luckless, and unprofitable in the show world."[30]

Wall Street's involvement in the affairs of Hollywood gave rise to the belief in film scholarship that Wall Street took over virtual control of the film industry during the Depression. The idea was formulated by two Britishers, F. D. Klingender and Stuart Legg, in their book *Money Behind the Screen,* which was published in 1937. The gist of Klingender and Legg's argument, in Janet Staiger's words, is as follows:

> The introduction of sound equipment (controlled by the electrical and telephone companies) gave the Morgan and Rockefeller [banking interests] virtual control over the major film companies. This was accomplished indirectly through their control of sound equipment and patents and directly through the number of their key executives on the boards of directors. . . . Writing in the middle of the 1930s depression, they claim: "Whether the movies will regain their former financial success ultimately depends on whether the Morgans and Rockefellers will find it in their best interest in the unceasing change of American life to provide the masses with the type of pictures that alone will induce them to flock to their cinemas." (David Bordwell, Janet Staiger, and Kristin Thompson, *The Classical Hollywood Cinema: Film Style and Mode of Production to* 1960 [New York: Columbia University Press, 1985], p. 315)

Popularized by Lewis Jacobs's *The Rise of the American Film* in 1939, the argument became dogma in film scholarship until Douglas Gomery and others offered alternative models for understanding the modern business enterprise. These revisionist accounts rest more or less on contemporary critiques of finance capitalism that focus on corporate hegemony—in other words, on management rather than ownership. Robert Sklar succinctly summarized the new thinking when he said that it is not so important "who owns the movie companies but who manages them."[31]

Investment bankers exercised financial control of motion-picture companies during the Depression, but failed to revive the sick firms. The revival of the industry occurred only when the majors behaved like modern business enterprises. Alfred D. Chandler, Jr., has defined the modern business enterprise as having two specific characteristics: "It contains many distinct operating units and is managed by a hierarchy of salaried executives."[32] Motion-picture firms took on the first characteristic during the teens and twenties when they integrated both horizontally and vertically. As they grew in size, these firms became managerial, which is to say, they rationalized and organized operations into autonomous departments each headed by a professional manager. The founders ran the companies at first, but over time as death and economic convulsions took their toll, the founders were replaced by salaried executives. When this occurred, motion-picture firms took on the second characteristic of a modern business enterprise. At this point in a firm's development, said Chandler,

> the management of the enterprise became separated from its owner-ship. . . . Unless the owners or representatives of financial houses became full-time career managers within the enterprise itself, they did not have the information, the time, or the experience to play a dominant role in top-level decisions. . . . In time, the part-time own-ers and financiers on the board normally looked on the enterprise in the same way as did ordinary stockholders. It became a source of income and not a business to be managed. Of necessity, they left current operations and future plans to the career administrators. (Alfred D. Chandler, Jr., *The Visible Hand: The Managerial Revolu-tion in American Business* [Cambridge, Mass.: Harvard University Press, 1977], pp. 9–10)

As mentioned earlier, Warner Bros. and Columbia Pictures were still run by their founders. However, both firms qualified as modern business enterprises accord-ing to Chandler's definition because the founders had become full-time career managers, and very successful ones at that.

By the thirties, corporate operations were financed from within. To supple-ment internal financing, companies sometimes turned to commercial banks for lines of credit. Designed to be used for short-term loans, lines of credit evened out the cash flow to meet payrolls, to pay operating expenses, and to acquire raw materials for production, among other things. The amount of the line depended on a company's needs, its fixed debt, and other obligations—in other words, its overall financial health. The point is, commercial banks did not make production loans per se to the major motion-picture companies. Nor did banks review motion-picture projects and pass on their commercial viability or artistic merit. Money for production came out of earned income—and the designated amount depended on the discretion of management.

The Exhibition Market

In 1930 the domestic exhibition market consisted of twenty-three thousand theaters. The most important theaters in the group were the four hundred movie palaces located in cities of fifty thousand or more. According to government census figures, these cities contained 35 percent of the population or around 43 million people and were situated mainly in the large eastern states and in California.[33] (The vast majority of states outside these areas had fewer than ten such houses.) To take advantage of such concentrations of population, "delux-ers," as the palaces were called by the trade, offered an array of inducements, including large seating capacities, comfortable appointments, proximity to public transportation, and air conditioning.

In the largest cities—New York, Chicago, Detroit, and Boston—flagship theaters of Paramount-Publix, Loew's, and Warners combined first-run movies and live entertainment consisting of presentations (comedy or musical skits) and top vaudeville acts, among them such stars as Al Jolson, Eddie Cantor, Maurice Chevalier, George Jessel, Kate Smith, and the Marx Brothers, and such bands as those of Cab Calloway, Duke Ellington, Paul Whiteman, Guy Lombardo, and Fred Waring. This combination policy of film and live acts put the last nail into the coffin of big-time vaudeville and paradoxically forced most deluxers, with the exception of the Radio City Music Hall, the Capitol, and the Roxy in New York, to switch to a pictures-only policy by 1934.[34]

Fully 65 percent of the population, or nearly 80 million people, lived in small towns at the start of the decade. Hundreds of these towns had only a single theater, a house that changed bills as often as three times a week and charged 35 cents tops for a ticket. Individually such theaters yielded rentals of from $7 to $15 per film, but as a group, they could spell the difference between a profit or a loss for a picture.[35]

Theaters were forced to close their doors during the Depression because most of the pictures in release neither drew nor held patronage. It was not long before neighborhood houses and even deluxers started shortening the length of the runs for pictures "without legs." This practice consumed product so fast that even the largest chains had to forage around in the independent field for pictures. Contributing to the product shortage was the panic swing by exhibitors to double features.

Night sports such as miniature golf, baseball, softball, boxing, wrestling, and dog racing also took their toll. Early in the decade, miniature golf provided most of the worry. In 1930 nearly every town between San Diego and Vancouver had at least two miniature golf courses. These places stayed open until well after midnight and charged as little as 25 cents. Night baseball competed for the entertainment dollar throughout the decade. *Variety* estimated that in larger cities, night baseball games cut into receipts only 10–15 percent, but in smaller communities, games affected the box office by as much as 30 percent.[36]

The repeal of Prohibition in 1933 provided business a shot in the arm. As *Variety* explained, repeal drew people out of their homes: "In many cities there had been no downtown life to speak of for the 13 years of the Great Mistake, whereas repeal had the effect of immediately bringing life to hotels, restaurants and other places in such downtown zones where the larger theaters are located."[37]

To rekindle the moviegoing habit, exhibitors experimented with a "galaxy of appetizers" from stage shows to vaudeville. RKO tapped small-time vaudeville by presenting four-act bills along with motion pictures in some of its houses. This policy was credited with keeping the grosses up and the losses down in the circuit up to 1932. RKO played vaudeville out of necessity because of the weakness of the studio's pictures.[38] To attract patrons to its small-town theaters in Pennsylvania, Warners roadshowed band acts complete with lines of chorus girls and comedians for one-to-three-day stands. Paramount-Publix introduced live acts in its theaters in New England, Pennsylvania, and the Southwest. By 1933, however, small-time vaudeville had lost its effectiveness and was dropped from all the circuits.

As a substitute for the lure of vaudeville, exhibitors cut ticket prices. Before the

Depression, the difference in admission price between a first-run affiliated theater and a subsequent-run house owned by an independent was around 20 cents a ticket on the average. When moviegoers tightened their purses, first-run theaters reduced the price of a ticket to within 5 cents of the scale charged by independents. Houses that once charged 25, 30, and 35 cents going into 1931 were charging from 10 to 15 cents by the end of the year. The number of 10-cent houses increased as well to around two thousand by the end of 1931.[39]

But ticket prices could be lowered just so far. As a result, exhibitors resorted to other forms of price cutting, such as double features, two-for-one tickets, half-priced student tickets, free ladies' matinees, and prizes. Prizes were particularly popular with independents who had already instituted double features and were in need of an additional lure. Since offering a third picture would have been impractical, some exhibitors initiated "premium nights" and gave away dishes, hams, and even automobiles as prizes. Testifying to the popularity of such gimmicks, a theater might announce on its marquee, "Tonight Is Dish Night—Also a Feature."[40]

The majors did not follow suit in the belief that such measures would soon lose their effectiveness. And they were right. Within months, dishes, food, and the like had lost their pull. Ever resourceful, independent theaters then offered cash prizes. The first cash prize game to sweep the country was Bank Night, the creation of Charles U. Yeager, a Fox West Coast theater manager. After trying out the scheme in a few small towns in the Rocky Mountains, he copyrighted the game and marketed it to other theaters. *Time* described Bank Night as follows:

> In his lobby a theatre owner places a large book. Persons who wish to do so may enter their names in the book opposite numbers corresponding to which the box office keeps a book of tickets. On Bank Night, usually Monday, when receipts are normally lowest, the tickets are placed in a drum on the stage. One number is drawn from the drum and announced. If the person whose name is entered for that number in the lobby book appears on the stage within a specified time, usually three minutes, he receives a cash prize of, say, $150. ("Bank Night," 3 February 1936, pp. 57–58)

Since Bank Night could increase box-office receipts several fold, more than four thousand theaters adopted the game by 1936. Bank Night and kindred contests, such as Prosperity Night, Movie Sweepstakes, and Treasury Night, were used throughout the decade and were generally believed to have kept more theaters open during the Depression than any other device.[41]

The exhibition scheme that made the greatest impact on the industry was double features. Showing two pictures for the price of one was an old industry practice. As *Variety* put it, "every time theatre figures have lagged the two-for-one has bobbed up in spots." However, the shortage of talking pictures during the conversion to sound and the higher rentals they commanded would spell the death of the practice, predicted *Variety* in 1929. But the trade paper soon did an about-face: "Almost down and out six months ago, double features are suddenly staging a strong comeback. Houses everywhere, including important first runs in chains, are leaning toward two talkers for the price of one." Double features established a foothold in New England in 1930. By the middle of 1932, six thousand of the fourteen thousand theaters then operating, or 40 percent, had adopted the practice. In some situations, independents had combined a talkie or a silent produced by an independent producer with a sound picture produced by a major. In highly competitive situations, exhibitors even resorted to triple features.[42]

The economic rationale of double featuring was simple enough. In essence, indies used the practice to break down the barriers of booking protection, which is to say, excessive clearances enjoyed by first-run theaters. Indies reasoned that if they could not present hit pictures in a timely manner to their patrons, they would offer quantity instead. Legally, a distributor could do nothing to stop them. Because double features would inevitably break open the market for independent producers, the MPPDA outlawed the practice in drafting its version of the NRA Code of Fair Competition. But independent producers and exhibitors fought back and convinced the NRA to legalize dual billing in August 1934, nearly one year after the industry adopted the Code. *Variety* called the decision "the Blue Eagle's first truly revolutionary decree for filmdom."[43] By then, nearly every theater in competitive situations—the markets that generated the bulk of the domestic box-office gross—had fallen into line.

And by then, the biggest users of double bills were the affiliated theaters. There were several reasons for this. The widespread acceptance of double bills made it awkward for a first-run house without a stage show to charge a higher ticket price for a single feature than a subsequent-run theater offering a double bill. Those theaters that still relied on stage shows found talent more expensive and increasingly hard to find in the waning days of vaudeville. And lastly, the overall reduction in quality of pictures made it necessary to offer "two pictures, even of poor quality . . . to satisfy a bargain-hunting public."[44] Thus, in dealing with this practice during the days of the NRA, the majors adopted an anomalous position of fighting a policy that made a favorable impact on their own box office.

Legalizing double features had the direct effect of doubling the demand for product. Had the NRA mandated a single-feature policy, the eight majors could have easily satisfied the production demands of the market, even for theaters that changed bills three times a week. But double features doubled the demand: *Variety* estimated that a minimum of seven hundred features were needed each year.[45] Since the production facilities and talent even of the majors limited the number of pictures they could produce, a gap existed between supply and demand, which was quickly filled by Poverty Row.

Hollywood had always produced a full range of pictures in various price brackets. Budgets depended on the basic ingredients of the picture—the underlying property, the stars, the director, and the physical requirements, among other factors. Low-budget pictures often served as vehicles to break in young actors, new writers, and novice directors. In reacting to the new market conditions, studios divided production more or less into two groups—class A and class B—and formed special production units to handle the lower grade product. Class-B pictures cost anywhere from $50,000 to more than $200,000 to produce, whereas the average class-A picture cost roughly $400,000.[46] Producing more pictures did not necessarily generate more revenue for the simple reason that exhibitors could not afford to rent two expensive pictures for each double bill. The majors therefore used a differential pricing policy—flat fees for class-B features and percentages for class-A pictures. Although flat fees were low out of necessity, producers could predict with great accuracy the amount of revenues B features could generate and so could scale production costs accordingly.

By the end of the decade, double features had become an institution, prevailing either all or part of the week in an estimated 60 percent of the nation's seventeen thousand theaters. The practice, said Bosley Crowther, created "one of the most prolonged disputes ever to disturb the American public." Women's clubs, parent-teacher organizations, and the education establishment complained that double bills were too long for children, that they offered too much excitement for little ones, and that they were terribly hard on youngsters' eyes. No one was willing to defend the double features. Why, then, did the practice persist? As *Variety* explained it, bitter experience had shown exhibitors that so long as one of them in a community offered two pictures for the price of one, double-featuring would persist in that community.[47]

The Recovery

The U.S. Department of Commerce indicated that the recreation and amusement industries started to revive in 1934, although nearly all their employment, payroll, and earnings figures were still below 1929 levels. Motion pictures, the last business to feel the pinch of the Depression, was "in the vanguard of industries emerging the earliest," said *Variety.* "Thus, although severely struck when it was hit, the picture industry was bedridden a much shorter spell than many other members of big business." Box-office receipts and theater admissions rebounded in 1934, and one thousand theaters were said to have reopened. During 1935, Paramount and Fox had undergone reorganization and were clear of debts, although RKO was not stabilized until 1940. In 1936, Universal, after selling off the last of its theaters, came out of receivership. The majors had survived the Depression intact.[48]

The media attributed the turnaround to quality pictures that had struck the public's fancy. The *Magazine of Wall Street,* for example, stated that as a result of the Legion of Decency's drive for cleaner pictures in 1934, "the industry awoke to the fact that the public was much more interested in quality films which neither offended its taste or intelligence."[49] The type of picture the magazine referred to was the prestige picture—a big-budget film, based typically on a popular novel, a standard classic, a stage success, or an opera. Examples of such pictures would be Columbia's ONE NIGHT OF LOVE (1934), MGM's DINNER AT EIGHT (1933), RKO's LITTLE WOMEN (1933), MGM's DAVID COPPERFIELD (1935), and Warners' A MIDSUMMER NIGHT'S DREAM (1935).

The *Magazine of Wall Street* also reported that in 1936, motion-picture patronage "now equals within a few thousand a week its peak of six or seven years ago when over 100,000,000 persons per week pushed their silver across the glass slides of the box offices, and there is little competition on the horizon." The magazine grossly exaggerated the number of weekly admissions. Not even the film industry itself ballyhooed such inflated figures. The *Film Daily Yearbook,* for example, stated that average weekly attendance rose from 60 million in 1933 to 70 million in 1934, to 80 million in 1935, and to 88 million in 1936. However, a Gallup poll in 1940 indicated that weekly attendance at films had been averaging only

Katharine Hepburn, Joan Bennett, Frances Dee, and Jean Parker in LITTLE WOMEN *(RKO, 1933), directed by George Cukor.*

around 54 million. Regardless of the actual figures, a turnaround of sorts did occur. Box-office receipts rose steadily after 1934. Motion-picture stocks, led by Loew's, Paramount, and Warner Bros., "assumed something like their old positions as trading favorites," said *Variety*. And 20th Century–Fox, Loew's, and Paramount, among other companies, started earning hefty profits, although no company earned in one year as much as it had in 1930.[50]

Widespread unemployment continued throughout the decade: by 1937, an estimated 7 million workers were still without jobs, and of those in the work force, 60 million received less than $1,000 per year.[51] Since motion pictures were not luxuries, they did not depend on "great general prosperity for profitable operation." It took America's entry into World War II to break the back of the Depression, and then conditions on the home front created the best market Hollywood had ever seen.

Foreign Films and Foreign Markets

Prior to 1930, foreign markets generated 30–50 percent of a picture's worldwide gross. Of this gross, nearly half came from English-speaking countries, mainly Great Britain. During the Depression the foreign take fell to around 20 percent, but by mid decade the percentage rebounded to normal levels. Hollywood's commanding position in world markets is documented by the following figures: by 1930, Hollywood produced 75–80 percent of all the pictures shown throughout the world, which pictures collected about $200 million in film rentals out of a total annual world gross of $275 million.[52]

The film industry's entry into the principal overseas markets began in earnest after World War I. For a crucial five years in the postwar period, European nations devoted their limited capital and purchasing power to rebuilding their shattered economies; little was left to rehabilitate their home film industries.[53] Hollywood producers capitalized on at least three built-in, natural advantages over their foreign competitors. First, they utilized the natural scenery of the Pacific Coast to produce the tremendously popular Westerns and other action films. Second, they situated their studios in a climate that enabled work to continue year-round. Third, they functioned in a large domestic market with a high standard of living that ensured large revenues. In addition, American firms controlled the domestic market through theater ownership, which meant that European producers could not hope to obtain distribution except for an exceptional film.

European governments responded to these barriers to entry by establishing barriers of their own to protect their domestic film industries. Germany was the first European nation to react by instituting a contingent act in 1925. Designed to prevent a deluge of American films from overwhelming national producers, the law stipulated that for every film produced in Germany, a contingent, or permit, would be issued to its distributor to import and release a foreign (read "American") film of equal length. In practice, the act was designed to force American companies either to become producers of German films or to invest in German production. Rather than protecting the home film industry, measures such as this merely encouraged the production of cheap, low-quality pictures, which damaged the reputations of European producers.

Charles Laughton and Binnie Barnes in The Private Life of Henry VIII *(UA, 1933).*

The talkies impeded foreign distribution at first, since spoken dialogue seemingly introduced an impenetrable language barrier. Moreover, theaters overseas were slow to convert to sound. To service these theaters, American distributors used subtitling. To service theaters wired for sound, Hollywood produced foreign-language versions of its latest releases using native casts. Paramount established a studio in Joinville, France, outside Paris, to produce versions of its films in French, German, and Italian. In the days of silents, said *Variety,* any picture could be retitled for all foreign markets for $10,000; in 1930 the cost of making multilinguals cost a minimum of $70,000 for each language.

Dubbing soon became the accepted practice in international trade. But not without a fight. Claiming that dubbed pictures were cheap to produce and hence constituted unfair competition, France and Germany passed laws barring films dubbed outside their borders. American film companies therefore constructed dubbing studios in each of these countries. Not only were dubbed releases cheaper to produce than foreign-language versions, but they also retained the commercial value of the Hollywood stars. The combination of these factors restored foreign distribution to its former profit levels. By the mid thirties, American films were dubbed into practically all languages of the world. Said *Variety,* "Europeans accept them easily and without argument because dubbing has made such exceptional strides technically that flaws are the exception rather than the rule today. Thus, auditors frequently can't tell the difference between dubbed and straight screened product."[54]

As always, European films faced many obstacles breaking into the American market. They had to outperform Hollywood's best product, for one thing. For another, they had to wedge their way into the key theater chains—chains that were controlled by the majors' distributors and were well supplied with product as a result of reciprocal booking arrangements. To secure a playdate in a deluxe house, a foreign film had to be not only good but a smash hit. For these reasons, few foreign films gained access to the mainstream exhibition market.

During the 1930s, only around forty theaters in the United States played foreign films exclusively; an additional two hundred theaters played imports on occasion. German imports made the strongest impact on the foreign-language market. In 1931, *Variety* reported that Loew's, Publix, and RKO played German films one day a week in some of their neighborhood houses in metropolitan New York. Three German companies, UFA, Tobis, and Capital, had distribution offices in New York and handled around seventy pictures a year as a group. Their pictures played in German-speaking neighborhoods of New York, Milwaukee, and a few other cities. But demand for such pictures dropped when Hitler came to power in 1933. After the Nazis nationalized the German film industry, the Reich offered pictures to American exhibitors at no cost up front, just a percentage of the take, but only a half dozen or so German-language houses accepted the offer.[55]

Demand for French films hardly existed in the American market during the Depression, when only about a dozen pictures a year were imported. Interest picked up later in the decade, but only in Manhattan, which had six thriving art houses. A small market existed for Spanish-language pictures in Texas and California. These pictures, plus an occasional Russian film, constituted the foreign-language film market in the United States.

Only Great Britain had the ability to make films suitable for the American market. Most of the credit for this achievement goes to Alexander Korda. Korda's THE PRIVATE LIFE OF HENRY VIII premiered at the Radio City Music Hall on 12 October 1933 and grossed a respectable $500,000 in the United States; Charles Laughton won an Academy Award playing the title role; and Korda proved to the world that a British film could match the best that America could produce in spectacle and lavishness. Korda, a Hungarian, had been producing quota quickies in England for Paramount. On the basis of his SERVICE FOR LADIES (U.S. title: RESERVED FOR LADIES), United Artists awarded him a two-picture distribution contract. Korda's second UA picture, CATHERINE THE GREAT (1934), was another hit and earned Korda a long-term contract with United Artists and a partnership in the company in 1935.

Korda was soon heralded as the man who single-handedly put the British film industry on its feet. Production companies mushroomed after 1934, lured into existence by the prospect of making another HENRY VIII. Hoping to cash in on the American market, Gaumont British opened a sales office in New York in 1934. J. Arthur Rank, the prominent British film magnate, became a partner in Universal Pictures in 1936 when J. Cheever Cowdin bought out Carl Laemmle. Parliament tried to give British pictures a boost in this country by placing a reciprocity clause in the new Quota Law of 1938 relieving American companies of the obligation of distributing British films in Great Britain if they distributed British films in the United States.[56]

United Artists became a principal distributor of British pictures in the United States. UA was solely a distributor and did not finance films; therefore, the company did not have to give top priority to its own product. UA was always in search of quality product from anywhere to include on its roster. On the strength of his UA contract, Korda's London Films Ltd. became the leading motion-picture company in Great Britain by 1937. Among the films Korda released through UA were René Clair's THE GHOST GOES WEST (1935) and two H. G. Wells fantasies, William Cameron Menzies's THINGS TO COME (1936) and Lothar Mendes's THE MAN WHO COULD WORK MIRACLES (1937); in addition, UA released two films starring Vivien Leigh, DARK JOURNEY and STORM IN A TEACUP (both 1937), which were produced by Victor Saville.

As hostilities spread in Europe and in the Orient, revenues from foreign markets declined. Before the Nazis came to power, the German film industry had been second to the United States in prestige and sales in the major European markets. With the exception of the United States, no other country had an international film market to speak of. American film imports had been dropping steadily in Germany, from more than two hundred in 1929 to fifty in 1932. By 1936, Germany virtually ceased to exist as an outlet for American films. The Reich Film Law of 1934 had instituted rigid censorship. The German mark was frozen, and with the passing of the Enabling Act in 1936, all imported films had to be "German" in character, which meant they had to be produced, directed, and performed by persons of Aryan descent. In 1937 the German film industry was nationalized and placed under the supervision of Minister of Propaganda and Public Enlightenment Joseph Goebbels. American distributors had no choice but to leave the country.[57]

Hollywood faced similar obstacles in Italy, but with a few special twists. For example, Mussolini prohibited American film companies from operating distribution subsidiaries; all imports had to be handled by a government film monopoly called Ente Nazionale Industria Cinematografica. This was something new; here, for the first time, a foreign government had gone into the business of distributing foreign and domestic pictures for profit. Although the monopoly was established in 1938, Italy had laid the groundwork for it ten years earlier by instituting quota laws, dubbing restrictions, and currency restrictions to bleed, antagonize, and alienate American film companies. American companies did only a token amount of business in Italy after 1938. When the United States entered the war, Hollywood severed all relations with the country.

Meanwhile, American film distributors had withdrawn from Spain following the outbreak of civil war in 1936, from the Far East in the wake of Japanese expansion in 1938, and from Central Europe following the *Anschluss* in 1938. After England declared war on Germany in September 1939 and while Britain's theaters remained boarded up during the Nazis bombings of London and other English cities, Hollywood saw its overseas market virtually disappear.[58]

The Paramount *Case*

The industry's monopolistic trade practices remained in force without significant alteration after the demise of the NRA. But the debate over these practices continued unabated and culminated in the historic antitrust case *United States* v. *Paramount et al.* The suit was filed personally by trustbuster Thurman Arnold, the chief of the Department of Justice's Antitrust Division, on 20 July 1938. The government charged the majors with combining and conspiring to restrain trade unreasonably and to monopolize the production, distribution, and exhibition of motion pictures. The bill of particulars contained charges that were nearly identical to those heard during the days of the NRA. So were the remedies: the government's petition asked for the divorcement of production from exhibition, the elimination of block booking, the abolition of unfair clearance, and the quashing of many other producer-distributor trade practices.

The case was scheduled for trial in the Southern District Court of New York in June 1940, but after a period of negotiation, the government entered an amended complaint providing for the entry of a consent decree that was to run for three years. The majors again succeeded in warding off an attack on their industrial structure. During the war, the majors earned record profits. When the case was finally adjudicated in 1945, the decision was appealed all the way to the Supreme Court. In 1948, when the Court handed down its decision, which went against the defendants, the remedies were too little, too late, to help the supposed beneficiary of the case—the independent exhibitor. An era of motion-picture history had ended and, along with it, a place for the small businessman.

3

The Production Code
and the Hays Office

Richard Maltby

*O*n 24 August 1939, Joseph Breen, the director of the Production Code
Administration (PCA), wrote to Harry Cohn about the draft script for a
remake of THE FRONT PAGE, then called THE BIGGER THEY ARE. With a few
exceptions, he noted, the script "appears to be acceptable under the provisions
of the Production Code and reasonably free from the suggestion of difficulty at
the hands of political censor boards." The exceptions included a warning that the
British Board of Film Censors "will not approve any motion picture, in which any
of the characters are, even suggestively, insane," and advice that the studio
should shoot a "protection shot" of a gallows scene, since American states and
foreign countries that did not have capital punishment "almost invariably
deleted" such scenes. "Political" censor boards (as municipal, state, and foreign
censorship authorities were always described) were also likely to delete "the talk
about 'production for use only,' and 'doing away with the profit system.' " On his
own behalf, Breen merely wanted the word "lousy" eliminated, together with
any suggestion that the character of Mollie Malloy was a prostitute. In a separate
letter, Breen also noted that the script "suggests to our minds the possibility that
your story may carry an objectionable reflection on newspapers . . . and as such,
give serious offense to persons engaged in that profession."

Five days later, Breen met with producer Sam Briskin and director Howard
Hawks, and amiably resolved the difficulties Breen had raised: the character of
Earl Williams "will not be played as an insane man, but rather as a confused
soul"; the "drunken newspapermen will be cut out of the story entirely." The
smooth passage of HIS GIRL FRIDAY through the machinery of the Production
Code was unremarkable; Breen and his officials were simply checking that the
rough edges had been polished off the movie so that it would not snag on the
sensibilities of anyone, particularly anyone of influence, who might see it. The
studio knew the rules: leaving a word like "lousy" (the British always deleted
it) or a phrase like "a common streetwalker" in the script was little more than
carelessness on the writer's part. All the celebrated improvisation that went on
around Hawks's set was similarly circumscribed by a set of conventions that
were by 1939 completely assimilated within Hollywood's system of production.
The one issue about which HIS GIRL FRIDAY did cause concern was not to do

with the Code as such but with a question of "industry policy." Earlier in the decade, the American Newspaper Publishers Association and the American Society of Newspaper Editors had been much exercised by the movies' representation of their profession. The industry's own trade association, the Motion Picture Producers and Distributors of America (MPPDA, commonly called the Hays Office), was as concerned not to antagonize pressure groups and opinion makers as it was to anticipate, through "self-regulation," the likely actions of political censors.

HIS GIRL FRIDAY ran the risk of antagonizing newspapermen for two reasons. Its source, THE FRONT PAGE, had been one of the principal causes of upset when Howard Hughes had first filmed it in 1931, and Columbia had thoroughly antagonized the Washington press corps, as well as the Senate, by portraying them as "cynical but lovable drunkards" who "winked their eyes at political corruption" in MR. SMITH GOES TO WASHINGTON, released in October 1939. The MPPDA's president, Will Hays, had warned Breen of "the trouble that would flow" Columbia's way, were they to repeat the offense so soon. In the event, the newspapermen took the joke, but if MPPDA officials now seem to have been humorless, they were merely doing what they were there for—safeguarding the industry against organized criticism, wherever it might come from.[1]

The Code is best known for the trivia of its requirements that, for instance, married couples sleep in single beds. It has also been held responsible for the trivialization of American movies and blamed for Hollywood's timidity and lack of realism. These charges both overestimate and underestimate its influence. The Code contributed significantly to Hollywood's avoidance of contentious subject matter, but it did so as the instrument of an agreed industry-wide policy, not as the originating source of that policy. On the other hand, within its sphere of influence, it was a determining force on the construction of narrative and the delineation of character in every studio-produced film after 1931. Public arguments about the Code's application—over Clark Gable's last line in GONE WITH THE WIND, for example—have themselves tended to be over trivia and have therefore supported claims that the Code was a trivializing document. The agreements that underlay the Code, amounting to a consensus over what constituted appropriate entertainment for an undifferentiated mass audience in America and, by default, the rest of the world, have received less attention. That consensus embraced the major companies and civic and governmental organizations that either took responsibility or expressed concern for the moral wellbeing of cinema audiences in the United States and elsewhere. Hollywood's married movie stars slept in single beds to meet a requirement of the British Board of Film Censors.

As clearly as a comparison of LITTLE CAESAR and ANGELS WITH DIRTY FACES or of BLONDE VENUS and STELLA DALLAS, a comparison of THE FRONT PAGE and HIS GIRL FRIDAY charts the distance between films of the early and late 1930s: a political satire set in the "mythical kingdom" of Chicago, in which an audience who read the tabloids would have no difficulty recognizing the burlesque of Mayor "Big Bill" Thompson, was transformed into a romantic comedy of remarriage that could take place nowhere else except in the mythical kingdom of Hollywood—a comedy that was, by common critical consent, an improvement on the original. The history of Hollywood in the 1930s has often been characterized as having two distinct phases: Robert Sklar's terminology of "the Golden Age of Turbulence" and "the Golden Age of Order" remains the most elegant and concise expression of this account.

Until recently, histories of the Production Code have largely relied on the "official" descriptions of its development provided by Will Hays in his *Memoirs* and Raymond Moley in his laudatory account *The Hays Office*. Maintaining that despite the best intentions of the MPPDA and the producers, the Code was not effectively enforced in the early 1930s, Moley asserted that "the years 1930–1933 passed without a notable improvement in the quality of pictures and without the elimination of those objectionable themes and treatments which had brought about the creation and adoption of the Code." Although Hays suggested that "it would be oversimplification to say that the industry adopted a moral code and then promptly forgot it until a rearoused public threatened a boycott," he conceded that "as the steady pull-down of external forces went on" in 1932–1933, movie content "gradually took a turn for the worse." Their version of events adheres to the requirements of a familiar early Depression Hollywood story, in which the industry appears as a fallen woman, led by economic hardship into immoral behavior and a fall from grace. Being a Hollywood story, there is a happy ending when Hollywood, the fallen woman, is rescued from sin and federal censorship by virtuous hero Joe Breen riding at the head of the Catholic Legion of Decency. The culmination of the Legion's campaign against immoral movies, the July 1934 agreement between the MPPDA and the Roman Catholic hierarchy to fully implement the Production Code, is regarded in these "official" accounts as a watershed separating the two halves of the decade.[2]

Most subsequent histories of the period have reiterated the "official" account without fully recognizing the extent to which Hays and Moley chose to emphasize the success of the industry's 1934 "reformation" by accepting the most conservative criticisms of earlier films. Historians have, for instance, noted the existence of a vocal campaign against the purported moral viciousness of Hollywood movies, and tended to assume that Hollywood movies of the early 1930s must have been morally vicious, or at least socially and culturally disruptive. Edward Buscombe wrote,

> Suppose for the sake of argument that scarcely any Hollywood films of the 1930s were actively hostile to capitalism in a direct political sense. One could nevertheless make a case for saying that Hollywood was in certain ways strongly subversive of the dominant sexual ideology. How else can one explain the outrage of groups such as the League [*sic*] of Decency and Hollywood's attempts to censor itself through the adoption of the Motion Picture Production Code? ("Bread and Circuses: Economics and the Cinema," in Patricia Mellencamp and Philip Rosen, eds., *Cinema Histories, Cinema Practices* [Los Angeles: American Film Institute, 1984], p. 8)

The dominant critical paradigm has accepted and inverted the perspective of contemporary moral reformers, valorizing as subversive, for instance, what reviewers at that time denounced as "the fashion for romanticizing gangsters." In many accounts, such assumptions are confirmed by a critical interpretation of around twenty-five movies—roughly one percent of Hollywood's total output of feature films during the period 1930–1934—taken to be representative of

Hollywood's output during the early 1930s. With little justification offered for the particular selection beyond its familiarity, "pre-Code" Hollywood is represented by "Some Anarcho-Nihilist Laff Riots" featuring the Marx Brothers, the subversion of dominant sexual ideology by Mae West and Marlene Dietrich, Warners' social-conscience films, and a trio of gangster movies. The classical Hollywood narrative of *The Hays Office* is read against the grain, so that the happy ending of July 1934 is understood ironically as an instance of repressive closure.[3]

The account offered here revises this history in a number of respects. In suggesting that the issues and motivations behind "self-regulation" were more complex and were determined more by economic considerations than by matters of film content, it also argues that the events of July 1934 are best seen not as the industry's reaction to a more or less spontaneous outburst of moral protest backed by economic sanction, but as the culmination of a lengthy process of negotiation within the industry and between its representatives and those speaking with the voices of cultural authority. The differences between movies made in the early 1930s and those made later in the decade are undeniable, but the change was gradual rather than cataclysmic, the negotiation, by experiment and expedient, of a system of conventional representation that was constructed in the first half of the decade and maintained in the second. Only one of that system's two governing principles was stated in the Production Code itself: "No picture shall be produced which will lower the moral standards of those who see it." This was the law by which a strict moral accountancy was imposed on Hollywood's plots. Its antithesis, which Ruth Vasey has aptly called "the principle of deniability," was a particular kind of ambiguity, a textual indeterminacy that shifted the responsibility for determining what the movie's content was away from the producer to the individual spectator.[4]

As Lea Jacobs has argued, under the Code "offensive ideas could survive at the price of an instability of meaning . . . there was constant negotiation about how explicit films could be and by what means (through the image, sound, language) offensive ideas could find representation." HIS GIRL FRIDAY has a typical instance when Earl Williams is reported as having shot his psychiatrist "right in the classified ads"—an undistinguished example of the way in which the Code "forced writers not only to be cleaner but also to be cleverer." The rationale for this practice, inscribed in MPPDA policy as early as 1927, was articulated by Colonel Jason S. Joy, the director of the Studio Relations Committee (SRC, precursor to the PCA). Joy recognized that if the Code was to remain effective, it had to allow the studios to develop a system of representational conventions "from which conclusions might be drawn by the sophisticated mind, but which would mean nothing to the unsophisticated and inexperienced."[5]

Like other Hollywood conventions, the Production Code was one of several substitutes for detailed audience research. Having chosen not to differentiate its product through a ratings system, the industry had to construct movies for an undifferentiated audience. While the Code was written under the assumption that spectators were only passive receivers of texts, the texts themselves were, out of the straightforward economic logic of what Umberto Eco has called "the heavy industry of dreams in a capitalistic society," constructed to accommodate, rather than predetermine, their audiences' reactions. In its practical application, the Code was the mechanism by which this multiplicity of viewing positions was achieved. Once the limits of explicit "sophistication" had been established, the production industry had to find ways of appealing to both "innocent" and "sophisticated" sensibilities in the same object without transgressing the boundaries of public acceptability. This involved devising systems and codes of representation in which "innocence" was inscribed into the text while "sophisticated" viewers were able to "read into" movies whatever meanings they were pleased to find, so long as producers could use the Production Code to deny that they had put them there. Much of the work of self-regulation lay in the maintenance of this system of conventions, and as such, it operated, however perversely, as an enabling mechanism at the same time that it was a repressive one.[6]

Producers, however, saw the Code predominantly as an instrument of restraint. Passing on "another one of those silly letters from the Breen office" to producer Robert Lord in 1937, Warner Bros. head of production Hal Wallis observed, "they seem to be getting worse and worse and the only thing you can do is to have them come over for a meeting and unsell them on a lot of these ridiculous demands." But though the Code existed to control the content of movies, the cultural anxieties that had brought it into being were about more fundamental social issues than a few bawdy Mae West jokes, the length of a hemline, or the condoning of sin in an "unmoral" ending. What the Code was, what it did, and why it came into existence can only be partially understood by thinking of it in terms of its effects on production or, indeed, by assuming that the social crisis over cinematic representation in the early 1930s was caused by the content of motion pictures. The institution of censorship in Hollywood was not primarily about controlling the content of movies at the level of forbidden words or actions or inhibiting the freedom of expression of individual producers. Rather, it was about the cultural function of entertainment and the possession of cultural power.[7]

The Origins of the Code

Debates about the censorship of popular culture have always been debates about the social control of its audiences. Although these debates have focused on the content or structure of the entertainment form, their real concern has been with its effects on consumers and with underlying issues of class and cultural power. From amusement parks to rock 'n' roll, different sites and forms of popular cultural expression in the twentieth century have derived their innovative energies from culturally and socially disreputable sources, but they have also operated under systems of convention and regulation that keep contained the subversive potential of their origins and that ensure they endorse, rather than challenge, the existing distribution of social, political, and economic power. The issue has seldom been expressed in such overt terms: more commonly, it has been articulated as an anxiety about the effects of entertainment on children, and specifically on the criminal behavior of adolescent males and the sexual behavior of adolescent females. Partially concealed by the concern for youth has been a deeper, class-based anxiety about the extent to which the sites of entertainment provide opportunities for the heterogeneous mixing of classes.

Since the first motion-picture censorship ordinance was introduced in Chicago in 1907, public debate has revolved around the question of whether the motion-picture industry was morally fit to control the manufacture of its own products. The terms of this debate were established by Progressive reformers who regarded "commercialized amusements" as an ameliorated form of "commercialized vice" rather than an acceptable mode of "recreation." After 1921, state censorship, declared constitutional by the Supreme Court in 1915, operated in seven of the forty-eight states. In addition, from Vermont villages to Chicago, municipal authorities operated local censor boards, usually administered by the police with varying degrees of rigor, predictability, and frequency. More than 60 percent of domestic sales, together with virtually the entire foreign market, were made in territories under "political censorship." State censorship boards exerted an essentially negative power to cut or ban films; as both the industry and its critics acknowledged, they could not positively influence the quality of Hollywood production. By its nature, political censorship was concerned with what happened at the site of exhibition, not the site of production. Exhibitors often readily acquiesced in the practice of censorship as a means of ensuring that movies offended as few of their community's cultural and legislative leadership as possible and that their commercial operations might thereby continue unhindered. Exhibitor organizations had on a number of occasions supported the establishment of censorship boards as the best means of protecting their commercial interests.[8]

Attitudes toward censorship constituted only one among several issues that separated the interests of exhibitors and those of producer-distributor combines. Like most industries, the American film business was structured by a basic antagonism between manufacturers and retailers, exacerbated since the late 1910s by the emergence of a production-distribution oligopoly that dictated business terms to independent theater owners. The MPPDA was established in 1922 to safeguard the political interests of the emerging oligopoly, and while censorship and the regulation of content was an important aspect of its work, the Association's central concern was with the threat of legislation or court action to impose a strict application of the antitrust laws to the industry. The Association pursued policies of industrial self-regulation not only in regard to film content but also in matters of arbitration, intra-industry relations, and negotiations with the government, attaching the movies to the "associative state" fostered by Herbert Hoover's Department of Commerce.

Hays presented the MPPDA as an innovative trade association at the forefront of corporate organizational development, largely responsible for the industry's maturation into respectability, standardizing trade practices and stabilizing the relationship between distributors and small exhibitors through film boards of trade, arbitration, and the standard exhibition contract. The establishment of "the highest possible moral and artistic standards of motion picture production" was in one sense simply an extension of this practice, but it also implicitly accepted that "pure" entertainment—amusement that was not harmful to its consumer—was a commodity comparable to the pure meat guaranteed by the Food and Drug Administration. For all industry parties, issues of oligopoly control and trade practice were much more important than censorship. But questions of censorship were of greater public interest, and could also be resolved at less economic risk to the majors. These factors encouraged the MPPDA to displace disputes over the industry's distribution of profits onto another arena—quite literally, from the economic base to the ideological superstructure of movie content.[9]

As Lary May has suggested, Hays's strategy was to transfer "the old moral guardianship of the small city and town to the movie corporations." In constructing affiliations with nationally federated civic, religious, and educational organizations, Hays had aimed to make "this important portion of public opinion a friendly rather than a hostile critic of pictures" and to contain the threat posed by their lobbying power. There was, however, no dispute over the need to regulate entertainment and relatively little dispute during the 1920s over the standards by which it should be regulated. The question was rather who possessed the appropriate authority to police the ideological apparatus of representation. Although the MPPDA succeeded in preventing the spread of state censorship after 1922, its attempts to abolish existing boards failed, so that its mechanisms for self-regulation became an additional, rather than a replacement, structure.[10]

In 1924, Hays established a mechanism for vetting source material—called "the Formula"—in order "to exercise every possible care that only books or plays which are of the right type are used for screen presentation." In 1927 the Association published a code to govern production, administered by its Studio Relations Committee (SRC) in Hollywood. The "Don'ts and Be Carefuls," as this code was familiarly known, was compiled by a committee chaired by Irving Thalberg and synthesized the restrictions and eliminations applied by state and foreign censors. Although the Association was always careful to differentiate the "self-regulation" of its advisory activities from "political censorship," Hays recognized that the industry could gain autonomy over production only by voluntarily accepting the standards that external agencies would in any event impose on them.[11]

The extent to which any of these procedures were effective in regulating production is a matter of debate, but it is an oversimplification to suggest, as many accounts do, that so long as the MPPDA had no punitive sanctions, producers blithely ignored their suggestions. Films were modified after production but before release in order to assuage the concerns of civic, religious, or manufacturing interests. Until the publication of the Production Code in 1930, however, Jason Joy had only an advisory function, and the principal weapon in his persuasive armory was an economic one: the savings that would accrue to production companies if they avoided filming material they would be unable to use. Although producers had to gauge the costs and disruptiveness of censorship against the possibility of additional profit coming from the use of censorable material, they were less concerned about the principle of censorship than they were about the limitation of their legal liability for shaping public sentiment. "We do not create the types of entertainment," argued Thalberg, their most articulate spokesperson, "we merely present them." Thalberg viewed entertainment as a form of cultural barometer, in which "people see . . . a reflection of their own average thoughts and attitudes. If the reflection is much lower or much higher than their own plane they reject it." People, he insisted, "influence pictures far more than pictures influence people." However, in denying their responsibility for creating public taste, producers surrendered much of the ground over which the cultural function of movies was debated by the press, religious and civic groups, and legislators.[12]

Producers saw the need for a new code in the complexities of sound

Will H. Hays, president of the Motion Picture Producers and Distributors of America. Although Variety *called him "the czar of all the rushes," in practice the influence Hays possessed came from his skills as a negotiator and an expert in public relations.*

production. Silent film had been easily altered by local censors, regional distributors, or even individual exhibitors. Early sound technology drastically restricted this malleability, since any subsequent editing of a print would destroy synchronization. Accepting the imperatives of Joy's economic arguments, producers began to demand something firmer than advice from the SRC, but at the same time, they wanted to establish a more permissive code for sound, since, as Thalberg argued, with dialogue characters could "delicately" discuss subjects "the silent picture was forced to shun."[13] Such desires to accommodate the movies to the Broadway of Elmer Rice and Eugene O'Neill ran counter to the increasing hostility among vocal sections of the middle class toward the Broadway of Earl Carroll's *Vanities* and Mae West. An increasingly insecure Protestant provincial middle class sought to defend its cultural hegemony from the incursions of a modernist, metropolitan culture that the provincials regarded as alien—a word that was often, but not always, a synonym for Jewish. With the roadhouse and the dance hall, the movie theater was one site at which they felt their values and their children endangered by a newer, urban, immigrant, largely Jewish and Catholic culture. The movies were particularly threatening both because they were apparently owned by aliens and because their advertising (which was all many of their critics saw of them) suggested that their permissive representations of sex and violence were designed to cater to the baser instincts of "morons," a term widely used to refer indirectly to the immigrant working class. Combining hostility to monopoly with a barely concealed anti-Semitism, provincial Protestantism saw movies threaten the ability of small communities to exercise control over the cultural influences they tolerated.[14]

It was in 1929 that Hollywood brought Broadway to Main Street: seventy-five hundred theaters (more than 50 percent of the total) were wired for sound during the year. Throughout the 1920s, Broadway had been castigated for its "realism," particularly in its representation of sexual mores. Now its dubious dialogue and "sophisticated" plot material was playing on Main Street for the children to see. In April 1929 the *Washington Star* told producers titles such as UNDERWORLD, SYNTHETIC SIN, and OUR DANCING DAUGHTERS provoked censorship. If the problem were "killed at the source, in the studios," calls for censorship would vanish. In October, reviewing Paramount's backstage melodrama APPLAUSE, MPPDA Secretary Carl Milliken suggested that "the folks who represent the intelligentsia in the country towns and small cities are not yet prepared to view with approval a long series of scenes including close-ups which show the heroine clad only in breechclout and brassiere."[15]

In the fall of 1929 the MPPDA was the subject of heavy criticism for reasons only tangentially related to movie content. Its relationship with the federal government had been strained by the mergers and theater buying among the major companies and by their "steady policy of aggrandizement, discrimination and exclusion" in dealing with independent exhibitors. At the same time, the stability of the public relations edifice Hays had constructed during the preceding seven years was threatened by the Association's failure to construct a cooperative relationship with the Protestant churches comparable to the one they enjoyed with the International Federation of Catholic Alumnae (IFCA). In June 1929 the liberal Episcopalian journal *The Churchman* accused Hays of being selected by "shrewd Hebrews . . . as a smoke screen to mask their meretricious methods," and asserted that "the motion picture industry is concerned not at all about standards either of taste or morals. . . . The only thing that the industry is interested in cleaning up is box-office revenue by playing to the tabloid mind."[16]

The Churchman alleged that the Association had "retained" prominent figures in civic, educational, and religious organizations to use their influence "to see to it that nothing [was] done to interfere with the freedom of the motion picture producers." The campaign was adopted by much of the Protestant religious press, including the widely circulated liberal *Christian Century.* It provided an opportunity for independent exhibitors to combine their attack on the majors' trade practices with a morals charge. Confronted with local criticism about the moral standards of the movies they showed, small exhibitors often defended themselves by arguing that the majors' insistence on block booking obliged the well-intentioned but powerless independent exhibitor in upstate New York or the small-town Midwest to show "sex-smut," regardless of his own or his community's preferences. Their trade association, Allied States, insisted that the only way to secure decency on Main Street was through federal regulation of the industry, and the Protestant press joined them in what Hays regarded as an unholy alliance.[17]

In September 1929 the MPPDA held a conference with its "public relations family" on "The Community and the Motion Picture" in New York. This marked the end of its attempt to form alliances with opinion-forming groups, in the face of a barrage of hostile press comment, again directed at Hays and the Association's activities rather than at film content. The regulation of content, however, represented the one area of industry activity where the Association, under attack from all sides, might be able to demonstrate its usefulness to both the public and its members. During the conference Hays began discussing modifying the 1927 Code with Colonel Joy, who prepared several drafts in the remainder of 1929. A committee of producers chaired by Thalberg also worked on a draft. A quite separate document emanated from Chicago, where the Association's general counsel, Charles C. Pettijohn, was working to repeal the city's censorship ordinance by gaining the support of the city's Catholic archbishop, Cardinal George Mundelein. His campaign led to the involvement of Martin Quigley, a prominent Chicago Catholic and publisher of the *Exhibitor's Herald World* (later *Motion Picture Herald*), in the Code's rewriting. As an alternative to Pettijohn's plan, Quigley proposed a much more elaborate Code enunciating the moral principles underlying screen entertainment. He recruited the leading figure in the revival of the Catholic Sodality youth movement, Father Daniel A. Lord, S.J., to draft it.[18]

As a document, the Production Code can be distinguished from the processes by which it was implemented. The Code was a corporate statement of policy about the appropriate content of entertainment cinema and acknowledged the possible influence of movies on the morals and conduct of those who saw them. It represented the industry's acceptance of its difference from the book, magazine, or theater business. As Lord argued, it was difficult to confine films to "only certain classes of people. The exhibitor's theaters are built for the masses, for the cultivated and the rude, the mature and the immature, the self-respecting and the criminal." Small communities, "remote from sophistication and from the hardening process which often takes place in the ethical and moral standards of groups in larger cities," were particularly vulnerable, but Lord was concerned that cinema's "mobility, popularity, accessibility, emotional appeal, vividness, [and] straightforward presentation of fact" affected audiences more intimately and more powerfully than other forms of expression.

Lord's instrumentalist view of culture emphasized the industry's responsibility for the manufacture of "correct" entertainment, "which tends to improve the race, or at least to re-create and rebuild human beings exhausted with the realities of life." But Lord's voice was only one of several raised in the writing of the Code, and its history as a document is the history of the attempted and failed compromise of those competing voices. The most important figure overtly contending Lord's position was Irving Thalberg, and his and Lord's drafts could hardly have been further apart. Thalberg began by asserting that "there is a very general tendency to over-emphasize the moral and educational influence of the motion pictures" and that "the sole purpose of the commercial motion picture is to entertain. It cannot be considered as education or as a sermon or even indirectly as an essentially moral or immoral force."[19]

Thalberg and Lord were addressing different issues because they were concerned with different audiences. Thalberg's document spoke to the overwhelmingly adult audiences of the majors' first-run theaters, where 70 percent of revenues were generated. Lord and other reformers saw "the vital problem" as "the selection of entertainment for children," a small part of the first-run audience, but frequent attenders at neighborhood and small-town theaters. Their strategies were also at odds. Thalberg intended to do no more than make "a special effort . . . to include compensating moral values" in borderline cases while reiterating the "Don'ts." Lord required a more positive commitment to "the magnificent possibilities of the screen" for "the building of right ideals" and "the inculcation in story form of right principles." If movies "consistently held up high types of characters," he argued, "they could become the greatest natural force for the improvement of mankind."[20]

Joy spent January 1930 attempting to shape a compromise between the two drafts, with their differing ambitions. More closely than either of them or than the published document, Joy's draft encapsulated the pragmatic attitude that he brought to his dealings with the studios and that set the tone for the SRC's activities until 1932. With Lord, Joy felt that films should "build up . . . our national ideals of government, of family and social relations and religious reverence. . . . The trend of every picture should uphold the good and condemn evil." But he qualified this by adding that "more weight should attach to the tone and effect of the picture as a whole" than individual incidents. In arguing that the industry should produce at least some pictures targeted at specific audiences —some for children, others "that will appeal to a relatively smaller audience, which might be considered a vanguard leading the general public to more discriminating standards"—he was closer to Thalberg, whom he greatly respected. His understanding of "compensating moral values" also concurred with Thalberg's. In "debatable" cases, scenes upholding "accepted moral and spiritual standards" should be included, and "a sincere effort" made to "clean up" characters and situations "in every instance when the theme of the picture may present them in a temporarily dubious light." "Good taste" should be "the ruling factor." His main concerns—to eliminate profanity, the gratuitous use of liquor, and "the treatment of sex in such a way that it violates the standards of family relations"—came from his experience of external censorship.[21]

Joy's formulations represented the practical policy he would adopt in applying the Code, but his document proved too much of a compromise to be acceptable to Martin Quigley, who called Lord to Los Angeles to present his Code to the producers on 10 February. When he left Hollywood a week later, Lord was confident that his Code had been accepted by the producers. A committee had produced a "condensed" version, and he and Hays had rewritten his draft as the "Reasons Underlying the Code." With the consent of both parties, Catholic involvement in the Code was to remain secret, together with its implementation procedure, the Resolution for Uniform Interpretation. Hays understood self-regulation to mean that responsibility for Code implementation should be placed firmly on the companies themselves. It was for this reason that the Resolution for Uniform Interpretation did not make submission of scripts to the SRC compulsory, and placed responsibility for making changes in finished films with the companies concerned. It also appointed a "jury" composed of the heads of production of each of the member companies as final arbiters of whether a film conformed "to the spirit and the letter of the Code." As Quigley noted with distrust, since the Association position lacked what he regarded as adequate enforcement procedures, it carefully avoided any commitment to which producers could subsequently be held and permitted them to agree to a document they could then evade.[22]

The "Reasons" were not included in the Code published by the MPPDA on 31 March; the text provided a list of prohibitions rather than the moral arguments of Lord's original draft. The "Particular Applications" of the published Code elaborated the "Don'ts and Be Carefuls" and added only clauses addressing Joy's concerns with "the use of liquor in American life," "adultery and illicit sex," vulgarity, and obscenity. Its preamble also provided a rationale that compromised Thalberg's and Lord's positions: it saw motion pictures "primarily as entertainment without any explicit purpose of teaching or propaganda," but acknowledged that "within its own field of entertainment," a film could be "directly responsible for spiritual or moral progress, for higher types of social life, and for much correct thinking." Lord's contribution was most visible in the three "General Principles" that preceded the "Particular Applications":

1. No picture shall be produced which will lower the moral standards of those who see it. Hence the sympathy of the audience shall never be thrown to the side of crime, wrong-doing, evil or sin.
2. Correct standards of life, subject only to the requirements of drama and entertainment, shall be presented.
3. Law, natural or human, shall not be ridiculed, nor shall sympathy be created for its violation. ("A Code to Govern the Making of Talking, Synchronized and Silent Motion Pictures," MPPDA, 1930, repr. in Moley, p. 241)

The Code did not explain how these principles (specifically Catholic only in their reference to "natural law") related to the "Particular Applications." It was over the interpretation of this relationship between the "spirit" and the "letter" of the Code that the SRC negotiated with the studios for the next three years.[23]

Implementing the Code, 1930–1931

However compromised it may have been, the Production Code was a statement of principle, reluctantly accepting the industry's responsibility for the moral well-being of its audiences. The practical implementation of that principle was, however, a complex matter, involving extensive negotiation over procedure, enforcement, and interpretation at the level of textual detail. Hays's caution in publicly committing the Association to the Code's enforcement had as much to do with his recognition of the practical problems to be solved in the Code's application as it did with a skepticism about producers' intentions. Although a growing chorus of voices denounced the moral evils of the movies, it would be wrong to conclude that movies became more salacious or vicious between 1930 and 1934. With occasional exceptions, the reverse is the case, as both Joy and state censors applied increasingly strict standards. But the early 1930s was a period of increasing moral conservatism in American culture, in which the film industry, along with other institutions of representation, failed to keep pace with "the growing demand for a return to decency in all of our leisure pursuits." The industry was pedaling backward as fast as it could, but not fast enough for its opponents, who in 1933 found themselves, for the first time, in the ascendant.[24]

The calls for censorship were, as Martin Quigley argued, "an awkward expression of demand," a complaint that too much "sophisticated" product was being made, and not enough that was suitable for children or small-town audiences. But the issue of audience demand was most often couched in moralistic terms and under the anti-Semitic expectation that a Jewish-dominated industry had to be intimidated into decency. Joy told Darryl Zanuck in August 1930, "We are on trial as far as a large part of the vocal public is concerned and a decision as to whether or not they will allow us to run our own business . . . depends largely upon how they believe we live up to our own promises."[25]

On its publication the Production Code was received with much skepticism. The Protestant religious press, who were credited with forcing reform on Hays, remained unremittingly hostile. Quigley, too, provided only cautious support, in a distinctly double-edged Catholic publicity campaign approving the Code's purposes organized by Joseph Breen. Like Quigley, Breen was an active lay Catholic, well connected with the church hierarchy; he had managed the press relations of the 1926 Eucharistic Congress in Chicago. His campaign, which secured him a post as one of Hays's executive assistants, sought to bind the industry to a definite commitment to the Code, while avoiding committing any Catholic party to endorsing its effectiveness.[26]

Initially, the studios cooperated "pretty much as a matter of routine" in voluntarily submitting scripts to the Studio Relations Committee. Within a few months, however, cooperation had become intermittent and patchy, determined in large part by the attitude of the studio's head of production and the particular market at which the company aimed its product. In general, the more important subsequent-run theaters were to the company's distribution system, the more they cooperated. Under B. P. Schulberg, Paramount remained thoroughly cooperative; so did Universal, despite Joy's worries about "Junior" Laemmle's lapses in taste. Thalberg used Joy's respect for him to choose how much he would cooperate on any given project. But in October 1930, Joy complained that Fox was ignoring his suggestions on OH FOR A MAN, while Warner Bros. and First National were submitting neither scripts nor prints. Until 1934, Warners remained the most recalcitrant of the major companies in its attitude to the Code and the MPPDA in general. But at the end of the Code's first year of operation, the Association claimed that only a dozen films had been subject to "more than a scattering of criticism" and cited the reduction in the number of censor board cuts as evidence of its efficacy.[27]

Others disagreed. The industry's most vociferous critics judged the movies on their advertising far more frequently than on their content, and a small number of visible infringements were sufficient to fuel the flames of their righteousness. The Association's Advertising Code, passed in June 1930, relied entirely on the voluntary cooperation of publicity departments and was much less effectively applied than the Production Code.[28] Joy's approach to the improvement of content was gradualist. Like Thalberg, he saw the "small, narrow, picayunish fault-finding" censorship of censor boards over "little details" as inhibiting his attempts to negotiate strategies of representation that permitted producers "to paint the unconventional, the unlawful, the immoral side of life in order to bring out in immediate contrast the happiness and benefits derived from the wholesome, clean and law-abiding conduct."[29]

Censors, on the other hand, identified some disturbing developments in movie content. Faced with a cycle of "kept woman" films, including ILLICIT, THE EASIEST WAY, and STOLEN HEAVEN, James Wingate, the director of the New York board, demanded to know if the SRC had changed its standards. Lord shared Wingate's concern: "single scenes, words or actions" that were the principal source of anxiety in 1930 had been dealt with, but current films

> are now concerned with problems. They discuss morals, divorce, free love, unborn children, . . . single and double standards, the relationship of sex to religion, marriage and its effects upon the freedom of women. . . . [N]o matter how delicate or clean the treatment, these subjects are fundamentally dangerous. ("The Code—One Year Later," Report by Lord, 23 April 1931, Hays Papers)

Inside the SRC, there were prolonged discussions of nuances of plot or characterization, as to whether the basic situation of BACK STREET made it a kept-woman story or only presented "the triangle." Outside, they feared, "our constituents won't differentiate."[30]

In early 1931 the SRC completely misjudged reactions to Universal's DRACULA, which was condemned by the women's and educational organizations that previewed films under the Association's auspices. Its commercial success exemplified the Association's and the industry's dilemma as the effects of the Depression began to be felt at the box office. Some of the material most likely to produce immediate high returns in first-run theaters, and thus maintain company liquidity, also provoked reform groups to claim the Code was being ignored. Beginning in late 1930, the brief cycle of gangster films inspired by press coverage of Al Capone proved a public relations calamity for the Association. For some time, the MPPDA had successfully countered arguments that a link existed

Irene Dunne played John Boles's infinitely tolerant mistress in Universal's adaptation of Fannie Hurst's bestseller BACK STREET (1932). *Although the movie contained no objectionable dialogue or suggestive scenes, it was denounced in the Catholic press as "among the most vicious of the past season" for teaching "false principles of morality."*

between moviegoing and juvenile crime, but the popularity of DOORWAY TO HELL, LITTLE CAESAR, and several sequels in the spring of 1931 revived charges that the movies were encouraging young audiences to view the gangster protagonist as a "hero-villain," clear evidence of Lord's argument that some material was too dangerous, no matter how it was treated. Although the Association defended them as "deterrents, not incentives, to criminal behavior," their popularity provoked a "prairie-fire of protest." A plethora of municipalities established local censor boards, and there were calls for a congressional investigation of the industry.[31]

During 1931 it became clear that Joy's attempt to conciliate the divided voices behind the Production Code was failing, and content could not be made proof against reformers' criticism. Movie content and the concern with content were symptoms of a moral panic about social behavior, induced by the economic collapse. The Code had been adopted in a strategy of retreat from the previous scale of engagement with public relations, but it had exposed the industry to more criticism and put it constantly on the defensive in its public utterances. Within the association, it was argued that the increasingly unpredictable behavior of the censors resulted not from a breakdown in the SRC, since "the same pictures now held up would have passed, flying, two years ago," but the "agitation against gang pictures" led censors to believe "that they can go to almost any length and that on a showdown the public will accord us scant support."[32]

In September 1931 Code procedures were considerably tightened. The submission of scripts, as well as the approval of release prints, was made compulsory, to ensure that every film had "a moral argument" by which Joy could defend it to censor boards. The SRC was granted a right of appeal from a producers jury to the MPPDA Board. At the same time, in its first intervention in a general trend in production, the Association of Motion Picture Producers (AMPP) also passed a resolution prohibiting the further production of gangster films. The film most immediately affected was Howard Hughes's SCARFACE, which was reconstructed on four occasions before it passed both the MPPDA and New York's censorship board in May 1932.[33]

The prohibition of gangster films raised a problem elsewhere. In December, Joy worried that

> with crime practically denied them, with box office figures down, with high-pressure methods being employed back home to spur the studios on to get a little more cash, it was almost inevitable that sex, as the nearest thing at hand and pretty generally sure-fire, should be seized upon. It was. (Joy to Breen, 15 December 1931, PCA POSSESSED file)

Studios, forced by their financial position to seek immediate returns on their investment in production by concentrating on appealing to the first-run market, were using material as provocative as the SRC would allow. By devising plots like that of the "sordid" SAFE IN HELL, in which Dorothy Mackaill eventually sacrificed "her life rather than her virtue," they remained just within the letter of the Code. Joy hoped that a "new drive on sex films would partially, if not entirely, eliminate" kept-woman stories and discourage the further production of chain-gang and horror films. But the problem was more elusive, since it seemed that every time the Association responded to one kind of complaint, it was replaced by another. As soon as Joy was provided with the means to ensure the overall morality of a movie's narrative, reformers argued that the stories Hollywood told were not the primary source of its influence. The cinema's power to corrupt was now assumed to lie in the seductive pleasure of its spectacle: as one disturbed reviewer of POSSESSED reported, she overheard a "young girl" sitting next to her say of Clark Gable, "I would live with him too, under any conditions." Although the Code had reduced the number of censorship eliminations by 30–50 percent, Hays warned his members of the "folly" of ignoring "the classes that write, talk, and legislate, on the basis that the mass public, as reflected by the box-office, is with us in any event. Reform elements outside, not inside, the saloon, enforced prohibition upon the country." In its well-informed 1931 report *The Public Relations of the Motion Picture Industry*, the Federal Council of Churches suggested that if the Association tried less hard "to conceal their household problems and to put up a bold front to the public," it "might have gained greater public support and might also have been an effectual disciplinary measure within the organization." Their analysis, however, assumed that the problem was one of discipline rather than of dissonance in definitions of acceptable standards.[34]

The "Crusader":
Containing the Crisis, 1932–1933

In January 1932, Joseph Breen arrived in Hollywood to oversee publicity for the MPPDA. On an earlier visit he had decided that the job needed "a genuine *Crusader* with the vision before him of saving a great industry"; he had determined that if he was to achieve anything with the producers, it was more necessary to be feared than liked. His style constituted a significant shift away from Joy's attempts at consensus. During the next two years, Breen made himself increasingly indispensable to the Association's operations in Hollywood, at the same time that he contributed energetically to the Catholic movie campaign. Like Quigley, Breen held "the present bunch" who "hold sway in production" in contempt: they were, he thought, "simply a rotten bunch of vile people with no respect for anything beyond the making of money." Breen's attitude to Thalberg, in particular, was markedly different from Joy's. Even Joy, however, found Thalberg's proposed script for RED-HEADED WOMAN "the worst ever." Written by Anita Loos, the film depicted Jean Harlow's progression up the social ladder by a series of affairs, but it made comedy out of what had previously been the material for melodrama and left Harlow living in unpunished luxury at its end. Joy feared that hostile public reaction would not prevent other studios accusing the SRC of giving MGM favorable treatment and "trying to figure out ways of topping this particular picture" in competition for the sensational element of the urban trade. The most drastic change of studio policy came when Emanuel Cohen replaced B. P. Schulberg as Paramount's head of production. Cohen's decision "to put aside the conservative policy which has characterized the studio for years, and to be as daring as possible" resulted in the studio producing A FAREWELL TO ARMS, purchasing William Faulkner's novel *Sanctuary*, and signing a contract with Mae West.[35]

In June, Joy accepted an executive position in production at Fox. Quigley, disillusioned with the existing production system, felt that "the whole Code scheme has become practically a wash-out during the past few months" and had no confidence in Joy's replacement, the former New York censor James Wingate. When, in August, Hays deplored "the reported distribution department pressure" for the production of "sex pictures," Joe Schenck bluntly told him that the public who did attend were "not interested in namby-pamby subjects." If the Association attempted to "make the producers live up to the spirit and the letter" of the Code, they would abandon it, "even at the expense of having censorship in every State in the Union." In his valedictory statement on the operations of the Code in September, Joy warned Hays that of 111 pictures in current production, 24 of the most prominent dealt with illicit sex relations. Quantity was only one problem. Plots adhered to the letter of the Code, while violating its spirit. In BLONDE VENUS, among others, "prostitution is depicted as a 'sacrifice' on a woman's part in behalf of her child or her husband." Did such pictures, which seemed to suggest that "while adultery is wrong, under these given circumstances it is right," violate the Code, Joy wondered. He argued that together with the elimination of "sex situations which are not essential to the story," the screen had to withdraw from any suggestion that it was advocating a change in social or sexual mores. There was danger in creating such sympathy for the fallen woman "that the double standard shall be seriously affected." Whatever he and Hays, "as enlightened beings," might think of it, "we are not engaged, as an industry, in crusades, nor are we yet ready to be the spearheads in any assault on society's strongest fortifications."[36]

Breen was far more critical. Nobody in Hollywood, he claimed to Wilfrid Parsons, editor of the Jesuit weekly *America,* "cares a dam [sic] for the Code or any of its provisions. . . . I've heard it sneered at and laughed at; I've heard important people talk about its being a first-rate *gag* to fool the bluenoses and the 'church people' but I have yet to hear it discussed seriously." He presented Hays as well-meaning but "above all, the politician—the compromiser," who had "sold us all a first-class bill of goods when he put over the Code on us." Breen's virulently anti-Semitic correspondence with Parsons and other prominent Catholics was a tactical instrument in the campaign he and Quigley had nurtured since 1929: in suggesting that America's enfeebled Protestant Main Street was being debauched by Jews and pagans, he was proposing that the Catholic church take up the sword.[37]

In some respects, the church was ideally situated to mediate this site of cultural conflict. Opposed to legislative regulation that would foster "the growing notion of the State's right to supremacy in the realm of moral teaching," it was also empowered by a sense of moral certainty that, alone among the religious groupings of the interwar period, it appeared to possess. The involvement of the Catholic clergy with the movies was part of a general project of confident Catholic cultural assertiveness, expressed in the Catholic Action movement. A group of conservative Jesuit intellectuals, including Parsons and Lord, developed a specifically Catholic response to what they denounced as neo-humanism in a number of cultural fields between 1928 and 1935. This group saw the motion-picture industry as an ideal instance of their argument for the primacy of moral rather than economic reform.[38]

In October 1932, inspired by Breen's correspondence with Parsons, *America* published "An Open Letter to Dr. Wingate," in which Gerard Donnelly advised him that Catholics chiefly resented "the type of film which teaches false principles of morality," particularly "of sex conduct." Acknowledging that Pos-SESSED and BACK STREET "did not contain one objectionable line nor a single suggestive scene," he nevertheless denounced them as "among the most vicious of the past season": "It is not the material that we condemn in these films, but the treatment; not the theme, but the thesis, the unsound philosophy which the pictures illustrated and dramatized." They persuaded an audience to approve immoral conduct, he claimed, since the heroines' rebellions were "against only the current standards of society; nowhere in the action or dialogue was there the slightest reference to God or conscience or supernatural responsibility."[39]

While the reform lobby's demands increased, the studios continued to show little willingness to acknowledge them. In October, Paramount announced that they planned an adaptation of Mae West's play *Diamond Lil,* despite the Association's prohibition on it under the Formula. At Hays's orders, Wingate refused to give an opinion on the script, because Paramount was threatening "the whole inter-company relationship" on which the Association was built. A board of directors' decision, however, acquiesced in the project, with the spurious proviso that the film be "made in strict conformity to the Code" and avoid any reference to its source in its publicity or advertising. Wingate urged the studio to

I'M NO ANGEL *(Paramount 1933). The popularity of Mae West has frequently been held responsible for the creation of the Production Code Administration in 1934. In reality, West was more a symptom than a cause of the increasingly acerbic disputes over the limits of acceptable representation. The decline of her career also suggests the extent to which she was a victim of the climate of moral conservatism after 1934.*

"develop the comedy elements, so that the treatment will invest the picture with such exaggerated qualities as automatically to take care of possible offensiveness." Self-regulation played an important part in the creation of Mae West as a cinematic caricature of female sexual aggression, using comedy as an instrument of containment, a broad-beamed alternative to the "lightness" of "the Lubitsch touch."[40]

However, the success of SHE DONE HIM WRONG with all audiences only increased alarm among reform elements that West, notorious after her arrests for indecency in New York in 1927 and 1928, was now considered fit material for the screen. Other producers, with Quigley, saw the film as evidence of the failure of the Code machinery, but though Wingate was prepared to admit to occasional miscalculations when the SRC had been "too liberal," he denied that the current standard of production was worse "then the average of pictures heretofore produced." Rather, "the public and organized minorities have become more keenly critical and more expressive. . . . this is a moment of hysterical criticism."

State censor boards, riding the tide of public opinion, signaled that the range of permissible subject matter was being further restricted. As had happened before, however, the film that provoked the greatest volume of complaint was unexpected: Will Rogers's comedy STATE FAIR, in which one bedroom scene, suggesting a sexual encounter between the farmer's son and a city girl, in a film otherwise providing "unobjectionable humor for the entire family," provoked more protests than anything since the 1930 release of a synchronized version of THE BIRTH OF A NATION. With West, at least audiences knew what they were getting. Mistakes like STATE FAIR did more damage by provoking "righteous resentment from the father who has taken his wife and children to the movies."[41]

Joy's resignation coincided with the publication in *McCall's* magazine of the first extracts from Henry James Forman's *Our Movie-Made Children*, a sensationalized digest of the Payne Fund Studies. The studies, collectively titled *Motion Pictures and Youth*, were the result of a five-year program by the Motion Picture Research Council (MPRC), which had in the late 1920s become the focal point of Protestant and educational concerns about the cultural effects of the movies. The MPRC was an organization of some social and scientific prestige: its director, Congregationalist minister William H. Short, recruited prominent members of the WASP elite to its National Council and some of the nation's leading psychologists and sociologists to conduct its research. Twelve studies were undertaken, investigating children's attendance and emotional responses to the motion-picture situation, as well as several examinations of motion-picture content to establish its relationship to current "standards of morality." While the studies demonstrated that movies could provoke emotional arousal and influence their audiences' attitudes, they also revealed the extent to which their effects were tempered by the age and social situation of the audience; the movies' principal effect was to reinforce familiar values and ideas.

These results did not meet the requirements of the studies' sponsor, and MPRC publicity emphasized findings that came closer to endorsing its expectations. In *Our Movie-Made Children*, Forman, a former news editor of the *Literary Digest*, made exploitative use of "movie autobiographies" collected by Chicago sociologist Herbert Blumer, reproducing the most sensational confessions of criminal behavior and "sex delinquency" inspired by adolescent attendance. The Association had confidently dismissed comparable charges in the 1920s: its own weakened position and the scientific credibility of the "Payneful" Studies made the MPRC's demands for federal regulation a profound threat to the industry. As early as August 1931, Hays knew that their impact on public opinion would hold "infinitely more danger than any report the Federal Council might have issued" and that "some of the attacks cannot be defended." However much the Association might deride Short, the personnel of the National Council were too prominent, socially and politically, to be dismissed, and their lobbying power was considerable. By the end of 1932, nearly forty religious and educational organizations had passed resolutions calling for federal regulation of the industry.[42]

The early months of 1933 marked the low point of the industry's fortunes. In the atmosphere of uncertainty that preceded Roosevelt's inauguration, there was widespread fear that the entire industry was virtually bankrupt, and the immediate crisis deepened with the declaration of a bank holiday on 5 March.

The exact nature of Roosevelt's proposals for governmental control of industry were not yet clear, and legislation hostile to the majors seemed a strong possibility. Hays held an emergency meeting of the MPPDA Board of Directors on the evening of 5 March and made it clear that more than economic action was required to deal with the crisis. The industry's most compelling argument against an increased tax burden was that going to the movies was a necessary recreation, not a luxury. If legislators or the public accepted the reformers' opinion that movies were positively harmful, the industry's position became indefensible. Only a more rigid enforcement of the Production Code, Hays argued, could maintain public sympathy and defeat the pressure for federal intervention over its content policies and its financial operations. He persuaded the board to sign a "Reaffirmation of Objectives" acknowledging that "disintegrating influences" threatened "standards of production, standards of quality, standards of business practice," and pledged them to the maintenance of "the higher business standards developed through years of cooperative effort."[43]

The Reaffirmation became the implement with which Hays began to reorganize the Code administration, instructing Wingate to tighten up its application. Significantly, Breen's involvement in SRC operations was increased. Company heads wrote to producers that there was a "new deal in the matter of objectionable pictures from now on." In April the entire MPPDA Board entrained for California to enforce stringent economies. Hays threatened producers that if they continued to evade the Code, he would take the issue first to the company heads in New York, then to the bankers and stockholders, and finally to the public. His rhetoric was embellished with apocalyptic threats of the consequences of another aberrant production bringing down legislative chaos and the "straight jacket" of federal censorship. Although little of this action was made public, the firmness of Hays's stance was communicated to congressmen, producing the desired effect. Thalberg's interpretation of the Code was one victim of the assertion of East Coast management control that signaled the end of Hollywood's central producer system. His own illness and his absence from Hollywood from January to July made this change easier to accomplish.[44]

A number of productions then nearing completion, among them Paramount's adaptation of *Sanctuary*, THE STORY OF TEMPLE DRAKE, and Warners' BABY FACE, were held up for extensive revisions, in addition to those agreed on prior to the Reaffirmation. Other films, in earlier stages of production, were subject to equally drastic but less expensive insertions of "compensating moral values." The tone of SRC correspondence changed: as one studio official explained to his producers, "prior to this time, we were told 'it is recommended, etc.,' but recently letters definitely state, 'it is inadmissible, etc.' or something equally definite." In April, Wingate wrote to Merian C. Cooper, the head of production at RKO, about the new Constance Bennett picture BED OF ROSES, articulating the SRC's effective policy change in his insistence that they "show some positive qualities of retribution and regeneration that will counter-balance this apparent glorifying of an unscrupulous adventuress . . . if the picture is to meet the general, as well as the specific provisions of the Code."[45]

The imposition of a "new deal" in regulation, with its emphasis on the reestablishment of an explicitly patriarchal moral order, coincided with the start of Roosevelt's presidency. The new policy was evident in negotiations during the summer over RKO's adaptation of Sinclair Lewis's best-selling novel *Ann Vickers*.

Miriam Hopkins in THE STORY OF TEMPLE DRAKE *(Paramount, 1933), based on William Faulkner's most commercially successful novel,* Sanctuary. *The Studio Relations Committee regarded movies based on what Hays called "bad source material" as by far the most troublesome they had to deal with in the early 1930s.*

Breen's opinion that the script was "vulgarly offensive" was in line with the Catholic press's condemnation of the book's apparent endorsement of a female character who flouted moral convention. A defense arguing that the quality of the source material justified its technical infringement of the Code had been accepted by the producers jury over A FAREWELL TO ARMS in December 1932; the jury's willingness to accept such sophistry persuaded Breen and Quigley that it must be eliminated. ANN VICKERS was shown no such mercy: Breen's insistence that it have "a clear distinction between right and wrong" forced RKO to concede drastic plot changes and downgrade the production; its narrative coherence was damaged and its theme muddied to a point of internal contradiction.[46]

The industry's internal reformers, however, were far from satisfied. Although Breen had succeeded in asserting his interpretation of the Code in the first half of 1933, he recognized that it exerted an essentially negative authority. It had not yet instilled a "will to righteousness" among the studios, who still regarded it as "something to be 'got around' rather than an expression of fundamental purposes." Wingate's appointment had not been a success. He failed to establish a rapport with any of the studio heads and paid too much attention to details of elimination rather than the wider thematic concerns at the heart of Catholic objection.[47] Breen had established his usefulness to the companies by doing what Wingate apparently could not: providing practical solutions to a studio's problem in applying the Code, and thus protecting its investment. In a further reorganization of the SRC in August, Joy was recalled from Fox to deal with "the general flavor of the pictures," while Wingate attended to "the narrower considerations of the censor point of view." Breen relinquished his other work to concentrate full-time on self-regulation, and although Wingate continued in the position of director, Breen was in effect "responsible for the entire work" of the SRC from then on. Although he was now in a position to harass undesirable studio projects and eliminate the most objectionable material from Mae West's I'M NO ANGEL, Breen wanted to prevent such productions altogether. To achieve that would require external pressure.[48]

The Crusade: Staging the Crisis, 1934

Catholics hoped to incorporate the Production Code into the industry's NRA Code, so that the Production Code "will become part of the contract between the producers and the government and involve the usual penalties for violation." In the final document, the industry pledged itself "to maintain right moral standards in the production of motion pictures" and "to adhere to the regulations made within the industry to attain this purpose," but this "pledge" fell short of an unequivocal inclusion of the Production Code's enforcement procedures within the jurisdiction of the NRA Code Authority. Breen, in an almost constant conspiratorial correspondence with Quigley, Parsons, Lord, and others pursued a separate strategy, aiming for a public demonstration of Catholic Action. Their first proposal was for a "national protest week" in which Catholics would lead a boycott of theaters. Hays, they agreed, "can do nothing if the producers will not cooperate. . . . What we need to have is . . . direct action that will reach the producers . . . such action must be mass action by a large number of people at once, so that it will be felt and understood for what it is."[49]

By late August, Breen had persuaded Bishop Cantwell of Los Angeles to propose "that the Bishops come out with a definite condemnation of bad pictures" at their annual meeting in November. Anticipating that meeting and to some extent forcing the bishops' hands, Parsons arranged for the new apostolic delegate to the United States to call for "a united and vigorous campaign for the purification of the cinema, which has become a deadly menace to morals." In November the bishops established the Episcopal Committee on Motion Pictures, chaired by Archbishop McNicholas of Cincinnati, advised by Parsons and, through him, Breen and Quigley. Plans were evolved through a series of meetings in March 1934, and on 11 April the committee announced the proposal to recruit the Legion of Decency. The Legion constituted an extension of the national protest week plan: initially, it lacked any permanent organizational structure and amounted essentially to a publicity campaign, in which Catholics signed a pledge condemning "those salacious motion pictures which, with other degrading agencies, are corrupting public morals and promoting a sex mania in our land," and promising "to remain away from all motion pictures except those which do not offend decency and Christian morality."[50]

The Legion was in no sense a spontaneous expression of public feeling: although its principal weapon appeared to be the economic one of a threatened boycott of films or theaters, its real power lay in its capacity to generate anti-industry publicity across a broad front. The Legion campaign was delicately orchestrated to achieve a precise objective: the effective enforcement of the Production Code by the existing machinery. It was designed to intimidate producers, not to inflict major economic damage. It had three stages. First, the bishops had to be persuaded to adopt a strategy that avoided linking Code enforcement to block booking, differentiated the Legion from the MPRC, and made it clear that it had "no purpose or desire to tell the picture people how to run their business." Breen and Quigley were determined to get rid of the producers jury, but Hays rejected a proposal to replace it with a separate committee of Catholic laymen in Hollywood or New York. In March, Breen devised a plan by which the Episcopal Committee would threaten boycotts in Philadelphia, Chicago, and "half a dozen of the larger cities" where one of the major companies had large theater holdings. The fact that the only actual boycott of any size occurred in Philadelphia was not accidental: it was directed against the extensive theater holdings of Warner Bros., the last intransigent opponent of Breen's full implementation of the Code in the spring of 1934.[51]

The second stage, which started with the announcement of the Legion, involved convincing producers that they had to accede to the committee's terms and agreeing precisely what those terms were. Throughout May, Breen bombarded the studio heads with bulletins describing the activities of the Legion and other reform groups on an almost daily basis in an attempt to persuade them of the seriousness of their situation. The Episcopal Committee met on 20 May, after which the bishops both proposed terms to Hays and took further action, including initiating the Philadelphia boycott. This was reported as causing a 40 percent drop in receipts. It significantly increased the press attention paid to the Legion campaign and provoked the companies to action. On 13 June, Breen was called to New York for an emergency meeting of the MPPDA Board that changed the Resolution for Uniform Interpretation. The SRC was renamed the Production

Code Administration (PCA), with Breen as its director and an augmented staff. The producers jury was eliminated, leaving appeal to the MPPDA Board as the only mechanism for questioning Breen's judgment. Each film passed by the PCA would be given a certificate, displayed on every print. All member companies agreed not to distribute or release a film without a certificate. Breen and Quigley were authorized to present these proposals to the Episcopal Committee's next meeting on 20 June, and negotiate any further conditions the committee required. The one condition it added was the addition of a penalty clause imposing a $25,000 fine for violation of the new Resolution for Uniform Interpretation. The board agreed to this on 3 July, but gave it no publicity; although it was later assumed to be the "sanction" that Lord had long demanded the Code have, it was in practice no more than window dressing. Any attempt to collect it would probably have constituted a breach of the antitrust laws. None was ever made.[52]

The third phase, public implementation, began after agreement was secured on 21 June and corresponded with the height of public attention being paid to the campaign. The Association declared that if these changes did not "prove to be a finally effective method of securing the uniformly high standard of pictures toward which the industry has been working by trial and error for some years . . . some other method will be found." Its members would permit exhibitors the right to cancel any film released prior to 15 July, against which there was "a genuine protest on moral grounds." This action, which was widely but incorrectly interpreted as a temporary suspension of block booking, received more press coverage and favorable comment than the creation of the PCA. Meanwhile, Quigley, Breen, Parsons, and other prominent Catholics were acting to limit the economic effects of Legion action. In the triumphalism of Catholic discussion after the July announcements, there was much talk of Quigley having Hays under his thumb, but that considerably exaggerated the influence that Hays had conceded. If Breen and Quigley's role in orchestrating the Legion campaign had to be hidden from the producers, it was even more imperative that Hays's compliance with their activities be concealed. Hays had used Breen, Quigley, and their perception of his powerlessness to engineer the result he desired, without risking his own position.[53] In the aftermath of the July "victory," there was much internal dissension among the Catholics principally involved, particularly over the publication of "black lists," which Quigley, in keeping with long-term Association policy, strongly opposed. Lord and, less publicly, Mundelein felt that Quigley and Breen had sold the Legion out to the producers.[54]

As a meeting of heads of publicity and advertising pointed out, given the climax the crisis had reached by mid 1934, it was in the industry's best interests to make a show of atonement. Industry publicity emphasized the scale of the 1934 crisis in order to create a dividing line between "before," when the SRC had been unable to control production, and "now," when PCA "self-regulation" had really become effective. The establishment of this policy was more important than the maintenance of existing release schedules, which should be altered so as only to release "the strongest available pictures." As a result of this need for a public act of contrition, the history of the SRC's gradual implementation of the Production Code was concealed behind a more apocalyptic account. The immediate purpose behind this exaggeration was less to flatter the Catholics than to outmaneuver the MPRC, independent exhibitors, and other groups still demanding federal regulation. In that respect, it was highly successful, if only temporarily.[55]

In fact, Breen had largely won the internal battle by March, when Fox, RKO, Universal, and Columbia were showing "a definite willingness to do the right thing," and there was "some progress" at Paramount and Twentieth Century. In April, MGM's TARZAN was rejected by a producers jury; approval of other films was withheld until a number of major changes were made. In late March the MPPDA Board agreed that Production Code correspondence should be copied and sent to company heads in New York; and in April, Hays required each studio to appoint an individual to act as liaison between the studio and the SRC. These decisions reduced the extent to which studio management could resist Breen's demands, and although individual films continued to create difficulties, even Lord congratulated Breen on the overall standard of current releases in May. The major problems in the period around the Legion's formation were created by two Warner films, DR. MONICA and MADAME DU BARRY, and Mae West's IT AIN'T NO SIN, which Breen rejected on 2 June. Within four days Paramount had produced a substantially reedited version that Breen was prepared to pass. Quigley, however, was wary of the danger of releasing a West film with so provocative a title at precisely the moment that the new structure was being enacted. On 22 June, the day after the Cincinnati meeting, the New York censor board rejected IT AIN'T NO SIN. It went back to Hollywood for further reconstruction.[56]

With the implementation of the agreement in mid July, conditions tightened further. As in March 1933, a number of films were withheld from release, and drastic reconstruction undertaken: the conversion of Jean Harlow's 100% PURE into THE GIRL FROM MISSOURI and of IT AIN'T NO SIN into BELLE OF THE NINETIES were the most prominent instances. The modifications to IT AIN'T NO SIN made between its rejection by New York in June and its granting of a PCA Seal in mid August were much less drastic than the changes Paramount had agreed to in early June. The delay in the film's release had, however, achieved Quigley's goal of not immediately confronting the Catholic compromise with what other reformers might call a blatant transgression. A number of films then in circulation were withdrawn before the end of their release cycle: many more were refused certification over the next few years when companies attempted to re-release them. Other films in production, including THE BARRETTS OF WIMPOLE STREET, BORDERTOWN, and IMITATION OF LIFE underwent substantial modifications; proposed projects, including MGM's plan to adapt James M. Cain's *The Postman Always Rings Twice*, were rejected. The immediate impact was apparent, principally in that companies avoided submitting problem scripts. Breen told Hays in August that "never during the two and a half years that we have been writing these reports has the preponderance of scripts of the right kind over questionable ones been so noticeable."[57]

In another important respect, production policy had changed dramatically in early 1934. Hays had consistently tried to persuade producers to undertake large-scale productions designed to appeal to the public relations groups and to create "a new movie-going public recruited from the higher income earning classes . . . which better pictures would transform from casual to regular patrons." Most of these films, from OLD IRONSIDES to WITH COMMANDER BYRD AT THE POLE, were box-office failures. The policy's first substantial commercial success was RKO's LITTLE WOMEN: despite the film's not being released until 24 November 1933, *Motion Picture Herald* reported it as the fourth box-office champion of the year. Hays told RKO studio head B. B. Kahane that LITTLE WOMEN "may open a new type of source material." Less predictably, Ned Depinet, the president of RKO Distribution, declared that its success meant that "the public is hungry for something clean and wholesome—particularly fathers and mothers who have been worried about the movie entertainment that their children have been seeing." The film's success was in part brought about by a marketing strategy aiming it at school audiences via large-scale direct-mail advertising to teachers. This strategy became a crucial implement in the sales campaigns used on the "better pictures" produced after 1934. The wave of Hollywood adaptations of literary classics and historical biographies designed to appeal to the middle-class readers of *Parents' Magazine* and *Ladies' Home Journal* resulted directly from the requirements of the industry's public relations, but it relied on the discovery of a successful method of selling the films. The MPPDA's long-term policy of cooperation with teachers' organizations as a way to "improve the quality of demand" came to fruition in the 1934–35 production season, with the regular use of study guides sponsored by the National Council of Teachers of English. The guides became a regular attachment to the prestige productions of 1934–35 and subsequent seasons; they were widely circulated, with print runs of several hundred thousand. The educational tie-ins were also crucial to the economics of such productions, since they could be used by distributors to justify the film's exhibition in neighborhood and rural areas where such films were frequently canceled. In November 1934, Milliken announced that "the list of authors whose works will appear on the screen during the 1934–35 season is headed by Dante, Shakespeare, Dickens, Poe, Tolstoy and Dumas," and insisted, correctly, that these productions had been planned well before "the healthy, nation-wide discussion of clean pictures this summer."[58]

The cycle of these comparatively high-budget historical pieces continued through the middle years of the decade. Max Reinhardt's A MIDSUMMER NIGHT'S DREAM, Thalberg's ROMEO AND JULIET, and such movies as CHARGE OF THE LIGHT BRIGADE and THE BUCCANEER were also aimed at convincing middle-class America of the bourgeois respectability of the cinema. In January 1935, *Variety* correctly surmised that "the files of history" were less likely to offend "the Church and other busybody factions." For a while, at least, this partial retirement from the present pleased a much wider constituency than just the better-films councils. At the end of 1934, *New York Times* critic André Sennwald wrote,

> The Legion of Decency . . . has performed a service to filmgoers everywhere by crippling the manufacture of such feeble-minded delicatessen as *All of Me, Born to Be Bad* . . . and a number of others which will hurt nobody by their presence on the Legion's blacklist. . . . There has been an obvious improvement in themes and a noticeable diminution in the kind of appalling cheapness and unintelligence which filmgoers deplore without regard to private allegiance of faith or creed. (Quoted in Murray Schumach, *The Face on the Cutting Room Floor: The Story of Movie and Television Censorship* [New York: Morrow, 1964], p. 88)

The Code as Convention: 1935–1939

By late 1934, peace was breaking out almost all over: even *The Churchman* praised Breen and Quigley and accepted that, since 15 July, Hays had been given the authority that the MPPDA had previously claimed for him. More important was the evidence of a box-office recovery led by the neighborhood theaters and apparently responsive to the new production trends that elevated Shirley Temple to the box-office pinnacle from 1934 to 1938. The complex ideological phenomenon that Temple represented indicated a change in public sensibility as well as industry strategy, but the films in which she appeared were, as Graham Greene pointed out in 1937, hardly devoid of sexual sophistication, any more than were Astaire-Rogers musicals or screwball comedies. Rather, these genres contained the culmination of Joy's policy of encoding the representation of sexuality in such a way that a preexistent knowledge was required to gain access to it.

The career of Ginger Rogers follows this development more closely than most: from Anytime Annie in 42ND STREET ("She only said 'no' once—and then she couldn't hear the question"), she progressed, via RKO's musicals, to BACHELOR MOTHER (1939), where the comedy is constructed around the resolute failure of the central characters to recognize the sexual suggestiveness of the situations they are placed in. The *New York Times* reviewer attributed "the spectacle of Miss Rogers and David Niven struggling forlornly to prove their innocence of parenthood, and winning no credence at all," to the director Garson Kanin. But "the sobriety of their performance," which ensured that "the audience enjoys the joke alone," was in fact the work of the PCA and represented one instance of the fulfillment of Joy's strategy of "sophisticated" representational conventions that allowed for multiple audience response and interpretation.

The events of 1934 had produced a recognition in Hollywood, to match the belief established much earlier in New York, that the Production Code must be accepted as a convention of representation. Having conceded the limitations of its boundaries, in the second half of the decade producers and audiences alike could explore the possibilities as well as the constraints of the convention, much as they had done before, but with much less public hindrance. The Code's "General Principles" were the equivalent of a formal statement of generic convention, describing the "intended" effect of plot on audiences. The art in their application lay in the detailed negotiation, an often colorful process. Jack Vizzard reports an exchange between Breen and Josef von Sternberg, who, in expounding the plot of a film he was planning, observed, "At this point, the two principals have a brief romantic interlude." In blunt terms, Breen asked for clarification, and when Sternberg prevaricated, Breen told him to "stop the horseshit and face the issue. We can help you make a story about adultery, if you want, but not if you keep calling a good screwing match a 'romantic interlude.' "[59]

Breen argued that his style of giving back "as good as I got" demonstrated his earnestness of purpose; the speed at which the PCA was required to comment on scripts (within seventy-two hours) also encouraged a stentorian tone of certainty that disguised the fact that the PCA was not empowered to disapprove scripts as such. The only point at which the PCA had the authority to reject any element of a film was in refusing to issue a seal of approval on a release print. Despite the tone with which Breen did business, everything prior to that was advisory. But under these circumstances it is not surprising that Breen often chose to express himself as forcefully as possible in the first instance when he thought that proceeding with a script would be inadvisable. Writers and producers commonly left in material that they knew would be cut in hopes of negotiating something else through, and frequently shots or sequences that the PCA initially objected to survived into the final film. By the same token, when Breen informed Jack Warner that the story of EACH DAWN I DIE "in its present form, is thoroughly and completely unacceptable from the standpoint of the Production Code, and . . . enormously dangerous from the standpoint of political censorship, both in this country and abroad," he was merely opening negotiations over modifications.[60] On the relatively rare occasions when the PCA did reject a script, Breen's tone was clear:

> We have read with utter amazement the script . . . of your proposed production, *Killers on Parole*. This story is so completely in conflict with so many provisions of our Production Code that we are compelled to reject the story in toto. Any . . . story remotely resembling the story set forth in this script, is certain to result in a picture which we will have to reject entirely. . . . it hardly seems credible that you have seriously had in mind production of such a picture. (Breen to Harry Zehner, 8 August 1935, Censorship file, Universal Studios Collection, USC)

The dialogues over the Code were themselves conducted in a highly conventionalized language of absolutes, under which adjustments of nuance were engineered. Though they often took place at a high decibel level and in retrospect often seem bizarre (in order to dilute the "flavor suggestive of propaganda for radicalism" in WINTERSET, Breen suggested that RKO "substitute the word 'lunatic,' or some other word, for the word, 'capitalist'"), what took place between the PCA and the studios were genuine negotiations in which concessions were made by both parties in pursuit of a common objective. Breen's insistence that the PCA was "regarded by producers, directors, and their staffs, as participants in the processes of production" was perfectly accurate: in a typical minor instance, Wallis's assistant, Walter MacEwen, recognized that Breen's main aim in having Warners alter one word in Joan Blondell's final song in GOLD DIGGERS OF 1937 was to prevent the routine being "mutilated" by censor boards.[61]

Beyond the shared assumption that the PCA functioned as an aid, not a hindrance, to production, there were two underlying considerations that governed its working operation. "Compensating moral values," as understood by Breen, ensured not only that "no picture shall be produced which will lower the moral standards of those who see it" but also that a calculus of retribution or coincidence would invariably be deployed to punish the guilty or declare sympathetic characters innocent. But if plots had to be morally unambiguous in their development, dialogue, and conclusion, the site of textual ambiguity shifted from narrative to the representation of incident, in a manner that required the audience to construct an event that may or may not have taken place. In matters of sex in particular, a policy of ambiguity came to preside over Hollywood's representation. Lea Jacobs notes the case of Garbo's CAMILLE in 1936, in which "it is difficult for the spectator to pinpoint with certainty when or how the heroine's sexual transgressions occur." In DEAD END, Francie's past, fragments of dialogue, and a knowledge of Sidney Howard's play suggest she has venereal disease; her cough, however, offers the alternative of tuberculosis. Textual indeterminacy became a feature of Hollywood's representation of sexuality, emerging in complex and oblique codes that resembled neurotic symptoms or fetishes. Even under Breen, the censorship of sexuality remained an imperfect procedure of repression, with the repressed always returning, as Freud had promised, in distorted form, given a sufficiently imaginative audience. In 1935 the PCA insisted on the removal of one shot, of rain falling on a door, from THE DEVIL IS A WOMAN, because it signified prostitution. This mode of representation developed a life of its own in front of an audience willing to play a game of double entendre. The public, argued Harold J. Salemson, "has learned to supply from its own imagination the specific acts of so-called misconduct which the Production Code has made unmentionable." Elliot Paul pithily observed, "A scene should give full play to the vices of the audience, and still have a technical out."[62]

The establishment of the PCA did not abate the process of negotiation over what constituted satisfactory material for films. The first serious anxiety occurred in October 1934, with MGM's THE MERRY WIDOW. In 1935, disputes over the representation of crime resurfaced with the attempt by several studios to circumvent the prohibition on gangster films in the "G-Men" cycle, until British censors objected to the trend. The Code's provisions on crime were modified on a number of occasions during the later 1930s to eliminate themes of kidnapping or suicide and to prohibit scenes showing law-enforcing officers dying at the hands of criminals or the display of machine guns. In 1938–1939, too, there was a revival of concern about the volume of crime films, triggered by the "boys gang" cycle following from DEAD END and ANGELS WITH DIRTY FACES and by gangster retrospectives such as THE ROARING TWENTIES. Breen suggested in September 1939 that crime stories accounted for 53 percent of all films in production. On the whole, however, these questions of code enforcement were relatively minor: the studios had acquiesced in the PCA machinery and, with occasional displays of resistance, acquiesced in its decisions over details of representation, Breen's refusal to certify some pre-1934 films for reissue, and the PCA's advice not to undertake a project. More important, public opinion had, with few and inconsequential exceptions, recovered from its moral panic and accepted the Association's or the Legion's account of the industry's rescue from the abyss in 1934.[63]

However, disputes with independent exhibitors were intensified by the independents' failure to gain significant concessions from the distributors during the controversy. Allied States persisted in their efforts to gain redress over block booking and cancellation privileges. After the abandonment of the NRA Code machinery in 1935, their campaign switched its focus to an attack on chain and circuit theaters, echoing the charges made by independent retailers against chain stores such as A&P and Woolworth's. This line of attack proved more promising than their attachment to moral reform, and put anti-block-booking legislation on the congressional calendar and before most state legislatures after 1936. The Neely bill to prohibit block booking was passed by the Senate in 1938 and 1940, but held up in the House of Representatives. Although none of the federal legislation was passed, the independents' persistent agitation against the industry's unfair trade practices and their increasing use of private antitrust suits against distributors played a significant part in provoking the Department of Justice investigation into the industry that resulted in the Paramount suit of 1938.

The difficulties the Association faced over film content in the late 1930s were largely the results of its successes in imposing a definition of entertainment as recreation. Protestant criticism about Catholic domination of Code machinery was concerned less with theology than with the Code's preoccupation with sex at the expense of less individualistic concerns:

> The right of the cinema to portray vested evils and entrenched privilege in their true light, and to embody the struggle for social security and economic plenty, as in *Our Daily Bread*, is a kind of morality concerning which the Code gives insufficient attention. (Worth M. Tippy to Quigley, 14 March 1935, MPA 1935 Production Code file)

MGM's decision in 1936 to not to produce a film version of Sinclair Lewis's *It Can't Happen Here* after spending $200,000 on the screen rights led to accusations that the Hays Office was engaging in political censorship. But against Lewis's assertion that "this decision raises an extremely important and critical question concerning free speech and free opinion in the United States," Terry Ramsaye, the editor of *Motion Picture Herald*, suggested that it "has all of the vast significance that would attach to a decision by . . . Armour and Company to discontinue a brand of ham." Free speech was not a consideration: MGM's decision, like that to drop the "G-Men" cycle, was made on business grounds, because the industry depended "for its prosperity on being international merchandise" and was "vulnerable to, and on occasion menaced by, all the governments there are, abroad and at home."[64]

The industry's studied neutrality in party politics was itself a calculation of political interest on the part of an industry heavily embroiled in the practical politics of its self-interest. Part of the political protection of those interests involved the definition of its product—entertainment—as being outside the sphere of the political. In his annual report for 1938, Hays argued that the industry could afford "the soft impeachment" that it provided nothing more than "escapist" entertainment:

> Entertainment is the commodity for which the public pays at the box-office. Propaganda disguised as entertainment would be neither honest salesmanship nor honest showmanship. . . . The industry has resisted and must continue to resist the lure of propaganda in that sinister sense persistently urged upon it by extremist groups. (Quoted in Thorp, *America at the Movies* [London: Faber, 1946], p. 161)

The Association's definition of extremism was, however, very narrow. Hays averred that "propaganda" could be recognized "only through the process of common sense," embodied, in effect, in the PCA. As his dealings with the studios became more assertive after 1934, Breen's correspondence made fewer distinctions between a decision under the Code, advice regarding the likely actions of state or foreign censors, and the implementation of "industry policy" in response to pressure groups, foreign governments, and corporate interests. Industry policy was, like self-regulation, designed to prevent the movies from becoming a subject of controversy or giving offense to powerful interests. Breen defended his practice of linking this strategy with Code enforcement by arguing that the studio executives supported his "vigorous" tone in urging eliminations of any kind on producers. PCA activities were centered around protecting the industry from criticism, whether that came from censor boards, foreign governments, or pressure groups whose displeasure might lead them to call for government interference in the industry. Since he saw the PCA as representing a national consensus on political issues as well as moral ones, he denied that there was anything "sinister" in his rejecting material that characterized "a member of the United States Senate as a 'heavy'; or . . . in which police officials are shown to be dishonest; or . . . in which lawyers, or doctors, or bankers, *are indicated as a class.*"[65]

In 1936, as part of the MPPDA's lobbying campaign to defeat federal block-booking proposals and by way of demonstrating the effectiveness of its self-regulation, the PCA prepared bound volumes of some of its decisions and circulated them among legislators.[66] Against their celebratory intent, these volumes substantiated the accusations of political liberals that "self-regulation . . . has degenerated into political censorship." *It Can't Happen Here* was cited as an example, as were PCA decisions over THEY WON'T FORGET and two films dealing with the Spanish Civil War, THE LAST TRAIN FROM MADRID and BLOCKADE. It was the overt anti-Communism of official Catholicism, and its attitude toward Spain in particular, that led to the strongest accusations of an excessive Catholic influence in the PCA. BLOCKADE, approved while Breen was on vacation in Europe, was attacked by the Knights of Columbus as Communist propaganda in 1938. Although Breen defended the film, he did so with little genuine conviction. In December 1937 he had proposed to contacts in the Vatican a plan to prohibit films involving "divorce and the re-marriage of divorced persons" and films in which "Communist propaganda" had been "injected." Breen proposed using the power of the foreign market, via Catholic pressure on government censorship, to prohibit such films in enough countries as to render them unprofitable to the producers.[67] Breen was not alone in seeing that the suppression of Communist propaganda was a moral, not a political, issue. In the middle of the BLOCKADE controversy, Martin Quigley proposed an amendment to the Production Code:

> No motion picture shall be produced which shall advocate or create sympathy for political theories alien to, and subversive of, American institutions, nor any picture which perverts or tends to pervert the theatre screen from its avowed purpose of entertainment to the function of political controversy. (Quigley to Hays, 11 July 1938, MPA 1939 Production Code file)

Quigley's proposal contributed to the innuendo spread by opponents of Hollywood unionization about a left-wing conspiracy against the industry, but failed to address the exigencies of a moment when the PCA was becoming controversial precisely because of its success in keeping controversy from the screen. Earlier in 1938, Hays had initiated an internal investigation into the extent of the jurisdiction of the PCA conducted by his executive assistant Francis Harmon. To some extent, the investigation itself represented a reining-in of Breen's expansionist tendencies and an assertion by the Association's WASP leadership that Catholic influence should not overstep its boundaries. But it also dealt with what became known within the MPPDA as the "twilight zone" at the borders of the Code's jurisdiction. By 1937, there was a growing concern over the increasing presence of advertising in films, in the form of advertising shorts, tie-ins, and product placements. Another issue of Code jurisdiction had been raised by the exhibition in affiliated theaters of two documentaries that had not been certificated by the PCA. BIRTH OF A BABY was in clear breach of the Code, and THE RIVER worried both producers and distributors that the government was entering into competition with the commercial industry.[68]

The predominant concern, however, was with the PCA's jurisdiction over matters of "industry policy" outside the Code and drew its impetus from the antitrust suit filed by the Department of Justice in July 1938. Implicating the PCA in the majors' restrictive practices, it alleged that through the Code the majors exercised a practical censorship over the entire industry, restricting the production of pictures treating controversial subjects and hindering the development of innovative approaches to drama or narrative by companies that might use innovation as a way of challenging the majors' monopoly power. Coinciding with the BLOCKADE incident, Harmon's investigation suggested that

> very great care is needed on the part of the PCA to distinguish between its administrative functions under the Code (with its penalty provisions) on the one hand, and its advisory functions (without penalties) on the other. . . . A reasonably clear and predictable definition of the extent of the jurisdiction of the Production Code Administration, is urgently needed. Legal problems must be met and a course charted through the maze of confusing terminology now in current use. (Harmon memo, 5 July 1938, MPA 1938 Production Code file)

He classified groups of films, including newsreels, advertising, and sponsored and government films, as properly falling outside the authority of the PCA, as did questions other than a film's conformity "to standards of decency, morality and fairness embodied in the Production Code":

> If the film deals with a controversial subject, but is free from that which offends decency or is listed in the Code as morally objectionable, then the sole remaining question to be decided by the PCA should not be whether the film is "desirable" but whether the presentation deals fairly and honestly, and without deliberate deception, with the subject matter. ("Jurisdiction of Production Code Administration," MPA 1938 Production Code file)

Quigley was horrified. The changes proposed, he suggested, were "an invitation to disaster." But the federal government's redefinition of what constituted unreasonable restraint of trade in the Paramount suit required the restriction of the PCA's jurisdiction, in order not to embroil the Association in a violation of the antitrust laws.[69] The effect was to encourage, or at least acquiesce in, the use of politically more controversial content as a way of demonstrating that the "freedom of the screen" was not hampered by the operations of the PCA. Although PCA officials continued to voice concern over whether such subjects as CONFESSIONS OF A NAZI SPY constituted appropriate screen entertainment, they were much more circumspect in expressing their opinions. This was only indirectly in response to a change in public sentiment, if indeed such a change had taken place. It was, rather more directly, in response to immediate political pressures.[70]

In 1930–1934 the dominant voices to which the association was attempting to adjust film content were moral conservatives, most clearly orchestrated by the Catholic church, but by 1938–1939 they had become much more marginal because more extreme. In January 1939, Quigley warned Breen that the war against "Red propaganda" on-screen would make the battle for decency seem a skirmish: "In many places in the industry, especially amongst our Semitic brethren, there seems to be growing an acceptance of the idea of radical propaganda on the screen. . . . [Hays] has been side-stepping and pussyfooting." Against this kind of rhetoric and Breen's grandiose ambitions to include all production under the Code, MPPDA Washington bureau chief Ray Norr insisted that in the face of the antitrust suit, the object now was "to *limit* the jurisdiction of the Motion Picture Production Code in various respects." Quigley's notion of an entertainment kept pure from all political utterance was becoming increasingly difficult to sustain—less in practice than as a principle for the MPPDA to adhere to in public.[71]

The change can be measured in Hays's rhetorical support for "pictures which dramatized present-day social conditions" in his annual report in March 1939. Margaret Thorp identified Hays's changed tone as marking "the day the motion picture industry extended an official welcome to ideas." However, Hays was also addressing the Association's immediate political and legal situation. The Neely bill never came to a vote in the House, while the Paramount suit was engineered into a consent decree in November 1940. For the third time in a decade the Association's efficient political lobbying power had headed off a major crisis faced by the industry's oligopoly structure. On the two previous occasions, in 1929–1930 and 1933–1934, that crisis had been successfully diverted away from issues of trade practice into concerns about film content. The affairs of the late 1930s suggested that mechanisms for the control of content had become too extensive, so that it could not so effectively fulfill its function as the currency of negotiation among parties who felt that the movie business was their business. Rather, the censorship of the movies—as opposed to movie content—was in danger of becoming the issue. Hays's rhetoric in 1939 echoed that of Sinclair Lewis in 1936, but did so according to the changed agenda of the intervening three years and was part of an Association campaign to persuade the federal government to "recognize the 'special significance and peculiarly difficult problems of' the film industry as an international leader in providing 'good and necessary recreation at a moderate cost.'" This line of argument would allow the MPPDA to gain government acceptance as an "essential industry" during World War II.[72]

As an influence on production, the regulation of movie content through the Production Code might best be understood as a generic pressure, comparable to the pressure of convention in a romantic comedy or a Western. Relocating the

Toward the end of the decade, controversy was more likely to result from the movies' representation of political subject matter and questions of the "freedom of the screen." For instance, PCA officials doubted that Warners' production of Confessions of a Nazi Spy *(1939) was appropriate screen entertainment.*

Code and its administrators as integrated participants in Hollywood's processes of production, rather than its philistine and picayunish villains, is in itself a contribution to a deeper understanding of how the motion-picture industry operated in practice. In viewing the Production Code as part of the much larger overall activity of the MPPDA, this account also integrates issues around the control of content within the broader concerns of the period about the movies as a cultural institution. Using this broader perspective, we can offer some revisions to the accepted history of Hollywood in the 1930s that, in particular, allow us to recontextualize questions of whether films produced in the early 1930s were "subversive" either in their intent or effect. Rather than identifying a clear-cut distinction between films produced before 1934 and those produced after, a recognition that the Code as a system of conventions was gradually developed during the early 1930s suggests that it is more appropriate to see "the Golden Age of Turbulence" as a period in which a system of representation acceptable both to the industry and to the cultural authorities to whom it deferred was negotiated. Those negotiations were clearly not concluded with the agreements of July 1934; questions of detail remained subject to constant discussion, and issues of broad principle, including the implementation of the Code itself, were as open to revision in the late 1930s as they had been earlier in the decade.

Industry trade practices, which were to a large extent the hidden agenda behind much of the activity around censorship in the decade, were frequently alleged to have an inhibiting effect on the industry's preparedness to experiment "with less popular themes aimed at smaller, more specific audiences." Undoubtedly, the industry's oligopoly structure inhibited experimentation, and the Production Code contributed to that effect. But if the "insane and inane and outmoded" Code made Hollywood's product less able "to deal more frankly with controversial themes," the extent to which it also represented a kind of transparent conspiracy between movie and audience remains largely unexplored. The industry had a more sophisticated understanding of the preferences of its several audiences than it was given credit for. It did not produce experimental films of the kind critics like Creighton Peet or Elmer Rice demanded, not because it refused to differentiate among its audiences, but because there was an insufficiently large audience for such productions.[73]

The Production Code did not cause the lack of experimentation in Hollywood product. Rather, it was itself a symptom of the underlying cause. The Code was a consequence of commercialism and of the particular understanding of the audience and its desires that the industry's commercialism promoted. But to produce films that were radically different from those actually produced in Hollywood would have needed changes far more substantial than the alteration or even abolition of the Code; it would have needed a redefinition of the cultural function of entertainment, and that was a task beyond the limits of responsibility the industry set itself.

4

Feeding the
Maw of Exhibition

So far this book has implied that the vertically integrated structure of the major film companies profoundly influenced the quantity and quality of the motion pictures produced by Hollywood. Because real estate assets (theaters) rested on a base of intangibles (motion pictures), the production process of these companies had to be well organized to accomplish three goals: first, motion pictures had to appeal to a large cross section of the public; second, they had to attract audiences consistently over long periods of time; and third, they had to be produced in sufficient quantity and on a regular basis to permit quick audience turnover.

To meet these demands, Hollywood had honed an efficient means of producing large numbers of feature films containing stars called the studio system. In place since the mid teens, the system organized production around a central producer who oversaw a large, fully staffed studio containing talent, technical workers, and craftsmen. Using the continuity script as a blueprint, production was divided into discrete parts, such as script development, art and costume design, cinematography, directing, and editing, which corresponded to departments that supplied talent and material as needed. Harnessing this work force, Hollywood churned out from four hundred to five hundred films a year during the thirties in an attempt to satisfy every taste in every city and town. The following discussion will demonstrate four things about the studio system: (1) the growing domination of producers over the production process; (2) the diminished status of the director and the screenwriter in the system; (3) the ''authorship'' of distinctive studio house styles; and (4) the methods used by the majors and elite independent producers to rationalize production.

The Shift to the Producer-Unit System

To elucidate the nature of the studio system in Hollywood during the thirties, it is appropriate to begin by quoting Leo Rosten:

> Each studio has a personality; each studio's product shows special emphases and values. And, in the final analysis, the sum total of a studio's personality, the aggregate pattern of its choices and its tastes,

73

may be traced to its producers. For it is the producers who establish the preferences, the prejudices, and the predispositions of the organization and, therefore, of the movies which it turns out. (*Hollywood,* pp. 242–243)

Studios were organized hierarchically.[1] At the top sat an executive who typically held the corporate title of vice-president in charge of production. Moguls such as Louis B. Mayer at Metro-Goldwyn-Mayer, Jack L. Warner at Warner Bros., Y. Frank Freeman at Paramount, and Darryl F. Zanuck at 20th Century–Fox headed the most important studios and were perpetually in the limelight. However, within the larger corporate structures of their companies, the moguls were beholden to the chief executives who typically held the title of president or chairman. For example, at Warners,

> Jack L. Warner . . . the stereotype of the crude, rough, all-powerful movie mogul . . . ruled feature film-making with an iron hand. Yet his management style only mirrored his older brother Harry's wishes. The brothers Warner sought a cut-rate movie factory, which would produce the required number of features and shorts for Warners' theaters each year. Warner Bros. operated on a volume basis, trying to make a small profit on every film. Jack Warner supplied the films; Abe Warner routed them to appropriate theaters, but there was no question who mapped overall corporate strategy and had the last word in all decisions—Harry M. Warner. (Douglas Gomery, *The Hollywood Studio System* [New York: St. Martin's Press, 1986], p. 112)

Harry Cohn, the production chief at Columbia, was the only mogul to serve in the dual capacity as chief executive officer of the corporation and the studio.

To motivate its production chief, a company might give him a cut of the profits in addition to a handsome salary. Louis B. Mayer, for example, became the highest-paid American executive during the thirties as a result of his unique profit-sharing agreement with Loew's. When Loew's acquired the Louis B. Mayer Pictures Corp. in 1924, Mayer wanted neither cash nor stock for himself and his two partners, Irving Thalberg and Robert Rubin, but a percentage of the profits—to be exact, 20 percent of the profits (after a dividend set aside of $2 per common share) up to $2.5 million and 15 percent of the profits over that. In addition to receiving weekly salaries ranging from $1,000 for Rubin to $4,000 for Thalberg, the three executives divided up more than $1 million in profits in 1935 alone.[2]

Studio chiefs did not rule their empires single-handedly, but administered staffs of high-salaried managers who took care of the myriad business affairs of operating a studio plant, including payroll, security, industrial relations, maintenance, and food services. Production was delegated to a central producer. MGM's Irving Thalberg, the prototypical central producer, had no set daily routines; *Fortune* said, "His brain is the camera which photographs dozens of scripts in a week and decides which of them, if any, shall be turned over to MGM's twenty-seven departments to be made into a moving picture. It is also the recording apparatus which converts the squealing friction of 2,200 erratic underlings into the more than normally coherent chatter of an MGM talkie."[3]

To assist him in producing the forty or fifty pictures the studio turned out each year, Thalberg employed a group of ten associate producers. Each associate producer specialized in a certain type of picture—prestige pictures, sophisticated comedies, melodramas, action pictures, and so forth. Functioning as surrogates for Thalberg, these men worked on two or three pictures simultaneously. To begin a project, the associate producer conferred with writers on the story idea and worked with them to develop the shooting script. After submitting the script for Thalberg's approval, he coordinated the efforts of the designers, director, and cast. Describing the associate producer's job, *Fortune* said, "Without being able in most cases to act, write, or direct, they are supposed to know more about writing than either the director or the star, more about directing than the star or the writer."[4] Associate producers stayed with a picture until it was completed, while resolving whatever problems arose. Thalberg treated the finished film as raw material. Thalberg was noted for testing audience reaction to his films before they were released. If audiences did not like something or failed to respond in the appropriate way, he did not hesitate to have parts of the picture reshot.

Darryl Zanuck, the producing "genius" at Warners, ran the studio practically as a one-man show early in the decade. In addition to his regular responsibilities as head of a production, Zanuck acted as the chief talent scout, story editor, and head writer. Allen Rivkin, a Warner screenwriter recalled,

> I remember when I came to Warner Brothers [in 1930], Zanuck would read a story on Friday, think about it over the weekend, get it set in his head and call the writers into his office on Monday morning. He'd say, "Okay boys, here's the story, it'll have Jimmy Cagney in it. We'll start shooting four weeks from this morning and we'll open at Warner's downtown eight weeks from today." (Quoted in James R. Silke, *Here's Looking at You Kid: Fifty Years of Fighting, Working, and Dreaming at Warner Brothers* [Boston: Little, Brown, 1976], p. 64)

To keep tabs on actual production, Warner employed "supervisors" to visit the set each day to anticipate and stop any costly overruns. They worked anonymously until 1932, when the studio gave them a supervisor credit on the screen.

Weaknesses in the central producer system became apparent straight off. Placing a studio's entire annual output in the hands of one person minimized originality and the exchange of ideas. As Paramount's Jesse L. Lasky put it, "The output of a studio must of necessity cover the entire field of motion-picture entertainment, and the mind and creative instincts of no one man is able to encompass every type of motion picture." Another weakness of the system surfaced during the Depression when it became apparent that a single person could not monitor production costs on a day-to-day basis. Some studios therefore modified the central producer system to create what became known as the producer-unit system. As the term implies, production was apportioned among a group of producers, each of whom headed a core group of talent responsible for three to six pictures a year. Because a unit producer specialized in a certain type of picture, the new system was supposed to improve quality while greatly lowering overhead costs.[5]

MGM instituted the producer-unit system in 1933 after Thalberg suffered a heart attack. Restructuring the studio, Mayer assumed all the administrative chores, formed a production unit for his son-in-law David O. Selznick to produce prestige pictures, and then upgraded Thalberg's associate producers by giving them responsibility for their own films and by giving them screen credit as producers. Until his premature death in 1936, Thalberg thereafter functioned as a special-projects producer to sustain MGM's reputation for "polished elegant craftsmanship." Among these special projects were THE BARRETTS OF WIMPOLE STREET (1934), MUTINY ON THE BOUNTY (1935), and ROMEO AND JULIET (1936).[6]

Warners shifted to the producer-unit system in 1933 following Darryl Zanuck's walkout in protest over Harry Warner's decision to retain salary cuts after the national bank holiday. To replace Zanuck, the studio made Hal B. Wallis associate executive in charge of production under Jack Warner. Over the next several years, Wallis upgraded the authority of the supervisors, changed their title to associate producer, and gave them appropriate screen credit. Unlike the shift at MGM that dispersed control, the reorganization at Warners left Wallis with a good deal of centralized authority. *Fortune* reported that "Wallis initiates many scripts and passes on all of them, dickers with stars, assigns budgets, and in fact takes bows for the whole Warner picture program." Like their counterparts at MGM, Warners' six associate producers specialized in certain types of pictures. Henry Blanke, for example, was assigned "the most artistically ambitious" projects, such as the prestigious biopics JUAREZ, THE LIFE OF EMILE ZOLA, and THE STORY OF LOUIS PASTEUR. Lou Edelman had the job of producing two types of low-cost movies, "service" pictures "glorifying some branch of uniformed forces of the nation" and "headliner" stories plucked from the newspapers. And Bryan Foy was given all of Warners' B pictures.[7]

Paramount followed suit when it followed Joseph P. Kennedy's advice on restructuring the studio. Barney Balaban, Paramount's new president, appointed Y. Frank Freeman head of the studio. Since Freeman was basically an administrator, he placed William LeBaron in charge of production. LeBaron assigned all the B pictures, which amounted to half the studio's output, to a single producer who functioned autonomously. To handle the A pictures, LeBaron organized two types of production units, one around the talents of producer-directors Cecil B. DeMille, Leo McCarey, and Henry Hathaway and the other around the talents of unit producers Arthur Hornblow, Al Lewin, Barney Glazer, and others. As *Fortune* said, "With the available Paramount star material more or less in mind, they sooner or later find a story that blossoms in their minds into a successful film. They clear it with LeBaron, get a budget from [George] Bagnall, and are off."[8]

The shift from central producer to the unit-producer system grew out of the Depression and answered a need to maintain fiscal restraints. This slight restructuring of production at the executive level did not loosen the studios' grip on talent; rather, the shift further concentrated production into the hands of executives. A Screen Directors Guild survey published in 1938 revealed that in 1927, Hollywood used 34 producers to make 743 pictures; ten years later, Hollywood was using 220 producers to make 484 pictures. "In other words," said Leo Rosten, "800 percent more producers were used in 1937 to make 40 percent fewer pictures than in 1936!"[9]

The Status of the Director

The pressures of mass production continued unabated as the decade progressed. Because the necessity of meeting the needs of exhibitors was often at odds with the creative impulses of moviemakers, the moguls resisted any encroachment on their prerogatives. In fact, the shift to unit production resulted in greater specialization in the design and execution of motion pictures as studios attempted to satisfy a cross section of audience tastes, particularly interest in big-budget prestige pictures.

To keep artistic personnel in line, studio chiefs had formed the Academy of Motion Picture Arts and Sciences in 1927. Conceived by Louis B. Mayer, the Academy was created to "improve the artistic quality of the film medium" and embraced five categories of filmmakers—producers, directors, actors, writers, and technicians. These employees apparently were given sufficient financial rewards to forestall serious labor organizing among their ranks for five years. Labor problems with the rank and file during the Depression were solved quickly and expeditiously. Among the talent groups, art directors, cinematographers, and editors joined unaffiliated professional associations, such as the American Society of Cinematographers and American Cinema Editors, which kept them content throughout the decade. Directors, actors, and screenwriters formed unions. Working conditions for these groups somewhat improved as a result, but the control of production remained firmly in the grip of producers.

Describing the status of his profession, Frank Capra, in his capacity as the founding president of the Screen Directors Guild (SDG), sent the following open letter to the *New York Times* in early 1939:

> There are only half a dozen directors in Hollywood who are allowed to shoot as they please and who have any supervision over their editing. We all agree with you when you say that motion pictures are the director's medium. . . . [But] we have tried for three years . . . to have two weeks' preparation time for "A" pictures, one week preparation time for "B" pictures, and to have supervision of just the first rough cut of the picture. . . . We have only asked that the director be allowed to read the script he is going to do and to assemble the film in its first rough form. . . . It has taken three years of constant battling to achieve any part of this. I would say that 80 per cent of the directors today shoot scenes exactly as they are told to shoot them without any changes whatsoever, and that 90 per cent of them have no voice in the story or in the editing. (Quoted in Leo Rosten, *Hollywood: The Movie Colony, The Movie Makers* [New York: Harcourt, Brace, 1941], pp. 302–303)

Capra echoed a common complaint. Not only directors but most artistic personnel chafed at the demands of rigid production schedules. Once a dominant creative force behind the motion picture, the director did not retain even the right of the final cut by the thirties. Clearly, the decline in status of the director vis-à-vis the producer resulted from the efficiencies mandated by the

Frank Capra (1934).

reorganization of studios during the Depression. Wall Street's opinion of the director can be glimpsed from a piece by C. F. Morgan, who said,

> What is the biggest production obstacle? The director. Five years ago he was king; today almost generally he's a liability. Any man who is so unsure of what he is doing and so lacking in confidence that he has to shoot 100,000 feet of film to be sure of 7,500 for his resulting picture, should be sent back to whatever he was doing before he began to infest the picture studios. ("Sanity Reaches the Movies," *Magazine of Wall Street*, 11 November 1933, p. 98)

Describing the function of the director, David O. Selznick said that at MGM, for example, "the director, nine times out of ten, is strictly a director, in the same sense that the stage director is the director of the play. His job is solely to get out on the stage and direct the actors, put them through the traces that are called for in the script." Elaborating on his point, Selznick noted that at Warners, the director is "purely a cog in the machine" for "ninety per cent of the Warner films" and is "handed a script, usually just a few days before he goes into production." A similar situation existed at 20th Century–Fox. Zanuck became deeply involved in script development, but he backed off during the shooting. However, while watching rushes he gave comments to the director, dictated notes to the editor, and chose the takes he wanted for the picture.[10]

The concept of authorial freedom as it is understood today did not exist in Hollywood during the thirties. Not even when Paramount made Ernst Lubitsch head of production in 1935. Although Lubitsch's short tenure marked "the only time in Hollywood studio history that such a noted director was given full creative control of a major studio's product," Lubitsch, in his capacity as production chief, disregarded so-called directors' prerogatives and used previews and the "retake and remake" method to improve pictures.[11] At best, the top directors such as Frank Capra at Columbia, John Ford at Fox, Cecil B. DeMille at Paramount, King Vidor at MGM, and a few others enjoyed ample preparation time, participated in story conferences, and consulted with the editor and music director. In this manner, they were able to exercise a measure of influence over the entire production process.

In an attempt to reassert its prerogatives over production, a group of seventy-five directors organized the Screen Directors Guild on 16 January 1936 (the name was changed to the Directors Guild of America in 1960). The guild's manifesto stated, "It is the firm conviction of the Screen Directors' Guild that rehabilitation lies, first in changing the present 'system of production' which pervades the Industry, namely, eliminating the involved, complicated and expensive system of supervision which separates the Director and Writer from the responsible Executive Producers."[12] To lead the fight for recognition, the guild elected Frank Capra as its first president.

Capra undoubtedly enjoyed more authorial freedom than any of his fellow directors. Capra earned it by directing a string of enormously popular pictures, by parlaying this success into control over production, and by constructing with the compliance of Columbia Pictures what Charles Wolfe called "the notion of what a successful, yet self-respecting and in some sense 'autonomous' filmmaker in Hollywood might be thought to be like."[13]

When Capra joined Columbia Pictures in 1927, the studio serviced the low end of the market. A member of Poverty Row, the studio owned no theaters, had no stars under contract, and generally operated on shoestring budgets. To make it into the majors, Columbia had to produce an occasional class-A picture. Harry Cohn, Columbia's president, gave Capra this job. Capra responded by directing a series of inexpensive but well-received comedies. Trading on his value to the company, Capra insisted on having more authority over his work and on receiving public recognition for his labors. Columbia complied and, by the end of his first year of work, billed his films as "Frank Capra Productions."[14]

Going into the thirties, Capra's stature as a director of class-A pictures grew with each successive release. By the time he made AMERICAN MADNESS in 1932, critics were referring to him as "one of Hollywood's best." After IT HAPPENED ONE NIGHT (1934) swept the Academy Awards, Capra literally became a star and received top billing in Columbia's ads. "A New Frank Capra production" and other such heralds thereafter became standard. To promote LOST HORIZON (1937), Columbia's most expensive picture of the decade, "Columbia launched a promotional campaign that stressed Capra's direct supervision of all aspects of the lavish production. . . . By 1938 a special place for Capra as a filmmaker controlling all aspects of his work within the context of the studio system had been clearly established in popular commentary on the movies." The *Saturday Evening Post,* for example, published a profile by Alva Johnston entitled "Capra Shoots As He Pleases." *Time* featured Capra in a cover story about the status of the director in Hollywood. During the production of YOU CAN'T TAKE IT WITH YOU, *Life* ran a photo spread entitled "How Frank Capra Makes a Hit Picture," in which Capra is seen studying the set designs, discussing the script, directing the cast, viewing the rushes, and even physically cutting the film. Howard Barnes in the *New York Herald Tribune* proposed that Capra was "the most important figure in motion pictures today," by defining "the importance of the director in the complicated business of turning out a photoplay."[15] Columbia, which lacked big-name stars, had created a star out of its top director. In the process, the studio gave the illusion that it was possible for a talented director to achieve the status of an auteur within the studio system.

When Frank Capra was fighting for recognition of the Directors Guild, 244 contract directors were working in Hollywood. More than half had started out in silent pictures, and only twenty-one had come from Broadway. Using *Film Daily*'s annual poll as a measure of critical esteem indicates that Frank Capra and George Cukor led the pack with six pictures; followed by Sidney Franklin with five; Clarence Brown, William Dieterle, W. S. Van Dyke, and King Vidor with four; John Ford, Edmund Goulding, Henry King, Mervyn LeRoy, and William Wyler with three; and Richard Boleslawski, Frank Borzage, Jack Conway, Victor Fleming, George Hill, Robert Z. Leonard, Frank Lloyd, Leo McCarey, and Lewis Milestone with two.

The directors who won recognition in the Academy Award sweepstakes during the decade were Frank Capra, with three Oscars, followed by Lewis Milestone, Norman Taurog, Frank Borzage, Frank Lloyd, John Ford, Leo McCarey, and Victor Fleming. Every picture that won an Academy Award for best direction also appeared on *Film Daily*'s Ten Best.

The directors whose pictures as a group made it to *Variety*'s annual list of box-office winners were W. S. Van Dyke with four mentions; Frank Capra and

George Cukor with three; followed by David Butler, Michael Curtiz, George B. Seitz, and Norman Taurog with two. Victor Fleming was mentioned only in 1939, but that year his two pictures, THE WIZARD OF OZ and GONE WITH THE WIND, grossed more money in one year than any other group of pictures by a director in the decade. Practically all the above-named directors who were active in 1938 are listed in Leo Rosten's roster of the forty-five highest-paid directors, which is to say, directors with an annual salary of more than $75,000.[16] As might be expected, a close correlation exists between a director's compensation and the number of times his name appeared on the lists, particularly *Variety*'s. But more interesting is the correlation between a director's esteem as measured by the number of times his name appeared on the lists and the types of pictures he directed. This comparison reveals that the prestige picture most often constituted the prism through which a director's talents were measured.

Although contract directors were expected to be versatile and skillful technicians capable of directing up to six pictures a year, the elite corps also specialized in superspecials constructed around a studio's top stars. George Cukor made his reputation as a woman's director, eliciting remarkable performances from such famous stars as Katharine Hepburn, Greta Garbo, Norma Shearer, and Joan Crawford at such studios as RKO, MGM, and Columbia. Clarence Brown made his reputation directing Greta Garbo—two silents and five of her most successful sound films at MGM. Henry King was best known for his pictures recreating Americana, but Darryl Zanuck also entrusted him with Fox's top stars, Tyrone Power, Alice Faye, and Don Ameche, in two big prestige pictures, ALEXANDER'S RAGTIME BAND (1938) and IN OLD CHICAGO (1938).

Michael Curtiz's forty-two pictures for Warners during the thirties consisted of horror films, crime films, women's films, swashbucklers, and comedies, among other types. However, Curtiz also specialized in handling the studio's newest young stars, Errol Flynn and Olivia de Havilland, in a series of swashbucklers. W. S. Van Dyke, MGM's work horse, directed MANHATTAN MELODRAMA (1934), a gangster film; MARIE ANTOINETTE (1938), a historical drama; the Thin Man detective series; an Andy Hardy family comedy; and three Jeanette MacDonald–Nelson Eddy operettas.

The Directors Guild finally won recognition in February 1939 after Capra threatened to call a strike of all directors in Hollywood. The contract the studios signed with the guild gave most contract directors "greater freedom at the expense of the associate producers and supervisors who held power over them" and won for elite directors the status of producer-director. Unlike the contract director, the producer-director was allowed to select his own writers, cast, and cameraman, and to see his film through to the end. Moreover, he was allowed to concentrate on maybe two or three pictures a year instead of rushing through five or six. For his efforts the producer-director was paid a salary ranging from $90,000 to $300,000 a year and might even earn a share of the profits.[17] However, in every case the studio invariably retained rights of approval over the key ingredients of a production—namely, the underlying property, the script, the budget, and the stars—and, of course, over how the picture was to be marketed.

Rosten estimated that around thirty directors had achieved producer-director status in 1939, among them Ernst Lubitsch and Mervyn LeRoy at MGM; Cecil B. DeMille and Wesley Ruggles at Paramount; Frank Capra and Howard Hawks at Columbia; David Butler at RKO; and John M. Stahl and Rowland V. Lee at

Universal. Warners and 20th Century–Fox were the only studios that denied any director producer status.[18]

Capra, the leader of the pack, gained the most autonomy over his work by becoming an independent producer. Leaving Columbia at the end of 1939, he formed Frank Capra Productions in partnership with his screenwriter-collaborator, Robert Riskin. To make his next picture, he signed a production-distribution deal with Warners and secured financing from the Bank of America, a package that gave him rights of approval over the creative ingredients as well as authority over marketing.[19] By taking this step, Capra joined the vanguard of the industrywide shift to independent production that took place over the next ten years.

The Status of the Screenwriter

Talking pictures added a new dimension to the craft of screenwriting—the ability to write realistic dialogue. Numerous contract writers from silent films easily made it into the talkies. Anita Loos, for example, returned to MGM after temporarily giving up screenwriting to write SAN FRANCISCO (1936), SARATOGA (1937), and THE WOMEN (1939). Frances Marion, who wrote for Mary Pickford in the teens, continued her career at MGM, where she wrote THE BIG HOUSE (1930), MIN AND BILL (1930), THE CHAMP (1931), DINNER AT EIGHT (1933), and CAMILLE (1937). Jules Furthman, who started out selling stories to the movies in 1915, collaborated with Josef von Sternberg at Paramount on three major Marlene Dietrich films, MOROCCO (1930), the picture that launched Dietrich's career in America, SHANGHAI EXPRESS (1932), and BLONDE VENUS (1932). Furthman also wrote two pictures directed by Howard Hawks, COME AND GET IT (Goldwyn, 1936) and ONLY ANGELS HAVE WINGS (Columbia, 1939).

Nonetheless, Hollywood needed fresh writers after converting to the talkies and sent its agents to New York, where they scoured publishing houses, newspaper and magazine editorial offices, literary agencies, and Broadway in search of talent. One result of the search was that a large chunk of the eastern literary establishment boarded Santa Fe's Super Chief for the West Coast. Joining the exodus were Maxwell Anderson, S. N. Behrman, Robert Benchley, Charles Brackett, Sidney Buchman, W. R. Burnett, James M. Cain, Marc Connelly, Rachel Crothers, William Faulkner, F. Scott Fitzgerald, Dashiell Hammett, Moss Hart, Ben Hecht, Lillian Hellman, Sidney Howard, Nunnally Johnson, George S. Kaufman, Charles MacArthur, Dudley Nichols, Clifford Odets, Dorothy Parker, Samson Raphaelson, Robert E. Sherwood, Donald Ogden Stewart, Preston Sturges, and Thornton Wilder.

The experiences of these writers at the hands of producers generated the myth of Hollywood-as-destroyer, which Richard Fine described as follows:

> Novelists and playwrights of acute sensibility and talent . . . were lured to Hollywood by offers of huge amounts of money and the promise of challenging assignments; once in the studios they were set to work on mundane, hackneyed scripts; they were treated without respect by the mandarins who ruled the studios; and they were subjected to petty interferences by their intellectual inferiors. In the process, they were destroyed as artists. Hollywood was a loathsome

and demeaning place which invariably corrupted writers. Although writers prostituted themselves by accepting Hollywood paychecks, the film industry itself was the true villain of the tale. (*Hollywood and the Profession of Authorship, 1928–1940,* p. 3).

In analyzing the substance of the myth, Richard Fine discovered that the exodus of novelists, poets, playwrights, and newspapermen to Hollywood did not begin in earnest during the conversion to sound, as commonly believed, but in 1933 when the Depression forced half of Broadway's theaters to close and many venerable publishing firms to file for bankruptcy.[20] In other words, they were not necessarily lured to Hollywood by offers of fat paychecks but were driven there by economic circumstances.

Back east, relations between authors and publishers were surprisingly cordial. Writers who earned a measure of notoriety gained respect and prestige. From a business and legal standpoint, an author owned his literary output, functioned as an independent economic agent, and retained creative control in the publication process. In the theater, playwrights enjoyed similar rights and privileges, thanks mainly to the Minimum Basic Agreement of the Dramatists Guild.

Once these writers nestled into their studio offices, they encountered circumstances totally different from what they had left behind. They learned that motion-picture production was big business dominated by five vertically integrated corporations and that creative authority resided in the financial-managerial class—namely, producers. As Fine put it,

> For writers, Hollywood was New York turned topsy-turvy: instead of owning and controlling their work as independent economic agents, they found themselves employees, workers stripped of all proprietary rights; instead of their individuality and creativity being admired and rewarded, it was all too often prohibited or penalized; instead of editors, publishers and theatrical producers who acted as friends as well as business partners, they dealt with movie producers who were their absolute bosses in what was frequently an antagonistic relationship; and, finally, instead of receiving prestige because they were writers, they found themselves *denied* prestige because of their profession. The studio system, then, judged in terms of the world view of the New York literary marketplace, was an unmitigated disaster. (*Hollywood and the Profession of Authorship, 1928–1940,* pp. 127–128).

In terms of specifics, writers did not labor endlessly under long-term contracts; rather, they found employment "notoriously uneven, short-termed, and unpredictable."[21] Studios sometimes preferred using length-of-picture contracts, under which a writer was hired to work on a single script usually for around six months, or even short-term contracts lasting anywhere from one week to three months. In between jobs, writers went unemployed for long periods.

Studios paid higher salaries than New York—about $1,000 a week—but a writer seldom worked the full year. Fine reported that of the 238 writers under contract at the four largest studios in 1938, "only 165 earned more than $15,000 a year. The median salary of these 165 writers was approximately $25,000, or half

what a writer earning $1000 a week would make working a full year."[22] And
unlike back east, Hollywood contract writers more often than not had to keep
regular hours at the studio, normally from ten to five daily and a half day on
Saturday.

Once they found employment, eastern writers complained mostly about three
things: (1) the speed at which they were forced to work; (2) compulsory
collaboration; and (3) unfair assigning of screen credits. Said Fine, "Despite the
innumerable story conferences called by producers and the interminable delays
they engendered, and despite the long periods during which contract writers
waited to be assigned to projects, many writers felt pressured to work quickly."
They were also forced to collaborate with other writers by working as a team and
to take on projects that had been simultaneously assigned to others. Studios
rationalized compulsory collaboration by saying the practice "promoted efficiency and used the special talents of each writer to enhance the total effect of
the film—the whole being more than the sum of its parts," said Fine. But writers
disagreed and countered that team writing was the result of producers having a
compulsive need to control the writing process.[23]

The practice of assigning screen credits caused the most rancor. Before the
Screen Writers Guild achieved recognition, the producer of a picture decided
who would receive screen credit. Since more writers worked on the development
of a screenplay than could receive credit, writers who worked on intermediate
drafts could work for years without receiving recognition. "Writers constantly
complained that the system of granting credits was corrupt and counter-
productive in that it insidiously pitted writer against writer," said Fine.[24] As will
be explained below, writers had to wait until 1941 before studios accepted the
Screen Writers Guild's plan for fairly arbitrating credit decisions.

In the meantime, a writer finding Hollywood's norms distasteful had several
options. Top talents like Lillian Hellman, Dudley Nichols, Preston Sturges, and
Nunnally Johnson refused to collaborate with other writers. A few screenwriters
teamed up with elite directors who were sympathetic to their work. Dudley
Nichols, for example, acquired considerable creative control writing screenplays
for John Ford. Described as "the most successful sustained collaboration of
screenwriter and director in Hollywood's history," Nichols and Ford made
thirteen films together beginning in 1929, among them THE INFORMER (1935),
and STAGECOACH (1939).[25] THE INFORMER was nominated for best picture and
won Oscars for best screenplay and direction. STAGECOACH, of course, became
a Western classic. Another director-writer team to enjoy similar long-term
success was the Frank Capra–Robert Riskin unit at Columbia. Their collaboration resulted in the acclaimed pictures AMERICAN MADNESS (1932), IT HAPPENED
ONE NIGHT (1934), BROADWAY BILL (1934), MR. DEEDS GOES TO TOWN (1936),
LOST HORIZON (1937), and YOU CAN'T TAKE IT WITH YOU (1938).

A few writers even moved up to the producer ranks. Herman J. Mankiewicz
functioned as associate producer for two early Marx Brothers films at Paramount,
MONKEY BUSINESS (1931) and HORSE FEATHERS (1932). Sidney Buchman was
made a producer at Columbia after writing the original screenplay for Capra's
MR. SMITH GOES TO WASHINGTON in 1939, the unofficial sequel to MR. DEEDS.
Nunnally Johnson was promoted to writer-producer by Darryl Zanuck at 20th
Century–Fox in 1935, a position he held for twenty years. Preston Sturges
parlayed his writing credits into an opportunity to direct his own scripts. Doing

stints at Paramount, MGM, and Universal, Sturges wrote over a dozen hits, based mostly on his own ideas. Finally, in 1940, Paramount permitted him to direct his seven-year-old script THE GREAT MCGINTY and revived screwball comedy in the process.

For those writers who could not find relief within the system, the option of unionizing always existed.[26] As pointed out earlier, the salary cut instituted by the studios after the 1933 bank holiday precipitated a crisis in labor-management relations and resulted in the formation of the Screen Writers Guild (SWG) on 6 April 1933 and of the Screen Actors Guild (SAG) that June. The producers recognized the SAG on 15 May 1937, but recognition for the Screen Writers Guild came only after a protracted and acrimonious battle. Since the SWG platform went far beyond the bread-and-butter issues of the Actors Guild by demanding more creative authority over production and copyright protection that would make writers part-owners of the movies based on their scripts, the studios fought back with obstinancy and indiscretion.

Although the SWG won certification from the National Labor Relations Board as the sole bargaining representative of motion-picture writers on 10 August 1938, the result of studio-by-studio elections, producers stonewalled during bargaining sessions. A guild shop was finally established in May 1941. Needless to say, none of the goals of the original platform were realized. The studios agreed to ban speculative writing, set a minimum wage, and made the guild the sole arbiter of screen credits, but they would have nothing to do with elevating the creative status of the screenwriter. The means producers used to oppose the SWG provided "one of the less flattering commentaries on the men who control movie production," commented Rosten.[27]

Creating the Studio "Look"

A commonplace of film history states that during the thirties each studio developed a distinctive style, a special visual "look." The notion needs qualification. It is more accurate to say each studio typically developed a distinctive house style when it produced the most important films on its roster at the level where differentiation would normally be most effective. And the extent of this differentiation depended on a combination of factors, among them the stars on the payroll, the specialty genres of the studio, the creative personnel on the staff, and the size of the production budgets.[28]

Studio art departments potentially had the greatest impact on the look of a picture. Describing MGM's operations, Morton Eustis said the art department is responsible for "everything that can be seen on the screen, with the exception of the faces, the figures and the motion of the actors themselves. This includes settings and props, real or unreal, lights and costumes and other less tangible but no less important elements." Organized during the twenties, the great Hollywood art departments used a two-tier system of organization that divided responsibility between a supervising art director, who visualized the script, and a unit art director, who did the actual design and oversaw its construction. The most powerful supervising art directors in Hollywood, Cedric Gibbons at MGM, Van Nest Polglase at RKO, and Hans Dreier at Paramount, headed departments of between fifty and eighty people, among them unit art directors, architects, illustrators, model makers, and set decorators.[29]

Cinematographer James Wong Howe with Ronald Colman and David Niven on the set of THE PRISONER OF ZENDA *(UA, 1937)*.

Original sets were designed for class-A pictures; class-B pictures either reused older sets or were shot on standing sets to save money. As each class-A picture was placed in development, the art department broke down the script to determine the number of sets, costumes, exterior locations, and other requirements to physically produce the film. The studio wanted the breakdown not only to determine costs but also to inform each technical department (property shop, special effects, miniature shop) exactly what was required and in what sequence. After the front office approved the picture and its budget, the supervising art director gave the go-ahead to the unit art director who had been assigned the project.

Having created the basic design concept of the picture, the unit art director produced sketches of the master scenes. From these sketches would emerge the selection of locations and the final designs for the sets, miniatures, and special effects. Some unit art directors and sketch artists specialized in certain types of pictures, such as crime films or Westerns, but most had to be versatile enough to work in every historical style. The actual building of the sets was done by construction crews working around the clock, six days a week, with most of the work being done on the night shift. Afterward, the set decorator completed the process by dressing the set with furniture, draperies, and props acquired from the property department or from rental sources or by purchase.

From the point of view of studio investment, Hollywood's most ambitious efforts of the decade were prestige period pictures. Whatever the period— ancient Rome, medieval Paris, Elizabethan England, eighteenth-century Versailles, or Victorian London—films had to conform to commonly accepted norms of authenticity. Working hand in hand with art and costume designers, a studio's research department authenticated the setting, costumes, and other elements of the *mise-en-scène* that reflected the period of the picture. To aid them, specialists in the research department organized reference libraries containing art history books, prints and illustrations, and art and architecture magazines.

Although the unit art director did the designing, the supervising art director customarily received the main production credit above the name of the unit art director whether or not he personally contributed to the project. MGM's Cedric Gibbons may have initiated the practice. Joining the studio as head of the art department in 1924, he had a clause inserted in his contract stipulating that his credit would appear on every picture the studio produced, a stipulation that the studio respected with few exceptions until his retirement in 1956.[30]

Art directors, like other creative and technical personnel at the studios, worked under exclusive term contracts. For example, Anton Grot at Warners worked on year-to-year contracts. In 1932, Warners paid him $250 per week, about the same amount as Joan Blondell and other contract actors, but considerably less than James Cagney's $1,750 weekly salary. During this period Grot single-handedly designed as many as eleven productions a year. By 1939 his lot improved somewhat; he was earning $450 a week on a two-year contract and had to design only two pictures. Art directors were not unionized until the mid forties when the Society of Motion Picture Art Directors, which had been functioning as a professional organization, became affiliated with the International Alliance of Theatrical Stage Employees (IATSE).[31]

The famous MGM look was created mainly by one individual, Cedric Gibbons. "The nearest thing to a movie star that Hollywood art direction ever had," Gibbons was "one of the most powerful personalities in America's most powerful studio for thirty years."[32] Joining the newly merged MGM in 1924, Gibbons oversaw the construction of a vast assortment of permanent sets on the studio's backlot—a village, several town squares, city streets, a park, and a waterfront, among others. He also set up some of the finest ancillary departments in Hollywood, such as scene painting, models and miniatures, and special effects. Unlike those of other studios, MGM's ancillary departments were tightly centralized and existed to serve one person, and that was Gibbons. In one way or another, Cedric Gibbons's art department affected the work of 70 percent of the studio's forty-five hundred workers.

As the industry's most prestigious and financially secure studio, MGM became justly famous for the designs of award-winning period pictures and fantasies such as THE MERRY WIDOW (1934), DAVID COPPERFIELD (1935), MUTINY ON THE BOUNTY (1935), THE GOOD EARTH (1937), MARIE ANTOINETTE (1938), and THE WIZARD OF OZ (1939). But MGM is equally renowned for popularizing modernism in Hollywood art design. After attending the landmark Paris Exposition Internationale des Arts Décoratifs et Industriels Modernes in 1925, Gibbons came under the influence of art deco and art moderne. He first promoted these modernistic styles in OUR DANCING DAUGHTERS (1928), OUR MODERN MAIDENS (1929), and OUR BLUSHING BRIDES (1930), MGM's trilogy of carefree youth in the Jazz Age starring Joan Crawford. The designs for these pictures "were drawn in accordance with what he called his philosophy of the uncluttered—they were clean, functional and often highly stylized, a look that was to cause a major revolution in movie decor."[33]

Since modernism became associated with luxury, glamour, and affluence, it became the perfect visual style to complement Thalberg's urban strategy of producing pictures based on contemporary sources and themes. MGM's most famous modernistic set is undoubtedly the stunning art deco lobby of GRAND HOTEL (1932), which Gibbons designed in collaboration with Alexander Toluboff. Donald Albrecht described its design as follows:

> Circles are prominent in every aspect of the Grand Hotel's design— an appropriate image for the spinning-wheel-of-fortune scenario. The circular motif appears in the hotel's round, multilevel atrium with open balconies, in the continually revolving doors, and in ornaments on balcony railings. It also appears in the round reception desk, which acts as a pivot for the curving shots that follow the movement of the film's characters, who travel across the black-and-white floor like pawns in a chess game. Movie plot and architecture have seldom been so closely harmonized. (*Designing Dreams: Modern Architecture in the Movies* [New York: Harper and Row, 1986], pp. 139–140)

Influential exhibitions held in America such as the Museum of Modern Art's "Modern Architecture" in 1932 and the Chicago Century of Progress the following year marked the peak of modernism's popularity. By then, modernism had become the style of choice of Hollywood art directors when designing such perquisites of wealth as penthouses, nightclubs, executive suites, and ocean liners.

Some of the most dazzling modern set decor of the period was done at RKO. Under the leadership of Van Nest Polglese, RKO's art department was "second to none in stylishness, tasteful flights of fancy, and an enjoyably identifiable studio imprint." KING KONG (1933), THE INFORMER (1935), MARY OF SCOTLAND (1936), and THE HUNCHBACK OF NOTRE DAME (1939), to name a few, demonstrated the range and quality of RKO's atmospheric designs, but the studio's most polished work was done for the Astaire-Rogers musicals. Van Nest Polglase and unit art director Carroll Clark received credit for most of the pictures, but the designs were actually collaborative efforts that also used the talents of set designer Allan Abbott and illustrator Maurice Zuberano. This design team introduced what Arlene Croce has called "the fixed architectural institution . . . known as the

Cedric Gibbons and Alexander Toluboff's lobby set for GRAND HOTEL *(MGM, 1932)*. Courtesy of Museum of Modern Art/Film Stills Archive.

Richard Day's Art Deco steamship for DODSWORTH *(UA, 1936)*.

B.W.S. (Big White Set)." It appeared as grand hotels, nightclubs, and boudoirs in such pictures as THE GAY DIVORCEE (1934), TOP HAT (1935), and SWINGTIME (1936). Using art deco to "evoke a feeling of stark elegance," the B.W.S. characteristically incorporated streamlining, sharp contrasts of black and white in the decor, and geometric decorative motifs.[34] Describing their effectiveness, Ellen Spiegel said,

> The sets were simple enough to act as backdrops for the dance sequences, which were after all what the public came to see, and to highlight the costumed, elaborately-decorated bodies. But the attention given the design of the sets by Polglase and the art department shows that they were more than just rooms to be danced through. Their style had to co-ordinate with that of the costumes and the movement, since the sets formed an integral part of the action. Astaire and Rogers danced over the banisters, down staircases, over chairs, and around balconies in all their movies. ("Fred and Ginger Meet Van Nest Polglase," *Velvet Light Trap* 10 [1973], p. 19)

Working in the same architectural tradition as Gibbons and Polglase but using expressionism rather than modernism to create atmosphere and mood, Charles ("Danny") Hall designed Universal's most distinctive defining genre, the horror film. Hall's formula was perfected in DRACULA (1931), FRANKENSTEIN (1931), THE OLD DARK HOUSE (1932), THE INVISIBLE MAN (1933), and THE BRIDE OF FRANKENSTEIN (1935). Dracula's mysterious castle with its crumbling stone staircase and cobwebbed rooms and Frankenstein's modernistic laboratory housed in a decaying tower, among other sets Hall designed for these pictures, did more than differentiate Universal's films from its competitors; they also participated in the action.

Hans Dreier, supervising art director at Paramount, was even more concerned with individual shots and scenes. A Munich-born architect and former scene designer at the UFA studios in Germany, Dreier joined Paramount at the invitation of Ernst Lubitsch and served as the head of its art department from 1932 to 1952. Dreier ran a tight ship, but unlike Gibbons and Polglase, he encouraged his unit art directors to develop their own personal styles. In addition to his administrative duties, Dreier remained a practicing designer and developed a distinctive style as a master of "subtle and evocative atmosphere" collaborating with the studio's European-oriented directors. Among Dreier's most influential designs were the art deco set for Lubitsch's TROUBLE IN PARADISE (1932); the enchanting fairytale kingdom for Rouben Mamoulian's LOVE ME TONIGHT (1932); and a stylized expressionistic setting for Josef von Sternberg's THE SCARLET EMPRESS (1934). Dreier collaborated with Von Sternberg more closely than with any other director and was responsible for many arresting effects in Von Sternberg's pictures. Like Danny Hall's sets, Dreier's created mood for each scene and participated in the action. As Beverly Heisner described it, Dreier's sets "must be stepped through, seen through, they interfere with the actors. Curtains fall into faces, the camera moves with erotic intent through crevices in the wall—first blocking and then admitting the viewer. In a Von Sternberg film the surroundings engage the actors."[35]

Two designers, Anton Grot of Warner Bros. and the free-lancer William

Van Nest Polglase and Carroll Clark's Venice, the "Big White Set" for TOP HAT
(RKO, 1935) Courtesy of Museum of Modern Art/Film Stills Archive.

Cameron Menzies, had the most success in translating their ideas into completed
motion pictures. Born Antocz Groszewski in Poland, Grot worked as a full-time
art director for Warners from 1927 to 1948. An extremely prolific and imaginative
designer, Grot exerted a tremendous influence on directors Michael Curtiz,
Mervyn LeRoy, and William Dieterle. (Grot received four Oscar nominations,
but Warner's only Oscar for art direction during the thirties was awarded to Carl
Jules Weyl, for his storybook designs for THE ADVENTURES OF ROBIN HOOD
[1938].) Designing for Warners, Grot had to work with tight budgets, but he made
a virtue out of necessity by doing storyboards, frame-by-frame sketches in black
ink or charcoal containing finely detailed shadings of light and shadow. As Grot
did them, storyboards ensured that only the parts of the set that showed were
built, but they also had the secondary effect of limiting "directors to the camera
positions and angles he visualized."[36]

Fashioning sets seemingly "only of light and shadow," Grot created superb
designs for the studio's specialty genres, among them the horror film (SVENGALI
[1931]), the gangster film (LITTLE CAESAR [1931]), and the musical (GOLD DIG-
GERS OF 1935). When Warners moved into the prestige market in 1935, the new
studio look was largely of Grot's creation. His continuity sketches for CAPTAIN
BLOOD (1935) and THE PRIVATE LIVES OF ELIZABETH AND ESSEX (1939), for
example, were followed almost shot by shot. In addition to these pictures, Grot
designed A MIDSUMMER NIGHT'S DREAM (1935), ANTHONY ADVERSE (1936), THE
LIFE OF EMILE ZOLA (1937), and JUAREZ (1939).

Hired by David O. Selznick as production designer for GONE WITH THE WIND,

William Cameron Menzies made a major contribution by preplanning the color and design of the entire picture. To save money and to retain tight control over the shooting of the epic picture, Selznick wanted almost every last camera angle nailed down before production began. Working directly from the book—since a screenplay had yet to be written—Menzies created a "complete script in sketch form, showing actual camera setups, lighting, etc." Executed in color and with daring, Menzies's storyboards are the most famous of the period. The directors who worked on the film followed his storyboards slavishly. In recognition of Menzies's contribution to GONE WITH THE WIND, Selznick created the special credit "Production Designed by William Cameron Menzies." Since there was no precedent for what Menzies had done, the Academy awarded him a special plaque at the Oscar ceremonies to recognize his "outstanding achievement in the use of color for the enhancement of dramatic mood in the production of *Gone With the Wind.*"[37] Although storyboarding is a common practice today, Grot's and Menzies's influence over the visual look of their pictures confounds the notion of film authorship that is focused exclusively on the director.

Like the art department, the costume department of a Hollywood studio was hierarchically organized, supervised by a chief designer who was assisted by the head of wardrobe, several junior designers, sketch artists, period researchers, wardrobe assistants, and seamstresses. Responsible mainly for dressing the stars in a picture, the chief designer sketched their clothes and prepared a wardrobe plot indicating what they would wear in each scene. Costumes, like sets, served a narrative function; they helped define character, social status, and historical period.

Take the case of Scarlett O'Hara's costumes in GONE WITH THE WIND. Walter Plunkett's designs were among the most famous of the period. They were authentic in every detail and also had the distinction of revealing character in an original and complex way. Scarlett's costumes clearly reflected the two different periods of her life—"the petulant Southern belle, and later the postbellum woman who turns her back on her earlier life of picture-book elegance to face despair, poverty, and the bare necessity to survive." For the first period, Plunkett designed a wardrobe of organdy and tulle, light and sheer fabrics. For the second, Plunkett used velvets, a heavier and darker fabric. Costume reveals the start of Scarlett's second period of her life when she tears down the green velvet curtains in her mother's dining room and orders Mammy to sew a dress she can wear to ensnare Rhett Butler, who has the means to pay the property taxes on Tara and save it from foreclosure. Thereafter, as Scarlett rises to greater affluence, Plunkett dressed her in different colors and weights of velvet, creating a kind of motif.[38]

The fame of Hollywood's leading costumers—Adrian of MGM, Travis Banton of Paramount, Orry-Kelly of Warners, and Walter Plunkett of RKO—rested primarily on the clothing they designed for their studio's superstars. Undoubtedly, the most famous costume designer in Hollywood's history was MGM's Adrian, born Gilbert Adrian Rosenberg. "During his tenure at the studio [1928 to 1942]," Edward Maeder said, "he was treated like a star, and he was so well known that press releases would often trumpet his work as a special—sometimes the most important—element in a film."[39]

Adrian's most ambitious project was MARIE ANTOINETTE (1938), a vehicle Irving Thalberg conceived for his wife, Norma Shearer, the queen of the MGM

Adrian's costume for Norma Shearer in Marie Antoinette *(MGM, 1938).*

lot. Taking three years to produce, the film probably involved more period research than any other picture of the decade. Research experts were dispatched to Europe to gather antique prints, folios of drawings, actual garments of the period, and rare accessories. Adrian carefully studied the objects and made hundreds of sketches for his staff. The MGM costume shop turned out twenty-five hundred costumes; Max Factor and Company made more than two thousand wigs; and an international assemblage of artisans executed Norma Shearer's thirty-four costumes. Describing the effort that went into Shearer's costumes, W. Robert La Vine said,

> Special silk velvets and brocades were woven in Lyons, France's silk center, and hundreds of yards of gold and silver lace and intricate trimmings were imported from the few small factories in Austria and Italy that still manufactured them. Eight embroiderers were brought from Hungary to decorate the costumes with exquisite handwork, and a former milliner of the Imperial Russian Opera costume department, discovered in Paris, agreed to oversee the making of hundreds of hats and headdresses for the film. Sydney Guilaroff, MGM's famed

hairdresser, . . . made Norma Shearer's eighteen wigs, and Jack Dawn created her porcelainlike makeup. Dozens of copies of eighteenth-century buckled shoes were made by hand. Embroidered gloves and a fortune in jewelry, some set with genuine precious stones and diamonds, were assembled. Not even history's real Marie Antoinette had been dressed with a more lavish hand! (*In a Glamorous Fashion: The Fabulous Years of Hollywood Costume Design* [New York: Charles Scribner's Sons, 1980], pp. 44, 50–51)

Conceived in a modern idiom, Adrian's stylish outfits for Greta Garbo and Joan Crawford made a huge impact on women's fashions. For example, a white ruffled organdy gown Adrian designed for Crawford in LETTY LYNTON (1932) became all the rage and was widely copied by the fashion industry on New York's Seventh Avenue. Macy's claimed to have sold fifty thousand inexpensive copies of the dress. Even more influential was Adrian's famous design for Crawford, the wide-shouldered, narrow-hipped silhouette that became her most important fashion trademark.

Contrasting with the theatricalism of Adrian's designs, Travis Banton's designs for Paramount's stars such as Carole Lombard, Miriam Hopkins, Kay Francis, and Claudette Colbert were elegantly simple. La Vine said,

Travis Banton's understated and deceptively simple designs elevated motion picture costumes to the status of high fashion. His innate understanding of the bias cut . . . and his sense of exquisite balance in a garment perfectly captured the new sophistication that arrived with the thirties. A Banton gown, with a softness and sultriness that followed a woman's body, was Hollywood design at its most sublime. (*In a Glamorous Fashion*, p. 63)

For the likes of Mae West and Marlene Dietrich, Banton outdid himself. To underscore the campiness of Mae West's comedies, Banton's formula was "'Diamonds—lots of 'em' and huge hats, feather boas, fox stoles and vertical panels of light material or brilliants with darker side panels to slim her down." To complement the exoticism of Marlene Dietrich's Sternberg pictures, MOROCCO (1930), SHANGHAI EXPRESS (1932), and BLONDE VENUS (1932), Banton's formula consisted of "chiffon," "mountains of fur," "white tie and tails," and "lustrous black coq feathers."[40]

To costume Bette Davis, Warner's prima donna, Orry-Kelly used "utter simplicity and high fashion without theatricality." Unlike other superstars, Davis loathed being type-cast and insisted on changing her appearance from film to film—for example, from a spoiled Southern belle in JEZEBEL (1938), to a rigid spinster in THE OLD MAID (1939), to a headstrong and vulnerable queen in THE PRIVATE LIVES OF ELIZABETH AND ESSEX (1939). Bette Davis's rather plumpish figure presented problems, but "with the skill of an engineer, Kelly restructured her figure with cleverly cut, well-made garments that successfully created the desired image."[41]

The necessity of creating the desired image for a star was also a principal responsibility of the director of photography. The impact of new technology on cinematography during the thirties is discussed elsewhere. What is at issue here

Travis Banton's costumes for Kay Francis and Miriam Hopkins in TROUBLE IN
PARADISE *(Paramount, 1932).*

is the relationship of the director of photography to the studio look. Professionally, cinematographers were tied to the American Society of Cinematographers (ASC), which was neither a labor union nor a guild, but a tightly knit professional association that held a closed-shop contract with all the major studios. The first craft organization of any kind in the industry, the ASC was incorporated in 1919 for the interchange of ideas and technical information. Membership was by invitation and open only to accomplished directors of photography; later the ASC accepted second cameramen and assistant cameramen as members in a junior division. Firmly established by the thirties, the ASC became the only reliable talent pool from which producers could draw experienced cameramen. The ASC served as bargaining agent for all cameramen, but this function was taken over by the cameramen's union in the International Alliance of Theatrical Stage Employees during the mid thirties.[42]

The return of single-camera filmmaking following the conversion to sound reorganized the camera crew and more clearly demarcated the cinematographer's responsibilities on the set from the director's. The camera crew now consisted of the director of photography or cinematographer, whose principal creative input was to design the lighting for the shot and to oversee the camera setups in consultation with the director; the camera operator, who actually ran the camera, was "responsible for the mechanical perfection of the scenes"; and the assistant cameramen, who took care of the equipment, loaded and unloaded film and acted as focus pullers, among other jobs.[43]

A combination of factors influenced lighting style above and beyond the inclinations of the cinematographer: the house look, the star, and the story. A studio's specialty genres obviously dictated a certain look. Warners, for example, developed a somber house style for its social-problem pictures. To fit with the realism of these pictures, the style consisted of austere, flat lighting and highly contrasted images. To complement MGM's opulent and sophisticated house style, Gibbons imposed on MGM's pictures a consistency of style and mood; settings were bathed in brilliant high-key lighting that created a soft gray-white glossy look. In practice, this meant that Gibbons supervised the lighting of all the large, important sets, but left the lighting of close-ups entirely to the judgment of the cinematographer.[44]

Since the entire production process revolved around stars and since stars constituted some of the biggest investments of a studio, the prime responsibility of the director of photography in a picture was to safeguard the image of a star. Protection meant designing the lighting to present the star's image to best advantage. As cinematographer Gregg Toland pointed out, "The best angle, the most appropriate lighting for the scene, may have to be discarded in favor of the particular angle or light value most flattering to a star or principal. Such photo-flattery often means the subjugation of realism to personality." Karl Struss, director of photography at Paramount, put it another way: "We must strive to convey an impression, not alone of actuality, but of *perfected* actuality. Our aim is to show players and settings, not merely as they are, but as the audience would like to see them."[45] In practice, this meant that at MGM and Paramount, for example, cinematographers typically used a glamorous form of backlighting called "Rembrandt lighting" in close-ups of both its male and female stars.

Certainly the most famous star-cinematographer collaboration of the era was between MGM's Greta Garbo and William Daniels. Working with Garbo on her first U.S. picture, THE TORRENT (1926), Daniels was able to capture Greta Garbo's unique features, and after Garbo became a star, she had it written into her contract that the cinematographer on all her pictures would be Daniels. Lee Garmes collaborated closely with Josef von Sternberg at Paramount on a number of the most stunning Marlene Dietrich pictures. Ernest Haller was Bette Davis's favorite cameraman at Warner, but she also admired the work of Tony Gaudio and Sol Polito. Arthur Miller at Fox was entrusted with young Shirley Temple. Commenting on how he created her image, Miller said, "I always lit her so she had an aureole of golden hair. I used a lamp on Shirley that made her whole damn image world famous." And Joseph Valentine's handling of Deanna Durbin at Universal was described as "the difference between making a musical bright and fluffy or allowing it to settle like a cold soufflé."[46]

Efficiency would suggest that cinematographers be brought in early to consult with the art director, costume designer, and director. But cinematographers were seldom consulted in pre-production. Typically, they were required to move from project to project with little preparation time in between. Once production had begun, tight schedules and budgets kept expensive retakes and experimentation to a minimum. Because the system forced cameramen to fall back on conventional forms of shooting, Hollywood cinematography during the thirties all too often lacked individuality.

But the wonder is that so many cinematographers transcended these institutional constraints to imprint their visual signatures on their films. Gregg Toland's experiments with deep-focus photography working for independent producer Sam Goldwyn distinguished him as one of the most inventive and creative cinematographers of the period (see Chapter 5). MGM's most distinctive cinematography was done not only by William Daniels who photographed the studio's leading ladies—Greta Garbo, Norma Shearer, Jeanette MacDonald, and Eleanor Powell—but also by Hal Rosson, who shot THE WIZARD OF OZ (1939), and by Karl Freund and Joseph Ruttenberg, who won Academy Awards for their cinematography on THE GOOD EARTH (1937) and THE GREAT WALTZ (1938), respectively. Paramount's most distinctive cinematography was created by Karl Struss, who devised the filter work for the transformation process in DR. JEKYLL AND MR. HYDE (1932) and by Lee Garmes, Charles B. Lang, Jr., and Victor Milner, who won Academy Awards for SHANGHAI EXPRESS (1932), A FAREWELL TO ARMS (1933), and CLEOPATRA (1934). Warner's most distinctive work was done by Hal Mohr and Tony Gaudio, who won back-to-back Academy Awards for A MIDSUMMER NIGHT'S DREAM (1935) and ANTHONY ADVERSE (1936). Tony Gaudio also designed the cinematography for LITTLE CAESAR (1931) and the Paul Muni biopics. Sol Polito designed the effective black-and-white cinematography for I AM A FUGITIVE FROM A CHAIN GANG (1932) and the expressive lighting for the Technicolor THE PRIVATE LIVES OF ELIZABETH AND ESSEX (1939). Polito and Tony Gaudio together designed the lighting for another dazzling Technicolor production, THE ADVENTURES OF ROBIN HOOD (1938). After shooting JEZEBEL (1938), a Bette Davis vehicle, Ernest Haller co-photographed GONE WITH THE WIND (1939) with Ray Rennahan at Selznick and then returned to work with Davis again on DARK VICTORY and other pictures.

Other distinguished cinematographers include J. Peverell Marley, who established the lighting style for 20th Century–Fox's prestige pictures; Arthur Edeson and John Mescall, who designed the lighting for Universal's horror

pictures; and Joseph H. August, who created the atmospheric photography for
some of John Ford's most memorable films at RKO.

How the Big Five Rationalized Production

The discussion has so far implied that the majors rationalized production first of
all by dividing output into A and B groups and then by allocating a specified
amount of the total production budget to each group. The number and types of A
films produced in a season depended mainly on the financial health of the
company and the strengths of its personnel. For example, MGM budgeted
$500,000 on the average for each of its top-grade pictures during the Depression,
about $150,000 more per picture than any other company. MGM's outlay
reflected, of course, the financial status of its parent company, Loew's Inc. In
contrast, Warner Bros., which referred to itself as "The Ford of the Movies,"
produced its class-A films cheaply and efficiently, from $200,000 to $400,000 per
picture during the Depression. Reflecting Harry Warner's determination to pay
off company debts, Warner's class-A pictures consisted mostly of fast-paced
topicals based on stories plucked out of the day's news. The studio discouraged
costly retakes and rigidly cut costs to the bare bones. RKO's tenuous financial
condition during the Depression forced the studio to cap the production costs for
its top-grade product at around $200,000, but because of constant changes in
front-office personnel, RKO never succeeded in formulating a successful production strategy. When economic conditions improved, the gap in production costs
between MGM and the other majors closed somewhat, but Loew's remained the
most profitable company throughout the decade and in 1939 had allocated $42
million for production, the highest such budget in the industry.[47]

Average production costs, however, do not tell the entire story, because the
class-A output of the majors was actually divided into three tiers—superspecials,
specials, and programmers. Superspecials typically consisted of prestige pictures
and big-budget musicals with top stars, expensive production values, and running
times as long as two and a half hours. Costing $1 million and more to produce,
only a handful of such pictures would be produced by a studio in any given year.
Specials constituted the bulk of the class-A line. Like superspecials, they were
based on presold properties and contained popular stars, but they followed the
principal production trends, conformed to regular running times, and had lower
production budgets. Programmers had the lowest budgets of the group. They
were typically based on original stories and contained minor stars and running
times as short as fifty minutes. Such films were called programmers because they
could fill either the top or bottom of a bill, depending on the genre, size of
theater, and audience. A typical programmer, such as MGM's THE CHASER
(1938) featuring Dennis O'Keefe, was reviewed by *Variety* as follows: "Satisfactory programmer. Has fairly good plot, workmanlike script, capable direction and
lucid acting though weak in marquee rating. Okay for the duals."[48]

A prevailing myth states that the motion pictures produced by a studio
reflected pretty much the tastes of its chief executive.

> Hailing, as many of them did, from carnivals, nickelodeons, and
> amusement parks, studio executives compensated for any lack of

aesthetic criteria by a "feel" for what would sell. They claimed to possess a kind of anatomical Richter scale on which they relied for their pronouncements about the taste and salability of movies: a sinking in the stomach, a tug of the heartstrings, or Harry Cohn's oracular stimulus—a tickle on the buttocks. (Larry Ceplair and Steven Englund, *The Inquisition in Hollywood: Politics in the Film Community, 1930–1960* [Garden City: Anchor Press, 1980], p. 7)

But like everything else about production, the majors also rationalized story acquisition and development. All the companies had story departments with large offices in New York, Hollywood, and Europe that systematically searched the literary marketplace and the stage for suitable novels, plays, short stories, and original ideas. Scouts for the studios sometimes even secured new works in manuscript or galleys, which was how Selznick acquired the motion-picture rights to GONE WITH THE WIND.

The question is, what policy, if any, guided a studio in acquiring properties? Robert Gustafson has attempted to answer such a question in his analysis of story acquisitions at Warners from 1930 to 1949. Warners' story department may not be representative of all the majors; nonetheless, Gustafson's study provides unusual insight into this phase of the production process. Gustafson argues that "the pattern of source acquisition demonstrates two often contradictory goals: (1) the desire to base films on pretested material, that is, low-risk material that was already well known and well received by the public and (2) the desire to acquire properties as inexpensively as possible, especially during declining or uncertain economic circumstances."[49] In practice, this meant that in good times, Warners invested in pretested properties such as best-selling novels, hit Broadway plays, and popular short stories. In bad times, it offset the high costs of pretested properties by using original scripts written in its screenwriting department and by relying heavily on "the cheapest pretested material of all"—earlier Warner pictures.

Using its windfall profits from innovating sound, Warners splurged on Broadway hits, best-selling novels, popular nonfiction works, and short stories from popular magazines. From 1930 to 1934 these expensive pretested materials were used to produce nearly 50 percent of the studio's output, while original material, such as unpublished, unproduced, and untested short stories, novels, and plays created by Warners' writers, were used for 14 percent of the roster. Exploiting pretested source materials was an expensive but nonetheless conservative practice. But the remarkable thing about Warners' use of these pretested properties is that little relationship existed between acquisition costs and production costs. As Gustafson points out, "motion pictures that cost $200,000 or less to produce had an average source cost of $7,000. However, films that cost more than $200,000 to produce had an average source cost of $8,000."[50]

When the studio sank into the red, Harry Warner demanded a radical change in the operations of the studio to eliminate waste. The story department, in particular, was directed to tie acquisitions to the company's gross revenues; to be precise, Harry Warner mandated that the annual budget for the department was to be pegged at one-half of 1 percent of the company's gross for the previous year. Pegging the budget to revenues would prevent "wild" buying and link the department to the overall performance of the company.

Harry Warner's directive resulted in the story department moving away from expensive, tried-and-true properties to material written by salaried screenwriters working for the studio. From 1934, the first year of the pegged budget, to 1941, the last year before the World War II box-office boom, the studio relied on its writers for 40 percent of its source material, an increase of over 25 percent from the 1930–1933 period. Expensive, pretested properties were used for 21 percent of the studio's output in the same period, a drop of nearly 30 percent. In other words, Harry Warner's business plan reduced costs by substituting labor for capital.

Harry Warner's business plan had the effect of further rationalizing source acquisition formulas for A and B pictures. After 1934 the story department continued purchasing expensive properties at nearly the same rate as before to stay competitive, but Harry Warner added a new wrinkle to the process; all big-ticket items had to be sent to Jack Warner for approval. Jack insisted on being presented with a one-page synopsis of the property under consideration. If he liked it, he wanted to read a sixteen-page treatment before saying yea or nay.

The spending policy on properties for the class-A films seems to have been this; the higher the estimated production cost, the more that could be spent on the underlying property. On the average, class-A films in the $200,000–$400,000 range used sources that cost $12,000, while those above $400,000 used sources that cost $16,600. Having once acquired an expensive property, it seems reasonable that a studio would want to reuse it often. After all, it had great name value and would provide a cheap and easy way to replicate success. But the studio seldom recycled expensive properties (e.g., GREEN PASTURES) because they were by definition easily recognizable by many people and therefore were likely to make audiences feel cheated if reused. The number and percentage of remakes Warners produced increased significantly after 1934, but the majority of these pictures were Bs.

After the rise of double features, Warners boosted B production from 12 percent to 50 percent of annual output beginning in 1935, where it remained until the war. Since budgets for B pictures were between one-quarter and one-half the size of the A pictures, Harry Warner's business plan dictated that the cost of source materials for these pictures be scaled down accordingly. From 1934 to 1941, plays used in B pictures cost $8,400 on the average, compared to $42,500 for those used in A pictures; for novels, the ratio was $6,400 to $18,500; and for short stories, it was $1,500 to $10,500.

To stay within the new budget constraints, the story department tapped Warners screenwriters for original scripts. From 1934 to 1941, 44 percent of the B films were based on original sources compared to 18 percent of the A films. To save more money, the B unit also recycled previously purchased source material from films that had originally done "fair" or "poor" at the box office.

But how did a studio determine before the start of production what the public wanted? Howard T. Lewis noted in his 1933 study of the motion-picture industry that "no company has been able to develop to its own satisfaction any method by which it can guarantee in advance that a proposed picture will be a box office success." In deciding what to produce the next season, producers scrutinized box-office receipts; evaluated exhibitors reports, fan mail, and reviews; and watched newspapers, magazines, and books to keep abreast of public tastes. But no studio ever devised a "wholly satisfactory method of determining the probabilities of success of a proposed picture. . . . The method followed is still one of guessing; the producers don't know just what the public wants, and it is doubtful if they ever will know," Lewis concluded.[51]

The best a producer could do in the way of market research was to test a completed picture at a sneak preview before releasing it. Although it was a common practice, previewing did not help much; the producer had already committed himself to the basic concept of the picture, and all he could do after analyzing audience reaction was to trim here and there or to reshoot a scene or two to eliminate the dull moments and to highlight the good ones.

As a result, producers attempted to protect their investments by reducing risks. The most common way, of course, was to rely on stars, which is the subject of a later chapter. Another way was to diversify the roster. Although Warners is best remembered for its gangster pictures and films of social consciousness, a survey of its output during the 1930s and 1940s conducted by John Davis reveals that the studio produced close to thirty different types of pictures, which he categorized into six groups—crime, the American scene, love, comedy, musicals, and costumers.[52]

Another way to reduce risks was to follow trends. Production trends ran in cycles. Lewis described it thus: "What actually happens is that an outstanding gangster or war picture is produced. Immediately other directors imitate it in an effort to take advantage of the new idea conceived by someone else and to capitalize on the favorable publicity which the good picture has received. As a result a flood of such pictures, more or less copies of the original, inundates the screen." Thomas Simonet states this idea another way: "Cautious moviemakers might minimize their risks by emphasizing the familiar—recreating with slight changes films that have proven successful in the past. More risk-oriented moviemakers, on the other hand, might emphasize the original."[53] During the thirties, companies with the deepest pockets proved the most adventuresome, and the Little Three and Poverty Row studios, the most conservative.

The era is replete with examples of production cycles; but studios did more than imitate picture types; they even mimicked narrative structure. For example, the so-called "one locale" setting of MGM's GRAND HOTEL, which provided the basis for interweaving several unrelated narrative threads, inspired such pictures as Columbia's AMERICAN MADNESS, which is set in a bank, Warners' EMPLOYEES' ENTRANCE, which is set in a department store, and Paramount's BIG BROADCAST, which is set in a radio station.

The best way to hedge bets was to launch a series. Once successfully launched, a series creates loyal and eager fans who form a core audience. By keeping production costs in line with this ready-made demand, series pictures are almost guaranteed a profit. The problem, of course, is to hit upon a theme or subject that will keep an audience's interest beyond the sequel. Although series pictures were typically associated with B production, studios produced several important A series. For example, MGM's Thin Man series, starring William Powell and Myrna Loy as the husband-and-wife detective team of Nick and Nora Charles, sustained itself for more than a decade. Consisting of six pictures that came out every two or three years beginning in 1934, the thirties' pictures in the series consist of THE THIN MAN (1934), AFTER THE THIN MAN (1936), and ANOTHER THIN MAN (1939).

Warners' Gold Diggers musicals is another good example of a successful A series. The series had its roots in 42ND STREET (1933), a surprise hit staged by

Busby Berkeley, featuring two juvenile leads, Ruby Keeler and Dick Powell. The picture led to GOLD DIGGERS OF 1933 and a succession of Berkeley backstage musicals, including GOLD DIGGERS OF 1935, GOLD DIGGERS OF 1937, and GOLD DIGGERS IN PARIS (1938). Although the plots varied only a little from picture to picture, the series was unusual in that the original leads were not repeated in the subsequent pictures. Rather, the series was held together by Busby Berkeley's elaborately staged musical numbers.

Family series, particularly MGM's Andy Hardy series, starring Mickey Rooney, were popular at the end of the decade. A FAMILY AFFAIR, (1937), the first Andy Hardy picture, was a decidedly low-budget item, but the warm reception of the picture and the others it spun off earned the series class-A status, at least outside the largest metropolitan areas.

Representing 50 percent and more of the Big Five's annual output, B pictures enabled studios to operate at optimum capacity and to provide a training ground for young actors and actresses on their way up and a resting place for performers on their way down. B pictures cost anywhere from $50,000 to $100,000 to produce.[54] The majors reduced the risks of making these pictures by using the least expensive source material of all (mostly original stories ground out by studio screenwriters), by hiring supporting players on a per-day basis, and by adhering to rigid shooting schedules of from fifteen to twenty-five days.

Regardless of the quality of these pictures, they all found exhibition outlets for the simple reason that the majors block-booked the B pictures along with their A pictures. But unlike the percentage-of-the-gross rentals charged for the higher-grade films, B's were typically rented on a flat-rental basis. Although flat rentals prevented a producer from enjoying the extraordinary profits of an unexpected hit, the terms had the advantage of returning a predictable gross, meaning that if a studio kept costs in line, it could make a small but assured profit on its Bs.

To rationalize B production, studios relied extensively on the series. The economic rationale for B series was simple enough. As Thomas Schatz put it, "Not only the casting but the sets, props, music, even the story formula itself could be standardized, rendering what was already a low-budget enterprise that much more efficient and economical."[55] By the end of the decade, series pictures had become staples of double-feature exhibition and provided reliable entertainment for the intrepid moviegoer. Hollywood produced over seventy different series to reach every segment of the audience—the family trade, the Western buff, the adolescent set, and the horror aficionado, among others. Series Westerns were especially cheap to produce because they were shot outdoors using standing sets and contained scenes intercut from old pictures or from a studio's stock-footage library.

Warners' B unit was headed by Bryan Foy. Called "the Keeper of the Bs," Foy produced half the studio's pictures, around twenty-five a year on a total annual budget of $5 million. 20th Century–Fox's B unit was headed by Sol Wurtzel. Like Foy, he churned out half of the pictures on the studio roster. If Foy's strategy was to remake Warners' old silents and to produce cheap versions the studio's social-problem films to fill out the roster, Wurtzel sought to develop long-running series. Charlie Chan, for example, began in 1931 and lasted at Fox until 1942, even though its original star, Warner Oland, died in 1938 and had to be replaced by Sidney Toler. As Douglas Gomery noted, "This 'oriental' detective constantly changed locales in order to solve his mysteries, so in 1936 he went to the *Circus*, visited the *Race Track*, and attended the *Opera*."[56]

MGM, the most prestigious studio in Hollywood, with "More Stars Than in Heaven," never admitted publicly that it produced B pictures. MGM took this position despite the fact its parent, Loew's, Inc., announced that all its subsequent-run theaters were converting to double features in 1935. No one was fooled by MGM's posturing; MGM kept a stable of B-picture specialists busy like every other studio. Producers Lucien Hubbard and Harry Rapf divided up such pictures between them; the busiest directors were George B. Seitz and Edwin L. Marin. However, MGM's low-budget entries looked like no other B films. "When Metro goes out to make a Class B picture," said *Variety*, "they give it plenty of production, steady direction and a certain amount of class. It may not have big draw stars and the situation may be overdone, but it certainly will stand up on the second picture shelf in the theatres for which it was designed."[57]

How the Little Three Rationalized Production

The Columbia production policy was described by Harry Cohn:

> Every Friday the front door opens and I spit a movie out into Gower Street. . . . I want one good picture a year. That's my policy . . . and I won't let an exhibitor have it unless he takes the bread-and-butter product, the Boston Blackies, the Blondies, the low-budget Westerns and the rest of the junk we make. I like good pictures too, but to get one I have to shoot five or six, and to shoot five or six I have to keep the plant going with the program pictures. (Quoted in Joel W. Finler, *The Hollywood Story* [New York: Crown, 1988], p. 71)

Columbia mainly serviced the B-feature market. From 1930 to 1934, the studio produced thirty pictures a year; afterward, as a result of the spread of double features, the annual output increased to more than forty. The B films and programmers cost from $50,000 to $100,000; the better-grade pictures, around $200,000. To build a firm financial base, the studio also produced series Westerns starring Buck Jones, Tim McCoy, and Ken Maynard and a wide selection of cartoons, comedy shorts, and serials.

Columbia's policy was to follow trends and to churn out economy versions of hit class-A pictures produced by the Big Five.[58] During the first half of the decade, Columbia specialized in contemporary stories with realistic settings, such as crime pictures, mysteries, and comedies. Later in the decade, Columbia further rationalized its B output by initiating series, among them the Lone Wolf in 1935 and Blondie in 1938.

Shorts and B pictures paid the overhead, but Columbia needed a hit now and then to maintain its credibility as a principal player in the industry. Columbia could have existed without hits as a Poverty Row studio, but as a member of the Little Three, it needed box-office winners to strengthen its financial reserves, to pay dividends to stockholders, and to keep the interest of Wall Street. Since producing a hit was a difficult and elusive task, the studio needed stars. To secure them, the studio had three options: (1) it could develop stars by casting players in different roles and testing audience reaction; (2) it could borrow stars from other studios; or (3) it could pretend it had stars and hope that exhibitors and the public would play along. Early in the Thirties, the studio chose the third option. For example, the studio "starred" Jack Holt in over a dozen pictures. A typical Holt picture contained plenty of "love interest, melodramatics, outdoors and he-man stuff," said *Variety*. In its review of THE WOMAN I STOLE (1933), *Variety* said, "Jack Holt has been making pictures like this for years and has prospered. There's nothing especially distinguished in the output, but it is all eminently saleable material. Factory product, but factory product of a successful kind, with a ready market and satisfactory returns."[59]

Since developing stars required time and money, Columbia typically opted to borrow stars from the majors to produce its class-A pictures. The best example of this practice is Capra's great hit IT HAPPENED ONE NIGHT (1934), whose stars, Clark Gable and Claudette Colbert, came from MGM and Paramount, respectively. Columbia's A pictures were grouped mainly around its prize director, Frank Capra, and a few free-lance directors, such as Howard Hawks, Leo McCarey, and George Cukor.

Universal's principal market was the rural, small-town theater. Like Columbia, the studio specialized in series Westerns and inexpensive versions of popular class-A genres. Early in the decade the studio tried to break into the first-run market by producing a prestige picture, ALL QUIET ON THE WESTERN FRONT, and a number of horror films, such as DRACULA and FRANKENSTEIN, but after Carl Laemmle was bought out, the new owners reverted to the previous production policy of concentrating on the low end of the market.[60] To produce the occasional class-A picture, Universal borrowed talent from the majors, just like Columbia. The studio did not develop a top star of its own until it discovered Deanna Durbin near the end of the decade.

United Artists, the smallest company of the Little Three, was solely a distributor of quality independent productions. Independent producers had existed since the earliest days of the industry, but during the period of oligopoly control, three types did business: (1) indies that owned their own companies and produced quality product for release by United Artists; (2) indies connected with the majors as producers or directors; and (3) Poverty Row companies that worked outside mainstream Hollywood (see Chapter 8).

By the 1930s, UA had carved a secure niche for itself as a distributor of independent productions.[61] Of the four founders, only Charlie Chaplin remained active as a producer. Because the star system was now firmly controlled by the majors, the day of the actor-producer had passed. Chaplin was therefore an anomaly in the business. He not only produced his pictures using his own money, but he also wrote, directed, and starred in them as well—a one-man show. He produced two pictures during the decade, CITY LIGHTS (1931) and MODERN TIMES (1936).

UA's most active producers were Samuel Goldwyn, Alexander Korda, David O. Selznick, Twentieth Century Pictures, Howard Hughes, Edward Small, Walter Wanger, and a few others. Two members of the group, Goldwyn and Korda, were also partners in the company. These producers constituted a new breed of independent; such a producer typically headed his own production company and produced only a few pictures a year. What linked these producers to UA was the distribution contract, a document guaranteeing that in return for a fee, UA would sell and promote a picture in all the principal markets of the world. UA released relatively few pictures each year, from fifteen to twenty, but the pictures were consistently among the most acclaimed. Using *Film Daily*'s Top Ten as an indicator of public esteem during the decade, UA, with sixteen pictures, ranked second behind MGM, with thirty-five. Warners came in third with thirteen.

UA's archetypical producers, Goldwyn and Selznick, obtained production financing from commercial banks, such as the Bank of America, in the form of residual loans. To qualify for a residual loan, a producer needed a distribution contract in hand and completed pictures in release. In return for a loan, the producer had to mortgage his old pictures by pledging whatever residual revenues remained in them as well as the net producer's share of the revenue from the proposed picture. Such conditions made it extremely difficult to break into the business and help explain why so few first-class independents existed during this period.

In tailoring pictures for the high end of the market, first-class independents modeled their operations on the majors. Selznick operated out of the old RKO-Pathé studio in Culver City, which he renamed Selznick International Studios. Goldwyn operated out of the United Artists Studio in Hollywood, a rental facility originally owned by Mary Pickford and Douglas Fairbanks, which was renamed the Samuel Goldwyn Studios. Unlike the contract producer at one of the majors who was concerned mainly with the creative end of motion pictures and had an entire studio backing him, Selznick and Goldwyn also had to know the business end of motion pictures. Another difference was the way each type of producer interrelated with his staff. Playwright and screenwriter Sidney Howard described the collaboration process at Goldwyn as follows:

> The larger studios of Hollywood divide their picture making into various departments which have little contact with one another. Smaller production units, notably Mr. Sam Goldwyn's, are too clever for this. It is Mr. Goldwyn's custom to keep his highly gifted art director, Mr. Richard Day, in constant touch with the progress of the script. The result of this triple collaboration is a completely illustrated edition de luxe of the script which contains literally dozens upon dozens of thumbnail sketches both of photographic compositions and of camera angles. ("The Story Gets a Treatment," in Nancy Naumberg, ed., *We Make the Movies* [New York: W. W. Norton, 1937], p. 43)

Selznick said, "With me [the director] is in on the script as far in advance as it is possible for me to have him. He is in the story conferences with me and the writers, in the development of the script, and I always have my director in on the cutting right up to the time the picture is finished. That is not obligatory with me, nor is it the custom in most of the larger studios."[62]

UA's most prolific producer, Goldwyn made forty pictures during the decade, all of which he personally financed. His production staff included some of the best talent around—art director Richard Day; cinematographer Gregg Toland; music director Alfred Newman; directors John Ford, Leo McCarey, King Vidor, and William Wyler; and writers Sidney Howard, Elmer Rice, Maxwell Anderson, Lillian Hellman, Ben Hecht, Robert E. Sherwood, and S. N. Behrman. Goldwyn

Samuel Goldwyn and William Wyler on the set of WUTHERING HEIGHTS *(UA, 1939).*

specialized mainly in musicals and prestige women's pictures. His best musicals consist of six Eddie Cantor vehicles, starting with WHOOPEE! (1930), which was shot in two-strip Technicolor and marked Busby Berkeley's entry into the movies. Goldwyn's prestige women's films included three abortive attempts to launch his Russian-born protégée, Anna Sten, as another Garbo or Dietrich, and more-admired fare such as King Vidor's CYNARA (1932) and STELLA DALLAS (1937) and William Wyler's THESE THREE (1936), DODSWORTH (1936), and WUTHERING HEIGHTS (1939).

Selznick's production staff consisted of production manager Ray Klune; story editors Val Lewton and Katharine Brown; art director Lyle Wheeler; editor Hal Kern; and color cameraman Howard Greene. Selznick also specialized in prestige pictures and the women's market. The prestige pictures consisted of adaptations of literary classics, such as LITTLE LORD FAUNTLEROY (1936), THE PRISONER OF ZENDA (1937), and THE ADVENTURES OF TOM SAWYER (1938); the women's films, of such romantic dramas as A STAR IS BORN (1937), MADE FOR EACH OTHER (1939), INTERMEZZO (1939), and GONE WITH THE WIND (1939).

Conclusion

As modern business enterprises, the major film companies perfected a system of motion-picture production during the thirties that enabled them to meet market demand in a rational and relatively efficient manner. The principal changes in the mode of production were at the executive level. Greater executive control over production came mainly at the expense of directors who were relegated basically to staging the action. Although motion-picture production remained a collaborative art, the description needs refining. Actually, the studio system allowed little time for collaboration, not even for big-budget productions. Artistic personnel were expected to be versatile professionals capable of performing highly skilled and specialized tasks quickly and efficiently. This system of artistic production was at odds with norms in publishing and in the professional theater, but the necessity of supplying theaters with new product on a regular basis mandated tight production schedules and breakneck speed. That Hollywood produced such a wealth of entertainment in the decade is a testament to the system and especially to the vast pool of talented workers employed by the studios.

Subsequent chapters on production trends will highlight the importance of the prestige picture to the business. This chapter has also revealed that top-ranking independent producers distributing through United Artists specialized in this trend and tailored the production process to allow for greater collaboration, in order to carve a niche for themselves in the market. In so doing, they anticipated the era of the blockbuster, which has characterized the motion-picture business to this day.

John Cromwell, Carole Lombard, and David O. Selznick on the set of MADE FOR EACH OTHER *(UA, 1938).*

5

Technological Change and Classical Film Style

David Bordwell
Kristin Thompson

*T*he 1930s was an era of enormous technological development in the Hollywood cinema. This chapter considers major changes in the look and sound of the studios' product. That is, its concern is with the systematic use of film techniques that constitutes a film's style. It seeks to show how certain technological developments during the decade affected Hollywood's canonized style.

To explain such developments, we must take account of two broad factors. First, to a considerable extent, the aesthetic norms of Hollywood studio filmmaking as a whole constitute a group style. This style uses particular devices, such as three-point lighting and match-on-action editing. As might be expected, technology often creates new devices or reinforces or revises existing ones. The Hollywood style also embodies assumptions about how a film is constructed and the sorts of effects it should have. For example, the Hollywood style can be said to facilitate story continuity or to construct a unified space for a scene. Such assumptions can in turn guide technological changes. Filmmakers' beliefs about proper film technique make certain kinds of change more acceptable than others.

A second explanatory factor is nonstylistic. We must take account of the social processes that translate filmmakers' goals and standards into new materials, equipment, and procedures. In an industry as complex and wide-ranging as American movie production, these processes inevitably involve institutions. Just as the Hollywood style is a group phenomenon, so is technological change. In sum, the maintenance and development of this film style owes something to technological change. At the same time, technology is itself guided by both the characteristic devices and broader goals of that style. And both are subject to social practices within particular institutions.

A Specimen Scene

Consider a scene from THE CHARGE OF THE LIGHT BRIGADE (Warners, 1936), directed by Michael Curtiz. Late in the film, near the climactic charge, the scene shows Geoffrey (Errol Flynn), who has been made an officer in the Crimea, forcing his brother Perry (Patrick Knowles) to convey a dispatch to general headquarters. One aspect of the scene involves the historical action: Geoffrey has forged an order for the regiment to charge, and he needs to convey his decision to a sympathetic adviser. But there is a personal side to the scene as well. Since Perry is in love with Geoffrey's fiancée, Elsa, Geoffrey makes a noble sacrifice by sending Perry away from a suicidal charge. Perry, however, thinks that out of jealousy Geoffrey aims to shame him by sparing him from the fighting. Perry angrily accepts Geoffrey's order, not knowing that Geoffrey has already given Elsa permission to marry Perry. Geoffrey sacrifices his brother's honor and his own reputation as a judicious officer to make Elsa happy.

The scene, laid out in Figures 1–11 (pp. 111–112), provides a condensed example of some central stylistic features of the period.

THE CHARGE OF THE LIGHT BRIGADE
Scene 34

Dissolve to:

1. (Fig. 1) Long shot: Geoffrey at his desk in the foreground. Perry enters from rear and walks to desk; he starts to salute.
2. (Fig. 2) Medium close-up: Perry salutes, then starts. *Oh, I thought Sir Benjamin sent for me.*
3. (Fig. 3) Medium shot: Geoffrey at desk. *No, I sent for you. I want you to take this dispatch to general headquarters . . .*
4. Long shot, as 1: Geoffrey rises (Fig. 4) as he continues, *. . . and wait there for further orders.* As Geoffrey approaches and the camera tracks in (Fig. 5), Perry protests: *Wait at general headquarters! But I've learned the regiment's moving forward!* Geoffrey now faces him (Fig. 6). *If I have to wait at general headquarters, I'll be out of the fight altogether.* Geoffrey replies, *You'll deliver it personally to Sir Charles Macefield, do you understand?*
5. (Fig. 7) Medium close-up, Geoffrey's shoulder in the foreground: Perry glowers: *I believe you're trying to keep me out of this deliberately because of Elsa.*
6. (Fig. 8) Medium close-up, Perry's shoulder in the foreground: Geoffrey answers, *No; no, Elsa's got nothing to do with this. You're not in the diplomatic service now, you know. You're with your regiment at the front. You'll obey my orders immediately.* Perry replies, *If I refuse?* Geoffrey: *You'll be court-martialed.*
7. (Fig. 9) Medium close-up, as 5: Perry lowers his head.
8. (Fig. 10) Medium shot, as end of 4: Perry, looking down at the dispatch, takes it from Geoffrey. *I see. Disgraced either way.* He turns away toward the door. *Very well.* As he walks out the rear, track in to medium close-up of Geoffrey, who raises his head as if in pain and closes his eyes (Fig. 11). Dissolve.

Most fundamentally, the scene exemplifies what has come to be called the "continuity style" characteristic of Hollywood. In general, this style aims to present a coherent, stable, clearly defined space in which film technique is used to call the audience's attention to the most salient narrative information at each moment. In this style, lighting, costume, and figure placement will not change noticeably from shot to shot. Spatial continuity will be further assured by staging and shooting the action so that the camera is always on one side of the action.

Fig. 1

Fig. 2

Fig. 3

Fig. 4

Fig. 5

Fig. 6

Fig. 7

Fig. 8

Fig. 9

Fig. 10

Fig. 11

Sound will also aid temporal continuity by blending speech, music, and noise into an intelligible, smoothly modulated pattern. Music may lead into the action or underscore strong moments, while sound effects provide a background ambience. Nonetheless, dialogue is the principal carrier of story information, and it will dominate the other factors and stand out crisply.

This CHARGE OF THE LIGHT BRIGADE sequence shows that in many respects the continuity style of the 1930s continues traditions developed during the silent era. For instance, the staging of the action defines the interpersonal situation. Geoffrey is seated at his desk when Perry enters and salutes. Geoffrey rises, strides around the desk to him, and offers him the orders. When he threatens court-martial if Perry refuses his mission, Perry stalks out, leaving Geoffrey to agonize over what he has been forced to do.

Lighting serves to emphasize salient aspects of the staging. Throughout the Hollywood tradition, the human figure tends to be the center of the spectacle, and film technique serves to guide audience response by making aspects of that figure salient. Thus, lighting picks out the faces and the edges of the bodies (Figs. 7–8). The lighting also gives a soft sheen to the figures, eliminating blemishes from the faces and picking out highlights in the men's uniforms.

Similarly, when the human figures are framed in closer views, it is usually in order to emphasize what they say. For example, a cut-in to a medium close-up of Perry underlines his recognition of who his commanding officer is (Shot 2). Similarly, Geoffrey's reply is rendered during a closer view of him at his desk (Shot 3, Fig. 3). Sometimes the closer framing simply facilitates the audience's view of an unspoken reaction, as when Perry realizes the threat of court-martial and starts to look down at the order (Shot 7, Fig. 9).

The scene's editing is organized in terms of classical continuity's "axis of action," or "center line." This refers to the vector of movement, such as the direction of motion or the line of interaction between characters. In this scene, the line develops rather simply. At first, the line puts Geoffrey, sitting at the desk, in the foreground (Shot 1 to beginning of Shot 4). When Geoffrey rises and goes to Perry, he stops so as to place Perry slightly in the foreground (end of Shot 4). At one point (Shot 8), the line connecting the brothers is slightly diagonal to the camera.

Given a shot establishing an axis of action, the director assumes that no shot of either character can "break" it; that is, new camera positions will occupy any spot on one side of the center line. All the shots in this sequence respect such constraints. Shot 2, a medium close-up of Perry (Fig. 2), is taken from the same side of the line as was Shot 1. Shot 3, a reverse shot of Geoffrey (Fig. 3), is of the opposite end of the center line, but the camera position remains on the same side of the axis as it was in Shot 2. Such adherence to axis-of-action continuity ensures that when two characters face each other, their bodily orientations, facial orientations, and eyelines "match." Geoffrey is offscreen in Shot 2, but adherence to continuity editing assures that we understand that Perry is looking at him. Imagine, by contrast, if Curtiz had filmed Perry from the other side of the axis: he would now be facing and looking right, and the viewer might wonder if he had turned around.

Editing governs temporal factors no less than spatial ones. The sequence under discussion also reveals that unless there is an indication to the contrary, each cut is presumed to be durationally continuous. No moments of story action are left

out between shots. Two cuts display explicit temporal continuity by means of a
match on action. At the end of Shot 1, Perry salutes, and the next shot continues
his movement. A similar match connects Shots 7 and 8 when Perry lowers his
head. When some time must be elided, the Hollywood editing system handles
the matter in one of two ways: either by cross-cutting two actions in different
locales (so that when we leave one action to see another, time is skipped over in
the line of action we do not see), or by use of conventional "punctuations."
Instances of the latter frame the sequence under consideration: the scene begins
and ends with dissolves to indicate that some time has elapsed.

The bookended symmetry of the dissolves is echoed by repetitions within the
scene. The overall angle of view, along the diagonal running from the desk to the
door, is reiterated in three shots showing the two men facing each other (Shots 1,
4, and 8). In Shot 1, they face each other unmoving; in Shot 4, Geoffrey moves
from foreground to background; in Shot 8, Perry moves from foreground to
background. Interspersed with these three two-shots are three medium close-
ups of Perry (Shots 2, 5, and 7). The last two of these are from the same camera
set-up. Two shots give us closer views of Geoffrey, one at the desk (Shot 3), and
one when he forces Perry to take the dispatch (Shot 6). In a sense, there is a third
close view of Geoffrey—at the end of the scene when the camera tracks in on
him (Shot 8, Fig. 11). Shot 8, then, at first functions as a two-shot of the pair and
then becomes a close-up of Geoffrey. This creates a pattern:

Two-shots of two men	Close views of Perry	Close views of Geoffrey
1	2	3
4	5	6
	7	
8		8

This sort of balanced repetition has been pointed out by Raymond Bellour as a
basic principle of the classical style.[1]

In many cases, the repetition makes for greater efficiency in production. The
repeated setups of Perry (Shots 5 and 7) permit ease of filming: no adjustment of
lights or camera would be needed. More strikingly, the two-shots as edited (into
Shots 1, 4, and 8) are phases of what was probably during production a single
take, the "master shot." In the silent era, it was common practice to film all shots
with the same framing at the same time, but no continuous take of the entire
scene would typically have been taken. By the early 1930s, however, directors
usually made a master shot of the entire scene, with all dialogue and camera
movements played out. Closer framings of particular lines would then be shot, to
be inserted during the editing. The master-shot technique yields the sort of
repetition we see here. The setup at the end of Shot 1 is that seen in the
beginning of Shot 4; that at the end of Shot 4 supplies the framing for the
beginning of Shot 8. Here classical style pays double dividends: the repetitions
yield visual redundancy but also provide a financially economical filming
procedure.

Such tactics of staging, lighting, framing, and cutting emerged during the first
two decades of American film history and were by and large consolidated in a
systematic way by 1917. Thus, the LIGHT BRIGADE sequence relies upon stylistic
principles already firmly in place in the Hollywood silent cinema.

Yet the sequence also stands as a prototype of how the sound cinema of the 1930s could build upon these principles. Perhaps most notable is the rapid development of the action made possible by sound. The fairly complicated intrigue is developed in a scene employing merely 123 words and eight shots, and lasting for under a minute of screen time. In a silent film, the same lines would have required at least nine dialogue titles, each minimally five seconds long. Moreover, with sound the filmmakers can supply several pieces of story information at the same time by using different tracks. In Shot 4, while Geoffrey rises and approaches Perry (visual information), he continues issuing his order (auditory information). The sequence thus serves as a fair instance of the concision normally associated with studio filmmaking in the 1930s.

By the 1930s, "continuity" had come to connote a perceptually smooth conveyance of story information. Sound could enhance this sort of continuity in several ways. In the specimen sequence, beginning Geoffrey's line in Shot 3 and ending it in Shot 4 makes the cut itself less noticeable. Moreover, scriptwriters strove for a verbal continuity to match that on the visual track. The dialogue's flow from line to line proceeds from question and answer ("Do you understand?" "If I refuse?") and from echoing repetitions from one line to another:

> ". . . Sir Benjamin sent for me."/ "No, I sent for you."
> "Take this dispatch to general headquarters and wait
>   there . . ."/ "Wait at general headquarters! . . . If I
>   have to wait at general headquarters . . ."
> "If I have to wait . . ."/ "If I refuse?"
> "You'll deliver it . . ."/"You'll obey my orders . . ."/
>   "You'll be court-martialed . . ."

While some of these techniques can be found in the intertitles of the silent cinema, 1930s dialogue became a dense tissue of such repetitions.

Music yields a comparable auditory continuity. Here Max Steiner's score continues from the previous scene before fading out as the dialogue begins. Ten seconds later, when Geoffrey announces Perry's order, the line is followed by a two-chord "sting" in the woodwinds. The second chord is prolonged and provides a background for the next phase of the scene. After Perry's "Wait at general headquarters!" the two-chord motto is repeated in the brass. It recurs during pauses in the dialogue, before rising to a climax in the timpani under Geoffrey's "You'll obey my orders immediately." This line is further emphasized by the dead silence after it. With Perry's reply ("If I refuse?") the music resumes, underlining his resistance to the order. After his "Disgraced either way" comes a two-second pause. The music reappears, and as he walks out, a lyrical string theme (associated with Geoffrey and Elsa's romance) emerges to end the scene, underlining Geoffrey's closing his eyes in agony.

The sequence neatly illustrates the wide range of ways in which music can organize and point up patterns in the dialogue. Sometimes a line is delivered and music emerges in the pause after it. Sometimes the music continues underneath the line and continues during the pause. And sometimes the music runs under the line and abruptly halts to yield a few seconds of emphatic silence. In any event, few spectators will notice that about 80 percent of the scene has musical accompaniment. Steiner would write some years later that the "great problem" of film composing is "to give the scene continuity, to keep the audience unconscious of any break, yet to make the music perform its function of sustaining each mood and scene."[2]

The smooth flow of dramatic action is also aided by virtually unnoticeable camera movement. All the basic types of moving camera had been used during the silent era, and at several points camera movement had been a prominent stylistic device. Again, however, the 1930s gave certain stylistic options greater salience. When Geoffrey rises from his desk in Shot 4, the camera pans slightly right to reframe him. Such reframing movements, while not unknown in the silent era, were far more frequent in the sound period. As Geoffrey strides to Perry, the camera tracks (or "dollies") forward to frame them in medium-shot. The camera movement is quite unobtrusive because it follows the character's movement. At the end of the last shot, as Perry leaves, the camera tracks forward once more, stressing Geoffrey's pained reaction. Observe that again this movement is almost unnoticeable because its timing and pace coincide with the action of Perry stalking off in the background.

Our prototype is a very simple scene; a more complex sequence would require many more pages of analysis. But the CHARGE OF THE LIGHT BRIGADE passage does suggest that we can usefully consider the style of the 1930s Hollywood film to be a modification of certain devices and principles already established in the Hollywood tradition. Stylistic novelty during this period emerged within a frame of reference that valorized certain devices, such as matches on action and the 180-degree system, while also promoting certain broad goals: centrality of the human figure; spatiotemporal continuity; and a clarity and economy in emphasizing the ongoing dialogue, physical action, and psychological reaction.

The Interplay of Style and Technology

In any industry, one goal of technological change is efficiency—to make a process consume less time, energy, or money. The film industry is no exception. Many tools and procedures were introduced to cut the costs of film production, especially after the advent of talkies had raised expenses considerably. The 1930s was the era in which sound production came to be streamlined in a form that is recognizable today.

Technological change also has an aesthetic aspect. By canonizing a particular style of filmmaking, the Hollywood industry set engineers an agenda. Sound had to be integrated into an existing set of stylistic priorities. More specifically, the fluency and economy found in our specimen scene were goals consciously pursued during the early 1930s. Hollywood filmmakers strove to recover the stylistic flexibility that they had enjoyed during the late silent era and that had often been curtailed during the early days of sound. Technological change in the Hollywood studios thus had two goals: maximal efficiency and maximal integration with, or extension of, the classical stylistic norms.

These two goals came into sharp focus in the earliest days of talkies. Between 1929 and 1931 most filmmakers staged the action for the sake of sound recording. Getting a clear, complete soundtrack had the highest priority, and since microphones were heavy and hard to move, the picture track often became static and rather flatly lit. In addition, most scenes were shot with several cameras running simultaneously, all filming the scene in toto. By placing the cameras at various angles and by using lenses of different focal lengths, the filmmakers could preserve the changes of framing essential to Hollywood continuity editing.

A characteristic example is furnished by a sequence from MILLIE (RKO, 1931). Millie has just eloped with Jack, and they have checked into a hotel. The scene depicting her reluctance to go to bed is staged quite "theatrically" in a wide, fairly shallow set. The hotel room's parlor gives onto a curtained bedroom in the rear. In the course of the sequence, five cameras follow the characters around the room. After the couple check in, Millie sits down on stage right and Jack joins her; they are filmed in medium long shot (Fig. 12). After she goes out frame left (Fig. 13), a long-shot camera follows her walk to the door, panning right to reframe Jack as he approaches (Fig. 14). At the door, the couple are framed in medium shot as he tries to persuade her to come to bed (Fig. 15). In an extreme long shot he draws her to the bedroom in the rear (Fig. 16). As she resists, a medium shot enlarges them again (Fig. 17). The two medium shots are filmed with long lenses, while the other views are filmed with lenses of shorter focal lengths.

Multiple-camera filming guaranteed synchronization in an era when matching picture and soundtrack posed great difficulties. One cinematographer recalled, "In those days we didn't know how to cut sound, so we'd shoot the sound in one solid unit, and then cut the film from our twelve [!] cameras to fit the track."[3]

Yet the multiple-camera procedure had many drawbacks. It was inefficient, wasting time and film and requiring a large crew. Since most sound shots could not be made separately, any error in performance or recording necessitated starting the entire scene over. There were also aesthetic drawbacks. The cameras were frequently housed in soundproof booths, and the thick glass reduced photographic quality. Long lenses could not achieve the tight, precise framings of the silent era. In the cinema of the 1920s, the camera was frequently placed close to the players, and actors' glances and movements in a sense flowed around the spectator. In early talkies, however, the placement of the cameras outside the zone of action made the action seem more distant and uninvolving. In the MILLIE scene, in contrast with the sequence from THE CHARGE OF THE LIGHT BRIGADE, the viewer does not really enter the hotel room, either through camera movements or cut-in close-ups. Space becomes less voluminous, actors more distant. The analysis of the action is accomplished by enlarging portions of the scene, as if we were looking at a sporting event through binoculars.

Given the economic and aesthetic drawbacks of multiple-camera shooting, it is not surprising that technical personnel devoted a great deal of energy to returning to single-camera filmmaking. Filmmakers quickly learned that shots not requiring synchronized dialogue could be filmed silent and spliced into multi-camera sequences, perhaps with some sound effects added. Soon directional microphones and silenced cameras allowed closer framings and more nuanced lighting. New sound-editing equipment permitted picture and sound to be recorded and cut separately. Mobile camera carriages enabled filmmakers to recover and even enhance the fluidity of silent cinema. By the end of 1931, most studios were able to film with one camera again.

More generally, contemporary observers insisted that there was no going back to the plodding pace of most early talkies. Some writers foresaw a new cinematic rhythm born of a blend of talk, music, gesture, and silence.[4] One writer proposed

Fig. 12

Fig. 13

Fig. 14

Fig. 15

Fig. 16

Fig. 17

building smaller sets so that characters could pass through them more swiftly, eliminating "dead footage."[5] Another commentator asserted that film technique, instead of merely recording theatrical dialogue, was an intrinsic part of cinema's appeal. "And the tortuous way back to the old silent days' technique of many angles and rapid cuts, plus sound-camera equipment, was begun."[6] Yet another critic advocated increased tempo: more and shorter scenes, swift lap-dissolves and montage sequences, rapid-fire dialogue, and "an almost constantly moving camera."[7]

These writers were not calling for that "creative use of sound" by Mamoulian or Lubitsch canonized in film history textbooks. These directors' innovations often minimized speech, letting the audience grasp the situation by means of sound effects or purely visual cues. Rather, the commentators mentioned above foresaw a cinema grounded in dialogue. Nonetheless, the actors' performances would be enhanced by all the visual resources revealed in the silent era, as well as others yet to be developed.

Technological change thus fulfilled several roles. Not only was it aimed at greater economy or efficiency, but new technology could also help filmmakers maintain established standards of visual intelligibility, and it could enhance the appeal of what was essentially a dialogue-based cinema.

Sources of Innovation

While technological and artistic innovations can usually be attributed to individuals, those individuals operate within a broader context. The norms of Hollywood film style emerged and held sway within the routines of film production as fostered by the studios. Similarly, technological change and stability are processes that occur within particular institutions. The individual inventor works within a context of goals, constraints, and opportunities defined not only by the hardware's "state of the art" but also by the unspoken assumptions about what is needed for this particular mode of filmmaking.

During the 1930s, three types of institutions supplied filmmaking technology: the studios themselves, the large and small service firms, and professional organizations attached to the industry. A survey of these sources of technological innovation will illustrate how particular changes emerged.

The film studios were sometimes a source of technological innovation. At MGM, John Arnold oversaw a Camera Department whose job was not only to maintain equipment but also to solve technical problems. Douglas Shearer, head of the same studio's Sound Department, developed several pieces of recording equipment, as well as pressing for more uniform reproduction in theaters. At 20th Century–Fox, Daniel Clark, the Executive Director of Photography, devised a new camera and developed a useful system of standardizing f-stops. Less well endowed studios also put some resources into technology, most notably in the design of special-effects equipment and of camera carriages and cranes.

On the whole, however, the production companies were not well equipped for large-scale technical innovation. Most studio "research laboratories" seem to have been glorified machine shops, and the "experiments" sometimes referred to in the trade literature were seldom more than skillful tinkering. For basic and standardized innovation, two other sorts of institutions played more central roles.

Most visible are the firms, large and small, which served the industry's technological needs. Eastman Kodak, for example, had since late in the nineteenth century committed itself to an ambitious program of research and development. Recruiting outstanding graduates from the nation's engineering schools, Eastman undertook basic research into the optics and chemistry of photographic processes. Eastman supplied the movie industry with raw film, both positive and negative, and equipment, such as filters for cameras and sensitometers for laboratory work. Similarly, Eastman's Rochester neighbor, Bausch and Lomb, was the principal source of lenses for motion-picture cameras, projectors, printers, and other equipment.

With the coming of sound, other corporations entered the picture. Both the Radio Corporation of America and Bell Telephone had invested heavily in basic research, and, so, large and sophisticated laboratories stood ready to assist Hollywood in standardizing and improving sound processes.

Less committed to basic research were the more specialized companies serving the industry. Bell & Howell had been a mainstay since 1908, when its continuous printer helped standardize the industry's printing practices. During the 1920s, the Bell & Howell camera was considered the most sophisticated and precise available. The firm continued its triumphs with the introduction of new film gauges (16-mm silent in 1923, 16-mm sound in 1932, and 8-mm in 1936), of automated printers for sound (1930, 1935), and of perforators and splicers.[8]

Bell & Howell's chief competitor was the Mitchell company, whose camera also became widely used in the 1920s. The coming of sound gave the Mitchell NC (for "New Camera") a strong advantage, since the Bell & Howell camera's noise was picked up by microphones. Bell & Howell introduced a quieter version of its product in 1933, but it did not win out over the BNC (for "Blimped New Camera") that Mitchell introduced a year later. The BNC had a compact soundproof housing and other desirable features, such as a shutter that could be adjusted during a shot. By the end of the decade, Bell & Howell cameras were being consigned to newsreel and special-effects work, while the Mitchell was becoming the standard studio camera.[9]

Other specialized companies offered tailor-made engineering. The Moviola company had since the 1920s provided a variety of viewing machines, all of which obliged the cutter to view the film through a magnifying lens; in 1938 the firm created the Preview Moviola, which projected the film on a small screen. The firm of Mole-Richardson concentrated on supplying lighting equipment and mobile carriages for cameras and microphones. In 1928 the company won an Academy Award for its research into illumination, and in 1935, another for developing special spotlights. Mole-Richardson often built prototypes on demand and then manufactured the equipment that studios deemed most useful.

Along with such service companies—and there were many others—we can distinguish a third sort of institution that shaped technological change during the 1930s. During the teens and twenties there emerged several professional organizations that played important roles in the process.

A key instance is the American Society of Cinematographers (ASC), which grew from an informal club into the professional association of studio cinematographers. Chartered in 1919, it sought "to establish and maintain standards of professional and technical skill and integrity, and to bring into closer personal and professional fellowship all of the leaders of the motion picture camera profession."[10] During the thirties monthly ASC meetings became occasions for cinematographers to share discoveries and display new equipment. The results were often also disseminated in *American Cinematographer*, a monthly magazine.

The Society of Motion Picture Engineers (SMPE) took a more stringent approach to innovation. Founded in 1916 and composed of technicians from the supply firms, the SMPE was primarily devoted to establishing engineering standards for the motion-picture industry. The society served its members' companies by pressing for uniformity and efficiency in such matters as film dimensions, apertures, perforations, sound characteristics, screen materials and sizes, and so on. Research in the companies' laboratories was announced at twice-yearly conventions and in the *Journal of the Society of Motion Picture Engineers*. Relatively few employees of Hollywood studios belonged to the SMPE in the 1920s, but the arrival of sound filming gave engineering a new pride of place. In 1929 the SMPE opened its Pacific Coast section under the aegis of such major suppliers as Mitchell and Mole and with membership including major studio personnel.

The increased technological development of the decade required broad coordination, which could not be achieved by the rather specialized ASC and SMPE. The Academy of Motion Picture Arts and Sciences, founded in 1927, had many functions, but by the early 1930s it had taken on the role of coordinating technological innovation and its diffusion.

The Academy established its Technical Bureau in 1928, but it was not particularly effective until 1930, when the Motion Picture Producers Association transferred its technical office to the Academy and donated $15,000 to help coordinate the work of existing research facilities. In 1932 the Academy board of directors revamped the bureau and created the Academy Research Council, which announced that it intended "to coordinate motion picture research and standardization efforts and to function as a central bureau for the exchange of technical and artistic information."[11] The council's quarterly meetings brought together representatives of all branches of the membership, technical staff from each studio, and advisory engineers from supply companies. Across the years the council helped standardize apertures in cameras and projectors, process projection equipment, costume colors, and other factors. By representing the studios' interests, it provided a forum wherein producers could communicate their needs directly to the major suppliers.

During the early 1930s the supply companies developed close ties to these organizations. Not only did company employees become leaders of the SMPE, but in 1931 the society created the category of "sustaining member," which allowed firms to contribute money to collective efforts. Two years later, the ASC allowed representatives of Bell & Howell, Eastman, Bausch & Lomb, and other firms to become associate members, while some outstanding figures such as Howell and Mitchell became honorary members. Supply firms' innovations were often premiered at ASC meetings, and cinematographers were invited to try out new materials and equipment on the set. Similarly, when the Academy was reorganized in 1933, it created the category of "corporate member" to allow the suppliers to join and to help fund the council's activities. The Academy Research Council became heavily dependent upon the manufacturers; by 1937, its thirty-six committees were said to involve 180 different company representatives.[12]

Studios, supply firms, and professional associations were, then, the major innovators of technology during the 1930s. They cooperated closely with each other. When in 1931 new faster film stocks needed testing, the ASC cooperated with the Academy Technicians' Branch on the project. In 1936 the head of the SMPE's Sound Committee reported working with the studios' sound departments and the Academy to compare the recording frequencies of different studios.[13] As the following case studies show, most technological changes involved a degree of standardization that required a consensus among the product's users.

That consensus in turn rested on assumptions about what technology should be used for. Materials and equipment had to satisfy the criteria of efficiency characteristic of any industry: durability, low cost, portability, flexibility, uniformity, and so on. But more intangible were those requirements that bore on style and artifice. Studios proved startlingly uninterested in standardizing the most basic practices of their industry, such as perforation size and aperture dimensions; such issues would drag through the organizations' technical committees for years. But filmmakers had their own priorities. Peter Mole confessed that when he arrived in Hollywood, he discoverd that studios did not wholly share the engineer's gospel of efficiency. The most elegant technical solution would not always suit the studios' goals.[14]

In addition, the studios faced divisions within their own industry. Often the production sector's pursuit of novelty and spectacle would exceed exhibitors' willingness to adapt. Such innovations as the widescreen, 3-D, and stereophonic sound, all introduced during the 1930s, could not be developed on a large scale. The changeover to sound had required a huge investment in theaters, and exhibitors resisted attempts to revamp their facilities during the Depression years. Declining attendance in the late 1940s would make exhibitors more enthusiastic about 3-D, Cinerama, CinemaScope, and similar novelties in the following decade.

The dynamics of innovation are thus fairly complicated. Studios could make broad demands, such as for a greater fidelity of sound recording, or propose specific problems, such as the removal of unwanted equipment noise on the set. The Academy, the professional organizations, and the supply firms could investigate the matter. Possible solutions could be tested in various venues, often with studio cooperation. Reports from different agencies could sharpen the issues and suggest new prospects. Eventually a solution could be proposed, promulgated, and accepted, perhaps even becoming rigidly standardized. At every stage, contending factions within the motion-picture industry might have to be consulted.

In the course of the investigation, other technical issues might arise. Or an innovation in one area might have unexpected implications in another, such as improvements in rear projection. At certain points, the supply firms took the initiative and, anticipating filmmakers' needs, innovated in ways that offered filmmakers hitherto unexpected possibilities for improving production routines or exploring fresh options within Hollywood's characteristic style.

Here we can only suggest how this process worked in certain key instances. There is much that researchers still do not know about the dynamics of technology and style in Hollywood. It seems clear, however, that during the 1930s, Hollywood stabilized its sound-filmmaking practices by defining goals fairly clearly, pursuing them rationally, and integrating the efforts of various technical institutions. The case studies that follow show these processes at work in more detail.

Case Studies

What follows are case studies of five major technological developments over the decade. They have been chosen somewhat arbitrarily, since they are connected to each other and have links to still other developments that cannot be pursued here. For example, the increase in camera movement necessitated new instruments for racking focus, which drew in turn upon research undertaken for entirely different ends, the problems of focusing the bulky Technicolor camera. All this chapter can do is indicate how some important developments met the two central criteria: gaining greater production efficiency and fulfilling or extending norms of the classical storytelling style.

Innovations in Sound. Early sound-filming technology employed either sound on disk (the Warners Vitaphone system) or sound on film (the Fox Movietone system). Very quickly the problems with sound on disk—primarily related to synchronization—assured the dominance of sound on film. By 1930, most studios were using so-called double-system sound; that is, a separate strip of film ran through a recording device that registered sound impulses as optical patterns.

Since the Hollywood sound cinema was to be centered upon a narrative carried by dialogue, the crucial problem was that of recording the voice while retaining the flexibility of silent visual style. Here the purely acoustic difficulties were severe. Personnel, lights, and cameras created considerable noise on the set. Most microphones were "omnidirectional" and picked up such noise indiscriminately. They were also bulky and difficult to move around the set. In addition, the signal they captured was narrow in frequency range, muddy in texture, and often too low in volume.

Some of these difficulties were overcome by quieting the set. The camera was put in a booth or a soundproof metal casing ("blimp"). Noisy arc lighting was replaced by incandescents. Mole-Richardson designed lightweight microphone booms that replaced the crude rope-and-pulley system of the early days.

More complicated problems of recording required the help of RCA and Western Electric. For instance, in 1931, RCA introduced the "ribbon" microphone, which had a flat response, high sensitivity, and a bidirectional range of pickup. The ribbon microphone became widely used because it could be placed between conversing characters, and if it was perpendicular to the camera, little equipment noise would register. RCA's 1936 "cardoid" microphone yielded a unidirectional pickup over a heart-shaped field. This device was coming into wider use by the end of the decade, when Western Electric introduced a comparable series of directional microphones.

RCA and Western Electric engineers also strove to increase the range of sound that could be recorded. The most significant step here was the introduction in 1934 of "push-pull" sound recording. This procedure split the sound into two signals and recorded them 180-degrees out of phase, either by the variable-area method (the RCA design) or by the variable-density method (the Western Electric solution). This innovation increased the volume range of the recorded material by "pushing" the fundamental frequency and "pulling" overtones and equipment noise.[15] In addition, in 1936, RCA developed ultraviolet recording, which captured higher frequencies. Thanks to such innovations, by the end of the decade a Hollywood film could record a range of 50–8,000 cycles per second and could achieve up to sixty decibels in dynamic range.[16]

In the early days of talkies, nearly all sound recording took place during the shooting phase. Music had to be performed on the set, even if the source was never to be seen. If an actor had to be "dubbed," the dubber recited the lines off-camera. For the sake of efficient division of labor and greater control over the soundtrack, filmmakers strove to reduce the amount of sound recording occurring on the set. For this to be done, noise, music, and dialogue would have to be recorded and manipulated on separate tracks. The 1930s is thus the decade that established principles of multitrack sound that still govern film production.

The separation of tracks altered the handling of noise effects and music. By the end of 1932, most such sound was recorded independently of the image. At about the same time, prerecorded or "playback," sound came into use for musical numbers. A musical piece would be recorded on film or acetate disc and then played back during shooting so that songs and dances could be performed in synchronization. For the finished film, the sound staff would synchronize the piece with the footage. For ONE HUNDRED MEN AND A GIRL (1937), Leopold Stokowski experimented with recording on eight channels: six for different parts of the orchestra, one for the whole orchestra, and one for the soloist, Deanna Durbin. Although this was exceptional, it foreshadowed the multitrack recording of later decades.[17]

Rerecording dialogue lagged behind rerecording music and sound effects because vocal perspective was initially difficult to duplicate off the set. Soon, however, the improved microphones and recording equipment made dubbing voices feasible. By 1935, actors could rerecord voices guided by a track made during filming. Each stretch of dialogue was kept on a separate roll of film (a procedure still called "looping"). During the second half of the decade, the sound mixer might be handling as many as fifteen tracks for a scene. A 1938 observer commented that a finished eleven-minute reel could have a hundred sound cues.[18] For this reason, the sound department received the script before filming and, from it, built a "sound script" that would govern the search for music or effects.

These and other innovations in sound recording were coordinated by the Academy. Throughout the decade it held conferences and courses to train technicians in new equipment. In 1937 the Academy persuaded the major companies to standardize the frequency range of their release prints so that theaters could in turn establish a uniform sound characteristic.[19]

Developments in sound and picture editing proceeded alongside innovations in recording and reproduction. Double-system sound posed the problem of synchronizing picture and sound. This was solved through two procedures. At the start of every take, picture track and sound track were punched simultaneously so that they could easily be lined up. In addition, since 1918, Eastman negative stock had borne stenciled footage numbers on its edge; this enabled editors to distinguish various takes of the same shot. After 1930, the sound track was recorded on film with edge numbers identical to those on the picture track. Thus, the editor could immediately match any frame with its corresponding sound. The mechanics of the job were eased by the gang synchronizer, a mounted set of sprocketed clamps that allowed several reels of sound and image to be aligned in parallel. Precise editing was also assisted by the 1931 double-system Moviola, by a 1933 model with heads for three sound tracks, and by the 1937 Preview Moviola, whose 5.5-by-6.5-inch viewing screen replaced the peephole view of the film provided on earlier models.

Technology such as this, when integrated into the editing routines inherited from the silent era, enabled the filmmaker to time cuts quite exactly. What Barry Salt calls the conventional "dialogue cutting point" in sound cinema—cutting away from the speaker just before the last word or syllable has been spoken—became feasible with frame-by-frame matching of picture and sound.[20] Although the LIGHT BRIGADE example does not exemplify this tactic, the sequence does bleed one line over a cut, and it cuts on pauses in a way that shows how sound and picture editing cooperate in creating a scene's rhythm.

The new recording, mixing, and editing technology also permitted intricate manipulation of music. Silent films had had continuous musical accompaniment in the theater, but early talkies largely relinquished the use of nondiegetic (i.e., non-story-source) music. Once rerecording techniques could assure reasonable sound quality, however, Max Steiner, Alfred Newman, Erich Wolfgang Korngold, and others began to write long stretches of music. KING KONG (1933) contains an hour of original music, with some passages running for many minutes. Korngold's score for CAPTAIN BLOOD (1935) lasts over half of the film's running time. During the 115 minutes of THE CHARGE OF THE LIGHT BRIGADE, there are only about twenty-three minutes when Steiner's score is not heard!

Though these have come to be known as "symphonic" scores, they more closely resemble operatic accompaniment to vocal recitative.[21] As noted in the LIGHT BRIGADE analysis, the music ebbs and flows underneath the dialogue, emphasizing certain phrases, filling the pauses, linking scenes, or cutting off dramatically. The studio composer might write eleven- or twelve-minute passages, or bits only ten seconds long; the music might have to "sneak in" under dialogue or rise to mezzo forte very quickly.

The sound-recording and mixing techniques reviewed above made such split-second timing possible, as did some more specialized devices. The "click track" was originally a black leader punched with holes at intervals that matched the pacing of the action; these clicks gave the composer the rhythmic pulse of the music needed. Later, in recording the score, the conductor would lead the orchestra in time to the click track. The mixer could blend the score with other tracks with the help of Western Electric's "automatic balance regulator," which controlled the mixing balance between dialogue and music. Now the music could comment, moment by moment, upon the dramatic action without distracting from it.

In general, improvements in sound technology in the thirties reinforced the basic assumptions of Hollywood's stylistic tradition. Storytelling was enhanced by a variety of unobtrusive technical devices. The image track's emphasis on the human face was paralleled by an emphasis on the voice, and various technological innovations enabled clearer recording of speech. Certain canonized devices, such as the continuity cut, were strengthened by the judicious use of sound. Overall, the sound film gained a controlled economy and a brisk pace governed by dialogue.

Camera Movement. Camera movements had been part of Hollywood's technical repertory during the silent era, and the coming of sound did not eradicate
them. Many early sound films display rather complex camera movements, either
shot silent or filmed from wheeled booths. Some observers believed that THE
LAST LAUGH (1924), VARIETY (1925), and APPLAUSE (1929) had started a vogue
for flamboyant traveling shots.[22] In the course of the decade, more unobtrusive
camera movements became quite common, partly because of technological
factors that made them reasonably efficient and partly because they created a
fluidity that was considered valuable in the talking cinema.

In the silent era and in the early days of sound filmmaking, most shots were
made with the camera on a tripod. But the weight of a heavily blimped sound
camera strained ordinary tripods and made the camera difficult to move around
the set. It soon became evident that greater production efficiency and stylistic
flexibility could be achieved by retooling the sort of camera carts used in the
silent era.

The initial prototype was the Bell & Howell Rotambulator, introduced in 1932.
This was a seven-hundred-pound carriage about five feet long and four feet wide.
Using a central column on a turntable, the Rotambulator could set the camera at
any height between eighteen inches and seven feet. The seated cinematographer
could pan, tilt, track, rotate, or raise the camera on the vertical shaft. On the
most sophisticated model, hydraulics enabled the cameraman to control panning
with foot pedals while tilting by means of a hand lever.[23]

The Rotambulator, introduced in 1932 and disseminated in the following year,
was quickly revised. The Fox Velocilator (introduced in 1933 and manufactured
by the Fearless Camera Company) had many of the same features as the
Rotambulator, but it was only thirty inches wide and weighed only three
hundred pounds. Moreover, instead of a central column on a turntable it made
use of an angled boom arm that raised or lowered the camera. Cinematographer
John Seitz explained of the Velocilator, "While its primary purpose is, of course,
facilitating the making of traveling shots, it has proved equally valuable as a
means of saving time and effort in changing camera set-ups."[24]

Advantageous features of the Rotambulator and the Velocilator were combined
in the Fearless Company's Panoram Dolly, which debuted in 1936. The camera
was anchored to a boom arm, which in turn rested on a turntable on a
four-wheeled chassis. It could pass through a thirty-six-inch door, and two seats
were provided for camera personnel. The Fearless dolly, or copies of it, quickly
became standard studio equipment.[25]

Such standardized camera carriages naturally increased filmmakers' ability to
make lengthy tracking shots. During the mid 1930s some films utilized virtuosic
camera movements. The Velocilator appears to have been the basis of Erik
Charell's CARAVAN (Fox, 1934); the film's average shot lasts thirty-seven seconds,
and Charell uses camera movement to shift in and out of flashbacks within a
single shot. More orthodox films also made increased use of camera movements.
By 1938, one SMPE committee could report that the growing emphasis on camera
movement had made "a very definite contribution to the continuity and
smoothness of action of the motion picture story."[26]

But many cinematographers complained about the "orgy of indiscriminate
dollying": moving shots were complicated and expensive.[27] Most cameramen and
directors favored the unnoticeable tracking movements that followed the move-

ments of the players, as in the CHARGE OF THE LIGHT BRIGADE sequence. One observer spoke for many when he explained that the best talkies' style offered "a skillful blend of cuts and mobile camera, achieving the fullest cinematic effectiveness by an entirely unself-conscious 'participation' in the 'central emotional strain' threading rhythmically through the story."[28]

Highly noticeable camera movements did have their uses, however. Most often, they could be used at the beginning of a scene, as John Cromwell noted:

> Fundamentally [the director] has a choice of two kinds of technique: starting on a fairly close shot of some action that is either revelation of the characters or story, then proceeding back to a revelation of time and place, or establishing the locale first and then progressing up to the characters. Using the first method, the picture might open on a close shot of a newspaper lying on the pavement with the camera *tilting up* to the little boy who is standing over the newspaper reading it, and from there moving horizontally or *panning* over to a man standing on the street and watching the little boy, when the story begins. Using the second method, you might open on a long shot of the street, then move the camera towards the little boy in what is known as a *trucking shot*, and finally pan over to a shot of the man as the story begins. ("The Voice Behind the Megaphone," in Nancy Naumberg, ed., *We Make the Movies* [New York: Norton, 1937], p. 60)

While Michael Curtiz uses neither tactic at the start of the specimen scene, he does obey Cromwell's suggestion in other sequences. We can thus get a sense of the most common functions of 1930s camera movement: following figure movement or opening a scene by stressing a detail.

The new camera devices had other advantages as well. Hydraulic control of panning and tilting reduced the sort of jerky reframing that can be seen in some early talkies. Moreover, allowing the camera operator to sit comfortably and to manipulate reframing with feet and one hand represented an improvement over tripod heads that required the use of both hands. The new dollies made feasible the sort of tight, minute adjustments of framing seen in the LIGHT BRIGADE sequence.

The growth of the moving-camera style affected other equipment and procedures. Lighting units on the set floor hampered the dolly, so production became more reliant on hanging units. Since these put the light source farther from the action, spotlighting units became preferable to the broader units used on the floor. The new demand for spotlights in turn triggered a series of refinements in them, most notably the use of Fresnel lenses to focus the illumination.[29] Through such ripple effects, the preferred stylistic alternatives shaped the direction of technological innovation.

While various dollies were being designed and adopted, some practitioners experimented with larger camera carriages. The enormous Universal camera crane used on BROADWAY (1929), with its twenty-five-foot-long arm, had represented the summit of such efforts at the end of the silent era. The small sets in early talkies did not favor such equipment, but after 1931, cranes were proving feasible again. The BROADWAY behemoth was trundled out for ALL QUIET ON THE WESTERN FRONT (1930), and MGM and UA also began using cranes. In 1932, at an Academy equipment demonstration, Paramount displayed its "Baby" camera boom, which could rise from floor level to a height of about eight feet.

Often such cranes were used for transporting the camera from one setup to another and for taking static high-angle shots (thus obviating the need to build a special camera platform). But a 1931 article pointed out that filming from a moving crane yielded fluidity and spectacle. Citing an unspecified film, the writer noted that a powerful effect was achieved by tracking with the main characters as they entered a ballroom and then craning up to show the entire dance floor. "Such photography, interspersed throughout the more common-place scenes, does much to determine the success or failure of any motion picture. The problem of keeping the plot moving along and at the same time impressing the beauty and color of setting upon the spectator is solved in many instances by the camera crane."[30]

By 1936, most production companies had flexible dollies and either owned or rented large cranes that could rise twenty or thirty feet. In addition, the Velocilator had shown that a small unit could utilize a cranelike angled arm, so many firms sought to build middle-range cranes that could work between eight and twenty feet off the studio floor. One of the most noteworthy of these was John Arnold's MGM boom, introduced in 1939, which had a maximum height of sixteen feet. The crane's light weight, underslung camera mounting, and highly maneuverable wheels were designed to make it the preferred camera carriage for virtually any shot.[31] The boom won Arnold an Academy Technical Award.

Flamboyant crane shots are visible in several films of the early and mid 1930s, often being used to establish the setting in an arresting way (e.g., STREET SCENE, 1931). Crane shots are a major attraction of the musical numbers in such Busby Berkeley films as FOOTLIGHT PARADE (1933) and GOLD DIGGERS OF 1933. Stately crane movements are particularly in evidence in MGM's THE WIZARD OF OZ (1939) and GONE WITH THE WIND (1939). There was usually no attempt to make such shots as unobtrusive as the mild track-ins and reframings already noted. Instead, crane shots were used to impart a flow to ensemble musical numbers and to indulge in a momentary display of spectacle, as in GONE WITH THE WIND's legendary crane back through the railroad yard full of wounded soldiers, which utilized a sixty-foot construction crane.[32] On the whole, the crane shot remained a valuable but secondary tool in a cinema devoted to storytelling rather than camera pyrotechnics.

Technicolor. Although it would be some decades before most Hollywood films would be made in color, the 1930s saw a significant interest in color filmmaking, and this revolved chiefly around the firm of Technicolor.

In outline, the firm's history is fairly clear. The years 1929–1930 saw a boom in Technicolor, chiefly in such musicals as ON WITH THE SHOW (1929), GOLD DIGGERS OF BROADWAY (1929), and WHOOPEE! (1930). These films used the two-color Technicolor process, which favored reddish and greenish hues. After the box-office decline of the early 1930s and complaints about color quality, interest in the process waned. Technicolor developed its imbibition-printing method in 1930 and its three-color process in 1932. These greatly improved color techniques were tested in Disney's cartoon FLOWERS AND TREES (1932), in the short subject LA CUCARACHA (1934), and in the feature BECKY SHARP (1935). A new color vogue gradually emerged, signaled by the success of THE TRAIL OF THE LONESOME PINE (1936). This second wave of success gathered momentum in

1939, when a faster film stock was used on DRUMS ALONG THE MOHAWK, THE PRIVATE LIVES OF ELIZABETH AND ESSEX, GONE WITH THE WIND, and other major productions. Throughout the 1940s between twenty and fifty Technicolor features were produced every year.

The Technicolor camera used prisms to split the light beam and record different wavelengths on three strips of film.[33] As a result, the cameras were cumbersome and difficult to thread. Similarly, Technicolor's imbibition developing of color relied on a process akin to lithography and could not be accommodated by standard studio laboratories. Throughout Technicolor's history, it therefore had to convince the production companies that its technology was worth the trouble. Technicolor financed independent films to demonstrate various processes: THE GULF BETWEEN (1917) displayed the red-green additive process, and THE TOLL OF THE SEA (1922) exhibited the two-color subtractive method. After the decline in studio interest in the early 1930s, Technicolor used the Disney cartoons as a showcase for the three-component and imbibition processes. John Hay Whitney, a Technicolor stockholder, produced LA CUCARACHA and BECKY SHARP under the auspices of his own firm, Pioneer Pictures. Only then did the studios feel that Technicolor's increased cost (almost 30 percent over black-and-white film) might be justified for certain productions.

The Technicolor company exemplifies how a specialized service firm could be governed by engineering principles of standardization and efficiency. Founded in 1915 by two engineers from the Massachusetts Institute of Technology (MIT), Herbert Kalmus and Daniel Comstock, Technicolor was named after their alma mater. Kalmus and Comstock, along with W. Burton Westcott, had already served as scientific consultants for the chemical industry. The three men decided to ground their color-film enterprise in practical industrial research. They secured investment capital from New York lawyers, advertising agencies, and manufacturing companies. They also hired MIT students, one of whom, J. A. Ball, was eventually to devise the three-color system. In 1925, Comstock left the firm, making Kalmus the executive head of Technicolor. By 1930, he had a Hollywood laboratory said to employ six hundred people. Knowledge was kept compartmentalized for the sake of secrecy; only the executives had an overall view of the enterprise.[34]

Kalmus maintained that the quality problems in the two-color process had been due largely to inexperienced studio cameramen, so he insisted that the company had to supervise every phase of the process. For most 1930s productions Technicolor supplied not only the film stock but the cameras, the processing, the release prints, a company-approved cinematographer, the camera crew, and several advisers, notably the "color consultant" (usually Kalmus's ex-wife, Natalie). At the start of every shooting day, the crew would bring loaded camera magazines and the cleaned and inspected cameras from the company. Since threading a Technicolor camera did not go quickly, the production unit typically rented two cameras so that one could be shooting while the other was being reloaded.

For all his autonomy, Kalmus was obliged to work with related service firms. While his engineers knew physics and chemistry, their camera blueprints had to be turned over to other companies for realization; Mitchell produced three-strip cameras to Ball's design. The firm also depended upon Eastman, not only for supplying raw film stock but also for such innovations as the 1939 emulsion that cut required lighting levels in half.[35]

Also notable was the change in lighting equipment that followed from the mid-1930s color boom. Three-strip Technicolor was balanced for daylight, which was best matched by arc illumination. On the studio floor, however, arcs had largely been replaced by the quieter incandescents, which could be used with Technicolor in limited ways but could not deliver the intensity of light desired. Spurred by this new demand, Mole-Richardson devised silent, flickerless arc spotlights and broadsides for color production. These were in turn quickly adapted to black-and-white filming.

Technicolor created no radical changes in classical studio filmmaking. Instead, the process accommodated itself to the reigning aesthetic norms. For example, color risked calling attention to background details that would have gone gray in black-and-white filming. Natalie Kalmus therefore urged that backgrounds be darkened so that the warmer flesh tones would come forward.[36] This recommendation assumed that the human figure was the basis of the action. "The one key color present in every scene," wrote a Technicolor consultant, "is the face of the actor."[37] Technicolor aesthetics in the 1930s were governed by producer Edgar Selwyn's advice to Daniel Comstock: "The human being is the center of the drama. The face is the center of the human being. And the eyes are the center of the face. If a process is not sharp enough to show clearly the whites of a person's eyes at a reasonable distance, it isn't any good no matter what it is."[38]

At the same time, Technicolor provided an unrivaled degree of spectacle. Used for maximum intensity, as in THE WIZARD OF OZ (1939), it could yield bright, saturated hues suitable for fantasy. Cinematographers of the 1930s also learned to exploit Technicolor's rich shadows and subtle pastels, as in TRAIL OF THE LONESOME PINE (1936), THE GARDEN OF ALLAH (1936), and THE GOLDWYN FOLLIES (1938). Most circulating copies of NOTHING SACRED (1937), A STAR IS BORN (1937), and THE ADVENTURES OF ROBIN HOOD (1938) have lost the deep blacks and vibrant purples and greens that the process could render.[39]

Technicolor also had straightforward narrative uses. Like music and camera movement, it could underscore a dramatic moment: in DRUMS ALONG THE MOHAWK (1939) a gloomy medium shot bursts into red-orange when a rifleman is hit by a flaming arrow. And, like music, color could create motifs associated with a certain character or situation—a tactic developed in the green-faced Wicked Witch of the West. When Technicolor succeeded in making the splendors of color flatter the actor and intensify the ongoing drama, it proved itself suitable for adoption into the mainstream Hollywood style.

Special Effects. Although the term "special effects" conjures up thoughts of films of fantasy like KING KONG and THE WIZARD OF OZ, it is worth considering this characterization of special effects, offered in 1943 by William Stull, president of the American Society of Cinematographers:

> Ninety per cent of the trick and special effects shots in Hollywood movies are made with no thought of fooling or mystifying the audience. The great majority of camera trickery is used simply because filming the same action by conventional means would be too difficult, too expensive, or too dangerous. Virtually every picture that leaves Hollywood's major studios includes a greater or lesser propor-

tion of scenes made by one or more of the trick processes. Only in the rare instances of a film like DR. CYCLOPS, THE INVISIBLE MAN, or TOPPER is the process work done as a deliberate trick. ("Process Cinematography," in *The Complete Photographer,* vol. 8, edited by Willard D. Morgan [New York: New York Educational Alliance, 1943], p. 2994)

Because special effects offered economy, ease, and safety, as well as spectacle and fantasy, they were used extensively, and they affected the style of many films made during the 1930s.

During the silent era, the cinematographer and camera assistants created most special effects in the camera itself, without the aid of additional work in the laboratory. To make a dissolve between shots, the camera operator faded out at the end of one shot, wound the film back, and faded in at the beginning of the exposure of the second shot. Similar techniques were used for superimpositions, split-screen exposures, and other effects. If the two shots involved were not to be filmed in succession, the cinematographer often had to remove the film from the camera, carefully mark the footage already filmed, and replace it in the camera when the second shot was to be made. Such procedures were time-consuming and required enormous skill on the part of the camera staff, but they often yielded results that are still impressive. In Buster Keaton's 1921 comedy THE PLAYHOUSE, for example, multiple images of Keaton perform onstage in the same shot, as a result of great precision in winding the film back repeatedly to expose one tiny portion of the frame after another.

In general, during the silent era such effects were called "tricks." By 1928, however, the term *special photographic effects* came into common usage. By then, effects work was increasingly carried out by specialists working in separate special-effects departments in the main studios.

There are a number of reasons for this change. Most important, the introduction of sound took much control over the creation of the film away from the cinematographic team. In multiple-camera shooting, successive shots that might be linked by a dissolve would not necessarily be shot by the same camera; hence, the camera could not make the transitions. Moreover, shooting the whole scene straight through precluded stopping in the middle to rewind the camera and make a superimposition or a dissolve. (Even with the return to single-camera filming, the method of making a single master shot would inhibit in-camera effects.) Sound filming also called for less location shooting. Recording usually had to be done in soundproof studios; going on location to a busy street would make it difficult to exclude random noises. Instead, it was more practical to shoot the street scene separately and project it on a screen behind the actors in the studio as they were filmed speaking their lines. Such a procedure would also save money. Thus, for a variety of reasons, the blending together of images in the camera was minimized in the 1930s. Instead, a film became more of an assemblage of separate images (and sound tracks) shot and combined by specialists. This trend intensified over the decade.

Most types of special effects involved combining separate images in one of two ways. One familiar technique introduced during this era is rear projection (also called "process projection"). Here the background of a shot is filmed separately and projected onto a screen behind the actors. Alternatively, an optical printer might be used to expose a negative twice or more in order to create a composite image out of different components: painted settings, miniature landscapes, partially exposed positive prints, and the like. Such techniques cut costs and allowed filmmakers to redo the effect until they were satisfied—a choice usually not available to the silent-film cameraman.

Given these advantages, why were such techniques as back projection and optical printing not introduced earlier? Only in the late 1920s did a combination of technological factors make them possible. Farciot Edouart, head of special effects for Paramount, described how cinematographers had dreamed of using back projection: "Three key factors were lacking to make the dream into reality. We needed a simple, non-mechanical method of synchronizing the background projector and the foreground camera. We needed negative emulsions of sufficient sensitivity to enable us to record the back-projected picture. And we needed optics and light sources of increased power to enable us to get a brighter image through our background screens."[40] All three conditions were met within a short span of time. The introduction of sound brought motors to synchronizing camera and recording equipment, and these were easily adapted to link camera and back projector (so that the camera and projector shutters were open at the same instant). Highly sensitive panchromatic negative film, introduced in 1928, made it possible for the camera to pick up the relatively faint image thrown by the back projector. Rear-projection technology also made use of the powerful projector lamps manufactured for the big screens of the movie palaces and the wide-gauge formats that emerged in the late 1920s (e.g., the 70-mm processes Fox Grandeur and MGM Realife).

Since no commercial back-projection systems were available, studio personnel built their own equipment to suit their individual needs. Fox tried out the new technology in LILIOM and then on JUST IMAGINE (both 1930), a futuristic fantasy; the company received a special 1930–1931 Academy Award for this work.[41] By the middle of the decade, rear projection had become a common way to save money. In one shot from FURY (1936; Fig. 18), Spencer Tracy sits in a three-dimensional car, but the landscape and road that appear to recede behind him are projected on a flat screen. More elaborate is one scene from YOUNG MR. LINCOLN (1939; Fig. 19) that features a larger studio set, but the sky and river behind are a projection. A big battle scene in THE PLAINSMAN (1936) was staged primarily on a sound stage at Paramount, where footage of six thousand Indians and a cavalry regiment were added on two large screens at the rear, the gap between the two screens being hidden by a dead tree in the set.[42] The 1937 film CAPTAINS COURAGEOUS was set primarily on the deck of a fishing schooner at sea, yet again the main actors stayed in the studio, with real water in a large tank below them and seascapes and sky projected on a screen above. A film could even use miniature settings or animated figures as part of rear-projection footage, as in the complicated special effects in KING KONG (1933).

The industry made efforts to standardize the rear-projection process. In 1936 the studios agreed to cross-license almost fifty patents they had acquired on process projection. Out of its work for Technicolor, Mitchell created a rear projector possessing increased steadiness, and Eastman's Super-X panchromatic film was designed partly to improve rear-projection filming. In 1938 the Academy Research Council sponsored a committee of fifty experts to devise a set of standard specifications that all rear-projection systems should meet. After a year

Fig. 18   Fig. 19

of deliberations, the committee released a report detailing uniform rear-projection specifications.[43] Mole-Richardson, Bausch & Lomb, and Mitchell soon set to work furnishing the requisite equipment.

The optical printer was a more complex device than rear-projection equipment, and it offered several possibilities for rephotographing material. The main obstacle to the invention of the optical printer had been the lack of an adequate film stock for duplicate photography. Before 1927, all such stock yielded too contrasty an image; in that year, Kodak introduced the first successful negative duplicating emulsion. That made it possible for a machine to rephotograph portions of existing images onto one strip of film. As with rear-projection equipment, there was no standardized optical printer available commercially. Nevertheless, by the early 1930s most major studios were establishing effects departments centering on optical printers built by their employees.

Essentially an optical printer consisted of a camera, a lens mount, and a projection device facing the camera lens, all mounted to slide along a single track in a lathe bed. The projector displays an image, portions of which are photographed by the camera, usually with only part of the negative being exposed at one time. A second run through the camera exposes another portion of the negative by photographing a different image in the projector, and so on. The optical printer may be used to add a "matte painting" to a shot. A matte is simply a mask that blocks part of the negative while it is being exposed, either in the original camera or in the optical printer. When the matte is removed and a second matte covers the exposed portion, the unexposed portion is run through the camera to register a second image. In Figure 20, from QUEEN CHRISTINA (1933), a harbor scene has been created by exposing the original film of the actors and a three-dimensional portion of the set at the lower left and then by covering that part of the frame and photographing a painting of roofs, ships, sky, and water at the right and above.

Such an effect, in which the line separating the two portions of the image does not move, is called a "static matte." A "traveling matte" is far more difficult to execute, since the effects expert must make a whole series of pairs of mattes, each with a slightly different join line. Then the film must be exposed one frame at a time with only one of the mattes and then exposed again with only the other matte. The result is a moving joint between two separate images.

Fig. 20   Fig. 21

Fig. 22

During the 1930s, traveling mattes were commonly used to make "wipes," in which a line moves across a shot, bringing a new image gradually onto the screen without superimposing it over the previous one. Optical-printer virtuoso Linwood Dunn experimented with wipes of various shapes and directions in such RKO films as FLYING DOWN TO RIO (1933); sawtooth lines, starbursts, and spirals create elaborate transitions between shots. Dunn devised more subtle and virtually undetectable traveling mattes so that Cary Grant and Katharine Hepburn could appear to be in the same shots with a leopard in BRINGING UP BABY (1938).

Optical printers took over most of the functions originally performed in the camera in the silent era. Such printers easily provided fades and dissolves, made superimpositions and split-screen effects, and so on. For example, in LOVE ME TONIGHT (1932), a split-screen effect used mattes to join separate images of the hero and heroine in their respective beds; thus, the scene suggests that they are really together in the same bed (Fig. 21). A series of images could be linked through superimpositions, wipes, and split-screen effects into the familiar "montage sequence." Such a sequence offers a compressed account of passing time or large-scale processes, as in the newspaper montages in MR. DEEDS GOES TO TOWN (1936; Fig. 22).

As these examples suggest, optical-printer effects were extremely useful and quite common, and their impact is evident in the stylistic devices of many 1930s

Fig. 23   Fig. 24

films. Even the introduction of color caused only brief problems for experts in matte painting and other optical-printer effects. Experimentation soon revealed how the colors in the paintings could be matched to those in the photographed live scene. Matte work was first used extensively for a color production in THE GARDEN OF ALLAH (1936), and techniques devised at that point were ready to be expanded for GONE WITH THE WIND (1939), which depended heavily on matte paintings and other special effects.[44]

Although optical printers were generally built by the studios rather than the supply companies, America's entry into World War II created a need for them in military cinematography units, and Linwood Dunn, still at RKO, designed one that was manufactured by a small firm as the Acme-Dunn printer. Dunn's invention was significant enough to win his colleagues one Oscar in 1944 and another, for a later version of their device, in 1981.[45]

Cinematography Styles. Throughout the sound era, multiple-camera shooting never completely vanished. It remained a staple for coverage of unrepeatable action, such as burning buildings or cars careening off cliffs. It was sometimes considered an efficient way to shoot spectacular musical numbers.[46] Certain performers also required multiple-camera procedures. "Oh God, the Marx Brothers were difficult!" recalled Joseph Ruttenberg. "For one thing, you never knew what they were going to do, so you had to have a camera on each one of them. With the long-shot camera, that added up to four cameras, and lighting for four cameras is pretty dull."[47] The results can be seen in HORSE FEATHERS (1932): Groucho's cavorting with the college widow is framed from two slightly different angles (Figs. 23–24).

On the whole, though, the return to single-camera shooting allowed filmmakers to revive and refine tendencies that had emerged in the silent era. One of the most prominent of these was the "soft" style of cinematography, which had become particularly prominent in the late 1920s.[48] Cinematographers habitually diffused the lights or the lens in order to blur contours and lower contrast, yielding an image with muted highlights and more detailed shadow areas. By 1927, orthochromatic film had largely been replaced by panchromatic film, and the use of panchromatic stock and incandescent lighting in early talkies continued to produce rather soft images. After single-camera shooting was reestablished, many cinematographers sought to return to the soft style.

Eastman cooperated with the trend by introducing in 1931 its Super Sensitive Panchromatic, designed for use with incandescent light. Two to three times as sensitive as earlier stocks, the new panchromatic could also soften light values. The ASC formally recommended the new film because it enabled the cinematographer to lower the lighting levels on the set. The film was used on several major 1931 and 1932 productions, notably FIVE STAR FINAL, DR. JEKYLL AND MR. HYDE, and SHANGHAI EXPRESS. Soon Du Pont introduced its own panchromatic negative, and Bausch and Lomb designed its Raytar lenses for use with incandescent light and the new emulsions. By 1932, the more sensitive panchromatic became standard in most circumstances.

The new film stocks offered various possibilities. Most cinematographers used them to guarantee a somewhat soft image with more latitude in developing. As a rule, the soft style survived in only attenuated form in the 1930s; few films were as heavily diffused as those in the silent era. The sparkling image might be used to convey a romantic atmosphere, as in A FAREWELL TO ARMS (1932; Fig. 25); a more pervasive softness was reserved for fantasy, as in A MIDSUMMER NIGHT'S DREAM (1935; Fig. 26).

Cameramen also discovered that Super Sensitive Panchromatic yielded unprecedented definition. On exteriors, pointed out one cinematographer, the film was almost too crisp, piercing haze and revealing contours not visible to the naked eye.[49] The new emulsion's power was signaled when the ASC recommended using Eastman Super Sensitive: "With the present lightings and smaller lens openings, improved definition can be obtained without sacrifice of those qualities of softness which have always been the artistic aim of cinematographers."[50] The range of possibilities is spectacularly visible in SHANGHAI EXPRESS. For some shots, the Eastman stock enabled Lee Garmes and Josef von Sternberg to soften the highlights with relatively little diffusion (Fig. 27). In Figure 28, however, the new emulsion renders edges and planes razor-sharp. (Compare the much blurrier contours, partly a result of filming through the windows of camera booths, in MILLIE; Figs. 12–17 earlier.)

Some filmmakers were alert to the new possibilities of filming in depth, because this represented one option in the stylistic paradigm of the late silent era. In multiple-camera filming, however, staging and filming tended to create a flatter space of performance. During the 1930s, "deep-space" and "deep-focus" techniques reemerged.

Several stylistic choices are relevant here. A filmmaker can stage a scene in a relatively "shallow" fashion, putting all the relevant action on a single plane standing out against a background. The profiled two-shots from MILLIE exemplify shallow staging. Alternatively, the filmmaker can stage the action in greater depth by putting salient elements of the scene in two or more distinct planes. By choosing to stage in depth, the filmmaker faces a new set of alternatives. The filmmaker may adjust camera and lights so that only one of the planes will be in sharp focus, as in Figure 29, from William Wyler's JEZEBEL (1938). Or the filmmaker may opt for what was called "pan focus" or "deep focus"—that is, rendering all of the planes in sharp focus, as in THE PUBLIC ENEMY (1931; Fig. 30).

Most often, when deep focus depicted deep-space staging, the foreground plane was framed in a long shot or a medium long shot, as in the PUBLIC ENEMY example. This option simplified photographic control, since sharp focus was usually easy to carry from several feet to infinity. But in the cinema of the 1910s and 1920s one can find occasional examples of filmmakers setting one plane fairly close to the camera and seeking to carry focus all the way to the rear plane. A famous instance is Figure 31, from GREED (1924). If such a shot looks "modern," it is because CITIZEN KANE's close-up foregrounds helped launch a vogue for extreme deep focus in the 1940s and 1950s. In the context of 1920s cinema, however, the deep-focus style, with its hard-edged planar separation, was a functional alternative to the soft style.

During the early sound era, several filmmakers sought to present images with significantly deep focus. The art director William Cameron Menzies strove for closer foregrounds in BULLDOG DRUMMOND (1929) and CHANDU THE MAGICIAN (1932; Fig. 32). James Wong Howe's cinematography for TRANSATLANTIC (1931) also experimented in this direction. At Goldwyn studios during the early 1930s, there was something of a deep-focus vogue, typified by John Ford's ARROWSMITH (1931; Fig. 33).

Technological developments facilitated the trend toward depth. The film stocks already mentioned were the beginning of a series of faster and more sensitive emulsions from Eastman, Du Pont, and Agfa. These stocks facilitated the lowering of lighting levels on the set, and producers welcomed this as an efficiency measure. But inquiries by the Academy and the SMPE revealed that some cinematographers were keeping the lighting levels high and stopping down the camera diaphragm.[51] This raised the likelihood that the shot would render more planes in focus. In addition, during the mid 1930s, Mole-Richardson's arc lights developed for Technicolor began to be used with black-and-white, and these gave a harder, more directional light that favored the deep-focus approach.

Over the same period, cinematographers began gravitating toward lenses that could render several planes in focus. These "wide-angle" lenses were of short focal length (usually 35 mm or 25 mm). In the silent era they had been used principally for long shots, but Bausch & Lomb's improved Raytar lenses (introduced in 1931) enabled cinematographers to use them for closer views as well. In 1932 one cinematographer claimed that he was shooting 85 percent of a film with a 25-mm lens.[52] Late in the decade a new chemical coating increased the light-gathering capacities of the lens, and this, too, allowed cinematographers to stop down the apertures for greater depth of field.

Some cinematographers took advantage of these developments to cultivate a deep-focus look. James Wong Howe, for instance, designed VIVA VILLA! (1934) to have strongly foreshortened compositions, and he filmed all close-ups with wide-angle lenses.[53] Tony Gaudio's work in ANTHONY ADVERSE (1936) yielded a marked depth in certain images, with some exaggerated foregrounds (Fig. 34). Most famously, Gregg Toland cultivated a reputation as a cinematographer identified with deep-space staging and deep-focus filming. In his early 1930s work for Goldwyn, such as NANA (1934), there are strong foregrounds but without deep-focus treatment. In Toland's work with William Wyler later in the decade, however, we sometimes find a dense deep-focus style. DEAD END (1937), for example, is dominated by stifling foregrounds (Fig. 35). Such tactics would become central to Toland's work with Ford, Welles, and Wyler during the 1940s.[54]

Most deep-focus efforts were more subdued than the Wyler-Toland extravagance; the LIGHT BRIGADE sequence, with its mild diagonal entrances and exits in depth, is more typical of the period. Many directors sought to avoid obtrusive

Fig. 25

Fig. 26

Fig. 27

Fig. 28

Fig. 29

Fig. 30

Fig. 31

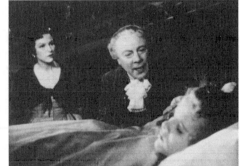

Fig. 32

Fig. 33

Fig. 34

Fig. 35

Fig. 36

Fig. 37   Fig. 38

Fig. 39

pictorial effects by staging in significant depth but framing the foreground plane
only in medium shot. Examples are Ford's YOUNG MR. LINCOLN (1939; Fig. 36)
and Howard Hawks's ONLY ANGELS HAVE WINGS (1939; Fig. 37). The technique
could also be used to intensify reverse-angle framings, as in the wide-angle
close-ups of King Vidor's STELLA DALLAS (1937; Fig. 38) and Raoul Walsh's THE
ROARING TWENTIES (1939; Fig. 39). By the end of the decade, the depth
approach had established itself as a significant stylistic alternative. It remained
for Welles, Wyler, Hawks, and Toland to push deep-space staging and deep-focus
filming to still greater extremes in CITIZEN KANE, THE LITTLE FOXES, and BALL
OF FIRE (all 1941).

Conclusion

The truly new technology of the 1930s, talking pictures, set the pace for much of
the technological change of the decade. Sound technology had to be made more
faithful and flexible, but it also had to be integrated into the stylistic priorities of
classical storytelling. Much of the research into microphones, recording media,
reproduction equipment, and editing instruments was therefore devoted as much
to problems of narrative coherence and spectacle as to strictly engineering
matters.

At the same time, filmmakers and researchers bent their efforts to recovering the visual and narrative dynamism that the early sound cinema was believed to have lost. Abandoning multiple-camera shooting, filmmakers sought to increase flexibility in editing, camera movement, special effects, and photographic qualities of the image. The industry and its professional organizations defined, often with considerable precision, the goals that technology had to meet, and the manufacturing and supply firms set out to achieve them. The ASC, the SMPE, and the Academy created channels of communication and promoted favored solutions. In sum, it was during the 1930s that the film industry fully realized its ability to standardize the very process of technological innovation.

At the same time, the pursuit of efficiency and stylistic standardization led to the exploration of new possibilities, such as the reintroduction of arc lighting and the devising of sophisticated back-projection equipment. Such developments could not have been predicted, but they were seized upon as ways to enhance the classical style.

During the 1930s, Hollywood recalibrated its filmmaking techniques, creating in the process many stylistic qualities that still endure. It also consolidated a systematic approach to technological innovation and assimilation that remains in force today.

Fredric March in ANTHONY ADVERSE *(Warners, 1936).*

6

Selling Stars

*T*he conversion to sound and the ordeal of the Depression left the star system firmly in the grip of the producers. As Alexander Walker put it, "the star system in the 1930s gradually took on the reality, if not the appearance, of a star serfdom. Glamour was its camouflage and fame its dazzling illusion. But behind the grandeur of being a movie star in these years lay all the gradations of servitude."[1] As Hollywood's most treasured assets, stars were among the most highly paid people in the country, but within the pecking order of the studio, they had to conform to the dictates of the front office.

Describing his treatment as a contract player at MGM, Clark Gable said,

> I have been in show business for twelve years. . . . They have known me in Hollywood but two. Yet as picture-making goes, two years is a measurably long time. Nevertheless, my advice has never been asked about a part in a picture. . . . I found out I was going into Susan Lenox [1931, with Greta Garbo] in Del Monte. Read it in the paper. . . . When I walked on the set one day, they told me I was going to play Red Dust [1932, with Jean Harlow] in place of John Gilbert. . . . I have never been consulted as to what part I would like to play. I am paid not to think. (Quoted in Walker, *Stardom: The Hollywood Phenomenon,* [New York: Stein & Day, 1970], p. 252)

Echoing Gable, Bette Davis described her status at Warners:

> I could be forced to do anything the studio told me to do. They could even ask a contract player to appear in a burlesque house. The only recourse was to refuse, and then you were suspended without pay. These original documents [option contracts] were so one-sided in favor of the studio that . . . when under suspension from your contract, with no salary, you could not even work in a five-and-dime store. You could only starve, which of necessity often made you give in to the demands of the studio. (Whitney Stine, *Mother Goddam* [New York: Hawthorne Books, 1974], p. 79)

This chapter enlarges the analysis of motion-picture production to encompass its most important component, the star system. The economic importance of stars had long been recognized by Hollywood and had influenced the development of the classical Hollywood style as well as the way the industry conducted its

Publicity poster for A STAR IS BORN *(UA, 1937).*

business. During the thirties, the majors retained tight control over their wards, but took advantage of vertical integration by manipulating star images at every level.

The Economic Imperative

In the era of vertical integration, the star system affected all three branches of the industry. A star's popularity and drawing power created a ready-made market for his or her pictures, which reduced the risks of production financing. Because a star provided an insurance policy of sorts and a production value, as well as a prestigious trademark for a studio, the star system became the prime means of stabilizing the motion-picture business. At the production level, the screenplay, sets, costumes, lighting, and makeup of a picture were designed to enhance a star's screen persona, which is to say, the image of a star that found favor with the public. At the distribution level, a star's name and image dominated advertising and publicity and determined the rental price for the picture. And at the exhibition level, the costs of a star's salary and promotions were passed on to moviegoers, who validated the system by plunking down a few coins at the box office.

In economic terms, stars created the market value of motion pictures.[2] To understand how this worked, we must remember three things. First, affiliated theater chains were located in different regions of the country, so that to reach a national audience the majors had to exhibit one another's pictures. Second, the majors rented their pictures to exhibitors a season in advance of production. And third, the majors used a differential pricing policy: flat fees for B pictures and percentage-of-the-gross terms for A pictures. No set price could be charged for the top-grade product because the market for this type of picture was difficult to ascertain. Charging a percentage was riskier than charging a flat fee, but in so doing, a distributor could reap the rewards of a box-office surge.

How did the majors determine the rental price for a picture, which is to say, the percentage terms for a new picture? They used star power—the ability of screen personalities to attract large and faithful followings. In practice, a distributor simply pointed to the past box-office performance of a star to justify the rental terms for his or her forthcoming pictures. An economist might say the distributor used star differentiation to stabilize the demand curve for class-A product.

Star differentiation did more than stabilize rentals; it also permitted the distributor to raise prices. Demand elasticity explains the phenomenon. "Demand elasticity measures the sensitivity of demand in relationship to quantity and change in price. Theoretically, if demand can be fixed by product differentiation, it then becomes less sensitive to increases in price."[3] Thus, if a new picture contained a star with a proven box-office record, an exhibitor would likely be willing to pay a higher rental for it, feeling certain that the risk was worth it.

The majors buttressed this method of pricing by instituting elaborate and costly publicity campaigns that revolved almost exclusively around stars. Because these campaigns were designed to peak simultaneously with the release of a new picture, as will be discussed later, they funneled audiences into first-run houses. Owned almost exclusively by the Big Five, these flagship theaters charged the highest ticket prices and generated 50 percent of the domestic rentals. Elaborate publicity campaigns served an added function; a successful launching of a new release helped establish its market value in the subsequent-run playoff.

The Contract Controls

The economics of the star system is a necessary prelude to understanding how the studios safeguarded their most precious assets. The studios devised an ingenious legal document to control their high-priced talent, the "option contract." This is how the contract worked. In signing an aspiring actor or actress, the studio used a contract that progressed in steps over a term of seven years. Every six months, the studio reviewed the actor's progress and decided whether or not to pick up the option. If the studio dropped the option, the actor was out of work; if the studio picked up the option, the actor continued on the payroll for another six months and received a predetermined raise in salary. Note that the studio, not the star, had the right to drop or pick up the option. The contract did not provide reciprocal rights, meaning that an actor or actress could not quit to join another studio, could not stop work, and could not renegotiate for more money. In short, the contract effectively tied a performer to the studio for seven years.

The option contract did more than that: it had restrictive clauses that gave the studio total control over the star's image and services; it required an actor "to act, sing, pose, speak or perform in such roles as the producer may designate"; it gave the studio the right to change the name of the actor at its own discretion and to control the performer's image and likeness in advertising and publicity; and it required the actor to comply with rules covering interviews and public appearances. Another restrictive clause concerned picture assignments. If the aspiring star refused an assignment, the "studio could sue for damages and extend the contract to make up for the stoppage."[4]

The studios argued that the option contract was not as inequitable as it seemed because developing talent was expensive and risky. If a new player clicked, the studio was justified in wanting to cash in on its investment. If a new player showed little or no promise, it made no sense for the producer to carry him or her for seven years. Be that as it may, stars exercised little control over production. Some stars had story-approval rights and could refuse to appear in an unsympathetic or unflattering role, but in that event, the studio simply assigned the role to another performer. And once into a picture, a star had no say in the interpretation of his or her role, let alone the script, since that was largely the prerogative of the director.[5]

The Top Stars

The notion that the talkies destroyed the careers of many stars is wrong. "Sound gave some fading stars a new if brief lease of life; it increased the artistry of some of the established stars once they had proved they could 'talk'; and it helped create new stars from among some, though by no means many, of the stage players whom Hollywood had recruited."[6]

Beginning in 1931, the *Motion Picture Herald* conducted an annual exhibitors' poll to determine the ten best box-office draws. During the first half of the decade, the polls indicated that "down-to-earth" stars were the most popular. And at the top of the list was MGM's Marie Dressler, who ranked number one in the polls for 1932 and 1933. A specialist in sentimental comedy, Dressler's appeal was universal. Her first big hit of the decade was MIN AND BILL (1930), in which she and Wallace Beery played "two old soaks making do." The role won her an Academy Award. MGM's Wallace Beery made it to the top-ten list every year until 1935. Like Dressler, Beery was an experienced character actor. He sustained a faltering career during the transition to the talkies by playing lovable old rogues with hearts of gold. MIN AND BILL made Beery a star, a position that he solidified in THE CHAMP (1931), playing a dirty rogue with a heart of gold, a role that earned him an Academy Award.

In 1934, Will Rogers became the first male star to rank number one in the polls. By then, his annual income as a cracker-barrel humorist in pictures, radio, lecturing, and writing came to $600,000, making him one of the best-paid entertainers of the time. A failure in silent pictures, Rogers reigned as Fox's biggest star, playing himself in a string of popular formula pictures from 1929 until his death in a plane crash with aviator Wiley Post in 1935. His biggest hits were STATE FAIR (1933) and JUDGE PRIEST (1934).

Child and adolescent stars led the polls throughout the decade. Fox's Janet Gaynor, who took over Mary Pickford's role as "leading waif," was one of the biggest stars of the early 1930s, trailing only Marie Dressler in the popularity polls. In 1934 she became Hollywood's box-office queen. Her biggest hits include DADDY LONG LEGS (1931) and TESS OF THE STORM COUNTRY (1932), two Mary Pickford remakes, and STATE FAIR (1933), in which she shared honors with Fox's box-office king, Will Rogers.

During the second half of the decade, child star Shirley Temple ranked number one four years in a row, from 1935 to 1938, and was "officially the biggest-drawing star in the world." Born in 1928, Temple started her movie career in 1932 at Educational Pictures, performing in a series of shorts called

Baby Burlesks, which were takeoffs on movies. Fox signed Shirley Temple to a contract for $150 a week in 1934. She was six years old. Her first conspicuous role in features was in STAND UP AND CHEER (1934), a revue in which she performed the song and dance number "Baby Take a Bow." Temple was billed seventh, but *Variety* called her the "unofficial star of this Fox musical." After a few small parts at Fox, she was loaned out to Paramount to play an orphan who reforms a bookie in the Damon Runyon film LITTLE MISS MARKER (1934). This is the picture that made her a star. Fox rushed her into BABY TAKE A BOW (1934) and gave her top billing for the first time. Temple appeared in nine pictures in 1934. During the Academy Award ceremonies that year, she received a miniature Oscar for bringing "more happiness to millions of children and millions of grown-ups than any other child of her years in the history of the world."[7] At the end of 1934, she ranked number eight in the polls. Afterward, her career took off.

By the end of 1935, Darryl Zanuck, the studio chief of the newly merged 20th Century–Fox, gave Shirley a revised contract that paid her $4,000 a week, fifty-two weeks a year. Under Zanuck's supervision at Fox, she remade several Mary Pickford silent hits based on children's classics—CURLY TOP (1935), a remake of DADDY LONG LEGS; POOR LITTLE RICH GIRL (1936); and REBECCA OF SUNNYBROOK FARM (1938), among others. HEIDI (1937), which was based on another children's classic, was possibly her best picture. From 1934 to 1938, she was the number-one box-office attraction in the world. Her pictures routinely grossed from $1 million to $1.5 million on their first run alone. According to Robert Windeler, "Her pictures did even better on second and third runs. What made her box-office appeal even more extraordinary was the fact that her pictures were cheap to make, costing between $200,000–$300,000. They had simple stories, few sets, mostly indoor, and small shooting companies." By 1939, she was earning $350,000 a year, the highest salary paid an adolescent star.[8]

Shirley Temple slipped to number five in the polls in 1939 and was replaced by teenage star Mickey Rooney as the number-one box-office draw. Rooney became a star in the Andy Hardy series. The series began with A FAMILY AFFAIR (1937), a modest B picture based on a minor Broadway play about a small-town judge and his family who lived in Carvel, Idaho. The picture was a sleeper, and soon a series was in the making. By 1939, nineteen-year-old Rooney had become MGM's "most valuable piece of talent," and the Andy Hardy pictures, "the biggest money makers, in ratio to investment, in plant's entire history."[9] Rooney's multiple talents enabled him to take on drama and musicals as well as comedy, and such hits as BOYS TOWN (1938) and BABES IN ARMS (1939) consolidated his success. In 1939, Rooney was earning over $2,000 a week.

Ranking alongside Mickey Rooney in public esteem was another teenage star, Deanna Durbin. In 1938 the two were awarded special Oscars for "their significant contribution in bringing to the screen the spirit and personification of youth." Born in 1921 and endowed with a remarkable singing voice, Durbin became nationally known performing on the "Eddie Cantor Radio Hour." Signing with Universal in 1936, she became a motion-picture star with her first picture, THREE SMART GIRLS (1936), and placed the studio on firm financial footing for the first time in the decade. Praised for her charm, spontaneity, and naturalness, Durbin made five more pictures for Universal during the 1930s, ONE HUNDRED MEN AND A GIRL (1937), MAD ABOUT MUSIC (1938), THAT CERTAIN AGE (1938), THREE SMART GIRLS GROW UP (1939), and FIRST LOVE (1939).

Shirley Temple receives the Oscar from humorist Irvin S. Copp, who presided over the Academy Award ceremonies in 1934.

Greta Garbo and John Barrymore in GRAND HOTEL *(MGM, 1932).*

The reigning leading ladies of the era were Greta Garbo, Joan Crawford, Norma Shearer, Claudette Colbert and Bette Davis. Garbo, said David Shipman, is "ultimately, the standard against which all other screen actresses are measured. Since the time of her second, if not her first, Hollywood film she has not been surpassed. For over 50 years the mystery, the enigma of Garbo has been a statutory feature of magazine journalism, her ability a source of wonder to critics." Born in Stockholm, Sweden, Garbo topped the list of early foreign imports that consisted of Marlene Dietrich, Elissa Landi, and Lili Damita. MGM delayed her talkie debut as long as possible, thinking that her Swedish accent would prove fatal, but ANNA CHRISTIE (1930)—which MGM advertised with the slogan GARBO TALKS!—"proved that Garbo talking was an even more magical figure than Garbo mute."[10]

Garbo reached her peak as a commercial property playing the role of prima ballerina Grusinskaya in GRAND HOTEL (1932). Her contract expired afterward, and there were rumors she might retire. MGM offered to raise her salary to $10,000 a week from $7,000, but she held out for an extraordinary contract "that would have caused an insurrection had it been published," said Alexander Walker. Although Garbo's box-office pull weakened in the United States, she remained enormously popular in Europe, where "her prestige was needed often enough to sell an otherwise indifferent package of films." Recognizing this value, MGM awarded her new contracts and continued paying her top dollar for her services. Garbo received rave critical notices for such pictures as QUEEN CHRIS-

TINA (1933), ANNA KARENINA (1935), and CAMILLE (1937), winning best-actress awards from the New York film critics and nominations from the film academy. However, a group of exhibitors listed her, among others, as "box-office poison" in 1938. Again her career was in peril, and again she threatened to retire. MGM revived her career by casting her against type in a Lubitsch comedy, NINOTCHKA (1939). MGM advertised the picture with the slogan GARBO LAUGHS! and the world queued up to see it. Although Garbo received another Oscar nomination, her career suffered a fatal blow when the war closed foreign markets and MGM failed to develop a successful formula for her in the domestic market.[11]

Joan Crawford easily survived the conversion to the talkies and, like Garbo, did not have to change her screen persona to do it. "The essential Crawford didn't change, whether as dancing daughter, sophisticated heroine or tragic lady. She played one sort of American woman for fifty years . . . the working girl from the wrong side of the tracks, clawing her way to the top."[12] As they say, the titles tell it all. Her hit films of the decade include OUR BLUSHING BRIDES (1930), PAID (1930), DANCE, FOOLS, DANCE (1931), THIS MODERN AGE (1931), GRAND HOTEL (1932), DANCING LADY (1933), and LOVE ON THE RUN (1936), all made by MGM. Crawford sustained her tremendous popularity until 1937, when for the first time she did not appear on the lists of top money-making stars.

Norma Shearer, "the epitome of glamour, of feminity, of beauty," was queen of the MGM lot. Thanks to brilliant handling by her husband, Irving Thalberg, she easily made the transition to the talkies by specializing in "restless, over-wealthy, over-sexed (by contemporary standards) women-of-the-world." Playing such a role in THE DIVORCEE (1930), she won an Oscar for best actress and thereafter figured prominently on the popularity polls by starring in diluted screen versions of hit Broadway and London plays, such as PRIVATE LIVES (1931), STRANGE INTERLUDE (1932), and THE BARRETTS OF WIMPOLE STREET (1934). Her screen appearances became rarer after Thalberg's death, but MGM ensured that each of them—ROMEO AND JULIET (1936), MARIE ANTOINETTE (1938), IDIOT'S DELIGHT (1939), and THE WOMEN (1939)—was an event.

After being plucked from Broadway by Paramount, Claudette Colbert won notoriety taking a bath in asses' milk as Poppaea in Cecil B. DeMille's THE SIGN OF THE CROSS (1932). She became a great star in 1934 playing the title role in another DeMille epic, CLEOPATRA, and on loan-out, playing in John M. Stahl's melodrama IMITATION OF LIFE at Universal and in Frank Capra's screwball comedy IT HAPPENED ONE NIGHT at Columbia. She picked up an Oscar for her performance in IT HAPPENED ONE NIGHT and was ranked number six in the polls. Specializing in screwball comedy thereafter, she became Paramount's biggest female draw, winning a new contract in 1938 that made her the highest-paid star in Hollywood.

Bette Davis was the only Warners actress to make it to the ten-best poll. Like many stars of the decade, history has appreciated her talents more than either her home studio or her audience. Today, Davis is remembered as "the First Lady of the Screen":

> She broke the old mould for female stars: she didn't want to get up on that screen and be decorative, to be glamorous like Garbo, to be sympathetic like Janet Gaynor, to pose as an actress like Norma Shearer: she wanted to *act,* to illuminate for audiences all the women

she found within her—waitresses, dowagers, spinsters, harridans, drunks. She fought to play them. All subsequent screen stars owe her a debt, in that she proved that an actress could be an excellent judge of material, and her dedication destroyed a lingering belief that stage acting was "superior" to film acting. (David Shipman, *The Great Movie Stars: The Golden Years* [New York: Hill and Wang, 1979], p. 149)

After a false start at Universal, Davis signed on at Warners as a contract player in 1932. Warners experimented to find suitable roles to fit her talents without much success. The correct formula was found—by chance really—when she was loaned to RKO in 1934 to play Mildred, "the vicious, grasping waitress who enslaves Leslie Howard," in John Cromwell's OF HUMAN BONDAGE. Inexplicably, the Academy failed to nominate Davis for an Oscar, which stunned the film community. Pressure from Hollywood notables forced the Academy to amend its rules to allow write-in candidates, and Davis was placed on the ballot. However, she was beaten out by Claudette Colbert for her performance in IT HAPPENED ONE NIGHT. Back at her home studio, she won an Oscar the following year playing "a dipso ex-actress who throws a jinx on anyone who comes near" in DANGEROUS. Although she had become the queen of the lot, she never received royal treatment. Davis won her second Oscar for JEZEBEL (1938), which was Warners' answer to Selnick's GONE WITH THE WIND, then in preparation. JEZEBEL marked the beginning of a great series of Davis vehicles that Shipman described "as smooth as limousines, elegantly crafted, designed to display every facet of her talents." Among these were DARK VICTORY (1939), THE OLD MAID (1939), and THE PRIVATE LIVES OF ELIZABETH AND ESSEX (1939).[13]

Clark Gable, MGM's first big male star of the era, represented a new type of leading man. Unlike the courtly and suave male stars of the twenties, Gable developed an image as a combination sexy lover and man's man. Signing with MGM at the end of 1930, Gable played a series of minor roles as tough guys or gangsters. MGM soon groomed him as a leading man playing rough and tough opposite the studio's leading ladies, as with Joan Crawford in DANCE, FOOLS, DANCE (1931), Greta Garbo in SUSAN LENOX (1931), Norma Shearer in STRANGE INTERLUDE (1932), and Jean Harlow in RED DUST (1932). In 1932 he made it to the top-ten poll 1932 for the first time, ranking number eight. On loan-out to Columbia, Gable starred opposite Claudette Colbert in Frank Capra's IT HAPPENED ONE NIGHT, and the Oscar it brought him revitalized his career. Starring in MUTINY ON THE BOUNTY (1935), SAN FRANCISCO (1936), and GONE WITH THE WIND (1939), he ranked near the top of the polls for the remainder of the decade.

Spencer Tracy, considered an actor's actor by his peers, was "one of the few actors whose career went only in an upward curve. Not all his films were hits, but his career had no reversals and he went from being a solid, reliable young actor to Grand Old Man of the movies." Making a name for himself on Broadway starring in a gangster melodrama, THE LAST MILE, Tracy signed on with Fox and was typecast as a tough guy, playing racketeers and brutish convicts. Playing such a role on loan-out in Warners' 20,000 YEARS IN SING SING (1933) made him a star. Moving to MGM in 1935, Tracy established himself as "the studio's consummate dramatic actor" who made it to the upper echelons of stardom by receiving an

Oscar nomination for best actor for FURY (1936) and by winning back-to-back Oscars for CAPTAINS COURAGEOUS (1937) and BOYS TOWN (1938). By the end of the decade, he was ranked number three in the polls behind Mickey Rooney and Tyrone Power.[14]

Although James Cagney became a star playing gangster and tough-guy roles at Warners early in the thirties, he did not make it to the top-ten polls until 1935. He ranked tenth that year and then dropped out until 1939, when he placed ninth. Cagney made a name for himself in THE PUBLIC ENEMY (1931), playing a thug with a taste for luxury who pushed a grapefruit in Mae Clarke's face. Afterward, Warners rushed him into a series of vehicles that were made quickly and cheaply and that contained implied social criticism: he played a "bellboy supplying broads and booze" in BLONDE CRAZY (1931), "a cabdriver fighting the rackets" in TAXI! (1932), a track driver in THE CROWD ROARS (1932), and a prizefighter in WINNER TAKE ALL (1932)—types of roles that Cagney called "dese, dem, and dose."[15]

After fighting Warners for better roles, Cagney was able to display a greater range of his talents, singing and dancing in the musical FOOTLIGHT PARADE (1933), playing Bottom in the Max Reinhardt production of Shakespeare's A MIDSUMMER NIGHT'S DREAM (1935), and performing in the Broadway farce about Hollywood, BOY MEETS GIRL (1938). But it was in his archetypal roles that he made it to the top-ten polls in 1939—ANGELS WITH DIRTY FACES (1938), about two boys who grow up together and part, one to become a hood (Cagney) and the other a priest (Pat O'Brien); EACH DAWN I DIE (1939), a prison film with George Raft as a fellow con; and THE ROARING TWENTIES (1939), a historical gangster film.

Tyrone Power and Errol Flynn ranked as the new romantic leads. Both made names for themselves in costume pictures. Power became famous in the 20th Century–Fox biopic LLOYD'S OF LONDON (1936). Afterward, Darryl Zanuck varied the formula by starring him in a musical biopic, ALEXANDER'S RAGTIME BAND (1938); a Western biopic, JESSE JAMES (1939); and a historical biopic, SUEZ (1938), among others. Power barely made it to the poll in 1938, but in 1939 he moved up to number two. Flynn became famous playing opposite Olivia de Havilland in CAPTAIN BLOOD (1935), Warners' first swashbuckler of the decade. Warners varied the formula by teaming the two stars in such costume-adventure pictures as THE CHARGE OF THE LIGHT BRIGADE (1936), THE ADVENTURES OF ROBIN HOOD (1938), and DODGE CITY (1939). Flynn made it to the box-office top ten for the first time in 1939.

RKO's Fred Astaire and Ginger Rogers were the most popular team of the decade. Performing together for the first time in FLYING DOWN TO RIO in 1933, Fred and Ginger went on to become an institution dancing and singing in a series of great musicals, including THE GAY DIVORCEE (1934), TOP HAT (1935), and SWING TIME (1936). Shipman remarked that "as a team, they balanced each other: he was debonair, an unassuming and somewhat innocent man-about-town, bent on winning her chivalrously if possible, but if not, not. She was bright, sassy and suspicious, her chorine background somewhat shaded by his interest. He gave her class, and she gave him sex-appeal. . . . Both seemed delightful people, humorous, intelligent and charming."[16] In 1935, Fred and Ginger made it to the top-ten polls, where they remained until 1937.

Forming the Screen Actors Guild

Actors had remained relatively docile employees until 1933, when producers responded to the bank moratorium by threatening to close the studios unless talent accepted a 50 percent pay cut for eight weeks. Following the lead of the screenwriters, a group of eighteen actors, among them Ralph Morgan, Alan Mowbray, and Boris Karloff, formed the Screen Actors Guild (SAG) on 30 June 1933. Over the next few months membership grew slowly to around fifty. But when producers drafted the Code of Fair Competition and blamed the financial difficulties of their studios on the star system, actors signed up in droves.

The moguls had written into the Code provisions barring star raiding, curbing the activities of agents, and limiting salaries. To prevent star raiding, a provision permitted a studio to keep a star in tow at the end of a seven-year contract by exercising the right of first refusal, which "amounted to professional slavery," said the guild. To curb agents, producers planned on organizing a general booking office to broker talent. "All agents, in order to deal with the booking office, would have to be licensed by the booking office. This would put the actors' representative completely under the thumb of the producer, make every contract a one-sided bargain, and in the end reduce compensation," said the guild. And to limit salaries, studios wanted to cap earnings at $100,000 a year.[17]

What really turned around SAG membership was a protest meeting held at the El Capitan theater in October 1933. Eddie Cantor, the new president of the guild, told the audience that the Academy was unable to represent the full interests of the actors and that the producers' salary ploy was unconstitutional. One of the highest-paid entertainers in the business, Cantor had endeared himself to actors at an organizational meeting held earlier when he said, "I'm here not because of what I can do for myself, but to see what I can do for the little fellow who has never been protected and who can't do anything for himself. If that's not the spirit of everyone here, then I want to leave." When Cantor called for "a 100% actor organization," five hundred actors out of the more than eight hundred in the audience "flocked to the stage to sign membership blanks in the new Screen Actors' Guild." Among the prominent names signing up were Adolph Menjou, Fredric March, Robert Montgomery, Jimmy Cagney, Miriam Hopkins, Jeanette MacDonald, and Paul Muni.[18]

Responding to the Code, SAG filed a brief with the NRA answering the charge that actors were being overpaid. By way of a preface, the brief said that "history shows that no agreement with producers is worth the paper it is written on"; that Hollywood's code of ethics "is the lowest of all industries"; and that "every dishonest practice known to an industry . . . has been resorted to by the producers against the actors." After this indictment, the brief presented statistics on actors' salaries. In 1933 one quarter of the employed actors made less than $1,000, about half made less that $2,000, and approximately three-quarters made less than $5,000. These salaries were gross incomes. Ten percent of an actor's salary went to an agent, and a significant amount went to maintain a proper wardrobe, which at the time was part of an actor's working tools. Concerning performers in the highest income brackets, the brief underscored the fact that earning power lasted a short while: "If one takes a glance at any group of extras of today, he will find many of the stars of yesterday."[19]

By way of contrast, SAG listed the high salaries and profit-sharing plans of the top movie executives, the purpose of which was

> not to show how much money executives make, but to give some idea of how ill it becomes these gentlemen to protest that the industry cannot afford fair working conditions for actors. It is even worse when we remember that most of the men who now run the business and assert that actors' working conditions cannot be bettered, dragged the industry to the verge of bankruptcy, took their employees' money for the purchase of stock at excessive figures, and made a record of financial ruin that has been seldom equalled in the annals of American business. ("Actors Report to NRA," *Variety,* 8 January 1935, p. 11)

Counterattacking, the producers tried to "fragment the actors' discourse of opposition" by asserting "their own morality, patriotism and commitment to quality motion pictures." Using the trade press, fan magazines, and even films as platforms, they accomplished this by simply reducing actors' complaints to the single issue of salaries. Producers argued that they, and not the actors, were the victims of unfair practices—that they "were victims of extravagance gone awry." The principal cause of the industry's financial problems was the astronomically high salaries demanded by stars, they said, and such greedy behavior was "out of step with the national recovery program."[20]

An example of these tactics is found in an article entitled "Figuring the Stars' Salaries" that appeared in *Screen Book.* The article quotes a fan letter allegedly sent to a prominent, though unnamed, star stating that she and other loyal fans are disturbed by the big salaries the stars earn when theaters are closing and when so many people have fallen on hard times: "I don't begrudge you your fine salary, but don't you think all *big* salaries might be lowered a bit—maybe to $1,000 a week? If what the paper says is true, you earn in one week five times what most of us earn in a year!"[21] Another tactic of the studios was to appropriate the NRA's WE DO OUR PART slogan and Blue Eagle insignia, using them in advertising and in pictures to garner favor with the public and the Roosevelt administration.

Eddie Cantor paid a visit to President Roosevelt, who was his personal friend, to plead the actors' case. To avert a highly publicized labor dispute that might adversely affect public acceptance of the NRA, the president suspended the obnoxious provisions in the motion-picture code by executive order. However, during the days of the NRA, SAG failed to receive recognition as bargaining agent for the actors. Nor did SAG receive recognition when the National Labor Relations Act was signed into law in 1935; Hollywood's response to the act was simply to ignore it.

But two years later, the Screen Actors Guild threatened to call a strike and finally won recognition on 15 May 1937. "The victories have been victories for the rank and file. For themselves the stars have asked and won next to nothing," said the *Nation.*[22] The rank and file won minimum pay rates, guarantees of continuous employment, and twelve-hour rest periods between calls. Although successive contracts won benefits for all classes of performers, the relationship of the actor to the production process remained unaltered; in fact, it was never an issue. The concessions had relatively minor economic impact on the studios, which explains why they were implemented.

The Star System in Place

The acting profession in Hollywood consisted of four classes of performers. Supporting players performed the least important parts in pictures. Employed for as short a time as a week, a supporting player did not receive screen credit or even the assurance that his or her part would not be cut before the picture was released. Stock players were either promising beginners or experienced old-timers and, as a group, formed a large talent pool from which the studio rounded out the cast of a picture. They received contracts of six months or longer and were paid from $50 to $350 a week. Featured players performed the principal roles and received screen and advertising credit. Their contracts went from year to year and specified a minimum and maximum number of pictures and a salary of so much a picture.[23]

Stars constituted the elite class. Like other classes of performers, they were required to play any part the studio designated, although the biggest names might have the right to refuse a specified number of projects they deemed unsuitable. Paul Muni, for example, used his considerable prestige to accept only those scripts that dealt in some way with social problems. Stars might also have the right to approve the cameraman, but rarely their directors. Greta Garbo, for example, would work with only one cameraman, William Daniels. Stars received option contracts that lasted as long as seven years and were paid on a per-picture basis. As privileged members of the studio, they received a range of perks that could even affect the paint on their dressing room walls. Examples of such perks are fixed working hours of not more than eight out of any twenty-four-hour period with time out for afternoon tea; a dressing room decorated to the star's satisfaction; arrangements for a personal maid or valet; and "greater prominence" in advertising, meaning that the star's name had to be placed above all others in all advertising, in letters larger and of greater prominence than any other name.

"Free-lance" actors, as the term implies, hired themselves out to any studio and worked on a picture-by-picture basis. Their ranks numbered about forty stars and featured players, among them Fredric March, Ronald Colman, Jean Arthur, Aline MacMahon, Adolphe Menjou, Edward Everett Horton, and Constance Bennett. These players were almost continually in demand, especially by independent producers.[24]

The total number of contract players in Hollywood during a given year came to around five hundred; the total on a studio's roster varied from around fifty to one hundred. Of the grand total, thirty or so received star billing. A similar number would fade out for a while or forever. As they faded, stars usually remained under contract, but inevitably they were dropped from the lists. Then they had the option of offering their services to independent producers or of becoming free-lance supporting players. Sometimes, a waning star received a new lease on life at another studio. "Countless players have made good on the second Hollywood bounce," said *Variety* and identified Warners as the "champ builder-

Fredric March and Norma Shearer in THE BARRETTS OF WIMPOLE STREET
(MGM, 1935).

upper." In 1935, Warners had working for it a dozen players dropped by other
studios, among them George Brent, Ricardo Cortez, William Gargan, Hugh
Herbert, Bette Davis, and Paul Muni.[25]

MGM had the largest and most prestigious stable of stars in Hollywood, which
enabled it to produce nearly a third of the top-grossing films every year. Taking
maximum advantage of MGM's talent pool, Irving Thalberg instituted a "galac-
tic" system of casting a picture, whereby two or more stars were teamed to
increase its box-office power. Among such vehicles are GRAND HOTEL (1932),
which starred Greta Garbo, John Barrymore, Lionel Barrymore, Wallace Beery,
and Joan Crawford; RASPUTIN AND THE EMPRESS (1932), which teamed the
three Barrymores; and DINNER AT EIGHT (1933), which listed eight top
names.[26]

After the economic shakeout of the Depression, stars' salaries rarely rebounded to the extravagant levels of the booming twenties. Leo Rosten's survey
of actors' salaries showed that in 1939 only 54 class-A actors out of 253 earned
over $100,000. Claudette Colbert topped the list, with earnings of $426,944,
followed in descending order by Bing Crosby ($410,000), Irene Dunne ($405,222),
Charles Boyer ($375,277), and so on down the line. However, in "startling
contrast" to these earnings, Rosten's survey revealed that the median average
salary for the group was $4,700, which meant that half the actors earned $4,700 or
less and that half earned $4,700 or more. Excluded from these calculations were

the pittances paid to movie extras. In short, the acting profession in Hollywood remained a poorly paid one.[27]

The fact that most directors, writers, and stars were temperamentally ill equipped to bargain with hardheaded producers explained the existence of the agent. Close to 150 registered agents worked in Hollywood. A dozen or so firms did most of the business, among them the William Morris Agency, Joyce–Selznick, Charles K. Feldman, and Leland Hayward. "In any business as sprawling, loose, and disjointed as show business," said *Fortune,* "there must be an intermediary between the possessors of talent and the users of talent." Agents represented actors, directors, and writers. As one agent described his job, "My occupation is representing clients, placing them advantageously, getting them the highest salaries I can, and maintaining the best possible working conditions for them." Other agents provided "personal representative" and "management" services pertaining to almost every facet of the client's career. Whatever his function, an agent took a 10 percent cut of all wages earned by his client during the term of the contract. This 10 percent fee, fixed by the Screen Actors Guild, was the maximum an agent could charge for his services.[28]

As might be expected, studios held agents in contempt. It was not unusual for a studio such as Warners to bar an agent from the lot because he tried to get too much for his client. Before 1930 the majors had tacit nonproselytizing agreements with one another. "The understanding was that one studio would not hire actors away from another studio. When his contract expired, the star had to negotiate a new contract with the same old company; if he tried to get bids for his services, he found the other companies not interested. The star could only accept the offer from his old employer or become a holdout," said Alva Johnston.[29]

This cozy relationship was broken up by Myron Selznick. Warners had gotten a headstart on its competitors by innovating sound, but it needed stars to maintain its lead. Understanding this, Selznick offered the studio three of his clients—William Powell, Kay Francis, and Ruth Chatterton, all of whom were working for Paramount. "Tempted beyond their strength, the Warners hired them away from the rival studio."[30] Paramount sued, but Warner quelled the controversy by agreeing to lend Francis to Paramount when it needed her. Clearly, nonproselytizing agreements were on their way out.

During the days of the NRA, producers tried to curb the power of agents by outlawing star raiding, but an executive order from the White House prevented them. The studios soon devised a way to get around the order. Talent was always scarce. *Variety* reported that "the complexities of casting . . . are so great that no single plant can cast its own productions from its contract list."[31] It gave as a reason talking pictures, which made individualized roles much more important to the acting ensemble than they had been in the silents. Studios developed young talent and recruited personalities from the stage and radio, both at home and abroad, but nothing proved sufficient to meet all their needs. Rather than raiding one another to bolster star rosters, the majors found it easier and just as effective to lend one another talent.

As always, economics played a role. Try as they might, studios found it impossible to keep high-priced talent busy all the time. An idle star was a heavy overhead expense. Why not "loan out" the idle star and recoup the overhead? Studios devised various formulas to determine the fee: the most common one was to charge a minimum fee of four weeks salary plus a surcharge of three weeks;

another was to charge the basic salary for however long the star was needed plus a surcharge of 25 percent.[32] Loan-outs kept RKO competitive and enabled Columbia and Universal to maintain their status as members of the Little Three. For example, Columbia borrowed most of the big names it needed for the Capra pictures—Claudette Colbert and Clark Gable for IT HAPPENED ONE NIGHT, Gary Cooper for MR. DEEDS GOES TO TOWN, and Jimmy Stewart for YOU CAN'T TAKE IT WITH YOU and MR. SMITH GOES TO WASHINGTON.

Top-ranking independent producers like Selznick, Goldwyn, and Wanger, who released through UA, also regularly borrowed players. The majors were willing to lend them stars because these producers had longtime connections with the industry and had successful track records. Myth has it that the majors used loan-outs to discipline stars and to keep difficult people in line. But this argument does not make much sense, because it implies that a studio would risk its investment in a star by allowing him or her to appear in a second-rate picture produced by an inferior company. Actually, most stars were on the lookout for challenging parts and wanted the right to play them anywhere. One agent reported, "I have secured for a number of my clients contracts which permit them to play in one outside picture a year, on terms which they negotiate independently. Usually such permission enables the artist to appear in some favorite story or work for some favorite director, and the novelty of an interlude on a different lot breaks the monotony of constant association with too-familiar faces."[33]

Loan-outs frequently revitalized flagging careers. For example, Clark Gable and Claudette Colbert were in lulls when MGM and Paramount, respectively, sent them to Columbia to star in IT HAPPENED ONE NIGHT. Because of the film's success, their careers took off. Bette Davis revealed her capabilities as a mature actress of great gifts when Warners loaned her to RKO to star in OF HUMAN BONDAGE. And on loan-out to Universal to star in MY MAN GODFREY, Carole Lombard found herself in her biggest success yet, which sent her asking price skyrocketing and won her contracts from several studios.[34]

The loan-out policy of the majors had antitrust implications. In pressing the *Paramount* case, the Justice Department tried to prove that the majors, by limiting loan-outs primarily to one another, restrained trade at the level of production. The department observed that from 1933 to 1939 the majors (including Columbia and Universal) loaned actors, directors, writers, and cameramen to one another over two thousand times and to independents less than two hundred times.[35] The loan-outs to independents were made principally to UA's affiliated producers.

Why might producers balk at loaning stars to Poverty Row studios or newly arrived independents? Clearly, the majors believed that loan-outs could easily impair the value of their properties, either because the overall production standards of the company would suffer or because the picture might not be handled properly. The majors also believed—correctly—that Poverty Row studios did not have the financial means to borrow high-priced talent. Furthermore, the majors knew that pictures produced outside the mainstream could rarely find first-run theater outlets and therefore had to be consigned to the low end of the market, which could ruin a star.

Periodically, courageous stars challenged the system by demanding bigger salaries, better roles, and more respect. The big battles took place at Warners and involved two issues: the right of a studio to treat a star as chattel, as a mere investment that could be milked for all he or she was worth (product maximization); and the right of the studio to tack on suspension time at the end of a contract.

James Cagney started the first battle when he walked out of the studio at the start of a picture in 1932, claiming he was working too hard for too little money. Cagney's original contract with Warners, which was negotiated by William Morris in 1930, paid him $350 a week to start and then rose in increments over the life of the contract. After Cagney made a name for himself in such pictures as THE PUBLIC ENEMY, TAXI!, and THE CROWD ROARS, Warners gave him a bonus that raised his base salary to $1,400 a week. But Cagney was not mollified; he wanted a new contract that started at $3,000 per week. Cagney said he based his stand "on the fact that [his] pictures, for the time being, are big moneymakers—and that there are only so many successful pictures in a personality. And don't forget that when you are washed up in pictures you are really through. You can't get a bit, let alone a decent part."[36]

After the dispute went to arbitration, Warners awarded Cagney a new contract that started at $1,750 a week. Warners also orally agreed that Cagney was required to make a maximum of four pictures a year. In 1935, Cagney again filed suit to break his contract. His stated rationale was that he had made fourteen pictures in three years and that contrary to the billing provision in his contract, he had received second billing on DEVIL DOGS OF THE AIR at certain theaters. Cagney was then earning $4,500 a week. Cagney told the court that "four pictures are enough for any actor whose career has advanced as far as mine. . . . When I signed the contract I understood my production schedule was to be limited to that number. . . . I feel an actor wears out his welcome with the public if he appears in too many pictures. In other words, the audiences get their fill, and turn in another direction."[37]

At the core of Cagney's discontent was the studio's practice of typecasting him in what he referred to as "dese, dem, and dose" roles and in inferior pictures in which he was teamed up with Pat O'Brien. The court ruled in favor of Cagney, stating that Warners had breached Cagney's contract.[38] Claiming that the so-called advertising breach was inadvertent and casual, Warners appealed the case to the California Supreme Court.

Pending the outcome, Cagney went to work for Grand National, a new Poverty Row studio. Cagney had approached the majors but had gotten nowhere because if the state supreme court were to reverse the decision, any studio that employed him would be subject to damages and might lose the entire amount it had spent on production. Cagney made two pictures for Grand National. Said Shipman, "Neither was outstanding, and he couldn't have been sorry when Warners made overtures—the case still not settled—to him to finish out his contract at $150,000 per film versus a percentage."[39] Cagney received better assignments afterward, among them BOY MEETS GIRL (1938), ANGELS WITH DIRTY FACES (1938), THE OKLAHOMA KID (1939), and THE ROARING TWENTIES (1939). However, Cagney remained recalcitrant and, when conditions were right, became one of the first stars to go into independent production.

Bette Davis, another Warners star, became dissatisfied with her roles and walked out on her contract in 1936. Bernard Dick described Davis's relationship with the studio as

one of the stormiest . . . that ever existed between a studio and its star;
graphically, it would resemble a fever chart. Davis would no sooner
make one good film than she would be assigned to a series of poor
ones. As if to punish her for making OF HUMAN BONDAGE (1934) on
loanout at RKO because she could not find a decent script at her own
studio, Warners released HOUSEWIFE (1934) immediately after her
triumph as Maugham's Mildred Rogers. After DANGEROUS [which
won her an Oscar for best actress] and THE PETRIFIED FOREST came
THE GOLDEN ARROW and SATAN MET A LADY (all 1936), which left
her "unhappy, unfulfilled." (Bernard Dick, ed., *Dark Victory* [Madi-
son: University of Wisconsin Press, 1981], p. 14)

Returning to the studio after OF HUMAN BONDAGE, Davis received a new
contract that raised her salary to $1,350 a week from $1,000, but the contract
merely guaranteed feature billing in her pictures and did not reduce the number
she had to make each year. Through her agent, she sent the following list of
demands to the studio: a five-year contract at a salary that escalated from
$100,000 to $220,000 per year; the right to make no more than four pictures a year;
star or co-star billing; the services of her favorite cameramen; and "three months'
consecutive vacation each year with the right to do one outside picture."[40]

Jack Warner suspended her, characterizing her demands "as exorbitant and
impossible." He added that "she would remain on the suspended list until she
returned to the studio to live up to the terms of her contract."[41] The studio cut off
her salary and announced its intention to tack on to her contract the time she
spent on suspension. To circumvent the ban, Davis accepted a leading role in a
picture to be produced in London by the independent producer Ludovico
Toeplitz. Warner took her to court by filing an injunction. After a brief hearing in
which the Warners lawyer characterized Davis as a "naughty little girl who wants
more money," the court granted the injunction, ruling that Davis must confine
her services exclusively to Warners.

Davis accepted the judgment and decided on another approach. Through her
attorneys she told Jack Warner that she would return to work without any
"modifications" of her existing contract, but she also politely reiterated her case.
Said Thomas Schatz, "[Jack] Warner held firm but he got the message; Davis
might have lost this skirmish, but the war would go on. And Warner himself,
having been without his top actress for nearly a year, was ready to compromise."[42] To demonstrate his good intentions, Jack Warner bought her a property
she had wanted, JEZEBEL. And Davis demonstrated her mettle by winning her
second Academy Award playing the lead role. But "just when she thought the
pattern of one mediocrity for every masterpiece had been altered," she was given
COMET OVER BROADWAY as her next picture. Davis refused the assignment and
went on suspension in April 1938. After a month, she and the studio resolved
their differences.

Now at the pinnacle of her career, Davis received a new contract that started
out at $3,500 per week and gave her star billing. However, "by explicitly detailing
her duties to the studio," the contract was in some respects more restrictive:
"Davis had to 'perform and render her services whenever, wherever and as often
as the producer requested.' Significantly, these services included interviews,
sittings for photographs, and the rest of the elements the studio could orchestrate

in its differentiation strategy." Thereafter, Davis would receive more money and would make fewer pictures, but "she never did earn the right to choose her roles or to have a say in her publicity. On the contrary, as Davis' name grew larger on theater marquees, the studio consolidated more control over her career."[43]

Not until Olivia de Havilland took Warners to court over its suspension practices was a star able to break any of the offensive terms of the seven-year option contract. Ruling in 1943 that Warners had violated the state's antipeonage laws, the court decided in de Havilland's favor, a decision the state supreme court affirmed in 1944. Schatz calls the decision "a watershed event in Hollywood's history, a significant victory for top stars and a huge setback for the studios. No longer could Warners or any other studio tack on suspension time to the end of a contract, thereby preventing an artist from sitting out and becoming a free agent."[44] It is difficult to attach such significance to the case, since every other provision of the option contract designed to keep stars in their place remained in force. It was not until the breakdown of the studio system itself during the fifties that the balance of power tipped in favor of the star.

Star Development

To build a roster of stars, a studio relied on what Douglas Gomery calls "the spillover effect" of personalities recruited from professional theater, vaudeville, radio, and other forms of entertainment. Hollywood's raid on Broadway began in earnest in mid 1928 and captured a new generation of actors that included James Cagney, Bette Davis, Claudette Colbert, Irene Dunne, Clark Gable, and Mae West, among others. By 1934, *Variety* reported that "Hollywood is now 70% dependent on the stage for its film acting talent up in those brackets where performers get screen credit."[45]

Although vaudeville was on its last legs, it supplied Hollywood with many early sound stars, among them Al Jolson, Eddie Cantor, the Marx Brothers, Joe E. Brown, George Burns and Gracie Allen, W. C. Fields, Bert Wheeler and Robert Woolsey, Will Rogers, and Mae West.[46] And radio, which was becoming increasingly popular throughout the decade, supplied the movies a steadily supply of its stars—Kate Smith, Rudy Vallee, Bing Crosby, and Ed Wynn. Even grand opera provided a few names. As musicals gained in popularity during the decade, studios widened their search and signed opera stars Grace Moore, Lily Pons, Nino Martini, and Gladys Swarthout, among others.

In her anthropological study of Hollywood, Hortense Powdermaker said she was surprised to learn that "while most executives swear by the star system, it is not a part of Hollywood custom to plan coherently even for the stars." She stated a commonly held belief, but it needs revising. During the conversion to sound, Warners and Paramount devised a cost-effective method to test stage and radio talent. After refurbishing their East Coast studios, the companies cast stage and radio personalities in shorts—for example, in "canned vaudeville" or comic skits. If they passed muster, they were offered long-term contracts and sent packing to California for exploitation in feature films. Mae West is the best example of this strategy. After a successful test, Paramount gave her a contract that permitted her to write as well as to star in her own vehicles. In such hits as I'M NO ANGEL (1933) and BELLE OF THE NINETIES (1934), she helped pull Paramount out of the Depression to become the highest salaried woman in the United States in 1934.[47]

Signing stars from other entertainment fields was one thing; making them palatable to movie audiences was quite another. Audiences did not necessarily overlap; in fact, they were often quite different. Moreover, an act in one entertainment form might not be easily adaptable to the norms of Hollywood narratives. Take the case of Eddie Cantor. A famous vaudeville and Ziegfeld Follies headliner and one of the very first radio stars, Eddie Cantor starred in a series of musical comedies produced by Sam Goldwyn from 1930 to 1936. A small, dapper performer with popping banjo-eyes who skipped and sang during his routines, Cantor established a persona built around a mixture of blackface comedy, Jewish jokes, and sketches of New York types that was tailored to entertain high-class Broadway audiences.

Cantor's first picture, WHOOPEE! (1930), was a literal transcription (in two-toned Technicolor) of his hit Ziegfeld show. Relating the adventures of a hypochondriac out West, the plot, in Henry Jenkins's words, "served as an excuse to allow the versatile comic to slip in and out of a variety of disguises (a Greek short-order cook, a black-face minstrel, a tough-talking western bandit, a commercially-minded Indian, and a fast-talking Jewish peddler), to spit forth a rapid-fire barrage of wisecracks and bad puns, and to perform a number of fast-paced and sexually-suggestive songs." Other production values included numbers choreographed by Busby Berkeley and performed by the Goldwyn Girls, which *Variety* once described as "glorified girl show[s] in celluloid." The picture did smash business in New York and broke house records in industrial cities with ethnic populations, but in the Midwest, South, and West the picture fared poorly. At the day's end, WHOOPEE! made money, but Goldwyn needed to develop a formula that would "broaden Cantor's appeal . . . without robbing his comedy of its energy and vitality."[48]

To make Cantor's next picture, PALMY DAYS (1931), Goldwyn borrowed some of the techniques studios were using to make former vaudeville clowns like the Marx Brothers, Wheeler and Woolsey, and Jack Oakie palatable to a broad-based audience. Out went the Yiddish references as Goldwyn and his writers constructed a vehicle designed for the masses containing plenty of slapstick, chases, and tricks. The promotional materials devised by United Artists, the distributor of the picture, changed Cantor's image by emphasizing his experience as a screen actor, by avoiding all references to his Jewishness, and by burying Cantor's on-screen joking about sexual infidelity beneath a "blizzard of publicity about his long-time marriage and his five daughters."[49] Cantor's new image disappointed New Yorkers, but PALMY DAYS did well outside the industrial Northeast, in those areas where WHOOPEE! had floundered.

Having devised a successful formula for his star, Goldwyn naturally repeated it in such pictures as THE KID FROM SPAIN (1932), ROMAN SCANDALS (1933), KID MILLIONS (1934), and STRIKE ME PINK (1936). All contained loosely woven plots that presented Cantor as a WASP character and that contained plenty of slapstick and stunts, such as a chariot race, a roller-coaster chase, and a bullfight. United Artists publicity campaigns tried to rekindle enthusiasm in the industrial North by touting the prestige and spectacle of the pictures, by hyping the Technicolor production numbers, and by sponsoring beauty competitions to discover new Goldwyn Girls for the pictures. These strategies worked to some extent, but as

Eddie Cantor with Ethel Shutta in Whoopee! *(UA, 1930)*.

Henry Jenkins noted, "with each subsequent Cantor vehicle, the gap, already visible in the box-office returns for Palmy Days, widened, with hinterlands engagements increasingly becoming the stable market for his comedies and his New York runs growing progressively shorter."[50]

Radio became a national pastime during the thirties. Some radio stars had enjoyed renown on the stage, and others became radio originals, created by the new medium. In either case, Hollywood wanted to absorb them. However, producers faced two problems: how to transfer a popular star from a medium that is primarily aural and that has its own set of performance conventions to a medium that is both aural and visual and that has a narrative tradition; and how to adapt a radio star to a motion-picture audience. Did the two audiences have the same demographic composition, age spread, and tastes? If they were different, to what extent? And how could one find out?

Hollywood devised two strategies to adapt radio stars to the movies. The first entailed building a full-length narrative around a radio personality and promoting the vehicle in the conventional manner—that is, by focusing all the attention on the star. Paramount tried this approach on Kate Smith after her appearance in The Big Broadcast (1932). In this picture, she played herself and sang a

number much like she did on her radio show. To launch her as a full-fledged
movie star, Paramount designed a vehicle, HELLO, EVERYBODY (1933), in which
she played a farm girl who breaks into radio as a singer in order buy off land
grabbers threatening to take her family's property. It flopped. Using a similar
strategy, Universal tried to launch Myrt and Marge, a popular mother-daughter
radio team, in a B musical called MYRT AND MARGE (1934). In its review of the
picture, *Variety* associated the team with "a whole list of radio folks who went to
Hollywood, made one picture, and apart from a piece of change, did themselves
little good."[51] With the single exception of Bing Crosby (see Chapter 7), this
strategy of star development failed because radio personalities either lacked the
acting skills to sustain a feature-length movie or performed roles that were out of
character.

The second strategy to adapt radio stars was devised by Paramount to make THE
BIG BROADCAST (1932).[52] A loosely woven musical inspired by the all-star cast
and multiple-plot structure of GRAND HOTEL, the film provided the minimum
excuse for a series of radio stars to perform their familiar routines. Using a radio
station as the motivation for guest appearances, Paramount showcased a series of
radio personalities—among them Bing Crosby, George Burns and Gracie Allen,
the Boswell Sisters, and Kate Smith—by having each star introduced on camera
by the same announcer who handled that function on the star's weekly show.
The formula had enough going for it to spawn a sequel, INTERNATIONAL HOUSE
(1933), and then a series (see Chapter 7).

Because the personas of stars in one medium did not always carry over into
motion pictures, studios obviously had to build personalities from scratch.
Describing the star-making process, W. Robert La Vine said,

> A star was not born, but made. Hair was bleached or dyed, and, if
> necessary, to "open" the eyes, eyebrows were removed and penciled
> in above the natural line. Studio-resident dentists, expert at creating
> million-dollar smiles, capped teeth or fitted them with braces. Cos-
> metic surgery was often advised to reshape the nose of a new recruit
> or tighten her sagging chin. A "starlet" was taught how to walk, smile,
> laugh, and weep. She was instructed in the special techniques of
> acting before a camera, perfecting pronunciation, and learning how to
> breathe for more effective voice control. Days were spent in wardrobe,
> situated in separate buildings within the studio communities. (*In a
> Glamorous Fashion: The Fabulous Years of Hollywood Costume Design*
> [New York: Charles Scribner's Sons, 1980], p. 27)

To devise an appropriate screen image for an aspiring star, a studio would cast the
player in a series of roles and test audience response to each by consulting fan
mail, sneak previews, reviews, exhibitors' comments, and the box office. In
essence, producers attempted to mold their protégés to fit consumer interest.
Once the correct formula was found, the ingredients would be inscribed in
narratives, publicity, and advertising. Take the case of Bette Davis. Davis
appeared in a series of unremarkable pictures from 1932 to 1935 as Warners
searched for the correct formula. In one of her first assignments, CABIN IN THE
COTTON (1932), Davis played a southern belle who attempts to titillate and cajole
a poor sharecropper (Richard Barthelmess) into betraying his friends. At one

point she tells Barthelmess, "Ah'd love to kiss you, but Ah just washed mah hair." Her vivid performance as a coquette elicited a strong audience response and led *Variety* to name her a box-office leader for 1932.

In her first starring role, Davis plays a liberated career woman in Ex-LADY (1933) who is forced to choose between remaining a free-spirited single "modern woman" or becoming an "old-fashioned" married woman. The picture was panned by the critics, and Davis was dropped from *Variety's* charts. In 1934, Warners loaned out Davis to RKO to play the part of Mildred, a mean, sluttish waitress who seduces and destroys a medical student (Leslie Howard) in OF HUMAN BONDAGE, a character that *Variety* described as a vamp. Audiences loved her in the role. Now that a successful match between narrative and actress had been found, Davis showed signs of becoming an unqualified star.

Returning to Warners, Davis was assigned to play a vamp in a Paul Muni vehicle, BORDERTOWN (1934). She received featured billing. Cathy Klaprat points out that "although *Bordertown* appeared on Warners' production schedule in June 1934, prior to the release of *Bondage,* . . . Davis was not cast as Marie until after her triumph." Ads for the picture asked, "Who will be the real star of the film: Bette Davis or Paul Muni?" Campaign books told exhibitors to place signs in their lobbies asking patrons if Davis should have received star billing. Fans must have answered yes because for her next assignment, Warner's starred Davis in DANGEROUS (1935) playing another vampish role, an alcoholic actress. Anticipating that DANGEROUS would be a hit, Warner's held up its release until the last week in December, the final week to qualify for an Oscar nomination. Warner's strategy was designed to keep the picture fresh in everyone's mind during the evaluation and voting period for the awards. It worked; Davis won her first Academy Award for best actress. Although Davis's Oscar was generally regarded as a consolation prize for not being nominated for OF HUMAN BONDAGE, the process of fitting actor to character as determined by audience demand had been a success.[53]

Having discovered the correct role, the next step was to create a fit between a star's personal life and his or her screen persona. The intent was to convince audiences that the star "acted identically in both her 'real' and 'reel' lives."[54] Fusing actor and character was the function of a studio's publicity department. To begin the process, the department manufactured an authorized biography of the star's personal life based largely on the successful narrative roles of the star's pictures. This material was disseminated to fan magazines, newspapers, and gossip columns. The department then assigned a publicist to the star to handle interviews and to supervise the star's makeup and clothing for public appearances. Finally, the department arranged a sitting for the star with a glamour portrait photographer to create an official studio image.

During Davis's blond coquette period, from 1932 to 1934, pressbooks touted her as a sexy blond and showed photos of her wearing bathing suits, low-cut gowns, and revealing blouses. Little personal information was revealed, indicating that Warners was still searching for the right image. After OF HUMAN BONDAGE, her publicity changed. Davis was no longer displayed as a blond in come-hither poses; her hair became darker and she wore tailored suits. Authorized stories also changed. *Modern Screen,* for example, "avowed that Davis was fiery, independent, and definitely not domesticated (all qualities she displayed in her films)." *Motion Picture Classic* portrayed her as "hard-boiled and ruthless, determined to get what she wants (all traits which motivate many of Davis' actions in her vamp films)."[55] Similarly, stories transposed character relationships from her films to her personal life. For example, one article asked, "Will Bette wed George Brent?" and displayed a publicity still from JEZEBEL showing the two in an embrace. The question would remain on everyone's minds because Brent played Davis's leading man ten times.

The influence of the star system on the narrative structure of classical Hollywood cinema was profound. Classical Hollywood cinema was protagonist-centered, and studio practice dictated casting a star in the principal role. The interrelationship of the two are described by Cathy Klaprat:

> The goals and desires of the protagonist generally motivate the causal logic of the action and, consequently, the structure of the narrative, the components of which included plot, the behavior of the characters in their relationship to the star, as well as the settings for the action. Thus, we can see that if the protagonist was constructed by the traits and actions of star differentiation, then the narrative was structured by the star. ("The Star as Market Strategy," in Tino Balio, ed., *The American Film Industry,* rev. ed. [Madison: University of Wisconsin Press, 1985], p. 369)

To illustrate this practice, take the case of JEZEBEL (1938). A vehicle designed for Bette Davis, JEZEBEL was based on the play by Owen Davis and produced to capitalize on the interest in David O. Selznick's GONE WITH THE WIND, which was in development. William Wyler directed. Like GONE WITH THE WIND, JEZEBEL takes place in the Civil War–era South and has a headstrong heroine as the protagonist. An examination of the development of the property from a play, through four screenplay drafts, to the finished film reveals how the studio tailor-made the project to fit Bette Davis's screen persona as a vamp.

Owen Davis's play is a historical drama depicting society in transition in the antebellum South; in contrast, the motion picture is essentially a character study. In the development of the shooting script, the structure of the story was changed from a late to an early point of attack that initiates the action at the moment of conflict. In essence, the studio de-emphasized the historical milieu and concentrated on the melodrama. The action has a bipartite structure built exclusively around Bette Davis's role of Julie Marsden. The first half shows us a reckless, daring, but basically sympathetic Bette Davis before her great mistake, appearing in a red dress at the Olympus ball. The second half shows us the results of that mistake; her apology to Pres (Henry Fonda) dressed in white, her revenge, and her redemption.

This structure allows us to witness character development in much the same way that the passage of time from the pre–Civil War era to Reconstruction reveals change in GONE WITH THE WIND. Take, for example, the way Julie is introduced. In the play, Julie simply walks on stage and is greeted by the other characters. In the film, Julie rides up to the plantation on a wild horse, which a young black servant has trouble controlling after she dismounts. Strutting up to the porch, she stops a moment to shout orders at the carriage driver and then whips her riding crop over her shoulder and hikes up her train before entering. We have been introduced to a confident and self-assured Julie Marsden. When

Bette Davis and Henry Fonda in Jezebel *(Warners, 1938). The Olympus Ball.*

she strides through the living room greeting the guests, the contrast between Julie's riding habit and her guests' more formal attire reveals her disregard for social conventions, an attitude that is upsetting to some of the women present.

Another early incident is the Olympus ball sequence. In the play, the dress incident is talked about, not enacted. Julie tells us it happened "one night" rather than at an important society event. The "wrongness" of the dress was simply a matter of personal taste—Pres simply did not like the daring low front of the dress—rather than a flaunting of social convention. And Julie's memory of the incident focuses on a personal hurt rather than a public scandal. In the film, the dress incident reveals not merely a conflict between two lovers but also a struggle between Julie and New Orleans society. Aunt Belle of the film tells us that wearing a red dress to the ball would "insult every woman on the floor." Thus, the Olympus ball sequence has taken on greater significance: it pits Davis against society in a way that is consistent with the "outcast" quality of Davis's roles in Of Human Bondage and her other films.

Davis earns the name Jezebel by manipulating the events leading to the duel that takes Buck Cantrell's (George Brent) life. In the play, Julie has a rather passive role in the affair. Pres tells her he still loves her and even kisses her, but when they are discovered by his wife, Amy, he is embarrassed and makes his apologies, at which point Julie slaps him, an understandable reaction. In the film, the incident has been substantially changed to make Pres an innocent victim of Davis's advances. Pres makes no declaration of love to Julie, nor does he reveal any romantic feelings for her; it is Davis who takes the initiative. She dominates the conversation and taking him unawares, kisses him passionately. Pres tears himself away from her, and as he stalks out of the room, a close-up shows the anger and contempt he feels. Humiliated and rebuffed, Julie decides to get her revenge. She manipulates Buck into challenging Pres to a duel by intimating that Pres, under the influence of brandy, improperly made advances. Narrative strategies similar to these were used to construct the Davis persona in pictures such as DANGEROUS, THE LETTER, IN THIS OUR LIFE, and DECEPTION.

After developing an effective narrative formula for a star, a studio would naturally want to cash in on its good fortune by repeating the formula in as many vehicles as possible. In this fashion a star could be "milked dry like a vein of gold is pinched out," said *Variety*.[56] The best performers chafed at being stereotyped. Repeating the same role deadened the spirit and prevented a talented performer from reaching his or her full artistic potential. However, studios justified this practice with the explanation that star development was risky and required an enormous amount of money. To tamper with success after having discovered an effective formula would be foolhardy. Yet, if a studio cast a star in the same role again and again, it ran the risk of satiating audience demand. The problem became how to extend the life of a star while simultaneously producing sufficient numbers of vehicles to diffuse the high salary costs.

To conserve resources, producers relied on product variation. As Darryl Zanuck put it, "there is no reason why, with proper care, a star cannot remain popular well beyond the traditional span of five years. To that end, care must be exercised in story selection. Vehicles must be varied." In practice, this meant diversifying character traits of roles "while at the same time invoking the familiar expectations associated with star differentiation"—the same-but-different principle.[57]

Warners had the most success varying Bette Davis's vamp roles by offcasting her as the good woman. The practice started in the forties. For example, THE GREAT LIE (1941) contains a triangle plot formula, but now Davis played a sympathetic woman with maternal and noble instincts. Mary Astor took the unsympathetic part, a brittle, selfish, and spoiled woman. However, publicity continued to refer to Davis as a vamp. One ad reads, "*Contrary* to the former Davis pattern, Bette Davis' new film does not find her killing anyone or acting nasty."[58]

Promotion at the Production Level

Nothing was too private if it interested the public, nothing was too trite if it got copy, and nothing was too exaggerated if it sold a ticket. It was this kind of material that freely found its way into any newspaper, magazine, or radio station in the country. Good, bad, or ridiculous, someone would be willing to read it, enter it, or buy it. No single audience was ever exposed to all the promotional material created for a motion picture. Publicity announcing a premiere drew an exclusive opening-night crowd. Previews of coming attractions whetted the appetites of loyal fans. Magazine articles, Sunday features, and news items stoked the interest of casual moviegoers. And, of course, movie ads in the local newspaper kept audiences in touch with the current fare. These were the common, expected ways to present the latest Hollywood feature to the audience and together with publicity stunts, trivia contests, merchandising tie-ins, and the like, they constituted motion-picture promotion.[59]

The publicity department of a major studio was organized like the city room of a newspaper. Publicity directors such as Howard Strickling at MGM, Edward Selzer at Warner's, Tom Bailey at Paramount, Harry Brand at 20th Century–Fox, and Russell Birdwell at Selznick-International functioned as editors who assigned stories and reviewed finished copy before it was released. They also personally handled front-office news concerning such matters as the hiring and firing of key studio personnel, the acquiring of important properties, and the financial affairs of the company. A suicide, a messy divorce, or a scandal turned their job into public relations with the goal of protecting the image of the studio or of salvaging the reputation of a star.

Working under the publicity director were the unit reporters, who covered the big pictures, and publicists, who were assigned to individual stars. Unit reporters were almost always former newspapermen and rarely earned more than $150 a week for the usual six-day week they put in. A unit reporter prepared a synopsis of the plot and special-interest stories about the production and its stars for use by newspapers. A publicist's job was to handle the public relations of a top star and sometimes even his or her private financial affairs.

To satisfy the huge demand for information about stars, other sections of the publicity department supplied fashion layouts for fan magazines and planted tidbits with gossip columnists Louella Parsons, Sheilah Graham, and Hedda Hopper, among others. Gossip columnists typically commented on affairs of the heart. They seldom dug up information on their own but relied on news from the studios. Studios and stars were happy to cooperate since even unfavorable publicity in a gossip column kept the name of a star in print and the myth of Hollywood alive.

The still-photography department supplied the iconography for promotion. Photographs were the physical artifacts of the motion-picture experience. During each major production, a still photographer took stills of every key scene to be used for lobby displays, advertising, and poster layouts. To service pulp magazines and newspapers, the studio needed high-contrast photos in shallow focus.

For fan magazines and glossy publications, the studio needed higher-quality photos, which were the special province of glamour portrait photographers. These photographers had the task of capturing in a single image the screen persona of a star. As John Kobal put it, "they had nothing to do with making movies, but everything to do with the selling of the dream that movies meant." The most skilled of these portrait photographers—Clarence Bull at MGM, George Hurrell at Warner Bros., Ernest Bachrach at RKO, and Eugene Robert Richee at Paramount—experimented with "backgrounds, shapes, textures, lighting, and produced a unique genre which not only served a specific function, but—unlike many of the films of the period—survives as an art form."[60] All photos were taken by an eight-by-ten-inch large-format camera. After a negative was processed, artisans retouched it to eliminate excessive weight around the waist, hips, throat, and shoulders by scraping the negative and stippling it (adding new dot patterns to the negative). They also removed lines and skin flaws from the face. After all physical imperfections were removed, the negative was airbrushed to give the face an alabaster appearance on the prints.

Glamour portraits served many purposes, but the main one was satisfying the needs of fans. Margaret Thorp observed the scene and said,

> Fan mail comes into Hollywood's studios daily by the truck load. Special clerks are needed to sort it on each lot. A conservative estimate puts the letters addressed to players at a quarter of a million a month. A top star expects about three thousand a week. . . . The bulk of the mail, at least 75 per cent, is made up of requests for photographs or for some personal souvenir. (*America at the Movies* [New Haven, Conn.: Yale University Press, 1939], p. 96)

Fan magazines were the most voracious consumers of publicity. *Photoplay, Modern Screen, Silver Screen,* and other such magazines had monthly circulations of nearly a half million each. Each magazine usually contained at least one signature of photos that were specially printed on gravure presses to ensure high-quality reproduction. Fans wanted color photos that were clear and suitable for framing on a bedroom wall or pasting in a scrapbook, and were willing to pay extra for such magazines.

Stories in fan magazines dealt with romance, marriage, children, divorce, and death. Adult stars such as Greta Garbo, Carole Lombard, and Errol Flynn made the best copy, along with such child stars as Shirley Temple, Deanna Durbin, Judy Garland, and Mickey Rooney. "Every aspect of life, trivial and important," said Thorp, was "bathed in the purple glow of luxury." The magazines revealed that Bing Crosby bred racehorses, that Shirley Temple had 250 dolls, and that Joan Crawford had a famous collection of sapphires and diamonds. Clothes were "endlessly pictured and described, usually with marble fountains, private swimming pools, or limousines in the background." Regardless of the luxury depicted, one purpose of these articles was to bring the image of the star down to earth: "She takes care today to make it known that she is really a person of simple wholesome tastes, submitting to elegance as part of her job but escaping from it as often as possible. It soothes the fans to believe that luxury is fundamentally a burden."[61]

.Hollywood's publicity machinery was thus designed to mesh comfortably with merchandising tie-ins. If advertising attempted to associate consumer products with romance, marriage, and sexual fulfillment, it found a handmaiden in the movies. Ranked second only to food products in the amount spent on advertising, the cosmetics industry signed stars to appear in literally hundreds of thousands of ads—"ads which dutifully mentioned the star's current film"—making cosmetics synonymous with Hollywood.[62] Stars also dutifully provided testimonials for ads hawking soap, deodorants, toothpastes, lotions, hair preparations, and other toiletries.

Fashion specialists tried to popularize the latest creations to come out of Hollywood's costume design shops. "*Vogue* printed Adrian's sketches for *Camille* (1936) and *Marie Antoinette* (1938). Luise Rainer primped for photos in a room full of spectacularly plumed hats from *The Great Ziegfeld* (1936). Marlene Dietrich appeared in layouts in splended Russian sables and brocades designed by Travis Banton for *The Scarlet Empress* (1934)." Gimmicks such as these were supposed to generate commercial spin-offs. For example, Adrian's "little velvet hat, trimmed with ostrich feathers," which Garbo wore "tilted becomingly over one eye," created a vogue for the Empress Eugénie hat. "Universally copied in a wide price range, it influenced how women wore their hats for the rest of the decade," said Edward Maeder. Walter Plunkett's wardrobe for GONE WITH THE WIND "produced a merchandising blitz unequaled in the history of period film publicity tie-ins. Brassieres and corsets, dress patterns, hats and veils, snoods, scarves, jewelry, even wrist watches, were marketed as 'inspired' by the film."[63] No dress in the 1930s was as copied as the Scarlett O'Hara's barbecue dress.

The power of the movies to popularize fashion styles was harnessed by Bernard Waldman and his Modern Merchandising Bureau. According to Charles Eckert, he played the role of fashion middleman for most of the major studios:

> By the mid-1930s Waldman's system generally operated as follows: sketches and/or photographs of styles to be worn by specific actresses in specific films were sent from the studios to the bureau (often a year in advance of the film's release). The staff first evaluated these styles and calculated new trends. They then contracted with manufacturers to have the styles produced in time for the film's release. They next secured advertising photos and other materials which would be sent to retail shops. This ad material mentioned the film, stars, and studio as well as the theaters where the film would appear. ("The Carole Lombard in Macy's Window," p. 8)

Waldman branched out by franchising a business called Cinema Fashions Shops. By 1937, more than four hundred official Cinema Fashion Shops were in operation (only one was permitted in each city) and an additional fourteen hundred stores were handling a portion of the star-endorsed style lines. As a result of Waldman's merchandising efforts and the studios' willingness to publicize costume designs, the names of the leading studio designers, notably Adrian of MGM, Orry-Kelly of Warners, Edith Head of Paramount, and Walter Plunkett of Selznick, became as familiar to shoppers as the stars themselves.

Hollywood added a new dimension to its advertising efforts during the thirties by taking full advantage of radio. If Hollywood wanted to exploit radio stars in the movies, radio also wanted to exploit movie stars for its own purposes. By the mid thirties the two industries had developed a symbiotic relationship. The radio audience had an "insatiable interest in the stars, scripts, and formulas developed by the movies," said Michele Hilmes, but the two networks could not effectively exploit this interest until 1935, when AT&T removed the double transmission rates, which required networks to pay for the transmission of a broadcast both to and from New York. When AT&T dropped the rates, NBC and CBS built new studios in Los Angeles and "produced a veritable deluge of programming."[64]

Hollywood talent and source material was used in four types of programming. Musical variety shows such as Maxwell House Coffee's "Show Boat," "The Rudy Vallee Show," and "Kraft Music Hall" combined big names, lesser stars, and regular performers in a mix of music, comedy, dialogue, and vignettes. Dramatic series such as Campana Balm's "First Nighter" and DuPont's "The Calvacade of America" showcased top dramatic stars. "Cavalcade of America," which presented historical dramatizations, "built up a reputation for thorough and accurate research as well as dramatic appeal," said Hilmes and "attracted stage and screen actors who had formerly remained aloof." Among the stars who

Omar Kiam's wedding dress worn by Merle Oberon in WUTHERING HEIGHTS
(UA, 1939). Window display.

portrayed historical figures on the program were Clark Gable, Raymond Massey, Charles Laughton, Lionel Barrymore, Dick Powell, Tyrone Power, and Edward G. Robinson. Hollywood gossip columns hosted by Louella Parsons, Hedda Hopper, Walter Winchell, and others found an eager listening audience for their tales of Hollywood life. From the studio's perspective, radio gossip and talk shows were found to be as effective as promotion in the print media.[65]

The movie adaptation was particularly effective as a publicity device. The "Lux Radio Theater," hosted by Cecil B. DeMille, represented "the culmination of its type" and remained one of the most popular shows on the air. The show was divided into three acts with breaks for commercial messages and interviews conducted by DeMille with that evening's stars. Most adaptations were broadcast after the release of a film and served to boost theater attendance. Among the hit pictures adapted for the program were DARK VICTORY, with Bette Davis and Spencer Tracy; THE THIN MAN, with William Powell and Myrna Loy; and MR. DEEDS GOES TO TOWN, with Gary Cooper.

Promotion at the Distribution Level

Promotion emanating from the studios was concerned primarily with creating and maintaining star images. Promotion at the distribution level was concerned mainly with advertising and publicizing new releases. The publicity campaign for a picture was formulated in Hollywood as it went into production and was developed and executed in New York at a company's distribution headquarters prior to its release. Hollywood and New York were both concerned with promoting stars and with hyping the new release, but promotion at the distribution level was aimed at motion-picture exhibitors as well as the public.

Vertical integration ensured that the majors controlled every facet of promotion in their attempt to funnel as many patrons as possible into their first-run theaters. To keep the process free from political or censorship harassment, the majors submitted all advertising materials to the Advertising Advisory Council (AAC), a wing of the Production Code Administration, for approval prior to its distribution. Advertising materials included posters, sketches, publicity stories, poster art, accessories, pressbooks, and exploitation ideas. The majors adopted the Advertising Code in 1930 and made the review process mandatory in 1933. The Advertising Code addressed many of the same concerns as the Production Code, such as respect for religions, national feelings, and the law. Similarly, both codes prohibited profanity, vulgarity, and nudity. But as Mary Beth Haralovich points out, "the Advertising Code is a general call for good taste and the honest representations of films while the Production Code is much more specific in what constitutes good taste."[66]

A promotion campaign began prior to the release of a new picture and was aimed at multiple segments of the audience. Although motion pictures were theoretically designed to reach an undifferentiated mass audience, a uniform campaign would be unsuccessful. Hollywood had already determined that a gala premiere could launch a picture with the biggest bang. And it was a longtime practice to stage such galas in New York and Hollywood. During the thirties, Hollywood added imaginative permutations to its stock of gimmicks.

Warners' launching of 42ND STREET in 1933 started the trend. Because this backstage musical boosted "the New Deal philosophy of pulling together to whip the depression" and because Warner Baxter, its star, "played a role that was a patent allegory of F.D.R.," the studio dreamt up the idea of linking the picture to the excitement surrounding Roosevelt's inauguration.[67] Near the eve of the inauguration, Jack Warner and a contingent of studio stars boarded a gilded and decorated train in Los Angeles, the 42nd Street Special, bound for Washington. General Electric put up money for the stunt in exchange for the advertising. As the train sped across the continent, "its radio broadcasted Dick Powell's jazzy contralto, GE ad-copy, and optimism. . . . When the train arrived at a major city, the stars and chorus girls motored to the largest available showroom and demonstrated whatever appliances they found themselves thrust up against. In the evenings they appeared at a key-theater for a mini-premiere." Describing the stunt as "unique in the history of 'personal appearances,'" *Motion Picture Herald* reported that "thousands have crammed railroad stations to get a glimpse of the trainload of stars. In small towns, where the train stopped only ten minutes, entire populations turned out to accord a welcome."[68]

Arriving in Washington in time for the inaugural parade and ceremonies, the stars made personal appearances later that evening at a local theater. The entourage then proceeded to New York in time for the premiere on 9 March. Charles Eckert has described these festivities:

> On March 9 bawdy, gaudy 42nd Street looked as spiffy as a drunkard in church: American flags and red, white, and blue bunting draped the buildings; the ordinary incandescent bulbs were replaced with scintillant "golden" GE lamps; a fleet of Chrysler automobiles (a separate tie-up) and GE automotive equipment was readied for a late afternoon parade which would catch those leaving work. In the North River a cruiser stood at anchor to fire a salute—a great organ-boom to cap off a roulade of aerial bombs. As the train approached New York from New Rochelle, a pride of small airplanes accompanied it. Once it arrived, the schedule was as exacting as a coronation: a reception at Grand Central by Forty-Second Street Property Owners and Merchants Association, the parade, a GE sales meeting at the Sam Harris Theatre, and the grand premiere at the Strand. ("The Carole Lombard in Macy's Window," p. 3)

By the end of the decade, studios regularly preceded the New York and Hollywood openings with a world premiere staged in a city or town connected in one way or another to the subject matter of the picture. GONE WITH THE WIND's premiere in Atlanta is the most obvious example of the practice, but such treatment was also given to DODGE CITY, UNION PACIFIC, and YOUNG MR. LINCOLN in 1939.[69]

To distribute its regular class-A product, the majors used tried-and-true practices and procedures. Prior to the release of a picture, the distributor placed ads in trade papers such as *Variety* and *Motion Picture Herald* to kindle exhibitor interest. After an exhibitor booked a picture, he received the official pressbook, containing order forms for posters, lobby cards, and stills and pre-written publicity stories that he could place in the local newspaper.

Advertising reflected the exchange values studios used to differentiate their products. According to Janet Staiger, these values consisted in part of stars, genres, "realism," authenticity, and spectacle.[70] The pressbook for Warners' CAPTAIN BLOOD (1935) illustrates just how these values were incorporated into motion-picture advertising. Directed by Michael Curtiz and featuring two up-and-coming young stars, Errol Flynn and Olivia de Havilland, CAPTAIN BLOOD initiated Warners' swashbuckler series. To call attention to the spectacle in the picture, catchlines on posters read,

> See—A Whole City Built in Splender to Show You How "Blood" Razed it with Cannonfire!

> See—The White Slave Markets of the Caribbean Reproduced in All Their Infamy to Show You Why "Blood" Hurled Defiance at an Emperor!

> See—Priceless Galleons Launched and Manned to Show You How "Blood" Blew Them to Bits!

To call attention to the novelty, a publicity release related that "the entire studio found itself struck with amazement over the quaintness of the costumes." To call attention to the authenticity, a story for a Sunday feature recounted the history of piracy and discussed legendary pirate heroes. Referring to the appeal of the genre, a catchline read "Exciting as Your Childhood Dreams . . . Thrilling as the Ring of Steel on Steel . . . Romantic as Red Sails in the Sunset!"

The pressbook promoted Errol Flynn as a "carefree adventurer and a rogue to opportunity." A pre-written story entitled "Errol Flynn's Life One of Astounding Adventure" revealed that Flynn was a former Olympic boxer, a wanderer, and a British stage actor. Described as "tall and handsome, lean and brown, with a flair for romance and a craving for excitement," Flynn is quoted as saying, "I would give a leg to play [the part of Blood], but I figure I haven't a chance. I'm an unknown." As Margaret Sullivan noted, "It was the perfect statement to follow two full columns extolling his exploits. He is the young unknown fighting for success against all odds. He expects nothing to be given to him but given a chance he will prove himself."[71]

The pressbook suggested a range of stunts an exhibitor might use to attract different segments of the audience. For example, to attract children, it suggested staging a pirate parade: "If you're having a pirate party for the kids, try to get them to parade to the theatre in their pirate costumes. By pulling a few strings, Boy Scout band may add a little music, while notables at theatre give ducats for best costume." To attract adolescents, it suggested holding a pirate song contest: "Using pop music alter the words into pirate song." And to attract educated men and women, it advised a music plug over radio: "On local radio get orchestra or choral group to perform numbers from *Pirates of Penzance*."[72]

In terms of advertising strategy, such promotional gimmicks avoided deep-seated attitudes and worked on curiosity and association. Because the choice of seeing a movie rarely involved an attitude change, a simple message with appealing language, content, and form was deemed enough to kindle interest in a picture. It was thought that once a film became a curiosity it was an easy matter to draw associations to it because there was no predisposition to avoid it.

Newspaper ad for CAPTAIN BLOOD *(Warners, 1935).*

Conclusion

In place for decades, the star system played a crucial role in the motion-picture business. The economics of the system explains in part the industry's resistance to unionization during the thirties. Contrary to public perception, Hollywood attempted to rationalize the development of stars just as it had attempted to rationalize other aspects of production. The methods were "unscientific," but no surefire way to create motion-picture personalities has yet been found. Why the public eagerly supported the star system is beyond the purview of this study. The point to be underscored is that the majors exploited this affinity for stars at every level of their operations.

Claudette Colbert in CLEOPATRA *(Paramount, 1934).*

7

Production Trends

The following analysis classifies the class-A feature films of the major Hollywood studios into six broad production trends: (1) prestige pictures; (2) musicals; (3) the woman's film; (4) comedy; (5) social problem films; and (6) horror films. The names given to the production trends are those used in the trade; the arrangement of the trends reflects a hierarchical ranking based on relative production costs, duration, and box-office performance. Individual trends are broken down into their component production cycles—comedy, for example, is broken down into sentimental, screwball, comedian-centered, and so on—and each is discussed from the perspective of product differentiation, studio by studio. As pointed out in the Introduction, the discussion is informed by contemporaneous polls and awards, especially *Film Daily*'s Ten Best, and industry discourse in the trade press and in reviews.

Prestige Pictures

The prestige picture was far and away the most popular production trend of the decade. Before defining the trend, some statistics are in order. From 1930 to 1933, the years of the Depression, fourteen of the forty films that made it to *Film Daily*'s Ten Best, were prestige pictures; from 1934 to the end of the decade, about half of the films on the lists fell into this category. Of the sixty-seven pictues on *Variety*'s Top-Grossing Films lists, close to thirty were prestige pictures. Compared to the total output of the majors, prestige pictures accounted for a small percentage, but compared to the total production budgets, they accounted for a lion's share. Moreover, prestige pictures played a crucial role defining the public image of a company.

The prestige picture is not a genre; rather, the term designates production values and promotion treatment. A prestige picture is typically a big-budget special based on a presold property, often as not a "classic," and tailored for top stars. *Motion Picture Herald* identified four types of properties used for these pictures: (1) nineteenth-century European literature, such as the novels of Charles Dickens, Leo Tolstoy, Alexandre Dumas *père*, and Victor Hugo; (2) Shakespearean plays, notably *A Midsummer Night's Dream* and *Romeo and Juliet;* (3) best-selling novels and hit Broadway plays written by Nobel and Pulitzer Prize–winning authors "that have been acclaimed by the classes and bought by the masses," such as Pearl S. Buck's *The Good Earth*, Hervey Allen's *Anthony Adverse*, and Marc Connelly's *The Green Pastures;* and (4) biographical and historical subjects taken "from originals or from books and plays produced by authors of known worth," especially biographies of European and American "great men," natural disasters (the San Francisco earthquake, the Great Chicago Fire), folklore (the adventures of Robin Hood and his Merrie Men), and war (Civil War, Crimean, and the Great War).[1] Thus, the prestige picture encompassed different genres, several motion-picture styles and other production trends—musicals, biopics, historical dramas, women's films, and even horror films.

Regardless of the genre, prestige pictures were injected with plenty of star power, glamorous and elegant trappings, and elaborate special effects. Irving Thalberg devised the concept of multistar vehicles to make MGM's top prestige pictures. Industry practices dictated that one or two names were necessary to carry a typical class-A picture, but MGM, having the largest roster of stars in Hollywood, infused some of its prestige pictures with a galaxy of stars to generate maximum impact at the box office. GRAND HOTEL (1932), for example, listed six stars, four of whom were among the biggest draws in Hollywood—Greta Garbo, John Barrymore, Joan Crawford, and Wallace Beery. RASPUTIN AND THE EMPRESS (1932) was designed as a vehicle for the three Barrymores—John, Ethel, and Lionel—the royal family of the American stage, and was the only picture in which they appeared together. DINNER AT EIGHT (1933) listed eight stars, five of whom lived up to their billing—Wallace Beery, the Barrymore brothers, Marie Dressler, and Jean Harlow.

Because of the technical difficulties and added expense of using Technicolor, prestige pictures were shot almost exclusively in black and white. Nonetheless, all prestige pictures were high-ticket items, ranging in cost from $1 million on the average to $4.1 million for the most expensive picture of the era, Selznick's GONE WITH THE WIND (1939). In addition to having bigger budgets, these pictures were longer than the 70–90-minute running time of the average feature. HELL'S ANGELS (1930), which was released with a 135-minute running time, held the record for sound films until MGM's THE GREAT ZIEGFELD (1936), which lasted 4 minutes short of three hours. Selznick's GONE WITH THE WIND lasted 220 minutes and set a new record.

At the exhibition level, prestige pictures were given splashy premieres and the roadshow treatment. Conventional class-A pictures lasted 80–90 minutes and were normally exhibited on a "grind" basis during first run—that is, on a continuous-performance basis. Prestige pictures, with their longer running times, were particularly suited to roadshowing, which entailed twice-a-day performance, intermissions, and reserved seats. Because the practice also meant higher ticket prices, higher film rentals, and extended runs, this pattern of release had the potential of recouping production costs much faster than normal. However, roadshowing had a downside. Because the practice required an expensive exploitation campaign to be effective, it increased a company's exposure when a picture met resistance at the box office. Roadshowing was popular during the 1930 season, dropped out of favor for two years during the Depression, and then resumed its privileged status for the remainder of the decade, when from six to ten prestige pictures were typically accorded this treatment each year.[2]

The prestige picture, having its roots in the earliest days of the feature film, was an established production trend at the very start of the decade. Nearly all the

Louis Wolheim and Lew Ayres in ALL QUIET ON THE WESTERN FRONT
(Universal, 1930).

titles on *Film Daily*'s Ten Best in 1930 were prestige pictures and ranged in style
from comedy of manners (Pathe's HOLIDAY), to drama (MGM's ANNA CHRISTIE),
to historical biopic (UA's ABRAHAM LINCOLN), to stage-bound melodrama
(Warners' OLD ENGLISH), to war pictures (Universal's ALL QUIET ON THE
WESTERN FRONT). The war picture, with three examples, was the most popular
cycle on the list: Tiffany-Gainsborough's JOURNEY'S END (directed by R. C.
Sherriff) and United Artists' HELL'S ANGELS (Howard Hughes), in addition to
ALL QUIET. This last film, which ranked number one, made a strong pacifist
statement. Based on Erich Maria Remarque's classic antiwar novel, the picture
signaled Universal's intent to carve a niche for itself in the first-run market. To
help adapt the novel, Universal hired the playwright Maxwell Anderson, the
author of the famous antiwar drama *What Price Glory?* Produced at a cost of
$1.45 million by Carl Laemmle, Jr., the picture starred Louis Wolheim and Lew
Ayres and was acclaimed for its vivid and graphic portrayal of trench warfare. To
make this landmark picture, Universal constructed a small town consisting of
thirty-five standing sets and staged the battle scenes over a thousand acres of the
studio's Irvine ranch. Lewis Milestone, the director, enhanced the realism of the
spectacle by bringing "all the fluidity of silent films to the camera—which freely
tracked and panned and soared over the battlefields or the little German
town. . . . At the same time Milestone imaginatively explored the possibilities of

sound." Universal's first entry into the prestige market, ALL QUIET won Oscars for best picture and best director.[3]

Declining admissions during the Depression put a damper on the production of silent-style epics, musical extravaganzas, prestige costume pictures, and other expensive productions. Going against the grain of the market, RKO risked $1.5 million in 1931 to produce CIMARRON (Wesley Ruggles), an epic Western starring Richard Dix that was based on the Edna Ferber best-seller. The picture began with an awe-inspiring re-creation of the 1889 Oklahoma Land Rush that used thousands of extras racing pell-mell on horseback, in wagons, and on foot to stake out claims on the millions of acres on the Cherokee Strip. Although the picture received rave reviews, won an Academy Award for best picture, and even made it to the top echelon of box-office winners in 1931, earning $1.38 million, it still lost money.

Paramount's THE SIGN OF THE CROSS (Cecil B. DeMille) fared better the following year. This, the first historical costume epic of the sound era, marked DeMille's return to the studio after a hiatus of seven years and revived his flagging reputation. Waldemar Young and Sidney Buchman adapted Wilson Barrett's play, which was first filmed in 1914. Charles Laughton gave an outstanding performance as a petulant Nero; Claudette Colbert, as his lascivious wife, Poppaea; Fredric March, as the prefect of Rome, Marcus Superbus; and Elissa Landi, as the Christian maid Mercia. DeMille spent eight weeks and $650,000 to make what the *New York Times* called "an opulent and striking pictorial spectacle."[4] The spectacle included Christians being fed to the lions, gladiator fights, revealing costumes, erotic dancing, and Poppaea taking a bath in a four-hundred-gallon pool of asses' milk. THE SIGN OF THE CROSS failed as a road-show attraction, but redeemed itself in general release.

In 1933, Fox released one of the most highly praised and successful prestige pictures of the period, CAVALCADE (Frank Lloyd, 1933). It was based on Noel Coward's pageant of the twentieth century, the hit of London's 1931–1932 season, and celebrated the experiences of a British upper-class family and their servants from New Year's Eve 1899 to the same evening in 1932. The film remained faithful to its source in most respects. Reginald Berkeley's adaptation repeated the episodic structure of the original and contained vignettes of Jane and Robert Marryot against backdrops of soldiers departing for the Boer War in South Africa, the funeral of Queen Victoria, the voyage of the *Titanic*, the Great War, the Jazz Age, and the Depression. The picture was produced in Hollywood, but the principals—Clive Brook, Diana Wynyard, and Frank Lawton—and other members of the cast were British. Period music was used to capture the spirit of each age, and William S. Darling's authentic-looking settings of Edwardian England—an upper-class home, a pub, a music hall, and Trafalgar Square, among others—evoked a strong sense of nostalgia. Produced by Winfield Sheehan at a cost of $1.25 million, CAVALCADE won Academy Awards for best picture, director, and art direction and grossed close to $4 million during its first release, much of which came from Great Britain and the Empire.

These few pictures were exceptions, for studios mostly had to devise cheaper, alternative ways to sustain prestige production. Warners fed the prestige market by releasing a series of vehicles designed around George Arliss, an aging British character actor. The series began with DISRAELI (Alfred E. Green) at the close of 1929. Making his American theatrical debut in 1902, Arliss played the title role of Louis N. Parker's *Disraeli* several times on stage and once in a silent film. By

CAVALCADE (*Fox, 1932*).

the time Arliss made the sound version, the role had became his trademark. DISRAELI was an enormous hit and enjoyed long runs in New York and other large cities worldwide.

Thereafter, Warners produced motion-picture versions of Arliss's other stage vehicles. OLD ENGLISH (Alfred E. Green), based on John Galsworthy's novel *The Stoic*, made it to *Film Daily*'s Ten Best in 1930. Arliss's subsequent prestige vehicles for Warners included two biopics, ALEXANDER HAMILTON (1931) and VOLTAIRE (1933), both of which were directed by John Adolfi. Arliss's pictures did not earn money: for one thing his acting style was considered old-fashioned; for another, his films were stage-bound. Nonetheless, Arliss was a public-relations success. As *Variety* put it, "allowing that none of this English star's films may have been dynamic successes, nevertheless, it may be said that the Arliss releases were an opening wedge and many a film will profit by the pioneering of this British actor and his type of work."[5]

United Artists released two noteworthy pictures by Samuel Goldwyn, STREET SCENE (King Vidor, 1931) and ARROWSMITH (John Ford, 1932). Prestige for Goldwyn meant Pulitzer Prize winners and Nobel laureates. STREET SCENE was based on Elmer Rice's 1929 Pulitzer Prize–winning play about big-city tenement life. Since the play was regarded as a masterpiece of American naturalism and had been produced in many countries, Goldwyn decided to respect the original and brought Rice to Hollywood to write the screenplay. Goldwyn signed Sylvia

Sidney to play the lead and hired nearly a dozen actors from the Broadway cast to reprise their roles in the film. Richard Day designed an authentic-looking single set of a Manhattan West Side street, complete with elevated tracks that preserved the unity of place of the original production. Alfred Newman added an extra dimension to the film by composing a main theme reminiscent of Gershwin's *Rhapsody in Blue* to conjure up the hustle and cacophony of city life. ARROW-SMITH was based on the 1925 Pulitzer Prize–winning novel by Sinclair Lewis, who in 1930 became America's first Nobel laureate in literature. Lewis's novel was an exposé of the medical profession. As adapted by playwright Sidney Howard, the film subordinated the exposé elements of the novel as it followed an idealistic young doctor and hopeful scientist, Martin Arrowsmith (Ronald Colman), and his unselfish wife, Leora (Helen Hayes), from a small-town practice in North Dakota, to a research institute in New York, to an isolated island in the West Indies, to a farm in Vermont. Richard Day's sets included an impressive streamlined modern research facility, the McGurk Research Institute, which is used "as a symbol for the sterile, antihumanistic values ascribed to in the 'pure' science idealism of Dr. Arrowsmith." In producing pictures such as these, the *New York Times* said, Goldwyn was a "pioneer picture producer who has quite often shown a desire to lead the public rather than follow it."[6]

MGM, the only studio to go through the Depression unscathed, had the most success exploiting the prestige picture. Describing the company's position in the industry, *Fortune* said in 1932 that "for the past five years, Metro-Goldwyn-Mayer has made the best and most successful moving pictures in the United States. No one in Hollywood would dream of contradicting this flat statement." To produce the yearly roster of pictures, Louis B. Mayer and Irving Thalberg operated without fiscal constraints. As Ronald Haver put it, they felt free "to spend as much as necessary to do it right. This lordly disregard for money was one of the things that made picturemaking at MGM such an obsession with the people who worked there during its years of greatness."[7]

Twelve MGM pictures made it to *Film Daily's* Ten Best in the years 1930–1933, four of which were prestige pictures—ANNA CHRISTIE (Clarence Brown, 1930), GRAND HOTEL (Edmund Goulding, 1932), THE GUARDSMAN (Sidney Franklin, 1931), and RASPUTIN AND THE EMPRESS (Richard Boleslawski, 1932). Practically all of the studio's twenty-two films on the list in the rest of the 1930s fell into this category. Going into the thirties, Irving Thalberg looked to the theater for story ideas and talent to make his prestige pictures. MGM had held back Greta Garbo's talking debut as long as possible, worried that her Swedish accent would be unacceptable for the new medium. Thalberg found the perfect vehicle in Eugene O'Neill's *Anna Christie*, a naturalistic drama about a waterfront prostitute that won a Pulitzer Prize in 1921. In one sense, ANNA CHRISTIE departed from the typical Garbo vehicle in that "Garbo wore only the drabbest of clothes amid the most sordid surroundings"; in another sense, it continued her established pattern. Garbo played a poor farm girl who runs away from drudgery, becomes a prostitute, falls for a seaman, loses him when she tells him of her past, but wins him back in the end. Garbo's accent sounded natural in the role because the heroine was also Swedish. Moreover, the adaptation built up suspense by delaying her entrance until well over thirty minutes into the film. And when she said her first lines, "Gimme a viskey. Chinger ale on the side. An' don't be stingy, babee," audiences applauded. *Variety* said, " 'Garbo talks' is, beyond quarrel, an event of major box office significance."[8]

Thalberg next signed the most glamorous and sophisticated couple of the American stage, Alfred Lunt and Lynn Fontanne, to make THE GUARDSMAN. Produced at a cost of $374,000, the picture was a faithful adaptation of Ferenc Molnár's comedy of manners, which the Lunts originally performed for the Theatre Guild in 1924. *Variety* said of the picture, "To the sophisticated it is all sublimated high comedy; to the commonality of gum chewers, it will be either a dark mystery or a sacrilege."[9] The failure of the picture convinced the Lunts to confine their considerable talents to Broadway.

Failing to develop the Lunts into motion-picture stars, Thalberg tried to transform his wife, Norma Shearer, into "the screen equivalent of a great lady of the theater." To begin, Thalberg teamed Shearer with Robert Montgomery in PRIVATE LIVES (Sidney Franklin, 1931), an adaptation of Noel Coward's sophisticated comedy, which he designed as a vehicle for himself and Gertrude Lawrence and which had enjoyed long runs the year before in London and New York. Thalberg then teamed Shearer with Clark Gable in STRANGE INTERLUDE (Robert Z. Leonard, 1932), MGM's second adaptation of a Pulitzer Prize–winning drama by Eugene O'Neill. This controversial play had been a hit starring Lynn Fontanne during its original 1928 Broadway run, but Thalberg's production was only politely received, mostly because of its unconventional use of voiceover to replicate the play's asides that were spoken directly to the audience to reveal a character's thoughts.

Thalberg's sorcery worked better for GRAND HOTEL, a multicharacter picture based on Vicki Baum's best-seller *Menschen im Hotel*. MGM acquired the motion-picture rights to the book for $6,000, but with the proviso that the studio would finance a dramatization of the novel on Broadway. William A. Drake did the adaptation, which was produced by Herman Shumlin for $55,000. The play was a big hit and earned MGM a handsome profit as well as the property. Drake wrote the screenplay with Frances Marion (uncredited). The all-star cast contained Greta Garbo as the world-weary ballerina Grusinskaya, John Barrymore as the luckless Baron von Geigern, Joan Crawford as the hotel stenographer Flaemmchen, Wallace Beery as the ruthless industrialist Preysing, and Lionel Barrymore as the downtrodden clerk Kringelein. In addition to the illustrious cast, the appeal of the picture resided in the art deco sets designed by Cedric Gibbons, in the gowns by Adrian, and the influential GRAND HOTEL narrative formula, which interwove the stories of a cross section of humanity within a single setting. Produced at a cost of $700,000, the picture was given road-show treatment and grossed nearly $2.6 million the first year of its release. It won the Academy Award for best picture and ranked number one on *Film Daily*'s Ten Best.

Producing RASPUTIN AND THE EMPRESS, Thalberg united the royal family of the American stage for the first and only time the Barrymores would appear together on the screen. Lionel had joined MGM in 1926; John had signed a non-exclusive contract with the studio in 1931; but Ethel had remained content with the theater. In getting her to do RASPUTIN, Thalberg hoped to entice her to sign a long-term contract. John, who was billed first, played Prince Chegodieff, Rasputin's assassin; Ethel played the czarina; and Lionel played the mad monk Rasputin. Written by Charles MacArthur and directed by Richard Boleslawski, a Russian-trained Polish expatriate, this historical epic of the tragic Romanovs cost $1 million. Although the Barrymores received good notices, the picture could not recover the huge outlay and became one of the studio's costlier failures.

Publicity poster for GRAND HOTEL *(MGM, 1932).*

Thalberg's heart attack in 1932 convinced Louis B. Mayer to reorganize the studio by creating autonomous production units to replace the central-producer system. To share responsibility for MGM's prestige pictures, Mayer hired his son-in-law, David O. Selznick, another "boy genius," who had just finished a successful production stint at RKO. For his MGM debut, Selznick followed in Thalberg's footsteps by producing DINNER AT EIGHT (1933), based on the George S. Kaufman–Edna Ferber 1932 comedy hit containing interlocking stories about the behind-the-scenes events leading up to a posh Manhattan dinner party. Envisioning a multi-star vehicle along the lines of GRAND HOTEL, Selznick chose Frances Marion and Herman J. Mankiewicz to write the screenplay. George Cukor, who had just finished LITTLE WOMEN for RKO, was brought in to direct. The picture cost only $387,000 to make, received excellent reviews, and returned more than $3 million in rentals to MGM.

Two prestige pictures released in 1933 forecast the future course of the trend. The first, UA's THE PRIVATE LIFE OF HENRY VIII, was a historical biopic produced and directed in Great Britain by Alexander Korda. Starring Charles Laughton in the title role, the picture premiered at the Radio City Music Hall on 12 October 1933. Produced at the modest cost of £60,000, the picture grossed about $500,000 in the United States, an enormous amount for a British picture, and much more abroad. Laughton's virtuoso performance won him an Academy Award, the first Oscar ever awarded to a British-made film. Korda also proved to the world that a British film could match the spectacle and lavishness of anything produced in Hollywood, which sparked a brief interest in the United States in British costume pictures and historical biopics in general.

The second 1933 prestige film, RKO's LITTLE WOMEN (George Cukor), was considered the first picture of the decade based on a literary classic to be turned into an artistic and commercial success. Initiated by David O. Selznick before he joined MGM, the project was revived by his successor, Merian C. Cooper, as a vehicle for RKO's newest star, Katharine Hepburn. Sarah Y. Mason and Victor Heerman adapted Louisa May Alcott's novel, winning an Oscar for their efforts. *Variety* described the picture as a superb "human document, sombre in tone, stately and slow in movement, but always eloquent in its interpretations. . . . There doesn't occur a picture in recent film history produced with so uncompromising a degree of sincerity, or one that so wholeheartedly aims at an honest realization of a significant novel of another era." Earning $800,000 in profits, LITTLE WOMEN became one of RKO's biggest hits of the decade.[10] It was nominated for an Academy Award as best picture and ranked number five on *Film Daily'* Top Ten list of 1934.

A second wave of prestige pictures hit the market early in 1934 "in numbers so thick as to constitute the champion of cycles since sound came in," said *Variety*.[11] They consisted mostly of historical biopics, among them MGM's QUEEN CHRISTINA (Rouben Mamoulian), VIVA VILLA! (Jack Conway), and THE BARRETTS OF WIMPOLE STREET (Sidney Franklin); Paramount's THE SCARLETT EMPRESS (Josef von Sternberg) and CLEOPATRA (Cecil B. DeMille); and UA's HOUSE OF ROTHSCHILD (Alfred L. Werker).

MGM's THE BARRETTS OF WIMPOLE STREET ranked number one on *Film Daily's* Ten Best. Based on Rudolf Besier's genteel dramatic biography of Elizabeth Barrett, which had enjoyed a long Broadway run with Katharine Cornell in the starring role, THE BARRETTS OF WIMPOLE STREET united three

Jean Harlow and Wallace Beery in DINNER AT EIGHT *(MGM, 1933)*.

Oscar winners—Norma Shearer, who played "the captive maiden" Elizabeth Barrett; Fredric March, "the dashing young knight" Robert Browning; and Charles Laughton, Elizabeth's "cruel ogre father." The *New York Times* said, "For the high-minded aspiration which went into the production, there can be nothing less than a shout of benediction. Hollywood could make no more fitting answer to her critics than this." The picture not only gave Shearer her most widely acclaimed great-lady-of-the-theater role but also earned a substantial profit.[12]

The number of prestige pictures rose dramatically thereafter, and for the remainder of the decade they constituted 50 percent of the pictures on *Film Daily*'s Ten Best. The traditional explanation for the revival of the prestige picture was that pressure from the Legion of Decency forced the industry to launch its Better Pictures Campaign of 1934. For example, during the height of the Legion of Decency campaign, *Variety* reported,

> Buffeted by church and reformer into the greatest amount of space ever concentrated in the country's newspapers over any other two months in its history, and faced with another accounting of its stewardship to the public in the fall, filmdom is taking advantage of the national recess on a clean screen to do some things it has never done before. It is delving furiously into major company archives for facts [to produce period pictures]. ("What the Public Wants," 7 August 1934, p. 1)

Looking back to the causes of the revival, the *Motion Picture Herald* observed two years later,

> An increasing demand for better pictures, crystalized in the Legion of Decency movement in 1934, led to the voluntary adoption by the industry of higher standards of production and the resultant success of a group of literary masterpieces, so-called, made into pictures has been so great that today a larger number of the "million dollar" productions than ever before are built around notable literary successes, either old or new. ("Producers Aim Classics," 15 August 1936, p. 13)

But these explanations ignore the economics of producing prestige pictures. The ability of prestige pictures to attract audiences was well understood by Hollywood. However, the heavy investments required to make these pictures placed them out of reach of most companies until general economic conditions improved and operations stabilized. Stated another way, the majors waited out the worst of the Depression and revived the trend when people had more disposable income to spend on entertainment.

Improved conditions at the box office meant that prestige pictures could resume their privileged places on production rosters. By 1936, the so-called million-dollar grosser was "no longer the rarity it [had] been during the long, lean years following the 1929 attack of indigestion in [the] industry," said *Variety*. Typically only a dozen or so pictures grossed $1 million in any given year. But in 1936 forty surpassed that mark. Concurrently, the million-dollar production became commonplace. *Variety* reported that at least thirty-five titles on the 1937–1938 release schedules cost more than $1 million, and of these, two or three had budgets of more than $2 million.[13]

To broaden the potential market for prestige pictures, Hollywood even flirted with producing Shakespeare. Educated middle-class Americans were not habitual moviegoers. In 1936 the Hays Office estimated that 36 million such people attended the movies infrequently, as little as once a year or only for special pictures. Warners spearheaded the crusade to capture this market by producing A MIDSUMMER NIGHT'S DREAM (1935), a decision that *Variety* described as "probably the biggest gamble ever taken by any picture company or producer." The decision to produce the first Shakespearean talkie also marked a switch in policy at Warners away from "its exclusive image as producer of popular realist films" to big-budget prestige pictures.[14]

Warners planned to re-create for the screen Max Reinhardt's outdoor production of the play presented at the eighteen-thousand-seat Hollywood Bowl during the summer of 1934. Germany's most important stage producer and director, Reinhardt had immigrated to Hollywood to escape Nazi persecution. Reinhardt's innovative staging of Shakespeare's play, which included "a lovely ballet of the fairies and a startling performance by a boy actor named Mickey Rooney in the role of Puck," attracted capacity crowds and prompted *Variety* to announce, "Shakespeare had made good in Hollywood!"[15]

Pulling out all the stops, Warners budgeted $1.3 million for the picture, an extremely large amount by the studio's standards, and scheduled a seventy-day shoot. Warners hired Reinhardt to direct the picture, but since Reinhardt had little experience with the ways of Hollywood, the studio assigned contract director William Dieterle, a former pupil of the impresario, to co-direct. Screenwriters Charles Kenyon and Mary McCall, Jr., preserved the play almost word for word. Anton Grot designed a fantastic fairy-tale forest on two large soundstages and magnificent interior sets and props. Because Grot's immense forest overpowered the actors, cinematographer Hal Mohr was brought in to redesign it and to devise a new lighting system. He won an Academy Award for his efforts. Erich Wolfgang Korngold arranged and elaborately executed the score, using Mendelssohn's incidental music for the play. The two ballet sequences were directed by Nijinska. The cast was drawn mainly from Warners' contract-player roster. Dick Powell played Lysander; James Cagney, Bottom; Victor Jory, Oberon; Joe E. Brown, Flute; Olivia de Havilland, Hermia; and Anita Louise, Titania. To play Puck, Mickey Rooney was borrowed from MGM.

Warners launched the picture simultaneously in New York and London on 9 October 1935 and then in other capitals around the world the next day. A gala opening at the Warners Theatre in Beverly Hills was set for the following week. To prepare audiences for the roadshow release in the United States, Warners distributed low-priced editions of the play to schools, literary societies, and cultural groups; planted stories and photographs of the principal cast at work in hundreds of magazines and newspapers; and gave away recordings of Mendelssohn's incidental music to radio stations. "Not a schoolchild lives in America today who hasn't heard about the picture, written essays about it, and then ducked seeing it, if possible," said *Variety*.[16]

The picture was a succès d'estime. For example, the *New York Times* said, "If this is no masterpiece, it is a brave, beautiful and interesting effort to subdue the

Olivia de Havilland and Dick Powell in A Midsummer Night's Dream *(Warners, 1935).*

most difficult of Shakespeare's works. . . . It is a credit to Warner Brothers and to the motion picture industry." *Variety* also praised the picture for its public-relations value and added that Warners would not be perturbed if it lost $500,000 on the project.[17]

Hollywood's next venture into Shakespeare, MGM's ROMEO AND JULIET (1936), surpassed Warners' A MIDSUMMER NIGHT'S DREAM in lavishness and scope. Starring Norma Shearer and Leslie Howard, the picture was produced by Irving Thalberg at a cost of $2 million. To assist Cedric Gibbons and Adrian in the design of the sets and costumes, the studio dispatched Oliver Messel, a British art expert, to Verona, Italy, where his staff took thousands of pictures so that the Renaissance could be captured on the screen as never before. Talbot Jennings created a cinematic adaptation of the play by trimming about a fourth of the verse and by opening up the action beyond the confines of the stage. George Cukor, who brought LITTLE WOMEN and DAVID COPPERFIELD to life, was entrusted with the direction. Choreographer Agnes de Mille staged the period dances at the Capulet ball.[18]

An ecstatic Frank Nugent of the *New York Times* said, "Never before, in all its centuries, has the play received so handsome a production . . . the picture reflects great credit upon its producers and upon the screen as a whole. It's a dignified, sensitive and entirely admirable Shakespearean—not Hollywoodean —production." MGM's exploitation campaign was even more extensive than Warners' and reached millions of people. However, when the picture posted a $900,000 loss, *Variety* concluded that the Shakespeare cycle was a "B.O. Washout . . . over almost before it got around the first curve. What started out to be the beginning of a new era of enlightenment at the studios and the propulsion that was to fill the theatres with new audiences has ended on a note of disappointment."[19]

Thereafter, biopics, costume-adventure pictures, adaptations of literary masterpieces, and even the class-A Western became the staples of prestige production. Of the group, the biopic was most esteemed. The motion picture most responsible for building this reputation was Warners' THE LIFE OF EMILE ZOLA (William Dieterle, 1937), starring Paul Muni. One of the most honored motion pictures of the era, THE LIFE OF EMILE ZOLA won an Academy Award and the New York Film Critics Circle Award for best picture and made it to the number-one spots on the *Film Daily* and *New York Times* Ten Best lists. Muni had won an Oscar the year before for his performance in the title role of THE STORY OF LOUIS PASTEUR (William Dieterle, 1936), which launched a series of biopics that made him, in Nick Roddick's words, "a kind of thinking man's Lon Chaney, impersonating the great men of history . . . aided by extensive make-up jobs." Muni and the Warners biopic set a high standard, and the appearance of a star in a biopic was taken as an index of his or her seriousness as an artist.[20]

Biopics depicted European personages at first, but by the end of the decade the focus shifted more to American heroes such as Alexander Graham Bell, Knute Rockne, Florenz Ziegfeld, and Abraham Lincoln. Hollywood preferred foreign biographies because they "carried with them virtually no audience preconceptions, and were thus more easily adjusted to contemporary values." For example, the *New York Herald Tribune* said that Twentieth Century's THE HOUSE OF ROTHSCHILD (1934) "belongs very definitely to the type of historical narrative that is concerned, not with escape, but with a parallel to present-day conditions.

With a shrewd eye on the current plight of the Jews in Hitler's Germany, the picture shows its Semitic family as the victims of race hatred and Nordic oppression." In an attempt to explain the shift to Americana in biopics, Paul Vanderwood noted that Hollywood was following the lead of historians, biographers, and writers who reacted to deteriorating world conditions by burrowing "backward into the national consciousness to discover how their predecessors had survived the pressures of their most difficult times."[21]

The costume-adventure film was revived by two 1934 hits—MGM's TREASURE ISLAND (Victor Fleming) and Reliance-United Artists' THE COUNT OF MONTE CRISTO (Rowland V. Lee). A spirited adaptation of Robert Louis Stevenson's classic, TREASURE ISLAND starred Wallace Beery as Long John Silver and Jackie Cooper as Jim Hawkins. Containing "as fine a lot of cutthroats as ever have infested a film," TREASURE ISLAND was one of the year's biggest box-office attractions. THE COUNT OF MONTE CRISTO, based on Alexandre Dumas's historical novel, had been made several times as a silent. Reliance's version, which was named to *Film Daily*'s Ten Best, starred Robert Donat as Edmond Dantès in his American film debut. "A walloping melodrama of revenge, conceived on the grand scale," MONTE CRISTO "is made in heaven for the manufacturers of the costume film drama," said the *New York Times.*[22]

Adventure films dealt "with make-believe, with soldiers-of-fortune, explorers, pirates, avengers, rescuers and trouble-shooters" drawn from Sir Walter Scott, Robert Louis Stevenson, Alexandre Dumas, Rafael Sabatini, and other masters of historical fiction.[23] The perfect escapist fare for an audience coming out of the Depression, the swashbuckler

> dealt with the heroic virtues. Usually there was an idealized hero defending the honor of a lady in a chivalrous and charming manner. Evil-incarnate villains were to be dispatched, but in a "romantically violent," stylized series of action set-pieces that were usually rendered with less than graphic reality. Color, dash, romantic order, and excitement prevailed, and in the end, of course, there was the triumph of good over evil. Here was audience wish fulfillment on a grand scale. (Rudy Behlmer, ed., *The Sea Hawk* [Madison: University of Wisconsin Press, 1982], pp. 13–14)

Warners became the leading purveyor of costume-adventure pictures by producing a series of Errol Flynn swashbucklers; however, just about every company tried its hand at the cycle.

The popularity of the costume-adventure picture also helped revive the prestige Western. Consigned mostly to the B ranks since CIMARRON went down to defeat in 1931, the class-A Western had been kept alive almost single-handedly by Paramount, which produced TEXAS RANGERS (King Vidor, 1936), THE PLAINSMAN (Cecil B. DeMille, 1936), WELLS FARGO (Frank Lloyd, 1937), and THE TEXANS (James Hogan, 1938). Beginning in 1939, as reported by *Variety*, there flowed from Hollywood "the rootin', tootin', shootin'est, bowie-knife-wielding bunch of ride-'em'-cowboy, major budget westerns the picture biz has witnessed in a decade."[24] According to the trade paper, it was a "tossup" whether Paramount's UNION PACIFIC (Cecil B. DeMille) or Fox's JESSE JAMES (Henry King) revived the cycle, but that season also saw the release of UA's STAGECOACH

UNION PACIFIC *(Paramount, 1939)*.

(John Ford), Warners' DODGE CITY (Michael Curtiz), Fox's DRUMS ALONG THE MOHAWK (John Ford), and Universal's DESTRY RIDES AGAIN (George Marshall), among others.

The comeback of the class-A Western can be attributed to fact that "oaters," as they were known in the trade, had never really lost their appeal. As *Variety* observed, "a good western picture never misses at the box office. From the earliest film days . . . the western has held its place against all other types of popular stories. There have been times when the majors have left the field to the independent producers. But they return. Then the western, produced on a grand scale, is revived and invariably, when well done, is handsomely rewarded." Another cause was the "surge of Americanism sweeping the country" as tensions in Europe increased. Hollywood no doubt wanted to boost national morale by producing these pictures; but it might also have anticipated the closing of foreign markets by tailor-making a cycle mainly for domestic consumption.[25]

Of note here is that two Westerns released in 1939 were accorded prestige treatment. Testifying to the potential drawing power of the cycle, Warners and Paramount launched DODGE CITY and UNION PACIFIC, respectively, with special premieres in locales, as *Variety* put it, "indigenous to the subject matter" of the pictures. Premiering its picture, Warners dispatched trains carrying 350 stars and studio executives from Hollywood and New York to Dodge City, Kansas. The trains stopped at cities along the way to promote the picture, making the "hinterland feel . . . as important and big with its $3 premiere as Hollywood in the past with its five- and ten-dollar openings." The festivities at Dodge City, which had a population of 10,000, attracted a crowd of 75,000. In total, Warners spent $75,000 on the premiere and considered the money well spent.

Paramount's premiere of UNION PACIFIC was even grander. President Roosevelt was enlisted to strike a telegraph key from his desk to start the celebration in Omaha, Nebraska, which included a banquet and parade that attracted over 250,000. Afterward, Paramount planned a ten-thousand-mile train tour carrying the film's stars and studio publicity men to coincide with the opening of the picture in first-run cities.[26] As will be discussed later, Selznick took this publicity practice to its apogee when he launched GONE WITH THE WIND.

The principal producers of prestige pictures after 1934 consisted of MGM, Warners, and United Artists in that order. 20th Century–Fox was a close runner-up and produced a series of biopics that included LLOYD'S OF LONDON (Henry King, 1936), THE PRISONER OF SHARK ISLAND (John Ford, 1936), SUEZ (Allan Dwan, 1938), JESSE JAMES (Henry King, 1939), STANLEY AND LIVINGSTONE (Henry King, 1939), THE STORY OF ALEXANDER GRAHAM BELL (Irving Cummings, 1939), SWANEE RIVER (Sidney Lanfield, 1939), and YOUNG MR. LINCOLN (John Ford, 1939). All were "romances of personal success and triumph over adversity."

Three Fox pictures made it to *Film Daily*'s Ten Best—IN OLD CHICAGO (1938), ALEXANDER'S RAGTIME BAND (1938), and STANLEY AND LIVINGSTONE (1939), all of which were directed by Henry King. The first two pictures are prestige musicals and are discussed in the following section. STANLEY AND LIVINGSTONE, an example of "Hollywood's fervent Anglophilia," owed much of its structure to Warners' LIFE OF EMILE ZOLA. Spencer Tracy played Henry Stanley, the American newspaperman, and Cedric Hardwicke, Dr. David Livingstone, the British explorer and missionary.

RKO and Paramount lagged far behind other members of the Big Five. RKO followed up LITTLE WOMEN (1933) with John Ford's THE INFORMER (1935), a "sleeper" starring Victor McLaglen that found its own way to the public. Dudley Nichols adapted Liam O'Flaherty's novel set in Dublin about a despicable drunk who would lie and betray anyone to save his own skin. Shot in seventeen days at a cost of around $260,000, the picture opened to adulatory reviews, but it withered at the box office. However, after being named best picture by the New York Film Critics and after winning Oscars for best director, best actor, and best adaptation, word-of-mouth advertising revived the picture.

Afterward, RKO had little commercial success with its prestige pictures until 1939. Among the many fine pictures released by the studio that year were two outstanding prestige pictures produced by Pandro S. Berman, THE HUNCHBACK OF NOTRE DAME (William Dieterle, 1939), a horror picture based on the Victor Hugo classic, starring Charles Laughton, and GUNGA DIN (George Stevens, 1939), a costume adventure picture based vaguely on a Rudyard Kipling poem, starring Cary Grant, Victor McLaglen, and Douglas Fairbanks, Jr.

Paramount produced only one prestige film that made it to the *Film Daily* list after 1934, LIVES OF A BENGAL LANCER (Henry Hathaway, 1935), a Kiplingesque adventure film produced by Louis D. Lighton about a gallant band of British fighting men who guard the northern frontier of Britain's empire in India. Cecil B. DeMille, Paramount's main purveyor of prestige films, faltered throughout much of the decade. After the conversion to sound, DeMille switched from

depicting "the marital misadventures of the leisured class" to historical and
frontier epics, such as CLEOPATRA, THE PLAINSMAN, and UNION PACIFIC.[27]
Although CLEOPATRA is best remembered today for its immense stylized sets,
writhing and gyrating dancers, gaudy showmanship, and Claudette Colbert's
provocative costumes, UNION PACIFIC, a saga of the first transcontinental
railroad, starring Joel McCrea and Barbara Stanwyck and complete with
spectacular train wrecks, Indian sieges, and colorful characters, was his most
successful picture at the box office.

Among the Little Three, Columbia was the only other studio besides UA to
produce a prestige picture. Columbia's only entry, Frank Capra's LOST HORIZON
(1937), was based on James Hilton's novel about a Utopian civilization hidden in
Tibet called Shangri-La and was produced at a cost of over $2.5 million, an
incredible sum for the studio. Coming nowhere close to recouping its production
costs, LOST HORIZON was responsible for the drop in Columbia's profits from a
high of $1.8 million in 1935, the year following the release of IT HAPPENED ONE
NIGHT, to a mere $180,000 in 1938.

Analyzing MGM a second time, *Fortune* reported in 1939 that the studio "has
for at least eight years made far and away the best pictures of any studio in
Hollywood. Metro's gross revenue from film rentals has been consistently higher
than that of other studios, and as a result Loews', Inc., has been and still is the
most profitable movie company in the world."[28]

Irving Thalberg, in his capacity as a special-projects producer, delivered three
prestige pictures before his untimely death in 1936—MUTINY ON THE BOUNTY
(Frank Lloyd, 1935), ROMEO AND JULIET (George Cukor, 1936), and THE GOOD
EARTH (Sidney Franklin, 1937). MUTINY ON THE BOUNTY was the most successful. Based on novels by Charles Nordhoff and James Norman Hall, this
adventure classic starred Charles Laughton as the sadistic Captain Bligh of
HMS *Bounty* and Clark Gable and Franchot Tone as his antagonists, Fletcher
Christian and Roger Byam. Produced at the then-astronomical cost of $2 million
and shot largely on location using life-size reproductions of the ships *Bounty* and
Pandora, the picture grossed $4.3 million, making it one of the biggest money-
makers of the decade. The *New York Times* called it "just about the perfect
adventure picture."[29] *Film Daily*'s poll ranked it number one. In the Academy
Award sweepstakes, all three leads—Laughton, Gable, and Tone—were nominated as best actor, a first in the history of the awards. They lost to Victor
McLaglen in THE INFORMER, but MUTINY ON THE BOUNTY captured the Oscar
for best picture.

Thalberg got the idea of doing THE GOOD EARTH after attending a Theatre
Guild dramatization of Pearl S. Buck's Pulitzer Prize–winning novel in 1932
that starred Claude Rains and Alla Nazimova. Thalberg spent three years and
$2.8 million on the picture, the most MGM had spent on a film since BEN-HUR
(1925). To make this epic about Chinese life as authentic as possible, Thalberg
dispatched a second unit to China, where it shot 2 million feet of footage to be
used for process shots to create the proper atmosphere. Cedric Gibbons and unit
art director Harry Oliver worked two years designing and constructing a replica
of a Chinese province, complete with peasant huts, palace, and rice paddies on
five hundred acres in the San Fernando Valley. Meanwhile, the script by Talbot
Jennings, Tess Schlesinger, and Claudine West underwent constant revision. Paul
Muni was borrowed from Warners to play the farmer Wang, and Luise Rainer was
chosen to play his wife O-lan.

Clark Gable and Charles Laughton in Mutiny on the Bounty *(MGM, 1935).*

Thalberg died early into the shoot, and Albert Lewin, his associate, took over. MGM released the picture with the dedication "To the memory of Irving Grant Thalberg," which marked the first time a Thalberg project at MGM carried his name. A. Arnold Gillespie's special effects depicting a plague of locusts attacking the crops and Karl Freund's camerawork created a picture of immense visual appeal. Frank Nugent of the *New York Times* called The Good Earth "one of the finest things Hollywood has done this season or any other."[30] A month after the picture's release, MGM scored a great publicity coup when Rainer and Muni were voted Academy Awards for their previous year's performances in The Story of Louis Pasteur and The Great Ziegfeld, respectively. At Academy Award time the following year, Luise Rainer won the best-actress Oscar for her performance as O-lan, which accomplished the seemingly impossible feat of winning back-to-back Oscars.

David O. Selznick, who had rapidly become Thalberg's equal as a producer of prestige pictures, specialized in translating literary masterpieces to the screen. Little Women had vindicated his "long-held belief that, contrary to industry tradition, classics were not taboo screen material, but could, with proper care and intelligent handling, be turned into artistic and commercial smashes."[31] Selznick put his ideas into practice in 1935, his last year at MGM, by turning out three such pictures, all of which made it to *Film Daily*'s Ten Best and were enthusiastically received.

David Copperfield (George Cukor, 1935), adapted from the Dickens classic by Howard Estabrook and Hugh Walpole, starred Freddie Bartholomew, Selznick's newest discovery, in the title role. In a bit of offbeat casting, W. C. Fields played Micawber, and Roland Young, Uriah Heep. Although Selznick and Cukor had scouted England for suitable locations, the film was ultimately shot on the MGM lot at a cost of little over $1 million. The *New York Times* hailed it as a "gorgeous photoplay which encompasses the rich and kindly humanity of the original so brilliantly that it becomes a screen masterpiece in its own right. The immortal people of *David Copperfield* . . . troop across the . . . screen like animated duplicates of the famous Phiz drawings, an irresistible and enormously heartwarming procession."[32] A great hit with the public, the picture ranked number one on *Film Daily*'s Ten Best.

Selznick next produced ANNA KARENINA (Clarence Brown, 1935), a vehicle designed for Greta Garbo. Playing opposite John Gilbert in 1927, Garbo had made a silent version of the Tolstoy novel for MGM entitled LOVE. In Selznick's remake, which was written by Clemence Dane, Salka Viertel, and S. N. Behrman, Fredric March played her lover, Vronsky; Basil Rathbone, her husband, Karenin; and Freddie Bartholomew, her son, Sergei. Mounted with a scrupulous regard for period authenticity, Selznick's picture emphasized the implicit social criticism in Tolstoy's novel by depicting Muscovite society of the 1870s as decadent and frivolous. Although ANNA KARENINA cost well over a $1 million, Brown's direction of this poignant, tragic story, which brought the best out of Garbo, made the picture a critical and commercial success.

For his final MGM entry, Selznick turned to another Dickens classic, A TALE OF TWO CITIES (Jack Conway, 1935), which "outdid even *David Copperfield* in spectacular scope and dramatic force."[33] Adapted by W. P. Lipscomb and S. N. Behrman, the picture had an impressive cast headed by Ronald Colman as Sydney Carton and dramatized memorable scenes of the French Revolution such as the storming of the Bastille, mass rioting for meat, and the kangaroo-court trials leading to the guillotine.

After Selznick left MGM to become an independent producer, the studio promoted Hunt Stromberg, one of Thalberg's associate producers, to the prestige ranks. Stromberg came through for the company by producing a string of commercial and critical successes that included the Thin Man series, the Jeanette MacDonald–Nelson Eddy operettas, and two big-budget prestige extravaganzas, THE GREAT ZIEGFELD (Robert Z. Leonard, 1936) and MARIE ANTIONETTE (W. S. Van Dyke, 1938). (THE GREAT ZIEGFELD is discussed in the following section.)

MARIE ANTOINETTE, which marked Norma Shearer's triumphant return to the screen after a two-year hiatus, was based on Stefan Zweig's biography. Produced with a running time of 160 minutes (trimmed to 149 minutes after the first runs) and at a cost of $2.3 million, MARIE ANTOINETTE was MGM's most lavish extravaganza of the decade. Bosley Crowther described why:

> Mayer and Stromberg instructed Cedric Gibbons, the studio's head designer, to prepare the most exquisite and impressive settings that could be conceived. Versailles itself was slightly tarnished alongside the palace Gibbons whipped up. He did some exquisite reproductions of the buildings of eighteenth-century France. Ed Willis, the head of the prop department, was sent to Europe to buy furniture and rugs. He stocked his department for all time with the antiques he bought

for *Marie Antoinette.* The costumes were nigh museum items. There were 152 roles to be garbed. The studio's great technical departments were triumphantly tested on this film. (*The Lion's Share,* p. 244)

As the queen of France who died on the guillotine during the revolution, Shearer gave the performance of her career. Fine support was given by Robert Morley, John Barrymore, Joseph Schildkraut, and Gladys George, among others. Tyrone Power, on loan from 20th Century–Fox, was the nominal leading man, but his presence was lost in the spectacle. Although the picture grossed a handsome $3 million, it was not enough to recoup the negative cost.[34]

Of the remaining MGM prestige pictures, several deserve mention. The first, SAN FRANCISCO (W. S. Van Dyke, 1936), was a disaster film with songs. Anita Loos wrote the screenplay from a story by Robert Hopkins, and John Emerson, Loos's husband, co-produced the picture with Bernard Hyman. Set on the Barbary Coast of San Francisco in 1906, the picture teamed Clark Gable, as Blackie Norton, the owner of a music-hall saloon, and Jeanette MacDonald, as Mary Blake, an aspiring prima donna torn between the cabaret and the opera house. MacDonald's numbers alternated between rousing popular songs ("Would You?" and "San Francisco"), religious numbers ("Hosannah" and "Nearer My God to Thee"), and operatic arias. A ten-minute earthquake sequence, the creation of special-effects artist A. Arnold Gillespie and editor John Hoffman, marked the climax, which the *New York Times* described as "a shattering spectacle, one of the truly great cinematic illusions; a monstrous, hideous, thrilling debacle with great fissures opening in the earth, buildings crumbling, men and women apparently being buried beneath showers of stone and plaster, gargoyles lurching from rooftops, watermains bursting, live wires flaring, flame, panic and terror."[35] Produced at a cost of $1.3 million, the picture was a huge hit, making it to *Variety*'s and *Film Daily*'s honor rolls, and inspiring a cycle of big-budget disaster pictures.

Louis D. Lighton, a new producer to MGM's ranks, produced the greatly admired CAPTAINS COURAGEOUS (Victor Fleming, 1937), an adventure picture featuring Freddie Bartholomew and Spencer Tracy that was based on Rudyard Kipling's tale about "an imperious and detestable young scamp who toppled from a liner's rail off the Grand Banks, was picked up by a Portuguese doryman . . . and became a regular fellow during an enforced three-months' fishing cruise."[36] Tracy, who won his first Oscar for best actor, became a star with this picture.

MGM's prestige lineup also includes two noteworthy British pictures, THE CITADEL (1938) and GOODBYE, MR. CHIPS (1939). Both were produced by Victor Saville at MGM's Denham Studios outside London to meet Great Britain's quota requirements for foreign film companies. The quota requirements specified that foreign film companies had to distribute a certain number of pictures each year produced in Great Britain by an all-British cast and crew, with the exception of the director and one star. The law assumed that the presence of these talents in a picture would be enough to make the it palatable for an American audience.

THE CITADEL (King Vidor) was based on A. J. Cronin's novel "about a young Scots doctor who changes objectives in mid-career and has to be jolted back into the line of humble medical service again." Ian Dalrymple, Frank Wead, Elizabeth Hill, and Emlyn Williams wrote the screenplay. Robert Donat

Spencer Tracy, Lionel Barrymore, and Freddie Bartholomew in CAPTAINS COURA-
GEOUS *(MGM, 1937).*

headed the British cast, playing Andrew Manson, M.D., a character whom
Cronin patterned after himself. The American contingent consisted of King
Vidor and Rosalind Russell, who played Donat's wife. According to the *New York
Times*, Vidor succeeded in making a film having "the pace of a Hollywood
production, the honest characterization typical of England's best films, and the
sincerity and depth which are proper to no country but are in the public domain
of drama."[37]

GOODBYE, MR. CHIPS (Sam Wood), another vehicle for Robert Donat, was
based on James Hilton's sentimental novella about a gentle teacher at an English
public school. The *New York Times* described the story as follows: "The Mr.
Chips of the Hilton [fictional] biography was the somewhat dull young pedant
who came to Brookfield's ivy-grown walls in his twenties, took quiet root there,
languished miserably for a decade or two and then, under the tender cultivation
of a woman's hand became such a human, quizzical and understanding person
that all Brookfield eventually began to regard him as an institution."[38] R. C.
Sherriff, Claudine West, and Eric Maschwitz wrote the screenplay. Greer
Garson, making her screen debut, played Chips's wife. Donat's tour de force
performance, in which he aged from twenty-four to eighty-three, was so moving
that he beat out Clark Gable in the Academy Award balloting for best actor. A
smash hit everywhere, the picture topped the *Film Daily* poll.

Warners ranked second in the number of prestige pictures that made it to *Film
Daily*'s Ten Best. After the failure of A MIDSUMMER NIGHT'S DREAM, the studio

turned to the American theater and produced a classic of quite another sort. THE GREEN PASTURES (1936) was based on Marc Connelly's Pulitzer Prize–winning folk drama, which told the creation myth in "terms that a southern black preacher might have used to explain Genesis to his Sunday school pupils." Opening in 1930, the play enjoyed a five-year run on Broadway and on the road with an all-black cast. Warners spent $800,000 to replicate the play. Connelly did the adaptation and shared the directing with William Keighley. And like its Broadway counterpart, the film had an all-black cast featuring Rex Ingram as De Lawd, Oscar Polk as Gabriel, Eddie Anderson as Noah, and Frank Wilson as Moses. Although the nation's press lavished praise on the picture, it did only moderate business. "American racial sensibilities had begun to change [by 1935]," explained Thomas Cripps, and "the movie could make only a fraction of the monumental impact of the Broadway production; it neither celebrated nor memorialized racial history; it merely repeated itself."[39]

Warners got the prestige formula right in 1936 when it produced THE STORY OF LOUIS PASTEUR, ANTHONY ADVERSE, and THE CHARGE OF THE LIGHT BRIGADE. "Thereafter the pattern was set for the rest of the decade," said Nick Roddick. "Energies were concentrated on one major prestige production per year, which almost invariably turned out to be Warners' most successful movie." The key production personnel who shaped the Paul Muni biopics consisted of associate producer Henry Blanke, director William Dieterle, cinematographer Tony Gaudio, and editor Warren Low. PASTEUR established the narrative formula for the pictures, which *Variety* described as follows: "As is usual with films using historical figures as protagonist the menace is the impersonalized symbolism of ignorance and redtape. . . . In each instance the farsighted and heroic central figure fought with narrow-minded and unimaginative defenders of things as they are and won a victory over the obstructive elements."[40]

The conflict in PASTEUR is between "crusading science, on the one hand, and entrenched medical stupidity, on the other," as personified by the French Academy of Sciences and its president. PASTEUR, like most biopics, played fast and loose with the facts. The *New York Times* noted that the picture ignored the work of such scientists as Lister and Koch, and made Pasteur "the only voice crying out in a wilderness of medical ignorance for physicians to wash their hands, boil their instruments and so avoid infecting their patients with puerperal fever." But in defense of the picture, Roddick said, "The screenplay's aim is to make the impact of the hero's discoveries accessible to audiences who know little and care less about preventive medicine in particular and scientific discoveries in general."[41] The Academy of Motion Picture Arts and Sciences seemingly made a similar assessment by awarding Sheridan Gibney and Pierre Collings an Oscar for their screenplay. Muni won the Oscar for best actor.

THE LIFE OF EMILE ZOLA (1937) was clearly designed as a sequel. "Pasteur fought bacteria, while Zola opposed lies. . . . Like Pasteur, who had to face obstacles, Zola had to suffer from defamation, prison, flight, and deportation." However, ZOLA was designed to make more of a political statement than PASTEUR. From the very inception of the project, "the Dreyfus affair" was to be the central focus of the story and Zola's literary career the "backstory." By highlighting Zola's fight to free Captain Alfred Dreyfus, who "was in 1894 accused on the flimsiest evidence (presumably because he was Jewish) of selling military secrets to the Germans and condemned to Devil's Island for life," Warners alluded to anti-Semitism and placed the picture squarely in its tradition

Paul Muni in THE LIFE OF EMILE ZOLA *(Warners, 1937).*

of social consciousness. The *New York Times* said of the picture, "Rich, dignified, honest and strong, it is at once the finest historical film ever made and the greatest screen biography, greater even than *The Story of Louis Pasteur,* with which the Warners squared their conscience last year."[42] Among the honors heaped on the picture, an Academy Award was given to Norman Reilly Raine, Heinz Herald, and Geza Herczeg for their screenplay. Paul Muni was edged out for the best-actor Oscar by Spencer Tracy in CAPTAINS COURAGEOUS, but Joseph Schildkraut, who played Alfred Dreyfus, received the award for best supporting actor.

JUAREZ (1939), the third Muni biopic, was a portrait of Benito Juárez, the Mexican patriot and liberator who overthrew Napoleon III's puppet regime in Mexico in 1867. The screenplay, written by John Huston, Wolfgang Reinhardt, and Aeneas MacKenzie, was based on a play by Franz Werfel and the novel *The Phantom Crown,* by Bertita Harding. Brian Aherne played Maximilian; Bette Davis, his wife, Carlotta; and Claude Rains, Napoleon III. Produced at a cost of $1.25 million, making it by far the most expensive biopic in the series, *Juarez* had far wider scope than the previous Muni biopics, and true to Warners' tradition of social consciousness, it made the most overt political statement of the series. As *Variety* remarked, the picture introduced "historical data that contains current timeliness. There is frequent mention of the Monroe Doctrine, of one-man rule over the lives and destinies of millions, and of the rights of the common man to possess land and work out his own salvation." However, the picture left audiences cool. JUAREZ "had more going against it than its obvious technical and artistic flaws," said Paul Vanderwood. "In 1939 most American were either confused by or unconcerned with international events; not many understood the ideological arguments at hand."[43]

Warners' costume-adventure films fared much better at the box office. Two pictures signaled the shift, CAPTAIN BLOOD (Michael Curtiz, 1935) and AN-THONY ADVERSE (Mervyn LeRoy, 1936). A remake of a 1923 Vitagraph silent, CAPTAIN BLOOD, described by *Variety* as "a lavish, swashbuckling saga of the Spanish main," was released in December 1935 on the heels of MGM's MUTINY ON THE BOUNTY. Casey Robinson adapted Rafael Sabatini's rousing historical novel set in the West Indies of the 1680s about a doctor-turned-pirate who leads his "Brotherhood of Buccaneers" to fight for the cause of England. Warners had originally signed Robert Donat for the lead, but for unknown reasons, he bowed out. The studio then decided to take a gamble on a relatively unknown contract player from Australia, Errol Flynn. Olivia de Havilland, who had come to Warners' attention in A MIDSUMMER NIGHT'S DREAM, was chosen to add romantic interest. The opening scenes dragged, there were inconsistencies in the plot, and the picture contained only one spectacular scene, the climactic sea battle; nonetheless, it was enthusiastically received. It also made stars out of Flynn and de Havilland.

If CAPTAIN BLOOD showed signs of Warners' economizing, ANTHONY AD-VERSE exhibited an uncharacteristic extravagance. Frank Nugent of the *New York Times* introduced the picture as follows:

> America has the tallest buildings, the longest subways, the most chewing gum, the hardiest flag-pole sitters, Hervey Allen's 1,224-page *Anthony Adverse* and the Warner's gargantuan film edition of it. If size is your deity and you feel you will be impressed to hear that eighty-odd speaking parts and a cast of 2,000 have shared the task of translating *Anthony* into film, then you will relish the Strand's new picture. (*NYTFR*, 27 August 1936)

Produced at a cost of more than $1 million, this 141-minute version of Allen's 1933 picaresque novel probably "set Warners on a course of large-scale costume pictures which would continue through to the end of the decade," according to Roddick.[44] Starring Fredric March in the title role, this episodic picture is set in the Napoleonic era and follows the adventures of a young man from Naples to Africa, the Caribbean, and Paris. Although it received mixed reviews, the picture became Warners' most successful picture of the year and even won four Academy Awards, including best supporting actress (Gale Sondergaard, receiving the first-ever Oscar in that category), cinematography, and score.

Having discovered a new star in Errol Flynn, Warners embarked on a cycle of costume-adventure pictures that combined the talents of Flynn with Olivia de Havilland and Michael Curtiz. In all these pictures, Flynn plays "a man for whom moral and political decisions are unambiguous, and who is provided with the chance to put these decisions into practice through direct physical action." Erich Wolfgang Korngold's lush musical scores added immense charm to the cycle.[45]

Basil Rathbone and Errol Flynn in THE ADVENTURES OF ROBIN HOOD *(Warners, 1938).*

THE CHARGE OF THE LIGHT BRIGADE (1936) solidified the cycle. Adapted from the Tennyson poem by Michel Jacoby and Rowland Leigh, the picture was probably inspired by Paramount's LIVES OF A BENGAL LANCER (Henry Hathaway, 1935), which starred Gary Cooper and Franchot Tone. *Variety* called LIGHT BRIGADE a "magnificent production" with countless exploitation possibilities in which Errol Flynn "lives up to the promise of previous film efforts as the youthful major [Geoffrey Vickers] who sacrifices all to avenge the slaughter of his comrades."[46] The "tremendous sweep" of the surging charge of six hundred cavalrymen riding into the "valley of death" with "sabers forward and lances leveled through a deadly thunder of cannon and rifle fire" provided the spectacular climax.

THE ADVENTURES OF ROBIN HOOD (1938) marked the triumph of the cycle. Originally planned for Jimmy Cagney, ROBIN HOOD is Flynn's finest picture, for he and his role are perfectly matched: "In Errol Flynn, Sir Robin of Sherwood Forest has found his man, a swashbuckler from peaked cap to pointed toe, defiant of his enemies and England's, graciously impudent with his lady love, quick for a fight or a frolic," said Frank Nugent of the *New York Times*. Olivia de Havilland as Maid Marian provided the love interest, which was "properly motivated and nicely woven into the plot fabric," unlike the usual clumsy and arbitrary treatment romantic scenes received in the typical costume-adventure picture.[47] The storybook cast featured Basil Rathbone as Sir Guy of Gisbourne and Claude Rains as Prince John.

Norman Reilly Raine and Seton I. Miller fashioned an original screenplay based on legend and lore that contained pageantry and color, a clearly articulated populist message, humor, and a spectacular climax. Warners spent close to $2 million to produce the picture, considerably more than Douglas Fairbanks's 1922 silent ROBIN HOOD, which at $1.5 million was the most expensive picture produced up to that time. Brilliantly photographed in three-strip Technicolor, the action shifted between scenes in Sherwood Forest, shot on location in Chico, California, and the town of Nottingham and its castle. Michael Curtiz's vigorous direction, together with Sol Polito's fluid camerawork and expressionistic lighting, articulated the picture's key moments. Carl Jules Weyl, who designed the monumental sets, was the first and only Warners art director of the decade to win an Oscar. Erich Wolfgang Korngold's score, which also received an Academy Award, added a stirring musical dimension. THE ADVENTURES OF ROBIN HOOD was named to several ten-best lists and has achieved the status of a classic.

Flynn's last swashbuckler of the decade, THE PRIVATE LIVES OF ELIZABETH AND ESSEX (1939), began the downward trajectory of the cycle. The picture was based on Maxwell Anderson's historical drama *Elizabeth the Queen*, which starred Alfred Lunt and Lynn Fontanne in the Theatre Guild production of 1930. The script by Norman Reilly Raine and Aeneas MacKenzie retained much of the poetic quality of the original. A Technicolor production containing stylized sets by Anton Grot and an outstanding score by Korngold, the picture was directed by Michael Curtiz as a series of tableaux rather than as an action film. However, the picture was really Bette Davis's. Playing an aging but still vital Elizabeth, she held the center of focus. Flynn, as the young Earl of Essex and a suitor, was not up to his role. As the *New York Times* put it, "Flynn is a good-looking young man who should be asked to do no more in pictures than flash an even-toothed smile and present a firm jaw-line. His Essex lacked a head long before the headsman got around to him."[48] Following THE SEA HAWK (1940), an almost entirely formulaic swashbuckler, Flynn specialized in Westerns and, after December 1941, war films.

United Artists ranked third as the company with the most prestige pictures to reach the *Film Daily* Ten Best in the 1930s. Twentieth Century Pictures was UA's principal producer of high-quality fare from 1933 until it merged with Fox Films in 1935. During its two-year association with UA, Twentieth Century delivered eighteen pictures, including two hit prestige pictures, THE HOUSE OF ROTHSCHILD (Alfred L. Werker, 1934) and LES MISERABLES (Richard Boleslawski, 1935).[49]

After 1935, UA's principal producers of prestige pictures were Sam Goldwyn and David O. Selznick. Goldwyn remained UA's most prolific partner, delivering twenty pictures to the company from 1935 to 1939. His biggest hit was THE HURRICANE (John Ford and Stuart Heisler, 1937), an adaptation of the novel by James Nordhoff and James Norman Hall that starred Dorothy Lamour and Jon Hall. The most memorable thing about the picture was the twenty-minute storm sequence at the end. The handiwork of special-effects expert James Basevi, this climax, said the *New York Times*, contained "a hurricane to blast you from the orchestra pit to the first mezzanine. It is a hurricane to fill your eyes with spindrift, to beat at your ears with its thunder, to clutch at your heart and send your diaphragm vaulting over your floating rib into the region just south of your tonsils. The Basevi hurricane, in a good old movie word, is terrific."[50]

But Goldwyn's reputation as a producer of class pictures was sustained by three he made in collaboration with William Wyler, DODSWORTH (1936), DEAD END (1937), and WUTHERING HEIGHTS (1939). All experimented with adaptation, and all made it to *Film Daily*'s Ten Best. Producing DODSWORTH, a prestige woman's film, Goldwyn again turned to Sinclair Lewis, but this time via a stage version by Sidney Howard that was produced in 1932 with Walter Huston in the title role. Howard's dramatization consisted of fourteen scenes interrupted by curtains. In adapting his play for the screen, Howard retained the "master scene" structure, but rewrote much of what took place off-stage into the action. "A story of the disintegrating marriage of a middle-aged couple" during a European grand tour, the film starred Walter Huston in the role he created on Broadway; Ruth Chatterton played the wife, "a silly, shallow, age-fearing woman of ingrained selfishness and vulgarity," and Mary Astor was "the other woman." "An attempt to explore a level of experience which the movies had shunned," DODSWORTH was hailed by *Variety* as "a superb motion picture which yields artistic quality and box office in one elegantly put-together package."[51] DODSWORTH was nominated for seven Academy Awards, including best picture and best director, but won only for Richard Day's art direction. The film did a respectable business of nearly $1 million.

To produce DEAD END, a prestige social problem picture, Goldwyn spent $165,000 to acquire the rights to Sidney Kingsley's long-running stage hit, a considerable amount for the time. Like Elmer Rice's *Street Scene,* which Goldwyn adapted in 1931, Kingsley's naturalistic drama depicted tenements as the breeding ground of crime. It starred Sylvia Sidney as Drina, "the same optimistic city-dweller she had played in Goldwyn's *Street Scene,*" and Joel McCrea as Dave Connell, who is sucked back into the slums after six years of studying to become an architect. Goldwyn borrowed Humphrey Bogart from Warners to play "Baby Face" Martin, an ex-con who returns to his old neighborhood after ten years unrepentant and unreformed. Leo Gorcey and five other players from the stage production (who became known as the Dead End Kids) were chosen to reprise their roles as juvenile delinquents. Lillian Hellman did a "near-literal film adaptation" of the play, and true to the original, confined the action to a single setting, the waterfront along New York's East River, to intensify "the claustrophobia felt by their trapped characters." Richard Day designed "a realistic set that jammed slums right up against a luxury apartment, wooden docks, and an inlet of the East River into which the Dead End Kids could dive. It offered many different levels and angles with which Wyler and Toland could create visual interest."[52] Considered an "important" picture of social protest, DEAD END grossed more than $1.4 million.

Goldwyn's WUTHERING HEIGHTS was one of the most widely admired pictures of the decade, winning the New York Film Critics award for best picture, among other honors. Based on Emily Brontë's strange tale of a tortured romance, it starred Laurence Olivier as the demon-possed Heathcliff and Merle Oberon as his beloved Cathy. Originally written on speculation for UA's Walter Wanger, the screenplay by Ben Hecht and Charles MacArthur did a major job of surgery on the novel by going "straight to the heart of the book," exploring its shadows and drawing "dramatic fire from the savage flints of scene and character hidden there." Art director James Basevi recreated an authentic version of the Yorkshire moors in the San Fernando Valley and, at Goldwyn's insistence, advanced the period of the setting from the Regency to the Victorian to better show off Merle Oberon and the women. William Wyler's sensitive direction, Gregg Toland's chiaroscuro lighting and deep-focus photography, and Alfred Newman's evocative score created "one of the most distinguised pictures of the year," in the opinion of *New York Times* reviewer Frank S. Nugent.[53] More attuned to popular tastes, *Variety* observed,

> *Wuthering Heights* will have to depend on class audiences. Its general sombreness and psychological tragedy is too heavy for general appeal. With that setup, and lacking socko marquee dressing, picture is more of an artistic success for the carriage trade. . . . Stark tragedy is vividly etched throughout. Tempo is at a slow pace, with many sequences devoted to development of psychological reactions of the characters. It's rather dull material for general audiences. (*VFR*, 29 March 1939)

WUTHERING HEIGHTS grossed $1.2 million in the United States, a respectable amount, but not enough to break even. Presumably, the uncompromising treatment of the story kept the masses at bay.

David O. Selznick joined United Artists in 1935. In forming Selznick International Pictures (SIP), Selznick described his production policy: "There are only two kinds of merchandise that can be made profitably in this business, either the very cheap pictures or the very expensive pictures." Concerning SIP, he said, "There is no alternative open to us but to attempt to compete with the very best."[54] Selznick produced nine pictures for UA before he made GONE WITH THE WIND. Prestige pictures based on literary classics figured prominently in his roster, among them LITTLE LORD FAUNTLEROY (John Cromwell, 1936), THE PRISONER OF ZENDA (John Cromwell, 1937), and THE ADVENTURES OF TOM SAWYER (Norman Taurog, 1938).

However, only A STAR IS BORN (William Wellman, 1937) made it to *Film Daily*'s Ten Best. Based partly on RKO's WHAT PRICE HOLLYWOOD? (George Cukor, 1932), which Pandro S. Berman produced when Selznick was executive head of the studio, A STAR IS BORN was essentially a celebrity biopic based on composites of Hollywood types. Effectively using Technicolor, the movie presented "the most accurate mirror ever held before the glitering, tinseled, trivial, generous, cruel and ecstatic world that is Hollywood," in the opinion of the *New York Times*.[55] Janet Gaynor played the Cinderella role of Vicki Lester, and Fredric March, Norman Maine, her alcoholic husband, who once was the biggest star in Hollywood. William Wellman and Robert Carson won an Oscar for their original story.

Selznick acquired the motion-picture rights to Margaret Mitchell's 1,037-page novel *Gone with the Wind* for $50,000 in June 1936, just as it hit the market. After the novel was accepted by the Book-of-the-Month Club, Macmillan, the publisher, boosted the original print order to forty thousand from ten thousand. Rave reviews, the Pulizer Prize, and word-of-mouth publicity made *Gone with the Wind*, the first novel of a thirty-five-year-old Atlanta housewife, the most popular American novel ever written to that time. By 1937, one year after publication,

Laurence Olivier and Merle Oberon in WUTHERING HEIGHTS *(UA, 1939).*

"sales of the novel had reached the astonishing figure of 1,375,000, with no let-up in sight, confirming the book's unofficial status as a modern classic." By the time of the film's premiere in December 1939, more than 2 million copies of the book had been sold.[56]

If there ever was a presold motion picture, GONE WITH THE WIND was it. As Roger Dooley put it, "*Gone with the Wind* seems never to have lost its grip on the public imagination since the novel was published. From 1936 to 1939 the amount of publicity it received, some promoted by Selznick, much spontaneous, was unparalled in this century."[57] American fans took over the job of casting the role of Rhett Butler. Clark Gable, named in a national poll as the "King of Hollywood," was the public's unanimous choice for the part of Rhett Butler. However, he was securely tied to MGM. To borrow Gable from the studio as well as money to complete the financing of the picture, Selznick approached his father-in-law, Louis B. Mayer. Driving a hard bargain, Mayer offered Gable's services and $1.25 million in financing, but demanded in return the distribution rights to the picture and 50 percent of the profits for five years. Selznick had no choice but to sign on the dotted line.[58]

Finding someone to play Scarlett was another matter. Of all the devices Selznick used to generate interest in the film, the talent search proved the most effective. Selznick had used the ploy before, but this time he received the cooperation of nearly "every female performer between the ages of Shirley Temple and May Robson" who had decided she must have the part.[59] Selznick's people toured the country, auditioning candidates from high school, college drama departments, and community theaters. Finally, on 13 January 1939, Selznick announced that the Scarlett O'Hara sweepstakes had been won by Vivien Leigh, a young British actress who was comparatively unknown in this country.

Developing the picture, Selznick was obligated to remain faithful to the source, yet the epic size novel presented enormous difficulties. Using the talent search to gain time, Selznick hired Sidney Howard, the Pulitzer Prize–winning dramatist, to develop the script. Starting on the mammoth project in 1937, Howard continued to work on the construction and dialogue of the second half while the picture was in production.[60] In addition to Howard, Selznick's production staff consisted of seasoned Hollywood professionals that included the distinguished production designer William Cameron Menzies, art director Lyle Wheeler, costume designer Walter Plunkett, special-effects designer Jack Cosgrove, cameramen Ernest Haller and Ray Rennahan, and composer Max Steiner. Selznick chose George Cukor to direct, but personal differences between Cukor and Gable shortly into the shoot forced Selznick to replace Cukor with Victor Fleming.

GONE WITH THE WIND "was innovative in many ways in the film industry: cost, length, fidelity to the source, and especially the way it pushed the frontiers of Technicolor photography to their limits of excellence."[61] It cost $4,085,790 to make—more than any picture had ever cost in the entire history of the American film industry. Running more than three and a half hours, the picture was nearly twice the length of a conventional feature.

Using a premiere to launch a picture was a common practice, but the GONE WITH THE WIND premiere in Atlanta on 15 December 1939 established a new high for motion-picture publicity. According to *Newsweek*, "Governor E. D.

Hattie McDaniel and Clark Gable in GONE WITH THE WIND *(MGM, 1939).*
McDaniel won an oscar as best supporting actress, the first ever given to a black
performer.

Rivers proclaimed Friday, the day of the premiere, a public holiday throughout
the state; all state buildings were closed and the Confederate banner flew from
the Capitol masthead beside the flag of the United States. Atlanta went the
governor two better; Mayor Hartsfield declared a three-day festival."[62] Half of
Atlanta's 300,000 population lined the streets to greet the motorcade that carried
the film's stars, feature players, and executives from the airport to their hotel.
The city presented an appropriate facade, celebrating the architecture and finery
of the 1860s, with its citizens dressed up in the hoop skirts and claw-hammer
coats of the antebellum era. The highlight of the festivities was a charity ball at
the City Auditorium the night before the premiere.

A few days after the Atlanta premiere, the picture opened in New York
simultaneously at the Capitol and the Astor on a reserved-seat basis. The
Hollywood premiere took place on 27 December 1939 at the venerable and
prestigious Cathay Circle Theater in the Wilshire District. January marked the
beginning of the national roadshow play-off, the most prestigious form of release.
In all the key cities, the picture was shown on a reserved-seat basis at top ticket
prices and with an intermission after an hour and forty-five minutes.

At Academy Award time, GONE WITH THE WIND won an unprecedented eight
Oscars in most major categories. Hattie McDaniel received an Academy Award
for supporting actress, which marked the first time a black had ever been
nominated, let alone honored. In recognition of Menzies's contribution, Selz-

nick created the special credit "Production Designed by William Cameron Menzies." Since there was no precedent for what Menzies had done, the Academy awarded him a special plaque at the Oscar ceremonies to recognize his "outstanding achievement in the use of color for the enhancement of dramatic mood." Clark Gable did not win the Oscar for best actor; that honor went to Robert Donat for his title role in GOODBYE, MR. CHIPS. Nor did Steiner win an Oscar for his score, oddly enough, because the Academy rules for the music category did not distinguish between dramas and musicals. The Oscar that year went to the musical classic THE WIZARD OF OZ. However, Selznick won the Irving G. Thalberg Memorial Award for his efforts as producer.

The box-office returns matched the picture's epic scope. By the end of May 1940, the picture had grossed an astonishing $20 million. No picture had ever come close to this. This gross was from the first roadshow play-off. Yet to come were the general release and the return engagements. When the results were in, GONE WITH THE WIND had established a box-office record that stood for more than twenty years.

Musicals

The musical, the only new production trend to grow out of the talkies, had become box-office poison by the summer of 1930. That season, said *Variety,* "marked the end of the gold rush west and the long portage back by many of the New York contingent. . . . They pushed the musicals beyond the pale of public acceptance, so they can't make pictures with tunes any more, or at least for a few months." Hollywood released sixty musicals in 1928 and over seventy in 1930, but by 1932, the number had fallen to less than fifteen. Musicals proliferated after the conversion to sound because the public, at least at first, grew tired of endless dialogue. Musicals, moreover, created ancillary profits for the music-publishing and phonograph companies newly acquired by the majors. As Alexander Walker pointed out, "between 100,000 and 500,000 sheets of a song could be sold, and an equal number of discs, within a month of a successful musical's release. (Without a film behind it, a song was usually lucky to sell 30,000 copies in three months.)"[63]

In its rush to capitalize on sound, Hollywood initially experimented with three types of musicals, the all-star revue, the Broadway adaptation, and the backstager. The revue was used by producers to showcase stars and contract players and to offer "proof positive that everyone could now talk, sing and dance at least passably well."[64] Modeled after vaudeville and burlesque and perfected by Florenz Ziegfeld, Earl Carroll, and other Broadway showmen, the revue was essentially a series of comic sketches, gaudy musical numbers, acrobatics, and even short dramas presented in a variety format, each introduced by a master of ceremonies. Elaborate routines, especially big dance numbers, might be photographed in two-strip Technicolor. Shot straight on in front of the proscenium, this type of musical was the most stage-bound of all. Among the more memorable revues are MGM's THE HOLLYWOOD REVUE OF 1929, Warners' THE SHOW OF SHOWS (1929), Fox's MOVIETONE FOLLIES OF 1929, Paramount's PARAMOUNT ON PARADE (1930), and Universal's KING OF JAZZ (1930).

The Broadway adaptation transferred operettas and musicals to the screen. Warners led the way with its production of THE DESERT SONG (Roy Del Ruth, 1929), which was based on the popular operetta by Sigmund Romberg; it was followed by MGM's THE ROGUE SONG (Lionel Barrymore, 1930) and Paramount's THE VAGABOND KING (Ludwig Berger, 1930), which were adaptations of Franz Lehár and Rudolf Friml operettas, respectively. The most successful adaptations, RKO's RIO RITA (Luther Reed, 1929) and UA's WHOOPEE! (Thornton Freeland, 1930), were based on Flo Ziegfeld hits.

RIO RITA, a musical western extravaganza, grossed an incredible $2.4 million. WHOOPEE! did even better and started a series. Produced by Sam Goldwyn at a cost of $1 million, the picture was an adaptation of a smash musical comedy built around Eddie Cantor. To bring Eddie Cantor to the screen, Goldwyn hired Ziegfeld to co-produce the picture and Busby Berkeley, the dance director, to restage his numbers. Goldwyn also hired most of the original Broadway cast to repeat their roles. Calling WHOOPEE! the best musical comedy to date, Variety liked just about everything in the picture—its effective use of Technicolor throughout; Cantor's comic antics and his songs, particularly "My Baby Just Cares for Me" and "Makin' Whoopee"; and Berkeley's numbers, particularly the Lady Godiva routine that was shot with an overhead camera. A personality-centered musical, WHOOPEE! made little attempt to integrate the comedy routines, songs, and story. Nonetheless, Cantor's feature-film debut grossed over $2.6 million worldwide and started a popular series that included PALMY DAYS (1931), THE KID FROM SPAIN (1932), and ROMAN SCANDALS (1933). All were released through United Artists.

The backstage musical was the most enduring cycle of the lot. MGM's THE BROADWAY MELODY (Harry Beaumont, 1929), the studio's first sound feature, set the pattern for all the show-business pictures to follow. Promoted as "All Talking! All Singing! All Dancing!" THE BROADWAY MELODY was "the first movie to use songs both within a story and as part of a Broadway show being performed, and it was the first to have an original score created specifically for its use." The songs by Nacio Herb Brown and Arthur Freed contained several hits—"You Were Meant for Me," "The Wedding of the Painted Doll," and the title song, "Broadway Melody." The screenplay by Edmund Goulding contained in pristine simplicity the main elements of the cycle—backstage romances, wise-cracking chorines, an imperious impresario, a dilettante backer, and big-hearted moments. Charles King played a song-and-dance-man, and Bessie Love and Anita Page, two sisters from the Midwest who try to break into show business. Chosen by exhibitors nationwide as their premiere sound attraction, the picture made over $4 million by the end of 1929 on an investment of $280,000. So many imitations of THE BROADWAY MELODY were rushed into production that within a year, Variety published an article entitled "Ingredients for Backstage Talkers" that satirized all the hackneyed elements of the cycle.[65]

Of all the early experiments to enliven the musical, none were as innovative as Paramount's continental fairy tales. These pictures eliminated much of the staginess that had characterized the early sound musical by shooting the musical scenes with some flexibility and by integrating story, locale, and scoring through editing. The cycle was short, consisting of three pictures directed by Ernst Lubitsch and one by Rouben Mamoulian. Built around Maurice Chevalier and/or Jeanette MacDonald, all are set in Europe rather than America and all are highly stylized.

Ernst Lubitsch's first sound film, THE LOVE PARADE (1929), started the cycle.

Jeanette MacDonald and Maurice Chevalier in Love Me Tonight *(Paramount 1932).*

A frothy operetta set in the mythical Central European kingdom of Sylvania, The Love Parade teamed Maurice Chevalier and Jeanette MacDonald for the first time. Chevalier, the international music-hall star whom *Variety* called the "'it' man from France," had starred in one other talkie; MacDonald, fresh from the musical-comedy stage, here made her motion-picture debut. Victor Schertzinger and Clifford Grey composed the score, and Ernest Vajda and Guy Bolton wrote the script, which was based on a French play. Lubitsch's use of the moving camera, editing, and off-stage business that inventively blended song and action led *Variety* to call The Love Parade "the first true screen musical."[66] A big hit, the picture made it to *Variety*'s list of top-grossing pictures in 1930 and made MacDonald a star.

Rouben Mamoulian's Love Me Tonight (1932), which concluded the cycle, was even more innovative in the way it expanded what Gerald Mast calls "the choreography of space." This Ruritanian operetta was written by Samuel Hoffenstein, Waldemar Young, and George Marion, Jr., from a French play. Richard Rogers and Lorenz Hart wrote the score, which contains three of their most memorable songs—"Isn't It Romantic?" "Mimi," and "Lover." Of the picture's many cinematic highlights, none is more inventive than the opening sequence. *Variety* described the sequence as follows:

It is dawn over the vacant, sunlit street of Paris. First a street worker hammers at the pavements, a cobbler pounds at his last, a vagrant snores in a doorway and a knife grinder grates over his grindstone. Gradually other sounds of the waking day work into a jazzy cadenza as the camera walks into the bedroom of the gay young tailor (Chevalier) waking to a new day with a song on his lips. Roulade is "Isn't It Romantic?" a rollicksome canticle that seizes everybody he passes on the street, until a squad of maneuvering militiamen out in the country bring it to the ears of the Princess heroine. (*VFR*, 23 August 1932)

Because the cycle contained so-called risqué, naughty, and salacious moments, it is commonly assumed that the continental fairy tale operetta was a casualty of the Breen Office. However, *Variety* offered another explanation for its demise when its review of Lubitsch's THE SMILING LIEUTENANT (1931) implied that the producers of the picture were out of touch with the audience: "Their trouble is gauging the fan mentality, which they constantly outdistance by that foreign flair for matters classing as politely risqué comedy. . . . what they do is funny at the Criterion, for $2, but may not register so solidly out of town." Its review of LOVE ME TONIGHT said the picture would probably "miss slightly for general release" because it was based on an original source "alien to American ideas" and the story was "innocent of that commodity called American hoke, and few pictures go to the heights without it within Mr. [Herbert] Hoover's borders."[67]

Warners discovered a formula to revive the musical in 1933 when it produced three Busby Berkeley musicals in a row, 42ND STREET, GOLD DIGERS OF 1933, and FOOTLIGHT PARADE. Motivated in part by exhibitors who demanded something to compete with music headliners on radio and by the poor box-office returns of revues, Darryl Zanuck decided to resurrect the backstage musical. Unlike the Lubitsch-type operettas, these Berkeley musicals were set in the very real world of Depression America and told gritty stories of backstage life spiced with platoons of chorus girls, upbeat music, and sex. The pictures were admired for their realism. *Variety*, for example, said of 42ND STREET, "Everything about the production rings true. It's as authentic to the initiate as the novitiate."[68]

What made the series distinctive, of course, was Busby Berkeley's production numbers. Berkeley had used chiaroscuro and kaleidoscopic camerawork—including traveling shots, rhythmic cutting, and his famous overhead shots (the "Berkeley top shot")—at Goldwyn in the dance numbers for the Eddie Cantor musicals. At Warners, Berkeley took advantage of the studio's enormous technical resources to perfect these techniques and made himself into a legend in the process.

The Berkeley musical contained two types of music, rehearsal numbers sprinkled throughout the film and the formal Berkeley pieces, which Gerald Mast calls "Big Musical Numbers," typically performed one after another at the climax in the following characteristic sequence: (1) a song built on a "sexually suggestive location"; (2) an "abstract-geometric number"; and (3) a "social-commentary number." The songs that form the basis for the numbers also follow a pattern: a fox-trot first, a waltz second, and a march third. The screenplays contained nothing to suggest the songs or how they might be staged. To produce the musicals, the songs came first, with lyrics by Al Dubin and then the music by Harry Warren; afterward, Berkeley took over.[69]

Berkeley's collaborators were director Lloyd Bacon, whose principal job was to keep the action moving at a fast pace; art director Anton Grot; costume designer Orry-Kelly; cinematographer Sol Polito; and songwriters Harry Warren and Al Dubin. In front of the camera, Warners used familiar faces from its stock company: Dick Powell and Ruby Keeler as the favored romantic team; Joan Blondell, Ginger Rogers, Una Merkel, Aline MacMahon, and Glenda Farrell as tough-as-nails gold diggers; and Ned Sparks, Guy Kibbee, Louise Fazenda, Frank McHugh, and Hugh Herbert as favorite clowns.

Launched by a coast-to-coast publicity campaign, 42ND STREET (Lloyd Bacon) became a smash hit, a milestone that *Variety* labeled "the *Broadway Melody* of 1933."[70] Adapted by James Seymour and Rian James from a novel by Bradford Ropes, the picture incorporates ingredients from such pioneering efforts as MGM's THE BROADWAY MELODY (1929) and Warners' ON WITH THE SHOW (1929). 42ND STREET follows a Broadway-bound musical comedy called *Pretty Lady* from its first rehearsals to its out-of-town tryout. Along the way, the audience is introduced to a slave-driving director (Warner Baxter), a lecherous financial backer (Guy Kibbee), an over-the-hill star (Bebe Daniels), juvenile leads (Ruby Keeler and Dick Powell), hard-boiled chorus girls (Ginger Rogers and Una Merkel), plus other assorted types.

The story uses a hoary Cinderella plot device: the temperamental leading lady sprains her ankle just before opening night and is replaced by an unknown chorus girl, who thereby becomes a star. Ruby Keeler, who plays the unknown chorus girl Peggy Sawyer, receives the following pep talk from Warner Baxter, the director, just as she goes on:

> Now listen to me—listen hard. . . . Two hundred people—two hundred jobs—two hundred thousand dollars—five weeks of grind—and blood and sweat—depend on you. It's the life of all these people who have worked with you. You've got to go on—and you've got to give—and give and give—they've GOT to like you—GOT to—you understand. . . . You can't fall down—you *can't*—Your future's in it—my future's in it—and everything that all of us have is staked on you—All right, now I'm through—but you keep your feet on the ground—and your head on those shoulders of yours—and go out—and, Sawyer—you're going out a youngster—but you've GOT to come back a star! (Rocco Fumento, ed., *42nd Street* [Madison: University of Wisconsin Press, 1980], p. 182)

Keeler goes on to perform the first big musical number of the picture, "Shuffle Off to Buffalo," a duet with Clarence Nordstrom staged on a honeymoon train to Niagara Falls. Although the number resembles a conventional theatrical prologue and could have been sung and danced on a Broadway stage, Berkeley added an impressive stunt: he breaks apart the Pullman car like a jackknife and moves his camera down the aisle to leer at amorous couples in their compartments. The second big number, "Young and Healthy," is a kaleidoscopic piece sung by Dick Powell and displays a bevy of chorines on a huge revolving platform. For "42nd Street," a spectacular six-minute finale, Berkeley used his full bag of tricks. After starting out with Ruby Keeler singing the title song and tap dancing atop a taxi, the number opens up into an expressionistic ballet that mixes

Busby Berkeley's abstract geometric staging for "The Shadow Waltz" number in GOLD DIGGERS OF 1933 *(Warners).*

melodrama, farce, and comedy, and concludes with a cutout of the New York skyline that parts to reveal Ruby Keeler and Dick Powell atop a skyscraper waving to the camera.

Warners had completed 42ND STREET by the end of 1932, but held up the release after the first preview until a sequel was put into production. Written by Erwin Gelsey and James Seymour, GOLD DIGGERS OF 1933 (Mervyn LeRoy) is based on Avery Hopwood's play *Gold Diggers*, a well-worn property Warners had used for a silent in 1923 and for a musical, GOLD DIGGERS OF BROADWAY, in 1929. GOLD DIGGERS OF 1933, like 42ND STREET, focuses on the difficulties of financing a show during hard times. In GOLD DIGGERS this problem is resolved by Dick Powell, an aspiring songwriter who puts up the cash to bankroll the show he has written. But as the title implies, the picture is also about gold-digging chorus girls. A subplot traces the efforts of Joan Blondell and Aline

Busby Berkeley's "Remember My Forgotten Man" number in GOLD DIGGERS OF *1933 (Warners).*

MacMahon to stymie the efforts of Powell's stuffy older brother and the befuddled family lawyer to break up Powell's engagement to show girl Ruby Keeler. A Cinderella plot device is also used in this picture; this time the juvenile lead suffers a bout of lumbago, and Powell goes on in his place.

Given a free hand by the studio, Berkeley created numbers that were longer and more elaborate than previously. The picture opens with a rehearsal number for a Broadway revue, "We're in the Money." Offered as a morale booster for Depression audiences, the song was performed by chorines (led by Ginger Rogers) clad only in large, strategically placed gold coins. The big musical numbers consist of "Pettin' in the Park," a risqué piece displaying girls in skimpy lingerie and in nude silhouette; "The Shadow Waltz," a pageant featuring a stageful of hooped-gowned dancers who play neon-lighted violins and create a series of geometric patterns; and "Remember My Forgotten Man," Berkeley's paean to America's unemployed inspired by the then-recent march on Washington of desperate World War I veterans.

Busby Berkeley's third musical of 1933, FOOTLIGHT PARADE, is based on an original screenplay by Manuel Seff and James Seymour. FOOTLIGHT PARADE remixes all the ingredients of the first two pictures and throws in James Cagney for good measure. To create jobs for out-of-work performers, Cagney gets the bright idea of producing live musical prologues to whatever picture a theater is showing. Of the three big musical numbers, "By a Waterfall," an elaborate aquacade showing a hundred girls diving, swimming, and cavorting, is the most elaborate in the three Berkeley pictures of 1933. The "Shanghai Lil" finale modifies the Cinderella plot device by permitting Cagney to replace a drunk actor at the last moment and thereby make his first appearance as a dancer on the screen. This finale concludes on a patriotic note; performing a series of military drills, the chorus holds aloft football-stadium cards to form the NRA eagle, the flag, and a likeness of President Roosevelt.

Warners sustained the series by producing GOLD DIGGERS OF 1935 (Busby Berkeley), GOLD DIGGERS OF 1937 (Lloyd Bacon, 1936), and GOLD DIGGERS IN PARIS (Ray Enright, 1938) and by producing spin-offs of the series such as WONDER BAR (Lloyd Bacon, 1934), FASHIONS OF 1934 (William Dieterle), and HOLLYWOOD HOTEL (Busby Berkeley, 1937), which featured Berkeley's typically elaborate routines. GOLD DIGGERS OF 1935 marked Berkeley's first effort as sole director and contains his most elaborate and complex creation, the white-piano number "The Words Are in My Heart." The picture also contains the most famous song of the series, Harry Warren and Al Dubin's "Lullaby of Broadway," which not only made it to the number-one spot on radio's "Your Hit Parade" but also won for Warren and Dubin an Academy Award for best song.[71] After this picture, Busby Berkeley's musicals lost their originality, and by 1939, the Warners musical had sunk so low that the studio allowed Berkeley, Dick Powell, and Harry Warren to walk off the lot when their contracts expired.

The Berkeley musicals naturally inspired other studios to develop formulas of their own to capitalize on the new interest in musicals. *Variety*'s annual list of top-grossing movies reveals that musicals reached the peak of their commercial popularity in 1936. In that year, four of the top seven hits were musicals: RKO's SWING TIME and MGM's SAN FRANCISCO, THE GREAT ZIEGFELD, and ROSE MARIE. The majors produced around thirty musicals in 1933, but by 1936, the number had risen to fifty.

While Warners was perfecting the Berkeley extravaganzas, RKO was working on a more intimate and sophisticated series of dance musicals built around Fred Astaire and Ginger Rogers. A newcomer to the movies, Astaire had performed in New York and London with his sister, Adele, in musicals specially designed for them by some of the greatest names of the American musical theater, among them the Gershwins, Cole Porter, and the team of Howard Dietz and Arthur Schwartz. Ginger Rogers, on the other hand, was a familiar face, having just played a sassy gold digger in Warners' first two Berkeley pictures. Unlike the Depression milieu of the Berkeley backstage musicals, the archetypal Astaire-Rogers picture is set in a fantasy world of luxury, elegance, and romance, where people spend their lives in evening dress and frolic the night long. Unlike the musical sequences of the Berkeley pictures, which are elaborate decorative appendages, the numbers in the Astaire-Rogers pictures are integrated into the narrative. Astaire and Rogers appeared in nine films together during the thirties, but the height of their popularity was 1935–1937, a period when their pictures made it to the annual lists of box-office champs. Describing the great appeal of their pictures, Arlene Croce said,

> Certainly no greater dance musicals exist. Oddly enough, the dance emphasis that made them unusual also made them popular. Although Astaire and Rogers did many things in their movies besides dance— the way they looked and read their lines and wore their clothes and sang in their funny voices has become legendary, too, and they could

make a song a hit without dancing to it—it was through their dancing that the public grew to love them and to identify their moods, the depth of their involvement, and the exquisite sexual harmony that made them not only the ideal dancing couple but the ideal romantic team. No dancers ever reached a wider public, and the stunning fact is that Astaire and Rogers, whose love scenes were their dances, became the most popular team the movies have ever known. (*The Fred Astaire and Ginger Rogers Book*, p. 5)

Fred Astaire and Ginger Rogers danced together for the first time in FLYING DOWN TO RIO (Thornton Freeland, 1933). RKO's answer to the Busby Berkeley backstager, the picture is a show-biz musical about an itinerant dance band. In an attempt to counter the Warners musicals, the picture combined Latin songs and dances with spectacular aviation production numbers, the most famous of which was the finale, a Berkeley parody that had "scores of chorus girls, anchored to the wings of airplanes, dancing and doffing their clothes for all Rio to see." The picture featured Dolores Del Rio; Astaire and Rogers, who perform with the band, received fifth and fourth billing, respectively. Fred and Ginger dance together only once, in "The Carioca," a group number that started a dance craze that swept the country. Although the story was slow and lacked humor, *Variety* pointed out, "the main point of *Flying Down to Rio* is the screen promise of Fred Astaire. . . . Not that Astaire threatens to become an ocean-to-ocean screen rage, but here he shows enough to indicate what he could do with good material. He's assuredly a bet after this one, for he is distinctly likeable on the screen, the mike is kind to his voice and as a dancer he remains in a class by himself."[72]

Now more sure of itself, RKO inaugurated the Astaire-Rogers series of musicals, which was to constitute the studio's most distinguished output of the decade. RKO assigned producer Pandro S. Berman to develop the series. It was Berman who organized the production unit and had the sense to give it plenty of room to maneuver. The core unit would consist of director Mark Sandrich; dance director Hermes Pan; screenwriters Allan Scott and Dwight Taylor; cameramen J. Roy Hunt and David Abel; art director Van Nest Polglase and associate art director Carroll Clark; costume designers Bernard Newman, Walter Plunkett, and Irene; and music director Max Steiner. The songs for the Astaire-Rogers pictures were written by Irving Berlin, Jerome Kern, Cole Porter, Vincent Youmans, and George and Ira Gershwin, to name only a few.[73] The distinctive visual look of these pictures was created by Hunt and Abel, who took advantage of new monochrome film stocks that could maximize contrasts in black and white, and by Polglase and Clark, who introduced "the fixed architectural institution that soon became known as the B.W.S. (Big White Set)." Berman hired Ginger Rogers, of course, and to round out the cast, he signed supporting players who were masters at the art of sophisticated farce—Edward Everett Horton, Eric Blore, Alice Brady, Helen Broderick, and Erik Rhodes.

The musicals were custom-built for Fred Astaire, who, by agreement with the studio, choreographed his solos and duets and outlined the ensemble numbers. He also controlled the development of a number. As Arlene Croce noted, "the songs did not pass through an arranger before they came to him. They came to him directly, and the arrangement was laid out, after weeks of rehearsal, at Hal Borne's piano. Astaire is himself a trained musician and knew how to manipulate a composition for maximum theatrical effect without distortion."[74] Preparing the dances, Astaire worked in seclusion, rehearsing only with his assistant dance director, Hermes Pan, and pianist Borne. After Astaire perfected a number, Hermes Pan taught it to Rogers. During shooting, Astaire oversaw the camera-work and afterward the editing of the numbers. Regardless of who directed the pictures, the shooting styles of the dances are identical: Astaire had the dances recorded in full shot and in long takes using the "Astaire dolly," which was specially constructed by Mark Sandrich so that it could track, glide, and turn with the pair perfectly.[75]

THE GAY DIVORCEE (Mark Sandrich, 1934) launched the series. It was based on Cole Porter's musical hit of 1932, *Gay Divorce,* which starred Astaire and marked the last time he would dance on Broadway. RKO changed the title of the original because the Breen Office would never permit the institution of divorce to be gay; however, it would allow a "gay divorcée." The adaptation by George Marion, Jr., Dorothy Yost, and Edward Kaufman contained the archetypal ingredients of the Astaire-Rogers musical: Astaire falls in love with Rogers at first sight, but his advances are thwarted by incidents involving mistaken identity. The complications are resolved through a series of song-and-dance numbers (usually three) performed by Astaire and Rogers that function as courtship rituals. Among the many charms of *The Gay Divorcee* are two Fred and Ginger duets—"Night and Day," perhaps the most effective seduction dance in the series, and "The Continental," a seventeen-minute follow-up to "The Carioca" that attempted to out-Berkeley Berkeley in spectacle. Although RKO unsuccessfully promoted the Continental as a new ballroom dance, the number (music by Con Conrad and lyrics by Herb Magidson) won the first Oscar awarded to a song.

In addition to the duets, the picture contained solos sung and danced by Astaire. They, too, are worked into the plot and function to showcase Astaire's brilliant phrasing of a song and the range of his dancing talent. Describing Astaire's opening solo in THE GAY DIVORCEE, "Looking for a Needle in a Haystack," *Variety* said that RKO "has a star whose libretto is written by his own dancing feet. The manner in which Astaire taps himself into an individual click with that 'Looking for a Needle in a Haystack,' a hoofing soliloquy in his London flat, while his man hands him his cravat, boutonniere and walking stick, is something which he alone elevates and socks over on individual artistry."[76]

RKO repeated this formula with slight variation in three pictures, TOP HAT (Mark Sandrich, 1935), SWING TIME (George Stevens, 1936), and SHALL WE DANCE (Mark Sandrich, 1937). Meanwhile, RKO produced two Astaire-Rogers pictures as spacers that reverted to the double-romance plot of FLYING DOWN TO RIO—ROBERTA (William A. Seiter, 1935) and FOLLOW THE FLEET (Mark Sandrich, 1936). ROBERTA, based on the 1933 Broadway hit by Jerome Kern and Otto Harbach, was intended as a showcase for the studio's newest star, Irene Dunne. Dunne and Randolph Scott play the romantic leads, and Astaire and Rogers revert to the secondary roles of comic and soubrette. Dunne sings three Harbach and Kern hits, "Yesterdays," "Smoke Gets in Your Eyes," and "Lovely to Look At," the last performed as a finale to accompany a lavish fashion show and musical entertainment. ROBERTA was a big hit, earning $770,000 in profits and boosting the careers of Dunne, Astaire, and Rogers.[77]

FOLLOW THE FLEET, the fifth film in the series, has a score by Irving Berlin. Fred and Ginger have center stage in this picture, but he is offcast as a gum-chewing sailor, and she, as a dance-hall hostess. Moreover, the locales—a battleship, a dance hall, and a schooner—are anything but continental chic. Not

Fred Astaire and Ginger Rogers in SWING TIME *(RKO, 1936).*

until the finale are Fred and Ginger returned to more familiar surroundings. Performing at a benefit, they don evening clothes to do "Let's Face the Music and Dance," a serious number resembling a one-act drama.

TOP HAT, the quintessential Astaire-Rogers musical, is essentially a remake of THE GAY DIVORCEE. Describing the similarity of the two pictures, *Variety* said, "It's like the Walla-Walla gag—they liked it so well they made it twice." TOP HAT is based on an original screenplay by Dwight Taylor and Allan Scott, and contains music and lyrics by Irving Berlin. Each of the five production numbers are gems: "No Strings (I'm Fancy Free)," Astaire's opening dance solo, introduces him as an American dancer in London who is footloose and carefree, and cleverly motivates his meeting with Rogers; "Isn't This a Lovely Day" and "Cheek to Cheek" are among the most appealing duets in the series; and "Top Hat, White Tie, and Tails," the title number, which Astaire sings and dances with a male chorus, is a classic of its kind. The picture concludes with "The Piccolino," a scintillating production number that had fun satirizing the exhibition dance. The playful spirit of the picture was nicely captured by the Big White Sets, especially the fantastic Venice set. After smashing box-office records at New York City's Radio City Music Hall during its opening run, TOP HAT went on to become the most profitable RKO picture of the decade, earning more than $3.2 million in film rentals. And for their efforts, Astaire and Rogers "rose to the number-four spot on the exhibitors' list of top star attractions."[78]

SWING TIME contains a score by Jerome Kern and Dorothy Fields and is based on a screenplay by Howard Lindsay and Allan Scott. Against a backdrop of glittering New York nightclubs, Fred and Ginger win acclaim as a dance team. The picture is noted for its fetching songs, particularly "The Way You Look Tonight" which won an Academy Award for best song, and a sensational dance number, "Bojangles of Harlem," an homage to the Broadway headliner Bill ("Bojangles") Robinson. In the dance number, Astaire danced in blackface against a triple silhouette, "a bravura example of creative special effects."[79]

SHALL WE DANCE, the only Astaire-Rogers picture with a score by the Gershwin brothers, varies the formula somewhat by casting Astaire as a ballet dancer who would rather be a hoofer, by introducing the pair on roller skates in "Let's Call the Whole Thing Off," and by using masks with the likeness of Ginger Rogers on them for an unusual finale, "Shall We Dance." The picture earned a profit, but familiarity with the plot formula was causing audiences to shrink.

RKO experimented further to sustain the series. CAREFREE (Mark Sandrich, 1938), "a clever spoof on psychiatry" that was just as much screwball comedy as dance musical, contained songs by Irving Berlin and fresh dance routines by Astaire. Nonetheless, it was the first Astaire-Rogers picture to lose money. THE STORY OF VERNON AND IRENE CASTLE (H. C. Potter, 1939), the least characteristic picture in the series, is a biopic that follows the adventures of a legendary husband-wife dance team from their first meeting in 1910 in New Rochelle to Vernon's death in an airplane training accident at the end of World War I. Unlike its predecessors, this vehicle does not contain an original musical score; instead, the picture uses more than forty authentic songs from the period to revive the dance routines created by the couple. This picture, too, lost money, and thereafter, Astaire and Rogers developed separate careers.

The Busby Berkeley backstager at Warners and the Astaire-Rogers dance film at RKO were the most innovative forms of the musical spawned by its revival. In the second half of the thirties, MGM dominated the production trend. The studio launched not only a popular series of operettas designed around Jeanette MacDonald and Nelson Eddy but also a series of dance pictures centered on Eleanor Powell. And for good measure, MGM produced a few blockbuster prestige musicals as well.

Credit for reviving the operetta should probably go to Harry Cohn at Columbia Pictures. In an attempt to cash in on the musical, Cohn fashioned a modest programmer in modern dress for the soprano Grace Moore, ONE NIGHT OF LOVE (Victor Schertzinger, 1934), about an aspiring American singer in Europe who falls in love with her voice teacher and who is transformed by him into a Metropolitan Opera star. Although Moore's first go at the movies four years earlier at MGM had flopped, ONE NIGHT OF LOVE became a surprise hit, and at Columbia its box-office returns were surpassed only by another sleeper, IT HAPPENED ONE NIGHT.

Grace Moore made four more musicals at Columbia; following the pattern established by ONE NIGHT OF LOVE, they combined opera and popular music. Jumping on the operetta bandwagon, RKO signed the opera star Lily Pons; Paramount hired Gladys Swarthout, Kirsten Flagstad, Jan Kiepura, and Mary Ellis; and Fox brought back Lawrence Tibbett and Nino Martini. As John Kobal said, "None of the men . . . and few of the ladies of the high C's ever established themselves as successful screen personalities."[80] The trend died out in 1938 almost as abruptly as it began—with the sole exception of MGM's Jeanette MacDonald–Nelson Eddy series.

The most successful singing team of the decade, Jeanette MacDonald and Nelson Eddy made eight operettas together. Five were produced during the thirties and based on beloved works by Victor Herbert (NAUGHTY MARIETTA, W. S. Van Dyke, 1935; SWEETHEARTS, W. S. Van Dyke, 1938), Rudolf Friml and Herbert Stothart (ROSE MARIE, W. S. Van Dyke, 1936), and Sigmund Romberg (MAYTIME, Robert Z. Leonard, 1937; THE GIRL OF THE GOLDEN WEST, Robert Z. Leonard, 1938). Describing the team, Ethan Mordden said, "The little-known Eddy shared billing with the famed MacDonald, his stolidity side by side with her vivacity. Eddy was the singing tree, immobile, and MacDonald the ornate kite trapped in its branches. Either one alone was a still picture; together they told a story."[81]

MGM had a series in mind from the outset and assigned producer Hunt Stromberg, a Thalberg protégé, to develop the formula. W. S. Van Dyke and Robert Z. Leonard alternated as directors. For the most part, the pictures were set in exotic locales—New Orleans in the eighteenth century, Paris during the Second Empire, and the Canadian north woods—at some indeterminate time. MGM discarded the original librettos and substituted new, streamlined scripts that were infused with wit, humor, and sentiment and that focused on central love plots. Naturally, MGM lavished all the resources at its command on the pictures. Herbert Stothart, MGM's music director, arranged the scores, excising outdated or unwanted songs and adding new ones. The numbers he chose for the films were integrated into the narrative and consisted of some of the most-beloved songs of the musical stage, such as "Ah, Sweet Mystery of Life" and "I'm Falling in Love with Someone" (NAUGHTY MARIETTA), "Indian Love Call" (ROSE MARIE), and "Will You Remember" (MAYTIME).

Although the pictures are considered high camp today, all were big commercial hits, especially ROSE MARIE and MAYTIME, which made it to *Variety*'s annual list of top grossers. The recognition the pictures received was consider-

Nelson Eddy and Jeanette MacDonald in MAYTIME *(MGM, 1937).*

able; NAUGHTY MARIETTA, for example, was nominated for an Academy Award as best picture and won *Photoplay*'s coveted Movie of the Year award.

In addition to launching the Jeanette MacDonald–Nelson Eddy series, MGM countered Warners' Gold Diggers series with a backstage musical series of its own. Taking its name from MGM's 1929 hit THE BROADWAY MELODY, the pictures were built around the virtuoso tap-dancing talents of Eleanor Powell. After a false start in her debut, Fox's GEORGE WHITE'S 1935 SCANDALS, she recovered and became known in Hollywood as the Queen of Tap. The pictures in the series were BROADWAY MELODY OF 1936 (1935), BORN TO DANCE (1936), and BROADWAY MELODY OF 1938 (1937). Nacio Herb Brown and Arthur Freed wrote the songs for the Broadway Melody pictures, and Cole Porter, the songs for BORN TO DANCE. All three pictures were directed by Roy Del Ruth and shared many

Eleanor Powell in Born to Dance *(MGM, 1936).*

of the same production staff, which included screenwriters Jack McGowan and Sid Silvers, choreographer Dave Gould, art director Cedric Gibbons, costume designer Adrian, orchestrator Roger Edens, and editor Blance Sewell.

Structurally, the Eleanor Powell pictures are a cross between the backstage musicals of Busby Berkeley and the dance films of Fred Astaire. Like the former, the films contain thin plots that furnish the pretext for the musical numbers, and like the latter, the films spotlight the virtuoso dancing of the star. To this formula, MGM added showmanship and spectacle. The staging of the production numbers is "brilliant, and the choral undertones and orchestral arrangements slick, and everything is treated with an air of understanding as to how a musical number should be presented."[82] Stylistically, the photography is influenced by René Clair and Berkeley. Concerning Powell's unusual dance style, *Variety* said,

> Buck dancing, which is Miss Powell's forte, is basically lacking in grace and anyone who tries it is apt to very often appear awkward. Miss Powell manages to overcome that by the inclusion of ballet work in her tap routine, and thus offers the most versatile display of solo hoofing that motion pictures have yet produced. As yet she lacks the "ideas" that background Fred Astaire's work and that all great dancers must have to go beyond the strictly dancing class, but the

"ideas" will come, because the ability is there in abundance. (*VFR*, 9 December 1936)

To broaden the appeal of these pictures, MGM provided Powell with plenty of backup. In BROADWAY MELODY OF 1936, her supporting cast included comedians Buddy Ebsen, Sid Silvers, and Jack Benny; in BROADWAY MELODY OF 1938, the cast included George Murphy and Sophie Tucker, and the fifteen-year-old Judy Garland, who sang "a plaint to Clark Gable's photograph" entitled "Dear Mr. Gable."

Exploiting the musical even further, MGM had other tricks up its sleeve. In 1936 it produced the first "disaster" musical, SAN FRANCISCO (actually a drama with songs, discussed earlier as a prestige picture), and the first big musical biography, THE GREAT ZIEGFELD (Robert Z. Leonard). A three-hour musical biopic loosely based on the life of the master showman Florenz Ziegfeld, THE GREAT ZIEGFELD was the most lavish Hollywood production up to that time. The *New York Times* said the picture "cost Metro about $500,000 an hour. . . . It is there . . . in the glittering sets, the exuberantly extravagant song-and-dance numbers, the brilliant costumes, the whole sweeping panoply of a Ziegfeld show produced with a princely disregard for the cost accountant." A highly romanticized version of Ziegfeld's life written by William Anthony McGuire, this backstage musical starred William Powell in the title role and Luise Rainer and Myrna Loy as his two wives, Anna Held and Billie Burke. A thin plot provided the excuse to introduce "a medley of guest stars impersonated or in the flesh" and "specialty numbers of no relevance to plot or characters." Roadshowed for five months in twenty-three theaters, THE GREAT ZIEGFELD grossed nearly $5 million worldwide during its first release, making it one of MGM's most successful pictures of the decade.[83] At Academy Award time, it picked up Oscars for best picture and best actress (Luise Rainer). As might be expected, it inspired imitations, which included MGM's own THE GREAT WALTZ (1938), a musical biopic about Johann Strauss; Paramount's THE GREAT VICTOR HERBERT (1939); RKO's THE STORY OF VERNON AND IRENE CASTLE (1939); and Fox's ROSE OF WASHINGTON SQUARE (1939), an homage to Fanny Brice.

Describing the appeal of MGM's Technicolor spectacle THE WIZARD OF OZ (Victor Fleming, 1939), *Variety* said, "There's an audience for 'Oz' wherever there's a projection machine and a screen."[84] Inspired by the success of Walt Disney's musical fantasy SNOW WHITE AND THE SEVEN DWARFS (1937), MGM turned to L. Frank Baum's popular children's saga *The Wonderful Wizard of Oz*, which was published in 1900 and had formed the basis for a hit Broadway musical and two silent films. Writers Noel Langley, Florence Ryerson, and Edgar Allan Woolf modified the story by introducing a crotchety but loving aunt, a busybody spinster witch, a Brooklyn-accented clown lion, and a midwestern medicine-show wizard.

Produced by Mervyn LeRoy at a cost of $2.8 million, THE WIZARD OF OZ made a star out of seventeen-year-old Judy Garland and contained a flawless cast that included Frank Morgan, Billie Burke, Margaret Hamilton, Ray Bolger, Jack Haley, and Bert Lahr. The picture's charms include the now-familiar songs by E. Y. Harburg and Harold Arlen, particularly the Academy Award–winning "Over the Rainbow," which Judy Garland sings in the opening sequence; the fanciful settings by Cedric Gibbons and William A. Horning, which used color

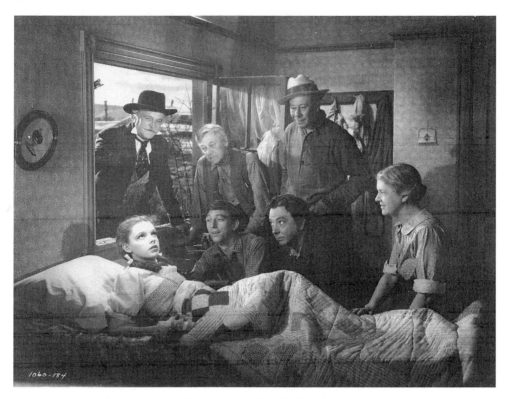

The Wizard of Oz *(MGM, 1939).*

in countless imaginative ways; and the special effects of Arnold Gillespie, which include "a cyclone made out of a woman's stocking and an army of flying monkeys suspended by thousands of piano wires."[85] The Wizard of Oz made it to the *Variety* and *Film Daily* honor rolls, but because of the record production costs, the picture did not break even the first time out.

Before its merger with Twentieth Century in 1935, Fox's musical production consisted of an assortment of production styles and themes. Happy Days (Benjamin Stoloff, 1930), Fox's contribution to the musical revue cycle, was presented at the New York Roxy in Fox's 70-mm Grandeur System wide-film process. Fox also produced a series of romances with songs that teamed Janet Gaynor and Charles Farrell. Delicious (David Butler, 1931) was noted for its Gershwin score and an imaginative seven-minute dream sequence, "New York Rhapsody," the music for which Gershwin later reworked into a concert piece for piano and orchestra, the Second Rhapsody.[86]

Shirley Temple took over as Fox's top box-office attraction in 1935. The new "Leading Waif," Shirley Temple ranked number one at the box office four years in a row, from 1935 to 1938. Most of the twenty-four pictures she made for Fox were essentially sentimental comedies, with songs and dances added. They told simple stories and contained little in the way of production values. And they were cheap to make, costing between $200,000 and $300,000.

The titles of her pictures say much about how she was marketed; she played in Bright Eyes, Curly Top, Dimples, and a series of "Little" pictures—The

Shirley Temple and George Murphy in LITTLE MISS BROADWAY *(20th-Fox, 1938).*

LITTLE COLONEL, THE LITTLEST REBEL, OUR LITTLE GIRL, POOR LITTLE RICH
GIRL, LITTLE MISS BROADWAY, and THE LITTLE PRINCESS. In these films,
Shirley suffered vicissitudes worthy of the most lurid Victorian melodrama. As
William Everson put it, "Shirley had an incredible traumatic history of mothers
who were run over by buses or done in by pneumonia, of fathers who were away
at war or awaiting execution, with long periods in stern orphan asylums in
between. Her problems ranged from the Victorian era and the Civil War to
being chased by a sex maniac in New York."[87] Typical of the child and
adolescent pictures of the time, Shirley played a fixer-upper, a matchmaker, or
a good fairy who invariably reunited her parents or straightened out the
romance of two young people. Two of her pictures made it to *Variety*'s annual
list of box-office champs—CURLY TOP (Irving Cummings, 1935), a musical
adaptation of Mary Pickford's DADDY LONG LEGS, which featured her singing
"Animal Crackers in My Soup" and "When I Grow Up," and THE LITTLEST
REBEL (David Butler, 1935), a comedy set in the Civil War that featured her
dancing with Bill "Bojangles" Robinson.

Shirley's songs have been described by John Kobal as "among the most vivid of the musical memories of the 30s." The songs that are most closely identified with her, such as "On the Good Ship Lollipop," "Baby Take a Bow," "Animal Crackers in My Soup," "When I Grow Up," and "That's What I Want for Christmas," became hits on their own, selling hundreds of thousands of copies of sheet music and placing her up there on the charts with Bing Crosby, Nelson Eddy, and Alice Faye.[88]

After fixing the formula for the Shirley Temple pictures, Darryl Zanuck devised a musical formula for his newest find, Sonja Henie. A three-time Olympic figure-skating champion from Norway, Henie appeared in nine movies for Fox, six of which were produced in the 1930s: ONE IN A MILLION (1936), THIN ICE (1937), HAPPY LANDING (1938), MY LUCKY STAR (1938), SECOND FIDDLE (1939), and EVERYTHING HAPPENS AT NIGHT (1939). Sidney Lanfield, Roy Del Ruth, and Irving Cummings directed her, and Don Ameche, Tyrone Power, Richard Greene, and Ray Milland played her leading men. Every film contained at least one spectacular number to show off her ice-skating skills. In MY LUCKY STAR, for example, she performed an ice version of *Alice in Wonderland,* a sequence that was shot in sepia. Of her acting skills, *Variety* said in its review of HAPPY LANDING,

> Obviously Miss Henie still hasn't heard about acting. But as long as she's given stories like HAPPY LANDING, handled so shrewdly and surrounded by such competent support, she continues to be a click. Roy Del Ruth has wisely minimized closeups and hasn't given the lady too many lines. Apparently her sole effective expression is an infectious smile, more than offsetting a rather monotonous way of reading dialogue. Still, she's cute, appealing and a genuine thrill on skates. (*VFR,* 26 January 1938)

Around the low, mellow singing voice of Alice Faye, Zanuck crafted a backstage musical formula that made her the studio's top musical star of the late 1930s. Zanuck placed her in modern stories at first, such as KING OF BURLESQUE (Sidney Landfield, 1936), SING, BABY, SING (Sidney Landfield, 1936), WAKE UP AND LIVE (Sidney Landfield, 1937), and YOU CAN'T HAVE EVERYTHING (Norman Taurog, 1937). Describing the formula for these pictures, *Variety* said, "Zanuck has developed a formula for this kind of entertainment . . . which is an expert piecing-together of story, melody, blackouts, nightclub specialties and production numbers. The fact that it looks as if it were easy to make is the best evidence that it is well done."[89]

Then, taking his cue from MGM, Zanuck produced two big-budget period musicals, IN OLD CHICAGO (1938) and ALEXANDER'S RAGTIME BAND (1938), leading some to rename the studio "19th Century–Fox." Directed by Henry King and designed as vehicles for Alice Faye, Tyrone Power, and Don Ameche, both pictures made it to *Film Daily*'s Ten Best. IN OLD CHICAGO was a disaster musical inspired by MGM's SAN FRANCISCO. Based on a script by Lamar Trotti and Sonya Levien, IN OLD CHICAGO, like MGM's disaster film, portrayed the bawdy and ostentatious life of a mighty American city in its youth, interwove musical numbers into the narrative, and featured a spectacular disaster sequence. Produced at a cost of $1.8 million, it was set in 1871, the

Jack Haley, Alice Faye, Don Ameche, and Tyrone Power in ALEXANDER'S RAGTIME BAND *(20th-Fox, 1938).*

year of the Great Chicago Fire. William S. Darling and Rudolph Sternad designed the sets, and H. Bruce Humberstone led a special-effects team that created a spectacular fire sequence lasting twenty-five minutes. One of the top-grossing films of the year, IN OLD CHICAGO was nominated for six Academy Awards and won the Oscar in two categories: the best supporting-actress award went to Alice Brady for her role as Molly O'Leary and the assistant-director award went to Robert Webb for his direction of the disaster sequence.

ALEXANDER'S RAGTIME BAND, like MGM's THE GREAT ZIEGFELD, was a musical biopic loosely based on the life of a great showman and started out early in the century and progressed to the present. THE GREAT ZIEGFELD was a tribute to Broadway impresario Florenz Ziegfeld; ALEXANDER'S RAGTIME BAND was a tribute to Tin Pan Alley's "most famous lodger," Irving Berlin. Produced at more than $2 million and containing twenty-six Berlin tunes, this "cavalcade of American jazz," as the *New York Times* described it, became one of the highest-grossing pictures of the decade. Knowing a good thing when he saw it, Zanuck followed up the picture with another period musical, ROSE OF WASHINGTON SQUARE (1939), a fictionalized biopic of Fanny Brice that starred Alice Faye and Tyrone Power.

After the demise of the Chevalier-MacDonald continental fairy tale, Paramount devised a completely new strategy. Influenced by the enormous success of

MGM's GRAND HOTEL, with its all-star cast and single setting that motivated the interweaving of multiple subplots, Paramount produced THE BIG BROAD-CAST (Frank Tuttle, 1932), a loosely structured musical that linked a number of radio stars: Bing Crosby, George Burns and Gracie Allen, the Boswell Sisters, the Mills Brothers, Kate Smith, Arthur Tracy, Cab Calloway and his band, and Vincent Lopez and his orchestra. George Burns, the harried station manager who is besieged by creditors, carries the story. Assisting him is his incompetent secretary, Gracie Allen. The radio station itself motivates the guest appearances, each of which is introduced on camera by the same announcer who handled that function on the star's weekly broadcasts. Bing Crosby played just himself, a happy-go-lucky crooner and a top name at the radio station. Paramount high-lighted his musical numbers and exploited the radio audience's familiarity with his material by giving him only one original song, "Please," written by Leo Robin and Ralph Rainger. His three other songs were hits he created on his radio shows, the best-remembered being his signature song, "Where the Blue of the Night."[90]

Paramount followed up the success of THE BIG BROADCAST with INTERNA-TIONAL HOUSE (Edward Sutherland, 1933). W. C. Fields and Burns and Allen headed the roster which included Rudy Vallee, Colonel Stoopnagle and Budd, Baby Rose Marie, and Bela Lugosi. INTERNATIONAL HOUSE, like THE BIG BROADCAST, has a loose, episodic structure that interweaves specialty and musical numbers, but it differs from its predecessor by relying on parody for much of the comedy. The target of the parody is the same GRAND HOTEL that provided the idea for the series. The Grand Hotel in the Paramount picture is located in Shanghai, where a group of quarantined travelers are shown specialty acts on an experimental television set perfected by a local doctor.

The formula had fully proved itself, and Paramount exploited it three more times by producing BIG BROADCAST pictures of 1936, 1937, and 1938 (released in 1935, 1936, and 1938, respectively). All are held together by nonsensical plots, and all are basically vaudeville revues spotlighting radio talent. The 1937 picture marked the beginning of Jack Benny's long association with Paramount, and the 1938 picture marked Bob Hope's movie debut. It is in this picture that Hope sings "Thanks for the Memory," which went on to become his signature song.

Bing Crosby was the only radio name who also became a motion-picture star. As a result of the warm reception he received in THE BIG BROADCAST, Crosby decided to branch out into the movies and signed his first multiple-picture contract with Paramount in 1933; he was already a top radio attraction and his records were selling in the millions. However, Crosby refused to take star billing in the movies until his third picture, TOO MUCH HARMONY (1933), believing that an unsuccessful try at movie stardom might damage his career. But Paramount surrounded him with top comic talent and glamorous leading ladies and tailor-made his roles, which allowed him to exude an aura of friendliness and easygoing charm that made him a durable star attraction.

Crosby made around three pictures a year, and although some were panned by critics, all were good box office. Today, the films are remembered primarily for their songs. For example, COLLEGE HUMOR (Wesley Ruggles, 1933) contained one of Crosby's biggest hits, "Learn to Croon," by Sam Coslow and Arthur Johnston; SHE LOVES ME NOT (Elliott Nugent, 1934), one of Ralph Rainger and Leo Robin's best-known songs, "Love in Bloom"; MISSISSIPPI (Edward Suther-land, 1935), a Rogers and Hart score studded with three hits, "Soon," "Easy to

Bing Crosby and W. C. Fields in MISSISSIPPI *(Paramount, 1935).*

Remember," and "Down by the River"; and WAIKIKI WEDDING (Frank Tuttle, 1937), which made it to *Variety*'s list of box-office winners and featured Crosby crooning Hawaiian songs, including the Oscar-winning "Sweet Leilani," by Harry Owens.

Concerning the musicals of the Little Three, Columbia's principal strategy was to devise vehicles for Grace Moore, as previously mentioned. Universal's principal contributions to the genre consisted of SHOW BOAT (James Whale, 1936), its second version of the Jerome Kern–Oscar Hammerstein II Broadway musical, and a series of Deanna Durbin pictures. SHOW BOAT was the last major production of the Carl Laemmle regime. (Universal's first version of the musical started out a silent, but was hurriedly turned into a part-talkie in 1929.) Believing the public had grown tired of the show-stopping songs in the original, Carl Laemmle, Jr., gave the order to strike all the numbers with the exception of "Ol' Man River." However, as the picture went into development, he had a change of heart and instructed Hammerstein, who was writing the screenplay, to restore the originals and even to add new songs. Starring Irene Dunne as Magnolia and featuring Allan Jones as Gaylord Ravenal, Charles Winninger as Captain Andy, Paul Robson as Joe, and Helen Morgan as the ill-fated mulatto Julie, this version of SHOW BOAT is generally regarded as one of the all-time great musicals.

Universal's new management had the good fortune to discover an adolescent star who almost single-handedly stabilized the shaky financial supports of the company. Of Deanna Durbin's box-office power, *Fortune* said, "It has long been a common Hollywood assumption that Durbin had been keeping that underprivileged studio [Universal] from bankruptcy single-handed." She was a teenage soprano "whose sweet, bell-like tones, pretty face, unspoilt personality and eye for fun" made her "the logical successor to the mantles of MacDonald and Dunne, in spite of the age difference."[91]

The architects of her pictures were producer Joseph Pasternak and director Henry Koster. Before coming to Hollywood, Pasternak and Koster worked as a production team at Universal's Berlin studios. Pasternak produced all ten of Durbin's earliest pictures, and Koster directed six. (Pasternak left Universal for MGM in 1941.) The other members of the production unit consisted of screenwriter Bruce Manning, cameraman Joseph Valentine, and music director Charles Previn. Called "Pasternak Specials," the Durbin pictures contained either Cinderella or Little Miss Fix-it stories. In all of them, she sang selections from the classical repertoire or grand opera and new pieces specially composed for her.

Playing Little Miss Fix-it in her first Universal picture, THREE SMART GIRLS (Henry Koster, 1936), the fifteen-year-old Durbin became a star and launched two hit songs, "My Heart Is Singing" and "Someone to Care for Me," by Gus Kahn, Walter Jurmann, and Bronislau Kaper. "Miss Durbin stands out not only as 'a darling child' personality, but as a winsome little dramatic actress whose talents do not end with an ability to hit the high registers," said *Variety*. Soon after, Durbin signed a new contract that paid her $1,500 a week and committed her to three pictures a year.[92]

To produce her next picture, ONE HUNDRED MEN AND A GIRL (Henry Koster, 1937), Universal budgeted $600,000, twice the amount spent on THREE SMART GIRLS. Since the goal was to spotlight Durbin's "classical" talents, Universal wrote in a part for Leopold Stokowski, the conductor of the Philadelphia Orchestra, who is enlisted by Durbin to form an orchestra of one hundred unemployed musicians. The task completed, Maestro Stokowski leads the orchestra as she sings Mozart's "Exsultate, Jubilate" and "Libiamo," from Verdi's *La Traviata*. After this picture, Universal doubled Durbin's salary to $3,000 a week.

Durbin's other thirties pictures are MAD ABOUT MUSIC (Norman Taurog, 1938), THAT CERTAIN AGE (Edward Ludwig, 1938), THREE SMART GIRLS GROW UP (Henry Koster, 1939), and FIRST LOVE (Henry Koster, 1939). *Variety*'s review of THREE SMART GIRLS GROW UP nicely sums up their reception:

> A warm, thoroughly delightful family entertainment that seems certain for big grosses and lots of holdovers. It will enhance Universal's standing in general and say the same for the film industry. Escape literature with smiles, heart-tug, lustre, and a collection of thoroughly nice people, the film is a welcome antidote to the front page headlines. It should tear up records like they tear up treaties in Europe. (*VFR*, 22 March 1939)

United Artists' producers released only a few musicals after 1934, among them THE GOLDWYN FOLLIES (George Marshall, 1938) and Walter Wanger's VOGUES OF 1938 (Irving Cummings, 1937). Walt Disney, a former UA independent producer who moved to RKO, produced a musical that was in a class by itself. SNOW WHITE AND THE SEVEN DWARFS (1937), produced by Disney for RKO release, was the first full-length animated feature and the most successful musical of the decade. Based on the Grimm fairy tale "Little Snow White," SNOW WHITE was the creation of teams of writers, composers, sequence directors, supervising

Deanna Durbin and Leopold Stokowski in ONE HUNDRED MEN AND A GIRL
(Universal, 1937).

animators, and sound-effects people, among others. It took the Disney organization three years and $1.5 million to make, but the expense and effort paid off. The
picture ran continuously at popular prices for five weeks in its New York run at
the Radio City Music Hall, playing to 800,000 persons and taking in over a half
million dollars, an unprecedented amount for the period.[93] At the conclusion of
its first theatrical release, the picture set another record—$8.5 million in film
rentals. The hit songs in the picture were "Some Day My Prince Will Come,"

"I'm Wishing," "Heigh-Ho," and "Whistle While You Work." *Variety* said of the picture,

> *Snow White* was a surprise, an animated, feature-length cartoon, which, the industry predicted, would be of mild and limited interest only; a jolt and a challenge to the industry's creative brains. Only reason why it wasn't followed up by a flood of similar cartoon features, merely on the basis of its astonishing grosses, was that elaborate animations of this kind are so staggeringly expensive to make. (Jack Jungmeyer, "Film Production Trends," 4 January 1939, p. 8)

By 1938, the series musical had just about run its course. Among the pictures that were conceived of as potential series were Paramount's ARTISTS AND MODELS (1937), Universal's MERRY-GO-ROUND OF 1938 (1937), RKO's NEW FACES OF 1937, and UA's VOGUES OF 1938 (1937) and THE GOLDWYN FOLLIES (1938), but none caught on. By the end of 1938, studios started closing down their musical production units. *Variety* reported that Warners purged all "contract cleffers from its music department"; let the option lapse on its "chief songster," Dick Powell; and cut its musical schedule "to lowest program in a long time." At Paramount, Boris Morros, the head of the music department, quit.[94] But when America entered the war, audiences welcomed back this trend.

The Woman's Film

Although the origin of the term *woman's film* is unknown, the cycle typically refers to a type of motion picture that revolves around an adult female protagonist and is designed to appeal mostly to a female audience.[95] Hollywood assumed that the motion-picture audience was mostly female, although the industry never collected the empirical evidence to substantiate this claim. Whatever the "true" composition of the audience, producers wanted to attract women and differentiated their product accordingly. Introduced as a production trend in the teens, the woman's film was enriched by the talkies and during the thirties it flourished. In the first half of the decade, the woman's film accounted for over a quarter of the pictures on *Film Daily*'s Ten Best. Although the percentage decreased thereafter, it remained a production staple and culminated in the biggest woman's attraction of them all, GONE WITH THE WIND.

Woman's film is a term of convenience to describe a range of pictures commonly referred to as fallen-woman films, romantic drama, Cinderella romances, and gold-digger or working-girl stories. The titles of such pictures are often taken from the names of their heroines or make some reference to women's conditions. The conflicts in the pictures involve interpersonal relationships that present the heroine with dilemmas the resolutions of which usually entail loss. According to Molly Haskell, the heroine in women's films must "sacrifice her own welfare for that of her children, . . . give up her (sometimes illegitimate) child for its own good, . . . abandon respectable marriage for her lover, . . . give up her lover (or possibility of one) because he is married, . . . relinquish her career for love, . . . [or] give up love for her career."[96]

Producers did not necessarily assign such projects to women writers. Like other artistic personnel, screenwriters were expected to be versatile. Sarah Y.

Mason, a writer on LITTLE WOMEN (1933), shared the Oscar with Victor Heerman for best screenplay, but Frances Marion, the most prominent woman screenwriter of the period, won Oscars for THE BIG HOUSE (1930) and THE CHAMP (1931), which were hardly woman's pictures. As it happened, the finest examples of the woman's film were written by men.

A few directors specialized in the trend. Dorothy Arzner, one of the few female directors in the history of Hollywood, made a half dozen pictures during the thirties, all of which were woman's films, among them CHRISTOPHER STRONG (RKO, 1933), NANA (Goldwyn, 1934), and CRAIG'S WIFE (Columbia, 1936). Among the men, John M. Stahl, for example, directed all three of Universal's big woman's films, BACK STREET (1932), ONLY YESTERDAY (1933), and IMITATION OF LIFE (1934). Josef von Sternberg handled all but three of Marlene Dietrich's thirties vehicles at Paramount, among them MOROCCO (1930), SHANGHAI EXPRESS (1932), and BLONDE VENUS (1932). Clarence Brown directed Greta Garbo's early talkies, including ANNA CHRISTIE (1930), ROMANCE (1930), and ANNA KARENINA (1935) at MGM. And George Cukor directed some of the better efforts of Greta Garbo, Katharine Hepburn, Norma Shearer, and other great female stars at several top studios. However, these directors were the exceptions; even so-called action directors such as Raoul Walsh, William Wellman, and Mervyn LeRoy, and horror-film specialist James Whale contributed to the trend.

The fallen-woman cycle dominated the woman's film early in the decade. A bifurcated cycle, the fallen-woman film consists of the kept-woman film, a type depicting a woman in an illicit sexual relationship who uses her sexuality to provide her with wealth and a rise in social status, and the maternal melodrama, a type depicting "an errant mother who comes back into contact with her child after many years and conceals her true identity for fear of her evil past."[97] "Sinful Girls Lead in 1931," said *Variety*, indicating the high-water mark of the cycle. "Important ladies of the screen . . . found smash films the wages of cinematic sin. The Great God Public, formerly considered a Puritan censor, voiced its approval with admission fees that fully endorsed heroines of easy virtue. . . . Public taste switched [from heroines on pedestals] to glamorous, shameful ladies, pampered by penthouses, coddled by limousines, clothed in couturier smartness." Commenting on the popularity of maternal melodramas, *Variety* added, "More babies were wrenched from their mothers' arms in 1931 than in any previous film year; more tears were shed over unofficial motherhood and the final renunciation that washed records clean. Every infant torn from a sobbing mother brought a happy smile to the box office."[98]

For ideas to make these pictures, Hollywood drew from continental sources, such as Tolstoy's *Resurrection* and *Anna Karenina* and Zola's *Nana;* American progressive literature, such as Theodore Dreiser's *An American Tragedy* and *Jennie Gerhardt,* David Graham Phillips's *Susan Lenox, Her Fall and Rise,* and Sinclair Lewis's *Ann Vickers.* From the stage, Hollywood tapped Eugene O'Neill's *Anna Christie,* Robert E. Sherwood's *Waterloo Bridge,* and Zoë Akin's *Morning Glory.* Turning to popular contemporary women's writers, Hollywood fed on the novels of Fannie Hurst, such as *Back Street* and *Imitation of Life,* and stories from *True Romance* to *Ladies Home Journal* by Adela Rogers St. John, Maurine Watkins, and Mildred Cram.

In adapting these works to the screen, Hollywood did not infuse them with a Victorian morality that punished the errant woman. According to Lea Jacobs,

In a whole body of films devoted to working-class girls in an urban milieu, the stereotype of the injured innocent or world-weary demi-mondaine gave way to any one of a series of self-consciously "modern" American types: flappers, gold diggers, chorines, wisecracking shop-girls. While the heroine could be a kept woman, a trickster, or simply out to marry a millionaire, the stories revolved around the problem of obtaining furs, automobiles, diamonds, and clothes from men. Thus, the downward trajectory of the fall was replaced by a rise in class. (*The Wages of Sin* [Madison: University of Wisconsin Press, 1991], p. 11)

Jacobs also argues that maternal melodramas typically "downplay the heroine's degradation and decline in favor of upward mobility" through work or marriage.[99]

It was just this plot structure that made reformers wince. Noting that the new Production Code in 1930 was supposed to outlaw immoral pictures, the *Outlook and Independent* said that Hollywood "is dedicated to the proposition that America is the most sex-conscious nation in the world. You question it? Examine a bouquet of successful movie titles snatched at random from the electric lights of Main Streets from Portland to Portland: *Single Standard, Street Girl, Half Marriage, Fast Life, His Captive Woman, Dangerous Woman.*" Movies such as these were supposed to have exercised "a pernicious influence upon women." For example, an editorial in the *Christian Century* appraising Hollywood's 1932 output said, "The leading ladies of the screen . . . sold themselves short in functions ranging . . . from noble prostitution to carefree concupiscence. When one considers the number of young girls who pattern their behavior after motion picture screen stars, we need not be surprised if there is an increase of strumpetry along our main streets in the near future."[100]

Noting that only a few fallen-women films were produced in the latter half of the thirties, it is tempting to point to the so-called stricter enforcement of the Production Code as the cause. After all, the Code was supposed to uphold the "sanctity of the institution of marriage" by condemning adultery and illicit sex and by outlawing "excessive or lustful kissing," among other things. A review of Hollywood's output from 1930 to 1934 reveals that the popularity of the cycle waned after 1931. Studios that produced seven or more fallen-women films in 1931 cut back to two or even one such film in 1932 and 1933. Moreover, parodies of the cycle appeared after 1931, for example, the vehicles MGM fashioned for Jean Harlow. Such reworkings of the formula "suggest that the cycle was beginning to pall and that its conventions were sufficiently (over-)familiar to warrant burlesquing." The fallen-woman films produced after 1934 conformed to the Code by treating potentially offensive material with greater ambiguity, but to repeat, the Code itself did not cause the cycle's decline.[101]

MGM produced more fallen-woman films than any other studio. In 1930 the studio released six fallen-women films; in 1931, ten; in 1932, three; in 1933, one; and 1934, two.[102] As a group, the MGM films are distinguishable from the output of other studios by their star power and by their special handling. Norma Shearer, Greta Garbo, Joan Crawford, and Jean Harlow generated the star power, and MGM's publicity machinery, the special campaigns and roadshow releases.

In 1931, the peak year of the cycle, fallen-woman films represented a remarkable 22 percent of the studio's output. THE SIN OF MADELON CLAUDET,

Helen Hayes in THE SIN OF MADELON CLAUDET *(MGM, 1931)*.

which starred Helen Hayes, generated the most interest, making it to the number-ten spot on *Film Daily*'s poll and winning the Oscar for best actress. *Variety* said, "Wistful Helen Hayes shot to meteoric success as Madelon Claudet, a besodden wretch of the Parisian by-ways. Buffeted from pomp to prison, slipping into pitiably made-up decrepitude—all because she loved unwisely and too well—she became the overnight sensation of cinema land."[103]

Norma Shearer and Conrad Nagel in THE DIVORCEE *(MGM, 1930).*

Beginning in 1933, MGM's big names were no longer associated with the cycle, suggesting that from the studio's perspective the cycle had gone downhill. Thereafter, MGM produced other types of women's pictures, ranging from sophisticated (but not sinful) dramas starring Norma Shearer, to contemporary romances starring Joan Crawford, to historical romances starring Greta Garbo.

Norma Shearer specialized at first in adult romantic dramas playing "ultra-emancipated heroines." Her first three thirties pictures—THE DIVORCEE (Robert Z. Leonard, 1930), LET US BE GAY (Robert Z. Leonard, 1930), and STRANGERS MAY KISS (George Fitzmaurice, 1931)—deal with infidelity and, according to Gavin Lambert, are "gift-wrapped in the conventions of the time":

> Each time she is finally reconciled with her husband, or the man who wants her to settle down and marry him, and each time an "excuse" is made for her infidelities, she feels neglected or misunderstood or the husband is unfaithful first. From Long Island to Paris, Mexico to Madrid, her partying takes Norma back to the Jazz Age; then, weary of pleasure, she accepts the post-Depression verdict of her suitor in *Strangers May Kiss:* "We like to mix our drinks, but we take our women straight." So the double standard continued to triumph, and audiences were equally delighted by a life of risk and a return to safety. (*Norma Shearer: A Life* [New York: Knopf, 1990], p. 137)

After this group of pictures, Shearer's theater-based vehicles range in style from the comedy of manners, to drama, to melodrama. The most adventuresome was STRANGE INTERLUDE (Robert Z. Leonard, 1932), a drama based on Eugene O'Neill's Pulitzer Prize play. Playing Nina Leeds, Shearer assumed the role Lynn Fontanne had created in the original Broadway production of 1928. C. Gardner Sullivan and Bess Meredyth compressed the five-hour play to less than two hours. Shearer plays a neurotic woman who has to confront loss of love, insanity in her family, and the shifting affections of several men in her life. A case study of Freudian sexuality, the role required her to age from eighteen to her late sixties, during which she has "a romantic fixation on her father, escapes from it into marriage and motherhood, still feels confined, liberates herself again with an affair, and ends up as a kind of Jocasta to her Oedipal son."[104]

O'Neill's play was experimental for its time, using asides to reveal the characters' thoughts and feelings. The picture handled this by having a character voice his or her actual words and then by having the character articulate his or her subconscious thoughts in a voice-over while adopting an appropriate facial expression. *Variety* called STRANGE INTERLUDE "a critic's and a woman's picture," but "the hinterland" was cool to the picture, and it ended up $90,000 in the red.[105] Thalberg's strategy did not really pay off until THE BARRETTS OF WIMPOLE STREET (Sidney Franklin, 1934), a widely acclaimed and profitable prestige picture.

Garbo invariably played either a vamp who broke men's hearts or a disillusioned woman of the world who falls hopelessly and giddily in love and suffers and sometimes dies when her lover deserts her on hearing of her past. After her sensational talking debut as a washed-out prostitute in ANNA CHRISTIE (Clarence Brown, 1930), Greta Garbo varied her image of a fallen woman playing an Italian diva in ROMANCE (Clarence Brown, 1930), a Parisian artist's model in INSPIRATION (Clarence Brown, 1931), a carnival kootch girl in SUSAN LENOX, HER FALL AND RISE (Robert Z. Leonard, 1931), a German spy in MATA HARI (George Fitzmaurice, 1932), and a chanteuse in a Budapest night club in AS YOU DESIRE ME (George Fitzmaurice, 1932). In GRAND HOTEL (Edmund Goulding, 1932), the only picture in this group that departs from this formula, she plays one of her most famous roles, the world-weary Russian ballerina Grusinskaya.

Reviewers fretted over her Swedish accent and her ability to read lines at first, but then complained that the stories Thalberg chose for her were unworthy of her talents. Reviewers also lamented the choice of her leading men. In her first talkies, she played opposite Charles Bickford, Gavin Gordon, and Robert Montgomery. Not until she teamed up with Clark Gable in SUSAN LENOX did her leading man have what fan magazines called "masculine S. A." Gable's presence revived the formula and helped make the picture one of Garbo's biggest successes. Her love scenes with John Barrymore in GRAND HOTEL were even more impressive.

Garbo's five-year contract with the studio expired in June 1932. Then at the height of her mass appeal, Garbo decided to vacation in Sweden, where she planned to remain until the studio gave her a new contract with a say in the choice of properties. After eight months, she agreed to return to the studio if she could make a picture based on the seventeenth-century Swedish monarch Queen Christina and if John Gilbert could be her co-star. QUEEN CHRISTINA (Rouben Mamoulian, 1933), a biopic produced by Walter Wanger, marked a new phase of

Greta Garbo in Queen Christina *(MGM, 1933).*

her career, in which she played tragic heroines in a series of prestige historical dramas.

Ranking behind Garbo and Shearer in status, Joan Crawford sustained her career playing the role of the "independent" woman, "who through choice or circumstance was forced to survive in modern society on her own." Although her social station varied from film to film, she played a kept woman in Possessed (Clarence Brown, 1931), a prostitute in Rain (UA; Lewis Milestone, 1932), and a woman on the make in CHAINED (Clarence Brown, 1934). In all her films, the problems she confronted "were what were thought to be 'women's problems' in the 1930s: finding the 'right man,' being in love with the 'wrong' man, raising children, and earning a living in a man's world."[106]

By the time Jean Harlow joined MGM in 1932, the fallen-woman cycle had just about run its course. But the studio used the cycle to good advantage by capitalizing on Harlow's flare for comedy. Her best pictures, RED DUST (Victor Fleming, 1932) and CHINA SEAS (Tay Garnett, 1935), contain hot-love-in-the-isolated-tropics plots in which she plays Sadie Thompson types opposite Clark Gable. She also played a memorable role as "a petulant, *nouveau riche* wife" in DINNER AT EIGHT (George Cukor, 1933).[107]

Following the pattern of MGM, Paramount's fallen-women films also peaked in 1931 and then went down to practically nothing by 1934. At first, the studio relied on Ruth Chatterton. Two pictures typify her work, SARAH AND SON (Dorothy Arzner, 1930) and UNFAITHFUL (John Cromwell, 1931). In the former, Chatterton repeated the MADAME X role she did for MGM in 1929 and played a "faithless wife who pays and declines and weeps and is at length defended in a murder trial by (unbeknownst to him!) her own son." *Variety* called this maternal melodrama a "three-handkerchief weepie." Of the latter picture, *Variety* said, "A first-class woman's story done in a modernized version of Arthur Wing Pinero; it's the sort of thing that Mrs. Pat Campbell used to moan through, only it has been jazzed up in the current style and if the femme fans don't go for it complete, the Empire State building is a bungalow."[108]

Paramount pinned its hopes on Marlene Dietrich. Like Greta Garbo, Marlene Dietrich was one of the biggest stars of the thirties, and like Garbo, she devoted herself mostly to playing vamps. Her image as a femme fatale became fixed playing Lola-Lola in von Sternberg's first talking film, THE BLUE ANGEL (1930), produced in Germany as a co-venture of UFA and Paramount. The picture was shot simultaneously in German and in English for worldwide distribution. In creating the Dietrich myth, von Sternberg said, "What I did was to dramatize her attributes and make them visible for all to see."[109]

After the success of the Berlin premiere, Paramount thought it had found a foreign star to rival Garbo and therefore signed Dietrich to a contract to work with von Sternberg on MOROCCO (1930). To introduce her to the American public, Paramount held back the general release of THE BLUE ANGEL in the United States until after MOROCCO hit the market. THE BLUE ANGEL was really Emil Jannings's picture, and besides, Paramount wanted to present its own version of the Dietrich persona first.

Playing opposite Gary Cooper in MOROCCO, Dietrich plays another cabaret artist, Amy Jolly, but unlike Lola-Lola, she is not a calculating destroyer of men; in a role reversal, it is she who falls hopelessly in love and is humbled by her lover. At the conclusion of the picture, Dietrich decides to be a camp follower and goes off into the desert (in high heels, no less) to her young French Legionnaire. Jules Furthman did the screenplay, which was based on the novel *Amy Jolly*, by Benno Vigny; Lee Garmes, the cinematography; Hans Dreier, the sets; and Travis Banton, the costumes. Released on a grind basis in New York rather than as a roadshow (Paramount knew the audience for this type of picture), MOROCCO was introduced by a huge publicity campaign that emphasized a rivalry with Garbo. *Variety*'s estimate of the picture was as follows:

Marlene Dietrich, Herbert Marshall, and Dickie Moore in BLONDE VENUS
(Paramount, 1932).

> The Dietrich girl has the Continental acting tricks, like Garbo. One is
> the tragic face—always tragic. Miss Dietrich perhaps smiles once in
> the entire picture, although in one section of it she's a cabaret singer
> and sings two songs, also in the Continental way. Otherwise the
> German girl looks quite nice and has an expressive face with features
> that photo well. But what she really holds in the talent line will have to
> be brought out by a stronger picture than *Morocco*. (*Variety*, 19
> November 1930)

The Dietrich–von Sternberg collaboration resulted in five additional pictures:
DISHONORED (1931), SHANGHAI EXPRESS (1932), BLONDE VENUS (1932), THE
SCARLETT EMPRESS (1934), and THE DEVIL IS A WOMAN (1935). In these pictures
she played, respectively, X-27, a World War I spy who sacrifices herself for her
lover by going to the firing squad; Shanghai Lily, China's most famous white
prostitute; Helen Faraday, a famous nightclub entertainer; a degenerate Cather-
ine the Great; and Concha Perez, a Spanish *fille de joie*. Following the precedent
established by MOROCCO, Dietrich performs suggestive songs more often than
not in bizarre costumes against exotic sets, courtesy of Travis Banton and Hans
Dreier. What made them distinctive, of course, was von Sternberg's unmistaka-
ble visual bravura.

The early Dietrich–von Sternberg films were considered art films and were accorded greater liberty in the depiction of "immoral" behavior. The National Board of Review, which commended films "for their artistic merit and for progress in the course of film art," named MOROCCO and DISHONORED to its list of Ten Best American Films. SHANGHAI EXPRESS, considered the finest of the group, received Oscar nominations for best picture, best direction, and best cinematography (Lee Garmes) and won in the latter category.

However, the Dietrich–von Sternberg magic began to lose its appeal with BLONDE VENUS. For one thing, von Sternberg's style became too mannered and too exotic for general tastes. For another, the plots become trite and fragmented. BLONDE VENUS was written by Jules Furthman and S. K. Lauren from a story by von Sternberg and combined tropes from the maternal melodrama and the fallen-woman film. Starting out a happily married wife and mother, Dietrich is taken on a downward trajectory to become first a cabaret singer, then a kept woman, and finally a prostitute; after bottoming out, her fortunes improve as she becomes a famous singer, the toast of Paris, and then a regenerated wife and mother as she is taken back by her husband. The nightclub number she performs in Paris, "Hot Voodoo," is one of her most unusual; she appears in a huge gorilla suit accompanied by spear-carrying chorus girls.

Disappointed by the poor showing of BLONDE VENUS, Paramount tried to revitalize Dietrich's image by assigning Rouben Mamoulian to direct her next picture and by developing Hermann Sudermann's *Song of Songs*, a novel that had presented "histrionic opportunities to Duse, Bernhardt, Modjeska, Pola Negri and Elsie Ferguson." In SONG OF SONGS (1933), Dietrich starts out an innocent peasant girl, becomes a sculptor's model, and then drifts from lover to lover. Paramount gave the picture a prestige send-off by arranging a roadshow engagement. *Variety*'s verdict: "Beautiful and artistic in montage and cinematography, but these elements have been permitted to eclipse the basic box-office intent. What matter the beautiful pan shots, idyllic scenes in the wildwood, the cinematic portrayal of the unsophisticated, peasant girl's amorous outpourings if it doesn't entertain?"[110]

The two Dietrich–von Sternberg pictures that followed, THE SCARLET EMPRESS (1934) and THE DEVIL IS A WOMAN (1935), were appreciated by the cognoscenti for their sophisticated themes and for the striking beauty of their settings and their photography, but what André Sennwald of the *New York Times* said of the latter probably held true for both: von Sternberg's work was "misunderstood and disliked by nine-tenths of the normal motion picture public."[111]

Trying to tap the woman's-film market using a foreign art-film model did not work. Devising another strategy, Paramount produced woman's pictures based on controversial American novels. AN AMERICAN TRAGEDY (Josef von Sternberg, 1931) and JENNIE GERHARDT (Marion Gering, 1933), were based on Theodore Dreiser novels and starred Sylvia Sidney. Both pictures deleted the social criticism and merely relied on the "lurid curiosity value" of Theodore Dreiser's name. THE STORY OF TEMPLE DRAKE (Stephen Roberts, 1933), an adaptation of William Faulkner's *Sanctuary* starring Miriam Hopkins, was "a sordid tale," said *Variety*. "No amount of seasoning to camouflage the basic rancidness of the theme can square it. It's hazy, befogged and replete with loose ends which, for obvious censorial reasons, can't be made to jell."[112]

Paramount's A FAREWELL TO ARMS (Frank Borzage, 1932), the first film adaptation of an Ernest Hemingway novel, fared best. Described by *Variety* as "the femmes' *All Quiet*—the romantic side of the great holocaust," the picture co-starred Helen Hayes as the English nurse in war-torn Italy and Gary Cooper as an American ambulance driver.[113] In its Broadway roadshow release, the picture ended with an "orthodox novel finish," in which Hayes dies with her unborn baby. For the general release, Paramount gave exhibitors a choice of two endings, the original or a happy, Pollyannaish fade-out. Nominated for the best-picture Oscar and voted into *Film Daily*'s Ten Best, A FAREWELL TO ARMS achieved prestige status.

With actresses like Constance Bennett, Ann Harding, and others on its roster, RKO tried to corner the woman's-film market, releasing six fallen-woman pictures in 1931 alone. RKO had so many box-office draws under contract that it differentiated its fallen-woman pictures by star and by type. For example, Constance Bennett typically played more sophisticated roles, whereas Helen Twelvetrees typically played working-class heroines. Capitalizing further on the woman's picture, the studio also produced maternal melodramas.

A free-lance actress, Constance Bennett worked for Warners and MGM in addition to RKO. In 1931, her peak year, she made five hit pictures and was ranked second only to Garbo in the polls. Her RKO films include BORN TO LOVE (Paul L. Stein, 1931), THE COMMON LAW (Paul L. Stein, 1931), LADY WITH A PAST (Edward H. Griffith, 1932), and WHAT PRICE HOLLYWOOD? (George Cukor, 1932). The first three are either fallen-woman films or maternal melodramas. The last one is a Cinderella story about a waitress who becomes a movie star. Produced by David O. Selznick, WHAT PRICE HOLLYWOOD? presented a romantic view of the movies and became the prototype for Selznick's A STAR IS BORN (1937).

Ann Harding became a star in Pathé's HOLIDAY (Edward H. Griffith, 1930), a comedy of manners based on the Broadway hit by Philip Barry. Harding received an Oscar nomination for best actress, and the picture made it to *Film Daily*'s Ten Best. After the studio merged with RKO, she starred in another Philip Barry comedy, THE ANIMAL KINGDOM (Edward H. Griffith, 1932). Her talents as a sophisticated actress were also used in a series of melodramas, imparting to them "a reality they didn't deserve." THE LIFE OF VERGIE WINTERS (Alfred Santell, 1934), in *Variety*'s opinion, was "one of those sobbers with the distinctive knack of drawing tears easily, naturally, and not forcing them. The women will go for it, and that's bound to mean business."[114]

The popularity of this group of female stars was short-lived. Constance Bennett, who was washed up at RKO by 1933, had several things going against her; she repeated the same roles in too many pictures too often. A star like Garbo made two films a year, but Bennett turned out four to six. Describing the quality of her scripts, *Variety* said that the formula of BORN TO LOVE "has been used by every film producer who could afford to buy a camera. . . . In *Born to Love* Constance Bennett is ruined again and has another baby. One of those war babies." Describing her acting style, *Variety* said that in THE COMMON LAW it was becoming as "stereotyped as the stories themselves."[115]

After the collapse of these stars, RKO pinned its hopes on a newcomer, Katharine Hepburn. The actress made a sensational motion-picture debut playing a devoted daughter opposite John Barrymore in A BILL OF DIVORCE-MENT (George Cukor, 1932), a role played by Katharine Cornell on Broadway. In

Constance Bennet and Joel McCrea in BORN TO LOVE *(RKO, 1931).*

her next picture, CHRISTOPHER STRONG (Dorothy Arzner, 1933), Hepburn played Lady Cynthia Darrington, a daring lady aviator who falls passionately in love with Sir Christopher Strong and commits suicide when she finds herself pregnant. The role, said Richard Jewell, "created a screen persona for Miss Hepburn that she would build upon for the rest of her career—independent, intelligent, courageous but, at the same time, vulnerable and sadly wistful due to her separation from orthodox life styles."[116] CHRISTOPHER STRONG died at the box office, but Hepburn had better luck with MORNING GLORY (Lowell Sherman, 1933), winning an Oscar in a Cinderella story about a struggling young actress who gets her big break and becomes a star. Hepburn solidified her reputation in LITTLE WOMEN (George Cukor, 1933) and helped revitalize the prestige picture.

Just when the fallen-woman cycle was thought to be dead, RKO released OF HUMAN BONDAGE (John Cromwell, 1934). Based on the novel by Somerset Maugham, the picture starred Leslie Howard as a clubfooted medical student who is obsessed with a "sluttish waitress." To play the role of Mildred, the waitress, RKO borrowed Bette Davis from Warners. Although the picture lost money, critics were awed by Davis's performance. *Life* called it "probably the best performance ever recorded on the screen by a U.S. actress." Davis returned to Warners a star, and RKO, prouder but poorer, concluded its fallen-woman cycle.

Kay Francis and William Powell in ONE WAY PASSAGE *(Warners, 1932).*

Warners relegated the fallen-woman film to programmers, a category some-where between the expensive class-A film and the low-budget B picture. During the early thirties, none of Warners' woman's films made it to *Variety's*, *Film Daily's*, or to anyone's list. Warners pinched pennies during the Depression, cutting production costs to the bone and investing in few big names. Rather than produce a few high-grade pictures, the studio relied on volume and concentrated on sensational stories to attract audiences. Such a policy accounts for the large number of fallen-woman films churned out by the studio well past the cycle's peak.

Warners released two fallen-woman films in 1930, eight in 1931, six in 1932, nine in 1933, and seven in 1934. Having no female names on its roster to speak of, Warners lured away two Paramount stars, Kay Francis in 1931 and Ruth Chatterton in 1932. Francis's biggest hit at Warner was ONE WAY PASSAGE (Tay Garnett, 1932), not a fallen-woman film but a poignant shipboard romance about two doomed lovers. Awarded the Oscar for best original screenplay (Robert Lord), the picture became a classic of its kind. Ruth Chatterton, a specialist in weepies, made six films for the studio, among them THE CRASH (William Dieterle, 1932) and FEMALE (Michael Curtiz, 1933). In the former, she played an unfaithful wife devasted by the stock market crash of 1929; in the latter, she played an executive of a large automobile company by day and an aggressive seductress by night.

Barbara Stanwyck served her apprenticeship at Warners and Columbia, having non-exclusive contracts at each studio. At Warners she was saddled with undistinguished material. In ILLICIT (Archie Mayo, 1931), she played an unconventional woman "unburdened by morals" who feels that marriage kills love and who seeks solace elsewhere. In LADIES THEY TALK ABOUT (Howard Bretherton and William Keighley, 1933), Stanwyck is an inmate in a women's prison, which *Variety* described as "a great retreat, the sort of a place where a lot of gals might like to spend a vacation until something or other blew over. They roam about as they please, play bridge, listen to the radio and have their cells fixed up like hotel rooms." In BABY FACE (Alfred E. Green, 1933), she is a working girl on the make. *Variety* said, "*Baby Face* is blue and nothing else. It possesses no merit for general or popular appeal, is liable to offend the family trade and can count only on juve attendance."[117]

Capitalizing on the popularity of the Busby Berkeley musicals, Warners produced a series of low-budget gold-digger films. They were designed for Joan Blondell and Glenda Farrell, who basically repeated their Berkeley roles in such pictures as HAVANA WIDOWS (Ray Enright, 1933), CONVENTION CITY (Archie Mayo, 1933), and KANSAS CITY PRINCESS (William Keighley, 1934). Unlike the typical fallen-woman heroine, the true gold digger was "as gaily amoral as Robin Hood," said Roger Dooley, and she "kept a wise-cracking tongue planted firmly in her well-rouged cheek. Since her willing victims were usually potbellied stage-door Johnnies played by actors like Guy Kibbee, Eugene Pallette and George Barbier, who could quarrel with such an equitable redistribution of wealth?"[118]

Ever resourceful, Warners produced another variant of the woman's film that depicted the working woman in the urban jungle who was *not* willing to trade on her sex. These pictures depicted successful business and professional women, but they did not compete directly for a man's job. Barbara Stanwyck is the title character in NIGHT NURSE (William Wellman, 1931); Bette Davis, a fashion illustrator in EX-LADY (Robert Florey, 1933); and Key Francis, a pediatrician is MARY STEVENS, M.D. (Lloyd Bacon, 1933). Although Ruth Chatterton played an executive of a motor car company in FEMALE, her role reflected the times in its characterization of women; Chatterton, having inherited the company from her father, runs it only until she falls in love and marries, after which she turns the company over to her husband so that she can remain home to raise a family.

Fox produced only a few fallen-woman pictures during the early thirties. Its biggest female draw was Janet Gaynor, one of the "purest" stars in Hollywood. For her talents, Fox attempted to exploit the Cinderella romance. Her first effort, DADDY LONG LEGS (Alfred Santell, 1931), a remake of a Mary Pickford silent, was a "smash," said *Variety:* "It is one of those rare talkers with universal appeal. . . . The picture will attract the women. It has everything for them from motherless children to a Cinderella-like romance. As such the film looks like happy matinee harbinger and something theatres have been looking for." Although the picture "threatened to unloose a series of similar productions from the coast studios," *Variety* observed that this anticipated cycle "never fully came to life."[119]

Columbia's principal contribution to the trend consists of two Barbara Stanwyck pictures directed by Frank Capra, THE MIRACLE WOMAN (1931) and THE BITTER TEA OF GENERAL YEN (1933). In the former, a combination of social criticism and romance, Stanwyck plays a con artist, the evangelist Florence ("Faith") Fallon, a role modeled on Aimee Semple McPherson and inspired by Sinclair Lewis's *Elmer Gantry;* in the latter, she plays a New Englander who is held by a Chinese warlord in Shanghai. Both repelled and fascinated by the artistic and villainous sides of the warlord's character, she ultimately succumbs to his spell and surrenders herself to him. Although he rejects the offer and commits suicide, the approval given to miscegenation by the movie raised the hackles of more than one censor.

Universal contributed three memorable pictures to the trend, all directed by John M. Stahl. BACK STREET (1932), based on Fannie Hurst's novel about a married man and his self-effacing mistress, featured Irene Dunne and John Boles. *Variety* called it "a winner. It's a tear-jerker, without being artificially sentimental, impressing in the main as a human document faithfully translated into celluloid and sound."[120]

IMITATION OF LIFE (1934), also based on a Fannie Hurst novel, starred Claudette Colbert, a young widow with a baby girl, who goes into the pancake business with her black maid, played by Louise Beavers, who also has a baby girl. Over time, the business makes both women wealthy, but neither derives much joy from the venture—all because of their daughters. Colbert discovers that she and her daughter, Rochelle Hudson, love the same man, Warren William; Beavers sees her daughter, Fredi Washington, a black born with white skin, "miserable being unable to adjust herself to the lot of her race and unable to take her place among the whites." Said *Variety,*

> Picture is stolen by the Negress, Louise Beavers, whose performance is masterly. This lady can troupe. She took the whole scale of human emotions from joy to anguish and never sounded a false note. It is one of the most unprecedented personal triumphs for an obscure performer in the annals of a crazy business. Fredi Washington as the white-skinned offspring was excellent in the funeral scene when overcome by remorse. (*Variety,* 27 November 1934)

Stahl's MAGNIFICENT OBSESSION (1935) co-starred Irene Dunne and Robert Taylor. Based on the best-seller by Lloyd C. Douglas, it was the studio's most prestigious picture of the year. Taylor, a playboy, is responsible for an automobile accident that results in Dunne going blind. Taylor's remorse turns to love for Dunne, and he becomes a reformed man. Inspired by a magnificent obsession to become an eye surgeon, he not only achieves his goal within six years but also wins a Nobel Prize. He then makes amends to Dunne by performing an operation on her that restores her sight.

The Breen Office did not kill the fallen-woman film, nor did self-censorship affect the durability of the woman's film in general. After 1934, mistresses and demimondaines were no longer found in modern dress, but they could be detected in period costumes. Garbo, for example, received her greatest acclaim playing a courtesan in CAMILLE (1937). Lea Jacobs has demonstrated how a little bit of ambiguity in the depiction of illicit sex could go a long way in satisfying the censors.[121]

Fewer women's films were produced after 1934, not because of pressure from bluenoses but because top actresses tried their hands at screwball comedy. A production trend without melodramatic excess, screwball comedy depicted a new relationship between the sexes, wherein the hero and heroine are social and intellectual equals. It is true the studios tried to revive the maternal melodrama in 1937 by producing THAT CERTAIN WOMAN, CONFESSION, and STELLA DALLAS. But *Variety* probably expressed the majority sentiment, saying that "all three are carefully and well made. What will happen if they are but forerunners of a cycle of films about renunciating mothers, however, is too horrible to contemplate."[122]

Paramount had no bankable female stars in the mid-thirties to replace Marlene Dietrich and Mae West. Following the success of LITTLE WOMEN, RKO saw Katharine Hepburn slip in the polls to the point where exhibitors labeled her box-office poison. Hepburn staged a brief comeback in ALICE ADAMS (George Stevens, 1935), an adaptation of Booth Tarkington's 1921 Pulitzer Prize–winning novel about a small-town girl who is snubbed by society, and tried to sustain it in QUALITY STREET (George Stevens, 1937), an adaptation of J. M. Barrie's play about "a lady teetering on the brink of spinsterhood and casting about for a husband before all hope is gone," but the picture bombed. RKO closed the decade by releasing one of the finest romantic dramas of the period, LOVE AFFAIR (Leo McCarey, 1939), which co-starred Irene Dunne and Charles Boyer. Co-authored, directed, and produced by Leo McCarey, the picture was described by Frank S. Nugent as having "the surface appearance of a comedy and the inner strength and poignance of a hauntingly sorrowful romance."[123]

The sheer power of MGM's top stars enabled the studio to coast along as the most important producer of woman's films. Garbo and Shearer made fewer and fewer pictures each year, but each one was an event that riveted media attention. Quantity was further affected by the death of Jean Harlow in 1937 and by the decline of Joan Crawford. As economic conditions improved in the second half of the decade, MGM declared Crawford's working-girl image outmoded and tried to convert her into a screwball heroine. The attempt failed. MGM checked her decline only temporarily by casting her as Crystal, a hard-boiled perfume clerk who steals the heroine's husband in THE WOMEN (George Cukor, 1939), a part that resembled her Flaemmchen role in GRAND HOTEL.

THE WOMEN achieved a status of its own in the woman's film. Based on Clare Boothe Luce's smash Broadway hit, which Roger Dooley calls a "comedy of *bad* manners," the picture was produced by Hunt Stromberg and adapted by Anita Loos and Jane Murfin. Containing not a single male role, the cast of one hundred and thirty was headed by a galaxy of stars, notably Norma Shearer, Joan Crawford, Rosalind Russell, and Paulette Goddard. Frank S. Nugent of the *New York Times* described the picture as "a sociological investigation of the scalpel-tongued Park Avenue set, entirely female, who amputate their best friends' reputations at luncheon, dissect their private lives at the beauty salon and perform the postmortems over the bridge table, while the victims industriously carve away at their surgeons. It is a ghoulish and disillusioning business."[124] Audiences loved it, nonetheless, even the five-minute Technicolor fashion show staged by Adrian that was inserted into the black-and-white footage. At year's end, the picture was named to the Ten Best lists of *Film Daily* and the *New York Times*.

By the end of the decade, Warners had nudged MGM from its lofty position as the preeminent producer of woman's films. Warners accomplished this feat by

Katharine Hepburn and Fred MacMurray in Alice Adams *(RKO, 1935).*

discovering the right formula for displaying the enormous and varied talents of its leading lady, Bette Davis. The actress introduced something new to the woman's film, the classical protagonist, described by Joanne Yeck as "neither the sacrificial mother nor the romantic lover," a "headstrong, intelligent, yet imperfect" woman who had to work through a particular problem.[125] The formula was introduced in rudimentary form in Dangerous (Alfred E. Green,

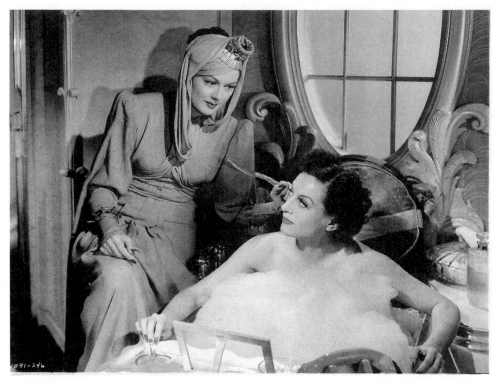

Rosalind Russell and Joan Crawford in THE WOMEN *(MGM, 1939).*

1935), a rickety melodrama written by Laird Doyle that reverses Davis's man-wrecking role of Mildred in OF HUMAN BONDAGE.

Davis won an Oscar for DANGEROUS, but she did not reach artistic maturity until JEZEBEL (William Wyler, 1938). In this picture, screenwriters Clements Ripley, Abem Finkel, and John Huston adapted Owen Davis's play to fashion a heroine to rival Margaret Mitchell's Scarlett O'Hara. As Julie Marsden, Bette Davis plays a willful, arrogant, and selfish Southern belle whose behavior has tragic results. She is rude to her guests by arriving late to her own party; she insults all of New Orleans society by insisting on wearing a shocking red dress to a ball and loses the man she loves to another woman; and she baits her suitor to a duel that costs him his life. Davis is hysterical, irresponsible, and even wicked, but when Pres, the love of her life, is stricken with yellow fever, she reveals a new dimension of her character—sacrifice. She begs Pres's wife, Amy (Margaret Lindsay), to let her accompany the dying Pres into quarantine with the promise that if he lives, she will send Pres back to her. Having fought hard for such a role, Davis was vindicated in her battle with Warners by winning her second Oscar for best actress.

Now at the height of her powers, Davis took on a series of roles that won her the title of First Lady of the Screen. She next did five pictures in little more than a year, in each giving a virtuoso performance of suffering and courage. Two of the pictures, JUAREZ (William Dieterle, 1939) and THE PRIVATE LIVES OF ELIZABETH AND ESSEX (Michael Curtiz, 1939), are prestige biopics. In the former, she plays a monarch, the Empress Carlotta, who goes mad, and in the latter, a monarch,

Bette Davis and Geraldine Fitzgerald in DARK VICTORY *(Warners, 1939).*

Queen Elizabeth, who sacrifices love for duty. However, Davis was more effective in DARK VICTORY (Edmund Goulding, 1939) and in THE OLD MAID (Edmund Goulding, 1939), vehicles specially crafted for her by producer Hal B. Wallis, director Edmund Goulding, and screenwriter Casey Robinson. DARK VICTORY was based on the hit Broadway play by George Emerson Brewer, Jr., and Bertram Block that starred Tallulah Bankhead; it is about a fast-living Long Island socialite who is afflicted with a malignant brain tumor and meets death finely. DARK VICTORY "brought the woman's film to its apogee," said Bernard Dick. "Nothing lay beyond it, for there is nothing beyond death met finely." Davis's honest approach and her craftsmanship transformed a potentially maudlin performance into "a great role . . . designed for a virtuosa," which was admired for its eloquence, tenderness, and "heart-breaking sincerity."[126]

Davis gave another outstanding performance in THE OLD MAID. A drama of rival motherhood set during the Civil War, THE OLD MAID is based on the Pulitzer Prize play by Zoë Akins adapted from Edith Wharton's novel. It co-starred Bette Davis and Miriam Hopkins. Charlotte (Bette Davis) has a daughter by a suitor (George Brent) who dies in the war and allows her childless cousin Delia (Miriam Hopkins) to rear the child as her own. As "Aunt" Charlotte, Davis watches her daughter grow up and has to endure the loss of motherhood, the resentment of the daughter and the rival mother, and the prospect of living out her life as an alienated old maid. The subtlety of Davis's interpretation revealed Charlotte's growth as a woman in accepting her lot and Davis's own powers as an actress.

United Artists came into its own during the second half of the decade, when its two most important producers, Sam Goldwyn and David O. Selznick, practically specialized in the woman's film. Goldwyn tried to create a continental star to rival Greta Garbo and Marlene Dietrich by grooming a young actress from the Ukraine, Anna Sten. After a two-year buildup during which she tried to learn English, Sten made her debut in NANA (Dorothy Arzner, 1934), a free adaptation of Emile Zola's classic. The picture failed miserably, partly because Goldwyn emasculated the story for American audiences and partly because Sten mangled her English. Goldwyn tried to launch her in a second vehicle and again failed.

To reach the woman's-film market, Goldwyn went another route and produced THESE THREE (William Wyler, 1936), which was based on Lillian Hellman's controversial Broadway play *The Children's Hour*. Because the play alluded to lesbianism, the Hays Office ruled that Goldwyn "could not use its title or its plot or even mention the fact that he had acquired it." To salvage something from the original, Goldwyn hired Hellman to adapt her own play. Having been given free rein, Hellman retained the psychopathic schoolgirl (Bonita Granville), her two teachers (Miriam Hopkins and Merle Oberon), and the girls-school setting, but changed the substance of the lies that destroy the lives of the two women from allusions to lesbianism to nonmarital sex. Frank S. Nugent said, "The film has preserved through the magic of Miss Hellman's adaptation, the very heart of the original" and named the picture to the *New York Times* Ten Best list.[127]

Goldwyn's STELLA DALLAS (King Vidor, 1937)—a remake of his 1925 silent starring Belle Bennett—was less sensational but more successful at the box office. It starred Barbara Stanwyck and proved the durability of Olive Higgins Prouty's novel of maternal love and sacrifice. Frank Nugent noted that "at the Music Hall . . . there were muted audiences that shed a communal tear and cleared their communal throat as Stella made the gallant gesture and abandoned her daughter to the proper influences and the wedding vows of Richard Grosvenor 3d."[128]

While Selznick was preparing GONE WITH THE WIND, he found time to produce two other woman's films, MADE FOR EACH OTHER (John Cromwell, 1939) and INTERMEZZO (Gregory Ratoff, 1939). The former starred Carole Lombard and James Stewart in a comedy-drama about the vicissitudes of a young married couple. *Variety* called it "an exquisitely played, deeply moving comedy-drama. It is a happy combination of young love, sharp cleancut humor and tearjerker of the first water."[129] The latter picture, which introduced Ingrid Bergman to American audiences and turned her into a star, tells the story of a famed concert violinist (Leslie Howard) who falls in love with his musical protégée.

In buying the motion-picture rights to Margaret Mitchell's GONE WITH THE WIND, Selznick had acquired not just a historical novel set during the Civil War but an epic that depicted the Civil War from the perspective of a female protagonist, Scarlett O'Hara.[130] By no means a sweet, domesticated heroine, Scarlett "symbolized a sassy restlessness with the twentieth-century arrangement of women's roles" and progressed through several stages of development:

> First, as a selfish socialite unrequitedly in love with Ashley Wilkes, the poetic dreamer who never comes to terms with the New South. Next, as the restless wife of three men—Charles Hamilton (for spite

Barbara Stanwyck and Alan Hale in STELLA DALLAS *(UA, 1937)*.

because Ashley is marrying Melanie), Frank Kennedy (to pay off the plantation Tara's postwar taxes), and Rhett Butler (for sexual pleasure, though eventual tragic separation). Most of all, as the pragmatist who moves with the times, getting on with delivering a baby single-handedly while the Yankees approach Atlanta, doing business with Yankees during Reconstruction in order to pay the bills, and then resolving to mend her broken heart by retreating to Tara to begin again. Like all of us, she has problems with everything and everyone: her parents, siblings, children, her sex life, her bank balance. And she is surrounded . . . by an array of complex, vital and comic characters who flesh out a historically acute and fictionally rich picture of the South at its greatest crisis. (Helen Taylor, *Scarlett's Women* [New Brunswick, N.J.: Rutgers University Press, 1989], pp. 16–17)

The women of the novel are familiar types. In addition to "the vain, proud, uppity Feminine Woman (Scarlett)," the novel contains "the capable, loyal, wise Female Woman (Mammy), the pure, genteel Real Lady (Melanie), and the trapped-in-the-past Fallen Woman (Belle Watling)."[131] Denigrated by the trade press but sustained by a loyal female audience, the woman's film revealed itself as a durable and venerable production trend throughout the decade. In transferring Scarlett O'Hara and her milieu to the screen, Selznick was amply rewarded by the woman's-film audience for his efforts.

Comedy

As America's principal purveyor of entertainment, Hollywood packaged comedy in many forms. In 1929, *Variety* surveyed the major studios and classified production trends into seven categories. Comedy was divided into two—comedy drama and comedy. The types subsumed under comedy drama consisted of society, rural, city, mystery, college, and domestic, and the types under comedy consisted of farce and action-adventure. A quarter of all the films produced by the majors in 1929 could be classified as comedies of one sort or another.[132] Although comic types metamorphosed into the sophisticated, low-life, anarchistic, sentimental, folksy, screwball, populist, or romantic, the production trend remained a key component of every studio's roster.

Because the talkies required "voiced verbal humor," the silent comedians of the twenties found themselves "being replaced by the invading, wise-cracking horde from vaudeville and burlesque."[133] The three greatest silent comedians, Charlie Chaplin, Buster Keaton, and Harold Lloyd, made the transition, but their careers were all affected. Chaplin fared the best, retaining his popularity not by capitulating to the talkies but by defying them. However, his production output dropped from seven films during the twenties to two during the thirties, CITY LIGHTS (1931) and MODERN TIMES (1936). Chaplin enjoyed the freedom to produce silents because as an independent producer he used his own money to finance his pictures and as an owner of United Artists he controlled their distribution.

Shortly before the release of CITY LIGHTS, Chaplin argued in an article for the *New York Times* that pantomine and comedy "represented a universal art which could not, or should not, be ousted by the current 'hysteria' for talkies." Pantomime, he claimed, "is a universal language, while speech as a form of communication is restricted to those who understand it."[134] The early talkies indeed seemed primitive compared to the beauty of late silent pictures, but Chaplin resisted dialogue also because his pictures typically did their best business in foreign markets, which would have been largely foreclosed to him had he used English.

CITY LIGHTS premiered on 6 February 1931, three years after the introduction of sound. Containing a musical score and sound effects, CITY LIGHTS was essentially a "film of the twenties," exhibiting "many of the narrative and comic conventions of *The Gold Rush* and *The Circus*." Acclaiming it as one of Chaplin's greatest achievements, *Variety* said, "He never talked . . . in vaudeville before going into pictures, and, having made himself the foremost exponent the world knows today, there doesn't appear any reason why he should talk. With his ability to create and take familiar situations to make them look differently he can go on making successful silent films until he chooses to retire—so long as they entertain." CITY LIGHTS grossed more than any other previous Chaplin picture and eventually earned a profit of $5 million, an extraordinary accomplishment for the time.[135]

MODERN TIMES premiered on 5 February 1936. In it, Charlie remains mute, but he sings some jabberwocky that he made up to the tune of a Spanish fandango. The picture contains a musical score, some sound effects, and a few vocal elements. Unlike Chaplin's earlier films, MODERN TIMES contains topical allusions to the Depression and to social problems, among them the dehumaniz-

Charlie Chaplin's CITY LIGHTS *(UA, 1931)*.

ing effects of the assembly line, the class struggle, unemployment, and homeless-
ness. "The critics welcomed back the well-loved figure and paid tribute to his
undiminished pantomimic skill, but found the film uneven," said Theodore
Huff.[136] Part of the problem was the ambiguity of the film's political message.
MODERN TIMES grossed $1.4 million domestically, placing it on *Variety's* list of
top-grossing pictures. Overseas, the picture fared even better. The picture was a
box-office hit, but compared to Chaplin's earlier efforts, it was a disappointment.

Buster Keaton fared the worst. Abandoning independent production during
the transition to sound, Keaton joined MGM as a contract player and thereby
turned over artistic control of his pictures to the studio. MGM experimented with
ways to use his talents, but the solution—teaming him with Jimmy Durante in
THE PASSIONATE PLUMBER (Edward Sedgwick, 1932) and WHAT! NO BEER?
(Edward Sedgwick, 1933)—finished his career. As Roger Dooley put it, "Durante's aggressive, verbal style of comedy virtually wiped Keaton's understated
deadpan humor off the screen."[137]

Harold Lloyd sustained his career by producing his own pictures as an
independent. Releasing mainly through Paramount, he turned out a picture
every two years: FEET FIRST (Clyde Bruckman, 1930), MOVIE CRAZY (Clyde
Bruckman, 1932), THE CAT'S PAW (Sam Taylor, 1934), THE MILKY WAY (Leo
McCarey, 1936), and PROFESSOR BEWARE (Elliott Nugent, 1938). At first, Lloyd
did not bend to the talkies to satisfy his fans. For example, Mordaunt Hall of the

New York Times said that MOVIE CRAZY, Lloyd's most effective picture, "hardly benefits by sound. It is essentially the old silent school technique."[138] However, beginning with THE CAT'S PAW, Lloyd adapted the techniques of sound production by subordinating gag development to story development, by relying on strong supporting casts to build up the comedy, and by adapting material from other media. In so doing, his pictures lost their individuality.

Sentimental comedy, or "folksy comedy," as it was sometimes called, was the popular favorite during the early thirties. Exploited mainly by MGM and Fox, the trend revolved around down-to-earth stars. At MGM the cycle actually began in the late twenties when Marie Dressler revived her fading silent-screen career by teaming up with Polly Moran to make a series of low-budget comedies. Over the next six years, they made eight pictures together and became a highly successful female comedy team. Playing plain older women of the type usually described as "battle-axes," the two were typically cast as "friendly enemies" in rough-and-tumble comedies "addressed to the banana-peel sense of humor" and containing a dollop of sentiment. These pictures appealed to "the mob" and did their best business away from the "class spots," said *Variety*. Among these pictures were CAUGHT SHORT (Charles Reisner, 1930), REDUCING (Charles Reisner, 1931), and POLITICS (Charles Reisner, 1931).[139]

MGM's cycle of sentimental comedies took off when the studio teamed up Dressler with Wallace Beery in MIN AND BILL (George Hill, 1930), a vehicle written by Frances Marion and Marion Jackson and based on the Lorna Moon novel *Dark Star*. Min is "a hard-boiled old gal, landlady of a fishing village inn, catering exclusively to sea rats but acting a lot tougher than she really is," and Bill, an old salt, is her sweetheart. Essentially a melodrama, the major thread of action concerns Dressler's attempt at keeping the abandoned child she has raised from her alcoholic mother. Discovering that her daughter is engaged to a wealthy young man from a prominent family, the mother returns and plans to insinuate herself back into her daughter's life. Just before she can reveal herself, however, she starts a fight with Dressler and ends up being shot dead. The ending of the picture shows Min watching the happily married couple sail away on their honeymoon and then being identified as the murderer and led off the dock by a policeman. Providing an antidote to these sentimental moments are scenes of broad humor, such as when Min catches Bill with the mother on his lap and "breaks up every loose article in the room in giving Bill a licking."[140] Not only did MIN AND BILL become the biggest box-office draw of the year, but it also earned Dressler an Oscar for her performance.

MGM teamed Dressler and Beery a second time in TUGBOAT ANNIE (Mervyn LeRoy, 1933), a sequel of sorts adapted by Zelda Sears and Eve Greene from a *Saturday Evening Post* series by Norman Reilly Raine. In this movie, Dressler plays "a game old woman, the captain of a tugboat, who is inordinately proud of her son (the captain of a liner) and has an ineradicable fondness for her husband (the tugboat's chief liability), who [she says] 'has never struck me except in self-defense.'" Said *Variety*, "Those who will be irritated or annoyed by the story's hokey, sobby, stale baloney nature are likely to be a very small minority. The average Dressler-Beery fan, of whom there are many, will eat it up as is without asking for Worcester sauce."[141]

Minus Beery, Dressler made EMMA (Clarence Brown, 1932), a vehicle designed for her by Frances Marion. In this picture, Dressler is a servant who

Marie Dressler and Wallace Beery in TUGBOAT ANNIE *(MGM, 1933).*

devotes her life to raising the children of a widower only to see them turn on her in her old age. "The hoke sympathy . . . has been laid on very thick," said *Variety*. "There is a courtroom scene that is the height of strong-arm bathos and some of the passages toward the end are absurd in their determination to pull tears by claptrap device. Nothing but Miss Dressler's astonishing ability to command conviction saves some of these sequences from going flat."[142] Dressler died of cancer in 1934, and her passing was deeply mourned by the public.

Wallace Beery made it to top-ten lists every year until 1935. An experienced character actor like Dressler, he sustained a faltering career during the transition to the talkies by playing lovable old rogues with hearts of gold. Given his looks, he had little choice. He once said, "Like my dear old friend, Marie Dressler, my mug has been my fortune." MIN AND BILL also made Beery a star, a position he solidified in THE CHAMP (King Vidor, 1931) by winning an Academy Award for best actor. Beery plays a broken-down ex-heavyweight fighter who is training for a comeback, a role written for him by Frances Marion. At his side is his young son, played by Jackie Cooper. A nine-year-old veteran of the Our Gang series, Jackie Cooper became the first child star of the decade in Paramount's SKIPPY (Norman Taurog, 1931), a kid's picture based on a popular comic strip that ranked number three on *Film Daily*'s Ten Best and that earned Taurog an Oscar for best direction. Using Cooper to good advantage, MGM pulled out all the stops at the conclusion of THE CHAMP. Describing the pathos of this scene, *Variety* said, "The tears are drawn by [Jackie Cooper] alone. The Champ, his father and his idol, dies at the finish. The kid goes into a crying panic. He walks from one sympathizer to another in the dressing room, rejecting each condolence with a scream for the Champ."[143]

Folksy comedy at Fox meant Will Rogers. Rogers was Fox's first important star in the sound era. A cowboy philosopher, cracker-barrel humorist, actor, and news commentator, Rogers was one of the best-loved Americans of his time. Starting out in show business in 1904, he performed roping acts and cowboy tricks in wild-west shows. Moving to vaudeville, he embellished his act with humorous comments expressed in an Oklahoma drawl. His Broadway career reached its zenith in 1917 when he became a star attraction in the Ziegfeld Follies. Performing off and on there until 1925, "his home-spun philosophy and cracker-barrel wit made him a surprising hit with New Yorkers: he spoke with seeming sincerity and without malice. He was Mr. Everyman—it was soon realized that he spoke for Mr. Joe Public."[144] In 1922, Rogers started writing a series of syndicated articles for the *New York Times* that were carried by some 350 newspapers with an estimated 40 million readers.

Rogers's stage character was transferred directly to the screen. The formula for his pictures was simple. What *Variety* said about HANDY ANDY (David Butler, 1934) can apply to just about all his pictures: "There's no doubt or hesitation about this one; it's all Will Rogers and all box office. There isn't any sophistication and there isn't any sheen—just Will Rogers." An insight into his act is found in *Variety*'s review of LIGHTNIN' (Henry King, 1930):

There is a scene where Lightnin' [Will Rogers] discourses solemnly with a bevy of fluttering Reno divorcees the ins and outs of alimony, and it's a gem for homely philosophy. There's also Lightnin's epic tale of how he "drove a swarm of bees across the prairie in the dead of winter without losing a single bee." The play is a mine of artless nonsense of the same sort, rising to the final scene, old Bill in court, where his devoted but headstrong wife has been inveigled into a divorce suit. Here is a bit of action that plays unerringly upon the heartstrings, with Rogers handling it for every ounce of appeal. (*VFR*, 3 December 1930)

Will Rogers in STATE FAIR *(Fox, 1933).*

Two of Rogers's pictures made it to *Film Daily*'s Ten Best and to *Variety*'s list of hits, STATE FAIR (Henry King, 1933) and JUDGE PRIEST (John Ford, 1934). STATE FAIR, his greatest success, was adapted from Phil Stong's best-seller by playwright Paul Green and Sonya Levien and featured Janet Gaynor and Lew Ayres. Said *Variety*,

> Henry King has nicely caught the spirit of the simple story and has turned in a production that has the charm of naturalness and the virtue of sincerity. No villain, little suspense, but a straightforward story of a rural family who find their great moments at the state fair, where paterfamilias captures the title for his prize hog, the mother makes a clean sweep in the pickle entries, the boy gets his first vicarious but satisfying taste of romance, and the girl finds a more lasting love. . . . *State Fair* promises to be a winner all the way down the line. (*VFR*, 31 January 1933)

After Rogers's death in 1935, Shirley Temple kept sentimental comedy alive at Fox for the remainder of the decade.

Sophisticated comedy, which was at the opposite end of the spectrum from sentimental comedy, practically glutted the market during the transition to sound. Used primarily to showcase glamorous female stars, these pictures typically received prestige treatment. Suffice it to say here that plays by Noel Coward, Somerset Maugham, and Ferenc Molnár satisfied Hollywood's perennial hunger for prestige and "represented the kind of distinction that studio heads could recognize without difficulty: the distinctions of rank and power and money. The 'classy' film is essentially an upper-class kind of film: a celebration of the elite and privileged," as James Harvey put it.[145] Although MGM specialized in the type, Paramount arguably produced the best example, TROUBLE IN PARADISE (Ernst Lubitsch, 1932). The film contains outstanding performances by Herbert Marshall, Miriam Hopkins, and Kay Francis; wonderful art deco sets by Hans Dreier; and a witty and clever script by Samson Raphaelson. Although Dwight MacDonald considered the picture a masterpiece, saying it "comes as close to perfection as anything I have ever seen in the movies," the picture found the going rough outside the biggest key cities.[146]

Explaining why even the best sophisticated comedies were coolly received, James Harvey said that these movies had "nothing to do with what Hollywood movies in general did best: evoking specifically American qualities of experience and consciousness. And that consciousness was programmed, whatever the actual and rampant injustices of American society, to a certain uneasiness on such subjects as class and wealth and privilege. . . . Such topics would nearly always be touchy, to some degree, in American films." *Variety* offered other explanations; its review of TROUBLE IN PARADISE stated, "Swell title, poor picture. Will have b.o. trouble. Despite the Lubitsch artistry, . . . it's not good cinema in toto." For one thing, "the mugg fans are sticklers for realism and the Continental abadabba, with which *Trouble* is flavored, doesn't click." For another, the plot is "predicated on a totally meretricious premise. Herbert Marshall is the gentleman crook. Miriam Hopkins is a light-fingered lady." And Kay Francis, "a wealthy young widow . . . decidedly on the make for Marshall," appoints him as her "secretary."[147]

Hollywood had better luck raiding Broadway and vaudeville for comic talent and developing various forms of comedian-centered vehicles to showcase their routines. During the shift to the talkies, Paramount signed the Marx Brothers, Mae West, and W. C. Fields; Goldwyn, Eddie Cantor; RKO, Bert Wheeler and Robert Woolsey; and Warners, Joe E. Brown, to name a few. The comedian comedies that made it to *Film Daily*'s Ten Best and to *Variety*'s top-grossing films lists are the Marx Brothers' HORSE FEATHERS (Norman Z. McLeod, 1932) and two Mae West pictures, SHE DONE HIM WRONG (Lowell Sherman, 1933) and I'M NO ANGEL (Wesley Ruggles, 1933). All were released by Paramount.

The Marx Brothers' pictures are examples of anarchistic comedy. A comic form that emerged when producers attempted to absorb certain aspects of the vaudeville aesthetic into the classical Hollywood cinema, anarchistic comedy, said Henry Jenkins, is anarchistic in both form and content: in form, such films "press against traditional filmic practice, moving from the classical Hollywood cinema's emphasis upon linearity and causality to a far more fragmented and atomistic textual practice," and in content, "they often celebrate the collapse of social order and the liberation of the creativity and impulsiveness of their protagonist."[148] In practice, anarchistic comedies are episodic, containing just enough connective tissue to string together sequences that enable the star to demonstrate his or her routines—for example, Eddie Cantor's blackface routines, Harpo Marx's harp solos, Bert Wheeler's female impersonations, and W. C. Fields's golf or pool tricks. Vaudeville stars are given names and social positions and play roles, but often they break loose from the constraints of the narrative by reverting to their stage personas. In so doing, they consciously break the "fourth wall" convention of classical Hollywood cinema by using such devices as direct address to the camera and reflexive gags.

In addition to borrowing from vaudeville, anarchistic comedy borrowed elements of slapstick from American silent comedy; the convention of incorporating songs, dances, and instrumental solos into the narrative from the musical stage; and comic forms of wordplay from "the lunatic school of writers" of the twenties, writers such as Stephen Leacock, Donald Ogden Stewart, and Robert Benchley.[149]

Two studios specialized in anarchistic comedy, RKO and Paramount. RKO developed a type of anarchistic comedy around the team of Bert Wheeler and Robert Woolsey. Between 1930 and 1937 the team turned out features like so many sausages, "with Woolsey a kind of road-company Groucho and Wheeler like a combination Zeppo and Harpo." Their comic formula included vaudeville patter laced with sexual double entendres, cavorting in drag, cardboard villains, romantic subplots, and songs. A favorite tack of theirs was to lampoon movie fads, for example, gangsters (HOOK, LINE AND SINKER, Edward Cline, 1930), prison (HOLD 'EM JAIL, Norman Taurog, 1932), costumers (COCKEYED CAVALIERS, Mark Sandrich, 1934), and Westerns (SILLY BILLIES, Fred Guiol, 1936).[150] Although their routines had gone stale after a couple of years, their following sustained them until the team ended with Woolsey's death in 1938.

Unlike Wheeler and Woolsey, the Marx Brothers caught the fancy of the critics and enjoyed media attention throughout their careers. The earliest Marx Brothers films included Groucho, a verbal comedian noted for his double entendres, wacky monologues, and sardonic asides who became identified with his crouched walk, painted mustache, leering eyes, and perpetual thick cigar; Harpo, a pantomimist and gifted harpist who communicates by honking a taxi horn and who became identified with his fright wig, crumpled top hat, oversized trousers, and capacious overcoat, "from which he could produce anything from a lighted candle to a cup of coffee"; Chico, a dialect comedian and pianist who resembles a vaudeville Italian; and Zeppo, a straight man and juvenile who typically played romantic roles.

The Marx Brothers in DUCK SOUP *(Paramount, 1933).*

The Marx Brothers' first two pictures, THE COCOANUTS (Robert Florey and Joseph Santley, 1929) and ANIMAL CRACKERS (Victor Heerman, 1930), were actually transcriptions of their hit Broadway shows and were shot at Paramount's Astoria Studio on Long Island by day while the team performed on stage by night. Afterward, the team moved to Hollywood and made a remarkable series of anarchistic comedies consisting of MONKEY BUSINESS (Norman Z. McLeod, 1931), HORSE FEATHERS (Norman Z. McLeod, 1932), and DUCK SOUP (Leo McCarey, 1933). Although DUCK SOUP is generally regarded today as their masterpiece, HORSE FEATHERS was the most successful. The butts of their satire are institutions, social fads, and the movies themselves. The Marx Brothers got away with subverting the law, government, international diplomacy, and other institutions not because of "their sheer madness" but because their pictures use satire "only as *New Yorker* cartoons do, lightly, echoing the popular consensus" and because their "comic method will not allow a sustained focus on any one thing."[151]

A blend of vaudeville, the musical stage, and slapstick comedy, the Marx Brothers style was a collaborative effort of producer Herman J. Mankiewicz; directors McLeod and McCarey; writers Bert Kalmar, Harry Ruby, S. J. Perelman, and Will B. Johnstone; and gagmen Nat Perrin and Arthur Sheekman. Kalmar and Ruby were also responsible for most of their songs. Concerning their routines, *Variety*'s jaded reviewers saw little that was new. For example, the reviewer of MONKEY BUSINESS considered the picture "mostly a patchwork of all previous Marx efforts. . . . Boys closely follow their established methods of reaching a point and immediately rushing for the next gag. . . . Show people will see nothing new in the film as regards the boys and much that is familiar. But that doesn't necessarily count in the majority of places this feature will play right now." Believing that the romantic subplots, songs, and musical specialties affected the pacing of their comedy, the Marx Brothers wanted to drop all vestiges of the musical stage from their pictures, but exhibitors apparently loved these elements, particularly Chico's and Harpo's solos, and pressured the studio to retain them.[152]

To showcase Mae West, Paramount developed a form of comedian-centered comedy that was closely allied to burlesque. A personality comedienne with a style all her own, West gained notoriety during the twenties in vaudeville and on the stage, writing, producing, and directing her own plays, several of which were either closed by the police or caused a commotion. Her trademark was a provocative walk with a toss of the hips, bawdy songs, and quips. In show-biz parlance, her routine was a two-act—a comedienne with a straight man—but in her case, a series of straight men feeding her quips. Describing the verbal humor of West's BELLE OF THE NINETIES, *Variety* said, "The Westian pepigrams are reeled off in orthodox variety manner; somebody, anybody (her maid, an admiring swain, the on-the-make muggs, a casual stooge) asks her a simple question and she never answers in straightforward manner. Always a wisecrack. But that's the West technique."[153] But West's comic style was not merely verbal; it also consisted of a special acting style:

> Miss West's acting style is at once both traditional and burlesque. Unfortunately, there is a certain confusion possible here because one means both that Miss West's style is in the tradition of American Burlesque, or "burleycue," and that it is a burlesque of that tradition. Whatever one may think of that tradition, it must be granted that Miss West has brought it to its classic culmination. One may use such a word as "classic" because of the extreme objectivity with which Miss West both recognizes and employs her materials. So perfectly does she now sum up in her own person—her speech, gestures, and carriage— the main elements of her tradition that she no longer requires a story or even a backdrop. She would be effective on a bare concert stage. (William Troy, "Mae West and the Classic Tradition," *Nation*, 8 November 1933, p. 548)

West's first two starring pictures for Paramount, SHE DONE HIM WRONG (1933) and I'M NO ANGEL (1933), grossed \$2.3 million and \$2.2 million, respectively, and became the studio's biggest hits of the decade. SHE DONE HIM WRONG was an adaptation by Harvey Thew and John Bright of West's smash Broadway play *Diamond Lil*. As *Variety* pointed out, "deletions in the script from its original 1928 legit form were few, with only the roughest of the rough stuff out. . . . The swan bed is in, but for a flash only, with Mae doing her stuff on the chaise lounge (*sic*) in this version." The songs—"Easy Rider," "I Like a Man What Takes His Time," and "Frankie and Johnny"—were "somewhat cleaned up lyrically."[154]

A Mae West craze swept the country and to capitalize on the notoriety of its

Mae West in BELLE OF THE NINETIES *(Paramount, 1934).*

new find, Paramount rushed I'M NO ANGEL into production. West wrote the story and dialogue. Said *Variety,* "Needless to say this opus will scarcely get on the reformers' recommended lists. But with the tide running the opposite way perhaps the spleen of the moralists isn't such a factor right now. And anyway, Mae West is today the biggest conversation-provoker, free space-grabber and all-around box-office bet in the country. She's as hot an issue as Hitler."[155] On the basis of these two pictures, West was voted the eighth-biggest box-office draw of 1933.

West planned on calling her third picture IT AIN'T NO SIN, but the Breen Office, no doubt reacting to the groundswell of protests against her films by women's clubs and civic and religious organizations, demanded a new title and revisions of certain scenes and dialogue. The result, BELLE OF THE NINETIES (Leo McCarey, 1934), was "sufficiently denatured from within and yet not completely emasculated." By the end of the year, Paramount had more than doubled West's 1933 salary of $220,000, which made her the highest-salaried woman in the country.[156]

To tailor vehicles for Joe E. Brown, Warners developed a special brand of comedian-centered comedy called affirmative comedy. Affirmative comedy, said Henry Jenkins, "subordinates performance almost totally to the demands of characterization" and depends "less upon extended sequences of comic performance or even upon individual verbal gags than upon small bits of character business and narratively integrated situations which display the comic protagonist's awkwardness or social ineptitude."[157] By emphasizing plot and character over performance and comic spectacle, affirmative comedy contrasts sharply with anarchistic comedy. If anarchistic comedy was most popular in big cities, affirmative comedy found its niche in rural areas.

Joe E. Brown's trademark was "his beady eyes, cavernous mouth, and air of amiable idiocy." Brown appeared in twenty-three films for the studio from 1929 to 1936, most based on the same formula "of the timid soul compelled to perform some impossible feat of daring or athletic prowess." Brown's top films include three baseball pictures—FIREMAN, SAVE MY CHILD (Lloyd Bacon, 1932), ELMER THE GREAT (Mervyn LeRoy, 1933), and ALIBI IKE (Ray Enright, 1935)—in which he plays "a bush league baseball player with phenomenal talent as a pitcher or hitter" and EARTHWORM TRACTORS (Ray Enright, 1936), which was based on the Alexander Botts character, a super-tractor salesman, who had been providing "entertainment fodder" for *Saturday Evening Post* readers for years.[158]

Comedian-centered comedies lost much of their appeal by 1934, which "the trade press attributed to their over-exposure and their failure to produce a consistently high-quality product." As Henry Jenkins notes, "Almost all of the comedians had long since exhausted the repertoire of 'tried and true' material they had developed through the years in vaudeville and were forced to venture into new territory without the benefit of audience-testing and revision."[159] Responding to decling ticket sales and exhibitor dissatisfaction, studios either pink-slipped fading stars or attempted to revamp their vehicles to conform to Hollywood entertainment norms.

Irving Thalberg tried the latter, signing the Marx Brothers to a contract in 1935. For their first MGM venture, A NIGHT AT THE OPERA (Sam Wood, 1935), Thalberg instructed writers George S. Kaufman and Morrie Ryskind to cut the number of gags and arranged for the team to pretest new material before live audiences in West Coast theaters. Thalberg also wanted to balance their routines with romantic subplots. Although their anarchy was tamed and their films resembled musicals with love plots, Thalberg's renovation worked. A NIGHT AT THE OPERA was a big hit, grossing twice as much as DUCK SOUP, and led to a series that included A DAY AT THE RACES (Sam Wood, 1937) and AT THE CIRCUS (Edward Buzzell, 1939), among others.

Mae West was not as fortunate. Revamping her act in 1935, she departed from her usual bawdy 1890s style to play a Western oil heiress who breaks into society in GOIN' TO TOWN (Alexander Hall, 1935). (The picture was originally titled *Now I'm a Lady.*) It was a "commendable attempt" that went awry. "No amount of epigrammatic hypoing can offset the silly story," said *Variety.* West returned to her ususal 1890s milieu in KLONDIKE ANNIE (Raoul Walsh, 1936), playing a character *Variety* called "a prostie and a murderess." "As a picture it is again Mae West with the usual formula of wisecracks. That is no longer enough," said *Variety*, which added, "Miss West really ought to let someone else have a word as to her stories."[160]

In 1934 a new comedy cycle struck the public's fancy, one variously labeled "madcap," "daffy," or "screwball." Launched by three surprise hits, Columbia's IT HAPPENED ONE NIGHT (Frank Capra) and TWENTIETH CENTURY (Howard Hawks), and MGM's THE THIN MAN (W. S. Van Dyke), the cycle peaked in 1936 with the release of Columbia's MR. DEEDS GOES TO TOWN (Frank Capra) and dropped out of fashion by 1938. According to *Variety*, "Changes in the taste of the candy that pours out of Hollywood have included a very definite trend away from screwball comedies. . . . This occurred early in the spring when a deluge of this type of picture finally started keeping people out of the theatres, with some very worthwhile comedies in this class going down to ignominious defeat at the box office."[161]

Influencing literally scores, if not hundreds, of pictures, the screwball comedy had its roots in silent slapstick comedy, in the satirical writing of Dorothy Parker, Alexander Woolcott, and Herman J. Mankiewicz, and in Broadway of the 1920s, particularly the carefully synchronized gag comedy of playwrights George S. Kaufman, Morrie Ryskind, Marc Connelly, and Moss Hart. In Hollywood the style was perfected by directors such as Frank Capra, Leo McCarey, George Cukor, Gregory La Cava, Wesley Ruggles, and George Stevens, by screenwriters such as Ben Hecht and Charles MacArthur, Albert Hackett and Frances Goodrich, Robert Riskin, Dudley Nichols, Norman Krasna, George Seaton, Claude Binyon, Charles Brackett, Billy Wilder, Preston Sturges, and by stars such as Cary Grant, Jean Arthur, Carole Lombard, Irene Dunne, Claudette Colbert, and Katharine Hepburn.

IT HAPPENED ONE NIGHT, which starred Clark Gable and Claudette Colbert on loan-out from MGM and Paramount, respectively, opened in February 1934 to positive reviews, but word-of-mouth made it one of the year's biggest hits. At Academy Award time, the picture swept the five most prestigious Oscars, including the one for best picture. Although this film has traditionally been considered the beginning of the screwball cycle, contemporaneous sources saw the picture as a continuation of ongoing trends. Noting that Robert Riskin's screenplay about a runaway heiress who falls in love with a tough reporter was based on a short story in *Cosmopolitan* by Samuel Hopkins Adams entitled "Night Bus," *Variety*, for example, identified the picture as the fourth version of the overland-bus cycle. Others considered the picture as just another version of GRAND HOTEL—a "traveling hostelry" film similar in structure to such GRAND HOTEL spin-offs as Fox's TRANSATLANTIC (1931), Paramount's SHANGHAI EXPRESS (1932), and Columbia's own AMERICAN MADNESS (1932). Seen from this perspective, IT HAPPENED ONE NIGHT did not pop out of nowhere, but materialized from Columbia's strategy of following trends.[162]

Clark Gable and Claudette Colbert in It Happened One Night *(Columbia, 1934).*

Capra's so-called breakthrough film, Lady for a Day, which Columbia had released the previous year, followed the same strategy. Based on a tale by Damon Runyan, the film combined elements of the Cinderella and sentimental comedy cycles. And its star, the seventy-five-year-old May Robson, who played Apple Annie, the whiskey-soaked street woman, came from the same mold as MGM's down-to-earth star Marie Dressler. The picture ranked number four on the *Film Daily* Ten Best and was nominated for four Oscars. IT HAPPENED ONE NIGHT, like LADY FOR A DAY, contained just the right combination of script, acting, and direction to make it special. Said *Variety,* "The story has that intangible quality of charm which arises from a smooth blending of the various ingredients. Difficult to analyze, impossible to designedly reproduce. Just a happy accident."[163]

Columbia's TWENTIETH CENTURY, produced and directed by Howard Hawks, was adapted by Ben Hecht and Charles MacArthur from their 1932 Broadway hit. Set on the Twentieth Century Limited en route from Chicago to New York, the picture starred John Barrymore, a Svengali-like theatrical impresario, and Carole Lombard, his protégée who walks out on him to go into the movies. Again, critics did not see the picture as a trendsetter but as another variation of satirical comedy. For example, *Motion Picture Herald* said, "Fundamentally, it's a ridiculous burlesque of stage people; a hare-brained egotistical producer and explosive temperamental star and the satellites around them." Barrymore, not Lombard, received most of the attention. For example, the *Film Daily* said, "Besides being refreshingly off the beaten path in the way of satirical comedies, this adaptation of the Broadway play has the value of the biggest and most versatile performance ever given by John Barrymore. Other choice morsels [include] hilarious situations, nifty dialogue, swell supporting work by Miss Lombard, Walter Connolly and Roscoe Karns."[164] The picture did well in larger cities, but in the rest of the country, only so-so. In popularity, it was eclipsed by MGM's THE THIN MAN.

A murder mystery with a comic romantic subplot, THE THIN MAN starred William Powell and Myrna Loy. MGM acquired the rights to Dashiell Hammett's novel soon after it was published in 1933, but because the story contained "sadism, masochism and kindred unfilmable stuff," screenwriters Frances Goodrich and Albert Hackett had to clean it up, while retaining "some of the flavor of the book that brought the advance plugs."[165] MGM probably got the idea of casting William Powell as Nick Charles after observing his success as Philo Vance in Warners' S. S. Van Dine detective series. The studio probably got the idea of teaming him with Myrna Loy after observing the chemistry they generated together in the recently released MANHATTAN MELODRAMA.

MGM apparently conceived the picture as a programmer by scheduling an eighteen-day shoot and by budgeting a modest $200,000 on the production. THE THIN MAN was a comic variation on a dramatic genre, as was IT HAPPENED ONE NIGHT.The film closely followed the basic plot of Hammett's murder mystery, but inserted into the narrative line a secondary plot involving Nick and Nora Charles. Describing the comic romantic interplay between Powell and Loy, *Variety* said,

> What appears to have been the most successful part of the Hackett-Goodrich team's adaptation is that they captured the spirit of the jovial, companionable relationship of the characters, Nick, retired detective, and Nora, his wife. Their very pleasant manner of loving each other and showing it was used as a light comedy structure upon which the screen doctors' performed their operation on the Hammett novel. . . . For its leads, the studio couldn't have done better than to

John Barrymore and Carole Lombard in Twentieth Century *(Columbia, 1934).*

William Powell and Myrna Loy in The Thin Man *(MGM, 1934).*

> pick Powell and Miss Loy, both of whom shade their semi-comic roles
> beautifully. (*VFR*, 3 July 1934)

Nick and Nora soon became a national craze and elevated Powell and Loy to
stardom.

Although every studio contributed to the screwball cycle, three specialized in
it, Columbia, Paramount, and MGM. Columbia followed up IT HAPPENED ONE
NIGHT with THE WHOLE TOWN'S TALKING (John Ford, 1935). If Columbia
varied the GRAND HOTEL formula to make the former picture, it varied the
LITTLE CAESAR formula by producing a parody of a gangster film to make THE
WHOLE TOWN'S TALKING. Written by Jo Swerling and Robert Riskin, the picture
starred Edward G. Robinson, who played a double role of villain and hero, and
contained the theme of lamb biting wolf, of David defeating Goliath, a theme
Capra would develop in the Deeds-Smith-Doe triolgy.

Capra followed up IT HAPPENED ONE NIGHT with BROADWAY BILL (1934).
Placed into production before IT HAPPENED ONE NIGHT caught on, BROADWAY
BILL can be considered a male version of LADY FOR A DAY. Robert Riskin's
screenplay was based on a Runyonesque story by Mark Hellinger about the
troubles and jams of Dan Brooks, played by Warner Baxter, "the hopeful owner
of a stout-hearted horse, Broadway Bill." BROADWAY BILL played on the
heartstrings like LADY FOR A DAY; *Variety* reported that when Broadway Bill
dropped dead after winning his race, the audience was left "bawling in the
Music Hall's $1.65 mezzanine."[166]

After IT HAPPENED ONE NIGHT's Academy Award sweep, Columbia continued following trends, but revised its production strategy by injecting madcap
elements into its comedies. The studio naturally wanted to capitalize on its
success with Claudette Colbert and borrowed her from Paramount again to
make SHE MARRIED HER BOSS (Gregory La Cava, 1935), a comic variation of the
traditional sob-and-hanky melodrama. Said *Variety*, "A couple of years ago the
same story would probably have been handled as a heavy, tragic domestic
treatise with everything sour until the sweet ending. But *It Happened One Night*
and *The Thin Man* have changed a lot of things and smashed numerous
precedents, among them stories such as this one."[167]

Although SHE MARRIED HER BOSS did only so-so business, Columbia decided
to use product variation a second time in designing two vehicles for Irene
Dunne. Dunne had previously specialized in melodramas and musicals, but
Columbia offcast her in THEODORA GOES WILD (Richard Boleslawski, 1936) and
THE AWFUL TRUTH (Leo McCarey, 1937). Playing opposite Melvin Douglas in
the former, Dunne played a "female Mr. Deeds" in a "distaff version" of Capra's
MR. DEEDS, noted a review. Playing opposite Cary Grant in the latter, a comedy
of remarriage, Dunne had better luck; the picture made it to *Film Daily*'s Ten
Best, McCarey won an Oscar for best direction, and Irene Dunne and Cary Grant
temporarily topped Myrna Loy and William Powell as the wittiest screwball
couple of them all.

After Katharine Hepburn bought up her contract with RKO, she convinced
Columbia to do a remake of HOLIDAY (George Cukor, 1938), a comedy of
manners based on the Philip Barry hit first filmed in 1930 by Pathé with Ann
Harding in the lead. Having understudied the lead in the original Broadway
production, Hepburn had a special affinity for the play and convinced Columbia

Cary Grant and Irene Dunne in THE AWFUL TRUTH *(Columbia, 1937).*

to produce it with Cary Grant as her co-star. *Variety* said of the picture, "Miss Hepburn, after a whirl at historical drama and a wild farce in her recent assignments, is back in her best form and type of role in *Holiday,* which is a modern drama. Her acting is delightful and shaded with fine feeling and understanding throughout."[168]

Columbia's reputation as a producer of comedies rests mainly on three big

James Stewart, Jean Arthur, Lionel Barrymore, and Edward Arnold in YOU CAN'T TAKE IT WITH YOU *(Columbia, 1938).*

Capra hits, MR. DEEDS GOES TO TOWN (1936), YOU CAN'T TAKE IT WITH YOU (1938), and MR. SMITH GOES TO WASHINGTON (1939). Capra's stature had grown to the extent that beginning with MR. DEEDS, Columbia placed Capra's name above the title of his pictures. Screenwriter Robert Riskin collaborated with Capra on the first two pictures, and Sidney Buchman, on the third. Columbia borrowed Gary Cooper from Paramount to star in MR. DEEDS and James Stewart from MGM to star in the others. Jean Arthur, Columbia's only contract star, co-starred in all three. If one line of screwball featured the madcap adventures of wealthy heroines in comedies of remarriage, these three Capra pictures followed another line by depicting "utopian fantasies" in which the little guy always comes out on top.[169] For example, the eponymous hero Longfellow Deeds, a rural innocent from Mandrake Falls, Vermont, inherits $20 million from a rich uncle and gets the happy idea of helping out needy farmers by giving each one a cow and two acres of land.

YOU CAN'T TAKE IT WITH YOU (1938), Riskin's adaptation of the Pulitzer Prize–winning Broadway comedy by George S. Kaufman and Moss Hart, depicted the wacky antics of the Sycamore family. Said *Variety*, "Lionel Barrymore plays the harmonica, his married, middle-aged daughter is typing plays that'll never sell, with a kitten cutely used as a paperweight; one of her daughters is practicing dancing; her husband is at the xylophone, and others are testing firecrackers or doing something else." Capra and Riskin rewrote the play by transforming the character of Anthony P. Kirby, a wealthy industrialist, into a principal part and by shifting the conflict from snobbish conventionality versus spirited self-expression to greedy capitalism versus the little guy. Graham Greene said of the film, "The director emerges as a rather muddled and sentimental idealist who feels—vaguely—that something is wrong with the social system."[170]

MR. SMITH GOES TO WASHINGTON pits Jimmy Stewart, a young senator, against the political machine and tears it to pieces. *Variety* described MR. SMITH as "typically Capra, punchy, human and absorbing—a drama that combines timeliness with current topical interest and a patriotic flavor blended masterfully into the composite whole to provide one of the finest and most consistently interesting dramas of the season."[171]

The three Capra pictures were named to *Film Daily*'s Ten Best and won numerous awards, including special recognition for Capra. YOU CAN'T TAKE IT WITH YOU, the most acclaimed of the group, was hailed by *Time* as "The Number 1 cinema comedy of 1938" and received Academy Awards for best picture and best direction. The box-office performance of these pictures was another matter. Columbia budgeted $500,000 for MR. DEEDS, double the amount it had spent on IT HAPPENED ONE NIGHT, and made money doing so. But for Capra's subsequent pictures, including LOST HORIZON, Columbia permitted budgets to escalate to $1.5 million and more, which went beyond the capability of the pictures to return profits. As a result, Capra's pictures earned Columbia enormous prestige, but little profits.[172]

Having had long experience in sophisticated comedy, Paramount was nicely positioned in the screwball-comedy sweepstakes. It started out with an offbeat entry, RUGGLES OF RED GAP (Leo McCarey, 1935), a comedy of displacement starring Charles Laughton as Ruggles, the British valet imcomparable, who is won in a poker game in Paris and is brought by his new master to the American frontier. McCarey's direction, Laughton's outstanding comic performance, and the support of an excellent cast, made RUGGLES a box-office leader and placed it on *Film Daily*'s Ten Best.

When Claudette Colbert returned to the studio a star after IT HAPPENED ONE NIGHT, Paramount attempted to recreate the Gable-Colbert chemistry by developing "in-house" vehicles that teamed her with Fred MacMurray. The job of developing these vehicles went to the studio's top director-writing team, Wesley Ruggles and Claude Binyon, who fashioned two love triangles, THE GILDED LILY (1935) and THE BRIDE COMES HOME (1935), in which Colbert chooses an average American guy over pampered and wealthy suitors. Unlike IT HAPPENED ONE NIGHT, in which she played a runaway heiress, these films cast Colbert as a working girl—a secretary in the first and a magazine editor in the second. Also unlike IT HAPPENED ONE NIGHT, which takes place mainly along a southern rural highway, these picture take place in an urban milieu of "skyscrapers, nightclubs, and fancy hotels favored by the rich . . . as well as the homely apartments, front stoops, spaghetti joints, park benches, and city buses frequented by the not-so-rich."[173]

Binyon and Ruggles enlarged the triangle to a quadrangle in I MET HIM IN PARIS (1937). In this picture, Colbert plays a working girl who goes to Paris for a hard-earned vacation and is pursued by playboy Robert Young, playwright Melvyn Douglas, and hometown boy Lee Bowman. Said *Variety*, "Long after audiences will have forgotten what this picture is about, the studio probably will be showing the film as one lesson in what a comedy picture ought to be. . . . But it's not the story. It's not the acting. It's not the production. It's the many infinitesimal touches stuck into the script and action by the adaptor, Claude Binyon, and the director-producer, Wesley Ruggles."[174]

After taking the triangle formula about as far as it could go, Paramount assigned writers Charles Brackett and Billy Wilder the task of getting extra mileage out of Colbert. They did so by placing the screwball conventions in a French milieu. In BLUEBEARD'S EIGHTH WIFE (Ernst Lubitsch, 1938), Colbert played opposite Gary Cooper, but the picture flopped. In MIDNIGHT (Mitchell Leisen, 1939), she played opposite John Barrymore. The picture received fine reviews, but was lost in the flood of great movies that year.

In addition to producing a virtual Claudette Colbert cycle, Paramount extended its range by creating vehicles for Carole Lombard and Jean Arthur. After winning recognition for her gifted performance in TWENTIETH CENTURY, Lombard's career stalled as she was loaned out by Paramount from studio to studio. She finally came into her own at Universal playing opposite William Powell in MY MAN GODFREY (Gregory La Cava, 1936). Commenting on her role as an endearing and zany heiress, *Variety* said, "Miss Lombard has played screwball dames before, but none so screwy as this one. From start to finish, with no letdowns or lapses into quiet sanity, she needs only a resin bag to be a female Rube Waddell. And she has no exclusive on eccentricity, for her whole family, with the exception of the old man, seem to have been dropped on their respective heads when young."[175] Powell plays the Bullock family butler. A tramp, he is collected in a scavenger hunt at the city dump by Lombard. However, it turns out that he is actually the scion of a blue-blooded Boston family who went on the bum as a result of a broken love affair. Attempting to straighten out the wacky Bullock family, Powell naturally becomes ensnarled by Lombard.

Returning to Paramount a star, Lombard played opposite Fred MacMurray in three pictures in a row: THE PRINCESS COMES ACROSS (William K. Howard, 1936), SWING HIGH, SWING LOW (Mitchell Leisen, 1937), and TRUE CONFESSION (Wesley Ruggles, 1937). None of the pictures clicked, and because Paramount tried to turn her and MacMurray into a regular team, she signed a non-exclusive contract with David O. Selznick.

Borrowing Jean Arthur from Columbia for EASY LIVING (Mitchell Leisen, 1937), Paramount produced its zaniest farce. A variation of the Cinderella cycle written by Preston Sturges, the picture was "reminiscent of those old custard pie and Keystone chase days," said Frank Nugent of the *New York Times*. Arthur plays a poor stenographer who, while riding to work on a Fifth Avenue double-decker bus one morning, is hit by a brand new sable coat that has been flung out of an apartment window by tycoon Edward Arnold in a fit of pique over his wife's extravagance. "Upon Miss Arthur's head it falls and with it, in one of those farce-illogical chains of circumstance, comes the reputation of being the tycoon's mistress, her lodgment in the imperial suite of the Hotel Louis (Luis Alberni, manager) and her unbeknownst encounter with the tycoon's son, Ray Milland, who has been earning a busboy's living in the automat."[176]

MGM was seemingly well positioned to exploit the screwball cycle, having on its roster Clark Gable and the William Powell–Myrna Loy team. IT HAPPENED ONE NIGHT revitalized Clark Gable's career, and he remained in the box-office top ten for the rest of the decade. However, he achieved this feat not by performing screwball comedy, since comedy was not really his strength, but by reverting to virile roles in romances and action pictures, playing opposite MGM's leading ladies, particularly Myrna Loy, Joan Crawford, and Jean Harlow.

MGM's first attempt at exploiting Powell and Loy following THE THIN MAN was EVELYN PRENTICE (1934), a courtroom melodrama. The picture was a bust. In the film, Powell and Loy are married to each other, but as the *New York Times* said, the picture provided them "with almost no opportunity for the kind of ripping and urbane humor at which they proved themselves so adept in *The Thin Man.*" MGM tried doubly hard the next time by mixing ingredients from IT HAPPENED ONE NIGHT and THE THIN MAN into a concoction called LIBELED LADY (Jack Conway, 1936). An heiress-newsman picture, it contained a galaxy of stars, among them Spencer Tracy as a newspaper editor, Jean Harlow as his fiancée, William Powell as a reporter, and Myrna Loy, as a millionairess. Said *Variety,* "Stripped of its encumbrances, picture seeks to tell of what befalls Powell when, as the trouble-shooter for a newspaper, he undertakes to frame a young millionairess and thereby compel her to drop a $5,000,000 libel suit. The expected occurs; he falls in love with her."[177] Taking another approach, MGM assigned Powell and Loy to DOUBLE WEDDING (Richard Thorpe, 1937), a pale imitation of Universal's MY MAN GODFREY, which had teamed Powell and Carole Lombard.

MGM discovered that Powell and Loy were not bankable as a team outside the THIN MAN context. MGM therefore initiated a series, which, during the thirties, consisted of AFTER THE THIN MAN (1936) and ANOTHER THIN MAN (1939). Like the original, both starred Powell and Loy and used the same director and writers—W. S. Van Dyke, and Frances Goodrich and Albert Hackett. AFTER THE THIN MAN topped the original, making it to *Variety*'s annual list of box-office winners, but ANOTHER THIN MAN failed "to measure up to the high entertainment standard set by its predecessors," said *Variety.*[178] The drawback—MGM domesticated the couple by giving them a year-old son.

In 1939, while MGM's Andy Hardy series had just about killed off the screwball cycle, the studio looked to the cycle for help. Greta Garbo, who had her largest following overseas, saw her career threatened by the spreading hostilities in Europe. MGM therefore assigned writers Charles Brackett, Billy Wilder, and Walter Reisch the task of devising a fresh formula that would increase Garbo's drawing power in the domestic market. The team fashioned NINOTCHKA (Ernst Lubitsch, 1939), a gem about a gloomy Communist envoy from Moscow who falls in love with a Parisian playboy (Melvyn Douglas). MGM's ads for the picture proclaimed, "Garbo laughs!"—a bookend to the "Garbo talks!" promotion that introduced her first talkie. Said *Variety,* "It's high-caliber entertainment for adult audiences, a top attraction for the key deluxers, and rates better grosses from the subsequent houses than has been the case in Garbo's last three pictures."[179] Although the picture received four Oscar nominations, it proved a disappointment at the box office.

RKO also looked to screwball comedy as a means of rehabilitating the career of its biggest star, Katharine Hepburn. RKO had trouble getting Hepburn's persona right after she made it to Hollywood's top echelons in 1933 starring in LITTLE WOMEN and MORNING GLORY. ALICE ADAMS (George Stevens, 1935) made money, but she then appeared in a series of flops that included MARY OF SCOTLAND (John Ford, 1936), A WOMAN REBELS (Mark Sandrich, 1936), and QUALITY STREET (George Stevens, 1937). Finally, the studio got it right by casting her opposite Ginger Rogers in STAGE DOOR (Gregory La Cava, 1937). Based on the Edna Ferber–George S. Kaufman play about a group of aspiring actresses living in a theatrical boardinghouse, the picture earned a modest profit, received four Oscar nominations, and became the only RKO comedy of the decade to make it to the *Film Daily* Ten Best. Actually, STAGE DOOR "didn't really change the Hepburn persona," notes Kathleen Kendall. "In fact, it sealed in the original Hepburn legend of the patrician heroine, entitled to put on airs and still be rewarded, because she's basically a good egg."[180]

In addition to rehabilitating Hepburn's career, STAGE DOOR indicated that Ginger Rogers could be effective without Fred Astaire. She would dance with Astaire in two more musicals in the thirties, but both understood that the series was winding down. To develop a separate persona for her in STAGE DOOR, RKO cast her as a wisecracking young hopeful, a role similar to those she had played early in her career at Warners. Rogers enlarged her skills as a comedienne in VIVACIOUS LADY (George Stevens, 1938), BACHELOR MOTHER (Garson Kanin, 1939), and FIFTH AVENUE GIRL (Gregory La Cava, 1939). BACHELOR MOTHER was the most successful; RKO's biggest sleeper of the decade, it earned over $800,000.

After STAGE DOOR, Hepburn made BRINGING UP BABY (1938). Inspired by THE AWFUL TRUTH and co-starring Cary Grant, BRINGING UP BABY was produced and directed by Howard Hawks and written by Dudley Nichols and Hagar Wilde from an original story by Wilde. Although the picture is regarded today as one of the most hilarious comedies of the era, it lost $365,000, partly because the public had grown tired of sophisticated comedies, but also because Hawks allowed the production to run far over budget.

Universal and United Artists also released screwball comedies of note, the best of which were tailored for Carole Lombard. Universal, as previously noted, produced MY MAN GODFREY, which teamed Lombard with William Powell. After joining David O. Selznick, Lombard made NOTHING SACRED (William Wellman, 1937), a screwball comedy of sorts written by Ben Hecht that satirized the newspaper business. Although *Variety* called it "one of the top comedies of the season," the picture did less than expected. The screwball cycle had played itself out.

Since Warners' stars lacked the urbane sophistication of Cary Grant or the daffiness of Carole Lombard, the studio hardly participated in the screwball comedy craze. Warners produced comedies, but looked to Broadway as a source. "Most of the Warners' stage-to-screen adaptations were comedies in the middle range: inoffensive, often veering towards farce, and studded with juicy roles for their 'stock company' players."[181] THREE MEN ON A HORSE (Mervyn LeRoy, 1936), based on the classic American farce by John Cecil Holm and George Abbott, started Warners' cycle. Frank McHugh, the studio's popular featured player, had the role of Erwin Trowbridge, "the simpleminded writer of greeting card verse who becomes entangled with horse racing gamblers because he can pick winners." TOVARICH (Anatole Litvak, 1937), based on Robert E. Sherwood's translation of the Jacques Deval comedy, starred Claudette Colbert and Charles Boyer on loan-out, playing former members of the czarist imperial household forced to take jobs as servants in the home of a Parisian banker. BOY MEETS GIRL (Lloyd Bacon, 1938), a spoof of Hollywood based on the 1935 Broadway smash hit by Sam and Bella Spewak, teamed up James Cagney and Pat O'Brien to play a pair of manic screenwriters.

Twentieth Century–Fox also lacked the wherewithal to produce screwball comedy. But, unlike Warners, "Fox kept trying, turning out great numbers of such films all through the time of their vogue. But Fox screwball always seemed imitative and pale, never first-rate or even quite convincing." The problem rested with its stars. Said James Harvey, "It's one of the oddities of Darryl Zanuck's tenure as studio production head that the contract stars—Loretta Young and Alice Faye, Tyrone Power and Don Ameche and Sonja Henie (the first ice-skating star)—were consistently less interesting than the stars at the other studios."[182] In an attempt to build Tyrone Power and Loretta Young into romantic leads, the studio rushed them into several co-starring vehicles in 1937—LOVE IS NEWS (Tay Garnett), a venture into the reporter-heiress cycle; CAFE METROPOLE (Edward H. Griffith), a mixture of the GRAND HOTEL and TOVARICH formulas; and SECOND HONEYMOON (Walter Lang), a variation of the familiar triangle drama. Afterward, Zanuck confined Tyrone Power and Loretta Young to Fox's prestige output.

The decline of screwball comedy in 1938 corresponded to the rise of sentimental comedy, particularly the family film. Direct ancestors of television sitcoms, the plots of these domestic comedies focused on minor incidents in a supposedly typical American family. Roger Dooley has noted, "The cast was often made up of convenient stereotypes—e.g., the henpecked father, the social-climbing mother, the daughter whose choice of the right young man determines the happy ending, perhaps a bratty younger brother, , , , and usually a peppery older relative, a grandparent or spinster aunt, to comment tartly on the others. A comic maid was also standard." Unlike the screwball family, which was noted for its eccentricities, the families in sentimental comedies were "considered in the main stream, reflecting more or less normal American folks at home."[183]

Twentieth Century–Fox probably inaugurated the family sitcom in 1936 when it introduced the Jones Family. A low-budget B series featuring Jed Prouty, a small-town druggist, as Pop; Spring Byington as Mom; Florence Roberts as Grandma; and Kenneth Howell and others as the youngsters, the Jones Family films were released at the rate of around three pictures a year. The series lasted from 1936 to 1940, and its principal director was Frank Strayer.

MGM's Andy Hardy series was by far the most successful. Mickey Rooney, the star of the series, became the number-one box-office draw in 1939. The series started out with A FAMILY AFFAIR (George B. Seitz, 1937), a B picture featuring Lionel Barrymore and Mickey Rooney that was based on Aurania Rouverol's play *Skidding*, about a small-town judge and his family in Carvel, Idaho. The warm response to the picture suggested a sequel, YOU'RE ONLY YOUNG ONCE (George B. Seitz, 1938), which focused attention on the judge's son Andy. In this picture, the Hardys go on a vacation to Catalina Island, where Andy discovers the excitement of kissing girls. Three changes were made in the cast: Lewis Stone replaced Lionel Barrymore as the judge, Fay Holden replaced Spring Byington as the mother, and Ann Rutherford was added to the cast as Polly Benedict, Andy's girlfriend.

Mickey Rooney in LOVE FINDS ANDY HARDY *(MGM, 1938).*

Four months after the release of this picture, MGM produced JUDGE HARDY'S CHILDREN (George B. Seitz, 1938), which developed the father-son relationship further. The fourth film of the series, LOVE FINDS ANDY HARDY (George B. Seitz, 1938), complicated the action by introducing Judy Garland as the young girl visiting next door. By now, said Bosley Crowther, "the word had got out that [the Andy Hardy pictures] were grossing three or four times their cost. And well they might, for they were genuinely charming, warm and likeable little films. Mickey Rooney was the new sensation and Andy Hardy was the all-American boy."[184]

LOVE FINDS ANDY HARDY earned the distinction of making it to both the *Film Daily* and *Variety* lists. By 1939, nineteen-year-old Rooney had become MGM's most valuable property, and his multiple talents enabled him to take on serious drama (BOYS TOWN, 1938) and musicals (BABES IN ARMS, 1939) as well as comedy. As other studios got on the family-picture bandwagon, the decade ended where it began—with sentimental comedy firmly in place.

Social Problem Films

In his social history of America during the thirties, Frederick Lewis Allen has described the extent to which movies mirrored the times:

As for the movies, so completely did they dodge the dissensions and controversies of the day—with a few exceptions, such as the March of Time series, the brief newsreels, and the occasional picture like "I Am a Fugitive from a Chain Gang" or "They Won't Forget"—that if a dozen or two feature pictures, selected at random, were to be shown to an audience of 1960, that audience would probably derive from them not the faintest idea of the ordeal through which the United States went in the nineteen thirties. (*Since Yesterday* [New York: Harper and Row, 1939], P. 222)

The social problem film, which includes the gangster and crime picture, played a minor role in the production strategies of the majors. However, it is misguided to condemn Hollywood for ignoring the economic and social upheavals created by the Depression and for concentrating instead on escapist fare for its survival. Defining itself as a purveyor of entertainment, Hollywood never considered it a duty to analyze society or the economy. Any attempt to do so would have opened the industry to the charge of producing propaganda. Moreover, any proposal to solve a social problem would carry a political liability and fragment the audience. Hollywood steered clear of this mine field and continued to do what it did best—provide "harmless entertainment" for the masses. Motion pictures might allude to the Depression or even exploit an issue, but the goal was always profits, not social justice. Journalists, do-gooders, and other civic-minded people believed Hollywood was shirking its responsibility, but no one offered to pick up the tab should attempts at producing message pictures fail.

One studio did devise a formula to capitalize on social problems, and that studio was Warner Bros. Considering itself "The Ford of the Movies," Warners pared budgets to the bare bones during the Depression in an attempt to pay off company debts. What better way to keep costs down than to produce fast-paced topicals based on stories plucked out of the day's news? Darryl F. Zanuck, Warners' head of production until 1933, called this cycle "headlines" pictures—which is to say a type of picture based on a story that had "the punch and smash that would entitle it to be a headline on the front page of any successful metropolitan daily."[185] The policy successfully differentiated Warners' roster from its competitors' even after Zanuck left the studio in 1933.

But in exposing gangsters, inhumane prison conditions, yellow journalism, and so forth, Warners did not meet the social problems head on; instead, the studio typically sidestepped issues by narrowing the focus of the exposé to a specific case or by resolving problems at the personal level of the protagonist rather than at the societal level. *Variety* called the process "Burbanking," referring to the location of Warners' studio in Burbank, outside Los Angeles.

A good example of Burbanking is found in I AM A FUGITIVE FROM A CHAIN GANG (Mervyn LeRoy, 1932), perhaps the most sensational social problem film of the period. Based on Robert E. Burns's lurid account of his experiences in a Georgia prison camp, FUGITIVE was named to *Film Daily*'s Ten Best and was voted best picture of the year by the National Board of Review. Written while Burns was in hiding, his exposé generated considerable notoriety when serialized in *True Detective* magazine in 1931 and then as a book in 1932. After acquiring the rights to the book, Warners hired Burns to work undercover in

Paul Muni in I AM A FUGITIVE FROM A CHAIN GANG *(Warners, 1932).*

Hollywood as a technical adviser on the screenplay, which was written by Howard J. Green, Brown Holmes, and Sheridan Gibney. Prison life in FUGITIVE is brutal: the workday begins at 4:30 in the morning and ends after dark, prisoners are shackled, the guards are sadistic, and the living conditions are squalid. Making such conditions even more horrific is the fact that the hero, James Allen (played by Paul Muni), a decorated World War I veteran who had been reduced by circumstances to wandering the country as a vagrant, is sentenced to ten years of hard labor for a crime he had been conned into committing.

The ending of the picture is the starkest of any social problem film of the period: Muni has escaped from the chain gang and become a successful engineer and civic leader in Chicago, but when his identity is revealed to the police by his spiteful wife, he is arrested and voluntarily returns to Georgia with the promise that the state will pardon him in ninety days because he had "rehabilitated" himself. After Muni is locked up, however, the warden suspends the pardon indefinitely. Escaping the chain gang a second time, Muni again becomes a fugitive. At the close, he appears from the shadows, a defeated and beaten figure, for a furtive meeting with his sweetheart. Describing life on the lam, he says, "I hide in rooms all day and travel by night. No friends, no rest, no peace." A distant police siren startles him, and as he disappears into the night, she asks him, "How do you live?" and he answers, "I steal."[186]

Highly regarded for its gritty realism at the time of its release, FUGITIVE is considered by some today as one of the "first true problem films" by going "beyond the brief putdowns of brutality and capital punishment to fully reveal what is wrong in the prison camps and who is responsible." It is true that the film indicts the courts, the penal system, and vengeful state officials, but American capitalism as a whole is depicted as fundamentally just. Because public sentiment up north was with Muni's character and social agencies there had worked on his behalf to clear him, the movie implies that if the chain gang is removed and the administration of justice in Georgia is reformed, all will be well.[187] Moreover, by focusing on the plight of the protagonist, the film obscures such issues in the story as why the state of Georgia tolerated the chain-gang system, why the federal government turned its back on World War I veterans, and why the economy had turned sour.

The gangster picture was the most popular social problem picture of the early thirties. It is easy to see why: first, the cult of the gangster had made headlines for a decade, ever since the start of Prohibition; second, gangster pictures were relatively cheap to produce and easy to mount; and third, the gangster picture could exploit the full possibilities of sound. Warners' LIGHTS OF NEW YORK (Bryan Foy, 1928), the first all-talking movie, introduced audiences to the distinctive, rough, argot-ridden dialogue of the gangster—words such as *molls, mugs, gats, rods,* and *cannons.* Audiences also heard the explosive rat-tat-tat-tat of the machine gun and the screeching of wheels as a car turned a corner to shoot at a cop or a member of a rival gang. The first sound gangster pictures depended on dialogue for their effectiveness, but producers soon realized that action was more important. By 1930, "every major had taken its crack at one or more gangland films," said *Variety,* and the "racketeer stuff was cold."[188]

The classic gangster cycle, consisting of such pictures as Warners' LITTLE CAESAR (Mervyn LeRoy, 1931) and THE PUBLIC ENEMY (William Wellman, 1931), and UA's SCARFACE (Howard Hawks, 1932), traced the rise and precipitous fall of the urban, often immigrant gangster involved in heavy racketeering and bootlegging during Prohibition. The protagonists of the pictures—Cesare "Rico" Bandello (LITTLE CAESAR), Tom Powers (PUBLIC ENEMY), and Tony Camonte (SCARFACE)—were suggested by notorious men of the era, Rico and Tony by Al Capone, and Tom Powers by Earl "Hymie" Weiss. The pictures also contained most of the iconographic characteristics of the genre. The milieu of the gangster was the city, in particular its dark streets, dingy rooming houses, bars, clubs, penthouse apartments, mansions, and precinct stations. The gangster typically wore nondescript and wrinkled clothing at first, but as he moved to the top, his clothing changed to flashy, custom-tailored stripped suits with silk ties and suitable jewelry, fedora hats, spats, and tuxedos. Being a modern man of the city, the gangster had at his disposal the city's complex technology, in particular firearms, automobiles, and telephones. The automobile was a major icon and had a twofold function: it enabled the hero to carry out his work, and like his clothes, it became the symbol of his success.

LITTLE CAESAR, starring Edward G. Robinson, "was unquestionably the foremost of the gang films for the money," catching "the public appetite for underworld stories at its height," reported *Variety.* The rise-and-fall structure of the picture was based on W. R. Burnett's novel about a small-time hoodlum climbing to near the top of a big-city racket and staying there briefly before sinking back into obscurity and death. Unlike other gangster pictures that had hit the market, *Little Caesar* became a standout because of its tightly structured narrative and an effective performance by Robinson. The *New York Times* said, "*Little Caesar* becomes at Mr. Robinson's hands a figure out of Greek epic tragedy, a cold, ignorant, merciless killer, driven on and on by an insatiable lust for power, the plaything of a force that is greater than himself."[189]

Warners' THE PUBLIC ENEMY stars James Cagney. Based on a story about gang lore by John Bright, and scripted by Bright, Kubec Glasmon, and Harvey Thew, it is structured as a semidocumentary about bootlegging that offers a sociological explanation for why Tom Powers grows up to become a "full-grown, vicious, minor hoodlum." Just as Rico's lust for power created a new type of screen gangster, so did Tom's thuggery. As *Variety* described him, Tom "is a bully behind his gun with men and the same with his fist toward his women. . . . Pushing a grapefruit into the face of the moll (Mae Clarke) with whom he's fed up, socking another on the chin for inducing him to her for the night while he's drunk, and spitting a mouthful of beer into the face of a speakeasy proprietor for using a rival's product are a few samples of Cagney's deportment as Tom, the tough in the modern gangster's dress and way."[190]

SCARFACE starred Paul Muni and was the only gangster picture to make it to *Film Daily*'s Ten Best. Howard Hughes's Caddo Corporation produced the picture for United Artists release. Ben Hecht, who adapted the novel by Armitage Trail, crafted a hero resembling Al Capone and wove into the plot famous gangster incidents of the twenties, such as the Saint Valentine's Day Massacre, the murder of "Big Jim" Colosimo in a telephone booth, and the assassination of "Legs" Diamond in his hospital room. In order to qualify for a Hays Office seal of approval and to satisfy state censorship boards, the picture underwent constant revision both during and after production. Among them was a change in the ending from a scene showing Camonte sentenced by the court and hanged, to one in which Tony is gunned down by the police on the sidewalk as he tries to make a break. The final release print carried the new title SCARFACE: SHAME OF A NATION and a prologue signed by Edward P. Mulrooney, police commissioner of New York City, condemning gangster rule and demanding that the audience do something about it. But such rhetoric probably fooled neither the reformer nor the film fan. As *Variety* described it, "*Scarface* . . . uses all the modern artillery tricks ever conceived by imaginative scenario writers who read newspapers and contributes a few more of its own. It bumps off more guys and mixes more blood with rum than most of the past gangster offerings combined." Although *Variety* noted that SCARFACE was "presumably the last of the gangster films, . . . it is going to make people sorry that there won't be any more."[191]

The classic gangster cycle flourished for one year only, 1931; as Richard Maltby put it, "the year 1931 was the best of times and the worst of times to release films about gangsters. They could hardly be more topical, but the climate in which they were released was one in which a generally tolerant press attitude had shifted to outspoken condemnation, expressed in editorial demands to 'end the reign of gangdom.'" The Production Code, which was officially adopted by the industry on 31 March 1930, stipulated, among other things, that crimes against the law should never be presented "in such a way as to throw sympathy with the crime as against law and justice or to inspire others with a desire for imitation"; that the "technique of murder must be presented in a way that will not inspire imitation"; and that the "methods of crime should not be explicitly

Wallace Beery, Robert Montgomery, and Chester Morris in THE BIG HOUSE *(MGM, 1930).*

presented."[192] Using the Code for leverage, the Hays Office helped convince producers to put an end to the classic gangster cycle. But the Hays Office was not the major cause of the cycle's demise. By 1931, the market had become saturated with such pictures. Thereafter, the number of class-A crime films of all types dropped markedly. Warners continued with the cycle all the way to the end of the decade, but the other majors cut back on crime-film production to one or at most two a year.

Unlike the gangster film, the prison cycle caused relatively little trouble with the censors. In fact, MGM's THE BIG HOUSE (George Hill, 1930), the picture that launched the cycle, was greatly admired as a social problem picture and made it to *Film Daily*'s Top Ten. Produced by William Randolph Hearst's Cosmopolitan Pictures, the film was inspired by actual prison riots in 1929 and by Broadway plays such as *The Last Mile* and *The Criminal Code*. Frances Marion crafted the screenplay and won an Oscar for her efforts. Chester Morris and Wallace Beery played two of the inmates, and Lewis Stone, the warden. Purporting to present a realistic portrait of prison life, THE BIG HOUSE depicted the processing of inmates, their mealtimes, and their routines in the yard. The picture also introduced what were to become prison stereotypes—the hardened criminal, the semihysterical weakling victimized by both guards and fellow prisoners, the informer, the ineffectual warden, the vicious guard, and the strong-willed leader. And true to form, the climax of the picture presented a thrilling revolt that graphically depicted how officials used hand grenades, barrages, stench bombs, tractor attacks, and other means "to deal with foolhardy prisoners." "Prison life on the half-shell," said *Variety*.[193] Although THE BIG HOUSE was a big hit, MGM had little interest in the cycle and produced only a few crime pictures thereafter.

Warners contributed two controversial pictures to the cycle, I AM A FUGITIVE FROM A CHAIN GANG (Mervyn LeRoy, 1932), previously discussed, and 20,000 YEARS IN SING SING (Michael Curtiz, 1933). Both were based on books that had caught media attention, and both were shot in a semidocumentary style. SING SING, which featured Spencer Tracy and Bette Davis, was released just a few months after FUGITIVE. The first of several screen adaptations of Warden Lewis E. Lawes's experiences as an enlightened penologist, the picture incorporated Lawes's controversial honor system, which allowed deserving prisoners to take furloughs to visit family and friends. In contrast to the brutal prison conditions in FUGITIVE, prison life in Sing Sing "wouldn't be a bad place at all to spend a vacation over the depression," said *Variety*.[194] FUGITIVE depicted a person being unjustly convicted of a crime and thrown into a convict camp; in SING SING, Spencer Tracy admits to a crime he did not commit and goes to the electric chair to vindicate the prison's honor system.

Other offshoots of the gangster film include the yellow-journalism, shyster-lawyer, and vigilante cycles. Most were hastily thrown-together exploitation films, concerned more with sensationalism than with examining any putative social problem. Warners' FIVE STAR FINAL (Mervyn LeRoy, 1931), the only other social problem picture besides SCARFACE and FUGITIVE to make it to *Film Daily*'s Ten Best, generated the most heat. A newspaper exposé based on the Broadway hit by Louis Weitzenkorn, the picture starred Edward G. Robinson as the editor of a scurrilous New York tabloid. Pressured by his publisher to build up circulation, Robinson runs a follow-up story to a twenty-year-old murder case. Unearthing the case results in a double suicide by the woman named in the story and her husband. Robinson becomes disgusted with his job, berates his publisher, and resigns from the paper in disgust. The picture ends with a "close-up of the *Gazette* lying in the gutter; a gob of dirt splatters down on to it, and a broom sweeps it down the gutter with the other garbage." *Variety* noted that FIVE STAR FINAL was a "hard rap at the readers of such tabs, . . . and while these readers will make up a large part of its audience, they won't mind." In other words, this picture contained social criticism, but the criticism was "well within the conventions of entertainment."[195]

The shyster-lawyer cycle, consisting of such pictures as Paramount's FOR THE DEFENSE (John Cromwell, 1930), Warners' THE MOUTHPIECE (James Flood and Elliott Nugent, 1932), and RKO's STATE'S ATTORNEY (George Archainbaud, 1932), typically featured unethical sharpies who front for gangsters. Vigilante pictures, such as MGM's THE SECRET SIX (George Hill, 1931), Warners' STAR WITNESS (William Wellman, 1931), and Paramount's THIS DAY AND AGE (Cecil B. DeMille, 1933), not so subtly advocated extralegal means to eradicate gangsters and their ilk. For example, STAR WITNESS, released as a rebuttal of sorts to THE PUBLIC ENEMY, depicted how "gangdom is undermining the U.S. citizenry." A normal middle-class American family that has witnessed an underworld slaying is "terrorized into perjuring themselves when followers of the captured gang leader learn that their evidence is sufficient to send the boss to the chair." However, the grandfather, a Civil War veteran (played by Chic

Sale, a vaudeville monologuist who specialized in Americana), is not intimidated and goes to the police. As the "star witness," he delivers a speech to the court complaining that organized crime is run by foreigners who are ruining the country. *Variety* predicted that Warners would produce a "follow-up film advocating deportation of all alien gangsters."[196]

As the Depression deepened, Hollywood offered various solutions to solve the country's economic problems. Columbia's AMERICAN MADNESS (1932), Frank Capra's first collaboration with writer Robert Riskin, offered a populist solution. Drawing on the GRAND HOTEL single-setting structure, AMERICAN MADNESS takes place in a bank—in the vaults, lobby, board room, cashier's office, and other parts of Walter Huston's First National Bank. After a cashier helps gangsters rob the vaults of $100,000, gossipers exaggerate the loss and start a run on the bank. To stem the flow, the board of directors adopts a tightfisted no-lending policy. Huston opposes the decision by stating "that a bank should serve all the people, not just a selfish few." The conflict is resolved in typical Capra fashion when hordes of "little people" come to Huston's aid by redepositing their meager savings in the bank. "It's swell propaganda against hoarding, frozen assets and other economic evils which 1932 Hooverism has created [and] should be the banker's delight. It's a natural for an A.B.A. tie-up on exploitation," said *Variety*.[197]

UA's OUR DAILY BREAD (1934), written, directed, and produced by King Vidor, offered a socialist solution. Inspired by policies of "such widely assorted persons as Walter Pitkin (Clearing House for Hope), Upton Sinclair (EPIC), President Roosevelt (subsistence farms), and the backers of the so-called Ohio plan," OUR DAILY BREAD dramatized the creation of a collective farm by a throng of desperate men and women who have fled the cities. Working together as a community, they vanquish bankruptcy, foreclosure, and drought, the implication being that "what the individual farmer could not stave off, the group can."[198]

MGM's GABRIEL OVER THE WHITE HOUSE (Gregory La Cava, 1933), produced by Walter Wanger for William Randolph Hearst's Cosmopolitan Pictures, offered a totalitarian solution. A fantasy designed as a tribute to Franklin Roosevelt and released to coincide with his March 1933 inauguration, GABRIEL OVER THE WHITE HOUSE starts out with the president of the United States (Walter Huston) advocating economic policies similar to Herbert Hoover's until an automobile accident knocks some sense into his head. Describing what happens next, *Variety* said,

> The resurrected President goes before Congress in a big scene, asks to be made a dictator to deal with the emergency, and when Congress refuses he declares martial law and takes control. He goes out to meet an army of hunger marchers at Baltimore, calms them and wins them to his policies in an address, sends the army out after the gangsters in an elaborate battle scene with tanks, and for the finish meets the diplomats of the world on the Presidential yacht, with the whole American navy assembled thereabouts, and talks them into paying the American foreign debt and agreeing to a new disarmament pact. (*VFR*, 29 March 1933)

King Vidor's OUR DAILY BREAD *(UA, 1934).*

Variety concluded, "A cleverly executed commercial release, it waves the flag frantically, preaches political claptrap with ponderous solemnity, but won't inspire a single intelligent reaction in a carload of admission tickets."[199]

After Roosevelt's inauguration, Warners changed its strategy for social problem films. Although fervent Republicans, the Warner brothers not only backed FDR's election efforts but also acted as major propagandists for the New Deal, designing morale boosters that presented "the administration—usually in the guise of federal judges, G-men, or benevolent civil servants—as the solution to all social problems."[200]

Notice, for example, how Warners dealt with the unemployment problem in WILD BOYS OF THE ROAD (William Wellman, 1933). Shot mainly in freight yards, a sewer-pipe city, and other locations, the picture realistically depicts how unemployment created displaced children who formed gangs and wandered the country. Said *Variety*, "The spiritual travails of these youngsters detached from their families and homes and left to roam the country, battered, rebuffed and hardened by adversity, is something to leave an impression of gloom not easily erased. Every incident, every character ceaselessly brings to mind the most gruesome underside of hard times." New Deal compassion solves the problem. The kids have run into trouble with the police and are brought before a judge with the Blue Eagle on the wall. (The Blue Eagle was the symbol of Roosevelt's National Recovery Administration.) The judge (Robert Barrat), who wears

Ward Bond and Frankie Darrow in WILD BOYS OF THE ROAD *(Warners, 1933).*

rimless spectacles and is a look-alike for the president, listens compassionately to Frankie Darro's brief on behalf of underprivileged children: "Jail can't be any worse than the street." Barrat responds by saying, "Things are going to get better all over the country. . . . I know your father will be going back to work soon." Although the judge offers words of comfort, nothing in the film indicates how the NRA or other New Deal projects will revive the economy.[201]

Warners treated labor unrest in BLACK FURY (Michael Curtiz, 1935). Militant unionism was at a peak in the mid thirties. The number of strikes in the United States increased dramatically during the Depression and abated only after the passage of the New Deal's Wagner Act (1935), guaranteeing labor the right to organize and negotiate. Perhaps the most tumultuous industrial strife involved the United Mine Workers and its flamboyant leader John L. Lewis.

BLACK FURY was based on the 1929 murder of a coal miner by company police in Imperial, Pennsylvania. Judge Michael A. Musmanno, who was involved in the case, wrote an original story about it that formed the basis of the film. The picture has a documentary look. Nick Roddick describes it: "Placard-bearing strikers march down the street of Coaltown and kids in the schoolyard shout 'Dirty scabs!' as replacement workers are brought in." Company police are depicted as thugs and the workers as "model representatives of the 'little man.'" However, after this initial presentation of industrial conditions, the narrative shifts to the personal vendetta of Polish coal miner Joe Radek (played by Paul

Muni), who heroically fights the company police force and triggers a federal investigation into its operations. New Deal bureaucrats in Washington expose the mob connections of the police, and the workers go back to their jobs, forgetting their former grievances. Another example of Burbanking, the picture switches focus from disgruntled labor versus capital, to labor versus strike-breaking syndicates. Thus, while flying the banner of political militancy, Warners maintained the status quo. "If anything," said *Variety*, "intelligent capitalism management is given a subtle boost."[202]

When the social and economic climate of the country improved, Hollywood decided that the time was ripe to revive the gangster film, but "to take the curse off these yarns," studios turned the gangster into a federal agent.[203] Warners led the pack with G-MEN (William Keighley, 1935), a surprise hit starring James Cagney. A semidocumentary in style, G-MEN depicts the making of an FBI agent. Seton I. Miller wrote an original screenplay that interweaves spectacular events from the headlines involving the most notorious characters of the time. The gangsters in G-MEN are modeled after "Pretty Boy" Floyd, "Baby Face" Nelson, and John Dillinger, who terrorized the Midwest; the good guys are patterned on J. Edgar Hoover, the director of the FBI, and Melvin Purvis, a colorful federal agent who helped engineer the gangster busts of the 1930s. James Cagney plays the Purvis character, James ("Brick") Davis. Born on the bad side of town, raised in state orphanages, and arrested for vagrancy and fighting, Davis is Tom Powers of THE PUBLIC ENEMY gone good.

Warners treated Cagney's conversion to the right side of the law as an event of national significance. An ad in the *New York Times* stated that the picture was dedicated to "the fearless Federal Agents whose heroic exploits and inspiration made this picture possible." Other promotion linking him to THE PUBLIC ENEMY declared that Cagney as a G-man was tougher than ever—"Cagney Is Now Public Hero No. 1!" and "Cagney Finds New Way to Sock Women." Undermining the intent, if not the spirit, of the Production Code, G-MEN glorifies violence by staging assaults using tear gas, rifles, pistols, and machine guns and by depicting Davis's motive for joining the Department of Justice as an obsession with avenging the murder of his G-man pal by a hoodlum.

G-MEN was a big hit and made it to *Variety*'s list of top grossers for 1935. By year's end, the trade noted that while the G-man cycle "has been considered constructive in presenting a picture of the Government's war on crime, at the same time films of this type were becoming so numerous as to create some resistance on the part of the public and hence an unhealthful condition at the box office."[204] Nonetheless, Warners decided to stretch its luck by assigning director William Keighley and writer Seton I. Miller to fashion a G-man type of vehicle for Edward G. Robinson. BULLETS OR BALLOTS (1936) substituted a police detective for an FBI agent and based the action on the activities of New York racketeer "Dutch" Schultz. The title of the picture refers to the duty every citizen has to support the political system or suffer organized crime. As Johnny Blake, a "tough, but honest dick," Robinson infiltrates the rackets and brings down a kingpin, but in doing so, he takes on their colors by organizing the most profitable and widespread racket of all, numbers. Thus, for a substantial portion of the film, crime fighter Blake is the city's greatest criminal, "playing the gangster role while not 'glorifying gangsterism.'"[205]

Not stopping there, Warners devised a gangster vehicle for its top female star,

James Cagney, Lloyd Nolan, and Robert Armstrong in G-Men *(Warners, 1935).*

Edward G. Robinson in Bullets or Ballots *(Warners, 1936).*

Bette Davis, inspired by New York's District Attorney Thomas E. Dewey's investigation into racketeering. Of particular interest to the studio was the conviction of gangster "Lucky" Luciano on charges of prostitution, a conviction that stuck as a result of key testimony from three prostitutes. MARKED WOMAN (Lloyd Bacon, 1937), written by Robert Rossen and Abem Finkel, changes the occupation of the women from prostitutes to hostesses in a clip joint and the setting from a brothel to a cheap nightclub to make it conform to the Production Code. Humphrey Bogart plays the district attorney, and Eduardo Ciannelli, the Luciano-like gangster, Johnny Vanning. Bette Davis and her friends do not feel exploited working for Vanning; on the contrary, they consider themselves lucky to have jobs. They testify against Vanning only after he murders Davis's kid sister and after his henchmen viciously beat up Davis. The resolution of the picture was particularly effective. Frank S. Nugent of the *New York Times* said, "The five shady ladies who take the stand and testify, with a ganglord's executioner waiting for them to leave the court room, are ennobled for that moment, but not glorified. When the fog swallows them up, there is no after-glow from their halos. Count that a point for realism on the screen."[206]

Influenced by American drama of social consciouness, the gangster cycle changed further to embrace a sociological analysis of the existence of crime. Sam Goldwyn's DEAD END (William Wyler, 1937), a prestige picture based on Sidney Kingsley's Broadway hit, which showed slums as the breeding ground for criminals, initiated the cycle. Treating the criminal "not as a heroic individual but as a social problem," these films, in Peter Roffman and Jim Purdy's words, "were populated by juvenile delinquents about to be initiated into big-time crime and ex-convicts struggling against an intolerant society to go straight. In both cases, sympathy is with the criminal and against the social institutions. But just as the unrepentant gangster had to die, so the reformed delinquents and cons are almost always reintegrated by a redeemer figure."[207]

At least two pictures anticipated the cycle, Warners' MAYOR OF HELL (Archie Mayo, 1933) and MGM's MANHATTAN MELODRAMA (W. S. Van Dyke, 1934). MAYOR OF HELL, a junior BIG HOUSE, takes place in a reformatory where James Cagney, a racketeer with a Jekyll-Hyde character, takes over as superintendent and changes the lives of kids. To explain the cause of juvenile delinquency, the picture tried to demonstrate how a poor environment fosters antisocial behavior. However, the plot muddled the message because, as *Variety* put it, "the big item which customers have to swallow is that while reforming kids, Cagney sticks to his trade as gang leader."[208]

MANHATTAN MELODRAMA, starring Clark Gable and William Powell, contained a Cain and Abel plot. Two orphans are raised together on the Lower East side and end up on opposite sides of the law, with Gable as a big-time gambler and Powell as a district attorney. To spare Powell from a mudslinging attack that might spoil his bid for governor, Gable kills the instigator and goes to the chair without revealing his motive. It is Powell as district attorney who convicts him and it is Powell as governor who will not commute the death penalty.

Warners' ANGELS WITH DIRTY FACES (Michael Curtiz, 1938), a vehicle for the Dead End Kids, stars James Cagney and Pat O'Brien. Like DEAD END, the picture shows the squalid living conditions—crowded streets and shabby tenements—that make petty criminals out of the kids. And like its prototype, the picture repeats the Cain and Abel motif: the kids have two models to look up to, a gangster (Cagney) and a priest (O'Brien), boyhood friends from the same neighborhood. The climax occurs in prison just as Cagney is about to go to the electric chair. O'Brien, who is at Cagney's side, wants to squelch the admiration the kids have for Cagney and talks him into turning yellow. After Cagney is strapped in, his screams and sobs are heard, but because the action occurs off-screen, the audience questions whether Cagney is truly frightened or just acting. Nonetheless, ANGELS ends optimistically, with the kids reconciled to society.

MGM's BOYS TOWN (Norman Taurog, 1938) implied that if big-city slums breed wayward children, then take the kids into the country. Starring Spencer Tracy as Father Flanagan and Mickey Rooney as Whitey Marsh, a supertough delinquent, BOYS TOWN depicts Father Flanagan's orphanage in Nebraska in its early, experimental stage; it is an idealized community in which "boys of all nationalities and faiths work side by side in harmony, under the benevolent care of a purposeful leader." Mickey Rooney is a cynical newcomer "with a pack of butts in his left-hand pocket, a deck of cards in his right, a Tenth Avenue Homburg cocked over one ear and his mind made up to blow the joint." Although he eventually succumbs to Father Flanagan's and the home's refining influences, *Variety,* which called the picture "a tear-jerker of the first water," pointed out that "the delinquents are reformed without any change in the slums or in the economic structure that produced them."[209] Spencer Tracy won an Oscar for his role as Father Flanagan, as did screenwriters Dore Schary and Eleanore Griffin for their original screenplay.

Warners squeezed extra mileage out of the gangster picture by producing two variants at the close of the decade. A SLIGHT CASE OF MURDER (Lloyd Bacon, 1938), a gangster comedy starring Edward G. Robinson, is based on the Damon Runyon and Howard Lindsay farce about "a retired bootlegger who has to get rid of four dead bodies left unceremoniously in his Saratoga home by his enemies in the rackets." Said *Variety,* "The underworld is turned inside out and scenes which once chilled the spectators with horror are the occasion here for hearty laughter."[210]

THE ROARING TWENTIES (Raoul Walsh, 1939), a quasi-documentary drama starring James Cagney, uses newsreel clips, montage sequences, voice-over narration, and music of the period to demonstrate how social conditions during Prohibition caused the rise of the gangster. Written by Jerry Wald, Richard Macaulay, and Robert Rossen from an idea by Mark Hellinger, the picture repeats the rise-and-fall structure of the classic gangster film and contains stock elements from major pictures of the cycle.

Variety observed at the end of 1939 that "underworld pics . . . are currently as poisonous at the b.o. as dictators are to peace."[211] The glut consisted mainly of B pictures. Beginning with the G-Men cycle in 1935, Hollywood adopted a two-tier production policy regarding crime pictures. Most crime pictures were assigned to B production units and consisted of spin-offs of class-A hits. The special-prosecutor film, for example, spun off imitations such as Warners' RACKET BUSTERS (Lloyd Bacon, 1938), which probed the trucking racket in New York, and RKO's SMASHING THE RACKETS (Lew Landers, 1938), which exposed the white slave trade.

The prison film spun off three imitations from Warners: ROAD GANG (Louis King, 1936), a remake of I AM A FUGITIVE FROM A CHAIN GANG; ALCATRAZ

ISLAND (William McGann, 1937), which introduces the Rock with the caption "America's penal fortress, grim and mysterious as its name, where cold steel and rushing tides protect civilization from its enemies"; and BLACKWELL'S ISLAND (William McGann, 1939), an exposé of a prison under the "virtual command of a ruthless criminal who ran it to enrich his own pockets by exacting tribute from its inmates."[212]

The class-B juvenile-delinquency cycle exploited the Dead End Kids. Unlike the bigger-budget versions, the sociological background is neutralized in these pictures and the kids' behavior becomes a source of comedy. Among the many films featuring the Dead End Kids are Universal's LITTLE TOUGH GUY (Harold Young, 1938) and CALL A MESSENGER (Arthur Lubin, 1939), and Warners' ANGELS WASH THEIR FACES (Ray Enright, 1939).

When the worst of the Depression was over, Hollywood turned to other sensational events besides crime to exploit. Early in the decade, the number of lynchings in the country rose alarmingly. Generally carried out by white middle-class conservatives, lynchings occurred predominantly in the South and in California with the tacit approval of local law agencies. The targets of the lynch mob were almost exclusively blacks, but Jews, Communists, and labor organizers were also singled out. Lynchings, of course, made grisly fodder for the tabloids. Although the frequency of lynchings dramatically declined after 1934, the result of federal legislation and national outrage with such behavior, "Hollywood joined the attack on mob violence at a time when it was still in the forefront of the public's consciousness."[213]

Hollywood turned out two important pictures involving lynchings, MGM's FURY (Fritz Lang, 1936) and Warners' THEY WON'T FORGET (Mervyn LeRoy, 1937). Since social problems just did not fit in with the studio's image of glitz and glamour, FURY was an unusual picture for MGM to produce. MGM made the picture only to secure the talents of the noted German director Fritz Lang, who had recently fled Nazi Germany. Lang waited around for over a year on payroll before the studio found a project fitting for his American debut. Norman Krasna's original screenplay, which was "elemental in its simplicity," satisfied him.

FURY did not involve a black victim, nor is the action set in the South; the central character is an auto mechanic, played by Spencer Tracy, who is stopped by the police on his way to visit his fiancée, Sylvia Sidney, in rural Illinois and is booked on suspicion of kidnapping a little girl. Lang was basically interested in mob psychology and presented the "great American institution" of lynching, in the words of the New York Times, "as the victim sees it, as the mob sees it, as the public sees it. We see a lynching, its prelude and its aftermath, in all its cold horror, its hypocrisy and its cruel stupidity."[214] However, the plot contrivances that turned the victim to victimizer and the happy ending placed FURY squarely in the tradition of Hollywood entertainment and undermined the social criticism. The picture was praised by the critics and established Lang's career in California, but it withered at the box office.

THEY WON'T FORGET took a different slant on lynching. The screenplay by Aben Kandel and Robert Rossen was based on Ward Greene's novel Death in the Deep South, about Leo Frank, an Atlanta Jew, who was charged with the murder of a fourteen-year-old girl and lynched in 1915. Like FURY, the picture depicts a small-town lynch mob and captures the boredom and frustration that "makes

Fury *(MGM, 1936)*.

lynching a perverted form of entertainment." Although THEY WON'T FORGET is set in the South, its focus is not on the criminal behavior of the lynch mob but on a cynical local district attorney, played by Claude Rains, who manipulates and inflames people to further his own career. In the tradition of Hollywood entertainment, the picture sidesteps the issue of personal responsibility by implicating the media for not merely sensationalizing the trial but using headlines to arouse the townspeople. However, unlike the ending of FURY, the ending of THEY WON'T FORGET is unsettling. After Robert Hale, a schoolteacher from up north, is convicted on flimsy evidence, he is rushed by train to another city to save him from the lynch mob. But the crazed mob is not to be denied; they board the train, drag Hale off, and hang him.

A group of pictures depicting native fascism were inspired by the Ku Klux Klan–like Black Legion, a secret organization operating in the Midwest in the thirties that cloaked "its cowardice, bigotry, selfishness, stupidity and brutality under the mantle of '100 per cent Americanism.'" Columbia's LEGION OF TERROR (C. C. Coleman, 1936), the first out of the gates, attempts "to sketch a story of local dementia plus an indictment of crackpot politico-fraternal organizations," said *Variety*. Two months later, Warners released THE BLACK LEGION (Archie Mayo, 1937). It was based on an original story by Robert Lord, who drew his information from accounts of the Legion's ritualistic murder in 1936 of WPA

Poster art for BLACK LEGION *(Warners, 1936).*

worker Charles Poole in Michigan. The picture featured Humphrey Bogart as
Frank Taylor, an embittered factory worker who joins the Black Legion because a
foreigner is promoted to foreman over him. Both pictures depict Legion leaders
as racketeers who use Americanism to enrich themselves. And both pictures
depict the bigotry and violence of the vigilante groups. However, neither probes
underlying social or economic causes for the social discontent.[215]

The spread of hostilities overseas stimulated a new war cycle in 1935. As
Motion Picture Herald put it,

> The thunder of hob-nailed marching feet of Mussolini's Italian
> infantrymen, mingled with the softer retreat of Haile Selassie's
> unshod but calloused tribesmen, echoes with the roar of bombing
> planes from Abyssinia across 3,000 miles of ocean and then 3,000 miles
> of land, and Hollywood is listening, even as the world listens to the
> newer rumblings of Mars on the Russo-Japanese border and on the
> waters at Malta and the Suez Canal. ("Hollywood Starts War Cycle,"
> 19 October 1935, p. 18)

But what did producers hear? Pictures in the first cycle of war films, such as ALL
QUIET ON THE WESTERN FRONT (1930), JOURNEY'S END (1930), and THE DAWN
PATROL (1930), expressed America's isolationist attitudes created by World War
I, but offered few insights into the causes of the war. The second cycle started out
with rousing adventure films, such as Paramount's THE LAST OUTPOST (1935),
Warners' THE CHARGE OF THE LIGHT BRIGADE (1936), and Fox's UNDER TWO
FLAGS (1936), which glorified militarism. When America's involvement in the
war became a possibility, Hollywood responded in typical fashion.

Paramount's THE LAST TRAIN FROM MADRID (James Hogan, 1937) was the first
picture to capitalize on the Spanish civil war. A melodrama featuring Dorothy
Lamour and Lew Ayres, it mixes elements of GRAND HOTEL and SHANGHAI
EXPRESS. *Variety* said, "Studio doesn't take any political chances with this one.
The war is on and a group of people are trying to escape on the last train. One is a
political spellbinder, another a newspaperman, one's a gigolo, there is a baroness,
a girl of the streets, a sweet young thing, a member of the Woman's Battalion. All
become vaguely mixed up, but everything works out after a murder, an arrest and
a jailing."[216]

Producer Walter Wanger tried to make a bolder statement about the Spanish
civil war in UA's BLOCKADE (William Dieterle, 1938), starring Madeleine Carroll
and Henry Fonda. John Howard Lawson fashioned a spy story set in Spain. The
picture failed, said *Variety*, because "it pulls its punches." The opening title
reveals that the setting is Spain in 1936, but the two opposing sides are never
identified and the real issues of the civil war are never discussed. "The stage and
the screen are potent vehicles for melodramatic propaganda," said *Variety*, "but
for a dramatist to take a middle course, in an evident attempt to spare tender
feelings, is to fire at his target with blank cartridges."[217]

Wanger was subjected to considerable pressure making the picture. The *Nation*
asserted that Hollywood waged a private campaign to intimidate the producer,
noting that some theaters refused to play the picture. The Catholic Knights of
Columbus and the *Catholic News* branded the picture as propaganda, making the
industry wonder whether the charge marked a change in the Legion of
Decency's policy of evaluating motion pictures primarily on the basis of moral
content. The intimidation did its job, forcing Wanger to change his message
picture into just another melodrama. *Variety* had observed earlier that BLOCKADE
was "the key to the opening-up of a vast source of screen material. Upon its
success financially revolves the plans of several of the major studios heretofore
hesitant about tackling stories which treat with subjects of international economic and political controversy."[218]

Warners' CONFESSIONS OF A NAZI SPY (Anatole Litvak, 1939) was the first
motion picture to portray the Nazis as a threat to America. The picture was based

on Leon G. Turrou's book *The Nazi Spy Conspiracy in America,* describing his experiences as an FBI agent who directed an operation that cracked a Nazi spy ring in the ranks of the German-American Bund. Warners acquired the movie rights to the book for $25,000 and hired Turrou to serve as technical adviser. Milton Krims and John Wexley wrote the screenplay, and Edward G. Robinson played Ed Renard, a character obviously based on Turrou. This picture also aroused intense hostility, and even Jack and Harry Warner received telephone threats. A theater showing the film in a German neighborhood of Milwaukee was burned to the ground by a group of outraged Nazi sympathizers. Hans Thonsen, the German chargé d'affaires, denounced the film to Cordell Hull, the U.S. secretary of state. Despite the publicity and favorable reviews, the public was not interested.

Like the Depression, the gathering tide of World War II was only dimly seen in motion pictures. Poor box-office returns, pressure from political groups, and an isolationist mentality nationwide convinced Hollywood to refrain from sending any more messages, at least for the time being.

Horror Films

Stylistically the least realistic of all the production trends and certainly the smallest in terms of quantity, the horror film left an indelible mark on the era. Although every studio tried its hand at a cycle, one studio, Universal, specialized in the genre in an attempt to break into the first-run market. No horror picture made it to *Variety*'s top-grossing films lists, and only one such picture made it to *Film Daily*'s Ten Best—Paramount's DR. JEKYLL AND MR. HYDE. Strangely, three horror films made it to the *New York Times* Ten Best list—Universal's FRANKENSTEIN (1931) and THE INVISIBLE MAN (1933) and Paramount's DR. JEKYLL AND MR. HYDE (1932).

Observing the reception of German expressionist pictures such as THE CABINET OF DR. CALIGARI (Robert Wiene, 1919), THE GOLEM (Paul Wegener and Carl Boese, 1920), and NOSFERATU (F. W. Murnau, 1922), Hollywood began to take the horror film seriously during the twenties and hired European talent skilled in the making of these films. Universal led the way by importing German motion-picture talent and by producing two celebrated vehicles for Lon Chaney, the Man of a Thousand Faces: THE HUNCHBACK OF NOTRE DAME (Wallace Worsley, 1923) and THE PHANTOM OF THE OPERA (Rupert Julian, 1925).

The first phase of the sound horror cycle, known as the classic period, lasted from 1931 to 1936, during which years around thirty horror films were produced by the eight majors. To be effective, these films had to have sinister settings, expressionistic lighting, evocative mood music, and specialized makeup. Because these elements were costly, most horror films in this period were produced as class-A pictures. In terms of narrative types, these pictures fall into four categories: the mad-scientist film, which constituted over half of the pictures; vampire movies; monster movies; and metamorphosis movies.[219]

The cycle fed on remakes of silent horror films, literary classics, and popular Broadway plays. For example, MGM's first horror picture of the decade, THE UNHOLY THREE (Jack Conway, 1930), was a remake that contained the same stars as the 1925 original, Lon Chaney and Harry Earles. Adaptations of literary works were based on Edgar Allan Poe, H. G. Wells, Victor Hugo, and Robert Louis Stevenson, and the results were often judged by critics on their fidelity or lack of fidelity to their sources. The stage provided not only models for such horror classics as DRACULA and FRANKENSTEIN but also acting and directorial talent. Universal's great horror stars Boris Karloff and Bela Lugosi started out in the theater, as did the studio's premier horror-film director, James Whale.

Universal retained its preeminent position as a producer of horror pictures as a result of Carl Laemmle, Jr.'s decision to use the cycle as an entrée into the Big Five's theaters. Horror films had high production costs and could easily qualify as a premium-quality product. And their popularity helped keep Universal afloat during the Depression. Universal built its first horror films around Bela Lugosi and Boris Karloff. The Hungarian-born Lugosi fled his native land for political reasons in 1919, appearing on the stage and in films in both Germany and the United States for over a decade, but did not achieve any real fame until at the age of forty-eight Universal offered him the lead in DRACULA, a part originally intended for Lon Chaney. His first line, "I am Dracula. . . . I bid you welcome!" made him famous and served as his artistic epitaph. At the height of his popularity, he reputedly received as many letters as any romantic screen idol, almost all of which, he said, came from women.

Born in London in 1887 and christened William Henry Pratt, Boris Karloff was forty-three years old when Universal offered him the part of the monster in FRANKENSTEIN. His performance earned him the sobriquet "the new Lon Chaney." Karloff made seven thrillers for Universal between 1932 and 1944 and, like Lugosi, numerous B versions at nearly every studio, major and minor.

DRACULA (Tod Browning, 1931) started the cycle. Although the origin of the character is found in Bram Stoker's British novel published in 1897, the inspiration for the picture was the stage adaptation by Hamilton Deane and John L. Balderston, which opened on Broadway in 1927 with Bela Lugosi in the title role and ran a year to packed houses. The production then toured for two years, also with Lugosi in the lead. Universal bought the rights to the play in 1929 as a vehicle for Lon Chaney, but Chaney's death in 1930 prompted the studio to hire Lugosi to recreate his stage role. The film featured Lugosi as Count Dracula, Dwight Frye as Renfield, and Edward Van Sloan as Professor Van Helsing. Karl Freund did the cinematography, and Charles Hall, the art direction. Promoted as "the Strangest Love Story of All," *Dracula* opened at the Roxy in New York on 14 February 1931 and quickly became Universal's biggest money-maker of the year. DRACULA became the prototype of the vampire picture. It contains a vampire who "terrorizes the surrounding countryside," in this case, Transylvania; "young innocents," particularly females, who "are caught up as potential victims"; "the expert [Professor Van Helsing], who is the only character capable of defeating the threat"; and, "all the familiar apparatus of movie vampire-lore," said Andrew Tudor. Count Dracula travels with coffins filled with the soil of his native Transylvania; he has a deranged and enslaved accomplice; he has the power to turn himself into a bat; and he is pursued by a vampire hunter who kills him correctly by driving a stake through his heart. *Variety* ascribed DRACULA's success mostly to the "horror tricks of sound and sight": "the spectral hand reaching out from the slightly raised lid of a coffin; a coffin that disgorges rat-like creatures, . . . the ominous flapping of ghostly wings as ghoulish bats circle about, . . . a madman who shrieks in demoniacal rage for

Bela Lugosi in DRACULA *(Universal, 1931).*

spiders to eat, and the stealthy creeping of the human vampire upon his sleeping victim."[220]

Although FRANKENSTEIN (James Whale, 1931) has its origins in Mary Shelley's Gothic novel published in 1818, the script by Garrett Fort, Francis Faragoh, and John L. Balderston was based on Peggy Webling's stage adaptation, which opened in London and toured the United States in 1930. The film was a collaboration of British artists, led by director James Whale, art director Charles "Danny" Hall, and a cast headed by Colin Clive as Dr. Henry Frankenstein. Boris Karloff as the monster received fourth billing. Universal had originally hired James Whale to direct a prestige version of R. C. Sherriff's *Journey's End*, a play that Whale had successfully directed in London's West End, but he stayed on to make four of the studio's most important horror films.

FRANKENSTEIN became the prototype of the mad-scientist horror film. A scientist "driven by a frenzy for knowledge," Dr. Frankenstein patches together a monster from "human odds and ends" in his laboratory hidden away in the mountains. He is assissted by a dwarf, who steals a brain from the dissecting room of a medical college. The creature is galvanized to life in the laboratory "during a violent mountain storm in the presence of the scientist's sweetheart and others, all frozen with mortal fright." The objects of the monster's malevolence are the townspeople, particularly young innocents. "A surrounding environment (Hollywood nineteenth-century mid-European) . . . provides both representatives of existing bourgeois authority (police chiefs, judges, physicians) and a population of potential victims who finally rise, en masse, against the threat." At the climax the monster is destroyed "when the infuriated villagers burn down the deserted windmill in which he is a prisoner," said Tudor.[221]

The laboratory in which Dr. Frankenstein conducts his grisly experiments was designed by Danny Hall. Frank Grove, Kenneth Strickfaden, and Raymond Lindsay created the incredible electrical machinery—conductors, switchboards, huge incandescent bulbs—that filled it. Jack Pierce was responsible for the makeup that transformed Karloff into the monster. A triumph of special effects, Pierce's achievement was described by the *New York Times* as follows: "Imagine the monster, with black eyes, heavy eyelids, a square head, huge feet that are covered with matting, long arms protruding from the sleeves of a coat, walking like an automaton."[222] Unlike Quasimodo in the silent version of HUNCHBACK, who was a repellent sight but basically a sympathetic creature, the monster in FRANKENSTEIN is malevolent, and his malevolence is no better seen than when he escapes from the windmill after killing Frankenstein's faithful servant and comes upon a little girl near a lake. When he finishes playing a little game with her, he runs amok and throws her into the water, where she drowns.

The *New York Times* said, "James Whale . . . has wrought a stirring Grand Guignol type of picture, one that aroused so much excitement at the Mayfair yesterday that many in the audience laughed to cover their true feelings. . . . No matter what one may say about the melodramatic ideas here, there is no denying that it is far and away the most effective thing of its kind." *Variety* also liked the way the picture delivered its "high-voltage kick" and considered the photography "the last word in ingenuity since much of the footage calls for dim or night effect and the manipulation of shadows to intensify the ghostly atmosphere."[223]

DRACULA and FRANKENSTEIN became Universal's number-one box-office hits of 1931 and 1932, respectively, and demonstrated that the cycle had staying power. The question was, how to tap it? The first thing Universal did was to organize its horror production around James Whale and other talented European directors. Giving Whale plenty of room to maneuver, Universal created a stable of distinguished writers such as R. C. Sherriff, John L. Balderston, and Philip

Wylie to improve the quality of the scripts and to hire seasoned British actors to support the casts, performers such as Charles Laughton, Elsa Lanchester, Ernest Thesiger, and Una O'Connor. Danny Hall and Universal's special-effects artists continued to supply the scenic and visual tricks.

Rather than immediately producing sequels, Universal opted for product variation. For Lugosi's next role, Universal cast him as a mad scientist, Dr. Mirakle, in MURDERS IN THE RUE MORGUE (Robert Florey, 1932), a picture loosely based on the Edgar Allan Poe story. For Karloff's next role, Universal cast him as a three-thousand-year-old resuscitated mummy in THE MUMMY (Karl Freund, 1933). Universal got the idea for this picture from accounts of the discovery of King Tut's tomb in 1921, an event that ultimately spawned countless B-horror pictures. Then the studio teamed the two stars in THE BLACK CAT (Edgar G. Ulmer, 1934) and THE RAVEN (Louis Friedlander [Lew Landers], 1935). Commenting on this pairing, *Variety* said, "Universal has proceeded on the theory that if Frankenstein was a monster and Dracula a nightmare, the two in combination would constitute the final gasp in cinematic delirium."[224] Although the two pictures were each touted as being based "on the immortal Edgar Allan Poe classic," they made only incidental use of the Poe sources. Regardless, these attempts at product variation generated little interest at the box office.

Whale devised other strategies to sustain the cycle. In THE OLD DARK HOUSE (1932), he introduced the "haunted house" formula. An adaptation of J. B. Priestley's novel *Benighted* by Benn W. Levy and R. C. Sherriff, it tells the story of an assortment of travelers motoring through the Welsh mountains during a dark, stormy night who find refuge in a strange mansion. There they meet the Femm family, consisting of a religious-fanatic hag sister, a pyromaniac-dwarf brother who is kept in the closet, and the head of the family, an insane 102-year-old baronet. Dominating them is a mute, brutish butler, Morgan, played by Boris Karloff. The remainder of the cast consisted of Melvyn Douglas, Gloria Stuart, Charles Laughton, Raymond Massey, and Lilian Bond.

THE INVISIBLE MAN (James Whale, 1933), adapted from the H. G. Wells novel by R. C. Sherriff, introduced a new character to the horror cycle. Claude Rains, making his motion-picture debut, plays a young chemist who discovers a drug that can make a person invisible. However, after taking the drug, he is unable to concoct an antidote to bring back his flesh and blood, which drives him mad. "No actor has ever made his first appearance on the screen under quite as peculiar a circumstance as Claude Rains does," said the *New York Times*. "Mr. Rains's countenance is beheld for a mere half minute at the close of the proceedings. The rest of the time his head is either completely covered with bandages or he is invisible, but his voice is heard." A "Roman holiday for the camera aces," THE INVISIBLE MAN was one of Universal's most creative horror efforts.[225]

BRIDE OF FRANKENSTEIN (James Whale, 1935) initiated Universal's cycle of horror sequels. Since the monster had died in a blazing fire at the conclusion of the original, screenwriters John L. Balderston and William Hurlbut had to devise a way to revive him. BRIDE OF FRANKENSTEIN begins with the same fire, but shows the monster taking refuge in the water-filled cellar of the tower. In this version, the monster is somewhat humanized. No longer is he just "a killer for the killing's sake"; now "he is slightly moonstruck" and yearns for a mate. Dr. Frankenstein therefore conducts an experiment to manufacture a woman for him, an experiment the monster is allowed to watch. Boris Karloff was joined again by Colin Clive as Frankenstein and Ernest Thesiger as the gin-sipping Dr. Praetorius. Elsa Lanchester played Karloff's mate, a "seven-foot, hissing and spitting virago" who looks quite a lot like the ancient Egyptian queen Nefertiti. A high point of Whale's career, the picture contains exceptional process shots by John Mescall and an eerie music score by Franz Waxman. Promoted with the slogan "The Monster Demands a Mate!" the film surpassed the original at the box office and in critical acclaim. The *New York Times* said, "Mr. Karloff is so splendid in the role that all one can say is, 'He is The Monster'" and added that "the monster should become an institution."[226]

DRACULA'S DAUGHTER (Lambert Hillyer, 1936), Universal's second sequel, combined elements of the Dracula legend with Sherlock Holmes mystery fare. Starring Gloria Holden in the title role, DRACULA'S DAUGHTER was promoted with the slogan "More Sensational Than Her Unforgettable Father!" Disguised as a Hungarian countess, this new vampire, the *New York Times* said, "manages to be lovely and deadly at the same time. She has not inherited the pointed canines of the late Count, but she wears a black cloak with equal effectiveness and she always manages to leave her bloodless victims with those two telltale marks on the throat, just over the jugular vein." Universal shut down horror-film production following the release of DRACULA'S DAUGHTER, giving as the reason censorship problems with the cycle in England and other European countries.[227] Regardless, by then, the cycle had lost much of its box-office clout.

Of the other horror films in the classical period, Paramount's DR. JEKYLL AND MR. HYDE (Rouben Mamoulian, 1932) has the distinction of being the only one to make it to *Film Daily*'s Ten Best. A prestige picture adapted from the Robert Louis Stevenson classic by Percy Heath and Samuel Hoffenstein, DR. JEKYLL AND MR. HYDE starred Fredric March in a dual role. The picture was noted for its use of sound montage, the subjective camera, scoring, and particularly the wizardry behind Karl Struss's camerawork, which gradually transforms the handsome Jekyll into the bestial Hyde. Describing Hyde, the *New York Times* said, "In physiognomy this Hyde has the aspects of an ape, with protruding teeth, long eye-teeth, unkempt thick hair leaving but a scant forehead, a broad nose with large nostrils, eyes with the lower part of the sockets pulled down, thick eyebrows and hairy arms and hands—a creature that would make the hairy ape of O'Neill's play a welcome sight."[228] Despite Hyde's appearance, the picture downplays horror and nicely motivates the transformation by linking it to Jekyll's suppressed sexual attraction for the barmaid Ivy, played by Miriam Hopkins. March's performance in the dual role won him an Academy Award for best actor in 1932.

RKO's KING KONG (Merian C. Cooper and Ernest B. Schoedsack, 1933) has the distinction of being the biggest box-office hit of the cycle. The second of a three-picture jungle series, which was RKO's response to the horror cycle, KING KONG was conceived of by Merian C. Cooper and Edgar Wallace and modeled in part on H. G. Wells's *The Lost World*. James Ashmore Creelman and Ruth Rose wrote the screenplay. Fay Wray and Robert Armstrong co-starred. Kong, a fifty-foot ape, and the other prehistoric monsters were the handiwork of puppeteer-animator Willis O'Brien and his staff of special-effects wizards. Establishing just the right mood for the picture, Max Steiner's music was a landmark of film scoring. KING KONG's premiere on 2 March 1933 marked the

Fredric March and Miriam Hopkins in Dr. Jekyll and Mr. Hyde *(Paramount, 1931)*.

King Kong *(RKO, 1933)*.

Olga Baclanova and Harry Earle in Freaks *(MGM, 1932).*

opening of the two largest theaters in the world, New York's Radio City Music Hall and the RKO Roxy, which had a combined seating capacity of nearly twelve thousand. Produced at a cost of $672,000, King Kong grossed close to $2 million during its first release and saved the studio from going under.

MGM responded to the demand for horror films by bringing Lon Chaney and Harry Earles out of retirement to remake their 1925 silent The Unholy Three (Jack Conway, 1930), about the feats of a trio of crooks—a transvestite ventriloquist, a dwarf, and a strongman. However, Chaney died one month after the release of the picture, frustrating MGM's plans to produce a series of Chaney remakes.

Reentering the horror market in 1932, MGM produced one of its most unusual efforts. Indeed, Freaks (Tod Browning, 1932) is probably the most sensational horror picture of the period. Written by Willis Goldbeck and Leon Gordon from the short story "Spurs," by Todd Robbins, the action takes place in a European touring circus. A midget from the sideshow falls in love with a "normal" trapeze artist, who then marries him with the intent of poisoning him for his money. When the freaks discover her motives, they chase the woman down one stormy night and change her into a legless giant hen. At the end of the picture, she is shown squatting in a pile of sawdust, a sideshow monstrosity like the other freaks.

Harry Earles played one of the midget leads and was supported by carnival performers imported from all over the world. Turning the conventions of the horror film around, Browning wanted the audience to respect and sympathize with the so-called abnormal humans and posed the real threat as coming from "normal" people. *Variety* said that "as a horror story, in the 'Dracula' cycle, it is either too horrible or not horrible enough. . . . It is gruesome and uncanny rather than tense, which is where the yarn went off track."[229] Others attacked the picture for being exploitative and tasteless, and after a short run, MGM withdrew it from circulation.

Browning directed two other horror films for MGM, both vehicles for Lionel Barrymore. THE MARK OF THE VAMPIRE (1935), a remake of Browning's LONDON AFTER MIDNIGHT (1927), combined detective elements with horror by teaming Barrymore as a criminologist and Bela Lugosi as a vampire. The novel thing about the picture, said *Variety,* was "that the characters suspected of being human vampires, rising from graves at night to attack, are actually a troupe of actors hired by a wily professor-criminologist in order to solve a crime."[230]

In THE DEVIL DOLL (1936), Barrymore plays a refugee from Devil's Island who disguises himself as an old lady and sells human dolls that murder the people responsible for his imprisonment. Barrymore, in a wig and skirt, hobbling on a crutch, provides some of the novelty, but most of the interest resides in a shrinking process whereby humans and animals are reduced to one-sixth their normal size. "Not since *The Lost World, King Kong,* and *The Invisible Man* have the camera wizards enjoyed such a field day. By use of the split screen, glass shots, oversize sets and other trick devices cherished of their kind, they have pieced together a photoplay which is grotesque, slightly horrible and consistently interesting," said the *New York Times.*[231]

MGM took another tack in the horror cycle when it signed Peter Lorre to MAD LOVE (Karl Freund, 1935). An international star who played the psychopathic child murderer in Fritz Lang's M (1931), Lorre had fled Nazi Germany and immigrated to the United States in 1935. In producing Lorre's first American film, MGM designed a study of "morbid psychology" by remaking a German silent based on the French novel *The Hands of Orlac,* by Maurice Renard. Lorre, a brilliant surgeon, is driven mad by his infatuation with a young actress in a *théâtre des horreurs* in Paris. She finds Lorre repulsive, but seeks his help when her husband, a concert pianist, mangles his hands in a train accident. Unable to save the husband's hands, Lorre grafts on the hands of a guillotined murderer. Although the picture was admired for the way Lorre illuminated the recesses of the doctor's mind, it fared poorly at the box office.[232]

Warners' answer to Universal's Karloff and Lugosi was John Barrymore. Just two months after DRACULA's release, Warners brought out SVENGALI (Archie Mayo, 1931), a costume picture based on the nineteenth-century British novel *Trilby,* by George du Maurier. By titling the picture SVENGALI, Warners shifted the focus to Barrymore, the mountebank and musical genius who turns Trilby O'Ferrall (Marian Marsh) into a great singer. Describing the photographic wizardry in the scenes when Barrymore hypnotizes Trilby, the *New York Times* said, "His eyes appear to lose the iris and become a luminous white. He wears a long dishevelled beard, and he seems to have put something into his shoes to make him even look taller than he really is." Perhaps not a horror film in the

Lionel Barrymore in DEVIL DOLL *(MGM, 1936).*

strictest sense, SVENGALI nonetheless resembles DRACULA in that both contain malevolent protagonists who exert a mystical influence over their victims.[233]

Finding the returns on the picture sufficient to make a sequel, Warners produced THE MAD GENIUS (Michael Curtiz, 1931). Based on Martin Brown's drama *The Idol*, the picture offered Barrymore another flamboyant role, this time as a crippled Russian ballet master who adopts a waif and turns him into a great

John Barrymore in SVENGALI *(Warners, 1931).*

dancer. The picture flopped, and Warners dropped its option on Barrymore's contract.

With DR. X (Michael Curtiz, 1932) and MYSTERY OF THE WAX MUSEUM (Michael Curtiz, 1933), Warners hit its stride. The studio differentiated these films from the competition's by setting the action in Manhattan in the present and by introducing inquisitive reporters into the action. Said Richard Koszarski, "Only at Warners could such films have been produced, for only there was the strain of newspaper realism powerful enough to yield no quarter in a struggle with the surreal requirements of the horror film."[234] Both pictures were designed around Lionel Atwill and Fay Wray, and because both arrived relatively late on the horror scene, Warners differentiated them further by using the two-color Technicolor process.

DR. X, a mad-scientist picture that interweaves strands of the murder mystery with the horror film, "almost makes *Frankenstein* seem tame and friendly," said the *New York Times*. Lionel Atwill as the clubfooted Dr. Xavier is "the head of a surgical research laboratory, under the roof of which several maniacal murders have been committed." During the investigation, suspicion points to many people until finally the murderer turns out to be Dr. Xavier's assistant, Preston Foster. Although Foster has only one hand, he is able to strangle his victims— always during a full moon—by creating a spare hand with synthetic flesh that he concocted in the laboratory. Lee Tracy, the reporter on the case, offers comic relief when he is "shut in a closet with dangling skeletons and skulls, hidden on a slab in a morgue under a sheet," and becomes "a victim of noxious fumes."[235]

MYSTERY OF THE WAX MUSEUM used the two-strip Technicolor process to create a splendid example of a metamorphosis picture. Atwill, a disfigured sculptor who conceals his hideously scarred face behind a mask, kidnaps people who resemble historical characters, dips them in boiling wax, and exhibits them in his wax museum. Glenda Farrell, a cynical, wisecracking reporter who discovers the source of his models, and Frank McHugh, her editor, provide the comic relief. The fire at the end, which was inspired by the destruction of Madame Tussaud's Wax Museum in London in 1925, destroys Atwill's waxworks, revealing the models "twisting and contorting into a chilling semblance of decaying flesh." At the climax, Fay Wray, the heroine, strikes at Atwill's mask and exposes "the ghastly face beneath it." *Variety*'s estimate: "It's one of those artificial things whose sole retrospection will inspire an uncomfortable feeling of the physically misshapen and little else. But it doesn't bore and should go well with the B-grade houses and nabes."[236]

A second horror-film cycle began in 1938 after Universal reissued DRACULA and FRANKENSTEIN as a twin bill. Remarking on the surprising business generated by the pair, *Variety* said, "Horror pix were presumably dead. But a double dose of the goosefleshers brought out the thrill-hungry customers in hordes." On the strength of the reissue, Universal rushed SON OF FRANKENSTEIN (Rowland V. Lee, 1939) into production. This sequel starred Basil Rathbone in the title role, Boris Karloff as the monster, Bela Lugosi as a mad cripple "who guides the monster on murder forays," and Lionel Atwill as the village police inspector who helps destroy the monster. Said *Variety*, "*Son of Frankenstein* will attract substantial business in those houses where audiences like their melodrama strong and weird."[237]

TOWER OF LONDON (Rowland V. Lee, 1939), inspired by Shakespeare's *Richard III*, is set in medieval England during the reign of Edward IV. Basil Rathbone plays Richard, Duke of Gloucester, and Boris Karloff, Mord, "a clubfooted and misshapen giant" who is Richard's chief executioner and torturer. The appeal of the picture, said *Variety*, resided mainly in the court pageantry and the political intrigue, which "neatly dovetailed with display of the various instruments of torture in vogue at the time."[238]

Jumping on the bandwagon, Warners released THE RETURN OF DR. X (Vincent Sherman, 1939), a sequel starring Humphrey Bogart as a doctor who is electrocuted but then keeps himself alive as a zombie by "sapping from the veins of others the same type of blood that once coursed through his own system." *Variety* said, "Hardly any device of the shocker school is overlooked. There's a succession of blood transfusion scenes, lots of laboratory abadaba, a couple of startling samples of the walking-dead and the usual anti-climax where the ingenue is saved in the nick of time from the morbid surgery of the scientific friend."[239] Paramount did what it knew best and produced a horror comedy, THE CAT AND THE CANARY (Elliott Nugent, 1939), starring Bob Hope and Paulette Goddard. Twentieth Century–Fox produced a mystery-chiller, THE HOUND OF THE BASKERVILLES (Sidney Lanfield, 1939), which marked Basil Rathbone's first appearance as Sherlock Holmes. Columbia, true to form, made a series of four virtually undifferentiated B films starring Boris Karloff.

RKO topped them all by producing THE HUNCHBACK OF NOTRE DAME (William Dieterle, 1939), which *Variety* labeled a "super thriller-chiller." Based on the Victor Hugo classic, which Universal filmed as a silent in 1923 with Lon Chaney, HUNCHBACK was RKO's first horror picture since the Kong pictures. And like the Kong pictures, HUNCHBACK contained a monstrous character who generated both sympathy and fear. Charles Laughton played Quasimodo, the deformed and imbecilic bellringer of Notre Dame cathedral. Laughton's "twisted and distorted facial makeup" made him a "most repellent character," said *Variety*, but this pathetic figure ultimately wins audience sympathy when he is unmercifully pilloried, when he defends the church against the mob, and when he twice saves the life of the gypsy girl Esmeralda (Maureen O'Hara). Pandro S. Berman's final project for RKO, HUNCHBACK was conceived as a prestige picture. Bruno Frank and Sonya Levien adapted Victor Hugo's novel and created a screenplay that "painted the world of King Louis XI in broad strokes, emphasizing the contrast between rich and poor, freedom and repression, and medievalism and enlightenment that marked the era," said Richard Jewell. RKO lavished $1.8 million on the picture, which was reflected in the elaborate sets, particularly the cathedral and square, and thousands of extras for the crowd scenes. Opening at the Radio City Music Hall in time for the Christmas holidays, HUNCHBACK went up against GONE WITH THE WIND. Nonetheless, HUNCHBACK grossed a substantial $3.2 million.[240]

Conclusion

This survey of production trends reveals the dynamics of the motion-picture market and places in relief the most popular cycles. Studios reduced risk by producing a variety of pictures every season. Only a few pictures provided something different; whenever one struck the public's fancy, a new cycle began. The cycle lasted until either the producer ran out of fresh ideas to sustain product variation or until a flood of imitations hit the market. Usually, it was a combination of both.

Although each studio is said to have had a "house style" based on a "specialty genre," this survey indicates that the Big Five specialized in several trends at once and that these specialties changed in response to the market. For example, MGM started the decade concentrating on sentimental comedies and prestige pictures based on sophisticated Broadway plays and ended the decade concentrating on family films and musicals. Warners branched out from "topicals" during the Depression to biopics, woman's pictures, and swashbucklers. Universal made its mark with horror pictures during the first half of the decade and with Deanna Durbin musicals during the last half.

Since specialty genres represented a studio's most highly differentiated product, they became the responsibility of special production units. As might be expected, several successful units operated out of MGM and Warners, the largest and healthiest companies among the majors. More surprising, a tally of *Film Daily*'s Ten Best lists reveals that the production units connected with United Artists ranked second behind MGM in the number of films so honored. The fact that a handful of independent producers made some of the most highly regarded films in the business is in itself significant, but the point to be emphasized is that unit production propelled Hollywood into a new era of prosperity.

Having said this, production trends resist easy subdivision into historical periods, such as Depression-recovery or pre-Code–Code. The Depression definitely affected production budgets, but with few exceptions, it did not register as subject matter on the screen. Concerning the Code, let us ignore for a moment Richard Maltby's argument (Chapter 3) that the industry started to enforce the Production Code in 1930, which would render pre-Code–Code breakdown for the thirties nonsensical. Contrary to what the print media in the thirties said about the matter, the Legion of Decency boycott in 1934 terminated neither the controversial fallen-woman cycle nor the gangster cycle. Nor for that matter did it initiate the prestige cycle. The fallen-woman film peaked in popularity as early as 1931. The gangster film peaked in 1932 and would have remained a popular cycle, had not pressure groups interceded. Although the industry stopped producing gangster films, it found a way to inject the violence of the cycle into the G-Men films in 1935, a year after the alleged start of Code enforcement.

It is true that the prestige film played a greater role in the market after 1934 and was partly responsible for the industry's recovery. But prestige pictures had been a production staple since the origins of feature films. During the Depression, the few companies that could still afford to make prestige pictures relied mainly on Broadway hits, a strategy that Hollywood adopted when it converted to the talkies. Discovering that such films appealed mostly to urban moviegoers, Hollywood had to devise a different strategy to reach a wider audience. LITTLE WOMEN and THE PRIVATE LIFE OF HENRY VIII, which were produced in 1933, signaled the way. In retrospect, the Legion of Decency campaign gave prestige films a boost. Therefore, the decade is best regarded as a continuum.

That Hollywood used such trappings as "Pulitzer Prize," "Nobel laureate," "Theatre Guild," and "Shakespeare" to promote its prestige pictures should not imply that the industry catered to a mass, undifferentiated middle-class audience. Rather, Hollywood tailored pictures for specific audiences and simultaneously promoted them to reach as many people as possible. Certainly, MIN AND BILL and DUCK SOUP were not designed to satisfy similar tastes; the same is true for TOP HAT and BABES IN ARMS, STATE FAIR and THE WOMEN, ALL QUIET ON THE WESTERN FRONT and A FAREWELL TO ARMS, and so on. However, it is clear that women composed the largest group. The fallen-woman films, maternal melodramas, Cinderella romances, and working-girl films, plus the prestige films leading to GONE WITH THE WIND, all testify to this fact, but much more than this cannot be known with much certainty.

8

The B Film:
Hollywood's Other Half

Brian Taves

*B*eyond the industrial structures and the typical glossy Hollywood cinema described elsewhere in this volume, there is another entire category of American fictional feature films created and shown under different conditions. These are the B movies, also called "quickies," "cheapies," "low-budget," or simply "budget films," even "C" or "Z" films. Such terms imply pictures that were regarded as secondary even in their own time, and the "B" label has often been used to imply minor pictures or simply poor filmmaking, anything tacky or produced on a low budget.[1] However, B films occupied an equally important role in Hollywood; to concentrate upon the A would emphasize the art of a few films and elide the basis of production, the underlying commercial and artistic means by which the industry survived—as well as the vast quantity and range of films offered to spectators during the studio era.

The content, production, exhibition, and profit from A films were not typical of the material that made motion pictures a continuously viable business enterprise. With each studio releasing, on average, one feature every week of the year, big-budget films were the exception, a distinct minority of the motion pictures produced. B's filled out production schedules and encompassed approximately half the product of the vertically integrated majors. In addition, beyond the Big Eight, about three hundred films annually were made by smaller concerns, collectively known as "indies" or "B studios," geographically centered in Hollywood along "Poverty Row." Hence, roughly 75 percent of the pictures made during the 1930s, well over four thousand films, fall under the B rubric.[2] The sheer number of B films indicates their importance in fully understanding the 1930s; never before or since has low-budget filmmaking been so integral to the Hollywood industry.

With their prolific numbers, the enormous base of B filmmaking, not the occasional A's, fueled the engines of production, distribution, and exhibition, allowing all three to function steadily and smoothly. By facilitating the industrial basis of filmmaking, B's permitted each studio and its myriad personnel to remain active year-round. Turning out some fifty pictures annually allowed the studios to balance a large overhead by using sets, stages, ranches, and contract talent on a nearly continual basis.[3] B's fulfilled a similar function for audiences and

exhibitors, providing a sufficiently steady quantity of new material to alter
theater programs twice a week or more, constantly tempting patrons by continuously changing offerings. The following pages analyze the basic characteristics of
the B, provide an organizational structure for the analysis of its production and
distribution, indicate the career patterns of B filmmakers, and discuss the
stylistic traits of their movies. Finally, the focus shifts to one unique offshoot of B
filmmaking, movies for ethnic audiences, especially African-Americans.

Defining the B Film

First, some clarifications and basic parameters are in order. During the 1930s, the
B label was equivalent to the term *low-budget;* both implied films made on
limited resources and aimed at filling double bills. (However, B and Poverty Row
are not synonymous, as discussed in the next section.) Otherwise, B's have been
defined primarily on the basis of their difference from A's rather than by what B
films share in common. A's were made on budgets averaging $350,000 or more,
with stars who appealed to a wide cross section of patrons.[4] Such films were
intended to play the top half of a double bill, with a running time of seven reels or
longer, and were produced on shooting schedules that allowed time for rehearsals and retakes. Among the A's would be a few prestige films, or "specials," with
an extra investment of time, money, and star power, in anticipation of awards and
major box-office success at first-run theaters.

B's, by contrast, had their own basic prerequisites. First, they were to fill the
bottom half of a double bill. Second, B's had leads with moderate, questionable,
or unknown box-office appeal, such as second-string cowboy stars. Third,
budgets and shooting schedules were more limited, and B's were usually made in
three weeks or as little as one week.[5] Fourth, the running time ordinarily ranged
from fifty-five to seventy minutes. Averaging six reels, some B's could be as short
as five reels or less; a few Poverty Row films, including some of John Wayne's
"Lone Star" Westerns of 1934–1935, ran only about forty-five minutes. Yet, no
single aspect of the B is a definitive guide to A or B status, and there are no clear
lines of demarcation. For instance, to define a B by running time is deceptive
because of the different pacing among the studios; a Warners A might run no
longer than a more leisurely Paramount B.

A's and B's were rented to exhibitors on different bases. With much of the
studio's anticipated profit margin and leadership depending on A's and prestige
films, access was on a percentage basis. Consequently, their eventual profit was
difficult to gauge in advance, and hopes for a blockbuster might not materialize.
Nor could theater owners afford the simultaneous rental of more than one "big"
picture, necessitating that it be paired with a smaller, less expensive movie. B's
usually earned only a single prearranged flat fee, or at best a smaller percentage.
Their relative success or failure and the potential for a small windfall from an
unexpectedly popular B were up to the ingenuity of the exhibitor's publicity
expertise and the practicality of the campaigns outlined in pressbooks. However,
in contrast to the unpredictability of the A, the expected grosses to the studio
from a B could be more reliably determined in advance because of the flat fee.
The budgets could be kept low enough to invariably show a profit, and even when
B's had proved successful, they remained a stable commodity, with higher

THE PAYOFF *(Warners, 1935) was typical of the type of B which, by virtue of its quality, mix of popular generic elements, and a star (James Dunn, right, with Patricia Ellis) was boosted to A status in distribution.*

budgets always going into A's. Consequently, B's almost never lost money for producers, large or small, whether a major with its own exhibition outlets or a small company catering to independent exhibitors. If the season's A product proved weak or failed to achieve the expected success, a studio could rely on the profits of its B's to stay in the black. For instance, during the late 1930s, the reliable gloss and entertainment value of Paramount's B's helped the company remain viable at a time when its A's were of highly variable quality, often inferior to their B's.[6]

The budget, script, and performers often indicated in advance which pictures were intended to be B's, but the product of B units was not necessarily an accurate guide to the status a film achieved when placed in distribution and exhibition. A few B's turned out better than A movies and achieved unexpected critical and popular success; such films were boosted to A status and won a place at the top of the bill. Typical among these was a mixture of the sports and newspaper genres, THE PAYOFF (Warner Bros., 1935); the medical drama A MAN TO REMEMBER (RKO, 1938), which marked Garson Kanin's directorial debut; and Columbia's remake of THE CRIMINAL CODE (1931) entitled PENITENTIARY; and the studio's nearly all-female melodrama GIRLS' SCHOOL (both 1938). Fortuitous circumstances could also boost a picture: when a Flash Gordon serial was cut into a feature version entitled MARS ATTACKS THE WORLD (Universal, 1938), it was fortunate to open shortly after the infamous Orson Welles radio broadcast of another fictional Martian invasion, *The War of the Worlds*. Even low-budget films could prove steady money-makers, including jungle pictures like the feature and serial TARZAN THE FEARLESS (1933), starring Buster Crabbe, or even a pure exploitation movie like the Jed Buell midget Western THE TERROR OF TINY TOWN (1938), which became such a hit that it was picked up for distribution by Columbia. Other factors impinged on the status of A and B films. Sometimes players, such as Fred MacMurray and Mickey Rooney in the mid 1930s, rose so fast in audience favor that their recent, often B pictures were carried up with them, such as two Rooney vehicles for Monogram, THE HEALER/LITTLE PAL (1935) and THE HOOSIER SCHOOLBOY (1937). Nor were all of the films which today seem to be B's actually regarded as such in their own time. Many B series became their own stars, as with one of Fox's biggest attractions, the Charlie Chan series.

Similarly, many big-budget films intended for the top half of a double bill turned out so badly they could barely pass muster at the bottom. Adverse reaction, whether poor reviews or an initial weak performance at previews or the box office, could quickly cause an A to fall in regard and ultimately receive distribution as if it were a B. HOTEL IMPERIAL (Paramount, 1939) provides an example; it was the result of three years of on-again, off-again production, attempting to turn out a "special," first with Marlene Dietrich, then Margaret Sullavan, under the guidance of Ernst Lubitsch, Henry Hathaway, and Lewis Milestone. To avoid further costly entanglements, HOTEL IMPERIAL was eventually assigned to Robert Florey, because of his reputation for turning out quality films on time and within the budget. While still an A, shot on a two-month schedule, it was completed in more modest, eight-reel form, with the Italian lead Isa Miranda imported in an attempt to create a new star, playing opposite Ray Milland. The picture was a commercial and critical failure domestically and usually exhibited as a B. Nonetheless, HOTEL IMPERIAL became a top Paramount offering overseas, where Miranda's name had star caliber, and the film's self-consciously artistic, expressionistic style was admired.

The Organization of B Product

Low-budget filmmaking had long been a significant part of Hollywood production, but demand vastly increased with the rise of double bills. While theaters promised two films for the price of one, audiences actually received approximately one and a half times the entertainment for their money. The double bill usually paired an A and an inexpensive B, or two medium-budget "in-between" pictures, or even two B's. By 1935, with double billing standard practice throughout the nation, all the majors had opened B units, emphasizing a prolific schedule to fill the exhibitor demand cheaply, deliberately designing low-cost films for the second half of double bills.

However, beyond the prerequisites noted in the preceding section, conceptions of the B movie varied widely. Even among the majors, the budgets for B pictures often diverged by $100,000 or more. There is no budget or production schedule typical of all B's because of the wide variations among the different companies—a fact complicated by the changing ways of computing overhead under various management regimes. For instance, in the early 1930s, most Warner movies were shot in about three weeks for much less than $200,000, yet this hardly reduced them all to the B category. Furthermore, the same schedule and budget that resulted in a high-quality B at Paramount or MGM might approximate the investment for an A at Columbia or Universal.[7]

While the B label had one meaning to the eight principal studios, definitions varied even more between the majors and smaller studios. Factoring in quickies and other disparate types of B within the overall field of low-budget films reveals that it has several separate levels. To clarify these distinctions, a practical, multilevel taxonomy for the B film is offered below, where the B film is broken down into four categories, listed in order of prestige: (1) major-studio "programmers," (2) major-studio B's, (3) smaller-company B's, and (4) the quickies of Poverty Row.

(1) The first category, programmers, includes movies produced by the majors and occasionally such lesser companies as Tiffany that share characteristics of both A's and B's. Properly, programmers have a status of their own, but since they are seldom discussed separately and are usually lumped together with B's rather than A's, an analysis of them is appropriate here.

At the major studios and occasionally in the smaller companies, the stratification tended to be more complex than a simple division between A and B. Not only were there prestige films, A's, and B's, but many lower-level A's occupying an equivocal position, intended as major product but sharing aspects of B's. Whether previously called "shaky A's," "gilt-edged B's," "in-betweeners," or "intermediates," such films straddling the A-B boundary have been best labeled "programmers" by Don Miller in his valuable history *B Movies*.[8] The use of the programmer category eliminates a problem in the discussion of B movies, differentiating between a film made in less than twelve days and one shot in five weeks, or one with a cast of unknowns and one offering cast names that were quite recognizable, if not top-draw marquee value.

Indeed, programmers were actually more common during the first half of the 1930s, before B units became an important factor of production. Programmers had reasonably elaborate sets, with running times between sixty-five and eighty minutes, and could occupy the services of major stars or at least one or two well-paid performers. Depending upon the studio, budgets might range from about $100,000 to $200,000, or even as high as $500,000, but programmers did not attain the aura of prestige associated with the high gloss of the A movie. A programmer might contain minor stars, have a relatively short running time, or be photographed in just a few weeks. For instance, Warner Oland was unlikely to be a headliner in the 1930s outside the Charlie Chan films, but he was the star of the series. Although formula mysteries, running less than eight reels, and shot in under a month on modest budgets, the Chan movies were designed as programmers, but attracted major audiences and box-office grosses on a par with A's.

The term *programmer* indicates its principal characteristic: its flexibility in playing any part of the program, operating in between A and B and appearing in either category. Depending on the prestige of the theater and the other material on the double bill, a programmer could show up at the top or bottom of the marquee, especially if the show consisted of two programmers or if it were

playing a theater's split-week show. Programmers might or might not benefit
from a coordinated national advertising and publicity campaign, instead usually
receiving wide but scattered attention, but with neither the important press
notices of an A nor the indifference and critical disdain typically given a B.
Considering the relative expense of programmers, market conditions could make
them problematic. They could easily fade into quick obscurity or show a loss
unless more often exhibited as A's rather than B's. Yet programmers might also
turn out as box-office champions and even become major hits under the right
conditions.

Because of programmers' medium budget and ambiguous positioning in
exhibition, potential new stars were more likely to be cast in them than in B's.
Similarly, while B's were traditionally generic, programmers were more apt to
deal with prestigious or unusual topics, indicating the studio's willingness to
make a modest investment on a theme with uncertain popularity. Programmers
often relied on one of the best aspects of B films, the willingness to try novel style
and content, without the attendant drawbacks of meager budgets and brief
shooting schedules. For instance, after the success and awards given to THE
INFORMER (John Ford, 1935), many critics pointed to it as an example of what
could be done with a programmer budget; some even labeled it a B.[9]

(2) In the second category are the B films from the larger studios, aimed at
filling the exhibition needs of their theater chains and lowering overhead by
keeping facilities and contract talent constantly busy. B's of the majors were
usually made on schedules of two to five weeks, averaging three weeks at studios
from Warners to Paramount. Such B's took advantage of the existing lavish
facilities and standing sets, often utilizing their roster of top technical talent and
character actors. B's at the majors were never hasty or slapdash; the studios'
prestige rested on the quality of their B's as well as their A's, with the frequent
hope that a B might turn out well enough to be released as an A. Depending on
the studio, the budget might go as low as $30,000, for a Western, or as high as
$300,000; anything higher was almost certainly a programmer or an A.

The Fox B unit was typical of such operations among the majors. After the
merger with Twentieth Century, the unit was headed by Sol M. Wurtzel, who
had a $6 million annual budget for twenty-four B's per year, averaging between
$150,000 and $200,000 per film.[10] Two to three months would be spent on
preparation, and three weeks in shooting, with comparatively important directors like Allan Dwan, Mal St. Clair, George Marshall, Alfred L. Werker, or rising
talents like H. Bruce ("Lucky") Humberstone and Norman Foster. Fox B's were
inclined to be series films, whether mystery, domestic, or comedy, including
Charlie Chan, Mr. Moto, Sherlock Holmes, Michael Shayne, the Cisco Kid,
George O'Brien Westerns, the Gambini sports films, the Roving Reporters, the
Camera Daredevils, the Big Town Girls, the hotel for women, the Jones Family,
the Jane Withers children's films, Jeeves, or the Ritz Brothers.

The house style was as noticeable in the studio B units as in A's, with
substantial product differentiation found among the B's of the various majors. For
instance, B units did not preclude Paramount and Fox from bringing high
standards and even sophistication to their B's. Specializing in many types of
crime films, Paramount enhanced fast pacing and original plots with an artistic
treatment, indulging in the elaborate, atmospheric, and European-flavored art
direction and cinematography of its A's. On the other hand, Warner Bros., whose

Some stars became prominently associated with B's while still appearing in A's, such as Ralph Bellamy, appearing here in Columbia's THE FINAL HOUR (1936). *Other performers, like Marguerite Churchill (left), rarely emerged from the B's.*

A's already reflected the crime formulas and tough realism typical of B's, had a poorer reputation with its purely B product. MGM's B's were widely regarded as little different from its A's, graced with the same sets and stars. A similar statement could be made for Universal, except that in this case the comparison had the reverse effect and was less flattering. While both Universal and Columbia produced A's and B's, much of their A product resembled the programmers or B's of the majors, in productions made quickly and cheaply with stars of questionable magnitude. Columbia had responded to the rising demand for a double-bill product by lowering their quantity of A's and doubling production, all of the growth occurring in the B division on shooting schedules of two weeks or less.[11]

The B's in categories one and two came from the majors, as well as Universal and Columbia, and these pictures were aimed at a wide array of exhibitors. By contrast, in the lower tiers, categories three and especially four, audiences became steadily more specialized, in proportion to the decreasing corporate size. Smaller than Universal or Columbia, the so-called B studios ranged from Republic on down to the indies. Such firms were generally distinguishable by the absence of exhibition arms, with low-budget product accounting for nearly all their output. Many companies were so small and short-lived that they were

Richard Dix and Karen Morely in DEVIL'S SQUADRON *(Columbia, 1936). Many A's from Columbia and Universal often resembled programmers or B's of the majors.*

quickly absorbed by equally transitory rivals, their product often distributed second- or thirdhand from those who produced it.

The companies in categories three and four are covered by the label Poverty Row, a term almost as problematic as the label B. While appropriately referring to a distinct geographical portion of Hollywood (Gower Gulch), the territory encompasses many studios, and the location of a plant on Poverty Row did not necessarily imply a B studio. Durable, important enterprises like Columbia and Republic had offices there, although the more typical inhabitants included such deceptively named firms as Peerless and Reliable—some of the most underfinanced, transient, and truly poverty-stricken producers in filmmaking. Poverty Row turned out films made for $100,000 to $10,000, and often even less—a broad range of variables that covered even more product differentiation than was found among the major studio B's.

The coming of sound had posed a tremendous challenge for all producers, but especially for Poverty Row. While their silents had been made for $3,000–$4,000, versus $50,000–$60,000 for a modest film from the majors, talkies doubled these budgets. Yet, as with the majors, profits proved sufficient for many low-budget producers to continue or return to business, and small companies like Syndicate, Big Four, and Superior served an important function during this transition period. They not only continued to supply silents to many smaller theaters without the resources to convert to sound, but also took up much of the challenge of adapting sound to outdoor pictures, with their prolific output maintaining the popularity of the B Western during these years.[12]

Later, the demand for B's to fill double bills and Saturday matinees created a voracious exhibitor need for quantity that was initially more than the majors could handle, leaving an opening for the product of various smaller companies. As a result, these concerns proliferated during the 1934–1936 seasons, until every lot in Hollywood was busy. However, the slack was soon taken up by the majors and Columbia, until there was a glut of B pictures, resulting in a merging of minor studios.[13] The B's of the majors came to dominate the market, and smaller companies again had problems finding financing, causing many marginal ones to vanish by 1937. With the secondary concerns dominated by Republic and Monogram, once more the majors preserved their basic hegemony over Hollywood.

(3) The third category is the B product of secondary studios who still commanded respect within the industry, from Republic, Monogram, Grand National, Mascot, and Tiffany on down to Ambassador-Conn, Chesterfield, Invincible, Liberty, Majestic, Sono Art, Educational, and World Wide. While they did not have the quality or resources of the majors, they were far from the quickies made in a week for a few thousand dollars, a type reserved for the next category.

Although such B companies generally lacked exhibition outlets, some, like Republic and Monogram, could afford exchanges equivalent to the majors in large cities.[14] These studios were comparatively stable organizations, with access to capital and their own facilities, turning out films of satisfactory technical quality. Budgets rarely rose above $100,000 and were often substantially less, but such obstacles were overcome, often achieving a quality nearly equal to the B's of the majors in similar genres. For instance, Republic's first Ellery Queen whodunit, THE SPANISH CAPE MYSTERY (1935), offers probably the most effective location photography of any B thriller during the 1930s, and Chesterfield's DEATH FROM A DISTANCE (1936) cleverly uses the Griffith Park Planetarium to evoke a unique mystery atmosphere. Although largely confined to B product, occasionally Tiffany, Mascot, Monogram, Republic, and Grand National rivaled the majors with their own A efforts, including A STUDY IN SCARLET (World Wide, 1933), LAUGHING AT LIFE (Mascot, 1933), DANIEL BOONE (Grand National, 1936), GREAT GUY (Grand National, 1937), and HARMONY LANE (Monogram, 1935), easily as credible a Stephen Foster biography as 20th Century–Fox's SWANEE RIVER (1939). While the talents on both sides of the camera were rarely of star caliber, they were still known and reputable, not far below those of the majors, with many advancing to the larger studios. The players who starred in B studio films were skilled and often also worked at the majors; examples include Lionel Atwill, Mischa Auer, Sidney Blackmer, Johnny Mack Brown, Harry Davenport, Charlie Grapewin, Boris Karloff, Bela Lugosi, Douglass Montgomery, Ralph Morgan, Karen Morley, J. Carrol Naish, and Jean Parker.

The four best-remembered studios in this category, Mascot, Monogram, Republic, and Grand National, were all interrelated in chronological development. The Monogram label emerged in 1931, having evolved from its founding by W. Ray Johnston in 1924 as Rayart Productions, which transformed into Syndicate Film Exchange and Continental Talking Pictures between 1928 and 1930. The studio quickly earned an important place as a leader among the small companies, and affiliated with Pathé in England, each corporation releasing some of the product of the other in its own country. Trem Carr became chief of production in the early 1930s, turning out twenty or more pictures annually, many of them made for as little as $25,000, equivalent to such contemporaries as Chesterfield, Ambassador-Conn, Liberty, and Mascot.[15] Priding itself on versatility, by 1934 Monogram enhanced its schedule by offering cheaply made versions of such prestigious literary titles as JANE EYRE, THE MOONSTONE, OLIVER TWIST, and A GIRL OF THE LIMBERLOST.

Republic (also called "Repulsive") Pictures grew out of Monogram and Mascot, the result of an enormous step toward amalgamating the independent front that occurred in March 1935—a sign of the coming consolidation. Herbert J. Yates, already involved in the business for more than two decades, called in the debts owed to his Consolidated Film Industries laboratories, thereby merging Liberty, Majestic, Chesterfield, Mascot, and Monogram. Yates had planned carefully; Monogram, for instance, would bring its national distribution organization of exchanges to thirty-nine cities. Mascot had been founded in 1926 by Nat Levine and had its own studio, specializing in serials before branching out to features in 1933. Knowing that he needed a merger with Mascot to succeed, Yates offered to help Levine boost his sagging feature schedule, while taking advantage of his leadership in serials. The offer to join forces seemed to promise both quantity and quality; to make full use of its studio and to control distribution, Mascot needed to increase production, but Levine lacked access to the necessary capital.[16] Both Levine and Monogram's Trem Carr had experience heading production, and at Republic they took on this responsibility together. Republic thus began not only in a strong financial position but also with some of the best and most experienced independent talent in the business.

Republic quickly realized the potential of higher-grade B Westerns produced on modest budgets. For instance, Gene Autry's first starring vehicle, TUMBLIN' TUMBLEWEEDS (1935), was made for less than $18,000, and eventually grossed over $1 million; it was helmed by a novice, Joseph Kane, who became Republic's house director. Named for one of Autry's most popular songs, TUMBLIN' TUMBLE-WEEDS led the new form of the singing Western to such wide success that Republic soon introduced an equally popular rival, Roy Rogers. The desire for singing cowboys was so great that even John Wayne was dubbed crooning in WESTWARD HO! (1935), which premiered at the Pantages Theater on Hollywood Boulevard—indicating that Republic's Westerns had found an audience beyond the usual small-town and rural theaters. Stars like Wayne and Autry received around $1,000 per picture, and in a few years such Republic series as the Three Mesquiteers were budgeted at around $50,000, with shooting schedules sometimes as short as a single week.[17]

Within limits, Republic imitated the majors, particularly with action-oriented themes, including a color Zorro swashbuckler THE BOLD CABALLERO/THE BOLD CAVALIER (1935), and an adventure film set in India, STORM OVER BENGAL (1938), following the success of LIVES OF A BENGAL LANCER (Paramount, 1935) and THE CHARGE OF THE LIGHT BRIGADE (Warner Bros., 1936). Unlike most of its immediate competitors, and because of its emergence from Consolidated labs, Republic successfully mated low-budget material with a degree of polished Hollywood seamlessness never equaled by the other smaller studios. These technical standards allowed the majors to feel comfortable with Republic's existence in a way they never did with other such companies.[18] Republic provided little direct competition until the 1940s, when the studio advanced beyond Westerns, rural comedies, serials, and other escapist fare, in an ultimately failed attempt to expand to major status.

Among those joining Yates in 1935, only Nat Levine had any lasting impact on Republic, through his organization of the studio's prolific serials division.[19] After little over a year at Republic, Johnston and Carr withdrew and revived Monogram. The company acquired the services of many proficient personnel associated with various independents, developing an ambitious program of forty pictures annually, all of a high standard for a small studio. While avoiding serials, Monogram became expert in series product, for instance imitating Fox's Charlie Chan series in the form of six Mr. Wong mysteries, based on the *Collier's* magazine stories by Hugh Wiley. Although in its second incarnation the company never surpassed its previous level or achieved the glamour and prestige to rise above Republic, Monogram remained its closest competitor for fifteen years before transforming into Allied Artists in 1953.

Just as Johnston and Carr had left Republic to reenter independent production, so did Levine. He worked briefly for MGM and then went to the newly created Grand National in the spring of 1936, together with Edward Alperson, Spyros Skouras, George Hirliman, and Al Herman; B. F. Zeidman, Zion Myers, Douglas MacLean, and Max and Arthur Alexander soon joined the roster of producers. Grand National acquired the studio facilities of E. W. Hammons's Educational Pictures, and the exchanges of the now-defunct First Division served as their distribution nucleus. Grand National began with a tremendous coup, securing James Cagney for two pictures in 1937, GREAT GUY and SOMETHING TO SING ABOUT. At the time, Cagney was quarreling with Warner Bros. over his contract, but after the two pictures for Grand National, he returned advantageously to his old studio. Grand National, meanwhile, had spent too extravagantly on the Cagney pictures (more than $900,000 on SOMETHING TO SING ABOUT, directed by Victor Schertzinger) to secure the necessary profit margin, despite their popularity. The company aspired to imitate the majors and produce relatively prestigious pictures, along with the necessary action pictures typical of the B's, such as Tex Ritter Westerns budgeted at $20,000 apiece. Grand National even released some features in a Cinecolor process that was renamed Hirlicolor for the studio boss. The studio never succeeded along the lines of Monogram or Republic; by 1940, swamped in debt, Grand National was liquidated, with Astor Pictures buying the negatives and reissuing many of the films. Astor, often associated with the product of William Steiner, was an independent clearinghouse for assorted old and new films that had received minimal release.[20]

(4) Astor was typical of the concerns that form the fourth category of B films. These are companies who truly deserve and justify the name Poverty Row. With their transitory nature, lack of finance, and limited access to necessary facilities and equipment, they were the domain of the indies making quickies or cheapies that often do not even rank as B's but are instead labeled C or Z pictures. These movies usually received one or two reviews at most in the trades, and often none at all, forming what today might be called an underground economy on the fringes of 1930s Hollywood.

Low-budget fare of one type or another was the sole output of minor indies. These companies concentrated on features, most often Westerns, along with

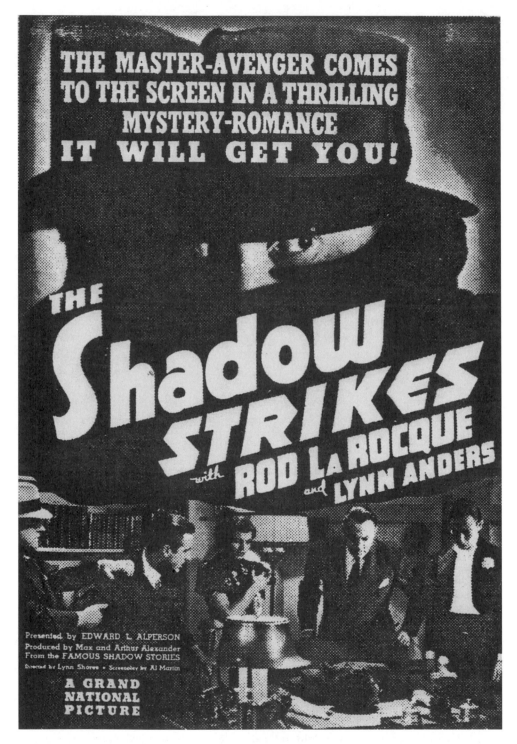

Newspaper ad mat for THE SHADOW STRIKES BACK *(Grand National). Secondary B studios adopted the series propensity of the majors, often featuring stars who were no longer popular enough to play the leads in the A's.*

occasional serials and such offbeat products as nature and expedition films and pictures for ethnic audiences. These companies obtained financing, commissioned lab work, and rented studio space as needed, usually by the day, at the RKO Pathé lot in Culver City, the Tec-Art, Prudential, the Talisman Studio on Sunset Boulevard, the General Service Studios on Romain, International Film Corporation's Television Studios, or the Larry Darmour Studios. Shooting schedules ranged from four to eighteen days, but most often were about a week. Sixty to eighty setups had to be averaged daily, often shooting from four in the morning until seven at night or later, and occasionally around the clock. There was no time for a day or two of added shooting; a quickie ran over budget with the brief illness of a leading player or a single afternoon's rain on location. Sudden storms or periods of drought in Southern California caused major difficulties, since favored locations could lose their scenic value or become temporarily impracticable. Yet the makers of such films were ingenious; when a drought hit, an Edward Finney screen version of James Fenimore Cooper's Leatherstocking classic *The Pioneers* was shot in a large garage at Newhall Ranch, opening the back doors to give an illusion of exteriors and adding some stock footage.[21]

Scriptwriters kept indoor shots to a minimum so that interiors could often be completed on a single day at a rented studio. For instance, one film was shot during a twenty-two-hour stint, completing 196 scenes, on a set rented for $2,500; the remainder of the film was shot using exteriors and only cost an additional $500. The producer quickly profited by selling the completed film to a "states'-rights" organization (see below) for $6,000.[22] With locations used whenever possible, Westerns were especially advantageous. To avoid the expense of accommodating a crew, most of the locations were within a fifty-mile radius of Hollywood, allowing cast and crew to return home each night. Consequently, a surprising number of Westerns were intentionally set in the present, with automobiles, telephones, and other indicators of modern life on the range. These settings gave many low-budget films a pictorial advantage over B's from the majors; for instance, Ambassador-Conn's VALLEY OF WANTED MEN and MEN OF ACTION (both 1935) offered stunning outdoor locations. By contrast, Universal's mystery YELLOWSTONE (1936), set in the national park, wastes its scenic opportunities through unconvincing rear projection and cramped studio shots unimaginatively directed by Arthur Lubin.

Quickies were often sold in advance at a specified rate to exchanges in order to raise initial financing. Budgets ranged from a low of $5,000 to as much as $20,000 per picture. A typical budget on an $8,000 picture allocated $250 for the script, often including a song, with $400 for the director. Often engaged for six-picture deals, at $1,000 per picture, were such B Western stars as Rex Bell, Johnny Mack Brown, Buffalo Bill, Jr., Harry Carey, Lane Chandler, Hoot Gibson, Raymond Hatton, Jack Hoxie, Tom Keene, Rex Lease, Ken Maynard, Kermit Maynard, Tim McCoy, Tom Mix, Jack Perrin, Reb Russell, Buddy Roosevelt, Fred Scott, Bob Steele, Tom Tyler, Wally Wales, John Wayne, and Guinn ("Big Boy") Williams. Personnel often had multiple jobs, doubling as actors, writers, directors, and supervisors. Some names were pseudonyms; for instance, Bernard B. Ray announced to the press that he had promoted an assistant, Franklin Shamray, to be Reliable's third director. In fact, Shamray was merely one more name under which Ray worked. Leading ladies had a fee of $75, and the supporting cast included many aspiring performers willing to take roles for little or nothing in the hope of being discovered. Some casting took place on the streets in front of Poverty Row, using whoever was nearby and available, and real cowpunchers were relied upon for extras because they could supply their own horses. The establishment of new Screen Actors Guild rules in 1937 raised the budgets of such pictures by about $1,100; this increase in expenses was too great to be recovered by many small companies, since a good profit margin for many Poverty Row producers was often a mere 10 percent, a few thousand dollars per picture.[23]

For some of the poorest studios in this category, five-reel films sufficed for the usual six-reel length. Expository material was often obviously missing, resulting in a fragmented, jumbled plot or even one that was simply incoherent, as in some of Weiss's Stage and Screen Westerns with Rex Lease, such as PALS OF THE RANGE (1935). With the budgets and schedules so limited, pictures were wrapped whether or not shooting had been finished on the script, regardless of the plot incongruities that might result. Just as often, footage was visibly padded, embellishing what had been shot through the use of stock footage that sometimes came to dominate a film. A typical case is provided by SKYBOUND (Puritan, 1935) episodically and nearly incomprehensibly composed largely of a jumble of disconnected aerial, nightclub, and chase footage, with little original material shot specifically for the movie.

Many of the B films in this category were directed toward specific theaters, audience groups, and classes of spectators. Such genres as B Westerns were, like serials, aimed at a quick payoff in minor houses attracting the Saturday matinee and juvenile audiences, especially in the small-town market. Although the theaters owned by the majors accounted for the best locations and the large majority of the profits, thousands of lesser houses proliferated across the country. These smaller, often independent exhibitors changed the double-bill programs two or three times a week, sometimes daily. At best, they showed subsequent, not first, runs, often utilizing quickies that would be shunned by critics and larger exhibitors. Many of the poorest theaters, such as the "grind houses" in the larger cities, screened a continuous program emphasizing action with no specific schedule, sometimes offering six quickies for a nickel in an all-night show that changed daily.[24]

Many of these small or rural theaters were served by an entirely different distribution system, one in which profits were so marginal that the majors bypassed it altogether. Nonetheless, there was sufficient money to be made in the "states rights" market to attract the producers of films ranging from low-budget Westerns to ethnic films. In the states rights system, movies were sold on a state-by-state or regional basis, with flat fees paid for the limited exclusive rights to distribute for exhibition in a particular area, allowing small but predictable profits. The distributors to such second- and third-rate houses absorbed the cost of release prints and publicity materials, paying a use fee to the producer that might range as high as $50,000. Such a system virtually guaranteed production, but had no incentive for quality, since the pictures were bought without regard to the care or expense that went into making them. Often packages of six or eight films with a single star were sold as a group, with the first or second result of such a sequence more frequently reviewed, regardless of quality, than the final pictures, usually issued later and without fanfare to fulfill the anticipated program. Many states rights producers had their own independent distributors;

for instance, Syndicate was a states rights concern specializing in low-budget Westerns. First Division Exchanges was the largest states rights distributor, virtually the United Artists of the small companies, handling product from Resolute, Weiss, and, depending on the region, Chesterfield, Invincible, Liberty, Monogram, Beacon, Olympic, and many others, as well as some British films and a few documentaries and other unusual films that were not picked up by others.[25]

To give a sample of the companies and their output in the fourth category, several are chosen from the pivotal year of 1935, the height of quickie filmmaking, with such prolific firms as Ajax, Beacon, Beaumont/Mitchell Leichter, Conquest, Du World, Empire, Hoffberg, Imperial, Kent, Peerless, Principal, Puritan, Reliable, Resolute, William Steiner, Spectrum, Victory, and Weiss. (All titles mentioned in the next several paragraphs are from 1935 unless otherwise noted.) Typical of Poverty Row production companies was one that distributed through Astor. Ajax Pictures had four specialties: the Four Leaf Clover series was their prestige item, such as the drama of a secretary climbing her way into society, $20 A WEEK. Their second group featured aging but still credible Harry Carey in above average B Westerns like THE LAST OF THE CLINTONS, RUSTLER'S PARADISE, WAGON TRAIL, and WILD MUSTANG. Ajax's third series, Our Young Friends, starred the quartet of grown Our Gang veterans David Sharpe, Gertrude Messinger, Mickey Daniels, and Mary Kornman. These satirical features, such as ADVENTUROUS KNIGHTS, ROARING ROADS, and SOCIAL ERROR, with stories and direction by Sharpe, together with C. Edward Roberts and William Berke, were amateurish and seldom won much notice. Ajax's fourth series used a similar approach; like Sharpe, Richard Talmadge's films again utilized a stuntman better remembered for his second-unit work and doubling than acting. However, unlike Sharpe's negligible results, Talmadge achieved a distinction to be discussed later in this chapter. His movies were sometimes released in conjunction with the Reliable banner, and the Ajax label was also on some of the B Westerns and other genre films, principally starring Bob Steele and Tom Tyler, produced by the prolific William Steiner.

Perhaps the lowest-budget firm was Weiss, an enterprise that continues to this day, maintaining in television release many of their low-grade 1930s films. The brothers Max, Louis, and Adolph Weiss entered production in the early 1920s with money earned from a New York lamp-and-fixture store, phonograph sales, and ownership of a theater that developed into a small chain.[26] Operating under such pretentious banners as Superior Talking Films, Stage and Screen Productions, Artcraft Productions, Exploitation Pictures, Consolidated Pictures, and International Pictures Corporation, the Weiss brothers produced a variety of supercheapies in which plot coherence was always the last priority. Most were so bad that they were never reviewed or copyrighted, apparently deliberately avoiding press attention; the only record of their existence is found in an occasional release chart, a few advertisements, and surviving prints. Though most Poverty Row producers averaged a six-reel length, or about sixty minutes, Weiss continually tried to pare that down to five reels, lasting just over fifty minutes.

In 1935, Weiss offered such series as producer Robert Emmett's Morton of the Mounted "northwest action thrillers" with Dynamite, the Wonder Horse and Captain, the King of Dogs receiving top billing over human star John Preston as Sergeant Bruce Morton, in COURAGE OF THE NORTH, FURY OF THE MOUNTED, ROARING RIVER, ROGUES OF THE ROCKIES, THE SILENT CODE, and TIMBER

Bruce Bennett in TARZAN AND THE GREEN GODDESS *(1938)*.

TERRORS. Weiss also produced a number of other more conventional Westerns, known as the American Rough Rider series (PALS OF THE RANGE, GOING TO TOWN, THE ROPIN' FOOL, TWO-FISTED GALLAGHER) and the Range Rider series (CYCLONE OF THE SADDLE, THE GHOST RIDER, SURE-SHOT SAM), the latter made in conjunction with Larry Darmour's Empire Film Distributors. Most of these starred Rex Lease, with George M. Merrick as producer and Elmer Clifton directing, both collaborating on the scripts. Weiss also sponsored Consolidated Pictures and producer Bert Sternbach's crime series of Melodramatic Dog Features, starring Tarzan, the Police Dog (CAPTURED, MILLION-DOLLAR HAUL, MISSING MESSENGER, ON PATROL, ON THE SPOT), and a four-reel special of the venerable temperance play *The Drunkard*.[27]

Not all the Poverty Row concerns were similar. Burroughs-Tarzan Enterprises arose from author Edgar Rice Burrough's dislike of the filmic treatment of his Tarzan character and the belief that he could earn a better share of their profits. He joined in sponsoring his own original story for the screen and chose Olympic champion Herman Brix for the role, according to his conception of the character as an educated man. However, the venture was doomed from the beginning; the majors had blocked the upstart firm from borrowing the most recent cinema Tarzans, Johnny Weissmuller and Buster Crabbe, and planned to keep Burroughs's films from playing in the major theater chains. Without access to studios, partner Ashton Dearholt, a silent-screen actor and RKO representative in Guatemala, suggested using that country as a location for their work. Twenty-nine cast and crew members spent four months around the Mayan ruins at Tikal, Guatemala, plagued by illness, bad weather, and other adverse jungle conditions aggravated by the low budget, until work was completed in March 1934. An introduction to the film tries to make a virtue out of these difficulties, noting, "The production of the film was carried out under conditions of extreme difficulty and hardship involving personal danger to the actors and technicians, to whom the producers owe a debt of gratitude. The sound recording was occasionally interfered with by the extremely variable atmospheric conditions and your kind indulgence is craved in this direction."

Meanwhile, needing cash and about to marry the former Mrs. Dearholt, Burroughs reoptioned MGM's film rights to his character. The Burroughs-Tarzan film was given the title THE NEW ADVENTURES OF TARZAN and eventually made available in three forms, a twelve-chapter serial, a feature, and the feature followed by a serial; it was the last Tarzan serial to be made. Bookings were limited to independent theaters in the United States on the states'-rights network, although it had more success overseas. In June 1938, a new feature was edited from the last ten chapters of the serial, together with some previously unused footage and titled TARZAN AND THE GREEN GODDESS. In 1940, billing was altered to reflect the change of Brix's name to Bruce Bennett, and the feature version THE NEW ADVENTURES OF TARZAN remained in almost continuous release until its sale to television in 1961. Burroughs-Tarzan Enterprises produced only four other, unrelated films, including TUNDRA (1936), but the saga of its Tarzan footage reflects the various release patterns typical of Poverty Row B films.

B Filmmakers

Just as B's were the product of the divisions noted above, from B units at the majors to the smaller companies along Poverty Row, filmmaking talent tended to be compartmentalized along similar lines, with their status reflecting the same taxonomy. While B's occasionally served as a training ground for directors, writers, cinematographers, designers, and performers, opportunities for promotions were the exception, rather than the rule.[28] Quickie filmmakers, especially, found little opportunity for upward mobility, and the prospect of talent emerging from the B's was far less likely than the reverse, a decline into Poverty Row. Once talent was identified with the A or B category, the person tended to be pigeonholed, even at the majors. Although an individual might be involved with an occasional A, he would still most often be considered for B's, just as a performer might typically play support in A's and leads in B's. Under contract, talent had to take the studio's assignments, regardless of personal preference, often with only a day or even less to prepare. Most B directors could not revise the script, had little say in choosing a cast or crew, and were seldom involved in the editing.

Many individuals were shunted into careers dominated by B's because of their consistent effectiveness in filming efficiently and smoothly. They became type-cast, in a sense, not for lack of talent, but precisely because of their demonstrated skill. Turning out pictures rapidly on low budgets required rare abilities: knowing exactly what shots were necessary, editing in the camera without

wasting footage on full coverage or more than a few takes, quickly arranging the
lighting and camera angles to conceal the cheapness of the sets, eliciting or giving
an effective performance with few rehearsals, and covering such disadvantages
with fast pacing and shadowy lighting. These abilities were highly prized and
might well lead to a continuation in the B realm, but seldom advanced one to the
A's.

B films became the domain of numerous individuals with long, prolific careers.
One individual who provides a perfect example of the career path and assignments of a major studio B director in the 1930s, and what could be accomplished
under such conditions, is Robert Florey.[29] As the form's premier practitioner and
exponent, the artistry he and others merged into the confines of B filmmaking is
one of the justifications for investigating the form. (His work will be discussed at
length in the next section of this chapter.) With thirty-five features to his credit
during the decade, his movies demonstrate the problematic nature of the term *B
director;* half of Florey's 1930s films were actually either programmers or A's,
including four box-office champions. After serving as assistant director on
big-budget productions, Florey directed three quality Poverty Row features in
1926–1927, but found they did not lead to directing for the majors. Next, he made
a quartet of shorts that firmly brought the avant-garde to American filmmaking
for the first time, including the renowned LIFE AND DEATH OF 9413—A HOLLY-
WOOD EXTRA. In quick succession, he was signed to direct the new talking
pictures at Paramount's Astoria studio, including the Marx Brothers's hit film
debut, THE COCOANUTS (co-director, Joseph Santley, 1929). He then traveled to
his native France to direct some of the first European talkies and returned to
America and co-authored (without any on-screen credit) the script of FRANKEN-
STEIN (1931) at Universal. At the same studio, his adaptation and direction of
MURDERS IN THE RUE MORGUE (1932) turned Poe's tale into a remake of the 1920
German classic THE CABINET OF DR. CALIGARI, revised into the form of a
Hollywood horror movie.

To continue both writing and directing, Florey joined his friend Sam Bischoff
in 1932 at KBS, the old Tiffany studio. However, after a few months he won a far
more lucrative directorial contract with Warner Bros., where, over the next two
and a half years, he directed thirteen films. These ranged from A's, to
programmers, to an occasional B. However, shunted from one type of film to
another, often given a negligible assignment after directing a hit, he left Warners
in frustration in mid-1935. Moving to Paramount for the next four years, Florey
found that the pattern of variable projects persisted, but he found far more
creative freedom, especially in camerawork and decor. Yet Florey was typecast
because of the continual need for B's and his reputation for skillfully fusing
artistic inclinations with a medium budget and shooting schedule as short as two
weeks. His unconventional technique and determination to adapt both German
expressionism and the avant-garde to Hollywood filmmaking became prized in
the B and programmer realm, especially in thrillers, but was less desired in glossy
A's. After seventeen Paramount B's, programmers, and A's, he wearied of the
pace and left in 1939. Briefly joining Columbia, he returned to Warners in 1941,
and thereafter nearly all of his pictures were A's. Florey renewed his contact with
B-type production when he became the initial significant director to switch to
the new medium of filmed television in 1951, winning the first Directors' Guild
television award.

A contrasting yet complimentary example is provided by Nick Grinde, whose career has been far more neglected. Grinde began as a vaudeville promoter before going to Hollywood; he and Florey first met in the 1920s as assistants to Josef von Sternberg, whom both sought to emulate. Neither man had industry connections to help him along, but Florey, unlike Grinde, was able to overcome this disadvantage with his reputation for fast yet artistic work. Although both worked quickly and cleverly, invariably producing a slick product on time, whatever the budget, Grinde did not bring Florey's intellectual and European bent to filmmaking. As a result, despite occasional box-office hits, such as the Barbara Stanwyck vehicle SHOPWORN (1932), Grinde was never able to graduate to A's, a goal Florey achieved in the 1940s. Grinde did not settle into a long-term contract, moving among MGM, Columbia, Universal, Hal Roach, Mascot, Warners, Republic, and Paramount, to complete some thirty pictures during the 1930s. Grinde was not employed entirely on features, for he also directed short films, documentaries, and animation; his work is so varied that his complete credits are uncertain because of the inadequate documentation of his career. Yet the care Grinde brought to his films has won them a place above most B product and allowed his name to endure. Grinde also had something of an experimental sensibility; during the late 1940s, he wrote an article urging the combination of animation with live action in feature filmmaking. Both Grinde and Florey were noted writers on the industry; Grinde wrote for such magazines as the *Saturday Evening Post* and penned the definitive filmmaker's article on the studio B, "Pictures for Peanuts," quoted below. Like Florey, Grinde eventually went into television, but much earlier, when Grinde's feature career sputtered in the 1940s.

Many other individuals could also be discussed. For instance, along Poverty Row, a typical director was Harry Fraser, one of the few B directors whose autobiography has been published (*I Went That-a-Way*, 1990). Fraser directed a wide range of movies, from Westerns to ethnic films, along with shorts and exploitation films. The trend of such a career in quickies is demonstrated by the fact that he worked when B's were at their most prolific, especially in the mid-1930s, but found jobs hard to come by when commercial conditions were more adverse. Further examples would tend to become repetitive; the basic challenges B filmmakers faced remained the same, and the odyssey of Florey, slowly upward, and Grinde, remaining stagnant, vividly indicate the problems and potential of a range of B filmmakers.

The Style of the B Film

For many years, B's were critically neglected in the belief that they were unworthy: necessarily formulaic, hastily and cheaply made. Yet this notion is at best reductive and an oversimplification. Not only were B pictures significant from an industrial perspective, but they were equally important from an artistic and cultural point of view. B's had many advantages over A's, stemming from the fact that they could target smaller audiences, such as youth or ethnic minorities, instead of the usual wide appeal of family entertainment A's. B's experienced many such contradictory pressures that both liberated and constrained the form, in both production and story. The following analysis of the narrative and visual characteristics of the B approaches the form both generally and in relation to the four-tiered structure outlined above, noting how the differences in production and exhibition result in divergent types of B filmmaking.

Recognizing the B style requires understanding it on its own terms, not in terms of A's. This involves acknowledging the disadvantages and the possibilities, judging the B as the separate commodity it was intended to be, not as a stunted or small-scale A. In his article "Pictures for Peanuts," Nick Grinde summarized it this way:

> "B" standing for Bread and Butter, or Buttons, or Bottom Budget. And standing for nearly anything else anyone wants to throw at it. . . . A "B" picture isn't a big picture that just didn't grow up; it's exactly what it started out to be. It's the twenty-two-dollar suit of the clothing business, it's the hamburger of the butchers' shops, it's a seat in the bleachers. And there's a big market for *all* of them. . . . When you are all through, you have a suit or a picture which goes right out into the market with its big brothers and gives pretty good service at that. The trick is to judge them in their class and not by "A" standards. (*Penguin Film Review*1, [February 1946], p. 41)

In practical terms, the B had little time for the leisure of care and retakes, preparations or planning; consultations between director, art director, cinematographer, and performer were minimal, and opportunities for rewriting scripts were rare. Grinde summarized the director's work this way: "He doesn't have time to do any one thing quite as well as he would like to, because he can't stop and do just that one thing. He is, for the moment, a juggler, and must keep his eye on all the Indian clubs." Many of the screenplays of quickies were penned in a week or less, and then shot in a similar time span, emphasizing quantity, not quality. B's often used plain or sparse decor; the best and most lavish sets, effects, or stock footage were usually left over from an earlier picture. Most B's made no effort to conceal their haste, shooting in uniformly high-key lighting throughout; only occasionally would the more creative B filmmakers partly conceal these drawbacks through the artistry of low-key lighting. For instance, Grinde noted that in contrast with an A film, the chase in a B concludes in a "scene shot in an alley with three cops and some dandy shadows. And if it's done properly, it can be plenty thrilling, even if it is mounted in cut-rate atmosphere."[30]

B's could be of any generic form, with probably as much diversity as was found among the A's. Nearly every genre was capably utilized in the B, whether animal, aviation, children's, college, comedy, detective, crime, domestic, gangster, horror, jungle, love story, medical, melodrama, musical, mystery, newspaper, Northwest, political, rural, satire, social problem, sports, war, Western, woman's, or youth films. Outside of the considerable number of Westerns, male-oriented action films did not dominate B output. B's were expected to offer not only action but also comedy, with a homey, folksy tone, and an important love interest, all considered useful in advancing its position on a double bill.[31] Many B's moved toward this goal by merging conventions of several forms, such as the gangster-woman's film THE GIRL WHO CAME BACK (Chesterfield, 1935). Evidence of this inclination is that in contrast to the B filmmaking of later decades, horror was a comparatively scarce genre among B's in the 1930s. The Universal efforts were A's

Shadowy lighting could disguise the sparse decor of Poverty Row sets, as in this scene from THE MAN CALLED BACK *(Tiffany, 1932), with Doris Kenyon and Conrad Nagel* (at left).

or at least programmers; not until after the successful reissue of DRACULA (1931) and FRANKENSTEIN (1931) in 1937 did the genre really begin to enter the B realm, with the Frankenstein, Dracula, Wolf Man, Mummy, and Invisible Man characters combining into a B series in the 1940s.

However, there was also pressure leading toward formulaic narratives, particularly those accenting mystery and the old West. Low-budget efforts were most often successful as entertainment when emphasizing fights and chases; consequently, the B became associated with the term *action pictures*. B's reflected the strains of pulp fiction—for instance, supplying fast-moving detective mysteries for audiences unsatisfied with the more fully rounded, slower-moving, character-driven A's, such as MGM's Thin Man series. Like the pulps, the B's had plots that were often simple, standardized, and repetitive, almost obsessively so, giving the audience the same situations over and over, deliberately remaining unoriginal. The least prestigious type of B, the quickie, is most remarkable in this respect. Their producers sought to exclude nearly all complexity or variation, since the familiarity of the most undemanding and rigid formulas was both expected and desired. In the words of a *New York Times* article, "Generally the stories told are of a routine character, written in bold fashion and played with directness. No time is wasted on fine writing or delicate direction. Villains are villains and heroes are heroes, and there is no mistaking it after the first 500 feet." Quickies reveal their target spectator as unsophisticated, juvenile or rural, not conditioned to the gloss of studio product, with an almost endless ability to absorb extreme repetition, especially in Westerns. Nor was repetition confined to formula; pictures were overtly remade and plots recycled. Not only were A's recycled into new A's, but some B's were scaled down remakes of earlier A pictures; for instance, Paramount's WOMEN WITHOUT NAMES (Robert Florey, 1940) recycled the women's prison film LADIES OF THE BIG HOUSE (Marion Gering, 1931). Many other B's were looser remakes, either combining portions of two or more plots into one picture or making alterations in background or character.[32]

The principal audience for quickies was the same youthful matinee crowd that responded to serials. And indeed, the narrative traits of B films echoed not only the pulps but also movie serials, emphasizing thrills, pace, and low budgets over mood, coherence, and characterization. B's and serials have similar action-oriented heroes, displaying fisticuffs, athleticism, and cheery youthfulness. B's move rapidly, often at the expense of probability, loading the narrative with action-filled incidents and twists of plot and character. They typically pack an enormous amount of raw story material into their five-to-seven-reel length, often exceeding the quantity of events found in an A film of nine reels or more, despite the typical additional thirty minutes of running time. The difference is a matter of making the narrative compact in the B through compression more than ellipses. By contrast, the A pauses for the contemplative subtleties of nuance, atmosphere, and motivation, to make the tale more credible. Hence, a key difference is in pace and density, giving a furious quality to the B that A's, even when action-oriented, seldom strive for.

Exemplifying this characteristic were upward of two hundred Westerns made annually, most of them B's. The B Western was often perceived as such a separate commodity, with personnel unique to it on both sides of the camera, that the trades discussed Westerns separately from any other type. The genre was both the most profitable low-budget form and the cheapest to make. Most of these movies dealt with the same well-known stories over and over: the struggles of cattlemen against rustlers, nesters, or other greedy, would-be tycoons, with the cowboy usually saving a besieged ranch headed by a kindly widower whose demure daughter quickly falls in love with the hero. Variation was usually limited to a crooked foreman; a case of mistaken identity, such as the hero proving to be an undercover Texas Ranger; or the hero avenging the murder of his parents.

Yet notable exceptions to the tendencies of low-budget narratives are found, even among B Westerns. These include the films of Buck Jones, the premier figure in the genre during the 1930s, who used his popularity to vary the Western formula in ways that presage the changes of the late 1940s. Whereas Tim McCoy, Charles Starrett, and the other Western stars at Columbia had to be satisfied with brief shooting schedules, Jones strove for greater autonomy, introducing new themes into his films. He usually spent three weeks or more shooting his own films, a schedule equivalent for the studio's A's, and finally set up his own production unit, Coronet Pictures. HOLLYWOOD ROUND-UP (1937) is rare in the genre for its reflexivity, telling of Jones's own rise from stuntman to take the place of another Western star, with a cast whose careers were now in decline, including Helen Twelvetrees, Grant Withers, and Jones himself. The anticlerical UNKNOWN VALLEY (1933), similar to Sir Arthur Conan Doyle's novel *A Study in Scarlet*, tells of a religious cult in the West modeled on the early days of the Mormon church. CALIFORNIA FRONTIER (1938) explicitly details, through the photography and a social-consciousness manner, the cruelty shown the Mexicans as California joined the Union. Other Jones films also embody a revisionist view of the Old West. In WHITE EAGLE (1932) he plays an Indian who is in love with a white woman and encounters persistent racism; Jones treated the theme again in a serial remake.

In fact, despite the genre's narrow range of narratives, the B Western formula contained a wide opening for a key social theme of the 1930s, the loss of farms to foreclosure during economic hard times. Conventions were employed to comment explicitly on the situation in a direct way that remained embedded in generic expectations and could not have been overlooked by contemporary audiences. Foreclosures were portrayed in a straight good-versus-evil format, with greedy bankers against the cowboys, as in the 1932 and 1933 Columbia pictures TWO-FISTED LAW and THE FIGHTING CODE; both proposed methods of dealing with this Depression dilemma that attacked the economic status quo. A vehicle for Tim McCoy, BULLDOG COURAGE (Puritan, 1935), shifted the idea to the repossession of a mine, but bluntly sanctioned the hero taking the law into his own hands. In the socially conscious WYOMING OUTLAW (Republic, 1939), the Three Mesquiteers bring an end to political corruption and a crooked relief administrator. This is done on behalf of victimized dust-bowl farmers, who, the picture notes, were encouraged to invest in large harvests during World War I and then lost their land and money when demand quickly fell.

Some, particularly sociological critics, have tended to regard B's as the arena of affirmation, conservatism, and optimism, but the many exceptions invalidate this generalization.[33] For instance, many roles in B woman's films, such as the lawyer in DISBARRED (Paramount, 1938) and the secretary in $20 A WEEK (Ajax, 1935), a melodrama of women in the workplace, portray considerably more freedom of choice than those in their A counterparts. Topical themes had a potential box-office value in B's as well as A's. Columbia was typical; prior to the 1936 release of Warners' famous BLACK LEGION, the studio distributed the programmer LEGION OF TERROR, a similar exposé of the Ku Klux Klan, and SMASHING THE SPY RING warned of German espionage nearly a year before Warners' CONFESSIONS OF A NAZI SPY (1939). Indeed, while A's concentrate on the lives of the wealthy, lower-budget films provide a contrast. With their less ornate costumes and sets, and secondary stars, B's center more on day-to-day living, and their themes arguably constitute a better cultural and political reflection of the time. Monogram's MAKE A MILLION (1935), directed by Lewis D. Collins from a script by Emmett Anthony and Charles Logue, offers a curious commentary on the distribution of economic resources in the Depression. MAKE A MILLION tells of a wealthy student (Pauline Brooks) who has her professor (Charles Starrett) fired for his radical theories on how to revitalize the nation's trade through increased spending. However, the professor puts his ideas into practice by public subscription, creating a World Improvement League, and winning the heart of the remorseful heiress. MAKE A MILLION demonstrates that a small studio like Monogram was able to presage the populist direction of Frank Capra, offering a far more intense and complex discussion of current events than most big pictures attempted by the majors.

The 1930s B could be an unrealized progressive force, as exemplified in the

CHARLIE CHAN AT THE RACE TRACK *(1936). "Yellow peril" stereotypes were overturned in 20th Century-Fox's Charlie Chan series, which presented Warner Oland as a wise, humane, and familial detective.*

Charlie Chan series. While the films are justifiably criticized for not casting a Chinese lead, the role had been twice entrusted to Japanese actors, Kamiyama Sojin and George Kuwa, in several films made before Earl Derr Biggers's literary character achieved motion-picture popularity. Not until Warner Oland was given the role in CHARLIE CHAN CARRIES ON in 1931 did the part win acceptance in popular movie culture. The Swedish Oland had played both white and Oriental characters in the past and became increasingly absorbed in Chinese lore as the Chan role assumed a steadily larger share of his time. Indeed, just before playing Chan, Oland had been cast in a brief series of A pictures based on the menace of Sax Rohmer's paradigm of the "yellow peril," Fu Manchu. The transition from Rohmer's villain to Biggers's hero was no minor event: it indicated a fundamental reversal in Hollywood's treatment of Oriental characters, and the Mr. Moto and the Mr. Wong series later in the decade gave ample evidence of the extent of the change. Indeed, the film version of Mr. Moto so valorized John P. Marquand's decidedly ambivalent literary character, a Japanese secret agent, that the series had to be dropped with the dawning of World War II.

    The Chan series, lasting eighteen years and forty-four films, offered its hero as a wise and paternal humanistic figure. Despite popular misconceptions, Chan never spoke "Pidgin English"; his language was invariably elegant, that of a cultured immigrant. His "number-one," "-two" and "-three" sons (always enacted by Orientals, most notably Keye Luke and Victor Sen Yung) were depicted as assimilating into American culture and were used as foils to note the resulting generational and ethnic changes, through gentle comedy echoing the pattern of Dr. Watson and Sherlock Holmes. The Chan films, in a manner unique for the time, offered a warm portrayal of a family emerging from a very different culture. Chan was etched as a loving father and patient parent of a dozen children, and his concern for them, together with his intelligent detection and Oriental wisdom, embodied in the form of proverbs, offered a unique character and a major positive development in Hollywood's treatment of minorities.

The Chan series actually began as A's, straight adaptations of the Biggers novels. Not until five of the six books had been filmed did the studio decide to send Chan around the world in search of new story material, and the movies then acquired certain series accoutrements. The Chans became so successful as programmers that although made by the B unit, they were sold to exhibitors on a percentage basis rather than for the flat fee charged for typical B's. Indeed, the films with Oland have the indulgence and pacing typical of A's. Not until after the star's death in 1938, when the detective's role was taken over by Sidney Toler (and eventually Roland Winters), did the series acquire the B look, with much faster pacing and typically B mystery plots—which made for more exciting, if less unusual, films.[34]

As demonstrated by the Buck Jones Westerns, the Chan series, and many other B films, the lower-budget realm often went beyond juvenile concerns to present serious themes, maturely handled. B's are certainly formulaic, but outside of the quickies, no more so than A's of the time. Indeed, many B's contain surprising deviations from archetypal plots, concentrating on unconventional themes and offbeat or bizarre elements that almost certainly would have been shunned in the big-budget arena. Studio moguls and the Hays Office were primarily concerned with the A's, since they had major stars and big budgets at stake. With distribution virtually guaranteed on a flat-fee basis, the studios defined a B as successful, not by the standard A criteria of content, critical response, and box-office grosses, but simply by whether the film was finished on time and within the budget.[35]

Within the limits of the B form, resourceful filmmakers, especially directors and cinematographers, were sometimes allowed to be more creative than in A's. Even preset scripts and crews could not dictate such important elements as camerawork, lighting, performance, tone, and use of decor. Robert Florey recalled that "as long as I remained on schedule, I could shoot all the angles and set-ups I wanted, and move the camera whenever and wherever I wanted to, in the limited time I had." The exigencies of production frequently required inventive, on-the-spot solutions to problems of editing, performance, design, and camerawork, resulting in stylistic devices that competed and contrasted with the tenets of A Hollywood films. Nick Grinde noted, "The B director has to know more tricks than Harry Houdini did, and he has to pull them out of his hat right now—not after lunch. He has to know a lot about making pictures and be able to toss that knowledge at a situation and hope that some of it will stick."[36] While the financial limitations of quickies could vitiate much of the freedom, the B's, especially at the majors, could become an artistic endeavor, while avoiding the budgetary excesses that doomed the A endeavors of a Josef von Sternberg or Orson Welles. Despite the regimentation of censorship and studio domination, the prolific quantity of the B as a secondary form of filmmaking allowed a broad array of diverse approaches to moviemaking and spectatorial positions. (These tendencies are illustrated by several examples of different types of B's discussed below.) In earlier and later decades, this position was reflected in types of filmmaking that moved steadily further from the mainstream.

The differences are most striking in the quickies, such as those of Richard Talmadge and Bob Steele noted below. Such films offer an aesthetic problem in the paradigms of classical Hollywood cinema. They present an audacious nonconformity to accepted standards, unquestionably incompatible in many ways. While the quickies may not have been deliberately subversive of the modes of production and presentation offered by the majors, minuscule budgets often allowed, and required, filmmakers to develop a different style. The chutzpah that emboldened them to attempt filmmaking under adverse conditions resulted in circumstances of production that required them to vary and at times violate classical technique and generic formulas. Quickies often evade concepts of believability taken for granted in A films, with a cavalier attitude toward standards of seamless realism, constructing stories around obvious stock footage or effects that were unconvincing even in their own time. In "Pictures for Peanuts," Nick Grinde offered an anecdote:

> One director, who shall be nameless, but whom we'll call Nick, was given a $16.50 bit man [speaking parts cost more] who had so much to pantomime that he and everyone else ran out of ideas for suitable gestures. Nods, points, shrugs, smiles and scowls were all tossed to the camera, but there was still more plot and still the order to keep him frugally inaudible. So, like always, something had to be done. He was finally played as a character with laryngitis, and wrote his answers on slips of paper, which were then photographed and cut into the film. The part came out as a nice thrifty novelty. (*Penguin Film Review*, p. 50)

B's also offer different standards in their musical tracks, providing a clear contrast with the classical conventions of self-effacing construction, by using library music that was frequently jarring, intrusive, and inappropriately matched to a scene or unrelated to the rest of the score. While such a style fails to fully sunder the dominant modes of filmmaking, the technique is on a level that only lives up to the standards of its own class.

An example of nearly experimental characteristics in a major-studio B programmer is THE FLORENTINE DAGGER, a pre-*noir* thriller from Warner Bros. in 1935. The complex story goes beyond suspense to operate on multiple levels, with mystery verging on horror through the theme of the influence of the dead upon the living. Cesare (Donald Woods), a descendant of the Borgias, becomes so absorbed in the legends of his ancestors that he believes he has inherited their criminal tendencies through a dual personality. Preventing him from committing suicide, a psychiatrist (C. Aubrey Smith) suggests a prescription for his obsession —writing a play on the Borgias. Cesare discovers he is not alone in psychological turmoil, for each of the principal characters is controlled by ungovernable passions, behaving in a consistently strange and unnatural way. Cesare's prospective father-in-law, Victor, is slain in a maelstrom of revenge and viciousness.

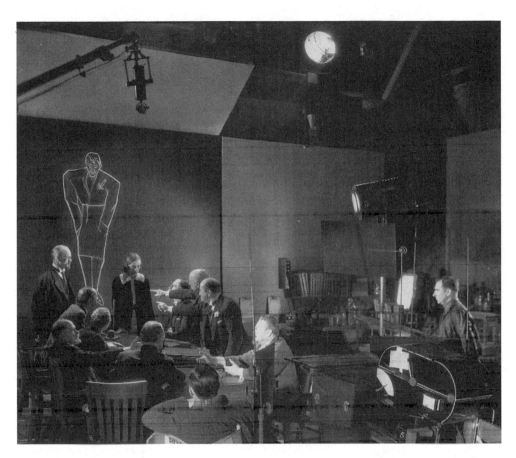

One of the expressionistic scenes cut from THE FLORENTINE DAGGER *(Warners, 1935). Margaret Lindsay at center.*

Victor had tried to kill his wife twenty years earlier by setting her dress afire, but she survived to conceal her scarred visage behind a lifelike mask. She worked as a servant to secretly protect her daughter by a previous marriage (Margaret Lindsay), upon whom Victor, as stepfather, is forcing his attentions. When the police realize why the mother murdered Victor, she and her daughter along with Cesare are allowed to escape. The morbid themes of incest, patricide, and suicide, not to mention the antipatriarchal tone and the lack of retribution for murder, are startling for a film made in the era of the Production Code and probably could only have appeared in a B.

The style is every bit as unusual as the content, with the psychological motifs enhanced by virtuoso expressionist treatment. The film is full of dark and shadowy lighting; bizarre, oblique camerawork and overhead shots; and frequent use of composition in depth, often emphasizing the distortion and imbalance created by the positioning of foreground and background objects. The direction of THE FLORENTINE DAGGER provides a forceful example of the adaptation and integration of expressionist and avant-garde styles into the American feature through the B. Yet the film was shot on a $135,000 budget in twenty days, and director Florey had barely a week to prepare. Tom Reed's script was still in revision during shooting, changing the original ending, which had called for the mother's suicide. In an outcome rare for a B, Florey was able to supervise the editing; Warners' indulgence of the style indicates their hope that THE FLOREN-TINE DAGGER could perhaps achieve A status through the richness of its presentation, and it won serious critical attention, along with some criticism of its unusual themes.[37]

While the content of a picture like THE FLORENTINE DAGGER was exceptional, a similar but more subdued style could still dominate a mainstream B mystery. Whereas expressionism explicated an unorthodox psychological thriller in THE FLORENTINE DAGGER, in A STUDY IN SCARLET (1933) the style is used to develop the eerie atmosphere of a classical English whodunit, with its distinctive bevy of suspects and highly intelligent detective. The sense of locale is enhanced by the use of a nearly all-British cast, something uncommon for a Hollywood-made Sherlock Holmes picture. With the film shot in the continental style, suspense is as much a factor of camerawork, lighting, and atmosphere as plot. Strange gatherings arranged by secret codes take place in out-of-the-way abandoned buildings; dark and oppressive dead-end streets are places of isolation and terror; fog and shadows hide murderers and their victims. A pervasive feeling of fear is created in the fogbound studio streets of the Limehouse section of London, heightening suspense through a number of cinematic devices unusual for 1933. For instance, the killer is kept unseen, while menace is suggested by having the crimes viewed through the murderer's eyes by use of a subjective camera. The silhouette of a giant shadow appears on a wall as the victim looks into the camera and screams, "It can't be you," followed by a close-up of a hand checking off the name of one more member of the Scarlet Ring who has been killed. The climax of this technique comes in a single take with the still-unknown murderer visiting the crooked lawyer (Alan Dinehart): the camera completely adopts the viewpoint of the killer as Dinehart opens the door and the unknown individual is offered a cigarette, puffs of smoke ascending in front of the lens.

These techniques again demonstrate the artistic potential of even the more traditional B. A STUDY IN SCARLET was an ambitious effort during the last days of the Tiffany studio. For only a small sum, producer Samuel Bischoff purchased the motion-picture rights to the title, but not the story, of Sir Arthur Conan Doyle's novel. He had also arranged to co-star the exotic Anna May Wong with Reginald Owen as Holmes. Owen and Robert Florey were given $1,000 and a week to compose a new Sherlock Holmes scenario to fit the title and utilize as many standing sets as possible. Edwin L. Marin finally directed (after Florey was enticed away by Warners), and like Florey, he shortly became a B director at the majors.

The schedules and budgets that allowed for the kind of stylistic and thematic innovation found in a major-studio B like THE FLORENTINE DAGGER, or even one from a secondary studio, like A STUDY IN SCARLET, seemed lavish by comparison with those found in quickies. However, while scarcer, such characteristics were still in evidence. Among the most unique examples are the Richard Talmadge "stunt films," especially the mid-1930s Reliable series, released through Ajax, with Bernard B. Ray, Harry S. Webb, and William Berke alternating or sharing producer and director duties, with such writers as Ralph Cusuman, Carl

Richard Talmadge (right) *performing a rooftop stunt in* Now or Never *(Reliable, 1935).*

Krusada, and Jack Natteford. The minimal production values facilitate the unmediated exhibition of the athleticism of the star, who was once Douglas Fairbanks's double and had a long career with second-unit action sequences. The aim in the Talmadge vehicles is to self-consciously draw attention to Talmadge's physical skill, often through unmotivated scenes, such as a series of Chinatown brawls in FIGHTING PILOT. Instead of the traditional means of involving the spectator in a story, the lack of artifice is emphasized, especially the thrill of Talmadge obviously performing his own acrobatics. Extended takes and long shots concentrate on exhibiting Talmadge's ability, avoiding the usual stunt effects of quick cutting and limited visibility. Simultaneously, Talmadge sophisticates the narratives by deliberately varying the genres and satirizing the action forms he used, but still offers the traditional highlights. For instance, FIGHTING PILOT spoofs the aviation film; THE LIVE WIRE, the adventure genre (including Talmadge's 1934 serial, PIRATE TREASURE); THE SPEED DEMON/HUNTING TROUBLE, the police film; THE SPEED REPORTER/DEADLINE, the newspaper film; and

NEVER TOO LATE/HIT AND RUN and NOW OR NEVER/TEARING INTO TROUBLE, the thriller. In a similar way, an Ajax vehicle for David Sharpe, ADVENTUROUS KNIGHTS, was a satirical reworking of THE PRISONER OF ZENDA.

Not all these deviations from the Hollywood norms were so fortuitous; the extent of the possible departures are revealed by BIG CALIBRE (1935), a William Steiner B Western shot in a single week. Typical of Robert North Bradbury's direction of his son, Bob Steele, BIG CALIBRE is minimalist to a startling degree, with astonishing lapses in continuity editing and no attempt whatever at seamlessness in technique or narrative. The film is preposterous, both visually and in plot line; in his own screenplay, Perry Murdock plays the misshapen chemist Otto Zenz, who uses acid smoke-bomb capsules to commit crimes and flees after murdering the father of the hero (Steele). In a nearby town, the bucktoothed Gadski menaces a rancher with foreclosure; Gadski, naturally, is Zenz, with the patently obvious disguise of a wig and false teeth. His smoke bombs help the hero escape jail, an idea conveyed not through a visual effect but simply through a cut between smoke and a broken lock. Zenz steals a motor stage in a chase, but accidentally poisons himself while trying to use his smoke bombs on the hero. Nearly every incident in BIG CALIBRE is equally bizarre, so patently unbelievable as to verge on surrealism.

Ethnic Films

Another aspect of B filmmaking revealing enormous differences from classical A's are ethnic pictures. Movies of special appeal to the small but definite market of ethnic minorities were an important offshoot of the fourth category, the quickie films of Poverty Row. The B label must not be regarded as a diminishment of these movies; instead, it simply recognizes the industrial conditions under which they were made and shown, and further indicates the rich possibilities inherent in the B form. Like other Poverty Row quickies, the intended audience is a defining factor, with the states'-rights distribution system used to target viewers. Ethnic films were aimed at the specific race, religion, or nationality they portrayed, just as many mainstream quickies were directed at juvenile and rural theatergoers. Many ethnic films were distinguished by language, being made for audiences whose primary tongue was not English; in a sense, they were the aesthetic successors to the multi-linguals made by the major studios at the beginning of the sound era for overseas audiences.

Ethnic movies shared the constraints of Poverty Row, with companies usually short-lived and underfinanced. Filmmakers had minimal access to facilities and equipment, frequently utilizing outmoded East Coast studios or private homes. There was little opportunity for care, rehearsals, or retakes on schedules lasting two weeks at most, with the completed films averaging six reels in length. Ethnic filmmakers were constantly confronted by a fundamental choice that went to the heart of their purpose and appeal. They could hire a Hollywood B director, who usually had little understanding of the subject matter, or make the movie with their own talent, despite an often poor grasp of film language and technique. When Hollywood talent was used, the personnel were usually already experienced in the unique challenges of quickies; a number of black, Yiddish, and

Cantonese movies had such directors as Harry Fraser, B. B. Ray, William Nolte, and Edgar G. Ulmer.

Since ethnic filmmaking did not share in the rising demand for double-bill material, the form took significantly longer to recover from the budgetary problems posed by the coming of sound, and not until the mid-to-late 1930s did the production of these movies flourish. Exhibition possibilities were always limited to segregated theaters, minority areas, or special occasions and off-hours. Unlike mainstream quickies, with their use of repetitious, formulaic genre stories, such as Westerns, ethnic films typically emphasized the group's traditional stories. Frequently the performers were not experienced movie players but non-professionals or stage actors identified with ethnic theater; the novelty of their film appearance served as a principal box-office draw. For instance, some of the early Yiddish films featured the best-known choirs and cantors of the day, before moving toward adaptations of venerable Yiddish plays. While this tended to limit their audience, it also captured its attention, often through notices in local and ethnic community newspapers. Ethnic films supported and perpetuated their respective heritage of customs and cultural identities, offering audiences one of the few opportunities to feel a wholly satisfying cinematic experience in unique rapport with their own people.[38]

There were, for instance, not only imported films for Hispanic audiences but also films originating in Hollywood, with Hispanics and Anglos collaborating for theaters catering to Spanish-speaking patrons. For example, in 1935 three Spanish-language films were produced in the United States, UN HOMBRE PELIGROSO/A DANGEROUS MAN, NO MATARAS/THOU SHALT NOT KILL, and CONTRA LA CORRIENTE/AGAINST THE CURRENT, the latter produced, written and directed by 1920s Hollywood star Ramon Novarro. Also during 1935, three American films were made in Yiddish, BAR MITZVAH, SONG OF SONGS, and YIDDISH KING LEAR; the decade's total was twenty-six features and twenty shorts. Yiddish production was also augmented by a substantial number of imports from Poland. Whether domestic or imported, the Yiddish cinema portrayed the preservation of Jewish traditions despite adversity and the surrounding gentile majority. The setting was most often Eastern Europe, where the rise of fascism was a contemporary threat.[39] Similarly, but almost forgotten today, were several films produced in Ukrainian, and another, ARSHIN MAL ALAN/THE PEDDLER LOVER (1937), in Armenian. There was at least one film in Cantonese, SUM HUN (1936), produced in Hollywood by a mix of Chinese and Anglo talent, for principal release in San Francisco's Chinatown district.

Another type of ethnic film, the most persistent, prolific, and best remembered, was set largely in the United States and differentiated by race. Black films, like other ethnic forms, can be defined through the principal audience.[40] This methodology isolates movies with a predominantly black cast and includes not only black-directed films but others with a mix of races behind the camera as cinematographers, directors, writers, or producers, with actual financing almost invariably white. Using this taxonomy, some three hundred features and an equivalent or greater number of shorts described as black films were made in the years 1910–1955, roughly the era of classical Hollywood. They were made during three principal cycles: one during the silent period (1916–1928), a second, which began in the late 1930s and paused for World War II, and a third cycle that

SUM HUN *(1936), the only Cantonese-language film produced in Hollywood during the 1930s.*

emerged with renewed vigor at war's end but quickly waned as the 1950s dawned. This pattern was reflected in the peak years for corporate formation and film production: 1918–1922, 1938–1940, and 1946–1947.

Black films grew largely out of an effort to find an independent cinematic voice, one that could rival Hollywood and respond to the prevailing stereotypes. Black filmmaking actually began back in 1910, with shorts made by William Foster in Chicago. Targeting the black middle class and avoiding stereotypes, Foster's success encouraged a number of other companies. However, exhibition remained sufficiently limited to constrain profits and investments, and the coming of sound harshly exposed the budgetary drawbacks.[41] Sound ended the first cycle of black filmmaking: while seven black features were released in 1928, in 1929 and 1930 there were only three each year, with two in 1931. Black feature filmmaking resumed slowly in the 1930s, and many of these productions, such as those by Harlem-based Paragon Pictures, remained silent or only part talking. The two independent 1933 features by Eloise and Robert Gist, HELLBOUND TRAIN and VERDICT: NOT GUILTY/NOT GUILTY IN THE EYES OF GOD, were shot silent on 16-mm film and had an amazingly fluid camera style. Replete with stunning metaphors and moral parallels, they received wide exhibition in black churches, enhanced by a live commentary.

Shooting on black features usually lasted a week, and budgets averaged

$10,000–$15,000 (some were made for as little as $3,500), but could be as high as $28,000, as with the Henry Armstrong boxing picture KEEP PUNCHING (1939). Profit for black films generally averaged $15,000, occasionally rising to $60,000, usually on the basis of rentals, which varied from $1,000 in a Harlem theater down to flat fees of $7 elsewhere.[42] The star system in black films reflected the form's emergence from Poverty Row as individuals like Ralph Cooper, Herb Jeffries, and Lorenzo Tucker dominated through their background in stage and recording. Since the teens, established Hollywood stars tended to make few appearances in black films. Although such performers as Louise Beavers, Bill ("Bojangles") Robinson, and Clarence Muse did play in black films, each appeared in only one or two movies, in contrast to the dozens of major-studio pictures in which they were credited. Salaries in Hollywood, even for the traditional black supporting roles, were far greater than could be achieved by starring positions in even the most lavish black movies. The importance of stars like Muse was strictly in proportion to black productions; for instance, Muse's 1940 feature BROKEN STRINGS was shot in four days. The star, Nina Mae McKinney, only became active in black films after her own Hollywood career had taken a downturn. Only one star, Mantan Moreland, actually emerged from black films to become a Hollywood contract player. By contrast, Josephine Baker was confined to appearing in French films, while the preeminent black actor Paul Robeson was in virtual exile after THE EMPEROR JONES (UA, 1933), pursuing his career in England with a number of films that presage Hollywood's use of Sidney Poitier in the 1950s. Other than THE EMPEROR JONES, only one other black feature was distributed by a major Hollywood company, Warners' 1936 adaptation of the stage hit THE GREEN PASTURES, a spiritual fantasy.

The most prolific and tireless voice in black filmmaking during the preceeding decade had been Oscar Micheaux. However, by the 1930s, his reputation was diminishing, since he was no longer a pioneer. Many of his early talkies were composed largely as silents, relying on long explanatory intertitles, such as A DAUGHTER OF THE CONGO (1930) and TEN MINUTES TO LIVE (1932). Micheaux's pictures were usually made in around ten days for between $10,000 and $20,000 dollars, with local actors, and shot in the New York area, often relying on the homes of friends for sets. Micheaux believed that profits were inevitably limited and hence saw no reason to increase his investment or quality.[43] His productions had increasing trouble finding exhibition as the black press decried the content of his films as well as his often primitive technique. Micheaux's sporadic output of one or two productions annually became clearly weak alongside those of other, similar companies; his fifteen movies in the decade were only a portion of black filmmaking during a period that saw approximately seventy-five black features.

The resurgence in black filmmaking in fact coincided with Micheaux's decline. While Micheaux Pictures Corporation of New York had been the pivotal concern of the 1920s, the better representative of the 1930s and beyond was Million Dollar Productions. Million Dollar, more than any other company, moved black filmmaking away from a marginalized form toward the mainstream, advancing considerably its reputation and ability to attract audiences. Although the Million Dollar name belied the firm's assets and budgets, for the first time blacks had substantial control over production in an integrated filmmaking corporation.[44] Million Dollar was the most financially successful such enterprise to date, and

HARLEM AFTER MIDNIGHT *(1935) with Lorenzo Tucker. Oscar Michaux's films emphasized the centrality of nightclubs in contemporary black life.*

the company sponsored a dozen prestigious productions between 1937 and 1940; at least six of these remained in release during the 1940s through one of its successors, Ted Toddy.

Million Dollar had its origins in 1936, when performer Ralph Cooper was brought to Hollywood by Fox but was immediately dropped when he did not fit the desired stereotype. Instead, Cooper united with another black, George Randol, to produce and star in DARK MANHATTAN (1937), which successfully adapted the Hollywood gangster formula to the ethnic screen. Cooper then broke with Randol and joined Harry and Leo Popkin to form Million Dollar Pictures. Over the next three years he co-produced and starred in such movies as BARGAIN WITH BULLETS/GANGSTERS ON THE LOOSE (1937), GANG WAR/CRIME STREET (1939), THE DUKE IS TOPS/BRONZE VENUS (1938), and AM I GUILTY?/ RACKET DOCTOR (1940). In addition, Cooper wrote GANG SMASHERS/GUN MOLL (1938), REFORM SCHOOL/PRISON BAIT (1938), LIFE GOES ON/HIS HARLEM WIFE (1938), and MR. SMITH GOES WEST (1940). Cooper, a bandleader, emcee, and musical entertainer, became the first black matinee idol of the movies; his skillful persona won him the appropriate sobriquet "the bronze Bogart."[45] Although his film career was brief, he had an enormous impact, and the black film cycle of the late 1930s was a direct result of the popularity of DARK MANHATTAN. Whereas twenty-three black features were made in the seven years 1930–1936, the next four years, 1937–1940, saw over fifty black movies.

The Cooper films in particular, and Million Dollar Productions generally, diverged from earlier black films. Narratives and performances were far more plausible than Micheaux's improbable and excessive melodramatics, yet still dealt with black issues. There was no trace of the homegrown aesthetic associated with Micheaux; Million Dollar films were equivalent in terms of style and quality with the better Hollywood B studios, on a par with the contemporary product of Monogram and Republic. For the first time a series of black films, not just a few isolated examples, sustained a polished, solid production style within the norms of classical production. Well-known stars were offered who could appeal to mixed audiences, such as Cooper, Louise Beavers, and Mantan Moreland. Although produced for only about twice as much as a typical Micheaux film, Million Dollar took advantage of a wide array of Hollywood talent, expertise, and equipment to increase production standards. For instance, DARK MANHATTAN was shot at the Grand National studios, a lot with superior facilities to those offered by Fort Lee and the private homes used in the Micheaux efforts. The consistent problems Micheaux and others had in achieving audible recordings, adequate lighting, smooth editing, and acceptable performances had always impeded their appeal to audiences. Indeed, despite the fact that Micheaux so often fell short, his rare exceptions, such as LEM HAWKINS' CONFESSION/BRAND OF CAIN/MURDER IN HARLEM (1935) and BIRTHRIGHT (1939), indicate that his unrealized hope actually was to achieve such standards.

Cooper's former partner, George Randol, was only slightly less successful, merging with the brothers Bert and Jack Goldberg to form International Road Shows in Hollywood. They produced a number of films that moved in the same direction as the Million Dollar efforts, without such smooth results. The Randol-Goldberg product included BROKEN STRINGS (1940), DOUBLE DEAL (1939), MIDNIGHT SHADOWS (1939), MYSTERY IN SWING (1939), PARADISE IN HARLEM (1940), and SUNDAY SINNERS (1940). The Goldbergs had previously been associated with black-cast stage productions, and films like HARLEM IS HEAVEN/HARLEM RHAPSODY (1932) and THE UNKNOWN SOLDIER SPEAKS/THE UNKNOWN SOLDIER (1934), and they remained active through the 1940s. Another mixed-race company, Hollywood Productions, headed by white director Richard Kahn, turned out THE BRONZE BUCKAROO (1938), HARLEM RIDES THE RANGE (1939), TWO GUN MAN FROM HARLEM (1939), and SON OF INGAGI (1940). Together, Micheaux, Paragon, Hollywood Productions, Million Dollar, and International Road Shows were responsible for more than forty features, well over half the black output during the 1930s. Most of the other companies of the period were responsible for only one or two films, tending to be small and focusing on a specific personality or picture; for example, Eddie Green's Sepia Art produced his own two featurettes.

The parallel cases of Cooper and Randol, and their separate development with the Popkins and Goldbergs, along with the example of Richard Kahn, indicate the direction of black production. Many of the companies, and certainly the most prolific ones, were neither all black nor all white, but integrated. Most often blacks collaborated in producing capacities, as writers and as leading performers, governing their personas, while whites, more experienced in B filmmaking, co-produced and directed. The cooperative black-white efforts succeeded, both as commercial ventures and in changing black images; Micheaux's one-man operation was hardly the only method.

These companies followed the lead of their mainstream counterparts by utilizing genre formulas, especially crime, musical, and comedy films. The crime film, encompassing gangster, underworld, mystery, thriller, and detective films, was one of the most prevalent escapist genres in black movies for the same reason it was popular in Hollywood generally: the formula allowed a suspenseful product, despite financial limitations. For instance, MYSTERY IN SWING (1939) is a typical B whodunit, little different from its white counterparts, and DARK MAN-HATTAN initiated a series of black gangster films by demonstrating the potential popularity of adapting an existing genre to the black milieu. Pictures like STRAIGHT TO HEAVEN (1939) went beyond the rise of a gangster or the solving of a murder to cover the impact of crime on the black community. Several musicals were successful, despite the need for more elaborate staging, including HARLEM IS HEAVEN, THE DUKE IS TOPS, and BROKEN STRINGS, starring Bill Robinson, Lena Horne, and Clarence Muse, respectively. Many other black films offered musical numbers in nightclub sequences only tangentially related to the main plot line, while individual musical acts were often the focus of shorts.

Other genres were also invoked. Horror films were represented by SON OF INGAGI, LOUISIANA/DRUMS O' VOODOO/VOODOO DRUMS/VOODOO DEVIL DRUMS (1933), and THE DEVIL'S DAUGHTER/POCOMANIA (1939), with the last shot in Haiti, a sharp visual contrast with black cinema's usual emphasis on cramped interiors or nightclubs. THE SPIRIT OF YOUTH (1937), KEEP PUNCHING/ WHILE THOUSANDS CHEER/GRIDIRON GRAFT/CROOKED MONEY (1940), and THE NOTORIOUS ELINOR LEE (1940) concentrated on the world of sports, featuring the noted athletes Joe Louis, Henry Armstrong, and Kenny Washington. Echoing Republic's success with Gene Autry, singing star Herb Jeffries was cast in a series of popular black musical Westerns: HARLEM ON THE PRAIRIE/BAD MEN OF HARLEM (1937), THE BRONZE BUCKAROO/THE BOLEY BUCKAROO (1938), HAR-lem Rides the Range (1939), and TWO-GUN MAN FROM HARLEM (1939). Although many of these pictures continued the Hollywood pattern of featuring stereotypical buffoons in comedic supporting roles, since all the characters were black, comics were no longer exclusively connected to race. Indeed, black comedians became a source of pride; for instance, in MR. WASHINGTON GOES TO TOWN (1940), Jack Benny is referred to as the fellow who appears on Eddie "Rochester" Anderson's radio show.[46]

Despite invoking the crime, musical, Western, sports, horror, and comedy genres, the social-conciousness type was the single form most frequently utilized, directly commenting on political issues facing the black community. For example, three films etch very different portraits of contemporary black leadership. THE BLACK KING/HARLEM BIG SHOT (1932) is a highly critical parable of Marcus Garvey and the back-to-Africa movement, with a sharp, satiric tone portraying him as a fraud and an exploiter of race. In THE EMPEROR JONES, an A picture produced for United Artists, an equally problematic portrait emerges of a self-absorbed leader. By contrast, in 1940 a film entitled GEORGE WASHINGTON CARVER presents a role-model type of biography in a near documentary style. THE UNKNOWN SOLDIER SPEAKS was a documentary to foster pride in the black contributions to American military history.

A common theme is how social problems created tensions within the family. In ONE DARK NIGHT/NIGHT CLUB GIRL (1939), Mantan Moreland leaves his family in frustration in order to find the wealth to support them properly and finally returns as the prosperous owner of a nightclub. Two 1938 films for Louise Beavers, LIFE GOES ON and REFORM SCHOOL, portray a widowed mother devoted to keeping her grown sons on the road to middle-class success and away from the temptations of crime. However, only Micheaux tends to portray blacks encountering white prejudice, as in THE EXILE (1931), LEM HAWKINS' CONFESSION, and BIRTHRIGHT. An equally frequent and unique theme in Micheaux's work is the internal divisions within the black community, found in A DAUGHTER OF THE CONGO and GOD'S STEPCHILDREN (1938), among others.

Through the use of generic conventions and an increasing adherence to the conventions of the classical Hollywood style, black movies expanded their potential audience with subject matter and presentation that addressed topics of wide interest. Black films had been clearly a separate form as the 1930s began, and the black press noted that the films fell below the standard that Hollywood norms led audiences to demand. By the end of the decade, the increasing distribution and emergence from the Hollywood states'-rights underground was reflected in scattered reviews in the trade press, which often explicitly mention that some black movies were considered acceptable for racially mixed audiences and white theaters. This prepared the way for the post–World War II cycle, when black independent production would resume with bigger budgets than ever before, concentrating on comparatively lavish musicals, such as BEWARE! (1946) and SEPIA CINDERELLA (1948). These were close enough to the Hollywood vein and gained sufficient commercial success, so that Hollywood realized that black concerns had become a potentially profitable form of screen entertainment, growing beyond a parallel shadow economy that could be ignored. This reaction was amplified by the desegregation of theaters and the increasing concern with integration, rather than the separation of the races, that black-audience films often embodied.

While the commercial results are clear, it is arguable whether this increasing use of genre formula and classical style was advantageous from an aesthetic or political standpoint. However, while reflecting Hollywood conventions, black films remained true to their social inspiration. Indeed, all 1930s black movies, even when ostensibly nonpolitical, have very strong overtones that were appreciated by their audiences. Even the films that did not deal with racial issues or specific contemporary events still have political content; the very fact of production and exhibition made a clear statement for filmmakers and audiences in the 1930s. The idealized blacks-only realm of the segregated cast reflected the general social reality of the time, yet casting blacks in a cinematic world of their own was also a powerful statement of equality. Within the context of entertainment, black films sought to overthrow, and serve as a haven from, Hollywood's demeaning stereotypes, creating a new mythology that contradicted the cinema's standard images.[47] Black pictures presented thoughtful, well-educated, moral, and highly motivated heroes who reflected credit on their race; even the villains behave with dignity and decorum. In etching a celluloid territory free of prejudice or white domination, the films may have also helped to show Hollywood new possibilities for black roles. For example, the Herb Jeffries cycle not only offered musical entertainment, but recognized the role of black cowboys in the settlement of the West. The black-cast film, by its very nature, offered a clear message of equality and esteem for black life, articulating a racial consciousness and establishing an aesthetic tradition that remains in force to this day. Separate but not financially equal, the films were a justifiable source of pride for black audiences and a reminder to Hollywood of possibilities overlooked.

Conclusion

With the end of the 1930s, the B film was rapidly changing. By 1939, small concerns making pictures for $20,000–$30,000 were having an increasingly difficult time selling their product, and though such films continued to be made, they were no longer so prolific.[48] The deliberate structuring of the major's annual product around the A and B polarities was steadily eroding. In the 1940s the content of B's altered under the influence of World War II; war and spy films had been all but nonexistent in the 1930s B. The box-office bonanza from 1942 to 1945 caused movie budgets to go up, and the majors were increasingly unwilling to burden their secondary or offbeat product with the B label. Studios claimed that their lower-budget pictures were made more carefully, on individual merit, and with less predetermination as to their eventual double-bill positioning. With the end of the vertical integration of the industry through the banning of block booking, and the consent decrees, theaters no longer had to accept a studio's lower-end product in order to get its A's. As the weekly national habit of "going to the movies" faded in the late 1940s, the economics of moviemaking changed from a priority on quantity and consumption to an accent on quality and individuation of product. Falling attendance eroded the faith in the B as an antidote; pictures intended simply to fill a program slot were no longer profitable without the guarantee of weekly patronage. Television adopted many B genres, such as crime and Westerns, taking advantage of the expected shorter running times and fast shooting schedules. These factors, together with declining enforcement of the Production Code and the increasingly youthful makeup of the audience, led to an explosion in new genres. Low-budget films appealed to a baby-boom market by turning toward horror/science fiction and exploitation, with formulas and exhibition strategies differing from Hollywood's previous approach.[49] Filmmaking changed enormously, and there is little comparison in either style or content between the 1930s B and the low-budget pictures of the 1950s and beyond; applying the B label to such widely different forms as exploitation, 1950s horror and sci-fi, and 1980s slasher films is a misnomer. Properly speaking, the historical context of the B belongs to the studio era of double bills, when such movies operated in relation to, and as a variation on, the principles of classical filmmaking.

9

The Poetics and Politics of Nonfiction: Documentary Film

Charles Wolfe

The document is a basis, and the document transfigured is the ultimate work of art in the cinema.

—Harry Alan Potamkin, "Movie: New York Notes," *Close-Up* 7, no. 4 (October 1930), p. 250

In today's troubled times, the documentary film has come into its own; it meets an urgent need for a medium of mass education and finds a highly receptive audience eager for the information, instruction, or propaganda it presents. Time, spirit and technique are well matched: the documentary film is on the march.

Lewis Jacobs, "Documentary Film Advances," *Direction* 3, no. 2 (February 1940), p. 14

*I*n the ten years between the above remarks, the term *documentary* for the first time gained wide currency among filmmakers, critics, and cultural commentators in America as films on diverse topics, produced under various circumstances, came to be thought of as kindred works constituting a vital development in the history of the medium. In 1930, Potamkin projected a future cinema born of experimentation with the filmic image as document; by the end of the decade, Jacobs was able to speak confidently of a full-fledged genre, the maturation and social relevance of which seemed amply evident. In the interim, a new generation of American filmmakers acquired professional identities as practicing "documentarists," "documentalists," or "documentarians." In 1938 the New School for Social Research in New York pioneered a course in documentary film, featuring screenings and lectures by leaders in the field. After introducing new British documentaries to American audiences in 1937, the Museum of Modern Art mounted international retrospectives of progressively wider scope in 1938 and 1939, with the last event timed to attract educators and students during the Christmas holidays. Through its circulating film library, the museum then proceeded to distribute programs on the history and art of documentary cinema to colleges, museums, and film-appreciation groups around the country. Government agencies, educational and philanthropic foundations, and blue-ribbon commissions now explored the civic function of work in this vein. Documentary thus emerged in the 1930s not simply as a widely recognized mode of film practice but as a conceptual category through which discussions concerning the history, aesthetics, and social value of cinema advanced.

Yet for all this talk and activity, there was little consensus on the precise boundaries or central characteristics of documentary as a genre. Was documentary fundamentally reportage, propaganda, or art? Did it require the application of specific techniques, or was it more like a general approach, an attitude, a perspective? Were certain subjects more appropriate to documentary treatment than others?[1] Capsule definitions struck a similar note—"the creative treatment of actuality" (John Grierson), "the dramatization of facts" (Richard Griffith), "an emotional presentation of facts" (Joris Ivens)—yet few commentators were prepared to explain what principles of inclusion or exclusion followed from these general descriptions.[2] In the pages of the *New York Times* in 1938, critic Frank S. Nugent compiled a list of common definitions of documentary, concocted a new one of his own (a film "which is—or successfully creates the illusion of being—an authentic representation of fact"), and then acknowledged what a careful reader had likely already concluded: "The trouble with all these definitions is that it is child's play to blast any one of them sky high."[3]

On two related points, however, there was general agreement. First, documentaries were distinguished from more prosaic forms of nonfiction (informational or instructional films, newsreels, travelogues) by greater formal ambition and higher social purpose. Second, measured against the fictional cinema of Hollywood, documentary possessed a privileged relation to contemporary social and political events. In standard accounts of the history of the genre, distinctions of this kind are commonly ascribed to Grierson, founder of the British documentary school, dating back to his critical appropriation of the French term *documentaire* in a review of Robert Flaherty's MOANA in 1926. But Grierson's use of the term on that occasion was unexceptional: the "documentary value" of *Moana*'s depiction of daily life in Polynesia, Grierson proposed, was secondary to a "poetic feeling for natural elements" emerging from Flaherty's "mastery of cinematic technique."[4] Only later, in a series of essays written in the early 1930s, did Grierson recast his notion of documentary (a noun now, not an adjective) to encompass this poetic dimension, proposing an elevated standard for "documentary proper" measured by qualities of observation and organization lacking in lesser works.[5] By this time, however, Grierson was simply one among several critics who— encouraged by the varied experiments of Flaherty, Dziga Vertov, Alberto Cavalcanti, and Walter Ruttmann in the 1920s—were searching for ways to account for, and promote, the particular perceptual effects, aesthetic power, and social impact of emergent documentary forms.

In February 1930, for example, Potamkin, an American critic steeped in the European "art" cinema of the 1920s who was seeking to ground film aesthetics in political terms, advised amateur moviemakers in America that "the film of *montage* and document offered fundamental, manifold, and independent opportunities," including "untried possibilities in the simplest relations of motion in familiar subjects." Two months later, inspired by Ruttmann's BERLIN, SYMPHONY

OF A BIG CITY (1927), Potamkin declared documentary "the wholesome basis for the new cinema."[6] Concurrently, L. Saalchutz, author of a brief treatise on motion pictures in the international film journal *Close Up*, described documentary as "the most exacting branch of constructive cinema" and "the ideal training ground for young producers."[7] Noting that such a cinema had inspired a wide range of contemporary artists, French critic and filmmaker Jean Dréville argued in 1930 that the concept of documentary encompassed the capacity of the medium to dissect the world and enhance the moral quality of objects represented on the screen. Through documentary practices, Dréville proposed, nothing less than "the soul of cinema" was revealed.[8] During the decade to follow, the idea that documentary filmmaking was a poetic activity emerged as a recurring critical theme: the force of cinematic composition, of patterns of light and movement, and of montage rhythms and juxtapositions was widely recognized as central to documentary forms. For American critics and budding documentarists on the Left, the work of Soviet filmmaker Dziga Vertov was especially influential: here was a cinema that promised, through the assemblage of shots filmed without staging, a creative role for a committed participant in the contemporary political scene. Filmmakers thus could approach documentary work as a dynamic, experimental process through which filmed events were granted conceptual structure or expressive force. The title of the 1939 Museum of Modern Art retrospective, The Nonfiction Film: From Uninterpreted Fact to Documentary, drew what for many was a crucial distinction between the simply "descriptive" function of earlier forms of nonfiction and the "interpretive" ambitions of true documentary. Soliciting emotional responses at the scene of a reconstructed social reality, documentary cinema was embraced as a vehicle for poetry, drama, history, and argument.

In the era of the Great Depression, these ideas resonated within broader debates concerning the role of social documentation in the arts and answered a call for new formal strategies responsive to the economic, political, and environmental crises of the decade. Along with proletarian novels, journalistic exposés, popularized casework studies, and experimental stage work that drew on headline news, documentary cinema was valued for its capacity to render dramatic the social trauma of unemployment, labor violence, and the erosion of the American farmland and to offer explanations for these disturbances and disasters. The "camera eye" emerged as a central metaphor in literature and the arts for a compelling accuracy and vividness to which chroniclers of the contemporary social scene or recent past might aspire. Motion pictures, moreover, could supply a causal or metaphoric logic to a collection of discrete photographs—"fractions of reality," Alfred Kazin labeled them—combining images with vocal commentary and music in a potent compound form.[9] Artists from other media were intrigued by the rhythmic, kinetic, tonal, and dramatic possibilities of such a form: composers Virgil Thomson, Aaron Copland, Marc Blitzstein, and Hanns Eisler, writers Ernest Hemingway, John Dos Passos, and John Steinbeck, and poet Archibald MacLeish, among others, lent their talents to documentary projects during this period.

As a distinct mode of film practice, documentary also gained definition by way of contrast with Hollywood. Filmmaking within the studio system was organized to maximize profits through principles of industrial management, such as division of labor and economies of scale. In contrast, documentary projects typically were undertaken by a small group of collaborators who owned their own equipment, worked on shoestring budgets, and performed a range of different tasks. Production was irregular, often inefficient, but also looser, less constrained. The commercial cinema's star system, with its emphasis on celebrity and glamour, also was shunned. In these respects, documentary filmmakers were heirs to efforts by amateur and avant-garde filmmakers in the 1920s to establish an alternative sphere of film activity outside the studio system, an inheritance most strikingly illustrated by the migration of some experimental filmmakers into the documentary fold over the course of the next decade. Photographer Ralph Steiner, for example, made a series of short abstract films (H_2O [1929], SURF AND SEAWEED [1930], MECHANICAL PRINCIPLES [1931]) on an amateur or experimental basis prior to joining the ranks of the Workers Film and Photo League, and he attempted to keep a playful dimension alive in his documentary work throughout the 1930s. In 1921 photographer Paul Strand collaborated with painter-photographer Charles Sheeler on an experimental short, MANHATTA, which anticipated the international cycle of symphonic "city films" to follow and helped pave the way for Strand's transition to social-documentary film projects in the 1930s. Dutch filmmaker Joris Ivens, having earned a reputation in the circles of the European avant-garde for *ciné-poems* such as THE BRIDGE (1928) and RAIN (1929), announced a shift to political documentary film work in 1931. Proposing that "in the present state of the cinema, the documentary is the best way to discover where the cinema's real path of development lies," Ivens stressed the shared struggle of all independent, artisan filmmakers for relief from economic domination by a profit-driven film industry. Upon his arrival in the United States in 1936, Ivens would in turn have a galvanizing impact on political American documentarists.[10]

Autonomy alone, however, could not ensure social impact. Some of the most spirited debates within the documentary community centered on the relationship of creative experimentation to social utility, as filmmakers and critics alike sought to justify aesthetic tastes in terms of social effects, and an unresolved tension between notions of documentary as a medium of artistic expression and an instrument of communication or persuasion informs much critical writing on the genre in the period. This may in part explain the appeal of definitions such as "the creative treatment of actuality" or "the dramatization of fact," which succinctly signaled both a commitment to the creative capacities of a filmmaker and an awareness of the pressing claims of social reality without specifying a relationship between the two or defining a role for the spectator within the process by which the "actual" or "factual" is creatively shaped or transformed.

Meanwhile, the problem of reaching, building, and motivating an audience remained a nagging concern. During the late 1920s "little cinemas," modeled in part after the *ciné-club* movement in Europe, had cultivated an audience for films off the commercial track. Amateur and avant-garde work, and foreign features that had not penetrated the commercial distribution network, on occasion found appreciative audiences in small, independent theaters located in metropolitan centers, notably New York. In the 1930s, documentary films from Europe and America often played in venues of this kind, sometimes attracting the attention of a reviewer in the mainstream press. Yet the social reach of films exhibited in this fashion remained limited. As late as 1937, Archibald MacLeish lamented that even the best documentaries in America were "apt to begin life in a smallish radical or art theater and end it in a lecture hall,'' a pattern of circulation that paled in comparison with the wide reception and potential impact of commercial movies.[11]

In response, some filmmakers and critics argued for a truly oppositional cinema, one that might not only offer a radically different perspective on economic and political events but challenge the infrastructure of Hollywood head on. Others targeted a nontheatrical market that Hollywood had not deemed lucrative enough to corner, in hopes of developing a parallel, secondary structure, with no illusions that such a network would supplant the one to which Hollywood laid claim. In the second half of the decade, moreover, efforts frequently were mounted to negotiate a relationship with the commercial film industry. The most sanguine documentarists thought Hollywood's priorities might be altered by a clear demonstration of the appeal of their work; at the very least, they hoped to tap into the powerful distribution system at Hollywood's command.

At issue across these different strategies was the definition of the public sphere that documentary served. In Great Britain, Grierson considered the mass audience to be documentary's natural constituency; to reach it, he eagerly accepted the power of the state government to counter or limit Hollywood's domination of Britain's theatrical film market. But Grierson's primary lever in this effort, the defense of the principle of a national cinema uncolonized by Hollywood, hardly had the same force in the United States, where the studio system could not easily be cast as an alien presence. If Hollywood was the enemy, it was an enemy within. Perhaps only the class argument of the radical Left had the power to define a distinct constituency, an unassimilated proletariat that a revolutionary cinema might unify across national boundaries in opposition to the "mass" audience for commercial movies. But the notion that a political avant-garde or "shock troop" of elite filmmakers could blaze the path for this new social order was largely spent by mid-decade, and filmmakers on the Left adopted a populist political stance that was less easy to distinguish from Hollywood's claim to a classless mass audience. One could argue, as critics on the Left were wont, that the commercial film industry created the appetite for the fictions it manufactured. One could plausibly speculate that, given a chance, audiences would respond to a radically different cinema that brought them into closer contact with the social forces governing the drift of their daily lives. But to the extent that the "public" was conceived as synonymous with a "mass audience" as constituted by media, commerce with Hollywood was inevitable, if only on the margins of the system it regulated. Hollywood was difficult to ignore, and it was a rare filmmaker, polemicist, or commentator on the general phenomenon of documentary cinema who attempted to do so.

A persuasive account of American documentary cinema in the 1930s thus requires an assessment of the conceptual field that the term *documentary* came to designate in relation to the particular institutions that shaped the development of nonfiction filmmaking as a concrete social activity. Julian Roffman, tutored under the auspices of the Workers Film and Photo League in the early 1930s and director of a variety of independent projects later in the decade, recalls that "groups formed and reformed like molecules," as friendships waxed and waned, disagreements splintered coalitions, and social conditions evolved.[12] As a way of charting this variegated and shifting pattern of activity, the account that follows is divided according to three institutional structures that buttressed the production and distribution of documentaries in the 1930s: labor and Left political organizations, the New Deal programs of the Roosevelt administration, and private foundation or social-welfare group sponsorship. Throughout, emphasis falls on how documentary practices were articulated and negotiated in specific circumstances. A final section then considers the influence of documentary on Hollywood, pursuing connections across spheres of filmmaking that historians have tended to treat as radically divorced, with a view toward locating thirties documentary within a broader history of American cinema during the dominant years of the studio system.[13]

Labor–Left Documentaries

Throughout the 1930s trade unions and cultural groups allied with the political Left provided a loose structure for the production and distribution of films outside the commercial mainstream. That workers' organizations could be used in this fashion was recognized as early as the teens, when newsreels and fictional melodramas encouraging working-class solidarity were sporadically produced by trade unions and socialist activists. By 1920, joint stock ventures for financing and distributing pro-labor films had been established on both coasts: the Labor Film Service in New York and the Federated Film Corporation in Seattle underwrote feature films and newsreels, available in the main to union halls and labor lyceums but on occasion exhibited theatrically as well.[14] Founded in Berlin in 1921 to coordinate relief efforts for a war-ravaged Soviet Russia, the International Workers Aid (IWA)—later renamed the Workers International Relief (WIR)—also distributed films in the United States as a means of generating interest in labor struggles abroad and a sense of international solidarity for socialist causes. On behalf of the IWA/WIR, William F. Kruse toured the United States between 1921 and 1927, screening compilation newsreels of revolutionary events in Germany and Russia for audiences in union and nationality halls, mining camps, schools, and rented movie houses. On an ad hoc basis, the WIR also sponsored film projects in support of textile strikes in Passaic, New Jersey, in 1926 and Gastonia, North Carolina, in 1929. In the decade to follow, harsher economic times and an emerging interest in documentary forms would galvanize efforts to develop full-time professional filmmaking units and a more regular system of production.

Crucial to this process was the formation of the Workers' Film and Photo League (FPL) in New York City at the initiative of the WIR in December 1930.[15] The league quickly became a magnet for aspiring filmmakers, many of them second-generation immigrants who had been politicized by contemporary economic events. At its peak in the early 1930s, about a dozen filmmakers and organizers staffed its core operation and as many as a hundred associate members paid annual dues of $2.50. By 1934, satellite Film and Photo Leagues had sprung up in Philadelphia, Detroit, Chicago, San Francisco, and Los Angeles, as well as smaller cities such as Marquette, Michigan, and Laredo, Texas. Filmmakers owned and shared 35-mm cameras (portable DeVrys or Bell & Howell Eyemos); additional equipment was donated or purchased with money raised from film screenings, photo exhibitions, and periodic fund-raising events. The WIR

BONUS MARCH *(Film and Photo League, 1932). The march to Washington.*

BONUS MARCH *(Film and Photo League, 1932). Gassed out in Washington.*

frequently supplied film stock and developing; by shooting with available light
and without sound, filmmakers kept production costs low. The league founders,
Lester Balog, Sam Brody, Leo Seltzer, and Robert Del Duca, trained less
proficient newcomers in an informal and ongoing production workshop. All
members worked without salary, and unemployed filmmakers often treated
league headquarters as home.

Film projects initially were keyed to strikes and demonstrations in which the
WIR or affiliated mass organizations of the Communist party participated.
Typically, footage was first screened for demonstrators to boost morale and then
sent back to league headquarters to be edited into a WORKERS' NEWSREEL,
sixteen issues of which were released between 1931 and 1934. Major events—
such as two national hunger marches organized by the Unemployed Councils in
the winters of 1932 and 1933, and the Bonus March on Washington by army
veterans in the summer of 1932—occasioned the production of longer proto-
documentaries that provided a rudimentary analysis of the reasons leading up
to these visible acts of social protest. At year's end, footage from these films
was edited into an annual compilation feature, AMERICA TODAY, which served
as an alternative to the "year in review" releases of the commercial newsreel
companies.

Distribution efforts, spearheaded by Thomas Brandon, were ingenious and
varied, yet a recurring source of frustration. From the outset, small art theaters
that showcased Soviet and European features (the Acme in New York, the
Filmarte in Los Angeles) booked FPL newsreels, but the irregularity of league
productions made it difficult for Brandon to negotiate long-term agreements with
independent exhibitors. The fact that all league films lacked a soundtrack also
diminished their appeal in theaters featuring films that now "talked." As a result,
much of Brandon's energy was devoted to expanding the old WIR circuit,
incorporating FPL newsreels into programs of Soviet or German features,
sometimes accompanied by an American comedy short or Soviet cartoon. Within
a hundred-mile radius of New York, Brandon also supplied lecturers and
projectionists from the ranks of the FPL. In industrial cities with substantial
immigrant and working-class populations, large auditoriums were rented, providing a middle tier of exhibition between commercial theaters and union halls,
schools, and rural camp settings. Meeting halls of European nationality groups
were considered especially reliable venues because they housed audiences
sympathetic to labor films and maintained silent 35-mm projection equipment
long after commercial theaters had converted to sound.[16]

The cultural impact of the Film and Photo League extended beyond its only
modest success in distributing and exhibiting films. Members wrote film criticism
for the *New Masses* and the *Daily Worker*, as well as new film journals, such as
Experimental Cinema (1931–1934), *Filmfront* (1934–1935), and *New Theatre and
Film* (1934–1937), the latter two of which had official ties to the league. Prior to
his death in 1933, Harry Alan Potamkin, a central figure in league planning,
drafted a proposal for a film institute where cinema could be studied; in
November 1933 the FPL established the Potamkin Film School in his name. Here
Sam Brody, Leo Hurwitz, David Platt, Lewis Jacobs, and Irving Lerner taught
courses in film history, criticism, and analysis. From the fall of 1933 through the
spring of 1935, the league also sponsored Saturday-night film screenings at the
New School for Social Research, including series devoted to the history of Soviet

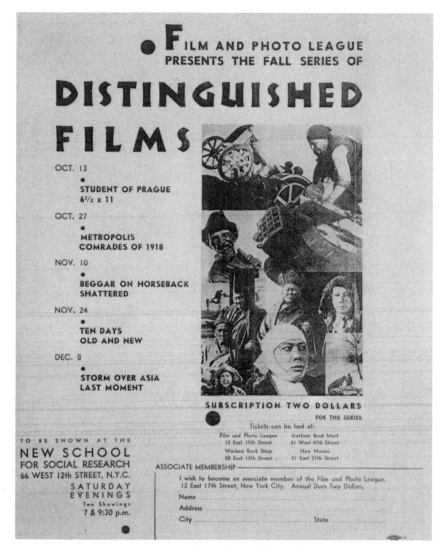

Film and Photo League flyer for "Fall Series of Distinguished Films" (1934).

cinema, recent amateur and experimental shorts from Europe and America, and acclaimed European features. On occasion, Hollywood films were screened as well, although accompanying program notes typically contrasted them unfavorably with foreign and experimental works on both aesthetic and political grounds.[17]

In print and in person, league members also protested the theatrical exhibition of Nazi films in Yorkville, the German section of Manhattan, and called for boycotts of Hollywood films and newsreels thought to espouse a fascist line or stimulate interest in war. Concurrently, censorship of pro-labor or pro-Left sentiments in American films by the Motion Picture Producers and Distributors Association or the Catholic Legion of Decency (the latter, in effect, a rival and more powerful pressure group) was vigorously denounced. Campaigns also were mounted against state and local officials who sought to suppress league films or jail league cameramen or projectionists. Members traveling in remote locales were especially at risk: in 1934, for example, Lester Balog spent six weeks in jail in Tulare, California, for screening footage he had shot of a cotton pickers' strike in the region the year before, accompanied by a celebrated Soviet film on homeless youth, Nikolai Ekk's THE ROAD TO LIFE (1931). In urban areas, however, group protests were promptly organized to call attention to acts of suppression of this kind. Efforts to establish a cohesive, alternative film culture thus proceeded on several fronts, with the WIR providing political expertise and muscle for collective action.[18]

The call for a working-class cinema had a compelling logic: if Hollywood ignored or appeared to distort the social experience of workers, films by and for workers could establish a new sense of community for a disenfranchised class. The Soviet revolution, moreover, could be interpreted as the harbinger of a new international confederation that a revolutionary, workers cinema in America might serve. From this perspective, building an audience for FPL films was fundamentally related to building a mass political organization, an activity at which the Communists, among Left groups, had proven most skillful. In 1934 the formation of the National Film and Photo League, with branches in major cities throughout the country, gave the organization a national reach that only the commercial film industry could match. Yet not all members of the Film and Photo League were, strictly speaking, of the working class, nor did all identify their political allegiances with the Communists. Moreover, in the absence of the domestic political revolution that hardliners predicted, the relationship of the "proletariat" to the "mass audience" for movies was never clearly articulated. As the New Deal gained momentum and the prospects of full-scale revolt on either the Left or the Right diminished, so, too, did the rhetorical power of the proposition that the working class would serve as the vanguard of a new, unstratified culture—of the *new* masses.

By 1934 the precise role of the league and its filmmakers had become a topic of intense internal debate. Members with ties to the WIR and a background in political organizing (Brody, Brandon) contended that the agitational work of the league remained primary: filmmaking was simply one among many activities in which all committed members were engaged, and the value of films—as the procedure of recycling footage in varied formats to different audiences suggested —resided solely in their immediate political function. Other members sought greater autonomy and time to develop their craft; only from a cadre of professional filmmakers, they argued, could a truly revolutionary cinema emerge. Hurwitz, Steiner, and Lerner, in particular, pressed hard for the chance to work closely and experimentally with writers and actors in search of a cinema of greater expressive power than editing unstaged footage allowed.[19] In the fall of 1934, a proposal by Hurwitz that the league set up a full-time, permanent filmmaking section was rejected on the eve of the first National Film and Photo League convention in Chicago. Although they acknowledged a need for special film units at local branches, representatives at the national convention then formally endorsed the league's commitment to newsreel coverage of topical political events.[20]

In the wake of these decisions, Hurwitz, Steiner, and Lerner, together with still photographer Sidney Meyers, left the FPL to form Nykino, an experimental film unit allied with the Workers Laboratory Theatre. Hence, just as the FPL consolidated its national base and mapped new strategies for the efficient exchange of films from coast to coast, the New York branch splintered. It was the first in a series of departures, as members accepted film work outside the league: Brody and Seltzer with the New Deal's Works Progress Administration in New York; Platt as full-time film critic for the *Daily Worker;* Edward Kern and Frank Ward as members of the executive committee of the New Film Alliance, a group with broad ties in the Left arts community and ambitions to coordinate independent film production throughout the country.[21] Returning from a tour of regional circuits in March 1935 with word that FPL production was still lagging, Brandon began to devote his own energies to developing Garrison Films, a small commercial distribution company that previously had handled WIR films in the United States. About the same time, the WIR was abolished by the Seventh Congress of the Communist International and the league's original political ties were severed. The photo section split off from the filmmakers in 1936 and was reconstituted as the New York Photo League, free of previous affiliations, in 1937. The same year, a lingering film contingent composed of Jules Roffman, Robert Del Duca, and Victor Kandel officially dissolved the league's cinema section. By this time, regional branches around the country had withered as well.

Out of Nykino, however, emerged the most stable and productive documentary group aligned with labor-Left organizations in the late 1930s. Hurwitz and Steiner cast wide nets in soliciting talented collaborators, including internationally renowned photographers such as Paul Strand and Henri Cartier-Bresson, and newcomers to the social-documentary scene, such as West Coast photographer Willard Van Dyke and a recent graduate of Columbia University, poet Ben Maddow. They also found natural allies in the Group Theatre, a Left drama troupe with whom Hurwitz and Steiner studied; in turn, they attracted Elia Kazan and Michael Gordon to Nykino's ranks. Devoid of outside funding, the film group scraped together money to complete two experimental shorts by Steiner and presented them with a mix of Soviet features and assorted short subjects at New School screenings in March and May 1935. Later that year, Steiner, Hurwitz, and Strand were hired by the New Deal Resettlement Administration to work on THE PLOW THAT BROKE THE PLAINS; although there was friction with director Pare Lorentz during filming, the Nykino group gained a measure of prestige for their labors. Eager to shift to sound film production, Nykino also embraced the new style of dramatic reenactments introduced in *Time* magazine's celebrated newsreel series, *The March of Time*, and completed two segments of a left-wing version, entitled *The World Today,* under Gordon's direction in September 1936.

The following spring, the group launched a new large-scale, nonprofit production company, Frontier Films. Strand was named president, Hurwitz and Steiner vice-presidents, and an advisory board was culled from the ranks of major cultural figures, including Aaron Copland, Malcolm Cowley, John Dos Passos, Waldo Frank, Lillian Hellman, Archibald MacLeish, and Clifford Odets. The Film and Photo League had been born amid the intensely sectarian politics of the Comintern's Third Period, inaugurated in 1928; anti-Socialist, later anti–New Deal, official policy had followed from the premise that capitalism soon would collapse. Frontier Films, in contrast, caught the crest of a wave of cultural support for the emergent Popular Front, an informal political alliance formed at mid decade by a spectrum of liberal-to-radical Left groups in common cause against fascism, with a new emphasis placed on the continuities between progressive politics and traditional American themes. The change in name by the filmmakers signaled this shift in tack: from Nykino—shorthand for *New York* plus *kino*, the Russian word for "camera"—to Frontier, the title of a recent film by Alexander Dovzhenko that many members admired, yet also evoking the era of American pioneers and a wider territorial expanse than a metropolitan center in which the contrast between Wall Street and immigrant neighborhoods was sharply drawn. That a broader coalition of this kind could grant the work of Left documentary filmmakers greater prominence was confirmed a few months later by the success—impressive by documentary standards—of Joris Ivens's THE SPANISH EARTH, a tribute to the heroism of Loyalist forces in the civil war in Spain. Underwritten by Contemporary Historians, a group formed by Ernest Hemingway, Dorothy Parker, Herman Shumlin, and several literary figures on Frontier's advisory board, THE SPANISH EARTH was screened for President Roosevelt at the White House and at a series of conspicuous fund-raising events in Hollywood in July 1937, enjoyed a lengthy and celebrated run at the Fifty-fifth Street Playhouse in New York, and subsequently was distributed to eight hundred theaters in sixty cities throughout the United States. The critical attention the film attracted could only have bolstered the confidence of Frontier's members as they sought to consolidate support for professional documentary filmmaking on the Left in the United States.[22]

Financially, Frontier relied primarily on loans and donations from wealthy contributors, with executive secretary Lionel Berman overseeing a variety of fund-raising initiatives. Local trade unions also provided modest support, but permanent funding from international unions was never established. All staff members were considered full-time salaried employees, but in practice, paychecks were not distributed during lean periods and the organization relied heavily on unpaid work time. Slow to get its own projects off the ground, Frontier established a high profile in 1937 by editing additional footage shot by Herbert Kline of the Spanish civil war and by Harry Dunham of the Japanese invasion of China, and successfully releasing the films under the Frontier banner as HEART OF SPAIN and CHINA STRIKES BACK. When in 1938 Maddow added English commentary to a third documentary on the Spanish conflict, shot by Cartier-Bresson and Kline, Frontier released the film as RETURN TO LIFE. Frontier also edited and added a sound track to UNITED ACTION, a documentary by the United Auto Workers about their strike at General Motors in 1939. In addition, nonpolitical assignments were accepted: Frontier edited a compilation film, HISTORY OF ROMANCE AND TRANSPORTATION, which was showcased by the Chrysler Motor Corporation at the 1939 New York World's Fair, and an Alaskan travelogue, WHITE FLOOD (1940), culled from footage shot by one of Frontier's benefactors and accompanied by Hanns Eisler's score. Frontier also supervised, from the moment of conception, PEOPLE OF THE CUMBERLAND (1938), an overtly political documentary on the Highlander Folk School in Tennessee, under the direction of Meyers and Leyda, with assistance from Kazan. Throughout this period, moreover, Strand and Hurwitz lavished attention on Frontier's prize project, an exposé of recent civil rights abuses suffered by labor unions, released as NATIVE LAND in 1942.

PEOPLE OF THE CUMBERLAND and the films on Spain and China all received theatrical distribution by Garrison Films, with Frontier receiving 65 percent of all earnings after the cost of prints, press sheets, and promotional material had been deducted. At a flat rate for shorts of $3 per week per theater and distribution restricted to independent theaters, little revenue was raised through commercial release, but the films were reviewed in the mainstream press and literary magazines, thus keeping Frontier in the public eye. A wider audience for the films was located through 16-mm rental and sales to a nontheatrical market—encompassing schools, churches, civic organizations, unions, and colleges—which Brandon now sought to centralize. Local unions were requested to pressure independent theaters to book individual films on a states'-rights basis ("Organize Your Audience—Get Your Share of This Market," read a Garrison flyer for PEOPLE OF THE CUMBERLAND), but there is no evidence that this strategy worked to an appreciable degree.[23] The solvency of Frontier thus depended principally on fund-raising.

The advantages and limitations of Frontier's mode of operation are illustrated by the production history of NATIVE LAND. Originating with the idea of a segment on labor espionage for *The World Today* in the summer of 1937, the project gradually evolved into an eighty-three-minute feature that interwove documentary and enacted passages in a history of labor struggle in the thirties and linked that history to a promise of personal and civil rights vouchsafed by America's Founding Fathers and the sacrifice of pioneers. In a period in which questions of national identity and historical roots were evident throughout much of American popular culture, NATIVE LAND thus staked a claim for labor's authentic inheritance of the Jeffersonian tradition. It was Popular Front historiography writ large, with the FPL's working class constituency reconceived as "we, the people," a democratic, classless force. Time and great care were devoted to the production of the film over the course of four and a half years. Footage shot by Gordon and Van Dyke was abandoned early on, and an entirely new script was drafted by Hurwitz, Strand, and Maddow in 1938. Filming continued at least through the summer of 1939, and a sound track scored by Marc Blitzstein and narrated by Paul Robeson was finally recorded in 1941. When funds ran out, endorsements were solicited and new contributors cultivated, with existing footage screened as an incentive.

Upon its release in 1942, NATIVE LAND was hailed by many critics for its pictorial beauty, intricate structure, and dramatic power, but these achievements had a price. Delays in production rendered the topic of the film less pertinent: amid calls for home-front unity in response to events abroad, NATIVE LAND's critique of labor espionage and repressive violence at home was widely viewed as out of date. Meanwhile, resources had been drained from other productions; the inability of Frontier to generate any new social-documentary projects after 1939 is especially telling. With no films in development and no national distributor for NATIVE LAND forthcoming, Frontier Films closed up shop in 1942.

Documentary filmmaking in support of labor-Left causes in the 1930s was not restricted to the activities of the Film and Photo League, Nykino, and Frontier. Notices of diverse productions in cities around the United States dot the pages of *Film Front* in the early 1930s, and it is likely that scores of other projects were undertaken, if not completed, without benefit of press coverage. This outburst of activity suggests the range of interest in social documentary in an era of economic

NATIVE LAND *(Frontier Films, 1942).*
Newsreel footage: violence against
steel-workers (Ambridge, Pennsylva-
nia, 1933).

NATIVE LAND *(Frontier Films, 1942).*
Reenactment: violence against share-
croppers (Fort Smith, Arkansas,
1936).

NATIVE LAND *(Frontier Films, 1942). Graphic match: the modern laborer as*
Lincoln.

and political crisis. Yet production in outlying regions, diffuse and remote, offered no answer to the fundamental question of how to construct a stable base for political filmmaking at the national level. Among labor-Left groups, Frontier Films constituted the boldest bid to secure a permanent place for social documentary production and distribution in the United States, and with the dissolution of Frontier in 1942, plans for this alternative network faded too. NATIVE LAND convincingly demonstrated that Frontier could match in formal terms—and decisively recast in an American idiom—a politicized art cinema from abroad, but not that existing structures could sustain a domestic cinema of this kind.

New Deal Documentaries

The two most acclaimed American documentaries of the 1930s were THE PLOW THAT BROKE THE PLAINS (1936) and THE RIVER (1937), films made by Pare Lorentz for the federal government with relief funds allocated to the Roosevelt administration by Congress. Enthusiastically endorsed by the president, studied by social scientists as instruments of persuasion, and the topic of wide critical discussion and political debate, these works in large measure bear responsibility for the term *documentary* passing into common parlance in the second half of the decade. They also paved the way for the establishment of a short-lived but active federal film agency, the U.S. Film Service, and introduced into popular culture the imagery of dust, erosion, and flooding that still informs historical accounts of the American heartland during the Depression years.[24]

At the time of Lorentz's arrival in Washington in the summer of 1935, motion-picture units had long been in place at the Department of Agriculture, the Department of the Interior, and the U.S. Army Signal Corps. A score of other federal departments and agencies also contracted with independent producers for instructional or informational films, most of which were used internally or distributed free of charge to schools, churches, professional groups, or community organizations—the nontheatrical circuit that labor-Left filmmakers also targeted. During World War I, moreover, newsreel shorts and features compiled by the government's Committee on Public Information had been distributed to theaters around the country by Pathé, establishing a precedent for quiet cooperation between Washington and commercial exhibitors.[25]

New Deal documentaries, however, aroused passions and sparked controversies that far outstripped public responses to previous ventures in nonfiction filmmaking by the federal government, a reaction attributable in large measure to the high public profile of New Deal programs and the campaigns attending their enactment. From its inception, New Deal filmmaking was bound up with the politics of economic and environmental recovery. Bolstered by Democratic victories in the 1934 election, Congress passed the Emergency Relief Appropriations Act (April 1935), which placed nearly $5 billion at the disposal of Roosevelt's administration. The heads of two agencies funded by the bill, Harry L. Hopkins of the Works Progress Administration (WPA) and Rexford Tugwell of the Resettlement Administration (RA), at once mapped plans to use motion pictures to explain relief activities to American voters. Access to this electorate, both concluded, required entry into the theatrical exhibition sector Hollywood dominated. By design, then, motion pictures were a prominent component of highly controversial programs concentrated in the executive branch of the government and subject to congressional inquiry. Conditions were ripe for media attention and partisan protest.[26]

Hopkins's mandate at the WPA was to move unemployed workers from government relief rosters to salaried jobs, either on government projects or in the private sector. In July 1935 he hired experienced newsreel cameramen to staff the Motion Picture Records Division, fulfilling two goals simultaneously. The relief activities of the WPA were to be documented by skilled workers who would otherwise be unemployed. By placing their footage in commercial newsreel programs, Hopkins also hoped to gain wide publicity for WPA projects. When newsreel editors resisted the informal lobbying of the WPA, Hopkins was forced to adopt a new strategy. In the spring of 1936, the WPA solicited bids from independent producers for a series of 35-mm shorts of "high entertainment standard," each to focus on regional WPA projects, with bidders required to guarantee monthly distribution to commercial theaters. In August a contract was awarded to Pathé News, which promised distribution through its new parent company, RKO, but the agreement immediately came under attack. In a complaint that was front-page news in the *New York Times,* Republican officials contended that relief money now was to be spent on New Deal propaganda keyed to the fall election campaigns. Independent producers protested that they had been prevented from bidding because they lacked distribution contacts, and several newsreel companies announced that they had refused to bid because the distribution requirement placed newsreel space up for sale, a violation of journalistic ethics. Independent theater owners joined the attack, arguing that such a contract could be construed as an attempt by the federal government to book its films in blocks, a contemporary practice of the major Hollywood studios that independent exhibitors strenuously opposed. In response, WPA officials cited the precedent of government newsreel production during World War I and noted the substantial use of newsreels by Republican administrations in earlier years. Given the political climate, however, it was not difficult for opponents to paint WPA "information" films as political propaganda and take particular offense at the fact that relief money was now to be routed into the production of films that taxpayers then had to pay to see.[27] Concerned about the WPA's public image, Hopkins did not push the issue hard; after the Pathé contract had run its course the project was abandoned.[28]

Lorentz, appointed motion-picture consultant at the Resettlement Administration, navigated equally turbulent waters with greater success. A film critic known for an irreverent and polemical style, Lorentz lacked experience either as a practicing filmmaker or a government insider, but he brought to his post a keen interest in movies and politics. In his criticism, Hollywood had often come under attack for its monopolistic control of commercial production and eviscerating censorship, themes Lorentz developed in detail in a book-length study of the film industry with Morris L. Ernst in 1930.[29] Lorentz's early and ardent support of Roosevelt and of New Deal agricultural policies further commended him to Tugwell, a liberal member of FDR's brain trust who now oversaw the government's program to resettle submarginal farmers on productive land and urban slum dwellers in suburban greenbelt communities.

With the aid of Arch Mercey, the RA's deputy information director, Lorentz designed a filmmaking policy that was more focused and provocative than that of the WPA. A tour of the dust bowl as a journalist in 1934 had convinced Lorentz that a powerful film could be made about environmental disasters in that region. In lieu of Tugwell's initial and more conventional proposal for a series of short information films, Lorentz outlined a plan for the production of a single, dramatic documentary on the abuse, erosion, and impoverishment of the Great Plains, a film that could circulate in commercial theaters and focus national attention on the urgent need for government action. With Tugwell's approval and a minimal budget ($6,000 at the outset, although three times that sum before the film was completed), Lorentz promptly charted a new course for government filmmaking. Locations were scouted using dust-bowl photographs taken by members of the RA's photo section. In search of seasoned assistants, Lorentz hired the Nykino trio of Strand, Hurwitz, and Steiner, paying them $25 a day and expenses for a seven-week tour of the dust bowl in the fall of 1935. Along the way Strand and Hurwitz, seizing an opportunity to put their ideas to the test, rewrote Lorentz's loose script to sharpen its political critique, but Lorentz survived the battle of egos, retaining control over the production. When Hollywood studios balked at providing him with stock footage for some historical passages, maverick director King Vidor came to Lorentz's aid. Editing the film in New York, Lorentz collaborated closely with celebrated composer Virgil Thomson, whose score was recorded by first-chair members of the New York Philharmonic under the direction of conductor Alexander Smallens. Poetic commentary written by Lorentz was read by Thomas Chalmers, veteran of the Metropolitan Opera Company and an editor with Pathé News. In sharp contrast to the typical information film released by the government, THE PLOW THAT BROKE THE PLAINS hence clearly bore the stamp of an innovative, artistic production.

In March 1936, Lorentz and his associates began a careful campaign to promote the film. Private screenings garnered support from President Roosevelt, sympathetic Hollywood directors such as Vidor and Lewis Milestone, and members of the New York arts community. On 10 May 1936, THE PLOW THAT BROKE THE PLAINS officially premiered in Washington, D.C., at the close of a program of European documentaries sponsored by the Museum of Modern Art, a prestigious debut for Lorentz as a filmmaker, with wide and enthusiastic coverage by the Washington press. Yet when distributors from the major studios were offered the film free of charge, they turned Lorentz down. Recalling the rebuff he had received when in search of stock footage, Lorentz took his case to his friends in the press, accusing Hollywood of an anti–New Deal bias and a fear of government competition—arguing, in short, that his work had been censored by the industry. Studio representatives denied the charge, claiming that the length of the film—at twenty-eight minutes, too long for a short, too short for a feature—prohibited easy distribution. Yet rumors of political uneasiness in Hollywood abounded, perhaps exacerbated by a circuit court ruling in April that challenged the very constitutionality of the Resettlement Administration and thus rendered Lorentz's project more vulnerable to partisan attack.

Instead of retreating, Lorentz went on the offensive. On 24 May, critic Frank S. Nugent drew on Lorentz's complaint to deliver a broadside against Hollywood and an encomium to the film in the pages of the *New York Times*. Four days later, independent exhibitor Arthur Mayer opened THE PLOW THAT BROKE THE PLAINS at the Rialto theater on Broadway, accompanied by a publicity campaign that promised viewers, "The film they dared us to show!" Bookings at independent theaters in other East Coast cities quickly followed. With favorable reviews in hand, Lorentz toured midwestern cities and towns to drum up support for the film. Principal distribution points were set up in New York, Chicago, Washington, D.C., and Lincoln, Nebraska, and RA information field officers served as distribution agents to regional communities. By the middle of July (just prior to the WPA-Pathé flap), independent theater chains in Ohio, Indiana, Illinois, Wisconsin, Arkansas, and Texas had booked the film. Mercey estimated it eventually played in more than three thousand commercial houses.[30]

Buoyed by this success, Tugwell granted approval for a second project, this one to focus on the erosion and flooding of the Mississippi Valley, a topic much in the news (and newsreels) in 1936. Production strategies on THE RIVER followed that of the first film, with a $50,000 budget allowing Lorentz a slightly less Spartan approach. After scouting locations in person, he hired a four-person camera crew: Nykino's Van Dyke; Stacy and Horace Woodward, an Academy Award–winning team of nature filmmakers; and Floyd Crosby, also the recipient of an Academy Award for his camerawork on F. W. Murnau and Robert Flaherty's TABU (1930), a South Seas idyll that Lorentz greatly admired. Filming took place over the course of a 2,100-mile journey up and down the Mississippi River in the fall of 1936. When a flood struck the valley in January 1937, cameramen from the

THE RIVER *(Lorentz, 1937). Down the Mississippi: deforestation and new cities, "but at what cost?"*

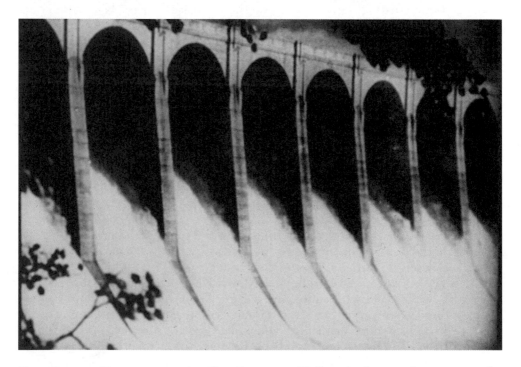

THE RIVER *(Lorentz, 1937). The Tennessee Valley Authority: harnessing the river's power.*

Department of Agriculture and Soil Conservation Service, and Coast Guard boats, airplanes, and facilities, were placed at Lorentz's disposal for additional filming. Reassembling his postproduction team of Thompson, Smallens, and Chalmers, Lorentz took even greater pains to cut the film precisely in rhythm to the score. Successful screenings of THE RIVER in New Orleans, Memphis, Saint Louis, Des Moines, Minneapolis, and Washington, and a three-week run in Chicago, led to a contract with Paramount Pictures for national distribution in the spring of 1938. A national exhibitor's organization, without apparent objection to the film's medium-length format, honored THE RIVER as the best three-reel film of the year. International acclaim followed when THE RIVER won first-place honors at the Venice Film Festival in the summer of 1938. Soon Lorentz's second production became the most requested government film in nontheatrical outlets as well.[31]

How might one account for the extraordinary reception of Lorentz's first two documentaries during this period? Clearly the institutional base from which he worked was a crucial factor. In contrast to labor-Left filmmakers, Lorentz had access to the resources of a federal agency with a regional "distribution" staff answerable to central headquarters in Washington. Furthermore, Lorentz's background as a combative journalist had taught him how to turn attacks to his own advantage, and he successfully marshaled the support of sympathetic reviewers and commentators to his cause. In the long run, moreover, Lorentz's ties to the Roosevelt administration not only attracted the attention of the mainstream press but may have earned him a measure of respect in Hollywood. When it was in their own interest to do so, studio executives warily courted those federal institutions empowered to regulate industry practices and were not inclined to aggravate existing tensions arbitrarily. It is logical to assume that the initial suppression—if it was that—of THE PLOW THAT BROKE THE PLAINS had less to do with organized opposition to New Deal policies per se than personal resentments inspired by Lorentz's earlier attacks, the ingrained reluctance of the studios to yield control over commercial screens, and an accurate perception that leaders in Congress were sharply divided on the merits of the film. Subsequent critical acclaim for THE PLOW THAT BROKE THE PLAINS, however, cast the film in a new light; in the absence of any immediate political liabilities attached to THE RIVER, Paramount then accepted the government's request that the film be distributed in first-run theaters throughout the country. Lorentz's documentaries thus acquired national prominence both despite and because of Hollywood—and inevitably in relation to Hollywood—however barbed his own criticism of studio policies and practices.

The cultural impact of THE PLOW THAT BROKE THE PLAINS and THE RIVER can also be traced to certain formal and thematic characteristics of the films that critics and commentators sought to identify, label, and assess. Were Lorentz's documentaries simply information films or government propaganda? Although lawmakers were attracted to this question, critics discovered other ways of approaching the films. They spoke of Lorentz's style, a unique admixture of powerful imagery and cadenced commentary and music, and noted a disturbing undercurrent that pressured even the New Deal antidotes to environmental and social catastrophe set forth at the close of the films. Rather than cheerful government ballyhoo, THE PLOW THAT BROKE THE PLAINS and THE RIVER were seen as stories of the tragic loss and tentative reclamation of the American heartland, told in a modern form that interwove familiar images and fragments of verse and folk tunes through incremental variations on a few powerful visual, verbal, and musical themes. "Without the benefit of Hollywood," declared reviewer Gilbert Seldes, "Pare Lorentz has created in *The River* one of the splendors of the American film. He has done it in a field more cultivated by the Europeans than ourselves, that is, the documentary film." If this was propaganda, Seldes among others argued, then so be it: dramatic effect could serve two masters or align them. "It fuses propaganda with art," claimed V. F. Calverton, "makes the river a thing of wonder, and conjures out of water and earth a magical symphony of design and motion."[32] Lorentz's documentaries thus called attention to a cinematic dimension inherent in a new body of cultural imagery central to the arts and literature of the 1930s. As a fit was found for Lorentz's work within critical discourses on the arts, a cultural space opened up that had been unavailable to previous government films.

Following the success of THE RIVER, Lorentz moved boldly again, winning approval from Roosevelt for the formation of a new federal film agency, the U.S. Film Service (USFS), and a commitment to feature-film production. An executive order issued in August 1938 authorized the USFS not only to produce its own films but also to coordinate the production and distribution of motion pictures throughout the federal government, maintain and distribute a library of films for educational institutions, and serve as a consultant to government agencies and educational organizations and foundations. One month later, additional responsibilities were assigned, including the drafting of minimum standards for government films, the ongoing review of all scripts and contracts, and the supervision of the use of federal personnel and property by commercial film producers. Named director of the agency, Lorentz embarked at once on an ambitious feature-length project, ECCE HOMO!, the fictional story of the migration of a jobless family from the Deep South during the Depression years. Floyd Crosby rejoined Lorentz as the agency's director of photography. The consolidation of distribution and educational activities proceeded largely under the supervision of Mercey, now the Film Service's assistant director. Consultant work for an interdepartmental committee on Latin America affairs also was undertaken in 1938 and 1939. When production of ECCE HOMO! bogged down in the fall of 1939, Lorentz set aside the project for THE FIGHT FOR LIFE, a dramatized account of the work of the Chicago Maternity Center, hoping to score a quick triumph with the press as well as the president, who was launching new public-health initiatives. He succeeded: released in March 1940, THE FIGHT FOR LIFE was featured in photospreads in *Life* and *Look* magazines, hailed by many critics as an original and powerful experiment in mixing documentary and fictional forms, and theatrically distributed by Columbia Pictures.[33]

Lorentz also sought to add luster to the USFS by importing renowned documentarists to work on other government projects. Joris Ivens was hired to direct THE POWER AND THE LAND, a film on the delivery of electricity to farmers cut off from private utilities, made at the behest of the Rural Electrification Administration. Focusing on the daily life of an Ohio farm family, Ivens's film was distributed by RKO in December 1940, reaching a general, as well as a specialized rural, audience. Less widely seen, but no less

POWER AND THE LAND *(Ivens, 1940). Rural electrification: from hand labor . . . to modern conveniences.*

THE LAND *(Flaherty, 1942).*
The human cost of mechanized
farming: displaced migrant workers.

THE LAND *(Flaherty, 1942).*
The benefits of modern planning:
terraced farming to protect the land.

suggestive of Lorentz's aspirations for the agency, was THE LAND, a plea for the conservation of farmland proposed by the Agricultural Adjustment Administration (AAA) and assigned to Robert Flaherty. Flaherty chafed under bureacratic restrictions, however, and the production dragged on for two years. When THE LAND was completed in the summer of 1941, AAA officials found Flaherty's critique of mechanized farm production out of tune with current government policy and limited distribution to some farmers. Following an official premiere at the Museum of Modern Art in April 1942, THE LAND was dropped from circulation entirely.[34]

By this time, however, the U.S. Film Service had disappeared from view as well. Throughout Lorentz's tenure as a government employee, his base of operation had been highly provisional and often under attack. Prior to the formation of the USFS, the Resettlement Administration had been declared unconstitutional, and its film and photo sections transferred to the Farm Security Administration at the Department of Agriculture, where THE RIVER was completed. Subsequent investigations by the General Accounting Office prompted Secretary of Agriculture Henry Wallace to rule in June 1938 that relief money could no longer be used for documentary films by his department. Two months later, Roosevelt established the USFS under the administration's National Emergency Council, with funding drawn from the Public Works Administration and the WPA, but the NEC, weakened by congressional scrutiny, was abolished in July 1939 and the USFS relocated in the Office of Education under the Federal Security Agency. Throughout these dizzying organizational shifts, Lorentz's power was sustained in large measure by the personal backing of Roosevelt rather than by any stable footing within the federal bureaucracy.

In February 1940, however, Mercey appeared before hearings of the House Subcommittee on Appropriations with a cautious proposal for the permanent funding of the USFS's distribution programs. The plan backfired: the committee not only denied Mercey's request but attached a provision to its 1941 relief bill that specifically prohibited the allocation of money to the USFS by any relief agency. In April an amendment to restore funding was debated on the floor of the Senate, but failed, 24–36, with the vote dividing along party lines. Roosevelt, facing a new set of challenges in his dealings with Congress concerning U.S. commitments overseas, publicly protested the defeat of the amendment, but decided not to fight to keep the agency alive.[35]

From the outset, New Deal filmmaking was a slippery operation: circuitously funded, it was also conceptually ambiguous, as New Dealers stressed in public the informational and educational value of works they clearly hoped fulfilled a political function, and Lorentz experimented with innovative documentary techniques while keeping FDR, his chief benefactor, satisfied that administration programs also were being served. Congressional deliberations in 1940, however, narrowed the terms for assessing the value of government filmmaking. In a lengthy (and some analysts think decisive) speech during the Senate debate, Robert A. Taft (R-Ohio) drew on what was by now a familiar distinction between information films, communicating scientific or technical knowledge, and the domain of social-documentary cinema, in order to place the latter category outside the pale of legitimate government activity. The Department of Labor, Taft pointed out, had produced an instructional film on prenatal care for $1,000; Lorentz's FIGHT FOR LIFE, in contrast, cost $150,000. How could it be argued, then, that the U.S. Film Service brought efficiency to government filmmaking? The dividend bought with the money—drama, rhetoric, the power to persuade and arouse constituents—was propaganda, an appropriate activity of private organizations but not the federal government.

Throughout the House and Senate hearings, moreover, unsympathetic interrogators frequently complained that documentaries financed through relief agencies—whatever their merits or professional craftsmanship—did not employ or train jobless workers. The complaint touched on an ambiguity at the foundation of agency policy. Whom did the U.S. Film Service serve? The unemployed, who might receive the direct benefits of a job? Officials, from FDR down, who tendered requests for particular projects? Documentary filmmakers with established reputations and new ambitions? Or an audience for new cultural works, whose vitality might be restored by film projects equivalent to those concurrently sponsored by the WPA in theater, literature, and the arts? Critics in Congress focused on the first two beneficiaries, at times unctuously alleging support for the unemployed while assailing the new power granted administration officials. Meanwhile, defenders of the USFS never mounted a far-reaching argument on aesthetic or cultural grounds. Linked together with a case for the funding of a new federal radio service in the Office of Education, the defense of the USFS was based upon a communications model: the efficient flow of information from the government to a diverse and remote populace. Detailed discussion of the aesthetic or cultural value of these films—central to critical commentary on them—perhaps seemed impertinent in this context. With elements of social advocacy and dramatic power factored out of the equation, defenders of the USFS fell back on narrow arguments concerning the legal language defining their authority, the economic advantages of a streamlined distribution system, and the sense of civic pride in government work that the Film Service fostered. With the social function of the agency thus circumscribed, New Deal filmmaking succumbed to a partisan vote.

During its brief existence, the U.S. Film Service was an inventive experiment in the development of a nonprofit, state-financed system of social-documentary production and distribution, with Lorentz briefly functioning as a de facto production chief, overseeing the development of projects, supervising the preparation of scripts, and hiring talent with the reputation of an Ivens or Flaherty. In keeping with his initial advice upon arriving at the Resettlement Administration in 1935, Lorentz focused resources on a few carefully crafted, innovative productions. Securing theatrical distribution was a cornerstone of USFS policy, designed to maximize public exposure and media interest in the films the agency released. Yet the very conspicuousness of the USFS as an autonomous film agency—heralded in the press, attracting prominent filmmakers into its ranks—may have contributed to its undoing by making it more difficult for Lorentz and his colleagues to go about their work behind the shifting, protective screens of parent agencies and departments. Given this political context, USFS policy appears to have been inevitably at cross-purposes with the agency's capacity to survive. House hearings in 1940 then afforded congressional opponents, long annoyed at the sub-rosa financing by the Roosevelt administration, an occasion to lower the ax.

Sponsored Documentaries

As social-documentary filmmakers gained recognition in cultural quarters in the second half of the decade, their services were increasingly solicited by private foundations and social-welfare or professional groups. When hiring filmmakers, the latter organizations typically had specific social objectives in mind—a problem to expose, a program to set forth. Foundations, in contrast, tended to justify their support of documentary production in terms of a broad mandate to fund programs in the "public interest," a concept that itself had a political dimension. Like labor-Left groups, educational organizations had used films as early as the teens to disseminate information to schools, factories, and community groups, and small companies specializing in the production of inexpensive instructional films flourished after the standardization of a nontheatrical 16-mm format in 1923.[36] New in the late 1930s, however, was an infusion of philanthropic money and an interest in sophisticated techniques that, unlike arid information films, could vivify social issues for general audiences. Often working in concert, foundations and special-interest groups thus came to sponsor a flurry of social-documentary projects as the decade drew to a close.

Precedent for privately funding the work of labor-Left documentarists was established in 1935 when Julian Roffman convinced the Consumers Union, a nonprofit advocacy group, to spend $500 on a film that explained product-safety testing and exposed fraudulent advertising. The popularity of the film led to the four-part GETTING YOUR MONEY'S WORTH and inspired Roffman, Del Duca, and Kandel to depart the weakened Film and Photo League to form their own company, Contemporary Films.[37] In 1937 an offer from the American Institute of Planners to work on THE CITY, backed by a $50,000 grant from the Carnegie Corporation, likewise emboldened Steiner and Van Dyke to cut loose from Frontier and form American Documentary Films.[38] Veterans of labor-Left filmmaking also were hired by Spencer Pollard's Educational Film Institute at the New York University Film Library, established in 1939 by the Alfred P. Sloan Foundation to produce and circulate documentaries on economic and educational themes. Under the aegis of the institute, for example, Roffman collaborated with John Ferno, Ivens's former cameraman, on a film on rural nutrition, AND SO THEY LIVE (1940). After completing THE POWER AND THE LAND for the moribund U.S. Film Service, Ivens and Crosby set out for Colorado on another Sloan/EFI project, NEW FRONTIERS. When work on THE CITY was concluded, Van Dyke formed his own company, Documentary Film Productions, under whose banner he directed two other Sloan sponsored projects, VALLEY TOWN and THE CHILDREN MUST LEARN (both 1940), as well as several promotional films for private companies.[39]

The broadest role of any philanthropic organization, however, was assumed by the Rockefeller Foundation, which as early as 1936 had funded research in educational film technique at the University of Minnesota and financed film projects by the American Council for Education and the Progressive Education Association. In the winter of 1937–1938, the foundation also subsidized a six-month visit to the United States by Paul Rotha, a prominent British documentary film producer, critic, and leading advocate of commercial sponsorship for social-documentary production. Lecturing extensively at the Museum of Modern Art and Columbia University during his tenure as a Rockefeller fellow, Rotha argued that in contrast to Great Britain's integrated system of government and private support, documentary film work in America was ineffectively administrated. The suggestion rankled Lorentz and many members of the Frontier collective, but Rotha's critique was to have an impact on Van Dyke and Steiner, whom he befriended during his stay, and on the Rockefeller Foundation itself, which shortly after his visit established the American Film Center as a link between sponsors and filmmakers.[40] Headed by Donald Slesinger, a former law professor at Yale and dean of social science at the University of Chicago, the American Film Center set up headquarters in August 1938 at Rockefeller Center, where it provided research space to film producers, awarded modest grants for selected projects, and kept filmmakers apprised of recent activity through a monthly newsletter. The American Film Center also investigated the possibility of documentary film production and distribution in Latin America, anticipating (perhaps not coincidentally) Nelson Rockefeller's role as coordinator of inter-American affairs for the federal government in the early 1940s. Although not to play as enduring a role as initial publicity predicted, the American Film Center nevertheless constituted the most far-reaching effort by a major foundation to promote the expanding field of documentary in the prewar years.[41]

The formation of the Association of Documentary Film Producers (ADFP) by Mary Losey in 1939 offered yet another mechanism to connect filmmakers with sponsors. A 1932 graduate of Wellesley, Losey had worked for noted advertising consultant Edward L. Bernays and headed the research department for *The March of Time* before traveling to Great Britain to study documentary production in that country. Upon returning to a post at the American Film Center in 1938, Losey launched a drive for a new association that would promote innovative documentaries, develop artistic and technical standards, and foster cooperation among professionals in the field.[42] Her idea at once struck a chord; within a year, the ADFP had nearly a hundred members. Although filmmakers with a background in labor-Left documentary played a leading role—Ivens, Strand, Van Dyke, Seltzer, and Leyda all served on ADFP's executive board—its membership was broad, encompassing representatives of government agencies, foundations, and private businesses. In 1940, Losey edited and published *Living Films: A Catalog of Documentary Films and Their Makers,* a reference guide to available documentaries with accompanying biographies of all ADFP members. In it political or institutional divisions were downplayed; films made for commercial companies (Eastman Kodak, Lockheed Aircraft, American Can Company, and the like) received attention equal to the political documentary projects of Frontier. The catalog, Losey noted in her introduction, sought not to classify or index works but rather provide a "who's who of documentary film in America." As for definitions of documentary, Losey simply observed, "This an art unlimited. The world is its studio and its people the actors." Under such a rubric, a vast range of films and filmmakers could be accommodated.[43]

Perhaps the greatest promotional achievement of the ADFP was a program of American and European documentaries organized by Losey and Philip McConnell for the 1939 New York World's Fair. Including works by Flaherty, Lorentz, Ivens, and Roffman, and highlighted by the fair's most popular film attraction, THE CITY, the ADFP program served as the focal exhibit at the Fair Corporation's Science and Education Building, placing the recent achievements of social-documentary filmmakers on conspicuous display. Between the 1939 and 1940 fair seasons, the ADFP also organized a twelve-part documentary retrospective, The Nonfiction Film: From Uninterpreted Fact to Documentary, at the Museum of Modern Art. Opening with a three-part chronology of the development of the genre, the series branched out into related forms such as travel and instructional films, and then settled into a sequence of programs built around specific social issues, such as housing, labor, and national affairs. Although the retrospective reached far fewer viewers than the show at the fair, the museum program generated favorable commentary in the press and shaped an emerging critical view of documentary as a genre with a discernible lineage, a record of distinguished achievement, and wide potential for future development.[44]

Despite these triumphs of promotion, the ADFP did little to counter the diffusion of political and economic energies that diverse sponsorship of documentary films fostered. The organization's base of support was broad but shallow; without institutional affiliation, capital resources, or even a core social philosophy, the ADFP lacked the muscle—and perhaps the will—to establish production priorities or otherwise intervene in contemporary political debates. Nor did it solve the chronic problem of documentary distribution. The *Living Films* catalog routed interested parties to the distributors of available films and offered the association's assistance in assembling film programs for a small fee, yet the ADFP itself did not emerge as an agency empowered to extend or streamline nontheatrical distribution networks. Theatrical distribution, moreover, was largely beyond its scope of concern. Thus, while art-house events like the museum retrospective helped secure a higher profile for social documentarists, the activities of the ADFP only had an indirect impact on developing a wider audience for their films.

In light of the ongoing problem of documentary distribution and exhibition, the New York World's Fair was an intriguing venue. Nonfiction films abounded at the various fair pavilions; estimates of the total number screened run as high as five hundred. In a sense, this showcase returned documentary to cinema's roots as a turn-of-the-century fairground amusement in which movies vied for attention among rival attractions. Yet unlike the typical fairground, the New York World's Fair combined hoopla with high purpose in a public celebration of the conquest of new technological frontiers; tourists from around the world were invited to Flushing Meadows to catch a glimpse of "the World of Tomorrow." Here the ADFP program at the Science and Education Building was surrounded by an array of new optical displays in the pavilions of corporate sponsors. Chrysler Motors, for example, presented a 3-D Technicolor stop-motion film in which the company's new line of automobiles, composed of mechanical parts that sang and danced, magically assembled themselves without benefit of human labor, a more cheerful view of industrial automation than would be found in social documentaries by, say, Van Dyke or Flaherty. At the General Motors Pavilion, an estimated 25 million visitors glided through "Futurama," a coast-to-coast aerial view of America, circa 1960, built by stage designer Norman Bel Geddes. Riding in upholstered armchairs, listening to a recorded commentary amplified through personal speakers, spectators peered down upon an immaculate system of arterial highways and planned communities, a social scheme devoid of the economic and political backdrop against which such a vision of the future might be assessed. As for a view of the past, historical accounts supplied in social documentaries could be compared with the variant treatment of Cecil B. DeMille's LAND OF LIBERTY, a compilation film culled from Hollywood's costume epics and regularly screened at the U.S. Pavilion. Surveying the full range of films at the fair (under the auspices of a grant from the American Film Center), Richard Griffith concluded that social documentarists outshone the competition across the board. But a poll of fairgoers, instead of critics, might have rendered a different verdict. Or perhaps no verdict at all: deposited amid this feast of sensory pleasures, documentaries may have been experienced as simply one among a host of audiovisual reports on the world—past, present, future. The fairground setting, in short, may have dulled distinctions rather than sharpened them.[45]

However perceived in this instance, sponsored filmmaking as a general phenomenon raised questions about the integrity of social-documentary practices. The shift toward sponsored financing was in part symptomatic of a broader trend toward professionalizing documentary production in the second half of the decade: filmmakers affiliated with both Frontier Films and the U.S. Film Service, for example, sought to establish standards for, and make a living from, the practice of their craft. But a different dynamic was introduced when social documentarists set up shop as filmmakers for hire, seeking clients, and following production money wherever it appeared. Devoid of a political base of their own, "independent" filmmakers were vulnerable to political pressures from the clients they served. A diffusion of documentary production could easily lead to an attenuation of the role of the filmmaker as a central participant in the shaping of social materials. Moreover, "public service," as defined by a private foundation bent on acquiring prestige, could quickly shade toward "public relations"—the projection of a favorable corporate image—robbing controversial topics of any political bite. Under these conditions, distinctions between sponsorship and self-promotion, between social documentaries and sponsored business films or "industrials," could become exceedingly fine.[46]

Films like THE CITY and VALLEY TOWN eventually bore the marks of these tensions and conflicts. Based on a scenario supplied to the Institute of American Planners by Pare Lorentz, THE CITY recounts the transformation of the American village into a modern metropolis, a story punctuated by stylistic and tonal shifts. A lyrical evocation of village life in the eighteenth century yields to a caustic indictment of poverty and pollution in industrialized cities, which in turn gives way to a playful and mildly satiric orchestration of urban movement and congestion in New York City and its vacation escape route into New Jersey. A solution is then offered: a decentralized greenbelt community, combining the security and open spaces of village life with the conveniences of modern engineering and planning. If reviews are an accurate index, THE CITY's indictment of industrial conditions pleased social critics, the humorous metropolis section delighted audiences at the fair, and the protracted greenbelt section (twice the length of any other) mainly satisfied the sponsors, who insisted, over the objections of Steiner and Van Dyke, that the conclusion promote their plan unequivocally and at great length. In the case of VALLEY TOWN, no such bargain was finally struck between filmmaker and sponsor. In his original version, Van Dyke employed an experimental sound track scored by Marc Blitzstein and commentary scripted by Ben Maddow to evoke a melancholic portrait of technologically induced unemployment in a Pennsylvania steel town. Displeased with Van Dyke's treatment of this economic theme, General Motors president Alfred P. Sloan (whose World's Fair Futurama transported tourists undisturbed) promptly blocked the film's release and then authorized its reediting and redubbing. Other Sloan/Educational Film Institute works were subsequently amended as well, and projects still in production (most notably Ivens's NEW FRONTIERS) were abruptly canceled.[47]

The pressures these filmmakers experienced followed in part from processes of collaborative judgment fundamental to all social-documentary production. Political or aesthetic ambitions often ran up against ideological and financial constraint; compromise came with the territory. But sponsored filmmaking resituated questions of compromise within a gray zone that had emerged between committed documentary film work, on the one hand, and labor for hire, on the other. Selected by sponsors for their past achievements in the field, documentarists who chose not to check their political baggage when accepting paid assignments often confronted difficult choices for which no guidelines had been drafted. Social-documentary practices were not introduced, fully codified, at the outset of the 1930s; rather, they were debated, tested, and refined in concrete situations. By the late 1930s, proposals for commercial sponsorship—vigorously opposed in some quarters—forced social documentarists to clarify

THE CITY *(Steiner, 1939). Two neighborhoods: inner city and the modern "greenbelt."*

their notion of the genre anew. For many filmmakers, boundary lines were drawn only after they had been crossed.

On the Margin: Documentary and Hollywood

Defenders of documentary in the 1930s frequently accused Hollywood of indifference or hostility to the values documentary filmmakers espoused. For many critics on the Left, this was axiomatic; the commercial film industry, owned by corporate interests and a purveyor of fantasy and escape, could not be expected to confront social realities or illuminate a path to social reform. The struggle of documentarists to produce and distribute their work in the face of Hollywood's massive domination of resources and theatrical markets lent credibility and a degree of moral fervor to the charge. Yet the political compass of the film industry was broader than the concerns of its financial backers; as a social institution, Hollywood was itself the site of conflicting interests and motives. Talent groups, for example, sought to influence studio practices in concentrated, if circumscribed, ways, and an ambition to earn prestige or a favorable hearing in Washington could counter the reflexive caution of studio executives. Bosley Crowther reported in 1940 that conservatives in Hollywood "bridled fiercely" at the very mention of documentary, a word that spelled "anathema, revolution or, at best, presumptuous 'art,'" but that the influence of documentary nevertheless was evident to a remarkable degree in recent Hollywood productions.[48] Indeed, it can be argued that the greatest threat posed to social documentarists by the studio system was less indifference or hostility than Hollywood's capacity to absorb the marketable aspects of this cinema in ways that cut documentary filmmakers out of the deal. Perhaps what these filmmakers most had to fear, then, was an embrace by Hollywood on its own terms.

Interaction between studio executives and documentary filmmakers, it is useful to keep in mind, dates back at least as far as the work of Robert Flaherty in the 1920s. Financed with money from a French fur company, Revillon Frères, and released in the United States by an independent distributor, Pathé Exchange, NANOOK OF THE NORTH (1922) enjoyed sufficient critical and commercial success to inspire Jesse Lasky at Paramount to back Flaherty's subsequent trip to the South Seas to film MOANA (1926).[49] Lasky also arranged distribution deals for two exotic travelogue features by Merian C. Cooper and Ernest B. Schoedsack— GRASS, filmed in Turkey and Persia in 1925, and CHANG, shot in Siam in 1927. Over the next few years, the expense of converting studios to sound drove some independent production companies out of business, but those specializing in narrative travelogues were less at risk, since their films could be shot silent, with sound effects, music, and commentary added during postproduction. Works of this kind continued to enjoy studio release on into the 1930s. Paramount, for example, heavily promoted Schoedsack's RANGO (1931), as well as films of Admiral Richard E. Byrd's first and second expeditions to the South Pole, WITH BYRD AT THE SOUTH POLE (1930) and LITTLE AMERICA (1935). Fox released H. A. Snow's THE GREAT WHITE NORTH (1928) and two African adventure films by veteran travelogue filmmakers Martin and Osa Johnson, CONGORILLA (1932) and BABOONA (1935). Columbia distributed AFRICA SPEAKS, filmed by the Colorado African Expedition in 1930. Universal produced and distributed IGLOO, modeled after NANOOK OF THE NORTH, in 1932. B. F. Zeidman's SAMARANG, a narrative documentary featuring South Seas natives, was distributed by United Artists in 1933. And Frank Buck's BRING 'EM BACK ALIVE, shot in the Malaysian jungle for the Van Beuren Corporation, was one of RKO's most profitable releases in 1932. Over the next few years, Van Beuren continued to supply RKO with exotic travel features, including INDIA SPEAKS (1933), ADVENTURE GIRL (1934), and two Frank Buck sequels, WILD CARGO (1934) and FANG AND CLAW (1935). Hollywood studios, in short, were not averse to marketing exotic documentaries, especially if independent filmmakers were willing to travel to remote settings and bear the risks of location shooting.[50]

Social documentaries, however, raised domestic political issues that exotic travel narratives did not and thus were likely to meet greater resistance from studio executives. Although support for labor-Left organizations grew among workers in Hollywood as the Depression took root, political film work by these groups was at first a marginal, if not at times subterranean, activity. Industry technicians in part staffed the Los Angeles branch of the Film and Photo League, and writers, directors, cinematographers, and editors sympathetic to left-wing causes lent their services to political projects such as THE STRANGE CASE OF TOM MOONEY (1933), a documentary account of the San Francisco labor leader's seventeen-year incarceration in San Quentin, produced by B-unit director Bryan Foy, or MILLIONS OF US (1936), a tale of labor solidarity filmed by studio workers who sought anonymity out of fear of reprisals from their employers.[51]

As Popular Front strategies shifted attention to anti-fascist causes, film work on the Left increasingly came above ground and gained a broader base of support. In July 1935, Joris Ivens screened his European documentaries in Hollywood, reportedly to great acclaim.[52] The Hollywood Anti-Nazi League, formed in 1936, attracted a wide membership, ranging from studio producers, such as Carl Laemmle and Jack Warner, to screenwriters affiliated with the Communist party, such as John Howard Lawson and Samuel Ornitz. For the next three years, the league provided an effective political base for coordinating a cluster of anti-fascist projects, including fund-raising initiatives for documentary films on the fascist threat in Spain and Czechoslovakia. The Motion Picture Democratic Committee, formed in June 1938 to support the California gubernatorial campaign of liberal Democrat Culbert Olson, also drew on industry talent for the production of a campaign film, CALIFORNIA SPEAKS. In the wake of Olson's election, the group committed itself to civil rights and antifascist causes, and established the Motion Picture Guild to produce ancillary films, with Floyd Crosby named president.[53] And the concurrent success of Pare Lorentz and the U.S. Film Service in gaining studio release of New Deal films augured a new era of cooperation between Washington and Hollywood in support of documentary production and distribution.

In the main, however, social-documentary filmmakers were not to benefit from these new alliances. This is attributable in part to the unraveling of Popular Front unity at the close of the decade. A mutual nonaggression pact between Germany and the Soviet Union signed in August 1939 fractured Popular Front coalitions, as pro-Soviet Communists abruptly reversed course and argued for nonintervention in the "phony war" in Europe. Liberal members of the Anti-Nazi League and the Motion Picture Democratic Committee openly sought to distance themselves from apologists for the Nazi-Soviet Pact, and an investigation of alleged Communist subversion in Hollywood, launched by Martin Dies's House Un-American Activities Committee the year before, gained new momentum. When congressional attacks on the U.S. Film Service mounted in the spring of 1940, the political affiliations of social-documentary filmmakers who had worked for the government were also called into question.

Meanwhile, film markets across the Atlantic closed, nullifying the impact of lost revenues that partisan political filmmaking could engender. Studio executives in greater numbers were hence willing to embrace the Allied cause in Europe, and "public service" at a time of international crisis became a new catchphrase in studio public relations. Following the fall of France in July 1940, producers from various studios formed the Motion Picture Committee Cooperating for the National Defense, under the direction of Darryl F. Zanuck, and offered the Roosevelt administration the assistance of the industry in the production and distribution of government films. Transformed into the War Activities Committee after Pearl Harbor, the group cleared the way for open collaboration between Hollywood and Washington throughout the war years. Thus, even as New Deal documentary production was curtailed by Congress, wartime filmmaking, targeting a foreign foe rather than domestic ailments, was undertaken in a spirit of national consensus.

Modest opportunities opened up for experienced social documentarists: Van Dyke, Lerner, Meyers, and Ferno all were recruited to make films for audiences overseas, first in support of the government's Good Neighbor policy in Latin America and then as part of a campaign by the Office of War Information (OWI) to present a favorable picture of American life to allies and conquered nations abroad. But prestigious military assignments were awarded to Hollywood directors (notably Frank Capra, John Ford, William Wyler, and John Huston), most of whom had no previous training on documentary films. Moreover, by 1943 the center of government filmmaking had shifted to the West Coast as Hollywood assumed primary responsibility for the production of all domestic films for the OWI.[54] With this shift, much of the rhetoric of the social-documentary movement of the 1930s—with its calls for political commitment and unified action, and testimonies to the power of cinema to vivify and explain social events—was taken up by the commercial film industry. Furthermore, the form and style of social documentaries from the 1930s served as models for many wartime productions, as experiments in narrative construction, vocal commentary, sound effects, and patterns of conceptual and rhythmic editing were absorbed and extended by filmmakers working on documentaries for the first time.

Fiction films, too, bore the stamp of documentary's impact on studio practices. Here again interaction with Hollywood can be traced back to the popularity of the travel documentary in the 1920s. Critics increasingly praised location cinematography for the enhanced sense of realism it supplied, and travelogue narratives, together with celebrated epic dramas such as THE COVERED WAGON (1923), served to establish new norms of verisimilitude for fiction filmmakers. For example, the industry's conversion from orthochromatic to panchromatic film stock, which rendered darkened skies and cloud formations with enhanced pictorial clarity and richness, was accelerated by its effective use by Flaherty on MOANA in 1926.[55] The following year, Karl Brown, cinematographer on THE COVERED WAGON and a long-term collaborator with D. W. Griffith, won the support of Lasky to film STARK LOVE, a story of rural mountain life, on location in North Carolina with a cast of native mountaineers in supporting parts and an amateur actor and actress as leads. With Robert Flaherty as consultant, MGM shipped a star cast and crew to Tahiti to film WHITE SHADOWS OF THE SOUTH SEAS in 1928, and again (without Flaherty) to Africa for TRADER HORN in 1931, forging a hybrid form out of travelogue footage and conventional Hollywood drama-turgy. In 1933, Cooper and Schoedsack, now under contract to RKO, embarked on their own variant of the jungle picture when they grafted special effects onto the genre with great commercial success in KING KONG.

Social-problem fiction similarly absorbed aspects of documentary form and style. While at Warners in the early 1930s, producer Darryl F. Zanuck, recognizing the potential box-office draw of contemporary political material, pressed for topical, "headline" stories told in a punchy journalistic style. In such films, passages shot in the manner of a documentary "city film" could quickly establish an urban location and set a dynamic pace for the drama to follow. Slavko Vorkapich, an avant-garde filmmaker, studio editor, and anonymous contributor to MILLIONS OF US, gained a reputation in Hollywood as a specialist in transitional montage passages, often constructed from stock footage and indebted to experimental documentary techniques. The climactic ending to King Vidor's OUR DAILY BREAD (1934), in which water pours through an aqueduct to irrigate the land of a new agrarian collective, likewise draws on a montage aesthetic, anticipating by three years Lorentz's use of rhythmic editing to evoke the rising power of floodwaters in THE RIVER.[56] When Zanuck undertook an adaptation of John Steinbeck's acclaimed novel THE GRAPES OF WRATH at 20th Century–Fox in 1939, the Farm Security Administration's documentary photo unit supplied Zanuck and director John Ford with pictures of the dust bowl and the westward migration of uprooted farmers to aid in the visual design of the work.[57] In a similar vein, an image early in Lewis Milestone's OF MICE AND MEN (1940), adapted from Steinbeck's novella and play of the same title, replicates a familiar photo by Dorothea Lange, FSA photographer and consultant to Lorentz on THE PLOW THAT BROKE THE PLAINS. CONFESSIONS OF A NAZI SPY, an antifascist treatise directed by Anatole Litvak for Warner Bros. in 1939 (and screened as the final film in the ADFP retrospective), interpolates newsreel footage and fabricates a documentary style to generate a sense of verisimilitude. By the end of the decade, topical imagery thus circulated through social-problem fiction and documentary photobooks and films.

The widespread impact of *The March of Time* at its debut in movie theaters in 1935 further blurred any hard and fast distinctions between the separate domains of pictorial journalism, social documentary, and Hollywood fiction. Produced in New York under the corporate sponsorship of *Time* magazine, with guaranteed distribution (from its fifth issue on) through the auspices of RKO, *The March of Time* occupied a position in the exhibition program roughly equivalent to commercial newsreels. Yet *March of Time* issues appeared monthly rather than twice weekly and typically were twenty minutes long, double the running time of conventional newsreels. Like social documentaries, *The March of Time* inter-preted and dramatized controversial political topics—most notably and consist-ently the rise of fascism abroad—and in 1938 adopted a single-story format that permitted subject matter to be probed in greater depth. Under the supervision of producer Louis de Rochemont, the series also ventured boldly into feature production in 1940 with THE RAMPARTS WE WATCH, a dramatization of the

THE PLOW THAT BROKE THE PLAINS *(Lorentz, 1936)* — *documentary.*

THE GRAPES OF WRATH *(20th-Fox, 1940)* — *fiction.*

impact of World War I on a small American city that was shot on location in New London, Connecticut, and mixed newsreel footage with scripted performances by townspeople. Three years later, de Rochemont left *The March of Time* to join Zanuck at 20th Century–Fox, where he oversaw the production of a feature-length documentary for the U.S. Navy, THE FIGHTING LADY (1944), and then wedded investigative journalism and foreign-espionage fiction in THE HOUSE ON 92ND STREET (1945), in pursuit of a new "semidocumentary" form.[58]

The war years in particular offered a fertile setting for experiments of this kind as numerous Hollywood producers, directors, writers, and cinematographers were assigned to documentary projects for the first time and borrowed elements of a documentary style for fictional works with wartime themes. Cinematographer James Wong Howe observed in 1943 that documentary coverage of the war had so powerfully shaped notions of pictorial realism for modern viewers that he now favored "natural" compositions and sources of lighting in his images and preferred actors to work without makeup. Furthermore, Howe declared "mechanical movements of the camera" and "shots from impossible angles" taboo on the ground that they violated a contemporary viewer's sense of filmic realism.[59] The social commitments of documentary filmmakers also occasionally were found compelling by wartime initiates to the genre. In 1946, recounting his experiences as a documentary producer for the OWI during the war, screenwriter Philip Dunne noted a trend in Hollywood "toward a more frequent selection of factual American themes, toward the theory that motion pictures should not only entertain and make money, but should also give expression to the American and democratic ideals, to 'the truth' as we, the citizens of democracy, accept it." The exposure of Hollywood filmmakers to the tenets and common practices of documentary production, Dunne predicted, would profoundly shape the course of the motion-picture industry in the postwar period.[60]

Only a few documentary filmmakers, however, found a new home in Hollywood. Indeed, for surviving filmmakers on the Left, the motion-picture industry in the era of cold-war politics and red-baiting was an even less hospitable environment than the Hollywood of the 1930s.[61] Nor did all documentary filmmakers aspire to acceptance in Hollywood: documentary stylistics, after all, could be diluted in a hybrid aesthetic concocted for mass commercial appeal, and the documentary filmmaker stripped of his or her power to mount a fundamental social critique. Yet, if we take as a measure not the trajectory of individual careers but rather the norms of institutional practice, the impact of thirties documentary looms large. Documentary films and photobooks were central to new representations of social reality—the way the world looked, sounded, seemed to hang together—serving as a benchmark against which verisimilar fictions were measured. Under the pressure of political events, as well as economic gain, Hollywood filmmakers would find attractive a style that seemed to bear a privileged relation to contemporary social life and would embrace the notion of the public interest that cultural discourses on documentary in the 1930s actively fostered. Moreover, Hollywood would mount an argument for the motion-picture theater—in lieu of the union hall, church basement, classroom, or chambers of Congress—as a logical site for civic enlightenment as well as popular amusement, with the neighborhood theater as the new American town hall.

The New York World's Fair of 1939 suggested other possibilities. The address of President Roosevelt at the opening ceremonies of a fair devoted to the World of Tomorrow occasioned the first live televised news event in the United States, as the new optical technology of the Radio Corporation of America was put into operation. A few months later Pare Lorentz, complaining of Hollywood's myopic disinclination to train new filmmakers or furnish funds for documentary work and anticipating a day when seed money from schools, foundations, and the federal government might render documentary production self-sufficient, added a deadpan afterthought: "Or, of course, perhaps by then we'll have television and won't have to worry about movies at all."[62] In a few short years, a system for televisual coverage of current events indeed would flourish under conditions of profitable corporate sponsorship. In the process, the attention devoted to motion pictures as the central instrument of mass enlightenment and propaganda would be displaced, and a system of corporate networks, emerging from television's direct antecedent, radio, would redefine production and distribution channels and transplant the site of reception of pictures of the world from the social space of the theater to the home. Broadcast journalism absorbed the topical register of documentary practices, but not those notions of artistic autonomy and expression that accompanied documentary theory and practice throughout the 1930s. With its emphasis on the spontaneous and instantaneous—the uncontrolled performance, the unrehearsed interview, the event caught "live"—television eventually altered a sense of social reality for a new generation of documentary filmmakers who, armed with new lightweight camera-microphone equipment, cast off many of the conventions of the 1930s and 1940s in pursuit of a new documentary style.

Yet much of the conceptual field first staked out by documentarists in the 1930s has remained pertinent to debates throughout the intervening decades. If broadcast journalism has emerged as the dominant mode for producing and delivering nonfiction images and sounds to a mass audience, documentary cinema (and now video) sustains work at the margins of this media system, sometimes penetrating it to inflect mainstream practices. Links between avant-garde and documentary filmmaking, articulated anew with the emergence of an "underground" cinema in the 1960s, have endured in the experimental work of film and video artists who engage unfamiliar or disturbing topics and rework familiar forms, sometimes mixing conventions of fiction and nonfiction. The evolution of political filmmaking in the 1930s from the radical work of the Film and Photo League to the Popular Front initiatives of Frontier finds an echo in the recent histories of newsreel collectives in New York and San Francisco, which emerged out of a culture of political agitation in the late 1960s, splintered under the pressure of competing factions in the 1970s, and have re-formed to cater to a liberal-Left educational film and video market in recent years. State, philanthropic, and corporate sponsorship for documentary films persists as well, reconfigured in a constellation of government agencies, foundations, and social-interest groups that underwrite, often in concert, documentary projects. An impulse to inform, enlighten, persuade, or provoke, to make visible the unseen or audible the unheard, still propels much work in this field. Moreover, patterns of institutional support and constraint, transformed by new technologies and the corporate structures that promote and adopt them, remain central to any effort to assess the social impact of documentary within histories of cinema more broadly viewed. From this perspective, the legacy of thirties documentary consists not simply of a body of films serving as historical artifacts of the Depression decade but of a set of concepts and questions about the possible forms and functions of documentary—indeed, the very name for one way of thinking about film images and sounds and the worlds to which we imagine they refer.

10

Avant-Garde Film

Jan-Christopher Horak

The evolution of avant-garde film, as articulated in the canonical texts of film historiography, has been teleologically structured as a chronological progression toward ever more sophisticated forms of film art. Divided essentially into three periods, each avant-garde has been connected to its predecessor by aesthetic and personnel continuities, constructing over significant gaps in time and space a discourse on the evolution of personal expression in the film medium. While appropriate for polemical argument and aesthetic legitimation, such a view of avant-garde film history has eliminated the gaps and fissures, discontinuities and dead ends, which necessarily mark a film form based on individual and essentially isolated modes of production.

The American film avant-garde established itself in the 1920s and 1930s, contrary to the standard histories, which date its beginnings to 1943 with Maya Deren.[1] While the 1930s were characterized by diminishing possibilities for the production of avant-garde film, because of the breakdown of infrastructures established in the latter half of the 1920s, numerous avant-garde filmmakers began or continued their careers. The list includes Roger Barlow, Josef Berne, Thomas Bouchard, Irving Browning, Rudy Burkhardt, Mary Ellen Bute, Joseph Cornell, Douglas Crockwell, Emlen Etting, John Florey, Roman Freulich, Jo Gerson, Jerome Hill, Theodore Huff, Lewis Jacobs, Jay Leyda, Hershell Louis, Ted Nemeth, Lynn Riggs, LeRoy Robbins, Henwar Rodakiewicz, Joseph Schillinger, Mike Siebert, Ralph Steiner, Seymour Stern, Paul Strand, William Vance, Charles Vidor, Slavko Vorkapich, James Sibley Watson, Melville Webber, Herman Weinberg, and Orson Welles. Supporting these filmmakers, at least in the early 1930s, was a network of exhibition outlets, including art theaters, galleries, and amateur film clubs, as well as film publications, all of which constituted an avant-garde movement.

The historical reception of the first American avant-garde is usually characterized by the judgment that it was essentially European in outlook and derivative of 1920s European models, aping expressionism, following the style of the constructivist documentaries, and filming American versions of European avant-garde ideas.[2] In fact, it was the reception of German expressionist films, like THE CABINET OF DR. CALIGARI, and Soviet revolutionary narratives, like BATTLESHIP POTEMKIN, in the mid 1920s that spurred American filmmakers to attempt the production of experimental films. In these American films, as well as in the

European avant-garde films trickling over to the United States, film lovers perceived a clear alternative to the generic conventions of Hollywood.

A crucial difference to understanding the dynamics of the 1920s and 1930s avant-garde in relation to its post–World War II American experimental film successors involves the self-images and material conditions of the two generations. Both defined themselves in opposition to commercial, narrative cinema, privileging the personal over the pecuniary. However, while the 1950s avant-gardists proclaimed themselves to be artists of cinema, actively engaged in the production of "art," those of the earlier generation viewed themselves as cineastes, as lovers of cinema, as amateurs willing to work in any arena furthering the cause of film art, even if it involved commercial productions.

In contrast, the second American film avant-garde's aesthetics, defined exclusively as means of personal expression, forced this generation to reject any collaboration with Hollywood or other commercial interests. Its aesthetics expanded into a political position opposing any utilitarian usage of the medium, be it commercial, instructional, or ideological. Ironically, such self-conscious declarations about the avant-gardist's role as film artist led to a professionalization of the avant-garde project. Of his own generation, Jonas Mekas noted, "To former generations film art was something still new and exotic, but for this generation it is part of our lives, like bread, music, trees, or steel bridges."[3]

This professionalization of avant-garde filmmaking was, of course, only possible because the institutions providing material support for the avant-garde had expanded to include university film courses (offering filmmakers a place to earn money while making their films) and nontheatrical film exhibition within the institutional framework of museums, archives, and media centers (offering filmmakers a place to show their work).

Earlier filmmakers, in contrast, thought of themselves much more as film amateurs rather than as professionals. Avant-garde filmmakers in the 1920s defined themselves in opposition to the professional, who was an employee of Hollywood, for hire to produce a profit benefiting the corporate hierarchy rather than the cause of film art. Given this self-image, the agenda of the first American film avant-garde was much broader: to improve the quality of all films, whether personal or professional. These cineastes moved freely between avant-garde film and other endeavors—documentary, industrials, Hollywood narrative, film criticism, film exhibition, painting, and photography.

Lewis Jacobs, for example, then a member of a Philadelphia amateur film club, noted of his group, "Our club is composed of painters, dancers, and illustrators. . . . It is our aim to emphasize a direction that will result in cinematic form."[4] As a paradigmatic example of the contemporary 1920s cineaste, one might fruitfully look at the career of Herman G. Weinberg. In the late 1920s and early 1930s he worked as a manager for a "little theater" in Baltimore, wrote film criticism for various magazines, and made avant-garde shorts.[5] His plethora of activity in different cinematic endeavors was also economically determined, since no single effort offered a livelihood.

As a result of such factors, it is extremely difficult, for example, to separate avant-garde film production from the production of documentary films in the 1930s. Numerous filmmakers, including Roger Barlow, Paul Strand, Willard Van Dyke, LeRoy Robbins, Henwar Rodakiewicz, and Ralph Steiner, not only earned their livelihood during the Great Depression through organizational, governmental, and private documentary film production but actually perceived such activity as a continuation of their experimentation with cinematic form.

Ironically, the desire to improve the status of the film medium on many different fronts was characteristic of both the 1920s European avant-garde—a fact that has been often suppressed by later historians[6]—and the first American avant-garde. Both European and American avant-gardists entered film as amateurs, because economics dictated it. At the same time, amateurs turned professionals, like Walter Ruttmann, Hans Richter, and René Clair, among others, thought of their contract and personal work as of a piece. Whether "city films" by Joris Ivens or Wilfried Basse or scientific views of sea life by Jan Mol, these documentaries were considered to constitute avant-garde cinema. Thus, both Europeans and Americans shared a broader, inclusionist, rather than exclusionist, view of good cinema.

While the first avant-garde pioneered alternative forms that survived on the fringes of institutional power, it was unable to support itself economically, because the avant-garde itself had not been embraced by institutions that could have created the material conditions for its continued survival. A history of early American avant-garde, then, cannot help but broaden its definition to include other noncommercial film forms, such as amateur film and documentary, as well as unrealized film projects, film criticism, and film reception.

Early American avant-garde film indeed identified itself with amateurism. As C. Adolph Glassgold wrote programmatically in *The Arts*, "The artistic future of the motion picture in America rests in the hands of the amateur."[7] The cause of both avant-garde and amateur film were advanced by the introduction in 1924 of 16-mm film by Eastman Kodak Company and the easy-to-use Cine-Kodak 16-mm camera, much as most World War II experimental film movements were technologically grounded in the less expensive 16-mm format. The new technology was not only cheaper and safer than 35-mm nitrate film but also in many ways more versatile, allowing for hand-held cameras, location shooting, and filming under ambient light conditions. The Cine-Kodak allowed every man and woman potentially to become a film artist.

For Herman Weinberg, the avant-garde constituted itself everywhere beyond the realm of Hollywood narrative. The amateur film enthusiast was seen as the most ardent supporter of an avant-garde. Even professionals could become amateurs, as Weinberg explained in the case of Robert Florey: "It was only when he was working on his own, after studio hours, with borrowed equipment, scanty film, a volunteer cast and the most elemental of props, that, released from the tenets of the film factories, he was able to truly express himself in cinematic terms."[8] Professionalism was thus equated with commercialism, while amateurism connoted artistic integrity. Such a discourse clearly identified personal expression with formal experimentation, a dualism repeated continuously in aesthetic manifestos and reviews. The emphasis on formalism is echoed by Frederick Kiesler: "In the film, as in every other art, everything depends on *how* its mediums (means) are utilized and not on *what* is employed."[9] Finally, according to contemporary observers around 1930, the total dominance of the professional and commercial sphere by sound technology meant that formal experimentation would necessarily migrate into the amateur realm: "If all the professional money goes into sound, the semi-professional and the amateur, with little money to spend, will carry on and exploit the purely cinematic qualities of the movie."[10]

The cause of the avant-garde and amateurs was given a concrete organizational form with the founding of the Amateur Cinema League in 1926, led in its early years by the inventor Hiram Percy Maxim. By June 1927, there were an estimated thirty thousand amateur filmmakers in the United States alone.[11] In 1928 there were more than 103 amateur cinema clubs organized in the United States and abroad, with more than twenty-three hundred members in the Amateur Cinema League, all of whom were producing amateur films.[12]

In any discussion of the role of the amateur in the growth of the first avant-garde, the role of the Amateur Cinema League (ACL) cannot be over-stated.[13] Undoubtedly, it was the most audience-rich center for the exhibition of avant-garde films. The league had begun to organize a lending library as early as 1927. Arthur Gale wrote of the library's purpose, "This will provide an adequate distribution of amateur photoplays, secure a dependable event for club programs and, as well, encourage new groups to undertake amateur productions."[14] The Amateur Cinema League became a major outlet for the exhibition of avant-garde films, since local clubs in countless American cities had an insatiable demand for films that could be screened at their monthly gatherings. The Amateur Cinema League's lending library included THE FALL OF THE HOUSE OF USHER (James Sibley Watson and Melville Webber, 1928), THE TELL-TALE HEART (Charles Klein, 1928), H$_2$O (Ralph Steiner, 1929), PORTRAIT OF A YOUNG MAN (Henwar Rodakiewicz, 1932), LOT IN SODOM (Watson and Webber, 1932), MR. MOTOR-BOAT'S LAST STAND (Theodore Huff and John Florey, 1933), and ANOTHER DAY (Molly Day Thatcher, 1934), all of which were screened extensively throughout the United States. THE FALL OF THE HOUSE OF USHER, one of the most popular, experienced literally hundreds of screenings in ACL clubs.[15] While the Amateur Cinema League's interests turned in the 1930s increasingly to travelogues and other forms of home movies, these avant-garde films were still available through the league in the early 1950s.

The Amateur Cinema League's yearly film contest was won by such avant-garde films as PORTRAIT OF A YOUNG MAN, LOT IN SODOM, and MR. MOTOR-BOAT'S LAST STAND. *Photoplay* and *Liberty* magazines and other organizations also staged amateur film contests, which offered public exposure to independent filmmakers. For example, in 1937 *Liberty* announced an amateur contest, sponsored by Metro-Goldwyn-Mayer's Pete Smith Specialties series, which led to the production of EVEN AS YOU AND I (1937) by LeRoy Robbins, Roger Barlow, and Harry Hay.[16]

Just as avant-garde film production created an alternative discourse on filmmaking, so, too, did the "little-cinema movement" provide both an exhibi-tion outlet for avant-garde and European art films and an alternative to the commercial cinema chains, dominated by the major Hollywood studios. The establishment of art cinemas was apparently first suggested in March 1922 by the National Board of Review magazine *Exceptional Photoplays*.[17] In that article, the founding of a little cinema movement was specifically tied to the growth of avant-garde cinema: "The showing of experimental pictures in a special theatre or series of theatres, and the building up of an audience, would naturally be

James Sibley Watson's LOT IN SODOM *(1934) typifies the crossover from amatuerism to avant-garde.*

followed by the actual making of experimental pictures. Directors and actors, stimulated by what they had seen in this theatre and encouraged by the reception of new work, would feel impelled to try their hand."[18]

Three years later, the little-cinema movement took off with the foundation of the Screen Guild in New York and a series of Sunday films at the Central Theater in New York, organized by Symon Gould. Within a few years little cinemas sprang up all over the United States. In spring 1927 the Little Theatre of the Motion Picture Guild, under the management of John Mulligan, was opened in Washington, D.C., the first little cinema outside New York City. This was followed by the Little Theatre of the Movies in Cleveland in late 1927, followed almost immediately by one in Chicago. A. W. Newman, director of the Cleveland cinema, specifically referred to the exhibition of short films, which "represent important experimentation," as a part of its mandate.[19]

In Hollywood the Filmarte was founded in 1928 by Regge Doran;[20] other little theaters were located in Boston (Fine Arts Theatre), Rochester (Little Theatre), New York (Carnegie Playhouse), Buffalo (Motion Picture Guild), Baltimore (Little Theatre), Philadelphia (Motion Picture Guild), Brooklyn (St. George's

LOT IN SODOM *mixed European modernism and American eclecticism.*

Playhouse/Brooklyn Film Guild), and East Orange, N.J. (Oxford Theatre).[21] The Motion Picture Guild, under the direction of Robert F. Bogatin, operated the theaters in Philadelphia, Buffalo, Cleveland, and Rochester.

Not surprisingly, art cinema programs often paired American avant-garde films with European, especially German and Russian features. This mixture was specifically commented on by Theodore Dreiser in the new Film Guild's inaugural program in February 1929: "The little cinema theatres, which should, and I hope will, act as havens for artistic American as well as European productions and such experimental efforts of 'amateurs' here as many have the real interests of the screen as art truly at heart."[22]

Likewise, Robert Florey's THE LIFE AND DEATH OF 9413—A HOLLYWOOD EXTRA (1928) played at the Philadelphia Motion Picture Guild with the German-Indian production, DIE LEUCHTE ASIENS (1926), while Florey's second film, THE LOVES OF ZERO (1929), was billed at the Los Angeles Filmarte Theater with Gösta Ekman's KLOVEN (1927). STORY OF A NOBODY (Jo Gerson and Louis Hirshman, 1930) was exhibited with Paul Fejos's arty Universal feature THE LAST PERFORMANCE (1929),[23] while Charles Vidor's THE SPY/THE BRIDGE (1931) premiered at the Hollywood Filmarte Theatre with another European feature.[24]

Watson and Webber's TOMATOES' ANOTHER DAY *(1930) parodied early sound cinema.*

Ralph Steiner's MECHANICAL PRINCIPLES *(1930) was also exhibited in an art gallery.*

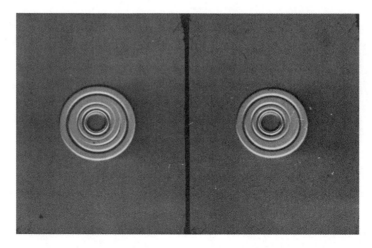

RHYTHMS IN LIGHT *(1934)*. *Mary Ellen Bute took up the legacy of Eggeling, Richter, and Ruttmann.*

John Florey and Theodore Huff's avant-garde short MR. MOTORBOAT'S LAST STAND *(1933), very much a document of the Great Depression, allegorized the economic rat race.*

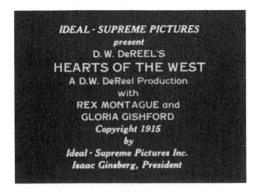 

HEARTS OF THE WEST *(1931). Theodore Huff's parody of D. W. Griffith and his Victorian melodrama.*

A debutante makes good in Ralph Steiner's PANTHER WOMAN OF THE NEEDLE TRADE . . .*(1931).*

PIE IN THE SKY *(1934)*.

Ironically, obituaries for the little-cinema movement appeared as early as 1929, when the movement was far from spent. John Hutchens's article in the September 1929 *Theatre Arts* noted, "That their bright day is done and they are for the dark, within only four years of their inception, is the unhappy comment on an art movement that from the first was characterized not so much by art as by a truly astonishing lack of foresight, and later by merely bad business methods."[25] Given the fact that Hutchens wrongly proclaimed the demise of at least two cinemas, it seems clear that another agenda was at work. In fact, the author found many of the foreign films distasteful, "static and inferior" (a consistent criticism of European "art" films from American film industry allies), noting that the little cinemas had "little or nothing to offer" and accusing Gould's Film Guild, for example, of showing too many Russian films. Indeed, it was not inferior foreign films, but rather the worsening economic climate that contributed to the demise of little cinemas. But that would take a few more years.

Art galleries were another potential site for avant-garde exhibitions. Paul Strand and Charles Sheeler's MANHATTA (1921) had of course been shown at Marius DeZayas's New York gallery. Jay Leyda's A BRONX MORNING (1931) was premiered at the Julien Levy Gallery in New York, as were Lynn Riggs's A DAY IN SANTA FE (1931), Henwar Rodakiewicz's PORTRAIT OF A YOUNG MAN (1932), and Joseph Cornell's ROSE HOBART (1936). Presenting European avant-garde films as well, Julien Levy in fact built up a substantial collection of avant-garde films, which he hoped "to display on request."[26] Rodakiewicz's and Leyda's films were also shown at Alfred Stieglitz's An American Place, another occasional showcase for American avant-garde films.[27]

Other kinds of distribution were haphazard at best, usually dependent on the filmmaker himself renting the film to individual exhibition outlets. Symon Gould, the founder of the Cinema Guild, did apparently set up some kind of distribution network, renting films to both the little cinemas and commercial theaters. However, any profits realized never made their way back to the filmmakers. Strand and Sheeler, for example, complained that their film MANHATTA disappeared after Gould got the print. Robert Florey was even more specific about promises made to him: "Early in 1928, Mr. Symon Gould, then manager of the 8th Street Cinema Playhouse in New York, offered to give World Wide exploitation to my experimental shorts . . . and to that effect I gave him *all* the negatives and prints that I had. I regret to say that I have not heard from Mr. Gould since 1929, and I have never received an account of the rentals or sales of my pictures."[28] When in 1950 Frank Stauffacher, programmer for the Art in Cinema series at the San Francisco Museum of Modern Art (1946–1951), asked Gould about the existence of certain avant-garde prints, Gould answered (on Film Guild letterhead) that he would be glad to undertake a search, for a $25 fee.[29]

Even by the late 1940s, the field of avant-garde film distribution had not changed substantially. Thus, both Stauffacher and Amos Vogel at Cinema 16 in New York could not fall back on established distribution outlets for avant-garde film, but were dependent on personal contacts to find films and filmmakers, usually borrowing films directly from the makers for about $10 per film.

Meanwhile, film magazines, including *Close Up*, published in Switzerland in English, and *Experimental Film*, edited by Seymour Stern and Lewis Jacobs, functioned as critical voices in the discourse around both European and American art film. *Close Up*, in particular through its American contributors, Harry A. Potamkin and Herman G. Weinberg, documented the achievements of the American avant-garde from 1927 to 1934. *Experimental Film*, which published between 1931 and 1934, concerned itself more with leftist filmmaking, but also wrote about avant-garde efforts. *Amateur Movie Makers*, the official organ of the Amateur Cinema League, also reported on the avant-garde, but became aesthetically more conservative in the mid 1930s.

The charge that early American avant-garde efforts emulated their European colleagues was not totally without merit, given the intense reception of European modernist films in America.[30] However, it is also true that American avant-garde films demonstrated a certain wild eclecticism, innovativeness, and at times naïveté, which made them qualitatively different from European films. Furthermore, the American avant-garde evidences antimodernist and romantic currents, which not only separate it from European models but also connect it directly to the later American experimentalists, like Stan Brakhage and Kenneth Anger.

While the American avant-garde film of the 1920s seemed to focus more on abstract and formalist experimentation, moving from the modernist vision of Strand and Sheeler's MANHATTA to the new realist abstraction of Steiner's H_2O, and from Warren Newcombe's animated dreamscapes in THE ENCHANTED CITY (1922) to Robert Florey's expressionist THE LOVES OF ZERO (1929), the 1930s avant-garde seemed, in general, to gravitate toward metaphor and parody, possibly a sign of the increasingly difficult times. Those filmmakers who eschewed the symbolic created documentary portraits or fiction shorts infused with lyrical realism, the latter often leading directly to a Hollywood career.

As a paradigmatic case of the amateur avant-gardist working in different genres, one can look Dr. James Sibley Watson. Born in 1894 to a prominent Rochester family, Watson was a medical doctor by profession. In 1928 he collaborated with Melville Webber on THE FALL OF THE HOUSE OF USHER, which was shot in his garage with a homemade optical printer.[31] His TOMATOES' ANOTHER DAY (1930) is a unique example of dadaist aesthetics in early sound cinema: a minimalist, virtually expressionless acting style on a claustrophobic set characterizes the melodramatic love triangle, with the actors verbalizing their every action, ironically commenting on the oververbalization of early sound films. After attempting to start a local newsreel—three issues were completed—Watson produced two industrial films that made heavy use of avant-garde techniques, THE EYES OF SCIENCE (1931, for Bausch & Lomb) and HIGHLIGHTS AND SHADOWS (1935, for Eastman Kodak). The EYES OF SCIENCE was in fact shown at amateur cinema clubs as an example of avant-garde filmmaking in the educational field.

Watson collaborated again with Melville Webber on LOT IN SODOM, which premiered at the Little Carnegie Theatre on 25 December 1933 along with Josef Berne's DAWN TO DAWN. It continued to play in gay theaters throughout the 1930s and 1940s, becoming in the process probably the most commercially successful avant-garde film of the era. Herman Weinberg wrote ecstatically about the film: "I have never seen light manipulated so eloquently as in these expressive lights and shadows which sometimes form men or fragments of a body."[32] While ostensibly a narrative of the biblical tale of Lot and his wife, who was turned into a pillar of salt while fleeing Sodom, the film is much more concerned with nonnarrative elements: the play of light and shadow, the balletic movement of bodies, the use of multiple exposures and optical tricks, and the poetic utilization of visual symbolism. The film's imagery is also highly erotic, especially in the scenes in which Lot offers his daughter to the angel, and homoerotic, especially in its light play on seminude bodies of numerous young men. Working without dialogue and with sparse titles superimposed in English and Latin, the film features atonal music by Louis Siegel that underscores the film's modernist construction.

Another important avant-garde filmmaker to emerge in the early 1930s was Lewis Jacobs, whose 1947 article on avant-garde filmmaking in America remains a seminal piece.[33] Jacobs helped found an amateur cinema club in Philadelphia in the late 1920s, with Jo Gerson and Louis Hirshman. Together they produced MOBILE COMPOSITION (1930), a film that apparently has not survived. Jacobs described the film as a story about a love affair in which "significant details, contrast lighting, double exposures, and large close-ups depicted the growing strain of disturbed emotions."[34]

Jacobs went on to work as a documentary filmmaker and as the founding editor of *Experimental Cinema*. While shooting footage for the Film and Photo League and working as a cutter for advertising films, Jacobs began a project, AS I WALK, which remained unfinished, except for a fragment, later called FOOTNOTE TO FACT (1934). It is a portrait of a young woman expressed in images ostensibly flashing through her mind, with documentary shots of street life in New York. Jacob's intercutting between shots of the woman and her subjective views of reality accelerates until the film comes to a climax.[35]

In the mid 1930s Lewis Jacobs collaborated with the photographer Thomas Bouchard and the dancer John Bovington to produce a dance film, UNDERGROUND PRINTER (1934). Bouchard, who was best known for his photographic portraits of well-known theater personalities, probably brought Jacobs and Bovington together. According to an ancient rental catalog, Bovington appeared in a solo dance in the film that could be interpreted as "an artistic attack on the type of machine-made thinking which produced the Nazi menace in Europe."[36] However, Bovington, who apparently financed the film, had a falling-out with the two filmmakers, because it was taken out of their hands and reedited by Bovington.[37]

Meanwhile, Gerson and Hirshman, who were both trained as painters, decided to remake MOBILE COMPOSITION without actors, calling it STORY OF A NOBODY (1930). They attempted to recreate the subjective views of the two lovers, defining them metaphorically through objects rather than actions.[38] Utilizing a symphonic structure, the film consisted of numerous close-ups edited together through dissolves, laps, and quick cutting, depending on the rhythm of the scene. The film was hailed as a revelation by critic Harry A. Potemkin and the National Board of Review.[39]

Best known as a painter and sculptor, Joseph Cornell produced his first film in 1936, ROSE HOBART. A nineteen-minute (at silent speed) reediting of Universal Pictures' EAST OF BORNEO (1931), a jungle adventure thriller that starred Rose Hobart and Charles Bickford, with a few snippets from scientific instructional films thrown in, Cornell's film is, like his famous collage boxes, essentially a creation out of *objets trouvés*. Completely eliminating any semblence of plot and dialogue, Cornell's montage of the ostensible heroine, hero, and villain has them moving in slow motion through empty rooms, caressing curtains, reacting to unseen events, never meeting. Their looks lead nowhere, their erotic desires careen into a void, while the audience is left with a mystery, with the film's purple-tinted eroticism masking an unfulfilled desire. Cornell thereby subverted not only the standard conventions of Hollywood filmmaking but also the viewer's expectations of finding meaning. True to the surrealist creed, ROSE HOBART is ambiguously meaningful without meaning.

Jerome Hill, later known for his film animation, began his career in the 1930s.[40] Born into a wealthy Minneapolis family, Hill moved to Europe in 1927, where he was inspired by French surrealist films. In 1932 he purchased a 16-mm Kodak Special and shot THE FORTUNE TELLER in Cassis, a fishing village in the South of France.[41] True to the title, the film has mystical overtones, its narrative constructed from seemingly unconnected images: a young woman hanging wash, a walk along the surf, a consultation with a gypsy fortune teller, a man rising up out of the sea. Apart from their pictorial beauty, the film's images seem to hold some primordial meaning connected to fertility rites, to mystical love and romantic fate, yet they remain ambiguous, like the old gypsy's fortune, as visualized in the cards. The film's overall romantic text thus seems to conflict with the modernist impulse of the film's construction.

In contrast to the earnest metaphors of Watson and Webber and others, parody was the preferred genre of Theodore Huff, another prominent Amateur Cinema League member. Later known as a film historian and Chaplin biographer, Huff directed 16-mm spoofs of Hollywood genre films in the early 1930s.

His first two productions, HEARTS OF THE WEST (1931) and LITTLE GEEZER (1932), starred children, burlesquing the conventions of Westerns and gangster films, respectively. (He shot them under the pseudonym of D. W. DeReel.) Both films imitated the conventions of silent film, its stereotypical characters and naive plots, the sentimentality of D. W. Griffith, and the innocence of the era. About his use of child actors, Huff wrote, "We have found children under twelve best suited as actors for these pictures. The contrast in size with the original adult actors brings out, more sharply, the incongruity necessary to satire."[42] Using children emphasized that the cinema was indeed in its infancy, but it also gave the films an ambiguous sexuality, implicating the subject in the director's slightly perverse gaze.

MR. MOTORBOAT'S LAST STAND (1933), Theodore Huff and John Florey's 16-mm silent Depression comedy, is a much less self-conscious work, an ironic comment on America's inability to deal with the economic catastrophe of the 1930s. The story of an unemployed black who lives in a junkyard, the film uses a garbage dump as a metaphor for capitalism's treatment of ordinary citizens. Living in an abandoned car that in fantasy is a limousine taking him to Wall Street, where his business is located (an apple stand), the hero suffers through the crash of 1929 and the Depression. MR. MOTORBOAT is, in fact, a humorous allegory on America's economic rise and fall, employing visual metaphor in the manner of medieval morality plays, where images communicate their meaning quite literally, such as a bursting bubble becoming the "exploding prosperity bubble" of the 1920s. After working as a film curator, Huff returned to filmmaking in the late 1940s.

The photographer Ralph Steiner, who had been making abstract avant-garde films in the late 1920s, contributed his own parody of American economic life with PANTHER WOMAN OF THE NEEDLE TRADES, OR THE LOVELY LIFE OF LITTLE LISA (1931). The film, which opens with Jehovah (Morris Carnovsky) creating the world out of a test tube, proceeds to present a short history of the universe before the birth of Elizabeth Hawes (1903), the heroine of the film's title. It then follows her career from childhood seamstress to Parisian designer of haute couture via a college education at Vassar. Reminiscent of Robert Florey's THE LIFE AND DEATH OF 9413—A HOLLYWOOD EXTRA (1928) in terms of its art direction and elliptical narrative style, PANTHER WOMAN is a parody of the all-American success story, a young woman's fantasy of a glamorous career in an age of diminishing possibilities.

Ralph Steiner also collaborated on PIE IN THE SKY (1934) with Elia Kazan, Irving Lerner, and Molly Day Thatcher. Produced by a left-wing collective around the Group Theater, PIE IN THE SKY is a parody of organized religion's efforts to convince the working classes that their day will come in heaven, rather than on earth, making any struggle for social improvement futile. In the film, two working-class heroes embark on a quest through society, again represented as a garbage dump, to find something to fill their empty stomachs, but are only served slogans by various authority figures, such as a socialite charity person, a priest, and a welfare bureaucrat. The "piece of the pie" remains elusive; the heroes die of starvation and go to heaven, where they encourage the audience to participate in a sing-along (a favorite Depression-era activity in movie theaters). Using polemical statements like just so many advertising campaign slogans, the film indicts the church, the state, and public figures, such as Father Charles Coughlin, as apologists for ruling-class neglect of poverty.

While most avant-garde films discussed here were parodies of mainstream commercial cinema, two films made in the 1930s were parodies of the avant-garde itself. The first was William Vance's THE HEARTS OF AGE (1934) with a nineteen-year-old Orson Welles (who also co-directed and wrote the script) playing a number of male characters. According to Welles, the film was a parody of Jean Cocteau's THE BLOOD OF A POET (1930) and the whole surrealist school.[43] Vance shot the film on 16-mm reversal, his second after completing a parody of DR. JEKYLL AND MR. HYDE in 1932. The film opens with a positive and negative image of a bell ringing in a bell tower. There follow a series of visual nonsequiturs: an old woman ringing a bell, an angel carrying a globe, death stalking corridors, a Keystone-like cop, a man hanging, a hand beckoning from the grave. Like earlier avant-garde films, THE HEARTS OF AGE favors obtuse camera angles, expressionist lighting, and narrative ellipses, utilizing these avant-garde techniques both seriously and with tongue in cheek.[44]

Near the end of the 1930s, Roger Barlow, Harry Hay, and LeRoy Robbins produced their own parody of the avant-garde, EVEN AS YOU AND I (1937). The film was shot in 16-mm, for the most part in the home of LeRoy Robbins, a photographer on a WPA Project in California that included Edward, Brett, and Chan Weston; Roger Barlow; and Hy Hirsh.[45] The three filmmakers began the project after *Liberty* magazine announced a short-film contest sponsored by MGM's Pete Smith Specialties series. The contest in fact became the frame for the film's narrative. EVEN AS YOU AND I, however, failed to win any prizes, although it was shown at the Los Angeles Carpenter's Local Hall, along with Paul Strand's REDES/THE WAVE (1936), and screened by Fred Zinnemann for MGM executives.[46]

Playfully ironic, almost dadaist in construction, the film narrates the attempts of three unemployed young men to make a film for an amateur film contest. After rejecting numerous boy-meets-girl script ideas, the three discover an article on surrealism and proceed randomly to construct a script out of paper scraps. The film within a film is an anarchistic montage of images, which acknowledges its debt to surrealism, Eugène Atget, Donald Duck, Buñuel's UN CHIEN ANDALOU, Hans Richter's GHOSTS BEFORE BREAKFAST, Eisenstein's POTEMKIN, René Clair's ENTR'ACTE, and Leni Riefenstahl's TRIUMPH OF THE WILL. It ends with the three would-be film artists realizing they have missed the deadline for the contest and then attempting to invent a useful gadget for another competition.

Almost postmodern in its use of quotation, EVEN AS YOU AND I also comments on the pressure toward originality when a canon of avant-garde works has already been established. Furthermore, the film refers to the difficulty of becoming a filmmaker and the need to survive economically in a Depression economy. Barlow and Robbins went on to become documentary filmmakers.

One of the preferred genres of both amateur and avant-garde filmmakers was the so-called scenic, which included both city films and more-abstract meditations on nature. Ralph Steiner's SURF AND SEAWEED (1930) fits into the latter category and was possibly a sequel to Steiner's H_2O (1929). A montage of close-up images of the ocean, low-angle shots of waves crashing against the rocks, and extreme close-ups of the swirling patterns of seaweed, the film's rhythm matches the endless to-and-fro of the surf, its images edited together abstractly, like music. In the 1960s this kind of film would be called structural, but in the 1930s they were considered attempts to find abstract patterns in nature, a tradition that had already established itself in Europe.[47]

In the documentary field, Jay Leyda's A BRONX MORNING (1931) is a tribute to one of his favorite photographers, Eugène Atget, a lyrical look at his Bronx neighborhood in the early morning hours before traffic and pedestrians crowd the street. The film opens with moving-camera shots, taken from the elevated train, images that hark back to Walter Ruttmann's BERLIN, SYMPHONY OF A BIG CITY (1927). The following images of storefronts, mannequins, signs, and other objects in the still-deserted streets are the most direct quotations of Atget's surrealistic photographs of Paris. Interestingly, the latter half of the film, beginning with a shot of a mother navigating a pram through the streets, switches to what is essentially a feminine perspective, a world of children, pets, and cleaning. Indeed, there are no images of men working, unlike earlier city portraits, which usually incorporate scenes of labor. Leyda's editing is strongly influenced by the formal and rhythmic patterns of the city films.

Another important city portrait from the early 1930s was Irving Browning's CITY OF CONTRASTS (1931). Released commercially by Sol Lesser with a completely superficial "comic" narration to improve its box-office potential, the film nevertheless merits recognition in terms of its cinematography and sophisticated montage. Browning, a photographer by trade, visually juxtaposes images both formally, contrasting light, shade, and form, and semantically, contrasting various ethnic neighborhoods, skyscrapers, and city parks, the wealthy on Riverside Drive and the shantytown at Hooverville on the Hudson. Its editing is thus much more ambitious than its sound track, yet ultimately the film fails to make any articulate statement.

The critic, film historian, and cinema manager of a little theater in Baltimore, Herman G. Weinberg produced at least two avant-garde films, although apparently the first, CITY SYMPHONY (1930), was cut up to provide footage for the second, AUTUMN FIRE (1931).[48] According to Weinberg, the latter film was a *romance sentimentale*, made as a means of courting a woman he then married, not for public exhibition.[49] The film subjectively portrays two lovers who suffer through their separation until they are reunited at the end. Utilizing a Russian montage style, Weinberg intercuts continually between the two, juxtaposing their environments, identifying the young woman symbolically with nature and the man with the city (New York). Their reunion in the train station is accompanied by an orgy of flowing-water images, an obvious reference to Freud. Thus, the film mixes elements of the city film with a portrait of nature.

Surprisingly, then, most American city films seem to lack the unequivocal celebration of modernism and urbanism found in European city films. In films such as RIEN QUE LES HEURES (Alberto Cavalcanti, 1926), BERLIN, SYMPHONY OF A BIG CITY (Walter Ruttmann, 1927), and MAN WITH A MOVIE CAMERA (Dziga Vertov, 1929), to name a few of the most well known feature films in this subgenre, the urban environment is celebrated for its excitement, speed, and modernity, with few references to nature, beyond its role in leisure-time activities for Sunday picnickers.

This ambivalent attitude toward urban spaces is nowhere as evident as in Willard Van Dyke and Ralph Steiner's government-sponsored documentary THE

CITY (1939), possibly the last of the real city films. In that film, the metropolis is seen as overcrowded, noisy, polluted, and unhealthy; images of smokestacks, traffic jams, and substandard industrial housing predominate. Ironically, the film's montage replicates the aesthetics of the earlier city films. However, the film advocates a form of city planning where living spaces and work spaces are strictly divided, offering residents of newly constructed, clean, green suburbs the nature they supposedly crave but are denied in an urban environment.

Like AUTUMN FIRE, Henwar Rodakiewicz's PORTRAIT OF A YOUNG MAN (1932) is an intensely romantic film, communicating a desire for man's union with nature. The young man of the title in fact never appears in the film; instead, the film presents an abstract montage of mostly close-ups of the sea, clouds, smoke, trees, and man-made machinery. According to Rodakiewicz, the meaning of the whole arises from the sum of its parts: "In creating a film of nature that represents the cameraman's individuality, the importance of selection cannot be overestimated."[50] Divided into three movements, the film owes a debt to Steiner's H_2O, but is indeed more romantic than analytic, its construction based less on formal than emotional values. Rodakiewicz, like Paul Strand and Steiner, went on to become a prominent member of the documentary movement in the 1930s.

Toward the end of the decade, Rudy Burkhardt, a Swiss-born photographer who would become an important figure in the 1950s and 1960s, made his first films with a 16-mm camera. In 1936, Burkhardt shot a little silent comedy about a domestic quarrel with some of his artist friends as actors, 145 WEST 21. That was followed by SEEING THE WORLD—PART ONE: A VISIT TO NEW YORK (1937), a spoof of travelogues.[51] His next film, HAITI (1938), was a travelogue of his ten-month visit to Port-au-Prince, but much more poetic. Using as music Erik Satie's *Trois Gymnopédies,* the film featured leisurely takes of street scenes, sweeping 180-degree pan shots of the town, and close-ups of architectural details and house furnishings. Burkhardt's camera eye is fascinated by the haphazard moment, by the calm surfaces of life in the tropical heat, by the unknowable facts of people caught unaware.

The 1930s also witnessed the emergence of Mary Ellen Bute, an abstract animator whose work has been unfairly neglected, possibly because it was screened commercially. Like Oskar Fischinger, Bute was interested in visualizing music, in creating abstract animated forms to accompany musical pieces. Born in Texas to a wealthy family, Bute began experimenting with animated abstract designs in 1934 when she collaborated with the composer Joseph Schillinger and Lewis Jacobs on an unfinished film.[52] Her second project, RHYTHMS IN LIGHT (1934), made in collaboration with Ted Nemeth (her husband) and Melville Webber, accompanied Grieg's "Anitra's Dance" and was a hit at the Radio City Music Hall. Through high-contrast lighting and multiple exposures of abstract objects, Bute produced an effective method of creating animation in the third dimension, the length of the individual shots and their internal movement worked out with mathematical precision to give visual form to music.

After producing a number of other films in this mode, including SYNCHRONIC-ITY NO. 2 (1935) and ESCAPE (1937), the latter employing Bach's Toccata and Fugue in D Minor, Bute turned to animated color drawings with SPOOK SPORT (1939), made in collaboration with Canadian animator Norman McLaren. Accompanying Saint-Saëns's *Danse Macabre,* the film utilizes anthropomorphic forms, as well as drawings of ghosts, bats, and skeletons. Bute continued producing animation until the early 1950s, when she turned to live-action films.[53]

Finally, a number of short, independently produced, 35-mm fiction films produced in the 1930s have been generally thought of as avant-garde. Charles Vidor's THE SPY/THE BRIDGE (1931) is an adaptation of Ambrose Bierce's short story "An Occurrence at Owl Creek Bridge." Vidor's film uses a flash-forward technique to visualize the escape fantasy of a man condemned to be hanged. Making use of real locations and nonprofessional actors without makeup, the film's quick cutting style, a montage of fantasy and grim reality, effectively creates a mixture of objectivity and inner subjectivity, stretching a few moments into a one-reel film.[54] Vidor went on to a generally undistinguished career as a Hollywood director.

Adapted by Seymour Stern (later a film historian), Josef Berne's DAWN TO DAWN (1934), was, at a length of thirty-five minutes, thought to be an "arty" featurette. It told the story of a young farm girl who comes into conflict with her authoritarian father over a young drifter, leading to the father's death of a stroke, after the young man leaves. Presented in only a few scenes with a cast of unknowns without makeup and virtually silent except for a musical score, the film's strength was its lyrical realism; its pastoral scenes on a real farm, which did not suppress the harsh reality of American agriculture before the age of electricity and machinery; and its explicit seduction scene. Berne remained a virtual unknown, directing Poverty Row productions.

Finally, the Hollywood still photographer Roman Freulich directed a remarkable one-reel short, BROKEN EARTH (1936). It relates the story of a black sharecropper whose son comes down with a fever and is miraculously revived through the father's fervent prayer. Shot in real locations with nonprofessional actors—except for the lead, Clarence Muse—the film's early scenes focus in a highly realistic manner on the incredible hardship of black farmers, with plowing scenes similar in power to those in DAWN TO DAWN, while the latter half demonstrates the centrality of religion to the rural African-American experience. Roman Freulich's earlier directorial effort, THE PRISONER (1934), is another apparently lost avant-garde film.[55]

An important, if isolated figure, whose work still needs to be reassessed is the painter Emlen Etting.[56] Born in Philadelphia in 1905, Etting graduated from Harvard in 1928 and then moved to Paris to study painting with cubist André Lhote. While in Paris, he shot ORLAMONDE (1931) with a 16-mm camera. He returned to Pennsylvania the following year, where he started teaching art at the Tyler School at Temple University and produced POEM 8. His third film, LAUREATE (1939), was shot on 16-mm Kodachrome.

Etting thought of all of his films as film poems "wherein the pictures, their sequence and development are used as in a poem as opposed to the customary story form. . . . In the film poem, music, the dance, the theater and the artist will all work together."[57] ORLAMONDE elaborates on the idea of Mélisande, using as music Alexander Scriabin's *Poem of Fire* and Gustav Holst's "Saturn" from *The Planets*. POEM 8 makes one of the earliest uses of the subjective camera and, according to Amos Vogel, has "retained a certain poetic vitality and verve."[58]

While it is true that material conditions for the production of avant-garde films diminished steadily throughout the decade, especially since exhibition sites became ever fewer, films continued to be made. The surviving films themselves point to the fact that American avant-garde films in the 1930s covered a broad spectrum, from highly symbolic, expressionist works to dadaist satires, from lyric documentaries to abstract animation, from subjective portraits to realistic narrative shorts. All of these genres would indeed be revived in the late 1940s when a new generation of American film avant-gardists would claim their place in the consciousness of art-film audiences.

Appendixes

APPENDIX 1

Variety's Top-Grossing Films
(* designates titles also listed among *Film Daily's* Ten Best.)

1930
*ANNA CHRISTIE (MGM)
BLUSHING BRIDES (MGM)
CAUGHT SHORT (MGM)
COMMON CLAY (Fox)
*THE DIVORCEE (MGM)
THE LOVE PARADE (Paramount)

1931
*CIMARRON (RKO)
DADDY LONG LEGS (Fox)
LITTLE CAESAR (Warner Bros.)
*MIN AND BILL (MGM)
THE SMILING LIEUTENANT
    (Paramount)
TRADER HORN (MGM)

1932
HORSE FEATHERS (Paramount)
BIRD OF PARADISE (RKO)
*BACK STREET (Universal)
WASHINGTON MERRY-GO-ROUND
    (Columbia)
RED DUST (MGM)
*GRAND HOTEL (MGM)
THE BIG BROADCAST (Paramount)

1933
*SHE DONE HIM WRONG (Paramount)
TUGBOAT ANNIE (MGM)
GOLD DIGGERS OF 1933 (Warner Bros.)
*42ND STREET (Warner Bros.)
*LITTLE WOMEN (RKO)
*STATE FAIR (Fox)

1934
I'M NO ANGEL (Paramount)
JUDGE PRIEST (Fox)
*DINNER AT EIGHT (MGM)
*IT HAPPENED ONE NIGHT (Columbia)
THE BOWERY (United Artists)

1935
*MUTINY ON THE BOUNTY (MGM)
TOP HAT (RKO)
*LIVES OF A BENGAL LANCER
    (Paramount)
CHINA SEAS (MGM)
CURLY TOP (20th Century–Fox)
G-MEN (Warner Bros.)
*DAVID COPPERFIELD (United Artists)

1936
MODERN TIMES (United Artists)
*SAN FRANCISCO (MGM)
SWING TIME (RKO)
*THE GREAT ZIEGFELD (MGM)
THE LITTLEST REBEL (20th
    Century–Fox)
ROSE MARIE (MGM)
UNDER TWO FLAGS (20th
    Century–Fox)

1937
MAYTIME (MGM)
*THE GOOD EARTH (MGM)
WAIKIKI WEDDING (Paramount)
*LOST HORIZON (Columbia)
*THE PRISONER OF ZENDA (United
    Artists)
AFTER THE THIN MAN (MGM)
THE PLAINSMAN (Paramount)
*A STAR IS BORN (United Artists)

1938
*SNOW WHITE AND THE SEVEN DWARFS
    (RKO)
*ALEXANDER'S RAGTIME BAND (20th
    Century–Fox)
TEST PILOT (MGM)
*IN OLD CHICAGO (20th Century–Fox)
*THE HURRICANE (United Artists)

*THE ADVENTURES OF ROBIN HOOD
  (Warner Bros.)
*MARIE ANTOINETTE (MGM)
*LOVE FINDS ANDY HARDY (MGM)

  1939
*THE WIZARD OF OZ (MGM)

*GOODBYE, MR. CHIPS (MGM)
*PYGMALION (MGM)
*BOYS TOWN (MGM)
*THE OLD MAID (Warner Bros.)
*DARK VICTORY (Warner Bros.)

Major Academy Awards

1930–1931

Picture	CIMARRON (RKO), produced by William LeBaron
Actor	Lionel Barrymore in A FREE SOUL (MGM)
Actress	Marie Dressler in MIN AND BILL (MGM)
Director	Norman Taurog for SKIPPY (Paramount)
Writing	
(Adaptation)	CIMARRON (RKO)—Howard Estabrook
(Original story)	THE DAWN PATROL (Warner Bros.)—John Monk Saunders
Cinematography	TABU (Paramount)—Floyd Crosby
Interior Decoration	CIMARRON (RKO)—Max Ree
Sound Recording	Paramount Studio Sound Department

1931–1932

Picture	GRAND HOTEL (MGM), produced by Irving Thalberg
Actor	Wallace Beery in THE CHAMP (MGM)
	Fredric March in DR. JEKYLL AND MR. HYDE (Paramount)
Actress	Helen Hayes in THE SIN OF MADELON CLAUDET (MGM)
Director	Frank Borzage for BAD GIRL (Fox)
Writing	
(Adaptation)	BAD GIRL (Fox)—Edwin Burke
(Original story)	THE CHAMP (MGM)—Frances Marion
Cinematography	SHANGHAI EXPRESS (Paramount)—Lee Garmes
Interior Decoration	TRANSATLANTIC (Fox)—Gordon Wiles
Sound Recording	Paramount Studio Sound Department

1932–1933

Picture	CAVALCADE (Fox), Winfield Sheehan, studio head
Actor	Charles Laughton in THE PRIVATE LIFE OF HENRY VIII (London Films, United Artists)
Actress	Katharine Hepburn in MORNING GLORY (RKO)
Director	Frank Lloyd for CAVALCADE (Fox)
Writing	
(Adaptation)	LITTLE WOMEN (RKO)—Victor Heerman and Sarah Y. Mason
(Original story)	ONE WAY PASSAGE (Warner Bros.)—Robert Lord
Cinematography	A FAREWELL TO ARMS (Paramount)—Charles Bryant Lang, Jr.
Interior Decoration	CAVALCADE (Fox)—William S. Darling
Sound Recording	A FAREWELL TO ARMS (Paramount)—Harold C. Lewis

1934

Picture	IT HAPPENED ONE NIGHT (Columbia), produced by Harry Cohn
Actor	Clark Gable in IT HAPPENED ONE NIGHT (Columbia)
Actress	Claudette Colbert in IT HAPPENED ONE NIGHT (Columbia)
Director	Frank Capra for IT HAPPENED ONE NIGHT (Columbia)
Writing	
(Adaptation)	IT HAPPENED ONE NIGHT (Columbia)—Robert Riskin
(Original story)	MANHATTAN MELODRAMA (MGM)—Arthur Caesar

Cinematography	CLEOPATRA (Paramount)—Victor Milner
Interior Design	THE MERRY WIDOW (MGM)—Cedric Gibbons and Frederic Hope
Sound Recording	ONE NIGHT OF LOVE (Columbia)—Paul Neal
Music	
(Song)	"The Continental" (THE GAY DIVORCEE, RKO)—Music by Con Conrad; lyrics by Herb Magidson
(Score)	ONE NIGHT OF LOVE—Columbia Studio Music Department, Louis Silvers, head; thematic music by Victor Schertzinger and Gus Kahn
Film Editing	ESKIMO (MGM)—Conrad Nervig

1935

Picture	MUTINY ON THE BOUNTY (MGM), produced by Irving Thalberg, with Albert Lewin
Actor	Victor McLaglen in THE INFORMER (RKO)
Actress	Bette Davis in DANGEROUS (Warner Bros.)
Director	John Ford for THE INFORMER (RKO)
Writing	
(Original story)	THE SCOUNDREL (Paramount)—Ben Hecht and Charles MacArthur
(Screenplay)	THE INFORMER (RKO)—Dudley Nichols
Cinematography	A MIDSUMMER NIGHT'S DREAM (Warner Bros.)—Hal Mohr
Interior Decoration	THE DARK ANGEL (Goldwyn, United Artists)—Richard Day
Sound Recording	NAUGHTY MARIETTA (MGM)—Douglas Shearer
Music	
(Song)	"Lullaby of Broadway" (GOLD DIGGERS OF 1935, Warner Bros.)—Music by Harry Warren; lyrics by Al Dubin
(Score)	THE INFORMER—RKO Radio Studio Music Department, Max Steiner, head; score by Max Steiner
Film Editing	A MIDSUMMER NIGHT'S DREAM (Warner Bros.)—Ralph Dawson

1936

Picture	THE GREAT ZIEGFELD (MGM), produced by Hunt Stromberg
Actor	Paul Muni in THE STORY OF LOUIS PASTEUR (Warner Bros.)
Actress	Luise Rainer in THE GREAT ZIEGFELD (MGM)
Director	Frank Capra for MR. DEEDS GOES TO TOWN (Columbia)
Writing	
(Original story)	THE STORY OF LOUIS PASTEUR (Warner Bros.)—Pierre Collings and Sheridan Gibney
(Screenplay)	THE STORY OF LOUIS PASTEUR (Warner Bros.)—Pierre Collings and Sheridan Gibney
Cinematography	ANTHONY ADVERSE (Warner Bros.)—Gaetano (Tony) Gaudio
Interior Decoration	DODSWORTH (Goldwyn, United Artists)—Richard Day
Sound Recording	SAN FRANCISCO (MGM)—Douglas Shearer
Music	
(Song)	"The Way You Look Tonight" (SWING TIME, RKO)—Music by Jerome Kern; lyrics by Dorothy Field
(Score)	ANTHONY ADVERSE—Warner Bros. Studio Music Department, Leo Forbstein, head; score by Erich Wolfgang Korngold
Film Editing	ANTHONY ADVERSE (Warner Bros.)—Ralph Dawson

1937

Picture	THE LIFE OF EMILE ZOLA (Warner Bros.), produced by Henry Blanke
Actor	Spencer Tracy in CAPTAINS COURAGEOUS (MGM)
Actress	Luise Rainer in THE GOOD EARTH (MGM)
Director	Leo McCarey for THE AWFUL TRUTH (Columbia)
Writing	
(Original story)	A STAR IS BORN (Selznick, United Artists)—William A. Wellman and Robert Carson
(Screenplay)	THE LIFE OF EMILE ZOLA (Warner Bros.)—Heinz Herald, Geza Herczeg, and Norman Reilly Raine
Cinematography	THE GOOD EARTH (MGM)—Karl Freund
Interior Decoration	LOST HORIZON (Columbia)—Stephen Goosson
Sound Recording	THE HURRICANE (Goldwyn, United Artists)—Thomas Moulton
Music	
(Song)	"Sweet Leilani" (WAIKIKI WEDDING, Paramount)—Music and lyrics by Harry Owens
(Score)	ONE HUNDRED MEN AND A GIRL—Universal Studio Music Department, Charles Previn, head
Film Editing	LOST HORIZON (Columbia)—Gene Havlick and Gene Milford

1938

Picture	YOU CAN'T TAKE IT WITH YOU (Columbia), produced by Frank Capra
Actor	Spencer Tracy in BOYS TOWN (MGM)
Actress	Bette Davis in JEZEBEL (Warner Bros.)
Director	Frank Capra for YOU CAN'T TAKE IT WITH YOU (Columbia)
Writing	
(Original story)	BOYS TOWN (MGM)—Eleanor Griffin and Dore Schary
(Screenplay)	PYGMALION (MGM)—George Bernard Shaw; adaptation by Ian Dalrymple, Cecil Lewis, and W. P. Lipscomb
Cinematography	THE GREAT WALTZ (MGM)—Joseph Ruttenberg
Interior Decoration	THE ADVENTURES OF ROBIN HOOD (Warner Bros.)—Carl J. Weyl
Sound Recording	THE COWBOY AND THE LADY (Goldwyn, United Artists)—Thomas Moulton
Music	
(Song)	"Thanks for the Memory" (THE BIG BROADCAST OF 1938, Paramount)—Music by Ralph Rainger; lyrics by Leo Robin
(Score)	ALEXANDER'S RAGTIME BAND (20th Century–Fox)—Alfred Newman
(Original score)	THE ADVENTURES OF ROBIN HOOD (Warner Bros.)—Erich Wolfgang Korngold
Film Editing	THE ADVENTURES OF ROBIN HOOD (Warner Bros.)—Ralph Dawson

1939

Picture	GONE WITH THE WIND (Selznick, MGM), produced by David O. Selznick
Actor	Robert Donat in GOODBYE, MR. CHIPS (MGM)
Actress	Vivien Leigh in GONE WITH THE WIND (Selznick, MGM)
Director	Victor Fleming for GONE WITH THE WIND (Selznick, MGM)

Writing
   (Original story)   MR. SMITH GOES TO WASHINGTON (Columbia)—Lewis R. Foster

   (Screenplay)   GONE WITH THE WIND (Selznick, MGM)—Sidney Howard

Cinematography
   (Black-and-white)   WUTHERING HEIGHTS (Goldwyn, United Artists)—Gregg Toland

   (Color)   GONE WITH THE WIND (Selznick, MGM)—Ernest Haller and Ray Rennahan

Interior Decoration   GONE WITH THE WIND (Selznick, MGM)—Lyle Wheeler

Sound Recording   WHEN TOMORROW COMES (Universal)—Bernard B. Brown

Music
   (Song)   "Over the Rainbow" (WIZARD OF OZ, MGM)—Music by Harold Arlen; lyrics by E. Y. Harburg

   (Score)   STAGECOACH (Walter Wanger, United Artists)—Richard Hageman, Frank Harling, John Leipold, and Leo Shuken

   (Original score)   THE WIZARD OF OZ (MGM—Herbert Stothart

Film Editing   GONE WITH THE WIND (Selznick, MGM)—Hal C. Kern and James E. Newcom

Special Effects   THE RAINS CAME (20th Century–Fox)—Photographic, E. H. Hansen; sound, Fred Sersen

SOURCE: Mason Wiley and Damien Bona, *Inside Oscar: The Unofficial History of the Academy Awards* (New York: Ballantine Books, 1986)

APPENDIX 3

Film Daily's Ten Best Films

(* designates titles also listed among *Variety*'s top-grossing films)

1930

ALL QUIET ON THE WESTERN FRONT
(Universal)
ABRAHAM LINCOLN (United Artists)
HOLIDAY (Pathé)
JOURNEY'S END
(Tiffany-Gainsborough)
*ANNA CHRISTIE (MGM)
THE BIG HOUSE (MGM)
WITH BYRD AT THE SOUTH POLE
(Paramount)
*THE DIVORCEE (MGM)
HELL'S ANGELS (United Artists)
OLD ENGLISH (Warner Bros.)

1931

*CIMARRON (RKO)
STREET SCENE (United Artists)
SKIPPY (Paramount)
BAD GIRL (Fox)
*MIN AND BILL (MGM)
THE FRONT PAGE (United Artists)
FIVE STAR FINAL (Warner Bros.)
CITY LIGHTS (United Artists)
A FREE SOUL (MGM)
THE SIN OF MADELON CLAUDET
(MGM)

1932

*GRAND HOTEL (MGM)
*THE CHAMP (MGM)
ARROWSMITH (United Artists)
THE GUARDSMAN (MGM)
SMILIN' THROUGH (MGM)
DR. JEKYLL AND MR. HYDE
(Paramount)
EMMA (MGM)
A BILL OF DIVORCEMENT (RKO)
*BACK STREET (Universal)
SCARFACE (United Artists)

1933

CAVALCADE (Fox)
*42ND STREET (Warner Bros.)
THE PRIVATE LIFE OF HENRY VIII
(United Artists)
LADY FOR A DAY (Columbia)
*STATE FAIR (Fox)
A FAREWELL TO ARMS (Paramount)

*SHE DONE HIM WRONG (Paramount)
I AM A FUGITIVE FROM A CHAIN GANG
(Warner Bros.)
MAEDCHEN IN UNIFORM (Filmchoice)
RASPUTIN AND THE EMPRESS (MGM)

1934

THE BARRETTS OF WIMPOLE STREET
(MGM)
THE HOUSE OF ROTHSCHILD (United
Artists)
*IT HAPPENED ONE NIGHT (Columbia)
ONE NIGHT OF LOVE (Columbia)
*LITTLE WOMEN (RKO)
THE THIN MAN (MGM)
VIVA VILLA! (MGM)
*DINNER AT EIGHT (MGM)
THE COUNT OF MONTE CRISTO
(United Artists)
BERKELEY SQUARE (Fox)

1935

DAVID COPPERFIELD (MGM)
*LIVES OF A BENGAL LANCER
(Paramount)
THE INFORMER (RKO)
NAUGHTY MARIETTA (MGM)
LES MISERABLES (United Artists)
RUGGLES OF RED GAP (Paramount)
*TOP HAT (RKO)
*BROADWAY MELODY OF 1936 (MGM)
ROBERTA (RKO)
ANNA KARENINA (MGM)

1936

*MUTINY ON THE BOUNTY (MGM)
MR. DEEDS GOES TO TOWN
(Columbia)
*THE GREAT ZIEGFELD (MGM)
*SAN FRANCISCO (MGM)
DODSWORTH (United Artists)
THE STORY OF LOUIS PASTEUR
(Warner Bros.)
A TALE OF TWO CITIES (MGM)
ANTHONY ADVERSE (Warner Bros.)
THE GREEN PASTURES (Warner Bros.)
A MIDSUMMER NIGHT'S DREAM
(Warner Bros.)

1937
THE LIFE OF EMILE ZOLA (Warner
    Bros.)
*THE GOOD EARTH (MGM)
 CAPTAINS COURAGEOUS (MGM)
*LOST HORIZON (Columbia)
*A STAR IS BORN (United Artists)
 ROMEO AND JULIET (MGM)
 STAGE DOOR (RKO)
 DEAD END (United Artists)
 WINTERSET (RKO)
 THE AWFUL TRUTH (Columbia)

1938
*SNOW WHITE AND THE SEVEN DWARFS
    (RKO)
 YOU CAN'T TAKE IT WITH YOU
    (Columbia)
*ALEXANDER'S RAGTIME BAND (20th
    Century–Fox)
*BOYS TOWN (MGM)
*MARIE ANTOINETTE (MGM)

*IN OLD CHICAGO (20th Century–Fox)
*THE ADVENTURES OF ROBIN HOOD
    (Warner Bros.)
 THE CITADEL (MGM)
*LOVE FINDS ANDY HARDY (MGM)
*THE HURRICANE (United Artists)

1939
*GOODBYE, MR. CHIPS (MGM)
 STANLEY AND LIVINGSTONE (20th
    Century–Fox)
 MR. SMITH GOES TO WASHINGTON
    (Columbia)
*THE WIZARD OF OZ (MGM)
*DARK VICTORY (Warner Bros.)
 WUTHERING HEIGHTS (United Artists)
*PYGMALION (MGM)
 THE WOMEN (MGM)
 JUAREZ (Warner Bros.)
*THE OLD MAID (Warner Bros.)

List of Abbreviations

AC   *American Cinematographer*
JSMPE   *Journal of the Society of Motion Picture Engineers*
IP   *International Photographer*
IPro   *International Projectionist*
MOMA   Museum of Modern Art
MPPDA   Motion Picture Producers and Distributors of America
MPH   *Motion Picture Herald*
NYTFR   *New York Times Film Reviews*
PCA   Production Code Administration
VFR   *Variety Film Reviews*

Notes

CHAPTER 1. Introduction

1. Larry Swindell, "1939: A Very Good Year, " *American Film* 1 (December 1975), p. 28.
2. Ronald Haver, *David O. Selznick's Hollywood* (New York: Bonanza Books, 1980), p. 311; Mary P. Ryan, *Womanhood in America: From Colonial Times to the Present* (New York: New Viewpoints, 1975), p. 218.
3. Margaret Farrand Thorp, *America at the Movies* (New Haven, Conn.: Yale University Press, 1939), p. 17.
4. *Ibid.*, p. 9.
5. Ian Jarvie, "The Social Experience of Movies," in Sari Thomas, ed., *Film/Culture: Explorations of Cinema in its Social Context* (Metuchen, N.J.: Scarecrow Press, 1982), p. 259; Thorp, *America at the Movies*, pp. 108, 117.
6. Thorp, *America at the Movies*, p. 50; Jarvie, "The Social Experience of the Movies," p. 256.
7. Richard Maltby, *Harmless Entertainment: Hollywood and the Ideology of Consensus* (Metuchen, N.J.: Scarecrow Press, 1983), p. 13.
8. Richard Randall, "Censorship: From *The Miracle* to *Deep Throat*," in Tino Balio, ed., *The American Film Industry*, rev. ed. (Madison: University of Wisconsin Press, 1985), pp. 510–536.
9. Lea Jacobs, "Industry Self-Regulation and the Problem of Textual Determination," *Velvet Light Trap* 23 (Spring 1989), pp. 6–8.
10. Mae D. Huettig, "Economic Control of the Motion Picture Industry," in Balio, *The American Film Industry*, p. 285; an abridgment of a chapter in Huettig's *Economic Control of the Motion Picture Industry* (Philadelphia: University of Pennsylvania Press, 1944).
11. Huettig, "Economic Control of the Motion Picture Industry," p. 294.
12. *Ibid.*, p. 295.
13. *Ibid.*, p. 291.
14. *Ibid.*, p. 295.

CHAPTER 2. Surviving the Great Depression

1. Tom Waller, "The Year in Pictures," *Variety*, 8 January 1930, p. 87.
2. Sean Dennis Cashman, *America in the Twenties and Thirties: The Olympian Age of Franklin Delano Roosevelt* (New York: New York University Press, 1989), pp. 118, 121, 217; Dixon Wechter, *The Age of the Great Depression, 1929–1941* (New York: Macmillan, 1948), p. 17.
3. Waller, "The Year in Pictures," *Variety*, 29 December 1931, p. 4; Joel W. Finler, *The Hollywood Story* (New York: Crown, 1988), p. 288; "'Movies' and the Investor," *Barron's*, 2 September 1935, p. 6; Sid Silverman, "What the Grosses Say," *Variety*, 29 December 1931, p. 169.
4. Sid Silverman, "What the Grosses Say," *Variety*, 29 January 1931, p. 1.
5. Cashman, *America in the Twenties and Thirties*, p. 320.
6. "Banks Bump Box Offices," *Variety*, 7 March 1933, p. 48; Silverman, "What the Grosses Say," *Variety*, 29 December 1931, p. 1.
7. "The Year in Pictures," *Variety*, 2 January 1934, p. 3.
8. "50 vs 156 Millions in 2 Yrs.," *Variety*, 14 March 1933, p. 7.
9. "6,500 Dark Theatres," *Variety*, 2 August 1932, p. 7; "U.S. Commerce Dept. Analysis," *Variety*, 18 November 1936, p. 6.
10. Finler, *The Hollywood Story*, pp. 286–287.
11. "RKO and Orpheum," *Variety*, 31 January 1933, p. 5; Waller, "The Year in Pictures," *Variety*, 8 January 1930, p. 87; "Theatre Receivership," *Variety*, 31 January 1933, p. 5.
12. "RKO's Stage Door Is Open," *Variety*, 26 April 1932, p. 7.
13. Roy Chartier, "The Year in Pictures," *Variety*, 1 January 1935, p. 3; "Paramount Pictures," *Fortune*, March 1937, pp. 87–96.
14. "The Case of William Fox," *Fortune*, May 1930, pp. 48–49; Douglas Gomery, *The Hollywood Studio System* (New York: St. Martin's Press, 1986), pp. 82–83.
15. *Ibid.*, p. 84.
16. *Ibid.*, p. 150.
17. "Loew's, Inc.," *Fortune*, August 1939, repr. in Tino Balio, ed., *The American Film Industry*, rev. ed. (Madison: University of Wisconsin Press, 1985), p. 340.
18. Gomery, *The Hollywood Studio System*, p. 110.

19. "Unique Motion Picture Enterprise," *Barron's*, 25 March 1935, p. 14; Stanley Devlin, "Movie Outlook Improving," *Magazine of Wall Street*, 20 July 1935, p. 355.

20. This discussion is taken from Chapter 5 of Tino Balio, *United Artists: The Company Built by the Stars* (Madison: University of Wisconsin Press, 1975), pp. 95–109. It is based on research conducted by Douglas Gomery that resulted in the following two articles: "Hollywood, the National Recovery Administration, and the Question of Monopoly Power," *Journal of the University Film Association* 31 (Spring 1979), pp. 47–52, and "Rethinking U.S. Film History: The Depression Decade and Monopoly Control," *Film and History* 10 (May 1980), pp. 32–38.

21. Gomery, *The Hollywood Studio System*, p. 7.

22. U.S. Temporary National Economic Committee, *The Motion Picture Industry: A Pattern of Control* (Washington, D.C.: U.S. Government Printing Office, 1941), p. 31.

23. Frederick Lewis Allen, *Since Yesterday: 1929–1939* (New York: Bantam, 1965), p. 132.

24. *Ibid.*, p. 155; Cashman, *America in the Twenties and Thirties*, p. 164.

25. "Harley Clarke's Career," *Variety*, 9 April 1930, p. 3; Gomery, *The Hollywood Studio System*, p. 86.

26. *Ibid.*

27. Balio, *United Artists*, pp. 119–126.

28. "Paramount Pictures," *Fortune*, March 1937, pp. 87–96.

29. *Ibid.*

30. Roy Chartier, "The Year in Pictures," *Variety*, 6 January 1937, p. 10.

31. Lewis Jacobs, *The Rise of the American Film* (New York: Teachers College Press, 1939), p. 421. For revisionist accounts, see Gomery, "Rethinking U.S. Film History," p. 32; Janet Staiger, "The Labor Force, Financing and the Mode of Production," in David Bordwell, Janet Staiger, and Kristin Thompson, *The Classical Hollywood Cinema: Film Style and Mode of Production to 1960* (New York: Columbia University Press, 1985), pp. 311–319; and Robert Sklar, *Movie-Made America: A Social History of American Movies* (New York: Random House, 1975), pp. 162–167. For the fullest contemporary account in support of the financial control thesis, see Janet Wasko, *Movies and Money* (Norwood, N.V.: Ablex, 1982), pp. 47–102.

32. Alfred D. Chandler, Jr., *The Visible Hand: The Managerial Revolution in American Business* (Cambridge, Mass.: Harvard University Press, 1977), p. 1.

33. "390 Cinema DeLuxers," *Variety*, 20 February 1934, p. 9.

34. Joe Bigelow, "End of 'Poor' Vaudeville," *Variety*, 3 January 1933, p. 70.

35. "Power of Small Towns," *Variety*, 22 April 1931, p. 5.

36. "Miniature Golf Courses All Over Map," *Variety*, 18 June 1930, p. 3; "Diamond Cuts into Pics," *Variety*, 7 August 1935, p. 7.

37. Roy Chartier, "The Year in Pictures," *Variety*, 1 January 1935, p. 3.

38. Joe Bigelow, "End of 'Poor' Vaudeville," *Variety*, 3 January 1933, p. 70.

39. "Bank Night," *New Republic*, 6 May 1936, pp. 363–365; "Go Wild on Price Cutting," *Variety*, 8 December 1931, p. 9; "Worry About 10 Cent Houses," *Variety*, 22 December 1931, p. 5.

40. "Coast Theatres' Suicide," *Variety*, 21 June 1932, p. 9.

41. "Bank Night," *New Republic*, 6 May 1936, pp. 363–365.

42. "Double Featuring Discussed by All Sides," *Variety*, 22 April 1931, p. 5; "Double Talkers on One Bill Coming Back," *Variety*, 2 April 1930, p. 12; "Indies and Twin Bills Out," *Variety*, 14 June 1932, p. 5; "Double Feature Playing More Plentiful," *Variety*, 8 October 1930, p. 4.

43. "Need Twice As Many Pix," *Variety*, 14 August 1934, p. 5.

44. Robert W. Chambers, "The Double Feature as a Sales Problem," *Harvard Business Review* 16 (Winter 1938), p. 231.

45. "Need Twice As Many Pix," *Variety*, 14 August 1934, p. 5.

46. Chambers, "The Double Feature as a Sales Problem," p. 227.

47. Bosley Crowther, "Double Feature Trouble," *New York Times Magazine*, 14 July 1940, p. 8; "Producers' Poll on Double Bills," *Variety*, 28 February 1933, p. 6.

48. "U.S. Commerce Dept. Analysis," *Variety*, 18 November 1936, p. 6; Roy Chartier, "The Year in Pictures," *Variety*, 6 January 1937, p. 10; C. F. Morgan, "Sixty Million Customers Weekly," *Magazine of Wall Street*, 14 April 1934, p. 662.

49. Stanley Devlin, "Movie Outlook Improving," *Magazine of Wall Street*, 20 July 1935, p. 354.

50. C. F. Morgan, "Picture Prospects and Profits," *Magazine of Wall Street*, 15 August 1936. p. 522; Dixon Wechter, *The Age of the Great Depression*, p. 241; Mike Wear, "No More Wall Street Eggs," *Variety*, 6 January 1937, p. 5; Joel W. Finler, *The Hollywood Story*, p. 288.

51. Cashman, *America in the Twenties and Thirties*, pp. 203, 217–218.

52. Sam Shain, "Problems of the Film Industry," *Variety*, 3 January 1933, p. 12; William Victor Strauss, "Foreign Distribution of American Motion Pictures," *Harvard Business Review* 8 (April 1930), p. 307.

53. Strauss, "Foreign Distribution of American Motion Pictures," p. 308.

54. "Dubbing Wins Out Abroad," *Variety*, 3 November 1931, p. 15; "Something of a Boom for Foreign Pix," *Variety*, 17 February 1937, p. 4.

55. "Foreign Films Over Here," *Variety*, 29 December 1931, p. 13; Wolfe Kaufman, "International Show Biz," *Variety*, 5 September 1933, p. 29, and "Foreign Films in the U.S.," *Variety*, 1 January 1935, p. 41.
56. Balio, *United Artists*, p. 134; Arthur Dent, "British Films in the American Market," *Variety*, 4 January 1939, p. 30.
57. Wolfe Kaufman, "Show Biz Around the World," *Variety*, 1 January 1935, p. 29; Balio, *United Artists*, p. 167.
58. "War Hits Hollywood," *Business Week*, 3 February 1940, pp. 49–50.

CHAPTER 3. The Production Code and the Hays Office

1. Joseph Breen to Harry Cohn, 24 August 1939; memo, 29 August 1939; Will Hays to Breen, 11 December 1939, Production Code Administration HIS GIRL FRIDAY file, Margaret Herrick Library, Academy of Motion Picture Arts and Sciences Library, Los Angeles (hereafter PCA). All researchers on the Production Code and Hollywood owe a great debt to Samuel Gill, archivist of the Academy Library, for securing the preservation of this archive, which has made possible a reassessment of the accounts of the Production Code and its origins provided by such "official" sources as Will H. Hays, *The Memoirs of Will H. Hays* (Garden City, N.Y.: Doubleday, 1955), and Raymond Moley, *The Hays Office* (Indianapolis: Bobbs-Merrill, 1945). The misfortunes of MR. SMITH GOES TO WASHINGTON are described in Charles Wolfe, "Mr. Smith Goes to Washington: Democratic Forums and Representational Forms," in Peter Lehman, ed., *Close Viewings: An Anthology of New Film Criticism* (Tallahassee: Florida State University Press, 1990), pp. 300–332.
2. Moley, *The Hays Office*, p. 75; Hays, *Memoirs*, pp. 445–446.
3. *Time* review of THE PUBLIC ENEMY, quoted in Garth Jowett, "Bullets, Beer and the Hays Office: *Public Enemy*," in John E. O'Connor and Martin A. Jackson, eds., *American History, American Film: Interpreting the Hollywood Image* (New York: Ungar 1980), p. 69; Andrew Bergman, *We're in the Money: Depression America and Its Films* (New York: Harper, 1971).
4. Stanley Cavell, *Pursuits of Happiness: The Hollywood Comedy of Remarriage* (Cambridge, Mass.: Harvard University Press, 1981), pp. 161–187; Gerald Mast, *Howard Hawks Storyteller* (New York: Oxford University Press, 1982), pp. 208–242; Robert Sklar, *Movie-Made America: A Cultural History of American Movies* (New York: Random House, 1975), p. 175; Ruth L. Vasey, "Diplomatic Representations: Mediations Between Hollywood and Its Global Audiences, 1922–1939" (Ph.D. diss., Exeter University, 1990).
5. Lea Jacobs, "Industry Self-Regulation and the Problem of Textual Determination," *Velvet Light Trap* 23 (Spring 1989), p. 9; Jacobs's argument is enlarged in *The Wages of Sin: Censorship and the Fallen Woman Film, 1928–1942* (Madison: University of Wisconsin Press, 1991); Joy to Col. John A. Cooper, MPPD Canada, Toronto, 21 February 1931; Joy to James Wingate, 5 February 1931, PCA LITTLE CAESAR file.
6. Umberto Eco, *The Role of the Reader: Explorations in the Semiotics of Texts* (London: Hutchinson, 1979), p. 9.
7. Hal Wallis to Robert Lord, 27 March 1937, THAT CERTAIN WOMAN production file, Warner Bros. Collection, Department of Special Collections, Doheny Library, University of Southern California (hereafter WB).
8. *Motion Picture Almanac* (Chicago: Quigley, 1931). See also Garth Jowett, *Film, the Democratic Art: A Social History of American Film* (Boston: Little, Brown, 1976), pp. 113–119.
9. Article 1, By-laws of the MPPDA, reprinted in Moley, p. 227.
10. Lary May, *Screening Out the Past: The Birth of Mass Culture and the Motion Picture Industry* (New York: Oxford University Press, 1980), p. 205; *The Open Door*, MPPDA pamphlet, New York, 1924, 1927; Will H. Hays, *The Motion Picture—1930*, MPPDA pamphlet, 1930, p. 4, Will H. Hays Archive, Indiana State Historical Society, Indianapolis (hereafter Hays Papers).
11. MPPDA Resolution, 24 June 1924. The formula is discussed in Richard Maltby, " 'To Prevent the Prevalent Type of Book . . . ': Censorship and Adaptation in Hollywood, 1924–1934," *American Quarterly* 43, no. 2 (Dec. 1992). The 1927 code was adopted as a "fair trade practice" at the trade practice convention held by the Federal Trade Commission in October 1927. As Garth Jowett has pointed out, there was a considerable similarity between the "Don'ts and Be Carefuls" and the code produced by National Association of the Motion Picture Industry in 1921. Garth S. Jowett, "Moral Responsibility and Commercial Entertainment: Social Control in the United States Film Industry, 1907–1968," *Historical Journal of Film, Radio and Television* 10, no. 1 (1990), p. 14. The Thirteen Points are reproduced in Ruth Inglis, *Freedom of the Movies: A Report on Self-Regulation from the Commission on Freedom of the Press* (Chicago: University of Chicago Press, 1947), pp. 83–84.
12. Francis R. Walsh, "*The Callaghans and the Murphys* (MGM, 1927): A Case Study of Irish-American and Catholic Church Censorship," *Historical Journal of Film, Radio and Television* 10, no. 1 (1990), pp. 33–45; Irving Thalberg, "General Principles to Govern the Preparation of a

Revised Code of Ethics for Talking Pictures," Reporter's transcript, board meeting, Association of Motion Picture Producers (AMPP), 10 February 1930, Motion Picture Association of America Archive, New York (hereafter MPA), 1930 AMPP Code file, pp. 97, 138–139.

13. John V. Wilson to Carl Milliken, 28 November 1928, MPA 1928 California office file; Thalberg, "General Principles," pp. 138–139.

14. The groups that remained most persistently opposed to the film industry during the 1920s, coalescing to an extent around the Federal Motion Picture Council, were Protestant clerics and women's groups. The FMPC was headed by Canon William Sheafe Chase, an inveterate Episcopalian critic of the movies. See Jowett, *Film*, pp. 176–179.

15. Douglas Gomery, "The Coming of Sound to the American Cinema: A History of the Transformation of an Industry" (Ph.D. diss., University of Wisconsin-Madison, 1975), pp. 269–270, 272; *Washington Star*, 1 April 1929; Carl Milliken to Hays, 9 October 1929, PCA APPLAUSE file.

16. John Lord O'Brien to Hays, 8 October 1929, Hays Papers; *The Churchman*, 6 July 1929; 29 June 1929, p. 1. For the MPPDA's relationship with the Protestant churches, see Richard Maltby, *"The King of Kings* and the Czar of All the Rushes: The Propriety of the Christ Story," *Screen* 31, no. 2 (1990), pp. 188–213.

17. "The Federal Council *Was* Retained," *The Churchman*, 5 April 1930.

18. Martin Quigley to FitzGeorge Dinneen, S.J., 26 November 1929, folder, Quigley, Martin— Movie Code 1927–1932, Daniel A. Lord, S.J. Papers, Jesuit Missouri Province Archive, St. Louis (hereafter Lord Papers). Quigley may also have separately proposed the idea of a more fully elaborated code, as an alternative to the "political censorship" that he believed had frequently broken down. Lord was already well known to the Association. He had acted as the Catholic adviser on THE KING OF KINGS and had attended the September conference. At various times after 1934 Quigley and Lord disputed authorship of the code. This issue is discussed in Stephen Vaughn, "Morality and Entertainment: The Origins of the Motion Picture Production Code," *Journal of American History* 77, no. 1 (1990), pp. 48–56.

19. "The Reasons Supporting Preamble of Code," repr. in Moley, pp. 243–244; Thalberg, "General Principles," p. 138.

20. Milliken to Hays, 20 December 1929, MPA 1930 Church and Drama League file; Thalberg, draft of "General Principles," Lord Papers, p. 5; Lord, draft of "Suggested Code to Govern The Production of Motion Pictures," Reporter's transcript, p. 123. The paragraph containing this statement, which comes at the end of "Reasons Underlying the General Principles," was subsequently omitted from all published versions.

21. Exhibit B, "Last draft by J [Jason Joy] and W [John V. Wilson]," 28 January 1930, folder, Motion Picture Code Publicity, Lord Papers.

22. Lord addressed a meeting of the Association of Motion Picture Producers (AMPP). For reasons relating to federal antitrust legislation, the AMPP was nominally an entirely separate organization from the MPPDA. In practice, however, it represented the junior, Hollywood arm of the New York–based Association, and the personnel of the two organizations were interchangeable. The subcommittee comprised Hays, Lord, Thalberg, B. P. Schulberg of Paramount, Sol Wurtzel of Fox, and Jack Warner. Lord to George, Cardinal Mundelein, 14 February 1930, folder, Movie Production Code, 1929–1930; Lord to Father Provincial, 17 February 1930, folder, Quigley, Martin, Movie Code, 1927–1932, Lord Papers; "Resolution Unanimously Adopted by the Board of Directors of the Motion Picture Producers and Distributors of America, Inc., on March 31, 1930," Hays Papers.

23. A comparison of the "Don'ts" and "Particular Applications" is in Inglis, pp. 131–138.

24. Hays, MPPDA Annual Report, 1931, p. 7, Hays Papers.

25. Quigley, editorial, *Motion Picture Herald*, 14 May 1932, p. 9; Joy to Zanuck, 6 August 1930, PCA ILLICIT Case File.

26. "The Movies Are 'Converted' Again!," *Christian Century*, 9 April 1930, p. 454; "Morals for Profit," *New York World*, 1 April 1930.

27. Joy to Hays, 16 April 1930, MPA 1930 AMPP Production Code file. Both the Chicago and Pennsylvania boards made only half the number of eliminations from films in 1930 that they had made in 1928. Joy, Report on the operation of the Production Code during its first year, 1 May 1931, PCA PUBLIC ENEMY; MPPDA Press release, 22 March 1931, Hays Papers.

28. An Advertising Code Committee, chaired by Joseph Breen, was established in July 1932. See Mary Beth Haralovich, "Mandates of Good Taste: The Self-Regulation of Film Advertising in the Thirties," *Wide Angle* 6, no. 2 (1984), pp. 50–57, and Janet Staiger, "Announcing Wares, Winning Patrons, Voicing Ideals: Thinking About the History and Theory of Film Advertising," *Cinema Journal* 29, no. 3 (1990), pp. 3–31.

29. Joy to Col. John A. Cooper, MPPD Canada, Toronto, 21 February 1931; Joy to Wingate, 5 February 1931. PCA LITTLE CAESAR file.

30. Lamar Trotti to Joy, 22 January 1931, PCA ILLICIT file; Trotti memo, 23 July 1931, PCA BACK STREET file.

31. "A Letter to Roger W. Babson from Carl E. Milliken, Secretary, Motion Picture Producers and Distributors of America, Inc." dated 7 May 1929, (New York: MPPDA, 1929); Carlton Simon to Hays, 15 November 1930, PCA THE DOORWAY TO HELL file; Hays to Joseph Melillo, secretary of the Hoboken Lions Club, 11 June 1931, PCA PUBLIC ENEMY file; Draft, Special Education Section, MPPDA Annual Report 1932, Hays Papers; *Christian Century*, 12 August 1931, pp. 1015–1016.

32. Lupton Wilkinson, "Observations on the Association's Publicity Situation and Proposals for Remedying It," 1 November 1931, Hays Papers.

33. This action was most directly brought about by Irving Thalberg's failure to submit a script for POSSESSED, a kept-woman picture starring Clark Gable and Joan Crawford. Before release, the film had to be reconstructed to provide it with a defensible "moral argument." Trotti to Joy, 22 October 1931, PCA POSSESSED file; Draft, MPPDA Annual Report, 1932, Hays Papers. The version of SCARFACE normally seen today is significantly different from the May 1932 release version. A fuller account of the production history of SCARFACE appears in Richard Maltby, "A Short and Dangerous Life: The Gangster Film, 1930–1932," in Giuliana Muscio, ed., *Prima dei codici 2: Alle Porte di Hays / Before the Codes 2: The Gateway to Hays* (Venice: : Fabbri Editori, 1991), pp. 159–174.

34. Joy to Breen, 15 December 1931, PCA POSSESSED file; Joy to Hays, 11 January 1932, PCA MURDERS IN THE RUE MORGUE file; "Mrs. R" (probably Mrs. Alonzo Richardson), Atlanta Board of Review, to Hays, 3 December 1931; PCA POSSESSED file; Hays, draft, MPPDA 1932 Annual Report, Hays Papers; *The Public Relations of the Motion Picture Industry*. A Report by the Department of Research and Education (New York: Federal Council of Churches of Christ in America, 1931), pp. 144–147.

35. Breen to Hays, 29 August 1931, Hays Papers; Breen to Father Wilfrid Parsons, S.J., 10 October 1932,. Wilfrid Parsons Papers, Lauinger Library, Georgetown University, Washington, D.C. (hereafter Parsons Papers); Joy to Hays, 15 April 1932; Joy to Milliken, 7 July 1932, PCA RED-HEADED WOMAN file; Joy to Hays, 25 July 1932, PCA A FAREWELL TO ARMS file.

36. Wingate took office in mid September. In late August, the SRC staff was augmented by one, in the person of Geoffrey Shurlock, previously of Paramount. Shurlock eventually became Breen's assistant and, in 1951, his successor. Quigley to Hays, 4 August 1932, Hays Papers; Hays to Joy, 20 August 1932; Joe Schenck to Hays, 29 August 1932; Joy to Hays, September 1932, MPA 1932 Production Code file.

37. Breen to Parsons, 10 October 1932, Parsons Papers.

38. "Notes" sent to bishops by Episcopal Committee, 16 May 1934, quoted in Paul W. Facey, *The Legion of Decency: A Sociological Analysis of the Emergence and Development of a Social Pressure Group* (New York: Arno, 1974), p. 138. See also "Federal Film Censorship," *America* 45 (11 April 1931), p. 7; William M. Halsey, *The Survival of American Innocence: Catholicism in an Era of Disillusionment*, 1920–1940 (Notre Dame, Ind.: University of Notre Dame Press, 1980) p. 5.

39. Gerard B. Donnelly, S.J., "An Open Letter to Dr. Wingate," *America*, 29 October 1932, pp. 84–86.

40. Hays to Zukor, 16 November 1932; Maurice McKenzie, memo, 28 November 1932; Wingate to Hurley, 29 November 1932, PCA SHE DONE HIM WRONG file. An excellent discussion of West's theatrical and early movie career can be found in Mary Beth Hamilton, "When I'm Bad, I'm Better: Mae West and American Popular Entertainment" (Ph.D. diss., Princeton University, 1990).

41. Wingate to Hays, 10 March 1933, MPA 1933 Production Code file; Milliken to Wingate, 21 March 1933, PCA STATE FAIR file; Trotti to Hays, 30 March 1931, MPA 1931 Production Code file; Hays to company heads, 19 May 1933, MPA 1933 Production Code file.

42. K. L. Russell to Hays, 2 May 1933; Ray Norr to Hays, 18 August 1931, Hays Papers; Hays, report to MPPDA Board of Directors, 8 October 1931, MPA 1931 Influence of Psychological Research file; Jowett, *Film*, p. 182. Although subsequent histories have followed Raymond Moley in rejecting the studies as unreliable, at the time of their publication they were widely taken as authoritative pieces of sociological or psychological research. See Kimball Young, review of Herbert Blumer, *Movies and Conduct*, and Henry James Forman, *Our Movie-Made Children*, in *American Journal of Sociology*, September 1935, pp. 250–255. Moley's first work for the Hays Office was a repudiation of Forman, *Are We Movie-Made?*, published in 1936. The best short account of the studies is in Shearon Lowery and Melvin L. De Fleur, *Milestones in Mass Communication Research: Media Effects* (New York: Longman, 1983), pp. 31–57. Forthcoming work in the studies by Clayton R. Koppes and Kathy Helgesen Fuller will allow a full reappraisal.

43. Reaffirmation of the Members of the MPPDA, signed 7 March 1933, quoted in Moley, pp. 250–251.

44. Hays to Wingate, 10 March 1933; R. H. Cochrane to Carl Laemmle, Jr., 29 March 1933; Hays, address to producers, 20 April 1933, MPA 1933 Production Code file; *Motion Picture Herald*, 29 April 1933, p. 9; John Callan O'Laughlin to Hays, 10 April 1933, Hays Papers.

45. Harry Zehner memo to producers and writers, 26 May 1933, in Universal Studios Censorship file, University of Southern California Special Collections Box 778; Wingate to Cooper, 12 April 1933; production file, BED OF ROSES, RKO Corporate Archive, University of California, Los Angeles, Special Collections (hereafter RKO). See Richard Maltby, "*Baby Face*, or How Joe Breen Made Barbara Stanwyck Atone for Causing the Wall Street Crash," *Screen* 27, no. 2 (1986), pp. 27–45.

46. Breen to Wingate, 5 May 1933; Wingate to Cooper, 27 May 1933; Cooper to Berman, 2 June 1933, RKO ANN VICKERS production file.

47. Alice Ames Winter to Hays, 10 July 1933, Hays Papers. On 17 May 1933, Quigley wrote to Lord, "Wingate is, indeed, a washout. Hays virtually acknowledged this yesterday. (On the telephone he threatened to fire him.) Hays is looking for more help from Breen. I don't think that Wingate can be taught the Code." Quigley to Lord, 17 May 1933, folder, Quigley, Martin, 1933–1936, Lord Papers.

48. The August reorganization took place after an AMPP meeting arranged by Breen at which Hays, Dr. Attilio Giannini of the Bank of America and Los Angeles attorney Joseph Scott berated producers for their continued production of dangerous pictures. Breen's seizure of power was officially confirmed when he went to New York in November, when the board appointed veteran publicity man J. J. McCarthy to administer the Advertising Code and gave Breen "complete control of the Code enforcement machinery." Breen began signing all SRC correspondence with the studios during Wingate's absence in December, and "it was decided that this procedure would be continued when Dr. Wingate returned." The arrangement was formalized on 4 January 1934, although no public announcements were made. In February, Joy returned to Fox, and Iselin Auster joined the SRC staff. There was no formal announcement that Breen had succeeded Wingate until June 1934. Breen to Quigley, 1 August 1933, folder, Martin Quigley 1933–1936, Lord Papers; Winter to Hays, 21 November 1933, Hays to McKenzie, 5 January 1934, Hays Papers; MPPDA press release, 22 June 1934; Milliken to Hays, 15 June 1934, MPA 1934 Production Code file.

49. Parsons to Dinneen, 9 August 1933; Parsons to Breen, 25 August 1933; Parsons to Lord, 16 October 1933, Boxes P-202-203, C-10, C-50, Parsons Papers; Louis Nizer, *New Courts of Industry: Self-Regulation Under the Motion Picture Code* (New York: Longacre, 1935), pp. 236, 299; Jowett, *Film*, p. 245; see also Douglas Gomery, "Hollywood, the NRA, and Monopoly Power," in Gorham Kindem, ed., *The American Movie Industry: The Business of Motion Pictures* (Carbondale: Southern Illinois University Press, 1982), pp. 205–214.

50. Quoted in Facey, p. 144. An initial proposal to have members pledge to abstain from all movie attendance was eliminated. Breen to Lord, 21 August 1933, folder, Breen, Joe, 1933–1942; Breen to Dinneen, 17 March 1934, folder, Movie Code Material from FitzGeorge Dinneen, S.J., Lord Papers. The pledge was rewritten in a shorter form in November 1934, and that version was subsequently used for the annual oral renewal of the pledge in all Catholic churches.

51. Quigley to Lord, 27 April 1934; Breen to Dinneen, 30 March 1934; Breen to Dinneen, 17 March 1934; Breen to Dinneen, 17 March 1934; Breen to Dinneen, 30 March 1934, folder, Quigley, Martin, 1933–1936; folder, Joe Breen, 1933–1942; folder, Movie Code Material from FitzGeorge Dinneen, S.J., Lord Papers.

52. Inglis, pp. 124, 141; Episcopal Committee press release, 21 June 1934; "Three Steps in Motion Picture Betterment," MPPDA press release, 27 July 1934, MPA 1934 Production Code file. There is a colorful account of this meeting, as related by Breen, in Jack Vizzard, *See No Evil: Life Inside a Hollywood Censor* (New York: Simon and Schuster, 1970), p. 50. Lord had first advocated a "sanction" for violations to Hays in March 1933. Lord to Hays, 25 March 1933, folder, Quigley, Martin, 1933–1936, Lord Papers; MPPDA Board Resolution, 3 July 1934, MPA 1934 Production Code file.

53. Coyly describing these events in his autobiography, Hays quoted his father: "I give Providence the glory, but I did the engineering." Hays, p. 448. In fact, the concession had been minimal, in that exhibitors were required to make their exemptions from the 10 percent cancellation they were already permitted under the NRA Code. "Suggested instructions by general managers to all branch managers in the United States," 10 July 1934, Hays Papers; *Boston Globe*, 27 July 1934.

54. These disputes were temporarily resolved in November 1934, when the bishops' annual meeting established the Legion as a permanent movement and settled on the Chicago list as its unofficial standard. By mid 1936, however, it had ceased publication, and the Legion adopted the list published by the IFCA in New York, effectively a reversal to the status quo prior to the Legion's creation. Facey, pp. 66, 161–164; Lord to Archbishop Curley of Baltimore, 31 May 1934, folder, Movie Production Code, Lord Papers.

55. 17 July 1934, MPA 1934 meetings, Advertising file.

56. Breen to Dinneen, 17 March 1934, folder, Movie Code Material from FitzGeorge Dinneen, S.J., Lord Papers; Breen memo, 3 April 1934, PCA HE WAS HER MAN file; Hays to Joe Schenck, 20

April 1934, MPA 1934 Production Code file; Lord to Breen, 11 May folder, Joe Breen 1932–1941, Lord Papers; Censorship notes, PCA BELLE OF THE NINETIES file.

57. Breen to Hays, 3 August 1934, PCA BELLE OF THE NINETIES file.
58. Ray Norr to Hays, 18 August 1931; Hays, MPPDA Annual Report, 1931, pp. 2–3, Hays Papers; Hays to Kahane, 10 November 1933, Depinet to Kahane, 20 November 1933; Depinet to All Managers, Salesmen and Bookers, 15 November 1933, RKO LITTLE WOMEN production file; Leon J. Bamberger to All Managers, Salesmen and Bookers, RKO ANNE OF GREEN GABLES production file; Carl Milliken, "Mr. Hays's Philosophy and Methods in Relation to Motion Picture Improvement," press release, 19 November 1934. William deMille Collection, University of Southern California, Box 8, folder 6.
59. Vizzard, pp. 63–64.
60. Vizzard, pp. 63–64. On 5 October 1934, Breen advised Vincent Hart, in charge of the East Coast office of the PCA, to "sneer back" at producers, "raise hell with them—threaten to punch them in the nose, etc. If you do this two or three times, I think you will have little trouble of this kind thereafter." PCA CRIME WITHOUT PASSION file. For a colorful contemporary account of Breen's behavior, see J. P. McEvoy, "The Back of Me Hand to You," *Saturday Evening Post*, 24 December 1938, pp. 8–9, 46–48. Breen to Jack Warner, 22 November 1938, WB EACH DAWN I DIE production file.
61. Breen to B. B. Kahane, 11 June 1936. RKO WINTERSET production file; Breen to Hays, 22 June 1938, MPA 1939 Production Code file; Walter MacEwen to Wallis, 12 October 1936, WB GOLD DIGGERS OF 1937 production file.
62. Jacobs, p. 13; Leonard J. Leff and Jerold R. Simmons, *The Dame in the Kimono: Hollywood, Censorship, and the Production Code from the 1920s to the 1960s* (New York: Grove Weidenfeld, 1990), p. 72; Harold J. Salemson, *The Screen Writer*, April 1946, quoted in Inglis, pp. 183–184; Elliot Paul and Luis Quintanilla, *With a Hays Nonny Nonny* (New York: Random House, 1942), pp. 63–64.
63. Gregory D. Black, "The Production Code and the Hollywood Film Industry, 1930–1940," *Film History* 3, no. 2 (1989) pp. 180–182; "Summary of Amendations and Interpretations of the Production Code on Crime," 20 December 1938, MPA 1938 Production Code file; the high volume of crime films resulted from the heavy use of crime formula stories in B features. Breen to Hays, 6 September 1939, MPA 1939 Production Code file.
64. "Whose Business Is the Motion Picture," *Motion Picture Herald*, 22 February 1936, pp. 15–16. According to the MPPDA, MGM's access to the British and French markets might well be affected in addition to the almost certain loss of the German and Italian markets to the company and possibly the industry as a whole.
65. Breen, 22 June 1938, MPA 1939 Production Code file.
66. These bound volumes were titled the "Opinions of the Production Code Administration," but they were never published. They were prepared by Charles R. Metzger and are referred to by Moley, p. 97, and by Vizzard, p. 10. To some extent they represented an attempted codification of precedent and case law in the PCA.
67. Morris L. Ernst, *The First Freedom* (New York: Macmillan, 1946), p. 203; *New York Times*, 26 June 1938; Thorp, p. 127; Memo attached to letter, Breen to Lord, 5 December 1937, folder, Joe Breen, 1933–1942, Lord Papers. For a discussion of the importance of the foreign market in this period, see Vasey.
68. Nancy Lynn Schwartz, *The Hollywood Writers' Wars* (New York: Knopf, 1982), p. 127; MPPDA internal memo, 31 August 1938, MPA 1939 Production Code file.
69. Quigley to Hays, 11 July 1938, MPA 1939 Production Code file; Harmon and Milliken memo to Hays, 20 September 1938; Norr to Harmon, 12 January 1939, MPA 1939 Production Code file.
70. Quigley, 10 January 1939, quoted in Leff and Simmons, p. 65; Norr to Harmon, 12 January 1939, MPA 1939 Production Code file.
71. Thorp, pp. 160–162; Wolfe, p. 304.
72. Jowett, p. 202; David O. Selznick to Jock Whitney, 6 September 1939, GONE WITH THE WIND Censorship File, Selznick Papers, quoted in Leff and Simmons, pp. 100–101; Walter Wanger, in *Time*, quoted in Kenneth Clark to Hays, 2 May 1939, MPA 1939 Production Code file.

CHAPTER 4. Feeding the Maw of Exhibition

1. This discussion is indebted to Janet Staiger's analysis of the studio system in David Bordwell, Janet Staiger, and Kristin Thompson, *The Classical Hollywood Cinema: Film Style and Mode of Production to 1960* (New York: Columbia University Press, 1985).
2. "Loew's Inc." *Fortune*, August 1939; repr. in Tino Balio, ed., *The American Film Industry*, rev. ed. (Madison: University of Wisconsin Press, 1985), p. 339; "File Details of Loew's $15,000,000 Plan," *Variety*, 8 February 1936, p. 4.
3. "Metro-Goldwyn-Mayer," *Fortune*, December 1932; repr. in Balio, ed., *The American Film Industry*, p. 313.

4. *Ibid.*, p. 316.
5. Howard T. Lewis, *The Motion Picture Industry* (New York: Van Nostrand, 1933), p. 103; Jesse L. Lasky, "The Producer Makes a Plan," in Nancy Naumberg, ed., *We Make the Movies* (New York: Norton, 1937), p. 5; Bordwell, Staiger, and Thompson, *The Classical Hollywood Cinema*, p. 321.
6. Douglas Gomery, *The Hollywood Studio System* (New York: St. Martin's, 1986), p. 70.
7. "Warner Bros." *Fortune*, December 1937, pp. 110–113; Bordwell, Steiger, and Thompson, *The Classical Hollywood Cinema*, p. 326.
8. "Paramount," *Fortune*, March 1937, pp. 87–96.
9. Leo C. Rosten, *Hollywood: The Movie Colony, the Movie Makers* (New York: Harcourt, Brace, 1941), p. 246.
10. David O. Selznick, "Then and Now . . . The Functions of a Producer," *Journal of the Producers Guild of America* 14 (December 1972), p. 24; "Stage Does Not Dominate," *Variety*, 31 March 1937, p. 5; David Gordon, "Mayer, Thalberg and MGM," *Sight and Sound* 45 (Summer 1976), p. 187; Samuel Marx, *Mayer and Thalberg: The Make-Believe Saints* (New York: Random House, 1975); "Metro-Goldwyn-Mayer," *Fortune*, December 1932; Bordwell, Staiger, and Thompson, *The Classical Hollywood Cinema*, p. 326.
11. Gomery, *The Hollywood Studio System*, p. 39.
12. Rosten, *Hollywood*, p. 303.
13. Charles Wolfe, *Frank Capra: A Guide to References and Resources* (Boston: G. K. Hall, 1987), p. 12.
14. *Ibid.*, p. 10.
15. *Ibid*, p. 11.
16. "Stage Does Not Dominate," *Variety*, 31 March 1937, p. 5; Rosten, *Hollywood*, pp. 283, 292.
17. *Ibid.*, pp. 265, 283; Arthur Ungar, "1939 Hollywood Toppers," *Variety*, 3 January 1940, p. 28.
18. Rosten, *Hollywood*, p. 265.
19. Wolfe, *Frank Capra*, p. 5.
20. Richard Fine, *Hollywood and the Profession of Authorship, 1928–1940* (Ann Arbor, Mich.: UMI Research Press, 1979), pp. 75–76.
21. Rosten, *Hollywood*, p. 323.
22. Fine, *Hollywood and the Profession of Authorship*, p. 92.
23. *Ibid.*, pp. 116–118.
24. *Ibid.*, p. 122.
25. *Ibid.*, p. 145.
26. Larry Ceplair and Steven Englund, *Inquisition in Hollywood: Politics in the Film Community, 1930–1960* (Garden City, N.Y.: Anchor Press, 1980), pp. 16–46.
27. Rosten, *Hollywood*, p. 318.
28. Thomas Schatz, *The Genius of the System: Hollywood Filmmaking in the Studio Era* (New York: Pantheon, 1988), p. 6.
29. Morton Eustis, "Designing for the Movies: Gibbons of MGM," *Theatre Arts*, October 1937, p. 785; Beverly Heisner, *Hollywood Art: Art Direction in the Days of the Great Studios* (Jefferson, N.C.: McFarland, 1990), pp. 25–40.
30. Heisner, *Hollywood Art*, pp. 61–62.
31. *Ibid.*, p. 38.
32. John Hambley and Patrick Downing, *The Art of Hollywood: Fifty Years of Art Direction* (London: Thames Television, 1979), p. 53.
33. Gary Carey, *All the Stars in Heaven: Louis B. Mayer's MGM* (New York: E. P. Dutton, 1981), p. 80.
34. Léon Barsacq, *Caligari's Cabinet and Other Grand Illusions: A History of Film Design*, rev. ed. by Elliott Stein (New York: New American Library, 1978), p. 233; Arlene Croce, *The Fred Astaire and Ginger Rogers Book* (New York: Galahad Books, 1972), p. 25.
35. Heisner, *Hollywood Art*, p. 172.
36. Hambley and Downing, *The Art of Hollywood*, pp. 29–35.
37. Rudy Behlmer, ed., *Memo from David O. Selznick* (New York: Viking, 1972), p. 151; Hambley and Downing, *The Art of Hollywood*, pp. 91–97; Ronald Haver, *David O. Selznick's Hollywood* (New York: Bonanza Books, 1980), p. 309.
38. W. Robert La Vine, *In a Glamorous Fashion: The Fabulous Years of Hollywood Costume Design* (New York: Charles Scribner's Sons, 1980), p. 94.
39. Edward Maeder, *Hollywood and History: Costume Design in Films* (Los Angeles: Los Angeles County Museum of Art, 1987), p. 81.
40. La Vine, *In a Glamorous Fashion*, p. 64.
41. David Chierichetti, *Hollywood Costume Design* (London: Studio Vista, 1976), p. 74; La Vine, *In a Glamorous Fashion*, p. 64.
42. "Six Decades of 'Loyalty, Progress, Artistry,'" *American Cinematographer* 60 (June 1979), pp. 576–577.
43. John Arnold, "Shooting the Movies," in Naumberg, ed., *We Make the Movies*, p. 157.

44. Eustis, "Designing for the Movies," p. 798.
45. Gregg Toland, "The Motion Picture Cameraman," *Theatre Arts Monthly*, September 1941, p. 652; Karl Struss, "Photographic Modernism and the Cinematographer," *American Cinematographer*, November 1934, pp. 296–297.
46. Charles Higham, ed., *Hollywood Cameramen: Sources of Light* (Bloomington: Indiana University Press, 1970), p. 142; "Little Fraternity Which Grinds Hollywood's Cameras," *Time*, 2 December 1940, p. 77.
47. "Metro-Goldwyn-Mayer," in Balio, ed., *The American Film Industry*, p. 312; Rudy Behlmer, ed., *Inside Warner Bros. (1935–1951)* (New York: Viking, 1985), p. 55; "Loew's, Inc.," in Balio, *op. cit.*, p. 343.
48. *VFR*, 10 August 1938.
49. Robert Gustafson, "The Buying of Ideas: Source Acquisition at Warner Brothers, 1930–1949" (Ph.D. diss., University of Wisconsin, 1983), p. 14.
50. *Ibid.*, p. 122.
51. Howard T. Lewis, *The Motion Picture Industry* (New York: Van Nostrand, 1933), pp. 83, 94.
52. John Davis, "Warners' Genres of the '30s and '40s," *Velvet Light Trap*. No. 15, pp. 56–60.
53. Lewis, *The Motion Picture Industry*, p. 108; Thomas Simonet, "Conglomerates and Content: Remakes, Sequels and Series in the New Hollywood," in Bruce Austin, ed., *Current Research in Film: Audiences, Economics, and Law*, vol. 3 (Norwood, N.J.: Ablex, 1987), p. 154.
54. "Twentieth Century–Fox," *Fortune*, December 1935, pp. 85–93; Schatz, *The Genius of the System*, p. 216; "Doubles Look In to Stay," *Variety*, 24 March 1937, p. 7.
55. Schatz, *The Genius of the System*, p. 257.
56. Gomery, *The Hollywood Studio System*, p. 97.
57. *VFR*, 6 October 1937.
58. Tino Balio, "Columbia Pictures: The Making of a Major Motion Picture Company, 1930–1934," paper presented at the Mostra Internazionale del Nuovo Cinema, Ancona, Italy, December 3-8, 1988.
59. *VFR*, 4 July 1933.
60. Gomery, *The Hollywood Studio System*, p. 155.
61. Tino Balio, *United Artists: The Company Built By the Stars* (Madison: University of Wisconsin Press, 1975).
62. David O. Selznick, "The Functions of the Producer and the Making of Feature Films," in Rudy Behlmer, ed., *Memo from David O. Selznick* (New York: Viking, 1972), p. 495.

CHAPTER 5. Technological Change and Classical Film Style

Most of the data for this chapter derive from material in the following publications: *American Cinematographer* (hereafter *AC*), *Journal of the Society of Motion Picture Engineers* (*JSMPE;* later, *SMPTE Journal*), *International Photographer* (*IP*), *International Projectionist* (*IPro*), *Projection Engineering, Sound Engineering,* and *AMPAS Bulletin.* More detailed discussion of many topics in this chapter can be found in Chapters 19–23 and 27–29 of David Bordwell, Janet Staiger, and Kristin Thompson, *The Classical Hollywood Cinema: Film Style and Mode of Production to 1960* (New York: Columbia University Press, 1985).

1. See, for example, Raymond Bellour, "Alterner/raconter," in Bellour, ed., *Le cinéma américain: Analyses de films,* vol. 1 (Paris: Flammarion, 1980), pp. 69–88.
2. Quoted in "Max Steiner Comments on Music Scoring," *Film Music Notes* 2, no. 4 (January 1943), p. 3.
3. Quoted in Lester Koenig, "Gregg Toland, Film-Maker," *Screen Writer* 3, no. 7 (December 1947), p. 27.
4. See, for example, Walter B. Pitkin and William M. Marston, *The Art of Sound Pictures* (New York: Appleton, 1930), pp. 121–126.
5. Morton Eustis, "Designing for the Movies: Gibbons of MGM," *Theatre Arts*, October 1937, p. 794.
6. A. Lindsley Lane, "Cinematographer Plays Leading Part in Group of Creative Minds," *AC* 16, no. 2 (February 1935), p. 49.
7. Tamar Lane, *The New Technique of Screen Writing: A Practical Guide to the Writing and Marketing of Photoplays* (New York: Whittlesey House, 1936), p. 37.
8. For historical surveys, see Laurence J. Roberts, "Cameras and Systems: A History of Contributions from the Bell & Howell Co.," *SMPTE Journal* 91, no. 10 (October 1982), pp. 934–946, and 91, no. 11 (November 1982), pp. 1079–1086; and John M. Ehrenburg and Laurence J. Roberts, "Seventy-Five Years of Motion-Picture Standards: Contributions of the Bell & Howell Co.," *SMPTE Journal* 92, no. 10 (October 1983), pp. 1058–1065.

9. For a history of the Mitchell company, see Laurence J. Roberts, "The Mitchell Camera: The Machine and Its Makers," *SMPTE Journal* 91, no. 2 (February 1982), pp. 141–152.

10. Quoted in Fred W. Jackman, "Birthday of the ASC," *AC* 23, no. 1 (January 1942), p. 5.

11. "Research in Hollywood," *Projection Engineering* 4, no. 11 (November 1932), p. 9.

12. William Koenig, "The Organization and Activities of the Research Council of the Academy of Motion Picture Arts and Sciences," *JSMPE* 29, no. 5 (November 1937), pp. 484–485.

13. "Report of the Sound Committee," *JSMPE* 28, no. 1 (January 1937), pp. 24–25.

14. Peter Mole, "Will There Always Be a Need for Carbon Arcs?" *AC* 31, no. 2 (February 1951), pp. 51, 72.

15. H. G. Tasker, "Slide-Rule Sketches of Hollywood," *JSMPE* 28, no. 2 (February 1937), p. 158; Frank T. Jamey, Jr., "The Push-Pull Sound Recording and Reproducing System," *IPro* 12, no. 4 (April 1937), pp. 19–20, 29–30; J. K. Hilliard, "Push-Pull Recording," *JSMPE* 30, no. 2 (February 1938), pp. 156, 161.

16. "The Influence of Sound Accompaniment on the Dramatic Value of Pictures," *IPro* 15, no. 4 (April 1940), pp. 20–21.

17. H. G. Tasker, "Multiple-Channel Recording," *JSMPE* 31, no. 4 (October 1938), pp. 381–385.

18. J. N. A. Hawkins, "Slyfield's New Mixers' Gallows," *IP* 10, no. 5 (June 1938): 18.

19. Leroy Chadbourne, "Effect of New Recordings on Theatre Sound Reproduction," *IPro* 12, no. 5 (May 1937), pp. 16–18.

20. Barry Salt, *Film Style and Technology: History and Analysis* (London: Starword, 1983), p. 285. This procedure is confirmed in Edward Dmytryk, *On Film Editing: An Introduction to the Art of Film Construction* (Boston: Focal Press, 1984), pp. 57–70.

21. A detailed study of operatic techniques in Hollywood film scoring is Robbert van der Lek, "Diegetic Music in Opera and Film: A Similarity Between Two Genres of Drama Analyzed in Works by Erich Wolfgang Korngold" (Ph.D. diss., University of Amsterdam, 1991).

22. See, for example, the discussion reported in Hal Hall, "Cinematographers and Directors Meet," *AC* 13, no. 4 (August 1932), pp. 10, 47.

23. Lewis W. Physioc, "Unterrified Inventors Show Work," *IP* 4, no. 5 (June 1932), p. 4; "New Perambulator and Camera," *AC* 13, no. 2 (June 1932), p. 16; "The New Bell & Howell Rotambulator," *IP* 5, no. 6 (July 1933), p. 13; Joseph Dubray, "The Rotambulator—A New Motion Picture Camera Stand," *JSMPE* 22, no. 3 (March 1934), pp. 201–202, 205.

24. John F. Seitz, "New Camera-Carriage Saves Time," *AC* 14, no. 1 (May 1933), p. 8.

25. Advertisement in *AC* 17, no. 3 (March 1936), p. 94; "Progress in the Motion Picture Industry," *JSMPE* 27, no. 7 (July 1936), pp. 11–12; "Technical Progress in the Industry During 1936," *AC* 17, no. 12 (December 1936), pp. 502–503.

26. "Report of the Studio Lighting Committee," *JSMPE* 29, no. 3 (March 1938), p. 294.

27. An example is Victor Milner, "Let's Stop Abusing Camera Movement," *AC* 16, no. 2 (February 1935), pp. 46–47, 58–60.

28. A. Lindsley Lane, "Rhythmic Flow—Mental and Visual," *AC* 16, no. 4 (April 1935), p. 138.

29. "Report of the Studio Lighting Committee," *JSMPE* 29, no. 3 (March 1938), pp. 294–298.

30. Gordon S. Mitchell, "The Camera Crane Used in Making Intricate Shots," *Projection Engineering* 3, no. 2 (February 1931), pp. 13–14.

31. William Stull, "MGM Builds Unique Camera Boom," *AC* 20, no. 12 (December 1939), pp. 539–540, 572.

32. Ronald Haver, *David O. Selznick's Hollywood* (New York: Knopf, 1980), p. 283.

33. A brief but authoritative explanation of the technology can be found in J. A. Ball, "The Technicolor Process of Three-Color Cinematography," *JSMPE* 25, no. 2 (August 1935), pp. 127–138.

34. Joseph V. Mascelli, "The Million Dollar Bubble," *IP* 23, no. 10 (October 1951), p. 8.

35. Through cross-licensing arrangements, Eastman and Technicolor were also cooperating in work on "monopack" color (the single-strip color negative in use today). A detailed discussion of Technicolor's relation to Eastman is George E. Frost and S. Chesterfield Oppenheim, "A Study of the Professional Color Motion Picture Antitrust Decrees and Their Effects," *The Patent, Trademark and Copyright Journal of Research and Education* 4, no. 1 (Spring 1960), pp. 1–39, and 4, no. 2 (Summer 1960), pp. 108–149.

36. Natalie Kalmus, "Colour," in Stephen Watts, ed., *Behind the Screen: How Films Are Made* (New York: Dodge, 1938), p. 122.

37. Lansing C. Holden, "Designing for Color," in Naumberg, ed., *We Make the Movies*, p. 240.

38. Quoted in Fred E. Basten, *Glorious Technicolor: The Movies' Magic Rainbow* (New York: A.S. Barnes, 1980), p. 30.

39. How contemporary archivists recovered the look of prime Technicolor is recounted in Robert Gitt and Richard Dayton, "Restoring *Becky Sharp*," *AC* 65, no. 10 (November 1984), pp. 99–106.

40. Farciot Edouart, "The Evoution of Transparency Process Photography," *American Cinematographer* 24, no. 10 (October 1943), p. 359.

41. George E. Turner, "The Evolution of Special Visual Effects," in Linwood Dunn and George E. Turner, eds., *The ASC Treasury of Visual Effects* (Hollywood: American Society of Cinematographers, 1983), p. 45.
42. Cecil B. DeMille, "A Director Looks at 'Process-Shots,'" *AC* 17, no. 11 (November 1936), pp. 458–459.
43. Edouart, "The Evolution of Transparency Process Photography," pp. 359, 380.
44. Clarence W. D. Slifer, "Creating Visual Effects for *GWTW*," in Dunn and Turner, *The ASC Treasury of Visual Effects*, pp. 121–122.
45. Linwood G. Dunn, "Historical Facts About the Acme-Dunn Optical Printer" and "Academy Scientific or Technical Awards Presentation," both *AC* 62, no. 5 (May 1981), pp. 476, 479.
46. MGM's ROSALIE (1937) was said to have used nine cameras for each scene, with some at ground level, some very high, and one on a perpetually moving crane. Cf. "Nine Cameras Film Huge Set," *International Photographer* 9, no. 12 (January 1938), pp. 24–26.
47. Quoted in Scott Eyman, *Five American Cinematographers: Interviews with Karl Struss, Joseph Ruttenberg, James Wong Howe, Linwood Dunn, and William H. Clothier* (Metuchen, N.J.: Scarecrow Press, 1987), p. 42.
48. Kristin Thompson discusses the soft style in silent cinematography in Bordwell, Staiger, and Thompson, *Classical Hollywood Cinema*, pp. 286–293.
49. Clyde De Vinna, "New Angles on Fast Film," *AC* 12, no. 2 (June 1931), 22; Oliver Marsh, "Super-Sensitive Film in Production," *AC* 12, no. 1 (May 1931), p. 11.
50. "ASC Recommends Fast Film," *AC* 12, no. 3 (July 1931), p. 19.
51. "What 1937 Has Shown in Technical Progress in Motion Picture Making," *AC* 18, no. 12 (December 1937), p. 494; "Pan and Sound Put Inkies on Top," *IP* 10, no. 3 (April 1938), pp. 43–48; "Lighting the New Fast Films," *AC* 20, no. 2 (February 1939), pp. 69–70.
52. "Riddle Me This," *AC* 13, no. 6 (October 1932), p. 16.
53. James Wong Howe, "Upsetting Traditions with 'Viva Villa!' " *AC* 15, no. 2 (June 1934), pp. 71–72.
54. A useful account of Toland's career is George E. Turner, "Gregg Toland, ASC," *AC* 64, no. 11 (November 1982), pp. 1144–1148, 1220–1228.

CHAPTER 6. Selling Stars

1. Alexander Walker, *Stardom: The Hollywood Phenomenon* (New York: Stein and Day, 1970), p. 240.
2. Cathy Klaprat, "The Star as Market Strategy: Bette Davis in Another Light," in Tino Balio, ed., *The American Film Industry*, rev. ed. (Madison: University of Wisconsin Press, 1985), pp. 351–376.
3. *Ibid.*, p. 354.
4. *Ibid.*, p. 375–376.
5. Leo C. Rosten, *Hollywood: The Movie Colony, the Movie Makers* (New York: Harcourt, Brace, 1941), pp. 331–332.
6. Walker, *Stardom*, p. 233.
7. Quoted in David Shipman, *The Great Movie Stars: The Golden Years* (New York: Hill and Wang, 1979), p. 530; "Stand Up and Cheer," *VFR*, 24 April 1934.
8. Robert Windeler, *Shirley Temple* (London: W. H. Allen, 1976), p. 34.
9. Bob Moak, "Heavy Run of Kid Films," *Variety*, 20 September 1939, p. 27.
10. Shipman, *The Great Movie Stars*, pp. 227, 229.
11. Alexander Walker, *Garbo: A Portrait* (New York: Macmillan, 1980), p. 132; Shipman, *The Great Movie Stars*, pp. 230, 232.
12. Shipman, *The Great Movie Stars*, p. 131.
13. *Ibid.*, p. 151.
14. *Ibid.*, p. 536.
15. *Ibid.*, p. 93.
16. *Ibid.*, p. 24.
17. David F. Prindle, *The Politics of Glamour: Ideology and Democracy in the Screen Actors Guild* (Madison: University of Wisconsin Press, 1988), p. 24; "Actor's Report to NRA," *Variety*, 18 January 1935, p. 11.
18. "100% Screen Actors Guild," *Variety*, 10 October 1933, p. 7; "Actor's Report to NRA," *Variety*, 18 January 1935, p. 11.
19. "Actors Lash Film Execs," *Variety*, 8 January 1935, p. 3.
20. Danae Clark, "Labor Discouse and (Extra)Textual Politics in New Deal Entertainment," Paper presented at the Society for Cinema Studies Conference, Iowa City, Iowa, 1989.
21. Jay Brien Chapman, "Figuring the Stars' Salaries," in Martin Levin, ed., *Hollywood and the Great Fan Magazines* (New York: Arbor House, 1970), p. 68
22. M. Thompson, "Hollywood Is a Uniontown," *Nation*, 2 April 1938, p. 383.

23. "Hollywood Middleman," *Saturday Evening Post*, 27 June 1936, p. 96.
24. "Only 10 Exclusive Stars," *Variety*, 3 July 1935, p. 23; "Less Than 2,000 Players Work," *Variety*, 7 September 1938, p. 2; "Hollywood Middleman," *Saturday Evening Post*, 29 August 1936, p. 68.
25. "Less Than 2,000 Players Work," *Variety*, 7 September 1938, p. 2; Joe Bigelow, "New, Old and Out Stars," *Variety*, 23 June 1931, p. 1; "H'wood's 2d Chance Stars," *Variety*, 24 April 1935, p. 3.
26. "Thalberg Claims Longer Life," *Variety*, 22 September 1931, p. 5.
27. Rosten, *Hollywood*, p. 345.
28. Alva Johnston, "Hollywood's Ten Percenters," *Saturday Evening Post*, 8 August 1942, pp. 10, 36; "The Morris Agency," *Fortune*, September 1938, pp. 71–73; "Hollywood Middleman," *Saturday Evening Post*, 27 June 1936, p. 94.
29. Johnston, "Hollywood's Ten Percenters," p. 36.
30. *Ibid.*, p. 36.
31. "Less Than 2,000 Players Work," *Variety*, 7 September 1938, p. 2.
32. *Ibid.*, p. 2.
33. "Hollywood Middleman," *Saturday Evening Post*, 29 August 1936, p. 17.
34. "Lively Trading Keeps Name Players on Move," *Variety*, 7 July 1937, p. 4.
35. Mae Huettig, "Economic Control of the Motion Picture Industry," in Tino Balio, ed., *The American Film Industry*, rev. ed. (Madison: University of Wisconsin Press, 1985), p. 309.
36. "Warners Adamant," *Variety*, 19 April 1932, p. 3; quoted in Shipman, *The Great Movie Stars*, p. 93.
37. "James Cagney Called Bad Boy," *Variety*, 11 March 1936, p. 3.
38. "WB Statement Characterizes Cagney Decision," *Variety*, 18 March 1936, p. 2.
39. Shipman, *The Great Movie Stars*, p. 94.
40. Thomas Schatz, *The Genius of the System: Hollywood Filmmaking in the Studio Era* (New York: Pantheon Books, 1988), pp. 219–220.
41. "Bette Davis in Salary Tiff with WB," *Variety*, 8 July 1936, p. 3.
42. Schatz, *The Genius of the System*, p. 220.
43. Klaprat, "The Star as Market Strategy," p. 376.
44. Schatz, *The Genius of the System*, p. 318.
45. "Star Changes up to Now," *Variety*, 18 February 1931, p. 28; "Film Names 70% Stage," *Variety*, 23 January 1934, pp. 1, 23.
46. "H'wood's Debt to Vaude," *Variety*, 24 June 1936, p. 3.
47. Hortense Powdermaker, *Hollywood, the Dream Factory* (Boston: Little, Brown, 1950), p. 246; Douglas Gomery, *The Hollywood Studio System* (New York: St. Martin's Press, 1986), p. 41.
48. Henry Jenkins III, "A Star Is (Re)Born: The Cultural Assimilation of Eddie Cantor" (Unpublished paper, University of Wisconsin, n.d.); "Kid from Spain," *VFR*, 22 November 1932.
49. Jenkins, "A Star Is (Re)Born."
50. *Ibid.*
51. "Myrt and Marge," *VFR*, 13 June 1933.
52. Kevin Heffernan, "Product Differentiation: Paramount's Use of Radio Talent, 1932–34" (Unpublished paper, University of Wisconsin, 1990).
53. Klaprat, "The Star as Market Strategy," p. 360.
54. *Ibid.*, p. 360.
55. *Ibid.*, p. 363.
56. "Funny Guys Last Longest," *Variety*, 30 June 1937, p. 5.
57. *Ibid.*, p. 29; Klaprat, "The Star as Market Strategy," p. 372.
58. *Ibid.*, p. 372.
59. Margaret Sullivan, "A Promotional Study of *Captain Blood*" (Unpublished paper, University of Wisconsin, 1974) and "The Art of Selling the Star System: A Study of Studio Publicity" (Unpublished paper, University of Wisconsin, 1977).
60. John Kobal, ed., *Hollywood Glamour Portraits* (New York: Dover Publications, 1976), pp. v–vi.
61. Margaret Farrand Thorp, *America at the Movies* (New Haven, Conn.: Yale University Press, 1939), p. 74.
62. Charles Eckert, "The Carole Lombard in Macy's Window," *Quarterly Review of Film Studies* 3 (Winter 1978), pp. 10-11.
63. Edward Maeder, *Hollywood and History: Costume Design in Film* (Los Angeles: Los Angeles County Museum of Art, 1987), pp. 81–82, 87, 88.
64. Michele Hilmes, *Hollywood and Broadcasting: From Radio to Cable* (Urbana: University of Illinois Press, 1990), p. 67.
65. Hilmes, *Hollywood and Broadcasting*, pp. 63–70.
66. Mary Beth Haralovich, "Motion Picture Advertising: Industrial and Social Forces and Effects, 1930–1948" (Ph.D. diss., University of Wisconsin, 1984), pp. 118–119.
67. Eckert, "The Carole Lombard in Macy's Window," p. 3.
68. *Ibid.*, "Warner Train Speeds Up Records," *MPH*, 4 March 1933, p. 35.

69. Roy Chartier, "The Year in Pictures," *Variety*, 3 January 1940, p. 5.
70. David Bordwell, Janet Staiger, and Kristin Thompson, *The Classical Hollywood Cinema: Film Styles and Mode of Production to 1960* (New York: Columbia University Press, 1985), p. 99.
71. Sullivan, "A Promotional Study of *Captain Blood.*"
72. *Captain Blood* Pressbook, Warner Bros. Film Library, Wisconsin Center for Film and Theater Research, State Historical Society of Wisconsin, Madison.

CHAPTER 7. Production Trends

1. "Producers Aim Classics," *MPH*, 15 August 1936, p. 13.
2. "Picture Biz Strong," *Variety*, 21 July 1937, p. 4; "Film Roadshows Drop," *MPH*, 20 August 1938, p. 15.
3. David Thompson, "All Quiet on the Western Front," in Ann Lloyd, ed., *Movies of the Thirties* (London: Orbis, 1983), p. 16; Thomas Schatz, *The Genius of the System: Hollywood Filmmaking in the Studio Era* (New York: Pantheon, 1988), pp. 83–85.
4. *NYTFR*, 1 December 1932.
5. Sid Silverman, "U.S. Film Field for 1930," *Variety*, 31 December 1930, p. 7.
6. Beverly Heisner, *Hollywood Art: Art Direction in the Days of the Great Studios* (Jefferson, N.C.: McFarland, 1990), p. 51; *NYTFR*, 8 December 1931.
7. "Metro-Goldwyn-Mayer," *Fortune*, December 1932, repr. in Tino Balio, ed., *The American Film Industry*, rev. ed. (Madison: University of Wisconsin Press, 1985), p. 312; Ronald Haver, *David O. Selznick's Hollywood* (New York: Alfred A. Knopf, 1980), p. 152.
8. *VFR*, 19 March 1930.
9. Bosley Crowther, *The Lion's Share: The Story of an Entertainment Empire* (New York: E. P. Dutton, 1957), p. 188; *VFR*, 15 September 1931.
10. "*Little Women* Taps New Movie Market," *Forbes*, 1 April 1934, pp. 14–15; *VFR*, 21 November 1933.
11. "Biographical Cycle," *Variety*, 13 February 1934, p. 3.
12. *NYTFR*, 29 September 1934.
13. Roy Chartier, "40 $1,000,000 Grossers," *Variety*, 21 July 1937, p. 3; John C. Flinn, "H'wood's $1,000,000 Cycle," *Variety*, 22 September 1937, p. 1.
14. "Producers Aim Classics," *MPH*, 15 August 1936, p. 13; Roy Chartier, "Shakespeare's B.O. in Stix," *Variety*, 4 March 1936, p. 23; Nick Roddick, *A New Deal in Entertainment: Warner Brothers in the 1930s* (London: British Film Institute, 1983), pp. 231–234.
15. John C. Flinn, "The Bard a B.O. Washout," *Variety*, 9 December 1936, p. 3.
16. *Ibid.*
17. *NYTFR*, 10 October 1935: *VFR*, 16 October 1935.
18. Roger Dooley, *From Scarface to Scarlett: American Films in the* 1930s (New York: Harcourt Brace Jovanovich, 1979), p. 186.
19. *NYTFR*, 21 August 1936; John C. Flinn, "The Bard a B.O. Washout," *Variety*, 9 December 1936, p. 3.
20. Roddick, *A New Deal in Entertainment*, p. 184.
21. Roddick, *A New Deal in Entertainment*, p. 199; quoted in Dooley, *From Scarface to Scarlett*, p. 172; Paul J. Vanderwood, ed., *Juarez* (Madison: University of Wisconsin Press, 1983), p. 18.
22. *NYTFR*, 18 August 1934; 27 September 1934.
23. Tony Thomas, *The Great Adventure Films* (Secaucus, N.J.: Citadel, 1976), pp. 1–3.
24. "Pic Cycle on Horseback," *Variety*, 3 March 1939, p. 5.
25. "Pic Cycle on Horseback," *Variety*, 3 January 1939, p. 5; John C. Flinn, "Film Showmanship," *Variety*, 8 March 1939, p. 8.
26. Arthur Ungar, "Hollywood Players Capture Dodge City at Record Premiere," *Variety*, 5 April 1939, p. 8; "Omaha, Noisy Host, Welcomes 250,000 for 'U.P.' Premiere," *ibid.*, 3 May 1939, p. 8.
27. Sumiko Higashi, *Cecil B. DeMille: A Guide to References and Resources* (Boston: G. K. Hall, 1985), pp. 32, 33.
28. "Loew's, Inc.," *Fortune*, August 1939, repr. in Balio, ed., *The American Film Industry*, p. 334.
29. *NYTFR* 9 November 1935.
30. *Ibid.*, 3 February 1937.
31. Haver, *David O. Selznick's Hollywood*, p. 156.
32. *NYTFR*, 19 January 1935.
33. Dooley, *From Scarface to Scarlett*, p. 183.
34. Gavin Lambert, *Norma Shearer: A Life* (New York: Knopf, 1990), p. 270.
35. *NYTFR*, 27 June 1936.
36. *Ibid.*, 12 May 1937.
37. *Ibid.*, 4 November 1938.
38. *Ibid.*, 16 May 1939.

39. Thomas Cripps, ed., *The Green Pastures* (Madison: University of Wisconsin Press, 1979), pp. 12, 25, 30.
40. Roddick, *A New Deal in Entertainment*, p. 179; *VFR*, 12 February 1936.
41. *NYTFR*, 10 February 1936; Roddick, *A New Deal in Entertainment*, pp. 184–185.
42. Quoted in Schatz, *The Genius of the System*, pp. 211–212; *NYTFR*, 12 August 1937.
43. *VFR*, 25 April 1939; Vanderwood, ed., *Juarez*, p. 40.
44. Roddick, *A New Deal in Entertainment*, pp. 29–30.
45. *Ibid.*, p. 235.
46. *VFR*, 31 October 1936.
47. *NYTFR*, 13 May 1938; Rudy Behlmer, ed., *The Adventures of Robin Hood* (Madison: University of Wisconsin Press, 1979), p. 39.
48. *NYTFR*, 2 December 1939.
49. Tino Balio, *United Artists: The Company Built by the Stars* (Madison: University of Wisconsin Press, 1975).
50. *NYTFR*, 10 November 1937.
51. *Ibid.*, 24 September 1936; *VFR*, 30 September 1936.
52. A. Scott Berg, *Goldwyn* (New York: Alfred Knopf, 1989), p. 278, 292; Richard Griffith, *Samuel Goldwyn: The Producer and His Films* (New York: Museum of Modern Art, 1956), p. 30.
53. *NYTFR*, 14 April 1939.
54. Quoted in Schatz, *The Genius of the System*, p. 178.
55. *NYTFR*, 23 April 1937.
56. Haver, *David O. Selznick's Hollywood*, p. 243.
57. Dooley, *From Scarface to Scarlett*, p. 611.
58. Haver, *David O. Selznick's Hollywood*, p. 243.
59. Helen Taylor, *Scarlett's Women: "Gone with the Wind" and Its Female Fans* (New Brunswick, N.J.: Rutgers University Press, 1989), p. 238.
60. Haver, *David O. Selznick's Hollywood*, p. 241.
61. *Ibid.*, p. 296.
62. "Three Years of Hullabaloo," *Newsweek*, 25 December 1939, pp. 26–29.
63. Sid Silverman, "U.S. Film Field for 1930," *Variety*, 10 December 1930, p. 7; Ethan Mordden, *The Hollywood Musical* (New York: St. Martin's Press, 1981), p. 43; Alexander Walker, *The Shattered Silents: How the Talkies Came to Stay* (New York: William Morrow, 1979), p. 179.
64. Walker, *The Shattered Silents*, p. 184.
65. Stanley Green, *Encyclopedia of the Musical Film* (New York: Oxford University Press, 1981), p. 38; "Ingredients for Backstage Talkers," *Variety*, 13 November 1929, p. 9.
66. *VFR*, 27 November 1929.
67. *Ibid.*, 27 May 1931; 23 August 1932.
68. *Ibid.*, 14 March 1933.
69. Gerald Mast, *Can't Help Singin': The American Musical on Stage and Screen* (Woodstock, N.Y.: Overlook Press, 1987), pp. 123–124.
70. *VFR*, 14 March 1933.
71. Roy Hemming, *The Melody Lingers On: The Great Songwriters and Their Movie Musicals* (New York: Newmarket Press, 1986), p. 273.
72. Richard B. Jewell, with Vernon Harbin, *The RKO Story* (New York: Arlington House, 1982), p. 69; *VFR*, 26 December 1933.
73. Jewell, *The RKO Story*, p. 69; Mast, *Can't Help Singin'*, p. 146.
74. Arlene Croce, *The Fred Astaire and Ginger Rogers Book* (New York: Galahad Books, 1972), pp. 90–91.
75. Jerome Delamater, "Performing Arts: The Musical," in Stuart Kaminsky, *American Film Genres: Approaches to a Critical Theory of Popular Film* (Dayton, Ohio: Pflaum, 1974), p. 128.
76. *VFR*, 20 November 1934.
77. Jewell, *The RKO Story*, p. 83.
78. *VFR*, 4 September 1935; Jewell, *The RKO Story*, p. 88.
79. *The RKO Story*, p. 98.
80. Arthur Unger, "Leading Film Names of 1935," *Variety*, 1 January 1936, p. 4; John Kobal, *Gotta Sing, Gotta Dance: A Pictorial History of Film Musicals* (New York: Hamlyn, 1971), p. 149.
81. Mordden, *The Hollywood Musical*, p. 94.
82. *VFR*, 9 December 1936.
83. *NYTFR*, 9 April 1936; "Top Pix and Stars for 1937," *Variety*, 5 January 1938, p. 12.
84. *VFR*, 16 August 1939.
85. Green, *Encyclopedia of the Musical Film*, p. 306.
86. David Shipman, *The Great Movie Stars: The Golden Years* (New York: Bonanza Books, 1970) p. 245.
87. Quoted in Dooley, *From Scarface to Scarlett*, p. 538.

88. Kobal, *Gotta Sing, Gotta Dance*, p. 175; Robert Windeler, *Shirley Temple* (London: W. H. Allen, 1976), p. 35.
89. *VFR*, July 28, 1937.
90. Kevin Heffernan, "Product Differentiation: Paramount's Use of Radio Talent, 1932–34" (Unpublished paper, University of Wisconsin, 1990).
91. "Deanna Durbin," *Fortune*, October 1939, pp. 66–69; Kobal, *Gotta Sing, Gotta Dance*, p. 157.
92. *VFR*, 27 January 1937; Schatz, *The Genius of the System*, p. 240.
93. "Snow White Reaches Theaters," *MPH*, 19 February 1938, p. 26.
94. Dennis Morrison, "What Is a Filmusical?" *Variety*, 16 June 1937, p. 10; Jack Jungmeyer, "Wane of Filmusicals," *Variety*, 4 January 1939, p. 35.
95. Andrea Walsh, *Women's Film and Female Experience*, 1940–1950 (New York: Praeger, 1984).
96. Quoted in *Ibid.*, p. 25.
97. "Dirt Craze Due to Women," *Variety*, 16 June 1931. p. 1; Lea Jacobs, *The Wages of Sin: Censorship and the Fallen Woman Film*, 1928–1942 (Madison: University of Wisconsin Press, 1991), p. 12.
98. Ruth Morris, "Sinful Girls Lead in 1931," *Variety*, 29 December 1931, p. 5.
99. Jacobs, *The Wages of Sin*, p. 13.
100. "Morals for Movies," *Outlook and Independent*, 16 April 1930, p. 612; Jacobs, *The Wages of Sin*, p. 3; "Another Year of 'Hays-Cleaned' Movies," *Christian Century*, 27 January 1932, p. 108.
101. Moya Luckett, "The Fallen Woman Film and Production Trends of the Early 1930s" (Unpublished paper, University of Wisconsin, 1990).
102. *Ibid.* To determine the number of fallen-woman films Hollywood turned out from 1930 to 1943, Luckett surveyed the Big Five studios by examining plot synopses and reviews from *Variety* and the *New York Times* and by viewing random samples of films.
103. Morris, "Sinful Ladies Lead in 1931," *Variety*, p. 5.
104. Lambert, *Norma Shearer*, p. 165.
105. *VFR*, 6 September 1932
106. Robert C. Allen and Douglas Gomery, *Film History: Theory and Practice* (New York: Alfred A. Knopf, 1985), p. 182.
107. *VFR*, 8 November 1932; Dooley, *From Scarface to Scarlett*, p. 9.
108. Ethan Mordden, *Movie Star: A Look at the Women Who Made Hollywood* (New York: St. Martin's Press, 1983), p. 94; *VFR*, 11 March 1931.
109. Quoted in David Robinson, "Marlene Dietrich," in Ann Lloyd, ed., *Movies of the Thirties* (London: Orbis, 1983), p. 36.
110. *VFR*, 25 July 1933.
111. *NYTFR*, 4 May 1935.
112. *VFR*, 9 May 1933.
113. *VFR*, 13 December 1932.
114. Shipman, *The Great Movie Stars*, p. 265; *VFR*, 19 June 1934.
115. *VFR*, 29 April 1931; 21 July 1931.
116. Jewell, *The RKO Story*, p. 59.
117. *VFR*, 21 January 1931; 28 February 1933; 27 June 1933.
118. Dooley, *From Scarface to Scarlett*, p. 19.
119. *VFR*, 9 June 1931; *Variety*, 5 January 1932, p. 14.
120. *VFR*, 30 August 1932.
121. Jacobs, *The Wages of Sin*, pp. 106–31.
122. *VFR*, 4 August 1937.
123. *NYTFR*, 17 March 1939.
124. *Ibid.*, 22 September, 1939.
125. Joanne Louise Yeck, "The Woman's Film at Warner Brothers, 1935–1950" (Ph.D. diss., University of Southern California, 1982), p. 54.
126. Bernard F. Dick, ed., *Dark Victory* (Madison: University of Wisconsin Press, 1981), p. 41.
127. Griffith, *Samuel Goldwyn*, p. 28; *NYTFR*, 19 March 1936.
128. *Ibid.*, 6 August 1937.
129. *VFR*, 1 February 1939.
130. Taylor, *Scarlett's Women*, p. 88.
131. *Ibid.*, p. 88.
132. "Various Classifications," *Variety*, 30 April 1930, p. 11.
133. Donald W. McCaffrey, *The Golden Age of Sound Comedy: Comic Films and Comedians of the Thirties* (New York: A. S. Barnes, 1973), p. 27.
134. Quoted in Roger Manvell, *Chaplin* (Boston: Little, Brown, 1974), p. 136.
135. Charles J. Maland, *Chaplin and American Culture: The Evolution of a Star Image* (Princeton, N.J.: Princeton University Press, 1989), p. 116; *VFR*, 11 February 1931; Balio, *United Artists*, p. 81.

136. Theodore Huff, *Charlie Chaplin* (New York: Henry Schuman, 1951), p. 253.
137. McCaffrey, *The Golden Age of Sound Comedy*, p. 32; Dooley, *From Scarface to Scarlett*, p. 395.
138. *NYTFR*, 15 September 1932.
139. Shipman, *The Great Movie Stars*, p. 176; *VFR*, 21 January 1931; 4 August 1931.
140. *VFR*, 26 November 1930.
141. *VFR*, 15 August 1933.
142. *VFR*, 9 February 1932.
143. *VFR*, 17 November 1931.
144. Shipman, *The Great Movie Stars*, p. 485.
145. James Harvey, *Romantic Comedy in Hollywood, from Lubitsch to Sturges* (New York: Alfred A. Knopf, 1987), p. 75.
146. Quoted in Harvey, *Romantic Comedy*, p. 47.
147. *Ibid.*, p. 76; *VFR*, 15 November, 1932.
148. Henry Jenkins III, "What Made Pistachio Nuts? Anarchistic Comedy and the Vaudeville Aesthetic" (Ph.D. diss., University of Wisconsin, 1989), p. 39.
149. Gerald Weales, *Canned Goods as Caviar: American Film Comedies of the* 1930s (Chicago: University of Chicago Press, 1985), p. 57.
150. Henry Jenkins III, "'Fifi Was My Mother's Name!': Anarchistic Comedy, the Vaudeville Aesthetic, and *Diplomaniacs*," *Velvet Light Trap* 26 (Fall 1990), pp. 3–27; Dooley, *From Scarface to Scarlett*, p. 406.
151. Weales, *Canned Goods as Caviar*, p. 77.
152. John R. Groch, "What Is a Marx Brother?: Critical Practice, Industrial Practice, and the Notion of Comic Auteur," *Velvet Light Trap* 26 (Fall 1990), pp. 30–41; *VFR*, 13 October 1931; 16 August 1932.
153. *Ibid.*, 25 September 1934.
154. Joel W. Finler, *The Hollywood Story* (New York: Crown, 1988), p. 153; *VFR*, 14 February 1933.
155. *VFR*, 17 October 1933.
156. *VFR*, 25 September 1934.
157. Jenkins, "What Makes Pistachio Nuts?" p. 285.
158. Ted Sennett, *Warner Brothers Presents* (Secaucus, N.J.: Castle Books, 1971), p. 177; Dooley, *From Scarface to Scarlett*, p. 402; McCaffrey, *The Golden Age of Sound Comedy*, p. 104.
159. Jenkins, "What Makes Pistachio Nuts?" pp. 209, 210.
160. *VFR*, 15 May 1935; 18 March 1936.
161. Arthur Ungar, "Best B.O. Pictures of 1936," *Variety*, 23 December 1936, p. 6; Roy Chartier, "The Year in Pictures," *Variety*, 4 January 1939, p. 9.
162. Heidi Kenaga, "Studio Differentiation of 'Screwball' Comedy" (Unpublished paper, University of Wisconsin, 1990).
163. *VFR*, 27 February 1934.
164. *MPH*, 21 April 1934, p. 35; *Film Daily* quote in Kenaga, "Studio Differentiation of 'Screwball' Comedy."
165. "Inside Stuff—Pictures," *Variety*, 30 January 1934, p. 52.
166. *VFR*, 4 December 1934.
167. *VFR*, 2 October 1935.
168. *VFR*, 18 May 1938.
169. Charles Wolfe, *Frank Capra: A Guide to References and Resources* (Boston: G. K. Hall, 1987), p. 22.
170. *VFR*, 7 September 1938; quoted in Weales, *Canned Goods as Caviar*, p. 162.
171. *VFR*, 11 November 1939.
172. Finler, *The Hollywood Story*, p. 75.
173. Elizabeth Kendall, *The Runaway Bride: Hollywood Romantic Comedy of the 1930s* (New York: Alfred A. Knopf, 1990), p. 58.
174. *VFR*, 9 June 1937.
175. *VFR*, 23 September 1936.
176. *NYTFR*, 8 July 1937.
177. *NYTFR*, 10 November 1934; *VFR*, 30 October 1936.
178. *VFR*, 15 November 1939.
179. *VFR*, 11 October 1939.
180. Jewell, *The RKO Story*, p. 111; Kendall, *The Runaway Bride*, p. 178.
181. Sennett, *Warner Brothers Presents*, p. 277.
182. Harvey, *Romantic Comedy*, p. 291.
183. Dooley, *From Scarface to Scarlett*, pp. 523, 530.
184. Crowther, *The Lion's Share* p. 256.
185. Rudy Behlmer, ed., *Inside Warner Bros.* (1935–1951) (New York: Viking Press, 1985), p. 9.

186. John E. O'Connor, ed., *I Am a Fugitive from a Chain Gang* (Madison: University of Wisconsin Press, 1981), pp. 186–87.
187. Peter Roffman and Jim Purdy, *The Hollywood Social Problem Film: Madness, Despair, and Politics from the Depression to the Fifties* (Bloomington: Indiana University Press, 1981), p. 29; *VFR*, 15 November 1932; Roddick, *A New Deal in Entertainment*, p. 125.
188. Fred Stanley, "Hectic Year in Studios," *Variety*, 29 December 1931, p. 6.
189. "Six Best Movie Stars," *Variety*, 5 January 1932, p. 1; *NYTFR*, 8 January 1931.
190. *VFR*, 29 April 1931.
191. Richard Maltby, "A Short and Dangerous Life: The Gangster Film, 1930–1932," in *Prima Dei Codici 2. Alle Porte di Hays* (Venice: Mostra Internazionale d'Arte Cinematografica, La Biennale di Venezia, 1991), p. 169; Stephen Karpf, *The Gangster Film: Emergence, Variation and Decay of a Genre, 1930–1940* (New York: Arno Press, 1973), p. 87; *VFR*, 24 May 1932.
192. "Hays' Film Regulation," *Variety*, 19 February 1930, p. 9.
193. *VFR*, 2 July 1930.
194. *VFR*, 17 January 1933.
195. Roddick, *A New Deal in Entertainment*, p. 95; *VFR*, 15 September 1931.
196. *VFR*, 4 August 1931.
197. *VFR*, 9 August 1932.
198. *VFR*, 9 October 1934; Roffman and Purdy, *The Hollywood Social Problem Film*, p. 124.
199. *VFR*, 29 March 1933.
200. Roffman and Purdy, *The Hollywood Social Problem Film*, p. 84.
201. *VFR*, 26 September 1933.
202. Roddick, *A New Deal in Entertainment*, p. 172; *VFR*, 17 April 1935.
203. "Gangster Cycle Up Again," *Variety*, 20 February 1935, p. 5.
204. "MPPDA Members Call a Halt," *MPH*, 2 November 1935, p. 27.
205. Karpf, *The Gangster Film*, p. 109.
206. *NYTFR*, 12 April 1937.
207. Roffman and Purdy, *The Hollywood Social Problem Film*, p. 135.
208. *VFR*, 4 July 1933.
209. *NYTFR*, 9 September 1938; *VFR*, 7 September 1938.
210. *VFR*, 9 February 1938.
211. Bob Moak, "Mothers Nix Crime Pix," *Variety*, 6 September 1939, p. 3.
212. *VFR*, 8 March 1939.
213. Roffman and Purdy, *The Hollywood Social Problem Film*, p. 166.
214. *NYTFR*, 6 June 1936.
215. *NYTFR*, 18 January 1937; *VFR*, 4 November 1936.
216. *VFR*, 23 June 1937.
217. *VFR*, 8 June 1938.
218. John C. Flinn, "Film Industry Watching *Blockade*," *Variety*, 24 June 1938, p. 1.
219. Andrew Tudor, *Monsters and Mad Scientists: A Cultural History of the Horror Movie* (Oxford: Basil Blackwell, 1989), pp. 27–33.
220. Tudor, p. 31; *VFR*, 2 February 1931.
221. Tudor, p. 29.
222. *NYTFR*, 5 December 1931.
223. *NYTFR*, 5 December 1931; *VFR*, 8 December 1931.
224. *VFR*, 29 May 1934.
225. *NYTFR*, 18 November 1933.
226. *NYTFR*, 11 May 1935.
227. *NYTFR*, 16 May 1936; "Horror Films Taken Off U Sked," *Variety*, 6 May 1936, p. 7.
228. *NYTFR*, 2 January 1932.
229. *VFR*, 12 July 1932.
230. *VFR*, 8 May 1935.
231. *NYTFR*, 8 August 1936.
232. *NYTFR*, 5 August 1935.
233. *NYTFR*, 1 May 1931.
234. Richard Koszarski, ed., *The Mystery of the Wax Museum* (Madison: University of Wisconsin Press, 1979), p. 11.
235. *NYTFR*, 4 August 1932.
236. Carlos Clarens, *An Illustrated History of the Horror Film* (New York: Capricorn Books, 1968), p. 81; *VFR*, 21 February 1933.
237. Jack Jungmeyer, "Film Production Trends," *Variety*, 4 January 1939, p. 8; *VFR*, 18 January 1939.
238. *VFR*, 22 November 1939.
239. *VFR*, 29 November 1939.
240. Jewell, *The RKO Story*, p. 138.

CHAPTER 8. The B Film: Hollywood's Other Half

1. The label B is often treated as if it were simply an abbreviation for "bad" filmmaking. See Leonard Maltin, "Foreword," in Don Miller, *B Movies* (New York: Ballantine Books, 1973), p. xi. In their own time, reviewers usually responded in kind to the notions of A and B, although programmers had a better opportunity to receive favorable recognition. Only rarely would dozing critics respond to a B, making it a sleeper.

    Although the bulk of B films survive, their imposing numbers have often discouraged study, in their own time through the present. Contemporary sources usually give a biased perspective; such standard reference tools as the *New York Times* and *Variety* highlight pictures regarded as significant by virtue of the money invested in them, both in choice of films to review and critical tone. Hence, not only are qualitative judgments skewed by economic biases, but no single journal is remotely definitive in listing total 1930s output or covering all of the product from smaller concerns. Whereas the B films of the major studios have left clear traces in the form of abundant reviews in contemporary journals, coverage given the product of Poverty Row was extremely variable. The films of such corporations as Republic, Monogram, and Liberty usually received attention nearly commensurate with the Bs of a major studio, but there were dozens of smaller companies, like Commodore or Empire, granted only sporadic notice in the trades. While more films were covered in *Variety, Film Daily,* and *Motion Picture Daily* than anywhere else, all missed a substantial percentage of product. Indeed, Poverty Row producers like William Steiner and the Weiss brothers avoided preview screenings, aware that critical reaction had no effect on their audiences and knowing they had nothing to gain from a review that was tepid at best and mocking at worst. The only record of their output is occasional advertisements or notations in the release charts of *Motion Picture Herald* and the annual advertisement previews of the forthcoming season's product in the trade yearbooks and almanacs. Confirmation of production is sometimes only made through the discovery of an existing print. Since few small companies took the trouble to copyright their work, many of these pictures have survived purely because of the public-domain market, frequently retitled and/or reissued in later years.

2. For instance, in 1937, Warners offered thirty-six B's alone; see "B Films Become Issue of Studio and Theater," *Motion Picture Herald,* 13 February 1937, p. 18. Paramount boss Y. Frank Freeman criticized the ratio of B's to A's in 1937, claiming B's outnumbered A's by three (or even five) to one, noting that many theaters were unfortunately being run largely on B's. By 1937, the *New York Times* and *Newsweek* estimated that at least two-thirds of screen product fell into the category of second- or third-rate B pictures. See Douglas W. Churchill, "Hollywood from A to Z," *New York Times,* 14 March 1937; "Screen Fans Organize to Bite Hand That Feeds Them Double Features," *Newsweek,* 4 October 1937, p. 25.

3. Edward Dmytyrk, in Barry Norman, *The Story of Hollywood* (New York: New American Library, 1987), p. 230.

4. Robert W. Chambers, "The Double Feature As a Sales Problem," *Harvard Business Review,* 16 (Winter 1938), p. 227.

5. Joan Cohen, "The Second Feature," *Mankind,* 5 (June 1976), p. 29.

6. *Ibid.,* p. 27; Maltin, "Foreword," p. xi; Chambers, "The Double Feature As a Sales Problem," p. 227; Robin Cross, *The Big Book of B Movies* (New York: St. Martin's Press, 1981), 7. For information on Paramount B's, see Cross, p. 9, and William K. Everson, "Introduction: Remembering PRC," in Wheeler Dixon, ed., *Producers Releasing Corporation* (Jefferson, N.C.: McFarland, 1986), p. 2.

7. William K. Everson, "Book Reviews: *B Movies,*" *Films in Review* 25 (November 1974), p. 564; Miller, *B Movies,* p. 175. As director Robert Florey noted, he had to shoot important pictures at Warners in 1932 as fast as he had earlier the same year at Tiffany, a much smaller Poverty Row studio; Florey, letter to Carlos Clarens, 13 December 1976, Florey collection (private). See also Brian Taves, *Robert Florey, the French Expressionist* (Metuchen, N.J.: Scarecrow Press, 1987), p. 222.

8. Don Miller, "The American B Film," *Focus on Film,* no. 5 (Winter 1970), pp. 31–32. However, the term *programmer* was used in a variety of different ways by reviewers of the time.

9. "B Films Become Issue of Studio and Theater," p. 13.

10. Douglas W. Churchill, "How Doth the Busy Little 'B,'" *New York Times,* 2 January 1938.

11. The problems with Warners B films are noted in Doug McClelland, *The Golden Age of B Movies* (Nashville: Charter House, 1978), p. 15, and Miller, *B Movies,* pp. 249–252. For an analysis of Columbia's economic use of the B film, see Brian Taves, "Columbia's Emergence from Poverty Row," in Robert Sklar and Vito Zaggario, eds., *Mr. Capra Goes to Columbia: Authorship and the Hollywood Studio System, A Case Study* (Philadelphia, Pa.: Temple University Press), in press.

12. Lewis Jacobs, "A History of the Obscure Quickie," *New York Times,* 30 December 1934; Les Adams and Buck Rainey, *Shoot-'em-ups* (Metuchen, N.J.: Scarecrow Press, 1985), pp. 41, 48.

13. D.W.C., "On the Leasing Lot," *New York Times*, 10 November 1935; "Quickies Not So Hot," *Hollywood Reporter*, 7 November 1935, p. 1.
14. Richard Maurice Hurst, *Republic Studios* (Metuchen, N.J.: Scarecrow Press, 1979), p. 4; Cross, *The Big Book of B Movies*, p. 13.
15. D.W.C., "On the Leasing Lot."
16. For analysis of how Yates pieced Republic together, see Hurst, *Republic Studios*, p. 2, and Jon Tuska, *The Vanishing Legion* (Jefferson, N.C.: McFarland, 1982), pp. 183–184.
17. For figures on *Tumblin' Tumbleweeds*, see Adams and Rainey, *Shoot-'em-ups*, p. 89, and Joseph Kane, in Todd McCarthy and Charles Flynn, *Kings of the B's* (New York: E. P. Dutton, 1975), p. 320. Autry had initially starred in the science fiction musical Western serial THE PHANTOM EMPIRE, later released as a feature under the alternate titles MEN WITH STEEL FACES and RADIO RANCH. Autry was actually not the first Western warbler; Ken Maynard has that distinction, but Autry popularized the form, continuing in features through the early 1950s. Data on the exhibition of WESTWARD HO! is given in Joe Collura, "Paul Malvern: Behind the Scenes—Part II," *Classic Images*, no. 191 (May 1991), p. 41, and information on the Three Mesquiteers is provided by George Sherman, in Norman, *The Story of Hollywood*, p. 232.
18. Hurst, *Republic Studios*, pp. 5–6, 8–9.
19. *Ibid.*, p. 17. Because of its absorption of Mascot, Republic became a major producer of serials, joining Universal, already well established in the field; Columbia also began competing in 1937. Annually, four 12–15 chapter serials were made at Republic on frenzied schedules, filming the entire thirty reels or more of footage (some five hours of running time) in three to eight weeks, on budgets from under $100,000 to more than four times that amount. The labor usually required two full-time directors, sometimes shooting different scenes simultaneously.
20. For data on Grand National, see Ted Okuda, *Grand National, Producers Releasing Corporation, Screen Guild/Lippert* (Jefferson, N.C.: McFarland, 1989), Gene Fernett, *Poverty Row* (Satellite Beach, Fla.: Coral Reef, 1973), pp. 41, 48, and Chuck Anderson, "The Tape Trail," *Classic Images*, no. 79 (January 1982), p. 20. Seventy-eight films were distributed, including some British imports and smaller domestic productions picked up regionally to fill the schedule. Information on Astor is provided by Don Miller, *Hollywood Corral* (New York: Popular Library, 1976), p. 236, and Adams and Rainey, *Shoot-'em-ups*, p. 91.
21. For information on feature production, see George Turner and Michael Price, *Forgotten Horrors* (New York: A. S. Barnes, 1979), p. 10; Fernett, *Poverty Row*, p. 135; Jacobs, "A History of the Obscure Quickie"; and Douglas W. Churchill, "More Vicissitudes of Turbulent Hollywood," *New York Times*, 13 June 1937. Location shooting is described by Cross, *The Big Book of B Movies*, p. 18; Douglas W. Churchill, "Little Drops of Water, Little Grains of Sand," *New York Times*, 19 December 1937; and Fernett, p. 130. In *The Great Movie Shorts* (New York: Crown, 1972), p. 27, Leonard Maltin indicates that Poverty Row avoided short subjects.
    During the first half of the decade, Poverty Row occasionally made serials, although by 1937 the field had been left exclusively to Universal, Columbia, and Republic, which essentially replaced the serial product that Mascot had been supplying. Independently made serials ranged from Syndicate's MYSTERY TROOPER and Metropolitan's SIGN OF THE WOLF in 1931, to Principal's TARZAN THE FEARLESS in 1933 and THE RETURN OF CHANDU and First Division's YOUNG EAGLES in 1934, to Screen Attraction's QUEEN OF THE JUNGLE, Burroughs-Tarzan's THE NEW ADVENTURES OF TARZAN, and Regal's THE LOST CITY (all 1935), to Victory's SHADOW OF CHINATOWN and BLAKE OF SCOTLAND YARD, to Stage and Screen's CUSTER'S LAST STAND, THE CLUTCHING HAND, and THE BLACK COIN (all 1936). The serials were frequently reedited and condensed at various times and reissued as features, often under different titles. The mid-1930s marked the end of serial making by small producers, however, except for commissioned productions. For instance, in 1937, Columbia decided to amplify its presence with the Saturday-afternoon audience, already familiar with the studio as a producer of B Westerns. For its entrance into the serial field, Columbia contracted with Poverty Row's Louis Weiss for production of THE JUNGLE MENACE, starring "Bring 'em Back Alive" animal documentarist Frank Buck in his first dramatic role.
22. Frank Condon, "Poverty Row," *Saturday Evening Post*, 25 August 1939, p. 64.
23. Jacobs, "A History of the Obscure Quickie"; Churchill, "More Vicissitudes of Turbulent Hollywood"; Fernett, *Poverty Row*, p. 134.
24. Miller, "The American B Film," p. 31; Fernett, *Poverty Row*, p. 118; Paul Seale, "'A Host of Others': Toward a Nonlinear History of Poverty Row and the Coming of Sound," *Wide Angle* 13 (January 1991), pp. 79, 97. For a grind review, see "On Probation," *Hollywood Reporter*, 5 June 1935, p. 3.
25. Hurst, *Republic Studios*, p. 4; Anderson, "The Tape Trail," p. 20; Miller, *B Movies*, p. 15.
26. Fernett, *Poverty Row*, p. 133.
27. Advertisements for the Weiss product are found in the *Film Daily Production Guide*, pp. 114, 133, 135 from the 1934 edition, and pp. 123, 125 from the 1935 edition.

28. Miller, "The American B Film," p. 31.
29. William K. Everson, "Book Reviews: *Robert Florey, the French Expressionist*," *Films in Review*, 38 (October 1987), p. 501. See Taves, *Robert Florey, the French Expressionist*. Florey used an apt French Foreign Legion metaphor in describing studio employment: "It was as the French say the marche ou crève—do or die—system." Florey, letter to Henry Hart, 12 June 1959, Florey collection (private); Taves, p. 5.
30. Cross, *The Big Book of B Movies*, p. 18; Nick Grinde, "Pictures for Peanuts," *Penguin Film Review* 1 (February 1946), pp. 46, 43.
31. Churchill, "How Doth the Busy Little 'B.'"
32. Miller, *B Movies*, p. 175; Seale, "'A Host of Others,'" pp. 79, 97; Churchill, "Hollywood from A to Z"; Cohen, "The Second Feature," p. 29; Hurst, *Republic Studios*, p. 64; Fernett, *Poverty Row*, p. 119. Remake patterns are noted by Sherman, in Norman, *The Story of Hollywood*, p. 237.
33. Hurst, *Republic Studios*, pp. 41–42.
34. For information on the sale of the Chan films, see Churchill, "How Doth the Busy Little 'B.'" Andrew Sarris notes the change in the pacing in "Beatitudes of B Pictures," in McCarthy and Flynn, *Kings of the B's*, p. 50.
35. Everson, "Book Reviews: *B Movies*," p. 564; Grinde, "Pictures for Peanuts," p. 51; Arthur L. Mayer, "The Reader Speaks Up," *New York Times*, 16 August 1942.
36. Taves, *Robert Florey, The French Expressionist*, p. 55; Hurst, *Republic Studios*, p. 65; Grinde, "Pictures for Peanuts," p. 46.
37. *Film Daily* (26 April 1935, p. 5) remarked, "General theme of the drama is not exactly wholesome." Reed's script departed greatly from Ben Hecht's novel, and the further changes that were made during production all made THE FLORENTINE DAGGER more original. All of these characteristics attest to the possibilities for divergence from classical norms in the B.
38. Eric A. Goldman, *Visions, Images and Dreams*, 2nd ed. (Teaneck, N.J.: Ergo Media, 1988), xviii.
39. J. Hoberman, *Bridge of Light* (New York: Museum of Modern Art/Schocken, 1991), p. 7.
40. This is a form Thomas Cripps has labeled "race" films, and the approach is also used by Henry Sampson, *Blacks in Black and White* (Metuchen, N.J.: Scarecrow Press, 1977). Another way is to look at Hollywood and European films, primarily aimed at white audiences but containing black images as diverse as the films of Lincoln ("Stepin Fetchit") Perry and Paul Robeson. This sociological point of view encompasses a vast number of pictures, most containing only incidental comment on blacks. The spectrum of pictures covered is ably represented in the catalog edited by Phyllis Rauch Klotman, *Frame by Frame: A Black Filmography* (Bloomington: Indiana University Press, 1979). While usually whites directed, discovering the ethnicity of all those who receive the various technical credits in such productions is problematic, since most are obscure individuals whose credits, in addition to their race, are difficult to determine. Data on the years of corporate formation and film production is from Sampson, p. 3.
41. This problem has been pointed out by Thomas Cripps, *Slow Fade to Black* (New York: Oxford University Press, 1977), p. 199. However, during the change to sound, the majors had accepted a popular myth that black voices recorded better than whites, and a wide range of performers appeared through the 1930s in short films, such as the Warner Bros. Vitaphone series. Some seventy black-related shorts were made during the decade, most tending toward musical numbers and comedy routines. Many of these were directed toward black audiences, including Oscar Micheaux's THE DARKTOWN REVUE (1931), Richard Kahn's THE TOPPERS TAKE A BOW (1940), and George Randol's DARKTOWN STRUTTER'S BALL (1939) and RHYTHM RODEO (1938). However, not all of the shorts were light entertainment; there were also newsreels and documentaries, often dealing with racial pride, such as COLORED CHAMPIONS OF SPORT (1940) or COLORED MEN IN WHITE (194?), or documentaries on the lives of famous black individuals, such as Booker T. Washington, George Washington Carver, and Florence Mills (all 1940), or LET MY PEOPLE LIVE (1938), starring Rex Ingram, a production of the National Antituberculosis Association.
42. Sampson, *Blacks in Black and White*, p. 83.
43. *Ibid.*, p. 84.
44. James R. Nesteby, *Black Images in American Films, 1896–1954: The Interplay Between Civil Rights and Film Culture* (Washington, D.C.: University Press of America, 1982), p. 89.
45. Sampson, *Blacks in Black and White*, p. 189; Daniel J. Leab, *From Sambo to Superspade* (Boston: Houghton Mifflin, 1976), p. 177.
46. W.R.W., "*Mr. Washington Goes to Town*," *Motion Picture Herald*, 20 April 1940, p. 35.
47. St. Claire Bourne, "The African American Image in American Cinema," *Black Scholar* 21 (Spring 1991), p. 16.
48. Douglas W. Churchill, "Doings in Hollywood," *New York Times*, 26 November 1939; Everson, "Introduction," in Dixon, p. 1.
49. Cohen, "The Second Feature," p. 35.

CHAPTER 9. The Poetics and Politics of Nonfiction: Documentary Film in the 1930s

1. The announced program for the course in documentary film offered by the New School in 1938 reflected the range of this debate. Lectures by Pare Lorentz and Paul Strand on their own films and by Paul Rotha, Jay Leyda, and Jean Lenauer on "factual films" from abroad were accompanied by a series of talks devoted to commercial newsreels, "newspicture magazines," and Hollywood fiction. The fifteen-week course opened and closed with lectures on THE BIRTH OF A NATION (Griffith, 1915) by cinematographer Billy Bitzer and FURY (Lang, 1936) by critic Gilbert Seldes. See *New York Times*, 23 January 1938, sec. 11, p. 4.

2. See John Grierson quoted by Paul Rotha in *Documentary Film* (London: Faber and Faber, 1939), p. 68; Richard Griffith, "A Note on Documentary Film," program note accompanying the Museum of Modern Art retrospective, The Nonfiction Film: From Uninterpreted Fact to Documentary, November 1939–January 1940, in File M257, Thomas J. Brandon Collection, Film Study Center, Museum of Modern Art [hereafter MOMA], New York City; and Joris Ivens, "Notes on the Documentary Film," *Direction* 3, no. 4 (April 1940), p. 15.

3. Frank S. Nugent, "Dragging 'The River,'" *New York Times*, 6 February 1938, sec. 10, p. 5.

4. John Grierson, "Flaherty's Poetic *Moana*," *New York Sun*, 8 February 1926; repr. in Lewis Jacobs, ed., *The Documentary Tradition* (New York: W. W. Norton, 1979), pp. 25–26.

5. Originally published in three issues of *Cinema Quarterly* (Winter 1932, Spring 1933, Spring 1934), these articles have been collated under the title "First Principles of Documentary" in Forsyth Hardy, ed., *Grierson on Documentary* (New York: Praeger, 1971), pp. 145–156.

6. Harry Alan Potamkin, "The Montage Film," *Movie Makers* (February 1930), repr. in Lewis Jacobs, ed., *The Compound Cinema: The Film Writing of Harry Alan Potamkin* (New York: Teachers College Press, 1977), pp. 70–73; and "The Rise and Fall of the German Film," *Cinema* (April 1930), repr. in Jacobs, ed., *The Compound Cinema*, pp. 304–309.

7. L. Saalchutz, "Mechanisms of the Cinema," *Close Up*, no. 8 (March 1930), pp. 303–305.

8. Jean Dréville, "Le Documentaire, l'âme du cinéma," *Cinémagazine* 10 (February 1930), pp. 28–32, trans. and repr. in Richard Abel, ed., *French Film Theory and Criticism*, vol. 2, 1929–1939 (Princeton, N.J.: Princeton University Press, 1988), pp. 41–45.

9. Alfred Kazin offers a contemporaneous view of the impact of documentary photography on the literature of the 1930s in the final chapter of *On Native Grounds: An Interpretation of Modern American Prose Literature* (New York: Harcourt Brace Janovich, 1982), originally published by Reynal and Hitchcock (New York) in 1942. Kazin's description of photographs as "fractions of reality" appears on p. 496.

10. Joris Ivens, "Some Reflections on Avant-Garde Documentaries," *La Revue des vivants* 10 (October 1931), trans. and repr. in Rosaline Delmar, ed., *Joris Ivens: Fifty Years of Film-making* (London: British Film Institute, 1979), pp. 98–100.

11. Archibald MacLeish, "The Cinema of Joris Ivens," *New Masses*, 24 August 1937, p. 18.

12. Julian Roffman, transcript of undated interview with Thomas Brandon, File J206, Brandon Collection, MOMA. For contemporaneous critiques of the dispersal of energies in documentary production and distribution in the United States, see Paul Rotha, "The Outlook for American Documentary Films," *New York Times*, 1 May 1938, p. 3; Ernestine Evans, "Much Could Be Done," *Virginia Quarterly Review* 14, no. 4 (Autumn 1938), pp. 491–501; and Theodore Strauss, "Documentary at the Crossroads," *Theatre Arts*, September 1941, pp. 683–689.

13. This, then, is not an exhaustive survey. Focus is largely fixed on social documentary, around which discussions of the genre largely centered in the 1930s. Dividing the field of documentary along institutional lines also means that idiosyncratic projects, like the remarkable MEN AND DUST, independently produced by Sheldon and Lee Dick in 1940, inevitably fall through the cracks. Filmmaking in New York, Washington, D.C., and Los Angeles, for which greater documentation survives, is foregrounded over regional initiatives, much of which never reached a national audience. As with amateur or experimental filmmaking, research into regional documentary activity would provide a different perspective on the notion of a national cinema and alternatives to Hollywood.

14. For a discussion of prewar labor films, see Kay Sloan, *The Loud Silents: Origins of the Social Problem Film* (Urbana: University of Illinois Press, 1988), pp. 53–57. On the Labor Film Service, see *New Majority*, 26 June 1920, p. 3, and 14 August 1920, p. 6; and *Liberator*, September 1920, p. 3. For a comprehensive survey of labor-Left film activity during the silent era, see Steven J. Ross, "Struggles for the Screen: Workers, Radicals, and the Political Uses of Silent Film," *American Historical Review* 96, no. 2 (April 1991), pp. 333–367. Unpublished manuscripts by Thomas Brandon on this topic also are held in the Brandon Collection, MOMA; see "Populist Film" (Files C38, C39) and an untitled book chapter on Left filmmaking in the 1920s (File D43).

15. Extensive interviews with surviving members of the Film and Photo League conducted by Thomas Brandon during the course of the 1970s are housed in the Brandon Collection, MOMA;

they provide the basis for much of the discussion here. Published articles by, and interviews with, former FPL members are included in the selected bibliography. Indispensable scholarly accounts of the Film and Photo League and its various offshoots are offered in William Alexander, *Film on the Left: American Documentary Film from 1931 to 1942* (Princeton, N.J.: Princeton University Press, 1981), and Russell Campbell, *Cinema Strikes Back: Radical Filmmaking in the United States, 1930–1942* (Ann Arbor, Mich.: UMI Research Press, 1982). Unpublished manuscript material on the FPL by Thomas Brandon is held in Files E59 and E60, Brandon Collection, MOMA.

16. Fred Sweet, Eugene Rosow, and Allan Francovich, "Pioneers: An Interview with Tom Brandon," *Film Quarterly* 28, no. 1 (Fall 1973), pp. 20–23; and Brad Chisholm, "Exhibition Practices of the American Film and Photo League" (Unpublished paper, University of Wisconsin-Madison, 1984). Late in 1932, Brandon and Sidney Howard, a noted playwright and league benefactor, founded Film Forum, modeled after workers' film groups in Germany, England, France, and Japan. Howard predicted regional branches would flower, forging a nationwide organization with ties to a world film culture, but despite Brandon's recruitment efforts throughout the Midwest, Film Forum had died a quiet death by 1934; see clippings and pamphlets, File Q332, Brandon Collection, MOMA.

17. Brochure, Harry Alan Potamkin Film School, Box CC 1042, MOMA; program notes, Film and Photo League Film Series, Box CC 1043, MOMA.

18. Balog's arrest is described in Tom Brandon, "The Movie Front," *New Theatre*, July-August 1934, p. 19, and discussed in detail in Brandon's 1974 interview with Balog, File I158, Brandon Collection, MOMA. For accounts of local protests by the New York FPL, see Leo T. Hurwitz, "Hisses, Boos, and Boycotts," *New Theatre*, July-August 1934, pp. 10–11; and Samuel Brody and Tom Brandon, "Epic of an Era," *New Masses*, 26 June 1934, pp. 29–30.

19. Samuel Brody, "The Revolutionary Film: Problem of Form," *New Theatre*, February 1934, pp. 21–22; Leo T. Hurwitz, "The Revolutionary Film—Next Step," *ibid.*, May 1934, pp. 14–15; Ralph Steiner, "Revolutionary Movie Production," *ibid.*, September 1934, pp. 22–23; Steiner and Hurwitz, "A New Approach to Filmmaking," *ibid.*, September 1935, pp. 22–23; and Ed Kennedy, "Three Workers Films," *Filmfront* 1, no. 2 (7 January 1935), pp. 10–11.

20. Leo T. Hurwitz, "Survey of Workers Film: A Report to the National Conference," *New Theatre*, October 1934, pp. 27–28; and David Platt, "The Movie Front: National Film Conference," *ibid.*, November 1934, p. 30.

21. As with most proposals of this kind, the plan to coordinate film projects was never realized. The New Film Alliance, however, merged with subsequent "audience" groups, such as Associated Film Audiences (1937), Films for Democracy (1938), and Film Audiences for Democracy (1939), forming more broadly based coalitions in support of pro-labor and antifascist filmmaking in the heyday of the Popular Front. See *Daily Worker*, 7 March 1937, p. 7, and 12 March 1937, p. 7; *Motion Picture Herald*, 13 March 1937, p. 9; *New York Times*, 15 November 1938, p. 25; and O. W. Riegel, "Press, Radio, Films," *Public Opinion Quarterly*, March 1940, pp. 149–150. Newsletters and announcements by Films for Democracy are held in File L234, Brandon Collection, MOMA.

22. John T. McManus, "Down to Earth in Spain," *New York Times*, 25 July 1937, sec. 10, p. 4, and [as J.T.M], "'The Spanish Earth,' at the 55th St. Playhouse," *ibid.*, 21 August 1937, p. 7; John Mosher, "The Current Cinema," *New Yorker*, 21 August 1937 pp. 51–52; *Time*, 23 August 1937, pp. 48–49; Ben Belitt, "The Camera Reconnoiters," *Nation*, 20 November 1937, pp. 557–558; Sidney Meyers and Jay Leyda, "Joris Ivens: Artist in Documentary," *Magazine of Art*, July 1938, in Jacobs, *The Documentary Tradition*, pp. 159–166; and Joris Ivens, *The Camera and I* (New York: International Publishers, 1969), pp. 103–138.

23. Copies of distribution contracts and promotional material for these films are held in Files F79, F98, and G123, Brandon Collection, MOMA.

24. New Deal documentary is broadly examined in Richard Dyer MacCann, *The People's Films: A Political History of U.S. Government Motion Pictures* (New York: Hastings House, 1973), chapters 3–5. Robert L. Snyder, *Pare Lorentz and the Documentary Film* (Norman: University of Oklahoma Press, 1968), focuses more narrowly on Lorentz's film work for the government between 1935 and 1940, drawing on Lorentz's personal files. Analyses of New Deal documentaries by Lorentz and Ivens also are offered by William Alexander in *Film on the Left*. For a contemporaneous survey of New Deal filmmaking by Lorentz's assistant, see Arch A. Mercey, "Films by American Governments: The United States," *Films* 1, no. 3 (Summer 1940), pp. 5–11.

25. Larry Wayne Ward, *The Motion Picture Goes to War: The U.S. Government Film Effort During World War I* (Ann Arbor, Mich.: UMI Press, 1985), pp. 106–108.

26. Government filmmaking in support of New Deal programs for nontheatrical release also continued throughout this period. In 1939 the *Motion Picture Herald* reported motion-picture production in support of administration programs or services by the Department of Agriculture, Department of the Interior, Department of the Treasury, Federal Housing Administration, National Youth Administration, U.S. Public Health Service, U.S. Housing Authority, Tennessee

Valley Authority, U.S. Maritime Commission, U.S. Post Office, and the Veterans Administration —all in addition to the films of the Works Progress Administration and the Resettlement Administration. See Francis L. Burt, "New Deal Held 'No. 1' Producer and Exhibitor of All Administrations," *Motion Picture Herald*, 25 November 1939, pp. 27–28.

27. *New York Times*, 13 April 1936, 7 August 1936, 9 August 1936, and 11 August 1936; *Motion Picture Herald*, 20 June 1936, p. 18, 18 July 1936, p. 13, 25 July 1936, pp. 13–14, and 1 August 1936, p. 15; *Literary Digest*, 8 August 1936, p. 32; *Newsweek*, 15 August, 1936, p. 18; Arthur W. Macmahon, John D. Millett, and Gladys Ogden, *The Administration of Federal Work Relief* (Chicago: Public Administration Services, 1941), pp. 291–300. Concurrently, right-wing opponents of the Roosevelt administration raised funds to finance anti–New Deal films; THE AMATEUR FIRE BRIGADE, for example, was circulated nontheatrically during the 1936 election. See *Motion Picture Herald*, 25 April 1936, p. 27; and Douglas W. Churchill, "A Stealthy Trend in Hollywood," *New York Times*, 23 August 1936, sec. 9, p. 3.

28. According to records in the National Archives, Pathé produced and released one-reel films on WPA activity in Chicago, Illinois, Massachusetts, Michigan, Minnesota, Missouri, New Jersey, New York City, New York State, Ohio, Pennsylvania, and West Virginia; a film on work programs for inner-city blacks in Washington, D.C., and New York (WE WORK AGAIN); two longer films on relief efforts in the dust bowl (RAIN FOR THE EARTH) and the flooded Ohio River valley (MAN AGAINST RAIN); and a thirty-six-minute survey of WPA projects across the entire country, WORK PAYS AMERICA. See Record Group 69, Motion Picture Collection, National Archives, Washington, D.C.

29. Morris L. Ernst and Pare Lorentz, *Censored: The Private Life of the Movie* (New York: Jonathan Cape and Harrison Smith, 1930). A selection of Lorentz's film criticism is collected in *Lorentz on Film* (New York: Hopkinson and Blake, 1975; Norman: University of Oklahoma Press, 1986).

30. Frank S. Nugent, "Raw Deal for the New Deal," *New York Times*, 24 May 1936, sec. 9, p. 3. See also *New York Times*, 15 May 1936, p. 28, 10 June, 1936, p.18, and 4 August 1936, p. 11; *Variety*, 13 May 1936, pp. 1, 52, and 3 June 1936, p. 15; *Literary Digest*, 16 May 1936, p. 22; *Time*, 25 May 1936, p. 47; Martin Quigley, "In the Raw," *Motion Picture Herald*," 30 May 1936, p. 7; Peter Ellis [Irving Lerner], "The Plow that Broke the Plains," *New Theatre*, July 1933, pp. 18–19; Snyder, *Pare Lorentz and the Documentary Film*, pp. 21–49; and MacCann, *The People's Films*, pp. 66–71. While this campaign for national distribution was mounted, THE PLOW THAT BROKE THE PLAINS continued to play at alternative venues, such as Women's Exposition of Arts and Industries at the Grand Central Palace, New York City, and the Cinema de Paris, a small New York art house, together with a French feature, MARIA CHAPDELAINE; see Mark Van Doren, "Further Documents," *Nation*, 10 June 1936, pp. 753–754; and *Motion Picture Herald*, 20 June 1936, p. 18. The challenge the film posed to conventional patterns of reception is suggested by a review of Otis Ferguson, who criticized efforts to promote PLOW as a suppressed film when it was "definitely ticketed for the experimental-amateur audience." See Ferguson, "They, the People," *New Republic*, 5 August 1936, pp. 381–382.

31. Hollywood producers had competing, sometimes contradictory, motives to consider in distributing New Deal films. Walt Disney, for example, reportedly not only sought to block THE RIVER from an Academy Award nomination as best short subject (a category Disney dominated) but also requested that the film play with SNOW WHITE AND THE SEVEN DWARFS during the animated feature's general release; see Snyder, *Pare Lorentz and the Documentary Film*, pp. 69, 79; Douglas W. Churchill, "Hollywood on the Wing," *New York Times*, 23 January 1938, sec. 11, p. 5; and Philip Sterling, "Following 'The River,'" *ibid.* 15 October 1939, sec. 9, p. 4. In 1938, THE PLOW and THE RIVER—together with two WPA shorts, HANDS (by Steiner and Van Dyke) and WORK PAYS AMERICA—were also the subject of a sociological study of documentary persuasion undertaken at Ohio State University; see Lloyd L. Ramseyer, "Factors Influencing Attitudes and Attitude Changes," *Education Research Bulletin*, 18, n. 2 (1 February 1939), pp. 8–14, 80, and "Measuring 'Intangible' Effects of Motion Pictures," *Educational Screen*, no. 18 (September 1939), pp. 237–238, 261.

32. Gilbert Seldes, "Pare Lorentz's *The River*," *Scribners*, January 1938, repr. in Jacobs, *The Documentary Tradition*, pp. 123–125; and V. F. Calverton, "Cultural Barometer," *Current History*, May 1938, p. 46. See also Mark Van Doren, "The Poetry of Erosion," *Nation*, 30 October 1937, pp. 485–486; *Time*, 8 November 1937, p. 49; and *Literary Digest*, 20 November 1937, p. 34.

33. "The Fight for Life," *Variety*, 6 March 1940, p. 11; Frank S. Nugent, "Grim Reality Note," *New York Times*, 10 March 1940; Bosley Crowther, "Lorentz Experiments," *ibid.*, 10 March 1940, sec. 10, p. 5; Franz Hollering, "Films," *Nation*, 16 March 1940, pp. 372–373; "The Fight for Life' Films a Story of Young Obstetrician," *Life*, 18 March 1940, pp. 98–99; *Time*, 25 March 1940, pp. 92–93; John Francis Crow, "Lorentz's *Fight for Life*," *Hollywood Citizen News*, repr. in Jacobs, *The Documentary Tradition*, pp. 189–190; and Snyder, *Pare Lorentz and the Documentary Film*, pp. 102–120. In 1943, THE FIGHT FOR LIFE was also selected for the anthology *Twenty Best Film Plays*, edited by John Gassner and Dudley Nichols (New York: Crown Publishers, 1943; repr. New York and London: Garland, 1977), pp. 1081–1111.

34. Snyder, *Pare Lorentz and the Documentary Film*, pp. 121–140; Ivens, *The Camera and I*, pp. 187–232; "Joris Ivens Interview with Gordon Hitchens," pp. 195–204; Arthur Calder-Marshall, *The Innocent Eye: The Life of Robert Flaherty* (London: W. H. Allen, 1963; repr. New York: Penguin Books, 1970), pp. 185–201; and Ben Achtenberg, "Helen Van Dongen: An Interview," *Film Quarterly* 30, no. 2 (Winter 1976), pp. 46–57.

35. *New York Times*, 7 May 1940, p. 15; Snyder, *Pare Lorentz and the Documentary Film*, pp. 79–95, 145–176; MacCann, *The People's Films*, pp. 87–117.

36. Gloria Walden, *The Information Film* (New York: Columbia University Press, 1949), pp. 9–12; F. Dean McClusky, "Public Schools," pp. 46–58, and Leo C. Beebe, "Industry," pp. 88–98, in *Sixty Years of 16mm Film, 1923–1983: A Symposium* (Evanston, Ill.: Film Council of America, 1954).

37. Transcript of undated interview with Julian Roffman by Thomas Brandon, File J206, Brandon Collection, MOMA; transcript of interview with Jean Lenhauer by Thomas Brandon, 28 January 1974, File J192, Brandon Collection, MOMA.

38. According to Steiner and Van Dyke, the split with Frontier Film was acrimonious; see transcript of interview with Steiner by James Blue, 12 July 1973, File K219, and transcript of interview with Van Dyke by Thomas Brandon, 15 July 1974, File K223, Brandon Collection, MOMA. Varying assessments of the breakup are offered in Alexander, *Film on the Left*, pp. 179–181; *Cinema Strikes Back*, Campbell, pp. 158–159; and Joel Zuker, *Ralph Steiner: Filmmaker and Still Photographer* (New York: Arno Press, 1978), pp. 249–263.

39. Alexander, *Film on the Left*, pp. 264–266; and Ivens, *The Camera and I*, pp. 235–237.

40. Paul Rotha, "The Documentary Method in British films, *National Board of Review Magazine*, November 1937, pp. 3–9; "The Outlook for American Documentary Films," *New York Times*, 1 May 1938; and *Documentary Diary: An Informal History of the British Documentary Film, 1928–1939* (London: Secker and Warburg, 1973), pp. 181–182, 208–212.

41. *Variety*, 17 August 1938, p. 29; *New York Times*, 14 December 1938, p. 32, and 5 May 1940, sec. 10, p. 5; and Waldron, *The Information Film*, pp. 80–81.

42. Jacobs, *The Documentary Tradition*, p. 188.

43. Mary Losey, *Living Films: A Catalog of Documentary Films and Their Makers* (New York: Association of Documentary Film Producers, 1940), copy held in File M257, Brandon Collection, MOMA; Richard Griffith, "A Big Year for Film Facts," *New York Times*, 17 September 1939; Bosley Crowther, "Realistic Stepchild of the Movies," *New York Times Magazine*, 25 August 1940, pp. 12–13.

44. Richard Griffith, "Films at the Fair," *Films* 1, no. 1 (November 1939), pp. 61–75; program for The Nonfiction Film: From Uninterpreted Fact to Documentary, 27 November 1939–6 January 1940, File M257, Brandon Collection, MOMA.

45. *The World's Fair of 1940 in New York: Official Guide Book* (New York: Rogers-Kellogg-Stillson, 1940), pp. 29, 58; *Exhibition Techniques: A Summary of Exhibition Practice* (New York: Museum of Science and Industry, Rockefeller Center, 1940), pp. 39–42; Alice Goldfarb Marquis, *Hopes and Ashes: The Birth of Modern Times, 1929–1939* (New York: Free Press, 1986), pp. 197–210; and Griffith, "Films at the Fair," pp. 61–75.

46. For a brief survey of industrial filmmaking practices during these years, see Daniel J. Perkins, "Sponsored Business Films: An Overview, 1895–1955," *Film Reader no.* 6 (1986), pp. 125–132.

47. *New York Times*, 21 May 1939, sec. 10, p. 3; Franz Hoellering, "The City," *Nation*, 3 June 1939, p. 39; Archer, Winsten, "*The City* Goes to the Fair," *New York Post*, 23 June 1939, repr. in Jacobs, *The Documentary Tradition*, pp. 126–128; *Variety*, 11 October 1939, p. 18; Willard Van Dyke, "Documentaries of the Thirties," *Journal of the University Film Association* 25, no. 3 (1973), p. 45; and Alexander, *Film on the Left*, pp. 247–270.

48. Crowther, "Realistic Stepchild of the Movies," p. 12.

49. On the relationship between Flaherty and Hollywood, see Mark J. Langer, "*Tabu*: The Making of a Film," *Cinema Journal* 24, no. 3 (Spring 1985), pp. 43–64.

50. These titles are drawn from Kenneth W. Munden, ed., *The American Film Institute Catalog, Feature Films, 1921–1930* (New York: R. R. Bowker, 1971) and *Variety Film Reviews*, vols. 2–6 (New York and London: Garland, 1983). The relation of travel narratives to conventional studio practices is explored in Dana Benelli, "*Inagagi*, the Travelogue Feature, and Hollywood (1930)" (Unpublished paper, Department of Communications, University of Iowa, 1986).

51. On THE STRANGE CASE OF TOM MOONEY, see Frank S. Nugent, "Seventeen Years After," *New York Times*, 24 July 1933, p. 11; William Troy, "Panorama," *Nation*, 2 August 1933, pp. 138–139; Robert Littell, "Sound Without Fury," *New Republic*, 6 September 1933, p. 102; and "The Strange Case of Tom Mooney," *International Literature Chronicle*, no. 4 (October 1933), pp. 158–159. On MILLIONS OF US, see Douglas W. Churchill, "A Stealthy Tread in Hollywood," *New York Times*, 23 August 1936, sec. 9, p. 3; and *New Republic*, 9 January 1937, p. 286.

52. Further interaction with Hollywood transpired: screenwriter Dudley Nichols wrote, and actor Fredric March spoke, the commentary for Ivens's 1938 documentary on events in China, THE 400 MILLION, and screenwriter Donald Ogden Stewart was briefly involved in Ivens's aborted

Sloan/Educational Institute project, NEW FRONTIERS. Ivens's impressions of Hollywood during the course of his visit in 1935 are recorded in "Notes on Hollywood," *New Theatre*, October 1936, pp. 8–10, 28.

53. John H. Winge, "Some New American Documentaries: In Defense of Liberty," *Sight and Sound*, Spring 1939, repr. in Jacobs, *The Documentary Tradition*, pp. 131–135; Griffith, "Big Year For Fact Films," p. 4; Douglas Churchill, "Autumn Leaves in Hollywood," *New York Times*, 22 October 1939, sec. 9, p. 5; and Larry Ceplair and Steven Englund, *The Inquisition in Hollywood: Politics in the Film Community, 1930–1960* (Berkeley: University of California Press, 1983), pp. 104–128.

54. Arthur L. Mayer, "Fact into Film," *Public Opinion Quarterly*, Summer 1944, pp. 206–225; Douglas W. Gallez, "Patterns of Wartime Documentaries," *Quarterly Review of Film, Radio and Television* 10, no. 2 (Winter 1955), pp. 125–135; and MacCann, *The People's Films*, pp. 118–172.

55. David Bordwell, Janet Staiger, and Kristin Thompson, *The Classical Hollywood Cinema: Film Style and Mode of Production to 1960* (New York: Columbia University Press, 1985), p. 284.

56. On the impact and modification of Soviet montage by Hollywood filmmakers, see Vlada Petric, "Soviet Revolutionary Films in America (1926–1935)" (Ph.D. diss., New York University, 1973).

57. MacCann, *The People's Films*, p. 61.

58. Developments in this direction may have been accelerated by Lorentz's THE FIGHT FOR LIFE, for which two scenes were shot on an MGM soundstage, and a score, composed by Louis Gruenberg, recorded in Hollywood. Reviewing the film for the *Nation* (16 March 1940, p. 372), Franz Hoellering noted that the label "semidocumentary" had recently been drafted to describe a hybrid work like THE FIGHT FOR LIFE.

59. James Wong Howe, "The Documentary Film and Hollywood Techniques," *Proceedings of the Writers Congress, Los Angeles, 1943* (Berkeley: University of California Press, 1944), pp. 94–97. Hollywood's notion of documentary and attendant norms of verisimilitude are also outlined in Herb A. Lightman, "The Technique of the Documentary Film," *American Cinematographer*, November 1945, pp. 371, 378, 402.

60. Philip Dunne, "The Documentary and Hollywood," *Hollywood Quarterly* 1, no. 2 (January 1946), pp. 166–172, repr. in Barsam, ed., *Nonfiction Film Theory and Criticism* (New York: E. P. Dutton, 1976), pp. 158–166. Also see Kenneth MacGowan, "A Change of Pattern?" *Hollywood Quarterly* 1, no. 2 (January 1946), pp. 148–153; and Parker Tyler, "Documentary Technique in Film Fiction," *American Quarterly* (Summer 1949), repr. in Jacobs, *The Documentary Tradition*, pp. 251–266.

61. Lorentz, for example, signed a contract as writer-director-producer at RKO in September 1941, but never completed a film for the studio. Exceptions included Irving Lerner, who was briefly employed at Paramount in 1938–1939 and returned to Hollywood after the war to work as an editor, director, and producer of low-budget films for the next three decades, and Ben Maddow, a successful screenwriter in Hollywood in the 1940s and 1950s and recipient of an Academy Award nomination for his screenplay for THE ASPHALT JUNGLE, co-authored with director John Huston, in 1950.

62. Lorentz, "The Documentary Film," *McCall's*, August 1939, repr. in *Lorentz on Film*, p. 171.

CHAPTER 10. Avant-Garde Film

1. See, e.g., P. Adams Sitney, *Visionary Film: The American Avant-Garde, 1943–1978*, 2nd ed. (New York: Oxford University Press, 1979), p. 29. See also Sitney, ed., *The Avant-Garde Film* (New York: New York University Press, 1978).

2. Ironically, the 1940s avant-garde also acknowledged the reception of the same European models, for example, through Museum of Modern Art film programs; however, in this case it was to legitimize their own efforts. See Jonas Mekas, "The Experimental Film in America," *Film Culture* 1, no. 3 (May-June 1955), p. 17.

3. Mekas, "The Experimental Film in America," p. 16.

4. Arthur L. Gale, "Amateur Clubs," *Amateur Movie Makers* 3, no. 2 (February 1928), p. 100.

5. Herman G. Weinberg, *A Manhattan Odyssey: A Memoir* (New York: Anthology Film Archives, 1982), p. 28.

6. Hans Richter provides a perfect case in point. While his early avant-garde films were initially produced as advertising films or prologues to commercial features, they were later exhibited and discussed by Richter and others as pure art films. See Jan-Christopher Horak, "Discovering Pure Cinema: Avant-garde Film in the '20s," *Afterimage* 8, nos. 1–2 (Summer 1980), pp. 4–7.

7. C. Adolph Glassgold, "The Films: Amateur or Professional?" *Arts* 15, no. 1 (January 1929), p. 56.

8. Herman G. Weinberg, "A Paradox of the Photoplay," *Amateur Movie Makers* 4, no. 1 (January 1929), p. 866.

9. Frederick Kiesler, "100 Per Cent Cinema," *Close Up* 3, no. 2 (August 1928), pp. 39–40.

10. Gilbert Seldes, "Some Amateur Movies," *New Republic*, 6 March 1929, p. 71.

11. "Cranking Your Own," *National Board of Review Magazine*, June 1927, p. 3.

12. Letter from Arthur Gale (Amateur Cinema League consultant) to Marion Gleason, 21 November 1928, Gleason file, Film Dept., George Eastman House.

13. Patricia Zimmermann, "The Amateur, the Avant-Garde, and Ideologies of Art," *Journal of Film and Video* 38, nos. 3–4 (Summer-Fall 1986).

14. Letter from Arthur Gale to Marion Gleason, 10 December 1927, Gleason file, Film Dept., George Eastman House.

15. Letter from James W. Moore to Frank Stauffacher, 28 January 1947, Art in Cinema files, Pacific Film Archives.

16. Interview with Florence Robbins and Harry Hay, Escondido, California, 23 May 1991.

17. O. Spearing, "A Valuable Service," *Exceptional Photoplays* 2 (March 1922); and John Hutchens, "L'Enfant Terrible, The Little Cinema Movement," *Theatre Arts* (Special Issue), September 1929, p. 696. See also Michael Budd, "The National Board of Review and the Early Art Cinema in New York: *The Cabinet of Dr. Caligari* as Affirmative Culture," *Cinema Journal* 26, no. 1 (Fall 1986), pp. 7–8.

18. Quoted in Hutchens, "L'Enfant Terrible," p. 697.

19. "More Anent the Little Theatre," *National Board of Review Magazine*, November 1927, p. 5.

20. "Hollywood Notes," *Close Up* 3, no. 1 (July 1928), p. 74. While there were reports of the closure of the Filmarte in April 1929, the theater did continue screenings until at least 1939. See "Hollywood Notes," *Close Up* 6, no. 4 (April 1929), p. 78.

21. Letter from Gale to Gleason, 21 November 1928 (George Eastman House).

22. See inaugural program of the 8th Street Film Guild Cinema, 1 February 1929, vertical file, New York Public Library, Performing Arts Library at Lincoln Center.

23. Harry A. Potamkin, *Close Up* 6, no. 2 (February 1930), p. 111.

24. *Close Up* 7, no. 6 (December 1930), 454.

25. Hutchens, "L'Enfant Terrible," p. 694.

26. Lincoln Kirstein, "Films: Experimental Films," *Arts Weekly* 1, no. 3 (March 1932), p. 52.

27. "Close-Ups," *Amateur Movie Makers* 7, no. 4 (April 1932), p. 179. See also Elena Pinto Simon and David Stirk, "Jay Leyda: A Chronology," published in memoriam of Leyda by the Tisch School of the Arts, NYU, December 1987.

28. Letter from Robert Florey to Frank Stauffacher, 27 February 1947, Art in Cinema files, Pacific Film Archives, Berkeley, California.

29. Letter from Symon Gould to Frank Stauffacher, 1 March 1950, Art in Cinema files, PFA.

30. See, for example, Sheldon Renan, *An Introduction to the American Underground Film* (New York: E. P. Dutton, 1967), pp. 75–76. Ironically, the 1940s avant-garde also acknowledged the reception of the same European models, for example, through Museum of Modern Art film programs; however, in this case, it was to legitimize their own efforts. See Jonas Mekas, "The Experimental Film in America," p. 17.

31. The optical printer, as well as Dr. Watson's films and papers, can be viewed in the Film Collections at the International Museum of Photography at George Eastman House, Rochester, New York.

32. Herman G. Weinberg, "Lot in Sodom," *Close Up* 10, no. 3 (September 1933), p. 268.

33. Lewis Jacobs, "Avant-Garde Production in America," *Hollywood Quarterly* 3, no. 2 (Winter 1947–1948), pp. 111–124, repr. in Roger Manvell, ed., *Experiment in the Film* (London: Grey Walls Press, 1949), pp. 113–152, and in Jacobs, *The Rise of the American Film* (New York: Teachers College Press, 1968), pp. 543–582.

34. *Ibid.*, p. 555.

35. Robert Allen, "Cine Experimenter," in *Home Movies* (1940). Clip in personal possession of Lewis Jacobs.

36. Film Classic Exchange, *16mm Art Films* (catalog, no date, presumably from the late 1940s). The film is now for sale through JEF Films.

37. Interview of Lewis Jacobs by J.-C. Horak, New York City, September 1989. See also letter from Eli Willis to Frank Stauffacher, 9 February 1947, Art in Cinema files, PFA.

38. This film was donated to the Museum of Modern Art in the late 1940s, but apparently decomposed before it could be copied.

39. Harry A. Potamkin, *Close Up* 6, no. 2 (February 1930), p. 111. See also unidentified clippings in Gerson file at the Theatre Collections of the Free Library of Philadelphia.

40. Cf. Jerome Hill, "Some Notes on Painting and Film," *Film Culture* 32 (Spring 1964), pp. 31–32.

41. Both THE MAGIC UMBRELLA and THE FORTUNE TELLER were incorporated in toto in Jerome Hill's autobiographical compilation-meditation FILM PORTRAIT (1972).

42. Theodore Huff, "The Mirror of Burlesque," *Amateur Movie Makers* 7, no. 10 (October 1932), p. 429.

43. Quoted in Joseph McBride, *Welles* (New York: Viking Press, 1972), p. 26.

44. A print of the film, 16-mm, black-and-white, 222 feet, can be viewed at the Museum of Modern Art.

45. In some sources (the original error seems to have been published in Stauffacher's Art in Cinema program notes in 1947), Hy Hirch is listed in the credits, but the film was produced by Barlow, Hay, and Robbins with Hirsh only appearing as an actor in two shots. Interview with Florence Robbins and Harry Hay, 23 May 1991, Escondido, California. See also letter to J.-C. Horak from Harry Hay, 14 September 1990.

46. Interview with Florence Robbins and Harry Hay, 23 May 1991.

47. SURF AND SEAWEED is comparable to such films as those of Jan Mol in Holland or Jean Painlevé in France.

48. See Robert Haller, "Autumn Fire," *Field of Vision,* Spring 1980.

49. Given Weinberg's penchant for generating publicity about the production of CITY SYMPONY, this seems too unlikely. See FIAF notes by Weinberg in *Travelling* (Lausanne, 1979); *Close Up* 5, no. 4 (October 1929), p. 339; and *Amateur Movie Makers* 5, no. 6 (June 1930), p. 377.

50. Henwar Rodakiewicz, "Something More Than a Scenic," *Amateur Movie Makers* 7, no. 6 (June 1932), p. 249.

51. Burkhardt went on to make numerous other portraits of his city, including THE PURSUIT OF HAPPINESS (1940), THE CLIMATE OF NEW YORK (1948), UNDER BROOKLYN BRIDGE (1953), EASTSIDE SUMMER (1959), and DEFAULT AVERTED (1975).

52. See Joseph Schillinger, "Excerpts from a Theory of Synchronization," *Experimental Cinema,* no. 5 (1934), pp. 28–31.

53. For a general introduction to Bute's work, see Robert Russett and Cecile Starr, eds., *Experimental Animation: Origins of a New Art* (New York: Da Capo Press, 1976), pp. 102–105.

54. For a shot-by-shot analysis, see Gerald R. Barrett and Thomas L. Erskine, eds., *From Fiction to Film: Ambrose Bierce's "An Occurrence at Owl Creek Bridge"* (Encino, Calif.: Dickenson, 1973), pp. 87–106.

55. The film is not mentioned by any of the standard histories of black film and is misdated by Henry T. Sampson, *Blacks in Black and White: A Source Book on Black Films* (Metuchen, N.J.: Scarecrow Press, 1977), p. 272.

56. At present Etting's films are unavailable, although they are known to have survived. Efforts are under way to guarantee their preservation.

57. Letter from Emlen Etting to Frank Stauffacher, 26 March 1947, Art in Cinema files, Pacific Film Archives.

58. Letter from Amos Vogel to Frank Stauffacher, 7 June 1949, Art in Cinema files, Pacific Film Archives.

Bibliography

The following selected bibliography lists publications the authors found most useful in the preparation of the respective chapters. A more comprehensive listing of the literature may be found in Frank Manchel, *Film Study: An Analytical Bibliography*, 4 vols. (Rutherford: Fairleigh Dickinson University Press, 1990); Richard Dyer MacCann and Edward S. Perry, eds., *The New Film Index: A Bibliography of Articles on Film in English*, 1930–1970 (New York: E. P. Dutton, 1975); *Film Literature Index* (Albany: Filmdex, 1973–); and *The Film Index*, 3 vols. (New York: Kraus International, 1985.)

CHAPTER 1

Huettig, Mae D. *Economic Control of the Motion Picture Industry.* Philadelphia: University of Pennsylvania Press, 1944.

Jarvie, Ian. *Movies and Society.* New York: Basic Books, 1970.

———. "The Social Experience of Movies." In Sari Thomas, ed., *Film/Culture: Explorations of Cinema in Its Social Context.* Metuchen, N.J.: Scarecrow Press, 1982.

Jowett, Garth. *Film, the Democratic Art: A Social History of American Film.* Boston: Little, Brown, 1976.

Leab, Daniel. *From "Sambo" to "Superspade": The Black Experience in Motion Pictures.* Boston: Houghton Mifflin, 1975.

Maltby, Richard. *Harmless Entertainment: Hollywood and the Ideology of Consensus.* Metuchen, N.J.: Scarecrow Press, 1983.

May, Lary. *Screening Out the Past: The Birth of Mass Culture and the Motion Picture Industry.* New York: Oxford University Press, 1980.

Sklar, Robert. *Movie-Made America: A Cultural History of American Movies.* New York: Random House, 1975.

Thorp, Margaret Farrand. *America at the Movies.* New Haven: Yale University Press, 1939.

CHAPTER 2

Balio, Tino. *United Artists: The Company Built by the Stars.* Madison: University of Wisconsin Press, 1976.

———, ed. *The American Film Industry.* Rev. ed. Madison: University of Wisconsin Press, 1985.

Cashman, Sean Dennis. *America in the Twenties and Thirties: The Olympian Age of Franklin Delano Roosevelt.* New York: New York University Press, 1989.

Chandler, Jr., Alfred D. *The Visible Hand: The Managerial Revolution in American Business.* Cambridge: Harvard University Press, 1977.

Conant, Michael. *Antitrust in the Motion Picture Industry: Economic and Social Analysis.* Berkeley: University of California Press, 1960.

Finler, Joel W. *The Hollywood Story.* New York: Crown, 1988.

Gomery, Douglas. "Hollywood, the National Recovery Administration, and the Question of Monopoly Power." *Journal of the University Film Association* 31 (Spring 1979): 47–52.

———. "Rethinking U.S. Film History: The Depression Decade and Monopoly Control." *Film and History* 10 (May 1980): 32–38.

———. *The Hollywood Studio System.* New York: St. Martin's Press, 1986.

Jacobs, Lewis. *The Rise of the American Film: A Critical History.* New York: Teachers College Press, 1968.

Kindem, Gorham, ed. *The American Movie Industry: The Business of Motion Pictures.* Carbondale: Southern Illinois University Press, 1982.

Lewis, Howard T. *The Motion Picture Industry*. New York: D. Van Nostrand, 1933.
"Paramount Pictures." *Fortune* 15 (March 1937): 87–96.
Sands, Pierre Norman. *A Historical Study of the Academy of Motion Picture Arts and Sciences (1927–1947)*. New York: Arno Press, 1973.
Thompson, Kristin. *Exporting Entertainment: America in the World Film Market, 1907–1934*. London: British Film Institute, 1985.
"20th Century–Fox." *Fortune* 12 (December 1935): 85–92.
Wasko, Janet. *Movies and Money: Financing the American Film Industry*. Norwood, N.J.: Ablex, 1982.
Wechter, Dixon. *The Age of the Great Depression, 1929–1941*. New York: Macmillan, 1948.

CHAPTER 3

Ayer, Douglas; Roy E. Bates; and Peter J. Herman. "Self-Censorship in the Movie Industry: A Historical Perspective on Law and Social Change." *Wisconsin Law Review* 3 (1970): 791–838.
Black, Gregory D. "The Production Code and the Hollywood Film Industry, 1930–1940." *Film History* 3, no. 2 (1989): 167–189.
Blumer, Herbert. *Movies and Conduct*. New York: Macmillan, 1933.
———, and Philip M. Hauser. *Movies, Delinquency, and Crime*. New York: Macmillan, 1933.
Carmen, Ira H. *Movies, Censorship and the Law*. Ann Arbor: University of Michigan Press, 1966.
Charters, W. W. *Motion Pictures and Youth: A Summary*. New York: Macmillan, 1933.
de Cordova, Richard. *Picture Personalities: The Emergence of the Star System in America*. Urbana: University of Illinois Press, 1990.
Ernst, Morris L. *The First Freedom*. New York: Macmillan, 1946.
———, and Pare Lorentz. *Censored: The Private Life of the Movies*. New York: Jonathan Cape and Harrison Smith, 1930.
Facey, Paul W. *The Legion of Decency: A Sociological Analysis of the Emergence and Development of a Social Pressure Group*. New York: Arno, 1974.
Forman, Henry James. *Our Movie-Made Children*. New York: Macmillan, 1933.
Haralovich, Mary Beth. "Mandates of Good Taste: The Self-Regulation of Film Advertising in the Thirties." *Wide Angle* 6, no. 2 (1984): 50–57.
Hays, Will H. *The Memoirs of Will H. Hays*. Garden City, New York: Doubleday, 1955.
Himmelberg, Robert F. *The Origins of the National Recovery Administration: Business, Government and the Trade Association Issue, 1921–1933*. New York: Fordham University Press, 1976.
Hunnings, Neville March. *Film Censors and the Law*. London: Allen and Unwin, 1967.
Inglis, Ruth. *Freedom of the Movies: A Report on Self-Regulation from the Commission on Freedom of the Press*. Chicago: University of Chicago Press, 1947.
Jacobs, Lea. "The Censorship of *Blonde Venus*: Textual Analysis and Historical Method." *Cinema Journal* 27 (Spring 1988): 21–31.
———. "Industry Self-Regulation and the Problem of Textual Determination." *Velvet Light Trap* 23 (Spring 1989): 4–15.
———. *The Wages of Sin: Censorship and the Fallen Woman Film, 1928–1942*. Madison: University of Wisconsin Press, 1991.
Jowett, Garth. "Moral Responsibility and Commercial Entertainment: Social Control in the United States Film Industry, 1907–1968." *Historical Journal of Film, Radio and Television* 10, no. 1 (1990): 3–31.
Koppes, Clayton R., and Gregory D. Black. *Hollywood Goes to War: How Politics, Profits, and Propaganda Shaped World II Movies*. New York: Macmillan, 1987.
Kuhn, Annette. *Cinema, Censorship, and Sexuality, 1909–1925*. London: Routledge, 1985.
Leff, Leonard J., and Jerrold L. Simmons. *The Dame in the Kimono: Hollywood, Censorship and the Production Code from the 1920s to the 1960s*. New York: Grove Weidenfeld, 1990.
Maltby, Richard. "*Baby Face;* or, How Joe Breen Made Barbara Stanwyck Atone for Causing the Wall Street Crash." *Screen* 27, no. 2 (1986): 27–45.

_____ . "*The King of Kings* and the Czar of All the Rushes: The Propriety of the Christ Story." *Screen* 31, no. 2 (1990): 188–213.

_____ . " 'Grief in the Limelight': Al Capone, Howard Hughes, the Hays Office, and the Politics of the Unstable Text." In James Combs, ed., *Movies and Politics.* Westport: Greenwood Press, 1992.

Martin, Olga. *Hollywood's Movie Commandments: A Handbook for Motion Picture Writers and Reviewers.* New York: Wilson, 1937.

Moley, Raymond. *Are We Movie Made?* New York: Macy-Massius, 1938.

_____ . *The Hays Office.* Indianapolis: Bobbs-Merrill, 1945.

Nizer, Louis. *New Courts of Industry: Self-Regulation Under the Motion Picture Production Code.* New York: Longacre Press, 1935.

Paul, Elliot, and Luis Quintanilla. *With a Hays Nonny Nonny.* New York: Random House, 1942.

Peters, Charles C. *Motion Pictures and Standards of Morality.* New York: Macmillan, 1933.

Peterson, Ruth, and L. L. Thurstone, *Motion Pictures and the Social Attitudes of Children.* New York: Macmillan, 1933.

Quigley, Martin. *Decency in Motion Pictures.* New York: Macmillan, 1937.

Randall, Richard S. *Censorship of the Movies: The Social and Political Control of a Mass Medium.* Madison: University of Wisconsin Press, 1968.

Shenton, Herbert. *The Public Relations of the Motion Picture Industry.* New York: Federal Council of Churches of Christ in America, 1931.

Staiger, Janet. "Announcing Wares, Winning Patrons, Voicing Ideals: Thinking About the History and Theory of Film Advertising." *Cinema Journal* 29 (Fall 1990): 3–31.

Vasey, Ruth L. "Diplomatic Representations: Mediations Between Hollywood and Its Global Audiences, 1922–1939." Ph.D. diss., University of Exeter, 1990.

Vaughn, Stephen. "Morality and Entertainment: The Origins of the Motion Picture Production Code." *Journal of American History* 77, no. 1 (1990): 48–56.

Vizzard, Jack. *See No Evil: Life Inside a Hollywood Censor.* New York: Simon and Schuster, 1970.

Walsh, François R. "*The Callaghans and the Murphys* (MGM, 1927): A Case Study of Irish-American and Catholic Church Censorship." *Historical Journal of Film, Radio and Television* 10, no. 1 (1990): 33–45.

Wolfe, Charles, "*Mr. Smith Goes to Washington:* Democratic Forums and Representational Forms." In Peter Lehman, ed., *Close Viewings: An Anthology of New Film Criticism.* Tallahassee: Florida State University Press, 1990.

CHAPTER 4

Albrecht, Donald. *Designing Dreams: Modern Architecture in the Movies.* New York: Harper and Row, 1986.

Barsacq, Léon. *Caligari's Cabinet and Other Grand Illusions: A History of Film Design.* Rev. ed. by Elliott Stein. New York: New American Library, 1978.

Behlmer, Rudy. *America's Favorite Movies: Behind the Scenes.* New York: Frederick Ungar, 1982.

_____ , ed. *Memo from David O. Selznick.* New York: Viking, 1972.

_____ , ed. *Inside Warner Bros. (1935–1951).* New York: Viking, 1985.

Carey, Gary. *All the Stars in Heaven: Louis B. Mayer's MGM.* New York: E. P. Dutton, 1981.

Ceplair, Larry, and Steven Englund. *The Inquisition in Hollywood: Politics in the Film Community, 1930–1960.* Garden City: Anchor Press, 1980.

Crowther, Bosley. *Hollywood Rajah: The Life and Times of Louis B. Mayer.* New York: Holt, Rinehart and Winston, 1960.

Chierichetti, David. *Hollywood Costume Design.* London: Studio Vista, 1976.

Eustis, Morton. "Designing for the Movies: Gibbons of MGM." *Theatre Arts Monthly* 21 (October 1937): 782–98.

Fine, Richard. *Hollywood and the Profession of Authorship, 1928–1940.* Ann Arbor, Mich.: UMI Research Press, 1979.

Hambley, John, and Patrick Downing. *The Art of Hollywood: Fifty Years of Art Direction.* London: Thames Television, 1979.

Haver, Ronald. *David O. Selznick's Hollywood*. New York: Bonanza Books, 1980.

Heisner, Beverly. *Hollywood Art: Art Direction in the Days of the Great Studios*. Jefferson, N.C.: McFarland, 1990.

La Vine, W. Robert. *In a Glamorous Fashion: The Fabulous Years of Hollywood Costume Design*. New York: Charles Scribner's Sons, 1980.

MacGowan, Kenneth. *Behind the Screen: The History and Techniques of the Motion Picture*. New York: Delacorte, 1965.

Maeder, Edward. *Hollywood and History: Costume Design in Films*. Los Angeles: Los Angeles County Museum of Art, 1987.

Marx, Samuel. *Mayer and Thalberg: The Make-Believe Saints*. New York: Random House, 1975.

Naumberg, Nancy, ed. *We Make the Movies*. New York: W. W. Norton, 1937.

Rosten, Leo C. *Hollywood: The Movie Colony, the Movie Makers*. New York: Harcourt, Brace, 1941.

Schatz, Thomas. *The Genius of the System: Hollywood Filmmaking in the Studio Era*. New York: Pantheon Books, 1988.

Thomas, Tony. *Music for the Movies*. New York: A. S. Barnes, 1983.

Toland, Gregg. "The Motion Picture Cameraman." *Theatre Arts Monthly* 25 (September 1944): 647–654.

Wolfe, Charles. *Frank Capra: A Guide to References and Resources*. Boston: G. K. Hall, 1987.

CHAPTER 5

Altman, Rick. "The Technology of the Voice." *Iris* 3, no. 1 (1985): 3–20.

Basten, Fred E. *Glorious Technicolor*. New Brunswick, N.J.: A. S. Barnes, 1980.

Bordwell, David; Janet Staiger; and Kristin Thompson. *The Classical Hollywood Cinema: Film Style and Mode of Production to 1960*. New York: Columbia University Press, 1985.

Dunn, Linwood, and George E. Turner, eds. *The ASC Treasure of Visual Effects*. Hollywood: American Society of Cinematographers, 1983.

Eyman, Scott, ed. *Five American Cinematographers: Interviews with Karl Struss, Joseph Ruttenberg, James Wong Howe, Linwood Dunn, and William H. Clothier*. Metuchen, N.J.: Scarecrow Press, 1987.

Higham, Charles, ed. *Hollywood Cameramen: Sources of Light*. Bloomington: Indiana University Press, 1970.

Hilliard, John K. "Basic Sound Recording and Reproducing Practices Between 1927 and 1940." *SMPTE Journal* 92, no. 2 (February 1983): 207–210.

Maltin, Leonard, ed. *The Art of the Cinematographer: A Survey and Interviews with Five Masters*. New York: Dover Publications, 1978.

Salt, Barry. *Film Style and Technology: History and Analysis*. London: Starword, 1983.

Sterling, Anna Kate, ed. *Cinematographers on the Art and Craft of Cinematography*, Metuchen, N.J.: Scarecrow, 1987.

Turner, George E., ed. *The Cinema of Adventure, Romance and Terror: From the Archives of "American Cinematographer."* Hollywood: American Society of Cinematographers, 1989.

Watts, Stephen. *Behind the Screen: How Films Are Made*. New York: Dodge, 1938.

CHAPTER 6

Affron, Charles. *Star Acting: Gish, Garbo, Davis*. New York: E. P. Dutton, 1977.

Bogle, Donald. *Toms, Coons, Mulattoes, Mammies and Blacks*. New York: Viking, 1973.

"Deanna Durbin." *Fortune* 20 (October 1939): 66ff.

Dyer, Richard. *Stars*. London: British Film Institute, 1979.

Eckert, Charles. "The Carole Lombard in Macy's Window." *Quarterly Review of Film Studies* 3 (Winter 1978): 1–21.

Gaines, Janet, and Charlotte Herzog, eds. *Fabrications: Costume and the Female Body*. New York: Routledge, 1991.

Gledhill, Christine, ed. *Stardom: Industry of Desire*. London: Routledge, 1991.

Griffith, Richard. *The Movie Stars*. New York: Doubleday, 1970.

Hilmes, Michele. *Hollywood and Broadcasting: From Radio to Cable.* Urbana: University of Illinois Press, 1990.

Jenkins, Henry, III. " 'Shall We Make It for New York or for Distribution?' Eddie Cantor, *Whoopee,* and Regional Resistance to the Talkies." *Cinema Journal* 29 (Spring 1990): 32–52.

Kobal, John. *Hollywood Glamour Portraits.* New York: Dover Publications, 1976.

Levin, Martin, ed. *Hollywood and the Great Fan Magazines.* New York: Arbor House, 1970.

"The Morris Agency." *Fortune* 18 (September 1938): 71–73.

Naremore, James. *Acting in the Cinema.* Berkeley: University of California Press, 1988.

Powdermaker, Hortense. *Hollywood: The Dream Factory.* Boston: Little, Brown, 1950.

Prindle, David F. *The Politics of Glamour: Ideology and Democracy in the Screen Actors Guild.* Madison: University of Wisconsin Press, 1988.

Ross, Murray. *Stars and Strikes: Unionization of Hollywood.* New York: Columbia University Press, 1941.

Shipman, David. *The Great Movie Stars: The Golden Years.* New York: Hill and Wang, 1979.

Walker, Alexander. *Stardom: The Hollywood Phenomenon.* New York: Stein and Day, 1970.

———. *Garbo: A Portrait.* New York: Macmillan, 1980.

CHAPTER 7

Allen, Robert C., and Douglas Gomery. *Film History: Theory and Practice.* New York: Alfred A. Knopf, 1985.

Altman, Rick. *The American Film Musical.* Bloomington: Indiana University Press, 1987.

Baxter, John. *Hollywood in the Thirties.* New York: A. S. Barnes, 1968.

Behlmer, Rudy, ed. *The Adventures of Robin Hood.* Madison: University of Wisconsin Press, 1979.

Buscombe, Edward. *The BFI Companion to the Western.* New York: Da Capo Press, 1988.

Clarens, Carlos. *An Illustrated History of the Horror Film.* New York: Capricorn Books: 1968.

Cripps, Thomas, ed. *The Green Pastures.* Madison: University of Wisconsin Press, 1979.

Croce, Arlene. *The Fred Astaire and Ginger Rogers Book.* New York: Galahad Books, 1972.

Crowther, Bosley. *The Lion's Share: The Story of an Entertainment Empire.* New York: E. P. Dutton, 1957.

Delameter, Jerome. *Dance in the Hollywood Musical.* Ann Arbor, Mich.: UMI Research Press, 1981.

Dick, Bernard F., ed. *Dark Victory.* Madison: University of Wisconsin Press, 1981.

Dooley, Roger. *From Scarface to Scarlett: American Films in the 1930s.* New York: Harcourt Brace Jovanovich, 1979.

Elsaesser, Thomas. "Film History as Social History: The Dieterle/Warner Brothers Bio-pic." *Wide Angle* 8, no. 2, pp. 15–31.

Feuer, Jane. *The Hollywood Musical.* Bloomington: Indiana University Press, 1982.

Green, Stanley. *Encyclopedia of the Musical Film.* New York: Oxford University Press, 1981.

Grouch, John R. "What Is a Marx Brother?: Critical Practice, Industrial Practice, and the Notion of Comic Auteur." *Velvet Light Trap* 26 (Fall 1990): 30–41.

Harvey, James. *Romantic Comedy in Hollywood, from Lubitsch to Sturges.* New York: Alfred A. Knopf, 1987.

Haskell, Molly. *From Reverence to Rape: The Treatment of Women in the Movies.* New York: Holt, Rinehart and Winston, 1974.

Heming, Roy. *The Melody Lingers On: The Great Songwriters and Their Movie Musicals.* New York: Newmarket Press, 1986.

Jenkins, Henry, III. " 'Fifi Was My Mother's Name!': Anarchistic Comedy, the Vaudeville Aesthetic, and *Diplomaniacs.*" *Velvet Light Trap* 26 (Fall 1990): 3–27.

Jewell, Richard, with Vernon Harbin. *The RKO Story.* New York: Arlington House, 1982.

Kendall, Elizabeth. *The Runaway Bride: Hollywood Romantic Comedy of the 1930s.* New York: Alfred A. Knopf, 1990.

Kobal, John. *Gotta Sing, Gotta Dance: A Pictorial History of Film Musicals.* New York: Hamlyn, 1971.

Koszarski, Richard, ed. *The Mystery of the Wax Museum.* Madison: University of Wisconsin Press, 1979.

Kreuger, Miles, ed. *The Movie Musical from Vitaphone to 42nd Street: As Reprinted in a Great Fan Magazine.* New York: Dover Publications, 1975.

Lloyd, Ann, ed. *Movies of the Thirties.* London: Orbis, 1983.

McCaffrey, Donald W. *The Golden Age of Sound Comedy: Comic Films and Comedians of the Thirties.* New York: A. S. Barnes, 1973.

Maland, Charles J. *Chaplin and American Culture: The Evolution of a Star Image.* Princeton, N.J.: Princeton University Press, 1989.

Mast, Gerald. *The Comic Mind: Comedy and the Movies.* New York: Bobbs-Merrill, 1973.

———. *Can't Help Singin': The American Musical on Stage and Screen.* Woodstock, N.Y.: Overlook Press, 1987.

O'Connor, John E., ed. *I Am a Fugitive from a Chain Gang.* Madison: University of Wisconsin Press, 1981.

Roddick, Nick. *A New Deal in Entertainment: Warner Brothers in the 1930s.* London: British Film Institute, 1983.

Roffman, Peter, and Jim Purdy. *The Hollywood Social Problem Film: Madness, Despair, and Politics from the Depression to the Fifties.* Bloomington: Indiana University Press, 1981.

Rossow, Eugene. *Born to Lose: The Gangster Film in America.* New York: Oxford University Press, 1978.

Sennett, Ted. *Lunatics and Lovers.* New Rochelle, N.Y.: Arlington House, 1973.

———. *Hollywood Musicals.* New York: Abrams, 1981.

Taylor, Helen. *Scarlett's Women: "Gone with the Wind" and Its Female Fans.* New Brunswick, N.J.: Rutgers University Press, 1989.

Tudor, Andrew. *Monsters and Mad Scientists: A Cultural History of the Horror Movie.* Oxford: Basil Blackwell, 1989.

Vanderwood, Paul J., ed. *Juarez.* Madison: University of Wisconsin Press, 1983.

Viviani, Christian. "Who Is Without Sin? The Maternal Melodrama in American Film, 1930–39." *Wide Angle* 4, no. 2 (1980): 4–17.

Walker, Alexander. *The Shattered Silents: How the Talkies Came to Stay.* New York: William Morrow, 1979.

Walsh, Andrea. *Women's Film and Female Experience, 1940–1950.* New York: Praeger, 1984.

Weales, Gerald. *Canned Goods as Caviar: American Film Comedies of the 1930s.* Chicago: University of Chicago Press, 1985.

CHAPTER 8

Adams, Les, and Buck Rainey. *Shoot-'em-ups.* Metuchen, N.J.: Scarecrow Press, 1985.

Chambers, Robert W. "The Double Feature as a Sales Problem." *Harvard Business Review* 16 (Winter 1938): 226–236.

Cohen, Joan. "The Second Feature," *Mankind* 5 (June 1976): 26–33.

Cross, Robin. *The Big Book of B Movies.* New York: St. Martin's Press, 1981.

Everson, William K. "Book Reviews: *B Movies.*" *Films in Review* 25 (November 1974): 564.

Churchill, Douglas W. "On the Leasing Lot." *New York Times,* 10 November 1935.

———. "Hollywood from A to Z." *New York Times,* 14 March 1937.

———. "More Vicissitudes of Turbulent Hollywood." *New York Times,* 13 June 1937.

———. "How Doth the Busy Little 'B.'" *New York Times,* 2 January 1938.

Condon, Frank. "Poverty Row." *Saturday Evening Post,* 25 August 1939: 30–64.

Cripps, Thomas. *Slow Fade to Black: The Negro in American Film, 1900–1942.* New York: Oxford University Press, 1977.

Fernett, Gene. *Poverty Row.* Satellite Beach, Fla.: Coral Reef, 1973.

Goldman, Eric A. *Visions, Images and Dreams.* 2nd ed. Teaneck, N.J.: Ergo Media, 1988.

Grinde, Nick. "Pictures for Peanuts." *Penguin Film Review* 1 (February 1946): 40–51.

Grupenhoff, Richard. *The Black Valentino.* Metuchen, N.J.: Scarecrow Press, 1988.

Hurst, Richard Maurice. *Republic Studios.* Metuchen, N.J.: Scarecrow Press, 1979.

Jacobs, Lewis. "A History of the Obscure Quickie." *New York Times,* 30 December 1934.

Klotman, Phyllis Rauch, ed. *Frame by Frame: A Black Filmography*. Bloomington: Indiana University Press, 1979.

McCarthy, Todd, and Charles Flynn. *Kings of the Bs*. New York: E. P. Dutton, 1975.

McClelland, Doug. *The Golden Age of "B" Movies*. Nashville: Charter House, 1978.

Mayer, Arthur L. "An Exhibitor Begs for 'Bs.'" *Hollywood Quarterly* 3 (Winter 1947–1948): 172–177.

Miller, Don. "The American B Film." *Focus on Film*, no. 5 (Winter 1970): 31–32.

———. *B Movies*. New York: Ballantine Books, 1973.

———. *Hollywood Corral*. New York: Popular Library, 1976.

Okuda, Ted. *The Monogram Checklist*. Jefferson, N.C.: McFarland, 1987.

———. *Grand National, Producers Releasing Corporation, and Screen Guild/Lippert*. Jefferson, N.C.: McFarland, 1989.

Sampson, Henry. *Blacks in Black and White*. Metuchen, N.J.: Scarecrow Press, 1977.

"Screen Fans Organize to Bite Hand That Feeds Them Double Features." *Newsweek*, 4 October 1937: 25–26.

Taves, Brian. *Robert Florey, the French Expressionist*. Metuchen, N.J.: Scarecrow Press, 1987.

Turner, George, and Michael Price. *Forgotten Horrors*. New York: A. S. Barnes, 1979.

Tuska, Jon. *The Vanishing Legion*. Jefferson, N.C.: McFarland, 1982.

CHAPTER 9

Achtenberg, Ben. "Helen Van Dongen: An Interview." *Film Quarterly* 30 (Winter 1976): 46–57.

Alexander, William. "*The March of Time* and *The World Today*." *American Quarterly*, Summer 1977, 69–73.

———. *Film on the Left: American Documentary Film from 1931 to 1942*. Princeton, N.J.: Princeton University Press, 1981.

Barnouw, Erik. *Documentary: A History of the Non-Fiction Film*. New York: Oxford University Press, 1974, 1983.

Brandon, Tom. "Survival List." *Film Library Quarterly* 12, nos. 2–3 (1979): 33–40.

Campbell, Russell. "'A Total and Realistic Experience': Interview with Leo Seltzer." *Jump Cut*, no. 14 (1977): 25–27.

———. *Cinema Strikes Back: Radical Filmmaking in the United States, 1930–1942*. Ann Arbor, Mich.: UMI Research Press, 1982.

Engle, Harrison. "Thirty Years of Social Inquiry: An Interview with Willard Van Dyke." *Film Comment* 3 (Spring 1965): 24–37; repr. in Richard Barsam, ed., *Nonfiction Film: Theory and Criticism*. New York: E. P. Dutton, 1976.

Fielding, Raymond. *The March of Time, 1935–1951*. New York: Oxford University Press, 1978.

Hitchens, Gordon. "Joris Ivens Interviewed by Gordon Hitchens." *Film Culture*, nos. 53–55 (Spring 1972): 190–194.

Hurwitz, Leo. "One Man's Voyage: Ideas and Films in the 1930's." *Cinema Journal* 15 (Fall 1975): 1–15.

Ivens, Joris. *The Camera and I*. New York: International Publishers, 1969.

Jacobs, Lewis, ed. *The Documentary Tradition: From Nanook to Woodstock*. New York: Hopkinson and Blake, 1971.

———. , ed. *The Compound Cinema: The Film Writings of Harry Alan Potamkin*. New York: Teachers College Press, 1977.

Kepley, Vance, Jr. "The Workers International Relief and the Cinema of the Left, 1921–1935." *Cinema Journal* 23 (Fall 1983): 7–23.

Klein, Michael. "*Native Land*: An Interview with Leo Hurwitz." *Cineaste* 6, no. 3 (1974): 3–7.

Levin, G. Roy. "Willard Van Dyke." In *Documentary Explorations: 15 Interviews with Film-Makers*. New York: Doubleday, 1971.

Lorentz, Pare. *Lorentz on Film*. New York: Hopkinson and Blake, 1975; repr. Norman: University of Oklahoma Press, 1986.

Losey, Mary, ed. *Living Films*. New York: Association of Documentary Film Producers, 1940.

MacCann, Richard Dyer. *The People's Films: A Political History of U.S. Government Motion Pictures.* New York: Hastings House, 1973.

Mercey, Arch. "Films by American Governments: The United States." *Films* 1 (Summer 1940): 5–11.

Nichols, Bill. "The American Photo League." *Screen* 23 (Winter 1972–1973): 108–115.

Rosenzweig, Roy. "Working-Class Struggles in the Great Depression: The Film Record." *Film Library Quarterly* 23, no. 1 (1980): 5–14.

Safford, Tony. "The Camera as a Weapon in the Class Struggle: Interview with Samuel Brody." *Jump Cut,* no. 14 (1977): 28–30.

Seltzer, Leo. "Documenting the Depression in the 1930s: The Work of the Film and Photo League." *Film Library Quarterly* 13, no. 1 (1980): 15–22.

Snyder, Robert L. *Pare Lorentz and the Documentary Film.* Norman: University of Oklahoma Press, 1968.

Stott, William. *Documentary Expression in Thirties America.* New York: Oxford University Press, 1973.

Sweet, Fred; Eugene Rosow; and Allan Francovich. "Pioneers: An Interview with Tom Brandon." *Film Quarterly* 28 (Fall 1973): 12–24.

Van Dyke, Willard. "Documentaries of the Thirties." *Journal of the University Film Association* 25, no. 3 (1975): 45–46.

Zuker, Joel. *Ralph Steiner: Filmmaker and Still Photographer.* New York: Arno Press, 1978.

CHAPTER 10

Curtis, David. *Experimental Cinema.* New York: Dell, 1971.

Dworskin, Stephen. *Film Is.* Woodstock, N.Y.: Overlook Press, 1975.

Fischer, Lucy. "The Films of James Sibley Watson, Jr., and Melville Webber: A Reconsideration." *Millennium Film Journal,* no. 19 (1987): 40–49.

Grierson, John. "Flaherty as Innovator." *Sight and Sound* 21 (October-December, 1951): 64–68.

Horak, Jan-Christopher. "Film and Foto: Towards a Language of Silent Films." *Afterimage* 7 (December 1979): 8–11.

Jacobs, Lewis. "Experimental Cinema in America, 1921–1947." In *The Rise of American Film: A Critical History.* New York: Teachers College Press, 1968.

Penley, Constance, and Janet Bergstrom. "The Avant-Garde: Histories and Theories." *Screen* 19 (Autumn 1978): 113–127.

Polan, Dana. *The Political Language of Film and the Avant-Garde.* Ann Arbor, Mich.: UMI Research Press, 1985.

Renan, Sheldon. *An Introduction to the American Underground Film.* New York: E. P. Dutton, 1967.

Russett, Robert, and Cecile Starr. *Experimental Animation: An Illustrated Anthology.* New York: Da Capo Press, 1976.

Singer, Marilyn. *A History of the American Avant-Garde.* New York: American Federation of the Arts, 1976.

Sitney, P. Adams. *Film Culture Reader.* New York: Praeger Publishers, 1970.

———. *The Essential Cinema: Essays on the Films in the Collections of Anthology Film Archives.* New York: New York University Press, 1975.

———. *Avant-Garde Film: A Reader of Theory and Criticism.* New York: New York University Press, 1978.

Tyler, Parker. *Underground Film: A Critical History.* New York: Grove Press, 1970.

General Index

Italic numerals signify illustrations.

Index of Films

Italic numerals signify illustrations.